CW01269730

Lijssenthoek Military Cemetery

Lijssenthoek Military Cemetery

In Memory and In Mourning

Paul Chapman

Pen & Sword
MILITARY

First published in Great Britain in 2016 by
Pen & Sword Military
an imprint of
Pen & Sword Books Ltd
47 Church Street
Barnsley
South Yorkshire
S70 2AS

Copyright © Paul Chapman 2016

ISBN 978 1 47385 095 8

The right of Paul Chapman to be identified as the Author of this Work has been asserted by him in accordance with the Copyright, Designs and Patents Act 1988.

A CIP catalogue record for this book is available from the British Library

All rights reserved. No part of this book may be reproduced or transmitted in any form or by any means, electronic or mechanical including photocopying, recording or by any information storage and retrieval system, without permission from the Publisher in writing.

Typeset in Ehrhardt by
Mac Style Ltd, Bridlington, East Yorkshire
Printed and bound in the UK by CPI Group (UK) Ltd,
Croydon, CR0 4YY

Pen & Sword Books Ltd incorporates the imprints of Pen & Sword Archaeology, Atlas, Aviation, Battleground, Discovery, Family History, History, Maritime, Military, Naval, Politics, Railways, Select, Transport, True Crime, and Fiction, Frontline Books, Leo Cooper, Praetorian Press, Seaforth Publishing and Wharncliffe.

For a complete list of Pen & Sword titles please contact
PEN & SWORD BOOKS LIMITED
47 Church Street, Barnsley, South Yorkshire, S70 2AS, England
E-mail: enquiries@pen-and-sword.co.uk
Website: www.pen-and-sword.co.uk

Contents

Author's Note — vii
Acknowledgements — x

Plot I — 3
Plot II — 16
Plot III — 33
Plot IV — 41
Plot V — 48
Plot VI — 62
Plot VII — 85
Plot VIII — 104
Plot IX — 129
Plot X — 137
Plot XI — 152
Plot XII — 158
Plot XIII — 163
Plot XIV — 173
Plot XV — 183
Plot XVI — 188
Plot XVII — 198
Plot XVIII — 206
Plot XIX — 211
Plot XX — 216
Plot XXI — 225
Plot XXII — 243
Plot XXIII — 254
Plot XXIV — 259
Plot XXV — 265
Plot XXVI — 275
Plot XXVII — 290

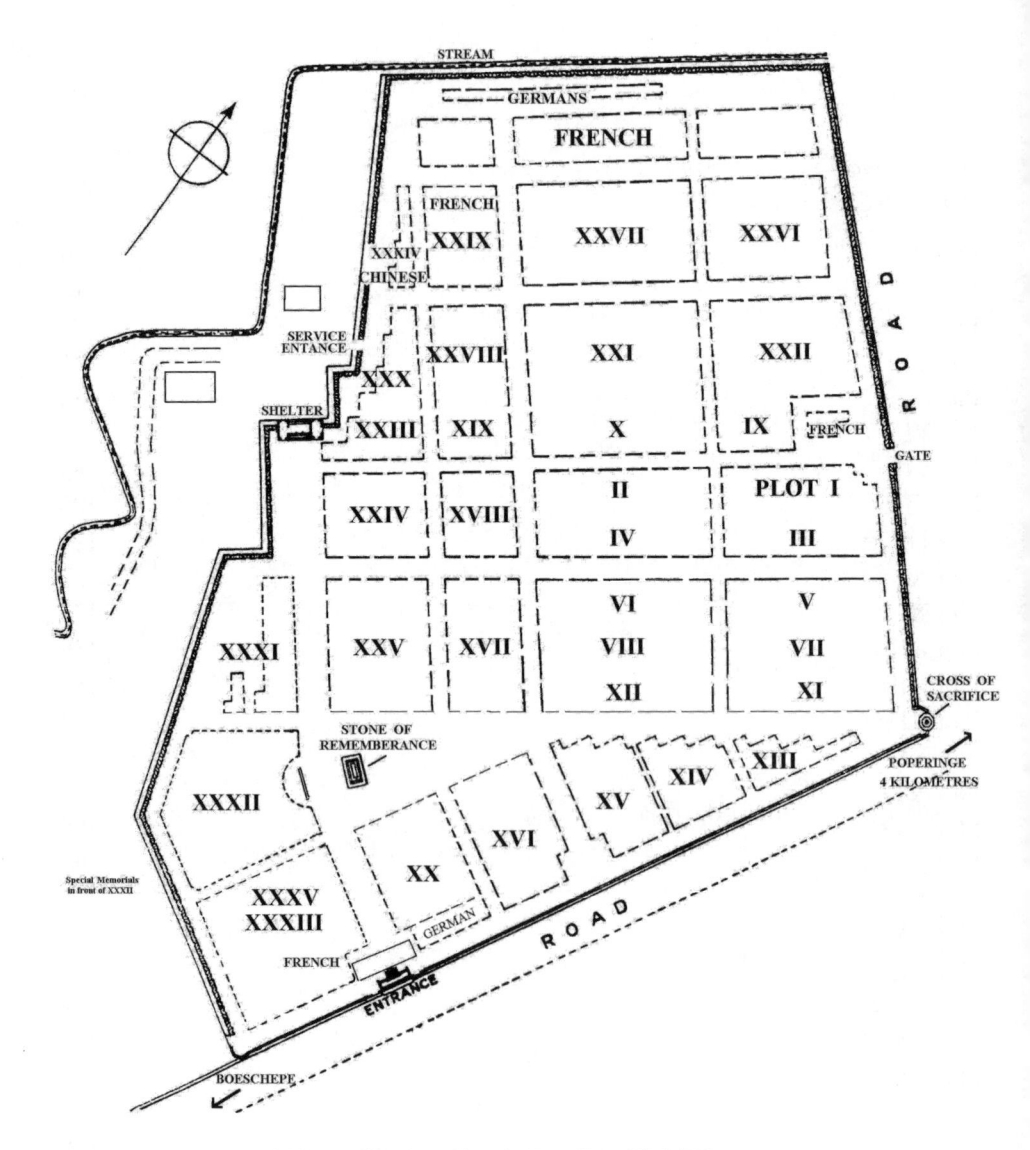

LIJSSENTHOEK MILITARY CEMETERY

Author's Note

The role of the historian is to study, draw upon and interpret the narrative for the perception of the future.

Bishop, 1969

No matter how many times one visits the Western Front of France and Belgium, one cannot fail to be awed by the number of Commonwealth War Graves Commission cemeteries encountered at almost every turn. Some cemeteries are considerably larger than others but they all have one thing in common – the serried ranks of headstones, silently guarding the land in which they stand, paid for in the blood and self-sacrifice of those who lie beneath; their lives given that we might live in freedom. Every headstone and name on a memorial represents a personal tragedy; collectively they represent a lost generation of husbands, fathers, sons and brothers who answered their country's call to duty.

The visitor to these silent cities of the dead (all are easily accessible be it by foot or vehicle) usually falls into one of three categories – personally related in some way to the casualty, historically minded, or casual. The relative, spurred by family connection, might be visiting for the first time, perhaps the very first time the casualty has received the comfort of a visit from home, or returning as part of an annual pilgrimage; paying their respects to someone unknown to them personally yet ever remembered by the family. The historian, documenting his or her findings for personal interest or publication, might be researching a particular individual or action in which a certain division, brigade, regiment or battalion took part. The casual visitor is invariably someone passing through the vicinity, mildly curious, taking a brief break from his or her journey. But, for whatever reason the visit is made – and one can spend hours walking round – those who fail to be touched emotionally are few and far between.

Uniform in size and design the headstone informs the visitor of the casualty's name, rank, regiment, service number, date of death and (sometimes) age. Poignant epitaphs abound, but few give any insight into the man. The memorials to the thousands of missing record only regiment, rank and name. Examination of the appropriate cemetery or memorial register for further details will, with the exception of Victoria Cross recipients, rarely reveal more than next of kin. Whatever terminology one chooses, without additional information a list is just a list.

After over forty year's association with the Western Front, and, in particular the Ypres Salient, I have frequently asked myself the question; who were these men? Where did they come from and what happened to them? The answer to these questions can never be fully answered, the detail herein recorded began purely out of personal interest; researching a considerable number of casualties whose graves I had photographed. Initially drawing on the Marquis De Ruvigny's Rolls of Honour, published at the time and shortly thereafter in a series of parts, in time this expanded into page upon page of information bringing a personal aspect to the casualty – explaining and answering much more of the who, what, where and why than the norm.

Almost one hundred years after the Armistice the death toll of the First World War remains as a Roll of Honour, commanding as much respect today as it did at the time. Dubbed the Great War for Civilization it was the first total war in British history to affect every aspect of national life, and stands as the supreme icon of the horror and inhumanity of armed conflict. Our picture of the war is still vivid, the poems speak just as freshly to A-Level students today as they did to older generations, and the poignancy of the many photographs and newsreel footage touches us still.

Those smiling, young, unsuspecting faces marching into Flanders; those exhausted, shattered bodies struggling through the mud, the squalor and filth of the trenches where the ever present sense of death and the macabre were just another facet of everyday life – they could be our faces and bodies, or belong to those we know and love.

Throughout Great Britain and the Dominions there were few families who did not know of a husband, father, son, brother or uncle killed or wounded in the conflict. Behind the bald statistics of every account written at the time or years afterwards lie countless stories of individual tragedy. Drawn from a vast variety of sources, the accounts and casualty details (many included at length) herein recorded, recount the gruesome horror of war in all its many facets. In an antidote to the brash adventure stories that pass for war in much of the literature of today, here we have mud, lice, rats, gas and death, presented in every manner imaginable (and unimaginable). The biggest killer – shellfire – often buried men alive, or completely vaporised them, leaving no trace of their existence. Jagged chunks of red hot metal sliced through flesh in an obscene fashion, removing heads and limbs with ease. Snipers, grenades and the scything machine guns, skilfully used by well-trained specialists, all contributed to the horror; all get their due.

How soldiers endured all this is beyond comprehension, any part of the thin veneer of civilisation they had left behind was quickly eroded after a short time at the front. Men became dehumanised by the war, they brutalised and stripped the corpses of their enemies for souvenirs; snipers took special enjoyment in knocking off members of burial parties. But, it was a different matter when it came to their own dead. Under strict orders to ignore wounded comrades in an advance, soldiers repeatedly strove heroically to protect their own. Time and time again they risked their own lives to go out onto the bullet and shell swept battlefield to search for wounded and fallen comrades; bringing in the latter that they might be given 'the dignity of a decent burial' – rites that all too often proved short-lived. Some, hastily buried, re-emerged from the earth during the next rainstorm; countless numbers were exhumed or blown to pieces by bombardments. On reflection the question arises: 'Why bother at all?' In part the answer lies with those of the battalion who, after the fighting, answered the roll-call, heard the repeated silences that followed the reading of the names, only to be informed from higher up the attack had failed due to 'lack of pluck' on their part. When one takes all this into account one realises the importance of remembering the dead was often as much an act of tenderness by their comrades as it was in defiance.

Within the confines of the Ypres Salient are to be found one hundred and sixty nine Commonwealth War Grave Commission cemeteries and three memorials to the missing, honouring the memory of British and Commonwealth servicemen who gave their lives in the defence of this relatively small yet strategically important region of Belgium. Of the 210,000 casualties buried or commemorated in the Ypres Salient extended details relating to over 20,000 were drawn upon to compose these books. A small percentage of the total, but who they were, where they came from, how they died – all these facts are just as important as those relating to precisely why they died. These men and the actions in which they gave their lives are a part of our history, our heritage; hopefully, by bringing something of the personal about them to the visitor, these books will ensure their memory never fades.

In Memory and In Mourning
Paul Chapman

Acknowledgments

First and foremost to my long suffering wife Sandra, who, without complaint over the almost thirteen years this work has taken, has not only put up with my spending days on end with my head stuck in one book or another, making copious quantities of notes (and leaving papers all over the house), typing or searching the internet at all hours, but has also endured alone my long periods away from home spent trekking the salient.

Secondly to the staff of the Commonwealth War Graves Commission, Maidenhead and Ypres, the Imperial War Museum, London, and the National Archives, Kew; for their many kindnesses and willing assistance. Also to the Australian War Memorial, Canberra, the Auckland Cenotaph, New Zealand and the Canadian National War Memorial, Ottawa, whose archival material greatly assisted in providing additional detail, clarified numerous points and answered many queries.

Special thanks to Gladys Lunn, MBE, for her continued interest and encouragement, without whose personal influence I would never have made the acquaintance of so many regimental associations: Royal Army Medical Corps; Royal Tank Regt.; Machine Gun Corps; Royal Berkshire, Wiltshire & Gloucestershire Regiments. Major A.R. McKinnell, Black Watch; Capt. A.W. Hughes – Cheshire Regt.; Corpl. Bingley and the late Major Louch – Coldstream Guards; Major T.W. Stipling – Duke of Cornwall's Light Infantry; Major P.R. Walton – King's Liverpool Regt., Manchester Regt.; Major C.M.J. Deedes – King's Own Yorkshire Light Infantry; Lieut.Col. G. Bennett – Lancashire Fusiliers; David Ball and Harry 'Aitch' Hogan – Prince of Wales's Leinster Regt. Association; Capt. Richard 'Dick' Hennessy-Walsh – The Life Guards; Major J.C. Rogerson – Middlesex Regt., Queen's Own (Royal West Kent Regt.); The Buffs (East Kent Regt.); George, Bob and J.P. – Northamptonshire Regt.; Leslie Frater – Northumberland Fusiliers; Major S.A. Kennedy – Prince of Wales's Own (West & East Yorkshire) Regt.; Major R.J.R. Campbell – Queen's Own Cameron Highlanders, Seaforth Highlanders; Capt. W.G. 'Bill' Sutherland – Royal Scots; Major A.W. Russell – Queen's Royal West Surrey Regt.; Major G. Correa – Royal Artillery; Lieut.Col. P.A. Roffey, Royal Army Veterinary Corps; Major R.G. Mills – Royal Warwickshire Regt; Major A. Ellingham – Royal Welch Fusiliers: And, Major John Baines and John Howells – New South Wales Lancers Museum

(Australian Light Horse); Capt. Gary 'Poppa Holdfast' Silliker, Royal Canadian Air Force (Engineers); and Alison Taylor, Auckland Museum.

Also a big thank you to the many people whose contributions to this work have in various degrees, enhanced the whole. In particular the members of the internet sites 'The Great War Forum,' 'World War 1 Remembered' and 'The Aerodrome' whose knowledge (and resourcefulness) never ceased to amaze: My friend and work colleague Dick Atkins who, when my computer crashed at 1500 pages and all seemed lost, completely restored everything including my sanity: Steve 'One Shot' Clews for his photographic expertise: Steve 'For Canada' Douglas, The British Grenadier Bookshop, Ypres, for his untiring assistance with queries regarding the C.E.F.; often closing shop to check names and panel numbers on the Menin Gate: Sue Cox, Richard 'Daggers' Daglish, Ian 'Scoop' Davies, Derek 'Del' Doune, Linda 'Linny' Carrier for inspiration, distraction and constructive criticism; Pete Folwell, Frank 'The Oracle' Grande, Sandra Hanley, Bryan Harris, Tim Harrison & Anna Parker, Patricia Healey, John & Elizabeth Holbrook, Clive Hughes, Patricia Jackson (Jamaica), Carol Johnson, Ken Jones, the late Dr. John Laffin, Brian Little, Tony 'Squirrel' Nutkins, Dave Pain, Col. Graham Parker, Paul 'Nationwide' Smith, the late Ted Smith and the late Tony Spagnoly, Jennifer Spooner, Sandra Taylor, Colin & Geraldine Ward, Sylvia Watkins, my many colleagues 'in the job' who over the years have supplied copious quantities of notes and peripheral information gleaned from personal research and war memorials throughout the length and breadth of the British Isles, and – too numerous to mention – the many visitors I have had the pleasure to meet who kindly entrusted their stories to me in Flanders Fields.

In the years it took to compile and prepare this work, the like of which has never been attempted before, there were many times when it became necessary to call on local assistance – 'over there.' Particularly deserving of special mention: Dries Chaerle and Jacques Ryckebosch whose combined knowledge of the region, the obscure and little known is second to none. And 'Brother' Bart Engelen and An 'Girly' Van Der Smissen who, in response to many email (and postal) enquiries, always managed to find time out to visit (sometimes in atrocious weather) various sites, accurately recording and promptly supplying the information required; and who willingly continue to accompany me on my travels.

And finally, a special thank you to Laura Hirst and Jonathan Wright, Pen & Sword, for their support, interest, advice and attention throughout the seemingly unending days of editing, proof-reading, checking and cross-checking, embedding the bits and pieces here and there that necessitated more than one delay: all this (and more) would have exhausted the patience of a saint. I thank you both.

Every reasonable effort has been made to trace copyright holders, but if there are any errors or omissions, the publishers will be pleased to insert the appropriate acknowledgement in any subsequent printings or editions.

Lijssenthoek Military Cemetery, Poperinghe

During the First World War the hamlet of Lyssenthoek was situated on the main communication line between the Allied military bases in the rear and the battlefields of the Ypres salient. Close to the Front, but out of range of most German field artillery, Lijssenthoek was ideally sited for the establishment of Casualty Clearing Stations. The Cemetery was first used by the French whose 15th Hopital d'Evacuation was sited here in late May 1915, and by June 1915 it was being regularly used by Casualty Clearing Stations of the Commonwealth forces, comprising:

July 1915–April 1918–No. 10 CCS
August 1916–October 1918–No.2 CCS
April 1916–October 1918 No.3 CCS July 1915–April 1918–No. 17 CCS
Early 1918–No. 54 CCS
Last months 1918–No. 62 CCS

No. 10 Stationary Hospital was still operating here in November 1919.

In early September 1920, having been reduced to fifty beds, the hospital complex was dissolved and the remaining patients removed to Calais.

During the period July – November 1917 there were many air raids over the CCS hereabouts; on 17 August No. 17 suffered 6 RAMC, 8 other ranks, 9 German prisoners killed and 37 wounded.

From April to August 1918 the Casualty Clearing Stations situated here were forced to fall back; Allied Field Ambulance Units (including 1 French) taking their place during that period. The cemetery contains 9,893 Commonwealth burials of the First World War (a few were brought in from the battlefields after the Armistice) and 883 graves of other nationalities, mostly French and German; it is the second largest Commonwealth cemetery in Belgium.

The earliest dated burials in the cemetery are from the period of French occupation (28 are of indeterminate date, including the brothers Jean and Louis Garach); the earliest dated French grave being that of Jean Baptiste Jarland, who died 6 November 1914 (XXXI.C.24): German, Josef Nowack, 7 July 1915 (III.D.3), and of the Allied burials the earliest dated is Capt. William A.M. Temple, 21 October 1914, (XXXI.D.19). The 3 American burials here are the only ones remaining in the salient – all the others who fell hereabouts were either repatriated to the United States or removed to the In Flanders Fields American Cemetery, Wareghem.

Immediately after the Great War a host of ex-soldiers became caretaker/gardeners with the newly formed Imperial War Graves Commission; one of these was Walter Sutherland, a Medical Orderly with 3rd Canadian C.C.S. At the end of the war Walter Sutherland was tending the field hospital at Poperinghe, the site of which would become the second largest war graves cemetery in Belgium. Sutherland married his Belgian sweetheart, Marie Lermyte, a local girl whose family owned the Café Boonaert opposite Remy Sidings. The couple settled in the town and began a family; their son George and grandson Alex both followed in Walter's footsteps as gardeners at Lijssenthoek.

> "They brought the men here from the fighting front. Hundreds of horse-drawn carts loaded with the wounded and the dead, were brought here over the cobblestones. The blood was dripping out of the wounded – the wounded soldiers – and then they were brought into the hospital. That's where my father had the job of selection – some of them to be taken into the hospital – some of them to the mortuary. On one occasion my father took what he thought was a dead person into the mortuary and he heard a groan, he looked – the chap was still alive, and he took him out and into the hospital where they saved his life. ... My father wanted to forget, but he couldn't. Those who were still alive after the war, such as my father, thought they had a duty to perform and to take care of the graves."
>
> George Sutherland,
> Head Gardener, Lijssenthoek, 1999.

Requiescant
In lonely watches night by night
Great visions burst upon my sight,
For down the stretches of the sky
The hosts of dead go marching by,

Strange ghostly banners o'er them float,
Strange bugles sound an awful note,
And all their faces and their eyes
Are lit with starlight from the skies.

The anguish and the pain have passed
And peace hath come to them at last,
But in the stern looks linger still
The iron purpose and the will.

Dear Christ, who reign'st above the flood
Of human tears and human blood,
A weary road these men have trod,
Oh, house them in the home of God.

Canon F.G. Scott, C.E.F.
Near Ypres, May 1915.

(I.A.1) 2nd Lieut. Philip Brydges Gutterlz Henriques, 8th (Service) Bn. The King's Royal Rifle Corps: only *s.* and child of Sir Philip Gutterlz Henriques, of 33, Grosvenor Place, London, S.W., and Normandy Park, Guildford, co. Surrey, J.P., D.L., Deputy Director-General of Munitions, by his wife Lady Beatrice Henriques, eldest *dau.* of Sir George Faudel-Phillips, Bt., G.C.I.E.: *b.* Grosvenor Place, 10 November 1894: *educ.* Eton, and New College, Oxford; member of the O.T.C. at both. Spending a long vacation in France when war broke out, he immediately returned and applied for a commission: subsequently gazetted 2nd Lieut. King's Royal Rifle Corps, 26 August 1914: went to France May 1915, and died at Ypres, 24 July 1915, of wounds received in action at Hooge earlier in the day: Age 20. *unm.*

Who Dies If England Live

On 30 July 1915, 6th K.O.Y.L.I. were ordered to take up support positions south of Hooge, owing to a German attack preceded by gas made on 41st Inf. Bde. The German artillery, searching the approaches by which reinforcements might come to the units in the front line trenches, inflicted several casualties on the battalion: Sergt. 11127, R. Callan killed, Capt. A.C.F. Elborough and Lieut. C.E.H. Knapp-Fisher mortally wounded, 24 other ranks wounded.

(I.A.4) Lieut. Cyril Edward Holme Knapp-Fisher, 6th (Service) Bn. The King's Own (Yorkshire Light Infantry): *s.* of Edward Francis Knapp-Fisher, of 16, Northwick Terrace, London, by his wife Winifred: gazetted 2nd Lieut. 25 August 1914: proceeded to France, promoted Lieut., 21 May 1915. Died of wounds received at Hooge, 31 July 1915: Age 21. A stained glass memorial window bearing the K.O.Y.L.I. regimental crest and inscribed "In loving memory of Lieut. Cyril E.H. Knapp-Fisher, 6th Battalion K.O.Y.L.I., died of wounds 31 July 1915, Interred in Lijssenthoek Cemetery" was installed in St. George's Memorial Church, Ypres, 1927.

Every morn we met together on our journey up to town,
Guyed the Government and weather, ran all other nations down;
And whenever (very seldom), strangers' visages were seen,
With indignant looks we quelled 'em
On the 9.17.

But today there's none remaining to bestow the crushing glance.
Down in Surrey Smith is training, Brown is somewhere out in France;
Going through his martial paces, Jones is billeted at Sheen;
Strangers sieze the sacred places
On the 9.17.

(I.A.5) Lieut. John Hyland Fosdick, 7th (Service) Bn. The Prince Consort's Own (The Rifle Brigade): only *s.* of the late Frederick Hyland Fosdick, and his wife Alice Anne ('Cullenswood,' Eastbourne, co. Sussex): *b.* Sproughton, Ipswich, 2 March 1895: *educ.* Rev. W.G. Price's Bowden House, Harrow; Charterhouse (gained a place in both the cricket and football teams); Pembroke College, Cambridge (gained his Blue, Freshman; Association Football), member of the O.T.C.: On the outbreak of war, August 1914, he had just arrived in the Argentine with the Corinthians cricket team; immediately returned to England and, having held commission 2nd Lieut., in his University O.T.C., joined South Wales Borderers (2nd Lieut., 12 October 1914): subsequently transf'd 7th Rifle Brigade, promoted Lieut.: served with the Expeditionary Force in France from 19 May 1915. Severely wounded (head) by a shrapnel shell, 30 July 1915, in the trenches at Hooge, and died at Abeele, 1 August 1915. Buried at Poperinghe: Age 20. A brass plaque to his memory was erected in Sproughton Parish Church.

God Takes Our Loved Ones From Our Homes But Never From Our Hearts

(I.A.6) Capt. Alfred Charles Ernest Elborough, 6th (Service) Bn. The King's Own (Yorkshire Light Infantry): eldest *s.* of Alfred Louis Elborough, of 'Holmead', King's Road, Lancing, co. Sussex, by his wife Mary Ann, *née* Eames: *b.* 2, Shardeloes Road, London, 4 May 1878: *educ.* Blair Lodge School, Scotland, where he was Head Boy, and Captain of the school cricket and football teams: Occupation – Bank Clerk; Hong Kong & Shanghai Bank, having worked for them in London, Hong Kong and Siam: enlisted 28th Bn. County of London Regt. (Artists' Rifles), 31 August 1914: commissioned 2nd Lieut. (Temp.) 6th King's Own Yorkshire Light Infantry, 7 December; promoted Capt. same month. In less than four months he had progressed from city gentleman to an officer in command of men in war. Went to France with his regiment, May 1915, and served with the Expeditionary Force there. At 4.30 a.m., 30 July 1915, the battalion, encamped at Vlamertinghe, received orders to 'Stand to' owing to an attack on 41 Brigade at Hooge. At 1.00 p.m. the battalion left their bivouac, arriving at their destination at 3 p.m to act as support to a counter-attack by 42 Brigade. As the battalion approached their positions a shell landed at the head of the column, killing the C.O.'s second horse and Sergt. Callan, and wounding eleven men. Shortly thereafter, another shell pitched over the parapet of the

battalion's trench, there being no parados, wounding Capt. Elborough, 2nd
Lieut. Knapp-Fisher, and twelve men. Evacuated to No. 10 Casualty Clearing
Station with wounds in the chest and left leg, Capt. Elborough died later the
same day. Buried at Poperinghe. On 16 August 1915 a brass plaque was unveiled,
and a service held in memory of Capt. Elborough, at St. James the Less: Age 37.

In Loving Memory

Sergt. Callan is buried in Railway Chateau Cemetery, Elverdinghe (C.4).
(I.A.7) 2nd Lieut. Brian George Casson Simpson, 'T' Howitzer Bty., Royal
Horse Artillery: *s.* of the late George Hamilton Casson Simpson, by his marriage
to Lilian Thompson (Sydney, New South Wales, Australia): *educ.* Sydney
Church of England Grammar School. Died of peritonitis, 29 July 1915, ensuing
from wounds received one week previously, *viz.* 22 July 1915: Age 22. *unm.*

Vital Lambada Tradunt

(I.A.12) Lieut. (Temp.) William Reginald Pryn, Royal Army Medical Corps
attd. 9th Field Ambulance, and Wiltshire Regt.: late of 25, Idmiston Road, West
Norwood, London, S.E.: eldest *s.* of Deputy Surgeon-Gen. William Wenmoth
Pryn, Royal Navy, Royal Naval Hospital, Gibraltar, by his wife Isabella Kate
('Yeoland,' Yelverton, co. Devon): and *gdson.* of the late Major John Cotter, The
Buffs: *b.* Ascension Island, 28 September 1892: *educ.* Kelly College, Tavistock,
co. Devon, and Guy's Hospital, London (M.R.C.S., L.R.C.P.): on the outbreak
of war was House Surgeon, Royal Surrey County Hospital, Guildford, but
immediately offered his services to the War Office: gazetted Lieut. (Temp.) Royal
Army Medical Corps, August 1914: proceeded to France, 23 August; initially
served at No. 11 General Hospital, Rouen, and St. Nazaire: apptd. Medical
Officer attd. 1st Lincolnshire Regt., September 1914–terminated May 1915:
immediately thereafter attd. No.9 Field Ambulance. Lieut. Pryn died at No. 10
Casualty Clearing Station, 27 June 1915, of accidental burning suffered while
on temporary attachment to the Wiltshire Regt., who were in the firing line at
the time. Buried in a Military Cemetery, nr. Poperinghe, Belgium: Age 22. *unm.*

Eternal Life

(I.A.13) Capt. Ralph William Homan, 1st Bn. (3rd Foot) The Buffs (East Kent
Regt.): *s.* of Ralph (& Amy A.) Homan, of Hadley, Culverden Down, Tunbridge
Wells: *b.* Hadley: *educ.* Rugby School (1906–10); Royal Military College,
Sandhurst: gazetted 2nd Lieut. 1st The Buffs, October 1911; promoted Lieut.
February 1913; Temp. Capt. February 1915: served with the Expeditionary

Force in France and Flanders from 7 September 1914; wounded Radinghem, October following; repatriated to England: returned to France, May 1915, and died of wounds (shrapnel, head), 11 August 1915, received in action at Hooge the previous day: Age 23.

As Straight As A Die
As True As Steel

(I.A.14) Lieut. James 'Jim' Francis Marsland, M.C., 'C' Coy., 2nd Bn. (109th Foot) The Leinster Regt. (Prince of Wales's Royal Canadians): *s.* of James Marsland, of Marine View, Helensburgh, co. Dumbarton: and *husb.* to Mary (25, Main Street, Tipperary): served with the Expeditionary Force in France from September 1914, and died of wounds (multiple), 15 August 1915, received 13 August; Menin Road, between Birr Cross Roads and Hooge. Sergt. T. Flaherty, who was with him on patrol, said they were lying out in No Man's Land, and Lieut. Marsland had withdrawn the pin from a Mills bomb; he was then shot in the head and had released the bomb which then exploded and blew his hand off. Removed to 13th Field Ambulance, died No.10 C.C.S. Poperinghe: Age 39. 'To the end Marsland raved about a boxing match he had been refereeing a few nights previously in billets.' (*ODGW record 18 August*)

We Loved Him In Life Let Us Not Forget Him In Death

(I.A.23) Major Harold John Fotheringham Jeffries, Comdg. 'D' Coy., 1/5th Bn. The Leicestershire Regt. (T.F.): *s.* of Edwin Forbes Jeffries, Solicitor; of High Street, Market Harborough, co. Leicester, by his wife Mary Frances, *dau.* of John Joseph Williams, of H.M. Dockyard, Pembroke: *b.* Bedford Park, co. Middlesex, 30 December 1883: *educ.* St. Edward's School, Oxford; Wadham College, Oxford, member O.T.C.; graduated B.A. (1905): subsequently became a Solicitor in his father's practice: gazetted 2nd Lieut. 5th Leicestershire Regt. February 1905; promoted Lieut. June 1906; Capt. 20 May 1911; Major (posthumous), 28 September 1915: volunteered for Foreign Service on the outbreak of war, August 1914: served with the Expeditionary Force in France and Flanders from the last week of February 1915, and was killed whilst leaving trenches nr. Hooge, 26 September 1915; almost at the end of the Division's tour in the Salient. Buried in the Military Hospital Grounds at Lyssenthoek, nr. Poperinghe. Capt. J.D. Hills, M.C., said, "Capt. Jeffries was leading and, hit almost at once, fell mortally wounded never again regaining consciousness..." Col. Jones wrote, "Our loss is great. As well as being an excellent Company Commander and capable soldier, socially he was always merry, and cheered us on all occasions." And one of his subalterns, "It was a nasty shock, because I liked Jeffries. He was a topping chap. He hated the war, but never tried to get out of things, and he often went into considerable danger to be with the men, when he might very well have kept out of it as a Company Commander." While at Oxford he was secretary, then captain of his College boat team, stroked the Eight in the Torpids and Eights, was in his College Rugby Football team and played for the Leicester Tigers. Before the war Major Jeffries commanded 'E' Coy. of the Territorials: Age 32. *unm.*

For God King And Country
Grant Him Lord Eternal Rest

(I.A.24) Lieut. Edward Joseph Weld, 72nd Bty., Royal Field Artillery: *s.* of Joseph Edward Weld, of Riversdale, Ware, co. Hertford, and his spouse, Frances Gertrude Weld: *b.* Mitcham, co. Surrey. Died of wounds, 27 September 1915: Age 17. Remembered on East Lulworth War Memorial.

Let A Perpetual Light Shine Upon Him
May He Rest In Peace

(I.A.25) 2nd Lieut. Archibald Ure Buchanan, 3rd Bn. (Royal Aberdeenshire Militia) attd. 1st Bn. (75th Foot) The Gordon Highlanders: *s.* of Robert Buchanan, Commercial Traveller; of 'Clarinnis,' Orton, Acocks Green, co. Warwick, by his wife Elizabeth Dunlop, *dau.* of Alexander Gartshore, of Spring Villa, Waterside, Kirkintilloch: and *gdson.* to the late Archibald Buchanan, of Scotsblair, Kirkintilloch: *b.* Dundee, 3 December 1895: *educ.* King's Grammar School, Birmingham: joined Warwickshire Yeomanry, June 1914: volunteered after the outbreak of war; gazetted 2nd Lieut. 11th (Service) Bn. Gordon Highlanders, 3 April 1915: went to the Front, being there attd. 1st Battn., and died 27 September 1915, of wounds received in action at Hooge on the 25 September. Buried in Poperinghe Cemetery: Age 21. *unm.*

(I.A.28) Capt. Frank Adams Bagley, 2nd Bn. (82nd Foot) The Prince of Wales's Volunteers (South Lancashire Regt.): 2nd *s.* of Charles John Bagley, of Westwood, Hartburn, Stockton-on-Tees, J.P., Managing Director, South Durham Steel & Iron Co. Ltd., by his wife Alice Jane, *dau.* of John Holmes: *b.* Hartburn, 15 April 1882: *educ.* Clifton College: served through the South African War, 1901–02, employed with the Mounted Infantry: took part in operations in Transvaal, April 1901–31 May 1902: operations in Cape Colony and Orange River Colony, April–August 1901: Queen's Medal, five clasps: gazetted 2nd Lieut. South Lancashire Regt. from the Militia, 28 January 1903; promoted Lieut. 25 April 1906; Capt. 17 June 1914: went to France with his battalion, 13 August 1914: took part in the Retreat from Mons, the engagement at Le Cateau, where he performed a fine piece of work when his company got cut off, by managing to bring it back with two machine guns: the fighting at Solesmes: the Battles of the Marne and the Aisne, and was seriously wounded at La Bassée, October 1914: returned to the Front, June 1915: was again wounded, 31 July 1915, but rejoined his battalion, 20 August, and died in the Field Hospital at Poperinghe, 2 October following, from wounds received eight days previously in action at the Battle of Hooge, 25 September, while leading his company in an attack. Buried in the Military Cemetery at Lyssenthoek. His Col. wrote, 'He again showed himself a very gallant English gentleman, and I have to-day received paper from Col. Ashworth recommending him for a Military Cross for gallantry on the Aisne. This should have been done ages ago. I have myself to-day added a recommendation for the D.S.O., which Frank most thoroughly deserves.' Mentioned in Despatches by F.M. Sir John (now Lord) French (*London Gazette*, 1 January 1916) for 'gallant and distinguished service in the field.': 2 October 1915: Age 33. *unm.* Remembered on Middlesbrough War Memorial.

Be Thou Faithful Unto Death And I Will Give Thee A Crown Of Life

(I.A.30) 2nd Lieut. Allan Muir Scougall, 3rd Bn. The Worcestershire Regt.: formerly no.1178, Honourable Artillery Company (T.F.): *s.* of Thomas John Scougall, of 'Redlands,' Park Hill, Bromley, co. Kent, by his wife Elizabeth: *educ.* Malvern House School, Lewisham Park, London, S.E.: served with the Expeditionary Force in France and Flanders from December 1914, and died, 7 October 1915, of wounds: Age 19. 2nd Lieut. Scougall was commemorated on his school memorial; it was destroyed during a bombing raid in World War II.

In God Is Our Trust

(I.A.31) Rev. Charles Edmund Doudney, Army Chaplain 4th Class, Royal Army Chaplain's Dept., attd. 18th Infantry Bde., 6th Divn.: 3rd *s.* of the Rev. David Alfred Doudney, formerly of St James, Carlisle, and Ore Rectory, Hastings, co. Sussex, by his wife Georgina Fry, *grandau.* of Elizabeth Fry, the noted prison reformist: *b.* Carlisle, 13 March 1871: *educ.* Hastings Grammar School; and Corpus Christi College, Cambridge, where he graduated B.A. (1892), M.A. (1896). At Cambridge he showed a keen interest in shooting, and rowing, being captain of his college eight and rowing the Head of the River; member of the Cambridge University Volunteers (Militia) 1890–1894: ordained Deacon, 1894, becoming curate of St. John the Evangelists', Penge, South London, assisting the Rev. W. Smyly: ordained Priest by the Bishop of Rochester, 1895: served as incumbent of Ororoo Mission, South Australia, 1896 becoming Rector of

St. Augustine's, Port Augusta, 1898: became Chaplain to the Commonwealth Troops, South Australia, 1901: Acting Curate for Christchurch, North Adelaide, 1902–04, and Rector, St. George's, Gawler, 1904: returned to England 1906: was for a short time at West Hampstead Church, before becoming Vicar of St. Luke's, South Lyncombe, Bath, May 1907: volunteered and enlisted as Army Chaplain 4th Class: went to France, April 1915; served with the Expeditionary Force there and in Flanders: returned to England, 12 July 1915, for treatment of eczema and, after two weeks, returned to the Front. Due to depart on leave, 14 October 1915, he was called upon on the evening of the 13 October to perform the burial of eight men in the front line trenches; with his leave papers in his pocket, he set out, remarking to his fellow chaplain, "Remember, whatever happens tonight is best." The following account, from *Keenes Bath Journal*, 6 November 1915, written by the Officer Commanding 18th Field Ambulance, describes what happened next, "It was just before 9 p.m. on 13th October that he turned in at our billet and asked me to take him up to one of our regimental aid posts to bury a soldier. He was in his usual cheery mood and I was delighted to have him for the sake of good company. There had been a heavy bombardment to the south and a few shells were passing over and around our village. He got on the front of the car with me, and said that he would like to sit on the left side. He was accustomed to sit in the middle between me and the driver, but after a few minutes he said that he would sit on the floor with his feet on the left step, obviously to give me more room, kindly soul that he was, and so we went on with him leaning against my knees. He talked to me about wireless telegraphy and X-ray apparatus that he had repaired or worked at the base, and about work which he said was divine. I wondered, indeed, what he thought his own work was. A few shells dropped some distance away, but otherwise things were quiet. Just after we had got into the ruined town (Ypres) which you know; and as he was turning round to talk to me, a shell burst to the right and in front of us. Immediately I asked if anybody was hit, and both he and the driver said 'No' and I told them to get off and take cover. I found all three in the front of the second car, 15 yards behind were wounded. On getting into the cellar of the nearest house Mr Doudney said he was bruised in the right side, and the driver, who had been sitting on my right was obviously wounded in the thigh. I first examined Mr Doudney, although he strongly protested saying I should examine the driver first, and found a small wound, but to my grief I could see that it was serious. Incessant shelling continued in our immediate vicinity and he begged me to go on and call for him on our way back. He asked me this time and time again, but two of our cars were out of action and I could not make him believe that in any case we were better where we were. Corpl. Wilkinson and Pte. Spedding got a stretcher for him and gave him morphia, of which he had a supply in his pocket. He was very comfortable, and I believe almost happy, or he would have been if he could have persuaded me to get away the men. At last things quietened, and I got him into a car which had come up. The last words that I heard him say to his driver, Ganley, who that night drove on the road three times under shell fire, 'Go as hard as you like driver, don't mind me.' At my request he was sent on immediately from our dressing station to the clearing station behind, whilst I went on my way to the aid posts." Taken to No.10 Casualty Clearing Station, Lyssenthoek, he was attended to by the Surgeon General; the 18th Field Ambulance officer continues – "…but it was of no avail and with him I know there left us the bravest and kindest of gentlemen, a good, self-sacrificing Padre, a true friend, and the most open and honest man it has ever been my lot to meet. He was borne to the grave only a few hundred yards from the field where I first saw his serious yet smiling face, by those stretcher-bearers who had carried him wounded to the ambulance and he was buried with a beautiful sun breaking through the Flanders mist and our heavy guns booming in the distance, and only a stone's throw away from that railway which, as he told me after he was wounded, should have carried him home the following day…." Canon F.B. MacNutt, C.F., ministered to him in his last hours and wrote, "We did so hope that he would pull through, and everything that skill could do was done. When it became apparent that he was passing, the Archdeacon (Southwell of Lewis), the sister (Thorold) and I knelt down and commended his spirit to God (9 p.m Saturday, 16 October 1915), and gave thanks for his life and ministry, and especially for his splendid service over here. The end came very quietly and peacefully, and as he was passing we repeated the words, 'Blessed are the dead that die in the Lord, from henceforth, yea, saith the Spirit, they rest from their labours, and their works do follow them.' There in the marquee, in the dim lamp-light, he passed into perfect peace to receive his Master's 'Well done, good and faithful servant, enter thou into the joy of thy Lord', the other side. I could hear the guns roaring in the distance and tried to picture the peace into which he had gone out of this scene here of pain and death. During Sunday his body lay in a coffin in the mortuary tent covered with the Union Jack, and in the evening Capt. G.E.L. Poulden, R.E. (Rev. Doudney's brother-in-law), who had hurried up on receiving a wire from London telling him that the Vicar was dangerously wounded, but only arrived in time for the funeral…On Monday we met there with some of the officers of his Division, the Major commanding his Ambulance, and the doctor officers from it, a bearer party of the men who had carried him when wounded from the house where they sheltered to the ambulance car, the Senior Chaplain of the 6th Division (Talbot), five or six of his fellow chaplains, and some of the officers of the Casualty Clearing Hospital. We had the full funeral service, at the request of Capt. Poulden. The senior chaplain took the opening sentences and read the lesson, and the Archdeacon, as chaplain of the hospital, took the committal. It was a beautiful autumn morning and all was peace except the roaring of the guns and we spoke all afternoon of what he had done and been here to so many men. ... Count him not dead, nor quenched the fiery spark of the Spirit which thus with duty kept its tryst. The swift shell struck – the pang – the mist – the dark! And then the Face of Christ!": Age 44. Whilst in Australia Rev. Doudney continued his interest in shooting as a member of the Adelaide Rifle Club, returning to England on one occasion to represent Australia at Bisley, where he took a number of prizes. He was also a member of the Interstate Team, and, as All Australia Champion, won the King's Aggregate in 1904; he was also renowned as a kangaroo hunter. Interested in yachting and rowing, for a number of years he coached the Adelaide University eight. He *m*. St. Augustine's, Port Augusta, South Australia, 16 June 1899; Joanna 'Zoe' Clara Schroeder Poulden ('Domremy', Old Headington, Oxford), *dau*. of Capt. Edward Poulden, R.N., of Blackheath, London, by his wife Katherine Gawler, *yst. dau*. of Lieut.Col. George Gawler (Second Governor of South Australia, 1838–41), by his wife Maria Cox (of Derby), and had four *daus*. – Esther Eirene 'Essie', *b*. 13 June 1900; Noelle Mary, *b*. 26 December 1904 (*d*. March 1907); Joy Poulden, *b*. 4 July 1908; Desiree Gawler, *b*. 5 November 1913. Had he not died it is highly likely Rev. Doudney would have been seconded by his superior – Senior Chaplain, Neville Talbot – to take over the day to day running of Talbot House, Poperinghe.

In Christo Et In Pace

(I.B.11A) Pte. 10813, John Bunting, 'H' Coy., 2nd Bn. (95th Foot) The Sherwood Foresters (Notts & Derbys Regt.): *s*. of John (& Ruth) Bunting: *b*. Bonsall, Matlock, co. Derby: enlisted Nottingham. Died 13 October 1915, of wounds (shell) received in action the previous evening while engaged in trench repair and improvement at Brielen: Age 25. He was married to Florence Mary Bradley, *née* Bunting (1, Ash Yard, Sherwood Street, Nottingham). See also Pte. W. Flint (I.B.21A).

(I.B.14A) L/Corpl. 12231, George Alderson, A.M., 10th (Service) Bn. The Durham Light Infantry: late *husb*. to Ethel Alderson (10, Stephenson St., Dunston-on-Tyne, Co. Durham): enlisted Gateshead, co. Durham: served with the Expeditionary Force, and died of wounds, 15 October 1915. Awarded the Albert Medal (posthumously): *London Gazette*, 19 May 1916, cites: "On the evening of 14 October 1915, Alderson, with two other non-commissioned officers, was moving some bombs into a room in a farmhouse where they were to be stored. While the bombs were being stacked, one of them fell to the floor and the percussion cap was fired. Alderson, knowing that the bomb would explode in four seconds, and that to throw it out of the window would endanger the men who were outside, picked it up and tried to reach the door. Before he could get out of the door the bomb exploded, blowing off his hand and inflicting other serious wounds, from which he shortly died. By his prompt action in picking up and carrying the bomb he probably saved the lives of the three men who were in the room with him, and by his presence of mind in not throwing it out of the window he probably saved the lives of those standing outside. This act was the more meritorious as Alderson was fully aware of the deadly nature of the bomb and the danger to himself that his act involved.": Age 31.

A Silent Thought, A Secret Tear, Keeps His Memory Ever Dear

At 7 p.m., 14 August 1915, 1/4th Duke of Wellington's (West Riding) Regt. relieved 5th West Yorkshire Regt. in trenches in the left Canal Bank sector, at Boesinghe; the Battalion War Diary records the relief was carried out without incident, and the following day (15th): "Quiet day. The Sector is somewhat improved since the battn. was here before. The communication trenches have been gridded. More dugouts built and Hd Qtrs improved." The 16th began quietly but: "About 1.30 p.m. the enemy commenced an artillery bombardment which was continued, at times with great intensity, until 6p.m. It was directed mainly on the dugouts in rear of our front line, on communication trenches and on second line. The Battn. stood to arms on the parapet. About 4 p.m. several of the enemy came forward and tried to cut their wire opposite E29. This party was fired on and some of the enemy dropped – three attempts were made by the enemy to enter the sap in E29. These parties consisted of about 12 men each and were bombed by our bombers and fired on by our men and machine guns – a party attempted to come down the hedge side to E29, but were also seen and fired on – the bombardment gradually fell away and at about 6 p.m. had subsided. The enemy fired a number of incendiary shells containing phosphorous – much damage was done to the parapets, dugouts and headquarters..." During the course of this action 1/4th Bn. suffered casualties of 1 officer and 13 other ranks killed, 23 wounded.

(I.B.21) Pte. 2607, Arthur Clee, 1/4th Bn. The Duke of Wellington's (West Riding) Regt. (T.F.): enlisted Halifax, 1 October 1914: proceeded to France, 18 August 1915: joined 4th Battn. In the Field, 9 October, and died of wounds, 17 October 1915, received in action the previous day (16 October); Canal Bank sector, Ypres: Age 34. He *m.* Halifax Parish Church, 18 December 1902; Amy, *née* Green, and leaves four children – Rose, Percy, William, Arthur. *(War Diary records Glee)*

(I.B.21A) Pte. 21412, Walter Flint, 2nd Bn. (95th Foot) The Sherwood Foresters (Notts & Derbys Regt.): *b.* Glossop, *c.*1890: Occupation – Calico Worker; Birch Vale: enlisted Buxton, co. Derby, January 1915: served with the Expeditionary Force in France from August following, and died, 18 October

1915, of wounds (shell) received while engaged in trench improvement and repair at Brielen six days previously (12 October): Age 25. He was married to Annie Longden, *née* Flint, *née* Meakin (16, Emily Street, Marple, Stockport), and left three children. See also Pte. W. Harrison, Ypres (Menin Gate) Memorial (Panel 41), and Pte. J. Taylorson, Potijze Burial Ground Cemetery (DI.10).

For the soldiers on both sides of the Western Front each day was heralded by the 'early morning hate' – an intense bombardment of one another's trenches, designed to negate any possibility of a surprise dawn attack. In August 1915, 6th Bn. Somerset Light Infantry were in the trenches at Hooge; L/Sergt. H.A. Foley wrote, "August 4th was no exception to the rule of early-morning hate. How we dreaded those cold, grey dawns, and waited with eyes almost hypnotically strained to the west to catch the first twinkle of the guns as they spat out in their fearful unison of sound. As the light slowly grew, we would feel just a glimmering of hope that perhaps this morning they would rest and let the day dawn in peace. And then those dreaded flashes, and in a moment hell would be loosened all round us. This morning, in the full blaze of the strafe, as seven of us sat crouched in the little shelter under the parados of our fire-bay, a high explosive shell pitched just in front of the parapet, blowing it to fragments. The air was filled with smoke and debris, and we had the sensation of experiencing a dozen concentrated earthquakes. Our doorway, luckily, was not blocked and we scrambled out, in spite of the entreaties of James, a miner from Wales, to "Hold the roof, for God's sake, hold the roof!" We squirmed out, over the tumbled ruins of our parapet, round into the neighbouring bay, and there awaited the next instalment. It came, but not so close; and gradually the bombardment slackened. It rained a good deal during the day, and, deprived of our home, we spent a pretty cheerless time. That night, however, sandbags were procured, we got to work with a will, and before dawn had erected a 'brand new Phoenix from the blaze,' in the shape of a new and greatly improved parapet. I was so tired next day that I slept through most of it, and at 11 p.m. that night (August 5th) a battalion of the 6th Division relieved us. To them had been given the job of retaking the lost trenches. They came in wearing "fighting order," and seemed in wonderful spirits. On our way out we lost Tincknell, a Bridgwater man, who was hit in the stomach by a stray bullet and died very soon afterwards."

(I.C.4) Pte. 10902, William Henry Tincknell, 'C' Coy., 6th (Service) Bn. The Prince Albert's (Somerset Light Infantry): *s.* of Charles Tincknell, of 102, Bristol Road, Bridgwater, co. Somerset, by his wife Bessie: *b.* Bridgwater: enlisted Taunton. Died of wounds, 9 August 1915, received in action four days previously. Dedicated – "In honour of the men of Bridgwater who gave their lives in The Great War, 1914–1918;" Pte. Tincknell is one among 364 men remembered on the Bridgwater War Memorial. It was unveiled by the Earl of Cavan, 25 September 1924.

Rest In Peace

(I.C.17A) Pte. 2122, Arthur George Flint, 1/7th (Robin Hood) Bn. The Sherwood Foresters (Notts & Derbys Regt.), (T.F): *s.* of the late George Flint, by his wife Annie (15, Medway Street, Old Radford, Nottingham): *b.* Old Radford: enlisted Nottingham: served with the Expeditionary Force in France and Flanders from 25 February 1915, and died of wounds, 4 August 1915: Age 18.

The Supreme Sacrifice
Duty Nobly Done

(I.C.28) Pte. 3366, Walter Adkin, 'C' Coy., 1/6th Bn. The Sherwood Foresters (Notts & Derbys Regt.), (T.F.): brother to Pte. 2040, J. Adkin, 6th Sherwood Foresters, killed in action, 14 October 1915: *b.* Staveley, co. Derby: employee Markham No.1 Pit; Staveley Iron & Coal Co.: enlisted October 1914: served with the Expeditionary Force in France and Flanders from 25 February 1915, and died of wounds, 1 October following, received in action 6.35 p.m. the previous evening (30 September) following the detonation of a German mine beneath his Company's position at The Bluff, nr. Hill 60. A comrade, Pte. G. Bytheway, wrote, "No doubt you will be surprised to hear from me but it is concerning your son Walter, my greatest friend. I am sorry to say that during a recent bombardment he was wounded in the head, but heedless of that he would go on, but alas he got another wound in the abdomen, and I am afraid you must be prepared for the worst for, as I left him at the dressing station, the doctor did not give much hope for his recovery. But, up to the time of writing, he was alive for all we could learn. He was always a keen trench worker, never shirked his duty, and whenever he took his post as sentry you could rely that no Hun would cross while Walter was there. If the worse should happen you will know he died like a hero for his country's cause." Dedicated – 'In grateful remembrance of the men...who fell in the war of 1914–1919' – the brothers are commemorated on Staveley Parish War Memorial. See account re. Pte. T. D'Arcy, Chester Farm Cemetery (I.B.2).

His brother Joseph has no known grave; he is commemorated on the Loos (Dud Corner) Memorial.

(I.C.28A) Pte. S/6836, Charles Butcher, 4th Bn. (77th Foot) The Duke of Cambridge's Own (Middlesex Regt.): *s.* of the late James Butcher, by his wife Jane (1, Balloon Yard, Blackfriars Street, Stamford, co. Lincoln): *b.* Stamford, 29 November 1894: *educ.* St. Martin's Boys' School, Stamford: enlisted Ponders End, co. Middlesex, January 1913: served with the Expeditionary Force in France from 11 November 1914, and died, 1 October 1915, of wounds received in action: Age 20. *unm.*

For King And Country
God Be With You Till We Meet Again
Love From Mother

(I.C.37A) Sergt. 2050, Thomas Edward Sedgwick, 1/4th Bn. The York & Lancaster Regt.: *s*. of William Henry Sedgwick, of 165, Eyre Street, Sheffield, by his wife Fanny, *dau*. of George West: and brother to Pte. 2215, J.H. Sedgwick, York & Lancaster Regt., who fell at St. Julien 28 July 1915: *b*. Sheffield, 24 July 1892: *educ*. St. Paul's School: Occupation – Jobbing Grinder; Mr Wood, Smith's Wheel, Sheffield: joined York & Lancaster Regt. 8 August 1914: served with the Expeditionary Force in France and Flanders from 13 April 1915, and died at the Casualty Clearing Station, Remy Siding, 5 October 1915, of wounds received in action at Marengo Farm the previous day. Buried at Poperinghe: Age 25. *unm*.

Beloved By All
Memory Clings

His brother John lies in Talana Farm Cemetery (II.E.6).

(I.D.5A) Sergt. 3484, Thomas Henry Webster, 10th Bn. (Scottish) The King's (Liverpool) Regt. (T.F.): late of Hoylake, co. Chester: *s*. of Henry Webster, by his wife Mary: *b*. Edge Hill, Liverpool: served with the Expeditionary Force in France and Flanders from 23 January 1915, and died of wounds, 1 August following: Age 26. A keen athlete, he was a member of Sefton Harriers Club.

Not Forgotten

(I.D.9A) Pte. 3/5442, Ernest Holloway, 6th (Service) Bn. The Duke of Cornwall's Light Infantry: *b*. Bermondsey: a pre-war member of the Reserve reported Lewisham, London, S.E., on mobilisation, August 1914; posted 3rd (Special Reserve) Battn., and proceeded to France with a draft of reinforcements to 1st Battn., 3–4 December following: subsequently posted 6th Battn. with which unit he was serving when he was severely wounded in the counter-attack to retake some lost trenches at Hooge on the afternoon of 31 July 1915. He died the following day (1 August).

(I.D.16A) Pte. 3566, Bernard Herbert Boseley, 1/7th (Robin Hood) Bn. The Sherwood Foresters (Notts & Derbys Regt.), (T.F.): *s*. of Henry Boseley, of 31, St. Paul Street, Old Radford, Nottingham, by his wife Euphemia: enlisted Nottingham: served with the Expeditionary Force in France and Flanders from 25 February 1915, and died of wounds, 1 August following: Age 16. Remembered on Radford (St. Peter's) Church War Memorial (Panel 2).

*Though I Walked Through The Valley Of Death My Lord
My God Was With Me*

(I.D.19A) Pte. 14853, Henry Thomas Cooper, 10th (Service) Bn. The Sherwood Foresters (Notts & Derbys Regt.): *s*. of Edward Thomas Cooper, of 15A, Hamilton Place, St. Paul's Road, Cheltenham, formerly of 25, Albert Place, by his wife Catherine: *b*. Cheltenham, 1893: *educ*. there: enlisted Sherwood Foresters, Derby: served with the Expeditionary Force in France and Flanders from July 1915, and died of wounds, 25 September following, received in action at Hooge. Pte. Cooper is remembered on St. Paul's Church War Memorial, Cheltenham; Salem Baptist Church Roll of Honour, and Cheltenham War Memorial: Age 22. *unm*.

(II.A.2) 2nd Lieut. William Jamieson McConnochie, 5th Sqdn. Royal Flying Corps: *s*. of Thomas McConnochie, of Ayr: prior to the outbreak of war was an Engineer: obtained his Flying Certificate, Hall School, Hendon, 16 March 1915. Killed in action, 8 November 1915: Age 28. On the day of his death 2nd Lieut. McConnochie was flying a BE2c (No.1728) on artillery observation patrol with 2nd Lieut. G.F. Harvey as observer. Shortly after taking off (12.10 p.m.) there occurred an explosion at an altitude of approximately 1,000 ft. The aircraft burst into flames, broke up and crashed to earth near Abeele: Age 28. (*IWGC record 8 October*)

(II.A.3) Lieut. Gerald Franklin Harvey, Royal Flying Corps and Royal Field Artillery: *s*. of the late Charles Harvey, of London: ward of Mrs Hancock (Bampton, co. Oxon, and 12, St. James' Square, Bath): *b*. London, 4 March 1893: *educ*. Lancing College, Shoreham: joined R.F.A., Special Reserve, January 1912: gazetted 2nd Lieut. Royal Field Artillery, 10 December 1913; promoted Lieut. June 1915: posted 21st Bty., R.F.A., 2nd Bde., on the outbreak of war, and proceeded to France as part of VIth Divn., reaching the Aisne, 13 September 1914: took part in the fighting around Armentieres, Ypres and Hooge but, in October 1915, when stationed at Abeele, near Poperinghe, was attached to Royal Flying Corps as Observing Officer, and was killed there 8 November following, by the falling of his aeroplane while returning from observation duty. Buried the next day in the cemetery at No.10 Casualty Clearing Station, on the Poperinghe – Boeschepe road. His Major wrote, "I cannot tell you how much I missed him in the Battery when he left me to join the Flying Corps. There is no one who can be trusted to carry out a difficult piece of work quite like him, and many excellent things he has done deserved the highest recognition but honours and rewards have frequently the unfortunate habit of missing the proper mark," and another officer, "He was such a fine upright, straight fellow – we all loved him.": Age 22. *unm*.

He That Dwelleth In Love Dwelleth In God And God In Him
John IV.16

(II.A.6) Capt. James Pitcairn Blane, 8th (Service) Bn. The King's Royal Rifle Corps: *s.* of the late Capt. Rodney Blane, Comdr., R.N.; of 44, Montpelier Street, Kensington, London, by his wife Mary Georgina: and elder brother to Capt. H.S. Blane, 19th Lancers (Fane's Horse), died of wounds, 31 October 1914: *b.* Norwich: proceeded to France, 19 May 1915; wounded at Hooge, 30 July following. Died of wounds 12.35 a.m. 23 November 1915, received in action (trench B16) north-east of Ypres, 5 p.m., 19 November, from the close explosion of a whizz-bang: Age 31. A member of Middlesex Cricket Club, he is remembered on Lord's Cricket Ground MCC Members War Memorial.

God Is Love

His brother Hugh is buried in Nieuwkerke (Neuve Eglise) Churchyard (I.1).

(II.A.7) Major the Hon. Sir Schomberg Kerr McDonnell, G.C.V.O., K.C.B., 5th (Service) Bn. The Queen's Own (Cameron Highlanders): 5th *s.* of Capt. Mark McDonnell, 5th Earl of Antrim, of Glenarm, Co. Antrim, by his wife Jane Emma Hannah, *dau.* of Major Turner Macan, and Harriet Sneyd, his wife: and *gdson.* to the late Vice-Admiral Lord Mark Robert Kerr: *b.* 22 March 1861: *educ.* Eton and Oxford University: was Principal Private Secretary to Lord Salisbury (Prime Minister), 1888–1902: gained his Captaincy with 1st London Rifle Volunteers, and Major, 5th Cameron Highlanders: served in the South African Campaign, 1900: Secretary to Commissioner of Works, 1902–12, and Chief Intelligence Officer, London District, 1914–1915: served with the Expeditionary Force in France, and died of wounds, 23 November 1915, received in action in the trenches at Ypres: Age 54. A Fellow of the Royal Society of Antiquities; he was married (1913) to Ethel Davis, *dau.* of Major Alexander Davis, of Naples.

Passed From Death Unto Life

(II.A.8) Capt. Philip Henry Milward, 7th (Service) Bn. The Prince Consort's Own (The Rifle Brigade): 4th *s.* of John F. Milward, of Southmead, Redditch, co. Worcseter: *b.* Southmead, 12 February 1873: *educ.* Uppingham School: sometime served with 2nd (Vol.) Bn. Worcestershire Regt.: in Natal at the outbreak of the South African War against the Boers, joined Durban Light infantry, under Sir Redvers Buller: took part in the Relief of Ladysmith and subsequent advance into the Transvaal: given a commission 2nd Lieut. 4th King's Own (Royal Lancaster Regt.) 1901; served with it until the end of the South African Campaign, 1902, when he resigned his commission: (Queen's

Medal, 3 clasps): engaged in business in Colombo at the outbreak of the European War, campaigned to raise a contingent of recruits from Ceylon for the New Army: enlisted 7th Rifle Brigade, gazetted Capt. (on strength of previous service) December 1914: proceeded to France, 19 May 1915; wounded during the heavy fighting at Hooge, 29–30 July following; rejoined his battalion after rapid recovery, and was again wounded, December following and died in No.10 C.C.S., Poperinghe, 7 December. 1915: Age 42.

(II.A.12) 2nd Lieut. Bertram Humphrey Collis, 3rd attd. 9th (Service) Bn. The Suffolk Regt.: *yr. s.* of William Robert Collis, of Heath Lodge, Nacton Road, Ipswich, by his wife Laura Lavinia, *dau.* of the late William Cooke, of Bury St. Edmunds: *b.* Ipswich, co. Suffolk, 28 November 1896: *educ.* Ipswich Grammar School, where he was a member of the O.T.C., and was studying to qualify as an optician when war broke out: joined Suffolk Yeomanry, 1 September 1914, obtaining a commission 2nd Lieut. 3rd Suffolk Regt. (Special Reserve) 17 February 1915: went to France, 30 September following: wounded in the thigh 19 December but, after having the wound dressed, returned to his platoon, and very shortly afterwards was again wounded by the bursting of a shell, and died at No. 10 Casualty Clearing Station, 20 Decmber following. Buried in Lyssenthoek Cemetery, 1½ miles from Poperinghe. His Colonel wrote, 'He was a promising officer, capable, popular, keen, and an excellent instructor. You will, I hope, find comfort in the thought that his life was not wasted; it was given in a good cause, and the good he did in the regiment still remains, and will remain.': Age 19.

Greater Love Hath No Man Than This

(II.A.13) 2nd Lieut. Frederic William Oswald Fleming, 4th Bn. The Duke of Wellington's (West Riding) Regt. (T.F.): *s.* of Frederick William Fleming, of Fern Dene, Halifax, co. York, by his wife Emily Blanche. Died of wounds (gas), 20 December 1915: Age 19.

In Loving Remembrance

(II.A.14) Lieut. Charles James Williams, 8th (Service) Bn. The Bedfordshire Regt.: late of 16, St. George's Road, Bedford: *s.* of Henry Clissold Williams, I.C.S., of 16, The Beacon, Exmouth, co. Devon; formerly of Ashridge, North Tawton, by his wife Mary: and brother to Lieut. R.L. Williams, 23rd Indian Cavalry (F.F.), killed in action, 27 October 1918, in Mesopotamia: *b.* North Tawton, 21 April 1887: *educ.* Oakhampton; Charterhouse, where he was a member of the O.T.C., graduated B.A., B.C.L. (Cantab.): a Solicitor prior to the outbreak of war, joined Inns of Court O.T.C. 5 August 1914: gazetted 2nd Lieut. 8th Bedfordshire Regt. 18 September following: proceeded to France with the battalion late August 1915, and died of wounds, 19 December following, on which date the enemy subjected the battalion's trenches (in the vicinity of Forward Cottage) to a series of gas attacks (phosgene) and heavy shellfire: Age 28. *unm*. Remembered on the North Tawton War Memorial; St. Martin's Church (Bedford) Roll of Honour; Lieut. Williams is also recorded in the TocH book of remembrance '*Liber Vitae.*'

The Souls Of The Righteous Are Into The Hands Of God
R.I.P.

His brother Robert has no known grave; he is commemorated on the Basra Memorial.

(II.A.15) 2nd Lieut. John Armitage Hartley, 4th Bn. The Duke of Wellington's (West Riding) Regt. (T.F.): late of Reigate, co. Surrey, formerly resident with grandmother (3, Parkside, Halifax, co. York): father was former Commanding Officer, Halifax Territorial Force: *educ*. Hunstanton, and Oundle, co. Cambridge: employee in his father's business Hartley & Sugden: served with the Territorials in which force, on the outbreak of war, he held the rank of Sergt.: volunteered for Foreign Service, Halifax, August 1914: received his commission 1915: joined 4th Battn. In the Field 17 June 1915; gassed in Ypres salient, and died in the hospital Poperinghe, 19 December 1915: Age 21.

'Phosgene, a derivative of chlorine, had eighteen times its power and could not be seen. Its insidiousness was that, even when inhaled in fatal doses, it was not always immediately irritating, just smelling faintly of mouldy hay and producing a slight sensation of suffocation. Then would come shallow breathing and retching, pulse up to 120, an ashen face and the discharge of four pints of yellow fluid from the lungs each hour for the 48-hour drowning spasm..." – Dennis Winter

(II.A.18) Lieut. Clarence Grosvenor Ridout, 9th (Reserve) attd. 1st Bn. (53rd Foot) The King's (Shropshire Light Infantry): *s*. of John Ridout, by his wife Ellen: late *husb*. to Elfreda Marie Ridout ('Clovelly,' The Hyde, Hendon, London, N.W.4): served with the Expeditionary Force in France from 7 December 1915; died of gas poisoning on the 22 December, received at La Brique on the 19 December. Age 30.

Trusting This May Find You Where Ere Thou Art In God's Great Universe

(II.A.20) 2nd Lieut. Cyril Shaw Shippey, 3rd (Reserve) attd. 8th (Service) Bn. The Bedfordshire Regt.: formerly Pte., Royal Army Medical Corps: *s*. of Frederic Shippey, of Pietermaritzburg, Natal, South Africa: and brother to 2nd Lieut. J.R. Shippey, 4th attd. 8th Bedfordshire Regt., died 14 October 1914, of wounds: served with the Expeditionary Force in France and Flanders; joined 8th Bn., Vlamertinghe, 8 October 1915, posted 'A' Coy., and died of wounds, 21 December 1915, received in action two days previously (19 December) on which date the enemy subjected the battalion's trenches (in the vicinity of Forward Cottage) to a series of gas attacks (phosgene) and heavy shellfire.

His brother is buried in Bethune Town Cemetery (I.D.27).

(II.A.26) Lieut. John Burrows Whitfield, 104th Field Coy., Royal Engineers: *yst. s.* of Thomas Whitfield, of 56A, Cambridge Road, Southport, co. Lancaster, by his wife Frances: and yr. brother to Lieut. R.H. Whitfield, 104th Field Coy., Royal Engineers, who fell four months later: *b.* Stoke Manor, co. Salop: served with the Expeditionary Force in France from 1 September 1915, and died of wounds, 20 January 1916: Age 26. *unm.* Erected by their widowed mother the brothers are commemorated by a stained-glass memorial window, depicting St. Michael and St. Gabriel, in St. Luke's Church, Hodnet, Staffordshire.

More Than Conquerors Through Him Who Loved Us

His brother Richard is buried in Maple Leaf Cemetery, Le Romarin (I.13).

On the night of 18–19 January 1916, Brigadier General H.G. Fitton, in company with Brigadier General Nicholson and, his Brigade Major (Captain B. Tower), was on a visit of instruction to 16th Infantry Brigade in the front line near Ypres. Owing to a portion of the communication trench having been blown in the party were forced to make their way across some open ground, whereupon they were spotted by an enemy sniper "…who got the General through both thighs…" His two companions "…were the only others present and had a difficult job in getting the wounded General, who was a big man, down the trench, though some stretcher-bearers of the K.S.L.I. came to their help. It was truly hard luck to be knocked over in this inglorious manner, before the troops he had trained so well had even got into the line." *The History of the 34th Division.*

(II.A.27) Brigadier General Hugh Gregory Fitton, A.D.C. to H.M. King, C.B., D.S.O., Comdg. 101st Infantry Bde., 34th Divn., late Princess Charlotte of Wales's (Royal Berkshire Regt.): *yr. s.* of the late Edward Brown Fitton, of Malvern, Barrister and H.M. Inspector of Factories, by his wife Harriet Margaret ('Fairlea, Graham Road, Malvern), *dau.* of George Gregory, of London, M.D.: *b.* London, 15 November 1863: *educ.* Eton (elected King's Scholar, 1877–1885); passed First on the list into Royal Military College, Sandhurst: gazetted 2nd Lieut. Berkshire Regt. 5 February 1884: served with Egyptian Army, 1894–1899: took part in the Sudan Campaign (Medal with clasp; Bronze Star): became D.A.A.G. Infantry Division: took part in the Expedition to Dongola, 1886, and was wounded (D.S.O. & Egyptian Medal, two clasps): served as Staff Officer to

G.O.C., Nile Expedition, 1897, and was present at the operations at Berber and the Atjabara River (Mentioned in Despatches; awarded the Fourth Class of the Medjidich, and clasp to the Egyptian Medal): as D.A.A.G., took part in the Battle of Khartoum (Mentioned in Despatches; Brevet of Major; Medal; two clasps to Egyptian Medal): served in the South African War, 1899–1902, (Queen's Medal, three clasps; King's Medal, two clasps). In 1905 he was given command of the Royal West Kent Regt.: was an A.D.C. to the King from 1907, being awarded the C.B., 1911: apptd. Asst. Adjt.-General, Eastern Command, 1910: became Director of Recruiting & Organization, War Office (1913); thereafter apptd. to a brigade on the North Coast: served with the Expeditionary Force in France and Flanders from 7 January 1916. Wounded nr. Ypres, 18 January 1916, by a sniper and died, without regaining consciousness, 1.20 p.m., two days later, in No.10 Casualty Clearing Station. Buried south of Poperinghe: Age 52. The news of his death reached his brigade as they were being inspected by General Haig and General Joffre. Letters of condolence from Lord Kitchener, Earl Beauchamp and many others were received. An officer wrote, Nothing was too much trouble to him as long as his men were thoroughly trained, and he had their love and respect;" another wrote, "his habit, which endeared him to all, of doing himself everything that the men were asked to do." The *Eton College Chronicle* said of him, "The country has sustained a heavy loss in the death of this distinguished soldier. With his long and exceptionally varied experience – on the staff, in regimental work, in action, in administration at the War Office…he would in all probability have risen to one of the highest commands in the field…No one who ever met him could forget his gigantic figure and the piquant contrast of his gentle voice, nor could fail to carry off the impression of a reserve of quiet strength. To his great ability our leading Generals have borne witness; about his own powers he was the most modest of men. As a friend he was incomparable – chivalrous, loyal and lovable: *multis ille bonis flebilis occidit*." He *m*. Kensington, London, W., 5 October 1910; May ('Island,' Petersfield, co. Hants), 6th *dau*. of Sir Alfred Hickman, Bart., M.P., of Wightwick, Wolverhampton. His family were connected to the composer Edward Elgar, his mother and sisters having many pieces of music dedicated to them. One of the Enigma Variations was inspired by his sister Isobel. *s.p.*

We Feebly Struggle, They In Glory Shine. Alleluia

Being three days after 34th Division's deployment to France; Brigadier General Fitton holds the somewhat unfortunate (and unique) distinction of being the only general officer to become his division's first battle casualty.

(II.A.29) Capt. Denis Henry Walker, 5th Bn. Princess Alexandra of Wales's Own (Yorkshire Regt.), (The Green Howards), (T.F.): *s*. of W.S. (& E.S.) Walker, of 'Milesden,' Newland Park, Hull: served with the Expeditionary Force in France from June 1915, and died of wounds, 26 January 1916, received in action the same day while superintending defensive work outside the parapet; Hill 60 – Sanctuary Wood sector: Age 26.

Much Beloved

(II.A.30) 2nd Lieut. William Henry Butland, 10th (Service) Bn. The Durham Light Infantry: elder *s*. of George Butland, Capt. Mercantile Marine; of 88, Bubbling Well Road, Shanghai, China, and Plymouth, co. Devon: and brother to 2nd Lieut. G. Butland, 2nd York & Lancaster Regt. dangerously wounded 29 July 1916; died of wounds, 21 May 1918: *b*. Norfolk, Virginia, U.S.A., 1 June 1890: *educ*. Chefoo College, North China: trained Shanghai and London for the profession of Architect & Civil Engineering (A.C.E.; Architectural Civil Engineer), and, at the time of the outbreak of war in 1914, was gainfully employed in Cornwall superintending bridge construction work: joined Artists' Rifles, January 1915, and after about nine months' training was gazetted Temp. 2nd Lieut. November 1915. He proceeded to the Front in France and died in the 10th Casualty Ward, Base Hospital, from the effects of a gunshot wound in the abdomen, received whilst in the trenches, 31 January 1916. Buried at Boeschepe, a village near Ypres: Age 25. Shortly before he was fatally wounded in action he had been recommended for a Mention in Despatches, for special machine-gun work, by his Commanding Officer, and thanked by his Brigadier-General: *unm*.

His brother George is buried in Nine Elms British Cemetery (XI.A.3).

"Since New Year's Day 1916, the 1/4th Battalion had spent the intervening period in trench warfare. But a close record for those eight (nearly nine) months reveals nothing of an outstanding character, for the battalion was not engaged in any attack on the enemy. Shelling, trench-mortaring, machine-gun fire and sniping occurred at all hours of the day and night, no part of the line was ever free from one or the other. Patrol work was assiduous; casualties were sometimes heavy and at other times extremely light, but speaking generally (and comparatively) those months spent in the Ypres trenches and at Kemmel may be written down as 'quiet.'" *Regimental History*.

Quiet or not, during the first eight months of 1916 4th East Yorks lost 3 officers killed, 5 died of wounds; among the latter, 25-year-old Samuel Quibell.

(II.A.31) Major Samuel Boyd Quibell, 1/4th Bn. The East Yorkshire Regt. (T.F.): *s*. of Oliver Quibell, of Shalem Lodge, Newark-on-Trent, co. Nottingham, by his wife Elisabeth: *educ*. Miss Wallis' School, Newark; Magnus Grammar School; Leys School, Cambridge: Occupation – Overseer, Messrs Thos Holmes & Son (Tannery), Hull: a pre-war member of 4th Bn. Territorial Force, held rank Lieut.; apptd. Capt. on the outbreak of war: proceeded to France, April

1915: hit in the jaw and neck by a shell January 1916; returned to duty within seven days. Hit in the chest by machine-gun fire on the 23rd of that month, and died in No.10 C.C.S., Poperinghe 5 February 1916: Age 25. *unm*. Mentioned in Despatches for his services in the Great War, on proceeding to France in April 1915 Mr Quibell was, at age 24, the youngest serving Major in the Territorial Force.

Make Him To Be Numbered With Thy Saints In Glory Everlasting

(II.A.32) 2nd Lieut. Frederick Charles Phillips, 'A' Coy., 5th Bn. The Northumberland Fusiliers (T.F.): *s*. of Frederick Phillips, of 204, Portland Road, Jesmond, Newcastle-on-Tyne, by his wife Margaret Jane: served with the Expeditionary Force in France from 1915, and died of wounds, 6 February 1916, received (vicinity Hill 60 – Mount Sorrel) the previous day from the bursting of a shell in the entrance to the elephant-iron shelter he was occupying in company with Capt. P.D. Forrett: Age 21. *unm*.

Capt. Forrett was killed outright and his grave lost in later fighting; he is commemorated in Maple Copse Cemetery (Sp.Mem.E.6).

(II.A.36) 2nd Lieut. Assheton Biddulph Cadell 10th (Service) Bn. The Devonshire Regt., attd. 8th Bn. The Queen's Own (Royal West Kent Regt.): only child of Dr. Nevil Pottow Cadell, of Foxlease, Camberley, co. Surrey, by his wife Gertrude Louisa, *dau*. of the late Francis Wellesley Marsh Biddulph, of Rathrobin, King's Co., J.P.: *b*. Tiverton, North Devon, 18 March 1894: *educ*. Woodcote, co. Oxon (Rev. J.H. Wilkinson), and Lancing College: obtained a commission Devonshire Regt. 17 March 1915: served with the Expeditionary Force in France and Flanders from 6 October following, attd. 8th West Kent Regt., and died in the ambulance on his way to hospital three hours after having been wounded in action at Chateau Belge, nr. Ypres, 19 February 1916. Buried in Lyssenthoek Soldiers' Cemetery, nr. Poperinghe: Age 21. *unm*.

In Thine Hands O Christ We Leave Him

"Lieutenant Bowden was wounded at the very beginning of the operation, as he scrambled out of his trench with the first wave, but he continued to lead his platoon. He was wounded again as he cut his way through the barbed wire, but still he carried on. When he reached the enemy trenches a German, who had succeeded in fixing his bayonet, lunged at him, but Bowden caught it in his hand. As they wrestled with the rifle, the German fired two rounds into Bowden's stomach at point-blank range. The stricken officer tumbled into the German trench, just as his batman came up and killed his assailant. Though unable to stand, Bowden insisted on supervising the consolidation of the position and only allowed himself to be carried to the rear when he was satisfied that everything possible had been done to withstand the expected counter-attack. On the way back, seeing the distress of the two men who carried him, Bowden asked them to put him down and rub his feet, as he thought that if they did he could walk a bit. His unconquerable spirit was an inspiration to the end, for his right arm was nearly blown off, he was riddled with lead and already his feet were cold with death. A few moments later he died." *Regimental History.*

(II.A.43) 2nd Lieut. Reginald Charles Bowden, 8th (Service) Bn. The King's Own (Royal Lancaster Regt.): *s.* of the late Charles Frederick Bowden, Official, Buenos Aires and Pacific Railway, by his wife Caroline Sarah (4082, Calle Navarro, Villa Devoto, Buenos Aires, Argentina): came to England shortly before the outbreak of war, and took up lodgings in Wargrave Road, Earlestown, co. Chester, having secured an apprenticeship at the Vulcan Foundry where 'he had a bright cheery disposition and a good word for everybody.': obtained a commission 2nd Lieut. 8th King's Own at the outbreak of war: served with the Expeditionary Force in France and Flanders, and died of wounds, 3 March 1916, received in action at The Bluff, nr. Ypres, the previous day. After assisting 2nd Lieut. Bowden to the Dressing Station, the Chaplain, M.P.G. Leonard, wrote, "Dear Mrs Bowden, I am writing to you at Reggie's request, to tell you he is very merry and bright. Our Battalion has just been through a very hard time. We attacked the German lines yesterday at dawn, and captured two lines and 250 Germans, but at the cost of many casualties. Poor Reggie, I am sorry to say, was among the number. He was hit in four or five places, but still went on; he was absolutely magnificent. His first wound was from shrapnel in the back, which knocked him onto the barbed wire. When he got off he found a German coming at him, so clutched hold of his rifle and tried to wrestle it from him. The Hun however managed to fire three times at him. Reggie still held on, and drew his revolver and shot the Hun dead. All the battalion are full of his pluck and courage. After he was wounded we got him on a stretcher, and managed to get him to the Dressing Station where he had to be left out in the open for some time, but he never complained, despite the pain of his wound and the bitter cold. I don't want to alarm you, but I must say that he is badly wounded, but he has youth on his side and infinite pluck, so I hope he will make a quick recovery. He asked me to send you his love, and to tell you to expect him soon in 'Blighty.' The whole Battalion is frightfully cut up that he should have been wounded, for he is the pride and joy of the whole Mess. All his brother officers, I know, join with me in expressing our sympathy in his wounds and our admiration for his courage and endurance." Three days later it was his duty to write a second, more painful, letter: "It is with the greatest sorrow and the deepest sympathy that I write to you again. We were all heartbroken when we heard the news that your boy had succumbed to his wounds. It was so crushing that we could hardly realise that he was gone. I cannot tell you how much we miss him, for we have all learnt to love him. He had one of those rare and loveable dispositions which attract all who come in contact with him. All the Battalion – officers and men alike – share your grief. Since we heard the sad news men have come to me with tears in their eyes and asked me if it was true that he was dead. Everybody loved him, for he was so full of life and good spirits, always so cheery and good natured, and above all, so sympathetic. Life is all the richer for having known him. As a friend and comrade his loss is irretrievable, but it is not only as a friend that the whole Battalion mourns his loss. As an officer he has left an imperishable mark. He was chosen for his intelligence and grasp of detail to be Brigade Pioneer Officer, and there is a strong point in the firing line which he built called 'Fort Bowden' after him. This was the only work in the whole of our line which stood the German bombardment in the assault in which poor Reggie received his wounds. I saw him after he was hit, in fact, I helped to carry him down to the Dressing Station, and he talked to me as we carried him back. Never once did he complain; his only thought was for his servant, Tom Boyes, who was killed at the commencement of the assault. I know well what a loss his death must be to you, and what a gap it will leave in your life, but don't think of him as gone forever, but only a little ahead on the Great Journey. He has made the greatest sacrifice a man can make. He has met his Pilot face to face, and passed with Him from the storm and stress of war to the peace and quiet of the inner harbour, where one day you will find him again, and resume in all its fullness and perfection your interrupted intimacy. He breathed his last at No.10 Casualty Clearing House, Poperinghe, and it is there that he is laid to rest. May he rest in peace, and may the God of All Comfort comfort you with His own consolations. In all true sympathy, in which every man and officer of the Battalion joins, believe me, very sincerely yours, M.P.G. Leonard.": Age 19.

In Loving Memory Of Reggie
Killed In Action
R.I.P.

Thomas Boyes has no known grave; he is recorded on the Ypres (Menin Gate) Memorial (Panel 12).

(II.A.45) 2nd Lieut. Terence Donough O'Brien, 6th Sqdn. Royal Flying Corps and 16th (Queen's) Lancers: only *s.* of Brig.Gen. Edmund Donough John O'Brien, C.B., C.B.E. (late 14th Hussars) and Florence H. O'Brien, of Buxted Rectory, Buxted, co. Sussex, dau. of Frederick Wheeler, of Worcester Park, co. Surrey: *educ.* St. Peter's, Broadstairs; Winchester; and Royal Military College, Sandhurst: apptd. 2nd Lieut. 16th Lancers, 14 August 1914; joined the regiment in Flanders, 23 October following (due to his age previous to this date);

took part in the fighting at Zillebeke, 21 February 1915, in which engagement the regiment, employed as dismounted infantrymen, suffered heavy losses – killed, wounded, missing – when the Germans, after exploding a mine beneath the Lancers trenches, attacked the position in force. And, with all the officers having been either killed, wounded or missing, 2nd Lieut. O'Brien assumed command of what remained of the squadron: transf'd. Royal Flying Corps September 1915 from which date until his death, in his capacity as Observer, his services were continuously called upon for aerial reconnaissance work. On 21 September 1915, while flying in BE2c, No.1784, he was involved in aerial combat at an altitude of 7,500 feet above Polygon Wood. Both he and his pilot, 2nd Lieut. Grey Edwards, were uninjured. On another occasion whilst flying in an FE2b with Capt. Ernest L. Gossage, on artillery observation duties near Ypres, 5 November 1915, he was involved in chasing a German Aviatik which they spotted about 1,000 feet above them heading toward the German lines; the Aviatik had no difficulty in out-climbing the FE2b and was last seen about 2,500 feet above them. Lieut. O'Brien was accidentally killed while landing at Abeele, 3 March 1916, following a mission over the front at Ypres; the pilot 2nd Lieut. R.A. Pierpoint was uninjured: Age 20.

A Very Gallant Officer And Gentleman
Truly Depicted In Psalm XV

Endnote: Shortly after 2nd Lieut. O'Brien's death Capt. Gossage returned to England on leave; he took with him O'Brien's personal effects to return to his family. During the course of this Capt. Gossage met O'Brien's sister, Eileen. They married in 1917 and had two sons, one of whom, Pilot Officer Peter L. Gossage, was killed as a fighter pilot, 31 May 1940. Capt. Gossage later became Air Marshal Sir Leslie Gossage; he was responsible for the manning of the fighter and bomber stations for the Battle of Britain. He died in 1949.

(II.B.10A) Pte. 3054, Arthur Brumby, 1/4th Bn. The Duke of Wellington's (West Riding Regt.), (T.F.): *s.* of Stephen Brumby, of 5, Wellgate, Greetland, Halifax, by his wife Annie: *b.* Swinton Bridge, co. York: prior to enlistment was employee, Messrs Sutcliffe's, West Vale & Dempsters, and member of the Territorial Force: undertook Active Service obligations, Halifax, August 1914: served with the Expeditionary Force in France from 15 April 1915, and died in a Casualty Clearing Station from gas poisoning received east of Ypres, 19 December following: Age 24.

(II.B.11A) Pte. 8866, William George Chambers, 1st Bn. (17th Foot) The Leicestershire Regt.: *b.* St. Mary's, Leicester, 1890: enlisted Leicester. Died of wounds (gas), No. 17 C.C.S., Poperinghe, 19 December 1915, received in action at Wieltje the same day: Age 25. He was married to Mrs L. McDonald, *née* Chambers (219, Farm Street, Hockley, Birmingham).

Thy Will Be Done

(II.B.12) Pte. 1920, Frederick Parker Furness, 6th Bn. The Duke of Wellington's (West Riding) Regt. (T.F.): *s.* of John Furness, of 28, Brougham Street, Skipton, co. York, by his wife Frances Mary: *b.* Skipton: prior to enlistment was employee, Messrs Marsden & Naylor, Iron Foundry: enlisted Skipton: served with the Expeditionary Force from 14 April 1915, and died 20 December 1915, of wounds (gas poisoning): Age 18. Sergt. F. Stork wrote, "Just a few lines on behalf of the gun section to express our sympathy with you in your sorrow. Fred and L/Corpl. Willan were in charge of two guns next to each other and they were both rather badly gassed as they were very near to the German line, and did not get much warning. Fred was an excellent gunner and for the last few months was in charge of a gun and was generally with me in the trenches. He always did his duty cheerfully and well, and we cannot express how sorry we are to lose him. He is one of the many victims of Hun Kulture, but we shall avenge them all if we get the chance again. Fred did his duty till the danger of attack was over and stuck to his gun until carried away to hospital, and it may comfort you to know he died a hero. He was a fine fellow, always ready for anything that turned up. Hoping you will be comforted a little by the section's sympathy and my own." And Sister M. Wharton, No.17 C.C.S., "It is with much regret that I send you very sad news. Your son, Pte. F. P. Furness, 1920, was admitted to this Hospital last evening, suffering from a severe attack of gas poisoning. He was unconscious and in a most critical condition, and although everything was done that could be done it was of no avail, and he passed quietly away at 1 am. There is one consolation, he did not suffer. He will be laid to rest in our soldiers' cemetery, and a cross will mark his grave, bearing his name, regiment, number, and the day on which he gave his life for his King and Country. He will have a military funeral and every respect. If any personal things were found in his possession they will be forwarded to you officially, but will take some time to come...."

He Is Not Dead But Sleepeth

(II.B.18) Pte. 17395, Samuel Hampson, 1st Bn. (53rd Foot) The King's (Shropshire Light Infantry): 2nd *s.* of James Hampson, of 16, Markland Hill Lane, Doffcocker, co. Lancaster, by his wife Maria, *dau.* of Absolam Haslam: *b.* Horwick, co Lancaster, 4 April 1890: *educ*. Markland Hill School, Doffcocker: Occupation – Stone Mason; Finch's Quarry, Horwick: enlisted

Bolton, 13 February 1915: served with the Expeditionary Force in France and Flanders from 27 July following, and died at No.10 Casualty Clearing Station, 22 December 1915, from wounds received in action in the Canal Bank Sector, Ypres, on the 20th. Buried in Lyssenthoek Cemetery, Poperinghe: Age 25. *unm.*

Thy Will Be Done

(II.B.43A) Pte. 20451, Joseph Ellison, 7th (Service) Bn. Alexandra, Princess of Wales's Own (Yorkshire Regt.), (The Green Howards): *s.* of Benjamin Ellison, by his wife Martha, *dau.* of John Heaton: *b.* Bingley, co. York, 5 September 1884: *educ.* National School, Bingley: Occupation – Stone Layer: enlisted 5 April 1915: served with the Expeditionary Force in France from 23 December following, and died in No.10 Casualty Clearing Station, 16 February 1916, of wounds received in action. Buried in the Military Cemetery on the Poperinghe Road: Age 31. He *m.* at Holy Trinity Church, Bingley, co. York, 24 August 1907, Charlotte Shackleton, *née* Ellison (3, Sun Street, Cullingworth, co. York), *dau.* of Joseph Chilton, and had three children – Eveline, *b.* 3 June 1908; Jack, *b.* 9 November 1909, and Robert, *b.* 3 March 1911.

(II.C.4) Pte. 2104, Bernard Gill, 1/1st Yorkshire Hussars: *s.* of William Gill, of 'Glenaire,' West Lane, Baildon, Bradford, co. York, by his wife Eliza Augusta: served with the Expeditionary Force in France and Flanders from 27 April 1915, and died of wounds received at Boesinghe, nr. Ypres, 27 November 1915: Age 19.

Bravest Heart And Best

(II.C.15) Corpl. 207, Stanley George Groome, 5th (City of London) Bn. (London Rifle Brigade) The London Regt. (T.F.): 2nd *s.* of William Groome, Boot & Shoe Manufacturer;of 317, Bethnal Green Road, London, E., by his wife Mary Ann, *dau.* of George William Wilcox: *b.* London, 10 February 1888: *educ.* Sir John Cass Foundation School, Minories: Occupation – Clerk; London Stock Exchange, but on the outbreak of war gave up his position and enlisted London Rifle Brigade, Bunhill Row, 31 August 1914: went to France, 13 January 1915, and during the spring and summer of 1915 was with his company in the trenches at Ploegsteert, St. Eloi and Ypres. Employed on the lines of communication (LoC) in the autumn of the same year, it was on returning to the trenches for the first time that he was accidentally shot at Poperinghe, 3 December 1915. He was buried in the soldiers' cemetery at Remy Siding, close to the main railway line between Hazebrouck and Poperinghe. An iron cross, sent out from England, subscribed for by the men in his old platoon, and engraved 'In memory of a good comrade,' marks the spot. Capt. C.W. Trevelyan, London Rifle Brigade, wrote, "I visited the grave, and when Sergt. Ford came back from leave he took out, and placed on the grave, a very nice iron cross as a small tribute of affection from some of the members of No.4 Platoon. We all felt that we had lost one of our best and most trusted friends." Groome was a good athlete, and was a member of the Leytonstone Rugby and Albion Rowing Clubs. He was a great lover of Nature and all Nature's gifts: Age 27. *unm.*

He Died For Us
Jesus Said Greater Love Hath No Man Than This

(II.C.19A) Pte. 1225, Herbert Briggs, 1/4th Bn. The Duke of Wellington's (West Riding Regt.), (T.F.): *s.* of the late James (& Mary) Briggs: late *husb.* to Emma Briggs (49, Green Lane, West Vale, co. York): *b.* Siddal, Halifax, 1880: *educ.* Blue Coat School & Almshouse, Harrison Road (orphan inmate): employee to Messrs Waller Brothers, Leighton: a pre-war Territorial, voluntarily undertook Active Service obligations Halifax, August 1914: served with the Expeditionary Force in France from 14 April 1915; gassed north-east of Ypres, 19 December 1915, and died at Number 10 Casualty Clearing Station, Poperinghe, the following day (20 December 1915): Age 35.

He Sleeps With England's Heroes In The Loving Care Of God

(II.C.23) L/Corpl. 2536, Sam Morton, 1/4th Bn. The Duke of Wellington's (West Riding Regt.), (T.F.): late *husb.* to Esther Garside, *née* Morton (41, Saddleworth Road, West Vale): served in France from 14 April 1915; gassed in the Canal Bank Sector, Yprcs salient, 19 December 1915, and died in the Casualty Clearing Station at Poperinghe the following day; 20 December 1915: Age 28.

(II.C.31A) L/Corpl. R/7355, Edward Ellison, 8th (Service) Bn. The King's Royal Rifle Corps: 2nd *s.* of James George Ellison, Painter & Decorator; of Alton, by his wife Elizabeth Fanny, *dau.* of the late Thomas Culverwell, of Basingstoke: *b.* Alton, co. Hants, 2 November 1893: *educ.* National School, there: volunteered and enlisted 17 November 1914: went to France December 1915, and died on 29 January 1916, of wounds (G.S. Head) received in action on the previous day whilst in charge of a carrying party at the Canal Bank, Ypres. Buried at Remy, nr. Poperinghe: Age 23. Sergt. Knight, of his company, wrote, "He was one of the best men I ever had under me." He *m.* Abbey Church, Minster, Sheerness, 22 July 1915; Susan ('Penlee,' Station Avenue, Walton-on-Thames, co. Surrey), 2nd *dau.* of Charles Hunt, of 33, Wratten Road, Hitchin, co. Hertford: *s.p.*

Faithful Unto Death

(II.C.33A) Corpl. 2068, Oliver William Risley, 1/16th (County of London) Bn. (Queen's Westminster Rifles) The London Regt. (T.F.): *s.* of the late L/Corpl. H.W. Risley, Royal West Kent Regt., by his wife Emily Sarah Risley (73, Raleigh Road, Richmond), *dau.* of Charles Ham: *b.* Hammersmith, London, W., 11 July 1893: *educ.* Richmond: joined Queen's Westminster Rifles, 4 August 1914: served with the Expeditionary Force in France and Flanders from 1 November 1914, and died at No.10 Casualty Clearing Station, 20 January 1916, from wounds received at Ypres the previous day. Buried in the Military Cemetery, Poperinghe-Boeschepe Road: Age 22. *unm.*

He Gave His All, His Life, For Us

His father Henry is buried in Richmond Cemetery, Surrey.

(II.D.1) Pte. 9155, John Lawrence Goring, 1st (Royal) Dragoons: *s.* of Harry Goring, of The Post Office, Bishops Cleeve, co. Gloucester, by his wife Elizabeth, *née* Staite: *b.* 1891: Occupation – Butcher's Assistant: enlisted Cheltenham: served with the Expeditionary Force in France from 19 October 1915, and died of wounds (GSW Lt. thigh), 21 November 1915: Age 24. Unveiled September 1919, dedicated 'To The Greater Glory Of God And In Loving Memory Of Those Men Who Laid Down Their Lives In The Great War. May They Rest In Peace;' Pte. Lawrence is one of 55 men remembered on the Bishops Cleeve War Memorial, Church Road.

(II.D.5) L/Corpl. 44050, Robert Swan Porter, 77th Field Coy., Royal Engineers: late of Elnor Street, Langley Mill, co. Derby: 3rd *s.* of Robert Porter, Self Employed Pianoforte Tuner, of 206, Crow Lane, Newton-le-Willows, co. York, by his wife Lucy Ann: *b.* Leeds, 1888: *educ.* Newton-le-Willows: on leaving school gained employ as Compositor's Apprentice, and was sometime Inspector, L.& N.W. Railway Coy., engaged at the Engineering Works, Messrs G.R. Turner & Co. Ltd., superintending the construction of carriages, later taking up employ with G.R. Turner 'which position he relinquished immediately on the outbreak of war in order to join the Colours': enlisted Nottingham: Died of wounds (G.S. multiple), 23 November 1915. During the time of his residence at Langley Mill he had made a large circle of friends: Age 27. *unm.* (*IWGC record age 28*)

(II.D.15) Pte. 3787, John Daglish, 11th (Service) Bn. The Highland Light Infantry: *s.* of Lieut. George Daglish, of 'West Lynne,' Dagshie, Simla, Punjab, India, by his wife Jessie: enlisted Glasgow, co. Lanark: served with the Expeditionary Force in France and Flanders from 6 July 1915, and died of wounds, 27 November 1915 received nr. Zillebeke, in the hospital at Lyssenthoek, nr. Poperinghe: Age 16.

He Answered The Call And Gave His Young Life

(II.D.22A) Pte. 3465, Frank Brown, 1/4th Bn. The Duke of Wellington's (West Riding) Regt. (T.F.): *s.* of Fred Brown, by his wife Alice, of Sowerby Bridge: late *husb.* to A. Horner, *née* Brown (2, Shaw Hill Lane, Halifax, co. York). Died of wounds (gas), 20 December 1915, received in the Canal Bank sector the previous day: Age 24.

(II.D.25) Rfn. 2512, Frederick Henry Browne, 16th (County of London) Bn. (Queen's Westminster Rifles) The London Regt. (T.F.): *s.* of Henry Frederick Browne, of 8, Harrow Rd., High St. North, East Ham, London, and Bertha his spouse: a pre-war Territorial, volunteered and enlisted 58, Buckingham Gate, Westminster, August 1914: proceeded to France, disembarked Le Havre, 19 February 1915. Died of wounds (G.S. head), 19 December 1915: Age 24.

(II.D.25A) Pte. 16624, Daniel John Hinton, 1st Bn. (17th Foot) The Leicestershire Regt.: late of Smeeton, Westerby, co. Leicester: *b.* Towcester, co. Northampton, 1890: enlisted Market Harborough: served with the Expeditionary Force from 4 May 1915, and died of wounds (gas asphyxiation), 20 December 1915, received at Wieltje the previous day: Age 25. He was married to Mrs A. Mason, *née* Hinton (3, Newland, Naseby, co. Northampton).

(II.D.29) Pte. 6271, John William Bushell, 8th (Service) Bn. The Queen's Own (Royal West Kent Regt.): 2nd *s.* of the late John Bushell, by his wife Esther, (27, Buckingham Road, Margate, co. Kent), *dau.* of Henry Bishop: *b.* Margate, 20 September 1892: *educ.* Salmestone Boy's School, there: voluntarily enlisted 22 April 1915; served in France from 1 October following. Died 16 January 1916, from wounds (fractured ribs, multiple contusions) received from shellfire. Buried between Poperinghe and Abeele, Flanders. A Lieut. of his battalion wrote, "He was one of my best men; a model man in many ways. With all the N.C.O.'s and men he was very popular.": Age 23. *unm.*

In God's Own Keeping

(II.D.32A) Pte. G/5326, Edward Ted Blackwell, 13th (Service) Bn. The Duke of Cambridge's Own (Middlesex Regt.): eldest *s.* of Edward Blackwell, Cab Driver; of 25, High Street, Barnet, by his wife Mary Jane, *dau.* of Richard Hamley: *b.* Barnet, London, 11 March 1897: *educ.* Public School, there: volunteered and enlisted 20 October 1914, aged 17 years: served with the Expeditionary Force in France and Flanders from October 1915, and died of wounds received in action, 15 January 1916. Buried at Poperinghe: Age 18.

Strictly speaking, at 52 years of age William Waple was exempt from active service. So what compelled him to serve? Did he have some special skill or knowledge that the Army required? Patriotism? A sense of duty? These are all questions to which the answers will never be known; he was destined to become another statistic and one of the oldest casualties in the Ypres salient.

(II.D.36A) Pnr. 115101, William Waple, 4th Labour Coy., Royal Engineers: *s.* of William Waple, of 10, Haberdasher Street, East Road, Hoxton, co. Middlesex, by his wife Elizabeth: *b.* Clerkenwell, co. Middlesex, *c.*1863: Occupation – Labourer: enlisted, 18 August 1915, London: served with the Expeditionary Force in France from the 26th of the latter month: admitted (acute appendicitis) No. 10 C.C.S., Remy Siding, 16 January 1916; died two days later (18 January 1916, peritonitis, septicaemia): Age 52.

George Coppard, Queen's (Royal West Surrey Regt.), described himself as "weighing over ten stone but very much a boy in heart and mind" when, in August 1914, he managed to enlist under-age. "There was a steady stream of men, mostly working types, queuing up to enlist. The sergeant asked me my age and when told replied, 'Clear off son. Come back tomorrow and see if you're nineteen, eh?' So I turned up again the next day and gave my age as nineteen. I attested in a batch of a dozen others and, holding up my right hand, swore to fight for King and Country. The sergeant winked as he gave me the King's shilling, plus one shilling and nine-pence ration money for that day. I believe he also got a shilling for each man he secured as a recruit…I was sixteen years and seven months old." No doubt the same scenario was repeated countless times up and down the country as young men, caught up in the euphoria and excitement of the moment, rushed to enlist. Young Donald Snaddon no doubt wanted to do his bit, the only difference being his age was even less than Coppard's. At enlistment Donald would have been about 13½ years of age.

(II.D.37) Pte. 17780, Donald McLeod Snaddon (*a.k.a* Sneddon), 1st Bn. (21st Foot) The Royal Scots Fusiliers: c/o Marion MacLeod (39A, Balallan Lochs, Stornoway); grandmother: *s.* of William Snaddon, of 3, White Street, Partick, Glasgow, by his wife Mary: and nephew to Q.M.Sergt. 545267, D. MacLeod, Royal Army Medical Corps, died 14 August 1918, of accidental injuries; Piper 103327, J. MacLeod, 67th Canadian Infantry, died 8 February 1919, consequent to wounds received (January 1918) in France; and L/Corpl. S/6100, R.D. MacLeod, 11th Argyll & Sutherland Highlanders, killed in action, 29 September 1915, at Loos: *b.* Govan, 2 June 1900: served with the Expeditionary Force in France and Flanders from 14 November 1915, and died of wounds, 18 January 1916, received in action at Scottish Wood, Ypres, on the 14th.: Age 15. Donald is remembered on the Kinloch, Laxay War Memorial.

I Give My All For You And For All

His uncle Donald is buried St. Pol British Cemetery (II.B.7); John, Victoria (Ross Bay) Cemetery, Canada (N.18E.T); Roderick has no known grave, he is commemorated on the Loos Memorial.

One of the youngest casualties buried in the Ypres salient; the attention of visitors is drawn to Pte. Snaddon's grave not only by virtue of his age, but also due to the fact that it lies beside that of 52-year-old William Waple.

(II.D.40A) Rfn. S/9750, Christopher Arthur Rivett, 3rd Bn. The Prince Consort's Own (The Rifle Brigade): s. of Albert Henry Rivett, of 86, Albany Road, Old Kent Road, Camberwell, London, by his wife Mary Ann: and elder brother to Rfn. S/27961, E. Rivett, 16th Rifle Brigade, killed in action, 31 July 1917: b. Peckham: enlisted Camberwell: proceeded to France, 1 September 1915, and died, 12 February 1916, of wounds received in action at Ypres: Age 21. unm.

His brother Ernest has no known grave; he is commemorated on the Ypres (Menin Gate) Memorial (Panel 48).

(II.D.45A) Pte. 15359, Edward Ball, 6th (Service) Bn. The King's (Shropshire Light Infantry): s. of Joseph (& Susannah) Ball, of No.6, Rookery, St. George's, nr. Wellington, co. Salop: b. St. George's: Occupation – Miner Granville Colliery: enlisted Wellington, November 1914; apptd. 9th (Reserve) Bn.: proceeded to France transf'd. 6th Bn., 22 July 1915: Died of wounds, 13 February 1916, received the previous evening when the hutted camp which he was in at the time was hit by German shellfire; 19 killed, 46 wounded. First visited by his greatnephew, 22 July 2012; he left a note – "In Loving Memory of Edward Ball. Your beloved sister Lizzie was always sad that no one had ever visited your grave, and that you had never had flowers. Today with great pride I put this right on behalf of her and all the family."

Rest In Peace

(III.A.3) Pte. 12122, Thomas Cox, 6th (Service) Bn. The King's Own (Yorkshire Light Infantry): late of 4, St. John the Baptist Street, Dewsbury, co. York: brother to Pte. 92010, M. Cox, 2nd Durham Light Infantry, killed in action, 24 September 1918: enlisted Dewsbury, 20 August 1914: served with the Expeditionary Force in France from 21 May 1915, and died of wounds (S.W., head), 30 July 1915, received in action at Ypres: Age 29. His brothers Francis, James and Joseph also served.

His brother Michael has no known grave; he is commemorated on the Vis-en-Artois Memorial (Panel 9).

(III.A.5A) Sergt. 978, Howard Davis, 8th (Service) Bn. The Prince Consort's Own (The Rifle Brigade): 2nd s. of Edwin Davis, Master Printer; of 'Trevosa,' Jockey Hill, Wylde Green, and Great Charles Street, Birmingham, by his wife Susan, dau. of the late Robert Andrews: b. Birmingham, 2 May 1888: educ. Aston Grammar School: Occupation – Works Manager: volunteered and enlisted, 1 October 1914, after the outbreak of war: served with the Expeditionary Force in France from 20 May 1915: wounded at Hooge, Flanders, 30 July 1915, and died in the Casualty Clearing Station, Poperinghe, following day (31 July). Capt. E.F. Prior, his Company Commander wrote, "I valued him very highly as a sergeant, and as a man of very strong character, and I placed a great reliance on him." And Lieut. E. Boughey, "I can't tell you what a good soldier he was, and what an enormous help to me.": Colour Sergeant Hill also wrote that he last saw him on 30 July, when the enemy used liquid fire, when he was wounded in the arm. In spite of this he crawled about in the open field, dressing other wounded men, before attempting to go into safety himself. He was hit in the chest later on by shrapnel bullets, which caused his death next day. He was a well-known footballer in the Midlands: Age 27. *unm.* (*IWGC record S/978*)

There Is A Divinity That Shapes Our Ends
Rough Hew Them How We Will

(III.A.7) L/Corpl. 16404, Charles Henry Hall, 3rd Bn. The Worcestershire Regt.: 4th & *yst. s.* of Edward Hall, Market Gardener; of New Row, Bretforton, Honeybourne, co. Worcester, by his late wife Sarah: *b.* Bretforton, 27 December 1894: enlisted, 2 September 1914, after the outbreak of war: served with the Expeditionary Force in France and Flanders from 19 December following, and died in No.10 Casualty Clearing Station, 29 July 1915, from wounds received in action at Hooge two days previously (27 July): Age 20. *unm.* Dedicated – 'In Memory of The Men Of This Village Who gave Their Lives In The Two World Wars,' L/Corpl. Hall is remembered on the Bretforten Memorial, St. Leonard's Church. (*IWGC record age 21*)

At Rest After Suffering

(III.A.18A) Pte. 2006, Ernest Askew, 6th Bn. The Duke of Wellington's (West Riding) Regt. (T.F.): *s.* of Mr (& Mrs) Askew, of 40, Westmorland Street, Skipton, co. York: Occupation – Engine Cleaner; Midland Railway Co., Skipton: a pre-war Territorial, volunteered for Active Service on the outbreak of war: proceeded to France, 14 April 1915, and died of wounds, 23 July following: Age 24. *unm.* Chaplain Southwell, No.10 C.C.S. wrote, "I deeply regret to say that Ernest Askew died early this morning. He will be laid to rest in our cemetery at 3pm, and the grave will be properly marked with a cross…"

(III.A.19) Pte. S/9701, James Cruickshank, 1st Bn. (75th Foot) The Gordon Highlanders: *s.* of James Cruickshank, of Auchnagatt, co. Aberdeen, by his wife Louisa: *b.* Fyvie, 22 August 1896: *educ.* Inverurie Academy, and Aberdeen University: enlisted 3rd Gordon Highlanders, Aberdeen, April 1915, proceeded to France with a draft of reinforcements to 1st Battn. 15 June following, and died, 24 July 1915, of wounds received in action at Ypres on the 22nd.: Age 19.

All He Has Given For Us, Life's Sacrifice

(III.A.28A) Pte. 6532, Thomas Knight, D.C.M., 1st Bn. (53rd Foot) The King's (Shropshire Light Infantry): eldest *s*. of John Knight, Foreman of Steel Works, by his wife Catherine, *dau*. of John Curnes: *b*. Bewsey, Williamstown, Co. Mayo, 1883: Occupation – Miner: served in the South African War; 1st King's Shropshire Light Infantry, 1899–1902 (Queen's and King's Medal): prior to the outbreak of war was a member of the Reserve: re-enlisted King's Shropshire Light Infantry, 5 August 1914; the day after the European War broke out: served with the Expeditionary Force in France and Flanders from 24 February 1915, and died at Lyssenthoek, nr. Poperinghe, 17 September 1915, from wounds (G.S.W., abdominal) received in action at the Battle of Hooge. Buried there: Age 32. He was awarded the Distinguished Conduct Medal. He *m*. Barnsley, 27 October 1910, Minnie (55, Cresswell Street, Pogmoor, Barnsley), *dau*. of Joseph Yeuill, and had three children – Honor, *b*. 11 August 1911, John Thomas Patrick, *b*. 26 June 1913, and Minnie, *b*. 15 August 1914. (*IWGC record age 39*)

(III.A.34) Dvr. 32264, Charles Turner, 53rd Bty., Royal Field Artillery: *s*. of Benjamin Turner, of Langton, Malton, co. York, by his wife Anna E.: *b*. Malton, 1899: proceeded to France, 12 April 1915, and died, 21 September 1915, of accidental injuries: Age 16.

In The Bloom Of Life God Called Him
Life's Work Well Done Then Comes Rest

(III.A.36A) Spr. 474, William James Hanson, 1st (North Midland) Field Coy., Royal Engineers (T.F.): eldest *s*. of James Hanson, Tool Maker; of 27, Station Road, Handsworth, Birmingham, by his wife Emma, *dau*. of William Cattell: *b*. Handsworth, 26 February 1894: *educ*. Wattville Road Council Schools: Occupation – Turner & Fitter; Messrs Archdale Ltd., Engineers, Birmingham: joined Royal Engineers, April 1914: volunteered for Foreign Service on the outbreak of war: went to France, 19 July 1915, and died, 22 September 1915, from wounds received in action at Ypres earlier in the day. Buried in Lyssenthoek Military Cemetery, nr. Poperinghe. 2nd Lieut. D.B. Dixon wrote, "I had only acted as officer of the section in which your son was serving for six weeks prior to his death, but out here one soon forms an opinion of individuals, and I can only say I had the highest esteem for Sapper Hanson's work, and also the manner in which he inspired others when work of a dangerous nature was in hand. We had been in the trenches for four days, and were to be relieved in the afternoon. About 5 p.m. the section was ready to commence the return journey; your son was in the last group of six, and had passed all dangerous places safely, when a bullet struck him in the head whilst the group were passing a stretch which had been thought safe. He was quickly carried to a dugout and a medical officer sent for, but he never recovered consciousness. How popular he was with the section will be understood by the fact that the N.C.O.'s and a sapper asked that they might be permitted to carry him on a stretcher to the motor ambulance, which meant that they would have to remain behind for another three hours, and then walk back for about nine miles instead of being driven.": Age 21. *unm.*

R.I.P.

(III.B.19A) Pte. 2587, George Ernest Hardy, 1/4th Bn. The Lincolnshire Regt. (T.F.): *s.* of George Hardy, of 'The Sycamores,' Crowland, co. Lincoln, by his wife Margaret: enlisted Luton, co. Bedford, 28 August 1914, after the outbreak of war: served with the Expeditionary Force in France from 1 March 1915, and died of nephritis, 1 September following: Age 26. *unm.* For nephritis see Rfn. G. Stephenson (X.C.43).

Safe In Jesu's Keeping

(III.B.23A) Pte. 23449, Sam Josh, 6th (Service) Bn. The King's Own (Yorkshire Light Infantry): formerly no.22072, 13th (Reserve) Cavalry Regt.: *s.* of Robert Josh, of 37, Scarboro' Terrace, Bootham, co. York, by his wife Sarah Ann: and brother to Pte. 51356, J. Josh, East Yorkshire Regt., died 10 September 1918: *b.* York: *educ.* Shipton Street School: enlisted York: served with the Expeditionary Force in France and Flanders from 12 August 1915, and was killed in action, 7 September following: Age 20. *unm.*

His brother John has no known grave; he is commemorated on the Vis-en-Artois Memorial (Panel 4).

(III.B.28A) Pte. 13372, Wilfrid Gant, 7th (Service) Bn. The Lincolnshire Regt.: 6th *s.* of William Gant, of Belchford, Horncastle, Farm Labourer, by his wife Biddie, *dau.* of William Parker: *b.* Tetford, co. Lincoln, 31 March 1893: *educ.* there: Occupation – Trainee Policeman; Lincolnshire Force: enlisted, 30 September 1914, after the outbreak of war: went to France, 29 July 1915, and died, 5 September following, from wounds received in action the previous day (4 September 1915): Age 22. *unm.*

(III.B.33) Spr. 6731, James Feltham, No.2 Siege Coy. (Royal Anglesey) Royal Engineers: elder *s.* of James Feltham, now (1918) serving with Royal Defence Corps: *b.* Holyhead, co. Anglesey, July 1896: *educ.* Cylie School, Holyhead: Occupation – Deck Boy; L. & N.W. Express Boat 'Scotia': joined Anglesey R.E., 3 September 1914, after the outbreak of war: served with the Expeditionary Force in France and Flanders from 14 December, and died of wounds, 7 September 1915 received in action earlier the same day. Buried near Ypres: Age 19.

Thou Art Gone But Not Forgotten, Never Shall Thy Memory Fade

(III.C.1A) Pte. 9893, Wallace Wonacott, 2nd Bn. (20th Foot) The Lancashire Fusiliers: *s*. of Walter Wanacott, of Swansea, co. Glamorgan, by his wife Frances: *b*. Crewe, co. Chester: served with the Expeditionary Force in France from 27 April 1915, and died of wounds, 12 July 1915. Buried in a Soldier's Cemetery nr. Poperinghe: Age 16. Remembered on Minshull New Road Methodist Church War Memorial, Crewe, Cheshire.

On 7 August 1914 German soldier poet Alfred Lichtenstein wrote:

> **Leaving For The Front**
> Before I die I must find this rhyme.
> Be quiet, my friends, and do not waste my time.
>
> We're marching off in company with death.
> I only wish my girl would hold her breath.
>
> There's nothing wrong with me. I'm glad to leave.
> Now mother's crying too. There's no reprieve.
>
> And now look how the sun's begun to set.
> A nice mass grave is all that I shall get.
>
> Once more the good old sunset's glowing red.
> In thirteen days I'll probably be dead.

Alfred Lichtenstein's war lasted precisely five weeks longer than he predicted, one would hope his death came swiftly and painlessly. For many thousands of soldiers death was destined to come not on the battlefield, but in some hospital tent far behind the lines. Despite receiving the best medical care and attention available 223 German soldiers died as patient prisoners of war here, for some the end would have come mercifully quickly; for others death would have been slow and painful. The first German soldier to die at Lijssenthoek is buried in Plot III. Row D., within four days he was joined by:

(III.C.4) Deutsche Krieger, Lieske, Emil; Musketier, R.J.R. 215: Gefallen fur Deutschland: 11 July 1915.

(III.C.7) Deutsche Krieger, Lambert, Hermann; Gefreiter, R.J.R. 215: Gefallen fur Deutschland: 10 July 1915.

(III.C.7A) Rfn. 5393, John Magee, 2nd Bn. (86th Foot) The Royal Irish Rifles: *s*. of Edward Magee, of Waringstown, Lurgan, Co. Down, by his wife Mary: and father to L/Corpl. J. Magee, 5th Royal Irish Fusiliers (surv'd):

b. Waringstown, 1869: a pre-war Regular, 'signed on for the duration,' served with the Expeditionary Force in France and Flanders from August 1914, and died, 29 August 1915, of wounds (G.S.W. thigh, compound fracture L. femur) received in action nr. St. Eloi four weeks previously (1 August): Age 46. He leaves a wife, Margaret Magee (Waringstown). A talented wood carver, a piece sculpted by Rfn. Magee (brought home to the deceased's family by Sergt. Reavey) was prominently displayed in a branch of Messrs Gilchrist & Sons.

Until The Day Dawn And The Shadows Flee Away

(III.C.9A) Pte. 9759, Harvey Bertram Carter, 1st Bn. (6th Foot) The Royal Warwickshire Regt.: *s.* of Annie Newbury (Childs Wickham, nr. Broadway, co. Gloucester): *b.* Childs Wickham, 25 February 1896: volunteered after the outbreak of war and enlisted, 9 December 1914: served with the Expeditionary Force in France from 2 May 1915, and died at Abeele, 9 July 1915, of wounds received in action on the previous day while carrying grenades to the firing line near Pilckem: Age 19.

(III.C.18) Pte. 4005, Joseph Ross, 2nd Bn. (109th Foot) The Leinster Regt. (Prince of Wales's Royal Canadians): *s.* of Thomas (& Bridget) Ross, of Carrickmacross, Co. Monaghan: enlisted Mosney Camp, Drogheda, Co. Louth: served with the Expeditionary Force in France from 26 October 1914, and died of wounds (shell) received in action at Ypres the same day, 20 August 1915: Age 23. See Ramparts Cemetery (Lille Gate).

(III.C.23) Pte. 9918, Joseph Griffen, 2nd Bn. (109th Foot) The Leinster Regt. (Prince of Wales's Royal Canadians): Died of wounds, 22 August 1915, received in action at Ypres on the 20th. See Ramparts Cemetery (Lille Gate).

(III.C.27) Pte. S/614, George Robert Baker, 1st Bn. (3rd Foot) The Buffs (East Kent Regt.): *s.* of the late John 'Jack' Baker, by his wife Emma Stickles, *née* Baker (Cesterham Cottages, Herne Bay): and brother to Pte. L/7059, W.H. Baker, 1st The Buffs, VIth Divn., who fell 30 October 1914: *b.* Herne Bay, co. Kent, about 1878: *educ.* Council School, Herne Bay: enlisted Margate: served with the Expeditionary Force in France from 9 February 1915, and died, 23 August 1915, of wounds received in action: Age 37. He leaves a wife Maud A. (33, Alexandra Road, Ramsgate) late of 5, Milton Square, Margate, co. Kent.

Just A Thought Of Sweet Remembrance And A Heartache Still For You

His brother William has no known grave; he is commemorated on the Ploegsteert Memorial (Panel 2.)

(III.C.30A) Pte. 1964, Matthew Booth, 1/6th Bn. The Sherwood Foresters (Notts & Derbys Regt.), (T.F.): formerly no.25062: 2nd *s.* of Henry Booth, of

6, Torrs Yard, Wirksworth, co. Derby, and Elizabeth, his wife: and brother to Pte. 21904, A. Booth, 6th Leicestershire Regt., died of wounds, 5 May 1918: Occupation – Plant Nursery Worker: *b*. Wessington, nr. Brackenfield, 1886: enlisted Wirksworth: served in France and Flanders from February 1915, and died of wounds, 26 August 1915: Age 29. *unm*. (*IWGC record age 27*)

On Resurrection Morn Father, Mother, Sisters, Brother Meet Once More

His brother Absolom is buried in Boulogne Eastern Cemetery (IX.B.44).

(III.C.31A) Pte. 7032, Peter Bent, 2nd Bn. (109th Foot) The Leinster Regt. (Prince of Wales's Royal Canadians): *b*. Manchester: enlisted there: proceeded to France September 1914, and died of wounds (G.S.W. abdominal), 27 August 1915, received in action at Ypres on the 20th. See Ramparts Cemetery (Lille Gate).

In the early hours of 30 July 1915 the Germans, using liquid fire for the first time against British troops, attacked and captured the front line trenches at Hooge. In support trenches at Maple Copse the 7th Bn. Sherwood Foresters ordered two companies to positions on the northern edge of Sanctuary Wood in readiness for a counter-attack later in the day. During the move to these new positions under heavy rifle, machine gun and artillery fire (which continued throughout the day and well into the night) the Robin Hoods suffered casualties in excess of 60 killed or wounded. Among the wounded was Arthur Daft who, after rudimentary treatment in a battalion aid post was later transported back to Remy Siding from whence, due to the severity of his wounds, evacuation to one of the coastal hospitals was not an option. He died 31 days later.

(III.C.38A) Pte. 3238, Arthur Gervase Daft, 1/7th (Robin Hood) Bn. The Sherwood Foresters (Notts & Derbys Regt.): elder *s*. of Arthur W. Daft, Coal Merchant; of 'Ivanhoe,' Woodhall Spa, co. Lincoln, by his wife Annie: *b*. Old Woodhall, co. Lincoln: Occupation – Waiter: resident in Canada at the outbreak of war, after enlisting in a Canadian regiment (which was subsequently disbanded), returned home and enlisted 7th Sherwood Foresters, Nottingham, 26 October 1914: went to France, 25 June 1915, and died of wounds (G.S.W. multiple), 1 September following, received in action nr. Hooge 30–31 July 1915: Age 23. *unm*.

Until The Day Breaks

The earliest dated German burial in Lijssenthoek Military Cemetery:

(III.D.3) Deutsche Krieger, Nowacki, Josef; Vizefeldwebel, R.J.R. 215: Gefallen fur Deutschland: 7 July 1915.

(III.D.6A) Pte. 1322, Samuel Turner, 1/6th Bn. The Sherwood Foresters (Notts & Derbys Regt.), (T.F.): s. of John William (& Mary) Turner, of Tom Lane, Whaley Bridge, Stockport: b. Chapel-en-le-Frith, Stockport: employee Messrs Frood's Brake-Lining Works: served with the Expeditionary Force in France from 25 February 1915, and died of wounds, 4 July 1915, received when, returning from fatigue duty near the front, a shell burst among the work party as they were passing through Ypres: Age 21. Buried by Archdeacon Southwell. A well-known sprinter in the Chapel-en-le-Frith and surrounding district, he won many prizes in local races.

Peace Perfect Peace

(III.D.7) L/Corpl. 3224, George William Lomas, 1/6th Bn. The Sherwood Foresters (Notts & Derbys Regt.), (T.F.): s. of James (& Mrs) Lomas: b. Dove Holes, Stockport: enlisted Chapel-en-le-Frith: served with the Expeditionary Force in France from 25 June 1915; died of wounds (shrapnel, leg), 4 July 1915: Age 20. Buried by Archdeacon Southwell. Capt. E. Heathcote wrote, "On the Saturday night we went up to the lines on fatigue, and travelled up a long way in motor lorries; it was quite an exciting journey for us after we left the lorries to march through Ypres, especially as for many of us it was the first experience of the war. Fritz was sending over a few gas shells and we were all sneezing and rubbing our eyes. We drew spades and set off after a short rest, landed at the work, finished off fairly quickly and started for home: Home consisting of bivvies made from water-proof sheets, and some of us hadn't even got those. We had a pretty rough journey coming through Ypres, had just downed tools and started the march towards the houses, when Fritz began shelling; of course he managed to get a lucky shot right in the middle of us, killing and wounding about half the party, many of whom had not yet even seen the trenches."

*"Went The Day Well? We Died And Never Knew
But Well Or Ill – England We Died For You" 1914–1918*

(III.D.14A) Pte. 1540, Bernard Donagh Carroll, 1/5th Bn. The Leicestershire Regt. (T.F.): late Altar Boy, Market Harborough Roman Catholic Church, co. Leicester: Occupation – Labourer; Messrs R. & W.H. Symington, Bodice & Hosiery Manufacturers, Market Harborough. Died of wounds, 10 August 1915, received whilst engaged in carrying rations to the trenches near Hooge when the guide lost his way: Age 18. His Commanding Officer, Major H.J.F. Jeffries, also of Market Harborough, lies nearby (I.A.23).

(III.D.19) Pte. 8297, Harry Frederick O'Leary, 2nd Bn. (84th Foot) The York & Lancaster Regt.: s. of Clr.Sergt. Arthur O'Leary, of Pontefract, and Sarah

Wesley, his wife: and yr. brother to Sergt. 12837, A.G.W. O'Leary, 6th York & Lancaster Regt., killed in action two days previously (9 August 1915) at Gallipoli: *b*. Pontefract, co. York: proceeded to France, September 1914, and died of wounds, 11 August 1915, received in action two days previously (9 August) in the attack to recapture some lost trenches at Hooge: Age 28. He leaves a wife, Elsie O'Leary (10, Radnor Road, Portmore Park, Weybridge, co. Surrey), in mourning. Remembered on Pontefract (All Saints Churchyard) War Memorial.

Rest In Peace

His brother Alfred has no known grave; he is commemorated on the Helles Memorial.

(III.D.21A) Pte. 10450, James Cohsall, 1st Bn. (3rd Foot) The Buffs (East Kent Regt.): *s*. of Thomas Cohsall, of 4, Blucher Row, Dover, by his wife Patience: *b*. Chatham, co. Kent, 1 May 1896: *educ*. National School, Dover: enlisted 23 February 1911: served with the Expeditionary Force in France and Flanders from 11 November 1914: employed with Battn. Machine Gun Section, and died at Abeele, Flanders, 11 August 1915, of wounds received in the Battle of Hooge. Buried in the cemetery nr. Poperinghe: Age 19. (*IWGC record S/10450*)

(III.D.27) Pte. 4733, Thomas Galligan, 2nd Bn. (109th Foot) The Leinster Regt. (Prince of Wales's Royal Canadians): *s*. of Lawrence Galligan, of Cavan, co. Meath, by his wife Julia: enlisted Navan: served with the Expeditionary Force in France from 26 October 1914, and died of wounds (G.S.W. head) received in action at Hooge, 13 August 1915: Age 19. See Birr Cross Roads Cemetery.

(III.D.33) Pte. 9469, Claude Connell, 2nd Bn. (109th Foot) The Leinster Regt. (Prince of Wales's Royal Canadians): *s*. of Thomas Connell, and Caroline Campe: Occupation – Waiter: *b*. Fairfield, Aughrim: enlisted Athlone, 19 August 1914: served in France from October following, and died of wounds, 14 August 1915, received at Hooge two days previously. See Birr Cross Roads Cemetery.

(IV.A.7A) Pte. 10/5493, George Bowman, 10th Bn. The Lancashire Fusiliers: *s*. of Joseph (& Elizabeth) Bowman, of 1, St. Cuthbert Street, Burnley, co. Lancaster: late husb. to Mary Bowman (101, Ardwick Street, Burnley), and father to one son: b. Colne, 1892: Occupation – Twister; Coronation Mill, Burnley: enlisted Burnley. Died 18 November 1915; pneumonia: Age 23. Shortly before his death he penned the following verse to his wife:

"To My Dear Mary"

Though far away I roam,
I often think of you at home;
And in my dreams I seem to see

Myself at home with a happy family.
But when I awake I feel so sad
When I think of you again and the lad,
And in my heart I often say,
May this dark cloud pass away.
But when the shells begin to roar,
This I think again and of home once more;
But duty first is our own way,
Be though death may be our pay.

It may be, dear wife, we have met for the last,
So I beg of you not to think of the past;
But look to the day when we will meet again,
Where wars no longer will remain.

We'll Meet Again O Happy Word
And Be For Ever With The Lord

(IV.A.11A) Pte. 12661, John 'Jack' Gold, 9th (Service) Bn. The Duke of Wellington's (West Riding) Regt.: *s.* of Henry Alfred Harcourt Gold, of 8, Lane Side, Luddenfoot, by his wife Florence B.: *b.* Liverpool: employee to Henry Sagar & Co., Mill House Dyeworks, Sowerby Bridge: served with the Expeditionary Force in France from July 1915, and died in a Casualty Clearing Station, 20 November 1915, of wounds received at Ypres the same day: Age 21.

(IV.A.14A) Corpl. 1876, Arthur Spencer, 'A' Coy., 1/4th Bn. The King's Own (Yorkshire Light Infantry), (T.F.): *s.* of Christopher Joseph Spencer, of Stennard Cottage, Wakefield, co. York, by his wife Elizabeth Ann: *b.* Wakefield, about 1896: Occupation – Electrician; Diamond Coal Cutter Works: joined Yorkshire Territorials, May 1913, attaining rank of Sergt.: on the outbreak of war was at Whitby Annual Training Camp: volunteered for Foreign Service, but was informed he was too young to go to the Front and serve as a Sergt., whereupon he relinquished his stripes: went to France, 13 April 1915, and died of wounds, 22 November following, received in action at Ypres: Age 18.

Until The Day Breaks And The Shadows Flee Away

(IV.A.21) Sergt. 1464, John Bolton, 'B' Coy., 1/9th Bn. (Dunbartonshire) The Argyll & Sutherland Highlanders (T.F.): eldest *s.* of Andrew S. Bolton, of Heath Bank, Heath Avenue, Lenzie, by his wife Sarah Gemmell: *b.* Partick, Glasgow, c.1893: employee to Messrs Andrews & Cameron, Engineers, Kirkintilloch: served with the Expeditionary Force in France and Flanders from February

1915: wounded March following and evacuated to England; rejoined his battalion September 1915. Severely wounded by shrapnel in various parts of his body, 13 December 1915, he was removed to the Clearing Station, Poperinghe, where he succumbed to his wounds three days later: Age 22. *The Kirkintilloch Herald*, 29 December 1915, recorded, "In letters of sympathy received by his parents, his officers speak very highly of Sergt. Bolton, who had proved himself a most efficient non-commissioned officer. At the morning service in Lenzie U. F. Church, when preaching from the words, "Neither count I my life dear unto me" (Acts XX., 24), the Rev. W. Purves Boyes referred to those who had made the great sacrifice, and in closing paid a brief tribute to the memory of Sergeant Bolton. What, he asked, are the issues of such a sacrifice? I might speak to you of the certainty for such of an ampler life in another world, but I am not thinking of the other world, but of this. I might quote the words, 'One crowded hour of glorious bliss is worth an age without a name;' but there is no question of winning a name. These men never posed as heroes, or thought of themselves as doing more than any man's duty when they went forth, before the days of pressure and compulsion, of their own noble impulse. The issue is this: that they have enriched the national life by their dying, more than even the most brilliant of them could have enriched it had they lived. Among such there has been numbered within the past week the first from our own Roll of Honour. A more conscientious, Christian lad than John Bolton it would have been difficult to find. I have had the privilege of reading a bundle of letters bearing testimony to his ability as a soldier from those competent to do so. But as his minister, I can speak today of his modest, yet sincere, Christian character, his affectionate and thoughtful regard for those nearest to him, and his sure persuasion that in going forth to serve his country he was following the will of God. In a quiet grave across the sea he has been laid to rest by loving hands, and a simple cross marks the place where a very gallant Scottish lad laid down his life for his friends. If he could speak to us today, would not his words, with those of so many who have made the same sacrifice, be the words of Homer, 'For our country 'tis a bliss to die?'"

For Those He Loved

(IV.A.23) Pte. 2575, Lyndon Hanson Hall, 6th Bn. The Duke of Wellington's (West Riding) Regt. (T.F.): *s.* of Luther Hall, of 22, Cross Street, Keighley, by his wife Elizabeth: served with the Expeditionary Force in France from 14 April 1915, and died 19 December following, of wounds (gas poisoning). In a letter to Mrs Hall 2nd Lieut. F. Longden-Smith wrote, "I cannot say how sorry I am to have to write and tell you that your son has died from the effects of gas poisoning received last Sunday. He was with the Machine Gun Section and close up in support, and the gas was on them before they could get their gas helmets on.

He was always a cheerful and willing worker. You could always be quite sure that if he was in charge of a gun team the gun would be in good working order and always well manned. On behalf of the N.C.O.'s and men let me offer you my deepest sympathy in your great loss.": Age 21. *unm.*

He Died That We Might Live

(IV.A.24) Pte. 2538, Charles Reading, 1/4th Bn. The Duke of Wellington's (West Riding) Regt. (T.F.): formerly of 29, Catherine Street, Elland: late *husb.* to Annie Reading (124, Pontrefact Road, Hopetown, Normanton, co. York): Occupation – Fitter; Messrs Dempsters, Rosemount Works, Elland: enlisted September 1914, after the outbreak of war: served with the Expeditionary Force in France and Flanders from 15 April 1915, and died in a Casualty Clearing Station, 20 December 1915, of gas asphyxiation received north-east of Ypres the previous day: Age 30.

Duty Nobly Done

(IV.A.29) L/Corpl. 15160, Robert Jones, 10th (Service) Bn. The Royal Welsh Fusiliers: *s.* of the late Robert Jones, by his wife Mary S. (8, Frankwell Street, Towyn, co. Merioneth), *dau.* of David Thomas: *b.* Bryncrug, co. Merioneth, 1 October 1890: *educ.* Council School, there: Occupation – Teamster: enlisted 11 September 1914, after the outbreak of war: served with the Expeditionary Force in France and Flanders from 27 September 1915; wounded in the front line trenches at St. Eloi, 2 January 1916, and died on the 6th of that month in the Casualty Clearing Station, Remy Siding (6 January 1916). Buried in the Military Cemetery on the Poperinghe-Boeschepe Road: Age 25. *unm.* (*IWGC record age 26*)

(IV.B.27) Pte. 15110, John William Oliver, 9th (Service) Bn. The Duke of Wellington's (West Riding) Regt.: late of 'Cringles,' Cliff Hollins Lane, Oakenshaw: Occupation – Miner; Cleckheaton Colliery: enlisted Cleckheaton: served with the Expeditionary Force in France from 16 July 1915, and died there, 16 December 1915 of wounds (G.S. head) received in the Canal Bank sector, Boesinghe, earlier the same day: Age 38. He was married to Minnie Lightowler, *née* Oliver (22, Union Road, Low Moor, Bradford, co. York), and leaves four children. Remembered on Oakenshaw (St. Peter's) War Memorial. His widow's nephew, Pte. F. Lightowler, lies nearby (XXVI.E.2).

At Rest

(IV.B.36) Bmdr. 1249, Arthur Bainbridge, 3rd (Northumbrian) Bde., Royal Field Artillery: *s.* of Thomas Bainbridge, of 8, Tempest Street, New Silksworth,

Sunderland, by his wife Emma: served in France from 19 April 1915, and died of wounds (G.S.W. back) received at Zillebeke Lake, nr. Ypres, 5 January 1916: Age 22.

(IV.B.38) Pte. 1977, William Kelly, 6th (Service) Bn. The King's Own (Yorkshire Light Infantry): *s.* of James Kelly, by his wife Maggie: *b.* Barnsley, co. York: *educ.* Roman Catholic School, there: enlisted 2nd King's Own Yorkshire Light Infantry (about 1902), and after serving 12 years service joined the Reserve and became a Chemical Labourer: re-enlisted Huddersfield on the outbreak of war: served with the Expeditionary Force in France and Flanders from 21 May 1915, and died at Ypres, 1 February 1916, being seized with a fit whilst in the trenches. Buried there. He *m.* at St. Patrick's Roman Catholic Church, Huddersfield, 26 April 1905, Elizabeth (37, Dock Street, Huddersfield), and had six children.

(IV.C.5A) Pte. 20491, Robert Edward Holt, 6th (Service) Bn. The King's Own Scottish Borderers: *s.* of the late Herbert Holt, of Robshire Yard, Cow Lane Bridge, Knottingley, co. York, and Hannah Mary Holt, his spouse (Tythe Barn, Knottingley): and brother to Pte. 12/1019, J. Holt, 12th King's Own (Yorkshire Light Infantry), killed in action, 13 April 1918, aged 23 years: *b.* Mirfield: enlisted Dewsbury: served with the Expeditionary Force in France and Belgium from 30 September 1915 and, severely wounded while on a working party before Zillebeke, died en-route to Poperinghe, 29 October following: Age 16. Remembered on Mirfield War Memorial.

Rest In Peace

His brother Jesse is buried in Outtersteene Communal Cemetery Extension (II.E.25).

(IV.C.16A) Pte. 10/5489, Henry Fawcett Halstead, 10th (Service) Bn. The Lancashire Fusiliers: late of Littleborough, co. Lancaster: 3rd *s.* of Joseph Halstead, of 13, Ormerod Road, Burnley, by his wife Frances Drusilla: *educ.* Carlton Road School; Burnley Grammar School, and Liverpool School of Navigation, from whence, after passing all the relevant examinations, he took up a position with Messrs Leyland, Mercantile Marine, as Ship's Capt. and Master, which appointment he held on the outbreak of war: enlisted Burnley. Died 6 November 1915, of wounds: Age 35. The Chaplain, Rev. John E. MacRae, wrote, "With deep regret I have to tell you that your son H.F. Halstead came in here badly wounded and received every possible skilled medical treatment at once. His strength, however, was not great and he passed away quite peacefully after speaking with me as his clergyman and telling me to send you word, and was buried in our soldiers cemetery here on Sunday afternoon. His grave is registered and marked with a cross and inscription, and his funeral service was conducted with military honours. His friends may well cherish his memory, for your son gave good services here, and one of them at least ought to come forward and fill his place for the work he did must not be left unfinished, and every man is needed."

In The Hour Of His Country's Direst Need He Rushed To Lend His Aid

(IV.C.24A) Spr. 33437, Edward Ernest 'Dits' Anderson, 56th Field Coy., Royal Engineers: *s.* of Charles Anderson, of 263, North Road, Prittlewell, Southend-on-Sea, by his wife Jane: *b.* Prittlewell, 1890: *educ.* Leigh Road School, where he was noticed for his ability as a footballer, was school team captain during his last four years there; and Southend Boy's School from whence he was selected to play both representative and championship matches – played two seasons for Southend United (Inside Forward), and enjoyed a number of games during Southend's tour of Germany 1910; also played for Woolwich Arsenal: enlisted Royal Engineers, Shoreditch, January 1915: served with the Expeditionary Force in France from July, and died, 11 December 1915 of wounds (G.S.W. multiple, back and head), received in action at Ypres the previous day: Age 24. *unm.* Shortly before his departure for France Spr. Anderson had become engaged to be married. Remembered on Southend-on-Sea (County Borough) War Memorial.

Ever In Our Thoughts Which Will Never Fade
From Mum & Dad

(IV.C.25A) Pte. 2567, Harry Marshall, 1/7th Bn. The Duke of Wellington's (West Riding) Regt. (T.F.): *s.* of George Marshall, of 20, Carr Cottages, Carrbrook, Stalybridge, co. Chester: and brother to Pte. 242470, G. Marshall, South Lancashire Regt., killed in action, 13 May 1917; and Pte. 266419, F. Marshall, Cheshire Regt., killed in action, 29 October 1917: *b.* Barnsley, co. York: enlisted Milnsbridge: served with the Expeditionary Force in France and Flanders from April 1915, and died No.17 C.C.S., Lyssenthoek, 11 December 1915, of wounds (septicaemia, consequent to fracture of the pelvis) received in the Canal Bank sector, Ypres: Age 20.*unm.*

Beneath The Soil In Sweet Repose Is Laid A Mother's Dearest Pride

His brother George is buried in Vlamertinghe Military Cemetery (V.M.11); Fred has no known grave, he is commemorated on the Tyne Cot Memorial (Panel 62).

(IV.C.37A) Pte. 3460, Edwin Pugh, 1/3rd Bn. The Monmouthshire Regt. (T.F.): *s.* of Elias Pugh, Maesmawr, Forest Coal Pit, Abergavenny, by his wife

Martha. Mortally wounded by an enemy shell in the vicinity of Elverdinghe Chateau, and died the same day, 29 December 1915: Age 22. See Ferme Olivier Cemetery.

Peace Perfect Peace

(IV.D.25) Pte. 20419, John Craven, 'A' Coy., 7th (Service) Bn. The Northamptonshire Regt.: *s.* of Charlotte Craven (Stanwick, nr. Wellingborough, co. Northampton): and yr. brother to Pte. 10161, T. Craven, 1st Northamptonshire Regt., who fell 9 May 1915, at Aubers Ridge, aged 44 years: *b.* Hargrave, nr. Wellingborough, about 1887: enlisted Northampton 1914: Died of wounds, 22 February 1916: Age 28. *unm.* In a letter to Pte. Craven's mother his commanding officer, Capt. Grierson, wrote, "…as you no doubt have heard, your son has died of wounds. He was badly hit by a sniper whilst returning from an important bombing post which he and three other picked men had been holding during the night. I had a chat with him as he was being brought down the trench, and he was very cheerful and brave though obviously suffering some pain. Although it had become light, stretcher-bearers volunteered to take him to the dressing station – a very dangerous business – so you may be assured everything possible was done for him. He died peacefully and he is buried with his comrades in a section of the cemetery reserved for the 7th Northants. His loss is a great one as he was a very fine bomber and quite fearless…"

To Part With Him Much Grief We Felt
Ever In Our Memory

His brother Thomas has no known grave; he is commemorated on the Le Touret Memorial.

(IV.D.28A) Spr. 2900, Leonard Kirkby Elliott, 459th (2/2nd West Riding) Field Coy., Royal Engineers (T.F.): eldest *s.* of Arthur Kirkby Elliott, of 108, Sackville Road, Crookes, Sheffield, French Polisher, by his wife Sarah, *dau.* of Robert Clark: *b.* Crookes, 24 May, 1895: *educ.* Western Road Council School: Occupation – Cabinet Maker & French Polisher: joined R.E., Sheffield, 22 July 1915: served with the Expeditionary Force in France and Flanders from 13 January 1916, and died in No.17 Casualty Clearing Station, 23 February following, from wounds (G.S.W. abdominal) received in action at Ypres on the 20 February. Buried at Abeele. His Major wrote, "Your son had only been with us a very short time, but he had already attracted my notice by the cheerful way in which he went about his work, and I deplore more deeply than I can say the loss of so gallant a soldier in the service of his King and Country.": Age 21. *unm.*

Greater Love Hath No Man Than This

(V.A.4) Lieut. George Edmund Heygate Fincham, 6th Sqdn. Royal Flying Corps: *s.* of the late Col. G.H. Fincham, Royal Army Ordnance Depot, and Mrs Fincham, of London: *b.* Guernsey, Channel Islands, 28 May 1890: *educ.* College of the Sacred Heart, Wimbledon: Occupation – Mechanical Engineer: obtained his Flying Certificate, Brooklands, 24 May 1915. Killed in aerial combat over Kruistraat (and crash-landed near there), 9 March 1916, while flying an artillery registration mission: Age 25. His observer, 2nd Lieut. G. Price, was also killed.

R.I.P.
Jesus Mercy, Mary Help

(V.A.5) 2nd Lieut. Graham Price, 6th Sqdn. Royal Flying Corps: *s.* of James Price, of 22, Bishopsthorpe Road, Sydenham, London, by his wife Martha: *b.* Penge, London: *educ.* Eaton House School, Anerley; St. Dunstan's College, London, S.E.: joined Royal Engineers, August 1914, and proceeded to France, Corpl. (no.29021), Motorcycle Despatch Rider, 26 October 1914: took part in the First and Second Battles of Ypres (1914–1915): subsequently obtained a commission, gazetted 2nd Lieut. October 1915: apptd. Observer, R.F.C., February 1916, and was killed 9 March 1916 when, flying an artillery registration mission over the front, the aircraft in which he was acting as observer engaged in aerial combat with (and was shot down by) a German Fokker: Age 29. His pilot Lieut. G.E.H. Fincham, was also killed.

Thou Livest O Brave Heart True Knight

(V.A.8) 2nd Lieut. Herbert Sykes Wooler, 12th (Service) Bn. The Prince of Wales' Own (West Yorkshire Regt.): 2nd *s.* of the late Ernest Octavius Wooler, Solicitor; of Balks House, Wortley, Leeds, by his wife Tabitha Louise ('Ashfield,' Pannal Ash, Harrogate), *dau.* of William Nowell, of Halifax, Surgeon: and brother to 2nd Lieut. C.A. Wooler, 10th West Yorkshire Regt., who died in the Herbert Hospital, Woolwich, 20 July 1916, from wounds received in action at the Battle of the Somme on the 1st: *b.* Morley, co. York, 28 November 1892: *educ.* Sedbergh Preparatory School; Sedbergh School (Dux), and St. John's College, Cambridge (Lupton & Hebblethwaite Exhibitioner); graduated with Classical Honours, 1914: although several years in the O.T.C., in preference to waiting for a commission, he joined 11th West Yorkshire Regt., Pte., no.12560, 6 September 1914, after the outbreak of war: obtained a commission in the same regiment 12 December following: transf'd. 12th West Yorkshire Regt.: served with the Expeditionary Force in France and Flanders from 5 October 1915 as

Intelligence Officer to his battalion. Died at No.10 Casualty Clearing Station 28 March 1916, from wounds (S.W. head) received in action at St. Eloi, nr. Ypres, the previous day, while watching the effect of our artillery fire. Buried in Poperinghe Cemetery. His brother, the late 2nd Lieut. C.A. Wooler, 10th West Yorkshire Regt., wrote, "Col. Leggitt, late Commanding Officer, 12th Battn. West Yorkshire Regt., motored over to see me the other day, and in the course of our interview spoke very highly of Bert, and said that he chose him out to observe some dead ground in front of the parapet, as it was a very responsible post. He said he was an excellent Intelligence Officer, and he was so very sorry about it all – he was a splendid fellow," and his servant, Pte. J.E. King, "I could not have had a better master. He was always so kind and considerate to me that it was a pleasure to attend to his wants. He was a fearless officer, Sir, and a great favourite with his men." Mentioned in Despatches (*London Gazette*, 15 June 1916) by General (now F.M.) Sir Douglas Haig, for 'gallant and distinguished service in the field.' He distinguished himself as a good all-round athlete, gaining his cricket and football colours at Sedbergh, and his College colours at Cambridge: Age 23. *unm.* Seven weeks before his death 2nd Lieut. Sykes visited Talbot House, Poperinghe and signed the visitor's book therein.

He Died For Freedom & Honour

His brother Charles is buried in Harrogate (Harlow Hill) Cemetery (F.7).

(V.A.9) Major Gerald Edgar Oliver Fortescue Lambart, 1st Bn. (21st Foot) The Royal Scots Fusiliers: elder *s.* of Col. Edgar Lambart, of 'Fouracres,' Harefield, co. Middlesex, C.B., late Royal Artillery, now (1918) Comdg. 55th Divn. Ammunition Column, British Expeditionary Force, by his wife Geraldine, *dau.* of Capt. James Stirling Stuart, of Castle Milk, Rutherglen: *b.* Dublin, 30 November 1885: *educ.* Laleham (Mr. Frank Buckland); Eton, and Royal Military College, Sandhurst: gazetted 2nd Lieut. 19th Hussars 25 January 1905; promoted Lieut. 20 February 1907; Capt. 2 September 1912: employed with West African Frontier Force from May 1910: took part in the attack on the German Cameroons, until invalided home December 1914: served with the Expeditionary Force in France and Flanders from May 1915: volunteered for the infantry August 1915, and transf'd. Royal Scots Fusiliers, in which regiment his paternal uncle, the late Major F.R.H. Lambart, had served in the Zulu and Boer Wars: promoted Major (Temp.) March 1916, and died in hospital at Poperinghe on the 28th of that month, from wounds received in action nr. St. Eloi the previous day. Buried in Lyssenthoek Military Cemetery, nr. Poperinghe: Age 30. *unm.*

Si Non Frustra Bene Est

(V.A.12) 2nd Lieut. William Hay, 12th (Reserve) Bn. The Cameronians (Scottish Rifles) attd. 1st Bn. Royal Scots Fusiliers: *s.* of William Hay, of 88, West Regent Street, Glasgow, and East Woodlands, Dyce, co. Aberdeen, by his wife Lizzie: *educ*. Glasgow High School; Glasgow University (O.T.C. member). Died of wounds, 1 April 1916: Age 20. Visited Talbot House, Poperinghe, 2 February 1916.

His Last Message
"I Am All Right Keep Cheery And Bright."

(V.A.13) Capt. John George Harter, 1st Bn. (68th Foot) The Durham Light Infantry: Brigade Major 151st Infantry Bde.: eldest *s.* of Charles B.H. Harter, Esq., of 5, Onslow Houses, Kensington, London, S.W.: *b*. London, 30 August 1888: brother to Lieut. C.J. Harter, 4th Royal Fusiliers, killed at Hooge, 16 June 1915: *educ*. Ladycross, Bournemouth; Beaumont College, Old Windsor; and Royal Military College, Sandhurst: joined Durham Light Infantry, 2nd Lieut. (from R.M.C. Sandhurst), September 1908; promoted Lieut. March 1912: apptd. Senior Subaltern 10th (Service) Battn. of his regiment on the outbreak of the Great War: joined 2nd Battn. in Flanders October 1914: apptd. A.D.C. to General Officer Commanding VIth Division, May 1915: apptd. Adjutant, 9th (Territorial) Bn. Durham Light Infantry, July 1915: apptd. Brigade Major 151st Brigade, Northumbrian Division, January 1916. While holding the latter position he was severely wounded in action at The Bluff, nr. Ypres, 3 April 1916, and died the same day at the Remy Casualty Clearing Station, Poperinghe. Buried in the cemetery there. The General Officer Commanding the brigade gave the following account of the circumstances to Capt. Harter's mother, "There was some very heavy shelling yesterday, and while he and I were walking from one headquarters to another a shell came and practically severed his leg. I gave him some morphia and sent him to a Dressing Station. We then got him down to the road, put him into an ambulance, and had him taken to the hospital. His leg was amputated and he died at 6 a.m. this morning. When he was hit his first thought was for others, and he said to me, 'I order you to go away out of danger. Don't stop with me.' He was so brave and plucky, and when I said good-night to him he was just like himself. The whole brigade talks of him with deep admiration and respect. I do so sincerely sympathise with you in your great sorrow. Everyone loved John, and to me he was more like a son than a Staff Officer, and I loved him very dearly. We buried him at 2.15 p.m. today, having got the priest to read the service." A Special Brigade Order of the Day was published announcing the Brigade Major's death. Rather fuller details were given by the Staff Captain of the brigade who wrote, "It was a glorious end, and what better and nobler than this can I say, that his end was a glorious example to us all? Our brigade had been, as you will probably know, holding a very important and difficult part of the line. Well, on the day before his death the enemy shelled our headquarters very heavily, and knocked in all the dug-outs except two. About ten of our servants, clerks and signallers were also knocked out at the same time. John had just come out of the office with the General when a small shell, known as a 'whiz-bang', hit him in the left thigh and severely wounded him. As he lay on the ground he said to the General, 'Go away, General, to safety. I order you to go away.' In a very short time he was carried into the signaller's dug-out, and, as he lay on the ground, he said to the men round about, 'Well, boys I am going to die, and I am quite ready. That's how you all should be.' Captain Harter had made a name for himself in India as a fine horseman, having won the Subaltern's Cup and Rose Cup two years in succession. He was also particularly successful in the training of polo ponies: Age 27. *unm.*

Brigade Major 151st Inf. Bde.
R.I.P.

His brother Clement has no known grave; he is commemorated on the Ypres (Menin Gate) Memorial (Panel 8).

(V.A.16) Capt. Francis Robert 'Frank' Heuston, 14th Bn. Canadian Infantry (1st Royal Montreal Regt. of Quebec), C.E.F.: elder twin *s.* of the late Francis Henry Heuston, M.D., F.R.C.S.I., by his wife Frances Letitia (St. David's, Greystones, co. Wicklow), *dau.* of the late Gibson Black, D.L., of co. Dublin: and twin brother to 2nd Lieut. F.G. Heuston, M.C., Princess Victoria's Royal Irish Fusiliers, reported wounded and missing in the fighting at the Dardanelles, 15 August 1915, now assumed killed in action on or about that date: *b.* Dublin, 17 June 1893: *educ.* Brynmelyn, Weston-super-Mare, and St. Columba's College, Dublin: went to Canada 1912: settled at Halifax, Nova Scotia, as Engineer: joined 66th Regt. (Militia), January 1914: volunteered for Imperial Service on the outbreak of war: apptd. Adjt., Halifax, August 1914: gazetted Lieut. 1st Royal Montreal Regt. 22 September following; Temp. Capt. August 1915: came over with 1st Contingent 1914: went to France, March 1915, and was killed in action nr. St. Eloi, Ypres sector, 7 April 1916. Buried there: Age 22. *unm.*

His twin brother Frederic has no known grave; he is commemorated on the Helles Memorial.

(V.A.18) Lieut. Frank Lawson, 18th Bn. Canadian Infantry (Western Ontario Regt.), C.E.F.: only *s.* of Francis James Lawson, of 504, 4th Avenue West, Calgary, by his wife Margaret: *b.* Inverness, Scotland, 30 March 1888: *educ.* McGill University (graduated 1914): Occupation – Architect: previously served Victoria Rifles (Montreal); 103rd Rifles (Calgary): obtained a commission Lieut. 56th Battn. C.E.F., 20 April 1915, enlisted Calgary, 24 April: subsequently transf'd. 30th Battn. promoted Major, but retained his Lieutenancy, and joined a draft to 18th Battn. that he might proceed more quickly to France. Shot by a German sniper while bringing in dead and wounded at St. Eloi, 10 March 1916, died at No. 10 C.C.S. two days later: 12 April 1916. Buried at Poperinghe. In a letter to his parents his Commanding Officer wrote, "It is with personal regret I am notifying you of the death of your son Lieut. F. Lawson of my battalion. To know him was to love his amiable disposition. He was devoted to his duty and to his men, was liked by his fellow officers, and we miss him. He did his duty and did it well, fearless, painstaking and cautious. He had led his men into a position under a bombardment that was simply hell on earth. He got through all right only to be shot by a Hun sniper when getting in the wounded and dead from 'no man's land,' between the trenches at night, after the battle was over. The bullet entered his right ear and lodged in the spine. When he left the aid post he was conscious and quite cheerful, not thinking the wound serious. He was wounded on the night of April 10, and was admitted to No. 10 Casualty Clearing Station the next morning. He was still conscious on arrival there. His wound was not considered dangerous. He became worse, however, and on being operated upon it was discovered that a clot of blood had formed on the brain. He survived the operation all right, but never rallied, passing peacefully away early the next morning, April 12. It seems hard that such noble young men are being sacrificed. Please accept my sincere sympathy, and rest assured he died a soldier; discharging his duty well.": Age 28. *unm.*

Cherished Memories Of One So Dear Oft Recalled By A Silent Tear

(V.A.24) Lieut. 26030, John Howe, 14th Bn. Canadian Infantry (1st Royal Montreal Regt. of Quebec), C.E.F.: *s.* of the late Arthur Howe, by his wife Beatrice (147, Victoria Avenue, St. Lambert, New Brunswick): gd.-nephew to the late Hon. Joseph Howe, of Halifax, Nova Scotia: *b.* St. John, 26 March 1890: Religion – Roman Catholic: Occupation – Accountant: 5′8½″ tall, blue eyes, brown hair: joined 3rd Victoria Rifles 1906, with which unit he obtained his commission: enlisted C.E.F. Valcartier, 22 September 1914; posted 2nd Battn.: served with the Expeditionary Force in France and Flanders, transf'd. 14th Battn.: Shot and killed by a sniper, 25 April 1916; The Bluff, nr. Hill 60: Age 25. *unm.* Two other ranks (Ptes. J.D.M. MacGillivray, T.J. Martin) were also killed.

We Have Loved Him In Life Let Us Not Forget Him Now
R.I.P.

Ptes. MacGillivray and Martin are buried in Chester Farm Cemetery (II.D.18-19).

(V.A.25) Lieut.Col. Donald Swain Lewis, D.S.O., 1st Sqdn. (2nd Wing) Royal Flying Corps and Royal Engineers: Brevet Major: *yst. s.* of Capt. Ernest Lewis, of Guildford, co. Surrey, and Maria Jane Lewis, his wife: *b.* 5 April 1886: held an appointment with Royal Engineers (from December 1904) gazetted Lieut. 1907; joined Royal Flying Corps, December 1913; promoted Capt. October 1914; Mentioned in Despatches same month: awarded Distinguished Service Order, January 1915 'for valuable information repeatedly furnished to the Royal Artillery in regard to the position of the enemies guns. His direction of our artillery fire, while flying, has constantly led to direct hits on the enemy's batteries and the silencing of their guns.': apptd. Comdr. No.3 Sqdn., April 1915: returned to duties in England, winter 1915–16: returned to France to take up command, 2nd Wing, February 1916, and was killed in action 11.30 a.m., 10 April 1916, when flying an Artillery Observation Reconnaissance Patrol east of Wytschaete, his aircraft (Morane, LA5132) was hit in the fuselage (by anti-aircraft fire from the battery he was co-operating with by radio) and was seen to fall from about 4,000 feet: Age 30. On 14 September 1914 Major G.S. Salmond, O.C. No.3 Sqdn. and Capt. Lewis carried out a successful experiment with a Royal Artillery battery using a radio transmitter to communicate the fall of artillery shells. D.S. Lewis is also credited with creating the "grid square" map system which revolutionized British wartime cartography. The following day (15 September) British IIIrd Corps assigned its R.F.C. squadrons to support of the divisional heavy and howitzer batteries. The radio-equipped aircraft successfully supported the artillery in destroying German positions during the Battle of the Aisne. The second highest-ranked British officer attd. Royal Flying Corps (Royal Air Force) to be killed in the Great War, he was married to Margaret Maitland, *née* Lewis (72, Addison Road, West Kensington, London, W.) His observer, Capt. A.W. Gale, D.S.O., was also killed.

(V.A.26) Capt. Arthur Witherby Gale, D.S.O., 2nd Life Guards (O.C. Trench Mortar Batteries, 3rd Divn.) attd. Royal Field Artillery (and Royal Flying Corps): *s.* of the late Alfred Christopher Gale, by his wife Sophia Eliza (2, Clifton Road, Winchester, co. Hants): enlisted Woolwich, August 1914: served with the Expeditionary Force in France and Flanders from 28 October 1914: awarded Distinguished Serve Order, March 1916. Killed in action, 10 April 1916 when flying as Observer on an Artillery Observation Reconnaissance Patrol east of Wytschaete, the aircraft fuselage was hit by anti-aircraft fire and fell from about 4,000 feet: Age 41. The pilot, Lieut.Col. D.S. Lewis, was also killed.

(V.A.31) Lieut. Gordon Knok Ross, 14th Bn. Canadian Infantry (1st Royal Montreal Regt. of Quebec), C.E.F.: *s.* of George D. Ross, of 102, St. Mark Street, Montreal, by his wife Jane C., *née* Finlay (411, Mackay Street): *b.* Montreal, 27 November 1884: Religion – Church of England: entered service Royal Trust Co., 1901; apptd. Co. Secretary 1913: joined 3rd Victoria Rifles 1914, obtained his commission April 1915; enlisted 9 July, posted 60th Battn. with which unit he proceeded to England. Offered, due to his experience in the banking profession, an appointment in Pay and Records Dept., but declined and proceeded to France with a draft to 14th Battn. March 1916, and was killed in action, 5.15 a.m., 30 April 1916, by a rifle grenade which fell into the trench where he was stationed at The Bluff, Ypres sector: Age 31. *unm.*

Until We Meet Before His Throne

(V.A.32) Lieut. Frank William Skinner, 7th Bn. Canadian Infantry (British Columbia Regt.), C.E.F.: *s.* of William Randall Skinner, of 'Tecumseh,' 44, Albion Road, Westcliff-on-Sea, co. Essex, by his wife Helen C.J.: *b.* Battersea, London, S.W., 5 February 1892: *educ.* Honeywell Road School; Emanuel School, Wandsworth Common (passed Cambridge Senior local examinations): entered service London City & Midland Bank Ltd., 1908; removed to Canada, 1912, to an appointment as Accountant, Head Office, Bank of British North America; transf'd. St. John branch, New Brunswick: previously served 1 year 16th London Regt. (Queen's Westminster Rifles); volunteered for Imperial Service and enlisted Valcartier, 23 September 1914; Spr. 5752, 1st Canadian Divn. Signal Coy. (Engineers): proceeded overseas with 1st Contingent, October 1914: trained Salisbury Plain, winter 1914–1915: joined Expeditionary Force in France and Flanders, February 1915; promoted Sergt. September following: rewarded with a commission, November 1915 – Lieut. attd. 7th Battn. – in recognition of his gallantry, efficiency and devotion to duty while on Active Service. Died of wounds (S.W. multiple, abdominal), 5 May 1916, received from *minenwerfer* fire near Hill 60 two days previously: Age 24. *unm.*

(V.A.33) Lieut. Henry Errol Beauchamp Platt, 'A' Coy., 3rd Bn. Canadian Infantry (Central Ontario Regt.), C.E.F.: *s.* of Arthur Thomas Platt, of 168, Balsam Avenue, Toronto, by his wife Helen A.C.: *b.* London, Ontario, 16 May 1891: *educ.* Talbot Street Public School there; Queen Victoria Public School; Parkdale Collegiate; University College, Toronto (Political Science), 1909–13, B.A., gained First and Second Rugby colours (played for Argonaut Rugby Team), member of XIII Club and Historical Club: on the outbreak of war was a law student, engaged with Messrs Rowell, Reid, Wood & Wright: Lieut. 2nd Regt. (Militia): obtained his commission with Queen's Own Rifles and took an active part in organising the University Coy. which trained with that unit during autumn 1914: apptd. 35th Battn. and, after a period of guard duty at Toronto Island, proceeded overseas with that unit June 1915; with him was his close friend and University colleague Lieut. G.L.B. Mackenzie, who served with him for several months and also fell at Ypres: joined the Expeditionary Force in France October 1915 and, with the exception of a brief period of training at St. Omer, spent the winter months and early spring in the trenches; south sector, Ypres Salient. At the time of his death he was Battalion Intelligence Officer, in command of the regimental scouts and snipers and, with a German attack before Ypres expected in early May, he, accompanied by two other men, went out on the night of 4 May to reconnoitre the ground near Hill 60. During the course of this work he was shot in the head by a sniper (12.30 a.m.) and such was the esteem in which he was held, there was no shortage of volunteers within his company to venture out and bring him in. Three men carried him back to the lines unconscious, from whence he was removed to Transport Farm, thence to Poperinghe where he died within a few hours (5 a.m.), 5 May 1916: Age 24. *unm.* Lieut. Mackenzie wrote, "5/5/16. Poor old Errol died this morning from a bullet wound in the head, received while he was patrolling at night with two of his scouts. I expect to be allowed to go to the funeral, the arrangements are not yet complete." And, in a letter to a friend, "Having lived with Errol in the last year in the closest intimacy, I learned something of his manly and lovable qualities, and, believe me, my sense of loss is very deep and real also. Errol's work as Battalion Intelligence Officer called for high qualities of mind and heart. As you, of course, realise his death from a rifle wound received when on patrol with two of his men only 20 yards from the enemy's lines, was in the highest sense honourable, and an ever shining example of cool devotion to duty. The work of gaining information about the enemy's line is and his movements is absolutely necessary and often dangerous in the extreme. Yesterday, two sergeants of his old platoon, No.4 (Sergts. Burger and Braddick), Lambert of his scouts, and myself, were given permission to leave the line to be present at his burial at Lyssenthoek Military Cemetery, which lies in a beautiful country 10 miles behind the trenches. Our Chaplain, Capt. Gordon, conducted the service. The afternoon sun shone brightly, and a crisp breeze rustled through the new leaves. The day was full of Spring, and the grain of poetry in every man's nature was stirred by thoughts too deep for tears, yet underneath all was a gladness unconquerable and a strong assurance." For their part in recovering Lieut. Platt's body Sergts. Burger and Braddick, and Pte. Lambert were awarded the Military Medal.

Oh True Brave Heart God Bless Thee Love Is Strong As Death

Lieut. George L.B. Mackenzie lies nearby (VI.A.17).

(V.A.37) Major George Edward Vansittart, 13th Bty., 4th Bde. Canadian Field Artillery, C.E.F.: only *s.* of the late John Pennefather (& M.I.) Vansittart, Public Works Dept., India (*d.* 1886): and *gt.-gdson.* to the late Vice Admiral Henry Vansittart, of Eastwood, Woodstock, Canada, and Bisham Abbey, co. Berks, and Mary Charity, his wife: *b.* Mussoorie, India, 7 October 1884: *educ.*

Royal Military College, Kingston, 1901–04 (Orderly Officer, 4th Cavalry Bde.); Upper Canada College (Applied Science), 1904–05; McGill University, Alpha Delta Phi fraternity: Occupation – Civil Electrical Engineer, Crane Falls Power & Irrigation Co., Boise, Idaho: attd. 9th C.F.A. (Militia); returned to Canada following the outbreak of war, enlisted Toronto, 8 December 1914, apptd. 13th Bty. 4th Bde. C.F.A.: promoted Major and O.C. prior to departing Canada: served in France from autumn 1915, on front south of Ypres and in the salient. Major Vansittart was wounded by the close explosion of a shell, 14 May 1916, while his battery was in action near Dickebusch, and died three hours later. Buried at Lyssenthoek, nr. Poperinghe. Posthumously gazetted; Mentioned in Despatches, April 1916: Age 31.

Only Son Of John Pennefeather Vansittart P.W.D. India
Faithful Unto Death

(V.B.21) Pte. G/64, Robert Bell, No.5 Squad, 'B' Coy., 8th (Service) Bn. The Buffs (East Kent Regt.): *b.* Blackburn, co. Lancaster: enlisted Folkestone, co. Kent: served with the Expeditionary Force from late September 1915, and died of wounds, 11 March 1916, received the same day, being shot by an enemy sniper while in the trenches between Sanctuary Wood and Hill 60. See also Pte. C. Phipps, and Corpl. J. Broom, Sanctuary Wood Cemetery (II.M.1 & II.K32 respectively). (*IWGC record S/64*)

(V.B.23A) Pte. 20127, Arthur Robertson, 1st Bn. (21st Foot) The Royal Scots Fusiliers: *s.* of Mrs M. Robertson (9, Bannermill Street, Aberdeen): enlisted Aberdeen, 1915: served with the Expeditionary Force in France, and died of wounds, 28 March 1916, received in the attack at St. Eloi the previous day: Age 16.

His Memory Remains

(V.B.24) Gnr. 83669, John Emerson Hill, 4th Bde., Canadian Field Artillery, C.E.F.: *s.* of James Hill, of Aurora, Ontario, by his wife Sarah J.: *b.* Goodwood, York Co., Ontario, 20 January 1891: *educ.* Whitchurch Public School; Aurora High School; University College, Toronto (Political Science), 1911–15, B.A.: member of the 'Varsity' staff, and C.O.T.C.: enlisted 14th Bty., 4th Bde. Canadian Field Artillery, autumn 1914: came over with Second Canadian Contingent: joined the Expeditionary Force in France, September 1915; served in the Ploegsteert – Ypres sector throughout the following months, and died at No.17 Casualty Clearing Station, Poperinghe, 28 March 1916, of wounds received in action the previous day. During the heavy fighting of 27 March 1916 at St. Eloi he went out to mend a broken telephone line and, while in a communication trench, was wounded in the spine (S.W. head, neck) by a shell. Recommended for a commission, the order for his return to England arrived the day after his death. A Freemason, Gnr. Hill was a member of Rising Sun Lodge No.129, Aurora: Age 26. *unm.*

(V.B.27A) Corpl. 942, John Arnold Shaw, 2nd (Durham) Bty., 1/3rd (Northumbrian) Bde., Royal Field Artillery (T.F.): *s.* of Joseph W. (& E.A.) Shaw, of 1, Waldon Street, West Hartlepool. Severely wounded (abdominal, 27 March 1916) by the detonation of a high-explosive shell which struck the position he was occupying with Lieut. J.R. Platt (died later the same day) and several other men while plotting artillery fire in the vicinity of Hill 60. Died in the Casualty Clearing Station, Poperinghe the following day; 28 March 1916: Age 21.

St. John Chap. 15 Ver. 13

Refers: 'Greater love than this no man hath, that a man lay down his life for his friends.'

Lieut. Platt is buried in Railway Dugouts Burial Ground (Transport Farm) (III.E.13).

(V.B.30A) Pte. 3469, Walter Scott, 'C' Coy., 7th Bn. The Northumberland Fusiliers (T.F.): *s.* of Ebenezer Scott, of Berwick-on-Tweed, by his wife Mary: *b.* Berwick: enlisted Alnwick: served with the Expeditionary Force from October 1915; wounded by retaliatory fire (S.W. multiple), 27 March 1916, consequent to a number of British mines being detonated beneath the German positions at St. Eloi, and died at No.17 Casualty Clearing Station, Poperinghe the following day; 28 March 1916: Age 27. *unm.*

He Fought The Good Fight

(V.B.31) Pte. 3037, Robert Todd; Officers' Servant, 'C' Coy., 7th Bn. The Northumberland Fusiliers (T.F.): *s.* of the late Robert Todd, of Chevington Drift, Acklington, co. Northumberland, and Catherine Todd, his wife (also deceased): enlisted Alnwick: proceeded to France, June 1915, and died of wounds, 28 March 1916; received from shellfire the previous day, vicinity St. Eloi – Hill 60: Age 19.

(V.B.35A) Pte. 460606, John Joseph Malone (*a.k.a.* Folinsbee), 13th (Royal Highlanders of Canada) Bn. Canadian Infantry (Quebec Regt.), C.E.F.: *s.* of the late Hugh Malone, and Alice W. Folinsbee (58, Allen Street, Buffalo, New York, U.S.A.); lately 364, West Avenue: *b.* Cleveland, Ohio, 2 October 1890: Religion – Presbyterian: Occupation – Clerk: joined C.E.F., Winnipeg, 21 June 1915; apptd. 17th Reserve Bn.: departed Montreal, 11 September: trained England; hospitalised (influenza) Shorncliffe / Dover, 26 November–3 December 1915:

proceeded to France, 17 February 1916, with a draft of reinforcements; joined 13th Battn., In the Field, 10 March. Wounded (SW Lt. side / abdominal) 2.30 a.m., 31 March 1916; while attached to a work party (Trench 47.S), admitted 3rd Field Ambulance, R.A.M.C., Dickebusch, transf'd. No.10 C.C.S., Poperinghe; died 4.30 p.m. same day: Age 25. (*IWGC record age 21*)

In Loving Remembrance From Mother

(V.B.39) Pte. 29412, Henry Aitken, 16th Bn. Canadian Infantry (Manitoba Regt.), C.E.F.: *s.* of Henry (& Elizabeth) Aitken, c/o Balfour Buildings, Stevenston, co. Ayr, Scotland: *b.* Aberdeen: Religion – Presbyterian: Occupation – Labourer. Died of wounds (GSW abdominal) No.17 C.C.S. 1 April 1916, received in action the previous day: Age 33. Correspondence c/o J. Buchanan, Esq., 21, Roslin Terrace, Aberdeen.

(V.B.39A) Sergt.Major 106, John Kirk, M.C., 1st Bn. Irish Guards: late of Bedford: *b.* Doddington, co. Cambridge: enlisted Chatteris. Died of wounds, 2 April 1916, being shot by a sniper in the vicinity of St. Jean earlier the same day. See Pte. D. O'Shea, Potijze Burial Ground Cemetery (E.17).

(V.C.4A) Pte. 19043, Aungier Ernest Peacocke, 7th (Service) Bn. The Northamptonshire Regt.: formerly no.98121, Royal Field Artillery: *s.* of Aungier Peacocke, of 124, Mill Road, Cambridge, by his wife Agnes E.: *b.* Leyton, co. Essex: enlisted Stratford: served with the Expeditionary Force in France from 25 November 1915, and died, 14 March 1916 of wounds (G.S.W. multiple) received in action; Menin Road – Hooge, nr. Ypres: Age 16.

There Is A Link Death Cannot Sever
Love And Remembrance Last For Ever

(V.C.7A) Rfn. B/2679, James Mitchell, 11th (Service) Bn. The Prince Consort's Own (The Rifle Brigade): *s.* of John Mitchell, of School Lane, Chandler's Ford, Southampton, by his wife Alice Jane: and brother to L/Corpl. 40743, E. Mitchell, 10th Lancashire Fusiliers, died of wounds, 14 November 1917, aged 22: enlisted Winchester: served with the Expeditionary Force in France from 22 July 1915, and died of wounds (G.S.W. head, abdomen), 14 March 1916. Remembered on Chandlers Ford War Memorial, St. Boniface's Churchyard; "Erected In Grateful Memory Of Those Who Fell In The Great War A.D. 1914–1919 These Died In War That We At Peace Might Live These Gave Their Best So We Our Best Should Live: Also To The Memory Of The Fallen In The '39–'45 War And Subsequent Campaigns."

Gone But Not Forgotten

His brother Ernest is buried in Dozinghem Military Cemetery (XIII.C.10).

(V.C.13) Pte. 17381, Edwin John Hewitt, 7th (Service) Bn. The Northamptonshire Regt.: *s.* of Edwin Hewitt, by his wife Mary: Occupation – Labourer; Excelsior Stoneworks, Finedon: enlisted Kettering, co. Northampton: served with the Expeditionary Force in France and Flanders from 1 September 1915; took part in the fighting at Loos later that month. Died of wounds (G.S.W., chest, abdomen), 14 March 1916, received in action at Hooge the previous day. *The Kettering Leader,* 14 April 1916, reported, "Kettering Soldier Family Again Broken: The regrettable news has been received that Pte. E. Hewitt, son-in-law of Mr T. Wright, 4, Carey Street, Kettering, has died as the result of wounds on the battlefield in France. Much sympathy is felt for the widow, and for Mr. T. Wright, the latter of whom had six sons and one son-in-law at the front. Of the sons, Pte. Herbert Wright, 1/4th Northants Regiment, was killed at the Dardanelles. The others are Pte. Walter C. Wright, 1/4th Northants; Pte. Thomas E. Wright, 3rd Northants; Pte. Wm. H. Wright, 3rd Northants; and Pte. Josh. Wright, 3rd Northants. The Deceased (Pte. E. Hewitt) was a native of Kettering, and 30 years of age. A year last September, he joined the 7th Northants, and up to that time he had been employed at the Excelsior Stone Works, Finedon. He went to France with his regiment at the latter end of August. The last time he wrote a postcard home was about March 14th (*q.v.*), and by the time it was received in England he had passed away, as the result of wounds." Chaplain D. Ellis Rowlands wrote, "Two days ago I wrote to you of your husband being wounded; I now regret to have to inform you that he passed away at 9.30 on the 14th. His case was quite hopeless from the first, but everything was done for him that possibly could have been done. I can only say that God will be with you and give you that there shall be no more parting.": Age 30. (*IWGC record Hewett*)

Herbert Wright is buried in 7th Field Ambulance Cemetery, Gallipoli (II.D.12).

(V.C.36A) Pte. 24856, Douglas Cameron McLaurin, 16th (Canadian Scottish) Bn. Canadian Infantry (Manitoba Regt.), C.E.F.: *s.* of John R. McLaurin Snr., of Vankleek Hill, Ontario, and his wife: and brother to Lieut. H.J. McLaurin, 16th Canadian Infantry, killed in action, 14 June 1916, at Sanctuary Wood: *b.* Vankleek Hill, Prescott Co., Ontario, 18 June 1892: Occupation – Student: enlisted 13th (Royal Higlanders), Valcartier, 23 September 1914: subsequently transf'd. 16th Battn.; came over with Second Canadian Contingent: served with the Expeditionary Force in France and Flanders; wounded at Ypres, May 1915. Died of wounds, 5 April 1916: Age 23. *unm.* (*IWGC record MacLaurin*)

Greater Love Hath No Man

His brother Howard lies nearby (VI.A.34).

(V.D.5A) Gnr. 1809, Arthur Clement Dibb, 1/2nd (Northumbrian) Bde., Royal Field Artillery: s. of Arthur Dibb, of 11, Pool Road, Otley, co. York, by his wife Jane: and brother to Gnr. 50559, H. Dibb, 107th Bde., Royal Field Artillery, died, 26 June 1917; and Pte. 36227, J.C. Dibb, 6th King's Own Yorkshire Light Infantry, killed in action, 12 October 1917: served with the Expeditionary Force in France, and died of wounds (gas), 19 March 1916: Age 21.

Duty Nobly Done

His brother Harold lies nearby (XIV.C.18); Joseph has no known grave, he is commemorated on the Tyne Cot Memorial (Panel 109).

(V.D.11A) Spr. 607, Charles Ross Morrison, 6th Field Coy., Canadian Engineers, C.E.F.: s. of William Stuart Morrison, of Wapella, Saskatchewan, by his wife Marjory Ross: *b.* Wapella, 24 September 1890: Occupation – Machinist: a serving member of the Militia, volunteered and enlisted Ottawa, 4 February 1915. Died of wounds (G.S.W. abdominal), No.10, C.C.S., 3 p.m., 21 March 1916, received at Zillebeke the previous day from the accidental explosion of an automatic revolver: Age 25. Charles and his brother – Spr. 608, H.K. Morrison, Canadian Engineers – with whom he enlisted, had been allocated leave two days later, and planned to spend part of it together; Hector had to proceed alone.

For Our Tomorrow He Gave His Today

(V.D.13) Pte. 14350, George Alfred Kiddle, 2nd Bn. Coldstream Guards: *s.* of Joseph William Kiddle, of Washingford Farm, Sisland, co. Norfolk, and his spouse Catherine: *b.* Sisland, 23 July 1894: proceeded to France, late October 1915. Died of wounds (G.S. chest), 22 March 1916, No.17 Casualty Clearing Station, Poperinghe. Buried in the Military Cemetery, Remy Siding: Age 21.

Brief Life Is Here Our Portion

(V.D.30) Sergt. 79660, George Wilson, 31st Bn. Canadian Infantry (Alberta Regt.), C.E.F.: *s.* of John Wilson, of Cellardyke, Anstruther, co. Fife, Scotland, by his wife Sophia: Occupation – Tinsmith: enlisted Calgary, 14 November 1914. Died of wounds, 6 April 1916, received in action at St. Eloi the previous day: Age 26.

(V.D.34) Pte. 80112, Arthur Currie, 31st Bn. Canadian Infantry (Alberta Regt.), C.E.F.: *s.* of Mr. E. Currie, of 607, 24th Avenue West, Mount Pleasant, N.W. Calgary, and Mrs Currie (Denmark Terrace, Harrogate, co. York, England): *b.* Harrogate, 11 December 1884: Religion – Church of England: Occupation –

Plasterer: 5'7" tall, dark complexion, brown eyes, dark hair: ¾" transverse scar across bridge of nose: previously served 7 years with West Yorkshire Volunteers; 1 year 5th (Territorial) Bn. West Yorkshire Regt.: enlisted Calgary, 19 January 1915, aged 30 years, 1 month: served with the Expeditionary Force in France, and died of wounds, 8 April 1916 received in action at St. Eloi five days previously: Age 31. *unm.*

(V.D.36) Pte. 5053, William John Hall, 2nd Bn. Scots Guards: *b.* Pittsburgh, United States: enlisted Edinburgh. Died 8 April 1916, of wounds: Age 31. He was married to Edith Hall (18, Waverley Park, Abbey Hill, Edinburgh), to whom Chaplain W.J. Baxter wrote, 'I regret to say that our fears were justified. Your husband passed away yesterday evening at 9.15. He had a peaceful end. The funeral took place this afternoon. At 2.15 he was borne out of the hospital on the little burial car wheeled by his comrades. No coffin is used at the Front, but instead a plaid or blanket is sewn round the body by a soldier's hand; and over all the Union Jack is spread. At the grave side the Union Jack was laid aside and 6 comrades lowered the body into the grave. Then we uncovered our heads and I conducted a simple Scottish ceremony. The grave is at Lijssenthoek, 1½ miles south of Poperinghe, and on the road to Boeshepe. A Cross is being erected to mark the spot so that it will never be lost sight of while men can admire a brave man's end.'

Until The Day Dawns And The Shadows Flee Away

(V.D.36A) Pte. 446440, Ernest Packwood, 27th Bn. Canadian Infantry, C.E.F.: c/o Miss Eleanor Packwood (46, Bourne Street, West Derby Road, Liverpool, England): *b.* 18 March 1893: Religion – Church of England. Occupation – Tailor: previously served 1 ½ yrs. 6th Liverpool Regt.; volunteered and enlisted Calgary, 30 April 1915: departed Quebec, S.S. 'Carpathia,' 16 May: disembarked Devonport, England, 29 May; trained Dibgate Camp, Shorncliffe; Otterspool, Liverpool: proceeded to France, night of 17 September 1915. Died of wounds, No.10 Casualty Clearing Station, Poperinghe, 9 April 1916; received in action at St. Eloi: Age 23. *unm.*

No.10 Casualty Clearing Station

> A bed at last, in a long low-roofed hall.
> Full of soft footfalls, moans and sharper cries.
> At intervals now I can see it all –
> White beds, red nurses, khaki orderlies.
> Then nightmare: dying, crushed by the victor Hun;
> Or struggling madly, shoulder-deep in mire.

Or straining demon horses until one
Rolls over me with breath and eyes of fire.

I waken from these horrors and thank Heaven.
Finding myself all safe in bed, but then
The real grows more clear and fearful
Even equals the dream.
Beside me lie two men
One young and fragile, with the bubbling cough
Of men shot through the lungs and dying slow;
A nurse is bending over to wipe off
The red foam from the quivering lips below.
The other, huge, grim, silent save for rare
Expostulation: "Why the hell can't he keep quiet like the rest of us?"
And there I almost break in to reprove him too.
But just refrain and later in the night
Someone steals gently to the strong man's bed.
And peers into his face in the dim light.
And brings the bearers to remove the dead.

Capt. Robert S. Smylie, Royal Scots Fusiliers,
Killed in action, 14 July 1916.
Flatiron Copse Cemetery, Mametz (Sp.Mem.3).

No.10. Casualty Clearing Station,
B.E.F. France.
23.5.16.

Dear Mrs Gamble, I am very sorry indeed to tell you that your son Lt. J.W. Gamble died in hospital here at 6.30 a.m. yesterday morning. He was brought here two hours before with a most serious wound in the abdomen. For a few moments he was just semi-conscious, and was able to give the nurse your address, but that was all he was able to say. The Doctors and Nurses spared absolutely no pains in their efforts for him, but they could not save his life and after a very short time he became unconscious and later passed quietly away without having been able to leave any message. I am so sorry that I was too far away to be able to get to see him before he died and the more so as I used to be in Derby and feel sure I remember your name. I would have given anything to have been able to get to him and receive some last message for you if only he had been able to give it. He did not suffer much pain. The shock of the wound prevented that. I do not know under what circumstances he received the wound but I hope I will hear from his

C.O. about that. I buried him late the same day in the military cemetery on the Poperinghe – Boescheppe Rd. one mile and a half from Poperinghe. His grave will be marked with a cross bearing his name and can always be easily found in future years. It will always be cared for and preserved and if you would like to send out some flowers or plants to me I will plant them myself on his grave. He lies well behind the firing line in the Belgian countryside. Any personal effects of his will be sent to you later by the authorities. Please accept my deepest sympathy and I hope you will feel that he was not alone, but with friends who did their very best for him. If there is anything at all that I can do for you do not hesitate to ask me. May God help and comfort you. Yours Sincerely, A.B. Brooker, Chaplain.

(VI.A.1) Lieut. John Walcot Gamble, 'B' Coy., 14th (Service) Bn. The Durham Light Infantry: *s*. of Ernest Thomas Gamble, of Derby, by his wife Constance: *b*. 1894: Occupation – Student: enlisted Derby, 15 September 1914: proceeded to France, October 1915. Died of wounds (abdominal), 22 May 1916, received in action at Ypres the previous day: Age 21. *unm*. (*IWGC record age 22*) See also Bard Cottage Cemetery.

(VI.A.3) Lieut. Edmund Arthur Brownsworth, 1st Bn. (17th Foot) The Leicestershire Regt.: *yst. s*. of the late David Brownsworth, Photographic Artist & Portrait Painter; by his wife Sophia (19, Otley Street, Skipton, co. York): and brother to Regtl.Sergt.Major 12701, S. Brownsworth, 7th Leicestershire Regt., died 5 November 1917: *educ*. Skipton National School, and, after a period of training, was apprenticed to (and entered) the Merchant Service from which, after numerous extended cruises, he departed on account of ill-health: subsequently joined the Army in which he rose to the rank of Sergt., Leicestershire Regt., and went to France in that capacity, November 1914: for distinguished service he was recommended for a commission by his Brigadier General, and gazetted 2nd Lieut. Leicestershire Regt. April 1915; apptd. Temp. Lieut. November following. Died of wounds, 27 May 1916, at No.10 C.C.S., Abeele, received in action three weeks previously consequent to the detonation of an enemy mine beneath his company's trench: Age 25. *unm*. On 2 November 2008 his father's 1886 scenic oil painting 'Skipton-in-Craven' sold at auction for £15.00.

His Life For His Country And His Soul To God

His brother Shearing is buried in Voormezeele Enclosures Nos. 1 & 2 (I.L.51).

(VI.A.6) Lieut.Col. Arthur William Tanner, 10th Field Amb., Canadian Army Medical Corps, C.E.F.: *s*. of the late Robert J. Tanner, by his wife Sarah Fanny: *b*. Watford, Ontario, 15 December 1876: *educ*. Victoria Public School,

Ottawa; University of Toronto (Medicine), 1895–99, M.B.: prior to enlistment was engaged in Railway Medical work; Practitioner, Moosomin, Saskatchewan. Holding a commission – Lieut., 16th Light Horse – in the autumn of 1914 he acted as Recruiting Officer, Moosomin District; apptd. Medical Oficer, 10th Canadian Mounted Rifles, January 1915; took command of Hospital Unit, Camp Hughes, rank Capt. July 1915: apptd. A.D.M.S., Military District No.10, August following: promoted Lieut.Col. apptd. Officer Commanding No.10 Field Ambulance, February 1916, and proceeded overseas: served with the Expeditionary Force in France, 3rd Divn. Front, Ypres, from April 1916. Severely wounded by shellfire while at the Advanced Dressing Station in the court-yard of the Sacré Coeur Hospital, Ypres, during the Battle of Sanctuary Wood, he insisted on continuing to direct and remove the wounded to a place of safety before seeking treatment for himself. Only when he had completed his work would he allow himself to be removed to No.10 C.C.S. where, despite an operation and the best possible care, he succumbed to his injuries two days later, 4 June 1916: Age 39. He leaves a wife, Flora Blanche Tanner, *née* Richmond (Moosomin, Saskatchewan), and family. (*IWGC record age 40*)

Be Thou Faithful Unto Death And I Will Give Thee A Crown Of Life

(VI.A.8) Capt. Harry James Pitts, 5th Bn. Canadian Mounted Rifles, C.E.F.: *s.* of Shadrach Pitts, by his wife Emma: *b.* Cambridge, England, 10 June 1876: Religion – Church of England: Occupation – Manager: 5'10¾" tall, blue eyes, fair hair: previously served 5th (Royal Irish) Lancers; a serving member of 6th (Duke of Connaught's) Hussars (Militia); enlisted Sherbrooke, 1 June 1915 (as Officer). Died of wounds, 3 June 1916, received in action at Maple Copse, shortly after 6.40 p.m. the previous day: Age 39. Capt. Pitts was mortally wounded in carrying out an order to proceed, with two platoons, to reinforce trench S.P.14 and gain touch with 10th Battn. on the right. His sister, Miss Rose Emma Pitts (4, Bassett Avenue, Montreal), will gratefully receive and acknowledge all correspondence regarding her dear departed brother.

(VI.A.10) Capt. Melville Greenshields, 13th Bn. Canadian Infantry (Quebec Regt.), C.E.F.: *s.* of James Naismith Greenshields, Lawyer, of Montreal, Quebec, by his wife Elizabeth Glass: Occupation – Founder & Associate Partner, Messrs Greenshields & Co., Stockbrokers: enlisted Valcartier, September 1914: embarked Quebec, 26 September, R.M.S. 'Alaunia': departed Wolfe's Cove, four days later: arrived Devonport, 14 October: underwent training Salisbury Plain throughout winter 1914–15: served with the Expeditionary Force in France and Flanders from 15 February 1915: took part in the fighting at St. Julien where, during an evacuation of the battalion's line (23 April), 'but for the gallant work of a small rear-guard under the command of Lieut. C.B. Pitblado, assisted by

Lieut. M. Greenshields, and supported by Lieut. J.G. Ross, it is almost certain the battalion would have been overwhelmed'; wounded the following day. Capt. Greenshields was killed in action, 3 June 1916, on which date 13th Canadians, in support to 3rd Brigade's counter-attack at Hill 62, received its share of enemy shell fire, which continued throughout the day. No fires could be lit for cooking, as the smoke would be seen. In the evening the companies altered their positions. No. 1 moved up to the position in the rear of Maple Copse, where the 14th (one of the leading battalion's in the attack) had been forced to dig in after coming under heavy rifle, machine gun and shell fire. This position the company set to work to consolidate, as they were to occupy it for the next twenty-four hours. No. 2 company moved to Zillebeke village. No. 3 remained in reserve in the old positions, and No. 4 moved to Valley Cottages. During these moves about fifty casualties were sustained through the continuous artillery fire poured onto the battalion's position by the enemy, Capt. Greenshields being killed instantaneously by a fragment of shell which hit him in the head: Age 32.

When the Battle of Mount Sorrel began on the night of 2 June 1916, 15th Canadians were in reserve resting in billets behind the lines and, after receiving orders to proceed to the front with all possible haste, hurriedly marched several miles through the night to take part in a counter-attack on Observatory Ridge on the morning of 3 June. The War Diary records: "3 June 1916: Attack 8.35 a.m. Upon the signal being given the officers and men behaved most courageously, immediately getting out, forming line and rushed forward in the face of a perfect HELL of Artillery and Machine Gun fire. It did not seem possible that anything could live through it, the right of the line was temporarily held up by a thick hedge and before a way was made through it the first line were all shot down..." Mike Malone – leading his platoon through this 'perfect Hell,' looking for a means to get through the hedge – was among those who fell.

(VI.A.12) Lieut. Maurice Edward 'Mike' Malone, 15th Bn. Canadian Infantry (Central Ontario Regt.), C.E.F.: *s.* of Edward T. Malone, of 85, Bay Street, Toronto, Ontario, by his wife Amy: *b.* Toronto, 2 April 1896: *educ.* Huron Street School; St. Andrew's College (1907–13), and University College, Toronto University (Beta Theta Pi, 1913–14), where he earned his Second Hockey Colours, and attained rank Colour Sergt. after only six months with the O.T.C.: previously served 3 months Lieut. 48th Highlanders (Reserve): enlisted Niagara, June 1915, posted 58th Battn.: proceeded Overseas, August following, joining 15th Battn. in France, 11 November 1915: served in the Ypres salient with his battalion throughout the winter and early months of 1916. When the Battle of Sanctuary Wood began on 2 June his platoon was back in billets resting. Immediately called up, they marched several miles through the night and, on arrival, advanced in the counter-attack at Observatory Ridge on the morning of the 3rd. Just as his platoon had reached the farthest point of their advance, and he was looking for a means to pass through a hedge, he was shot through the heart and, calling out "Never mind, it's alright," he fell. His Commanding officer wrote, "The Germans had effected a break in the line. We who were in reserve were suddenly called up and after a long night march made an advance in broad daylight under heavy shell and machine gun fire, which enabled us to take up a position which secured most of the lost ground and denied the enemy the advantages he had so nearly secured. It was at the farthest point of our advance, about half-past seven in the morning that Mike was struck down. He had been behaving most gallantly. Except for the manner in which he brought up his men to reinforce my line we should not have been able to reinforce as we did.".: 3 June 1916: Age 21. *unm.*

> *I Have Fought A Good Fight I Have Finished My Course*
> *I Have Kept The Faith*

Following a whirlwind bombardment of every calibre and large scale German infantry assaults, 2 June 1916 saw the Canadians in the region between Hooge and Hill 60 forced to give ground and a number of trenches up to the enemy. 3rd Canadians, who had only recently been withdrawn for a well-deserved rest, were but one of the units hastily rushed forward to restore the situation. 5 June found the battalion waiting in some shallow, hastily constructed, and totally inadequate trenches on the edge of Armagh Wood from where they would soon be attacking to retake a sector of the Mount Sorrel trenches on the other side of the wood. The trenches were in a vile condition, bodies lay everywhere in every stage of decomposition, and the well-known salient curse – mud – covered everything.

Although withdrawn on the night of 8 June the battalion were, during their period at the front, fully aware of the importance placed on information regarding the disposition of the enemy opposite, and accordingly made reconnaissances for this purpose. On the night of 6 June 1916, Lieut. George Mackenzie and Sergt. Fred Burger, an experienced scout, crossed no man's land, to reconnoitre the German lines which, if heavily defended, might prove serious problems to the Canadian advance. After successfully investigating one of the enemy positions the two men were spotted, fired on, and forced to retire. However, in the early hours of the following morning the two men stole out again and entered the German trench where it was known to be unoccupied and gained a complete insight into the system at that point. But while making their investigation of the system they encountered a sentry who, although dealt with, raised the alarm which in turn led to a lively five minutes for the two Canadians who, taking advantage of a momentary lull, departed the German trench with all haste and, during the course of this act, a third sentry shot Sergt. Burger through the thigh. By this time daylight had broken, but the Germans did not pursue the two men, and by taking advantage of the cover afforded by a number of bush thickets, Lieut. Mackenzie succeeded in getting the wounded sergeant back to the safety of the Canadian lines.

Those who saw Lieut. Mackenzie when he returned said he was soaked to the skin, plastered with mud, pleased with his adventure and in a very happy state of mind. Proceeding at once to impart the information he had gained – 'described as valuable and urgently required' – to Battalion Headquarters, some distance in the rear, he arrived safely and made his report. On his return, after a brief stop at Company Headquarters, where he spoke to his servant, he made his way toward the nearest platoon of his company. On passing an exposed spot in the trench, a spot that had so far escaped the attention of the enemy's sharpshooters, he was seen to sink to his knees, fall backwards like a person fainting, and lay still. He had been shot through the heart by a sniper, probably from somewhere on the heights of Observatory Ridge. A sergeant and private of the battalion, under fire of the Germans, crawled out and brought the lifeless body in to the nearest cover. There he lay all day until, under cover of darkness, his body could be removed to the rear where he was laid to rest in the cemetery at Poperinghe two and a half days later.

(VI.A.17) Lieut. George Lawrence Bissett Mackenzie, 3rd Bn. Canadian Infantry (Central Ontario Regt.), C.E.F.: *s.* of George Allan Mackenzie, of 665, Grosvenor Avenue, Westmount, Montreal, by his marriage to the late Ella Therese Mackenzie (*d.* 1900): *b.* 'Uplands,' Deer Park, Toronto, 4 January 1892: Religion – Church of England: *educ.* Private Institution for Very Young Boys, Northern Toronto; Upper Canada College, 1902–05, Harris History Prize winner; University College, Toronto, 1909–13, B.A., All Souls Prize winner, Phi Kappa Pi; Law School: Occupation – Law Student: 5'9" tall, grey eyes, brown hair: attempted to enlist on the outbreak of war, but was refused due to defective eyesight. Undaunted by this failure he proceeded to Valcartier, offering himself for a position in the Army Medical Corps; he reasoned it would far better suit him to save life than to take it. But, on discovering there was little opportunity to partake in any Active Service role for some considerable time, he returned to Toronto. Shortly thereafter, on learning of a need for officers within 12th (York Rangers) Regt. (Militia); successors to the 'brave York Volunteers' who Brock had cheered on to victory at the Queenston Heights, the premise being that officers from this unit would be drafted to some other unit for Active Service at the Front: joined 12th Rangers, appointed Temp. Lieut., trained throughout winter 1914–15; posted 35th Overseas Battn, Toronto, 20 April 1915, and proceeded overseas with a draft which included his close friend H.E.B. 'Errol' Platt, June following: trained Shorncliffe, attd. 23rd Battn. joined 3rd Battn in France 14 October 1915: served throughout the winter in southern sector, Ypres Salient.

During the interval between the loss of ground at Sanctuary Wood and the recapture of the line, Lieut. Mackenzie and an N.C.O. were sent to reconnoitre the trenches which (at the time) were being temporarily held by the enemy. After his companion became wounded Lieut. Mackenzie carried him back, but not without gaining valuable information first and, after making his report, he was returning to his company when he was shot by a sniper. Died en-route to the C.C.S., Poperinghe, 7 June 1916: Age 24. *unm.* Pte. 44167, R. McNee, 3rd Battn., wrote,"Just a few lines to extend to you my deepest sympathy in the loss of your son, George. I have been Mr Mackenzie's batman since last November, and looked after him as well as I could till the last. That morning he called me to make breakfast and, while I was preparing it, he went out down the trench, saying he would be back in five minutes. He had just seemed to have left when another officer brought in the news. Not only his platoon, but the whole company feel the loss, as he was so fearless, and could always be found on the job. Ever so many in the battalion have come to me expressing their sorrow at me losing my boss, so, Sir, you can be proud to know he was so popular, and may console to think that no one could have a finer death than for one's country. I have been shown many kindnesses from him and as a soldier it was a pleasure to obey and as a man a pleasure to serve, besides the more I knew of him the better I liked him. We have stirring times ahead of us and if I'm spared to come through this awful time, I shall always have fondest remembrances of your son. Trusting this finds you in the best of health and spirits, hoping you don't find it too hard to read this, Yours sincerely…". Buried Lyssenthoek Cemetery, close to Errol Platt who died a few days previously. Four other friends, Lieuts. H.R. Gordon and W.D.P. Jarvis, with whom he attended his very first school; Lieut. H.M. Grasett, a member of his university fraternity; and Capt. W.H.V. Van der Smissen, to whom he was more like a brother than a friend, also made the supreme sacrifice.

Till The Day Dawns

Lieut. H.E.B. 'Errol' Platt lies nearby (V.A.33); H.R. Gordon, W.D.P. Jarvis, H.M. Grasett, and W.H.V. Van der Smissen all have no known grave, they are commemorated on the Ypres (Menin Gate) Memorial (Panel 18).

(VI.A.19) Lieut. Harold Mackenzie Wilson, 15th Bn. Canadian Infantry (Central Ontario Regt.), C.E.F.: *s.* of Harold A. Wilson, of 15, Maple Avenue, Toronto, by his wife Elizabeth G.: *b.* Toronto, 10 October 1891: *educ.* Model School, Harbord Street Collegiate; Bishop Ridley College; University College, Toronto, 1908–09: previously Lieut., 48th Regt. (Militia), apptd. 15th Battn. August 1914: served with the Expeditionary Force in France and Flanders from May 1915: took part in the Battles of Givenchy and Festubert, thereafter served Ploegsteert sector: severely wounded 30 June 1915, near Hill 60, and, after convalescence and a period of home leave, returned to France February 1916: apptd. Bombing Instructor, La Clytte, nr. Dickebusch, he was chosen for a position on the Staff, 6th Bde. On the day of transfer to his new appointment, 9 June 1916, he was accidentally killed by the explosion of a bomb while instructing a class in the use of this weapon; having volunteered to take the place of another officer temporarily indisposed. Buried at Poperinghe: Age 24. *unm.* He was a member of the Zeta Psi fraternity, and Toronto Cricket Team.

Out Of Weakness Made Strong Waxed Valiant In Fight

(VI.A.23) Lieut. 85677, John 'Jack' Basil Hipwell, 5th Bty., 2nd Bde. Canadian Field Artillery, C.E.F.: *s.* of David Hipwell, of 98, Princess Street, St. John, New Brunswick, by his wife Margaret: and brother to Pte. 524892, H.D. Hipwell (surv'd.): *b.* Woodstock, 27 November 1893: Religion – Church of England: Occupation – Student: 5'10½" tall; blue eyes, brown hair: a serving member (1 year), Field Coy. Canadian Engineers (Militia); joined C.E.F. Fredericton, New Brunswick, 1 December 1914, posted 23rd Reserve Bty. C.F.A.: joined 5th Bty., Ouderdom, 11 June 1916; severely wounded in the leg on the evening of the 16th and removed to No. 10 C.C.S where he died the following day, 17 June 1916: Age 22. *unm.*

Graduate 1915 Forestry Class
University Of New Brunswick
Canada

(VI.A.24) Lieut. 77544, Ralph Featherstone Lake Osler, 16th Bn. Canadian Infantry (Manitoba Regt.), C.E.F.: *s.* of Francis Lake Osler, and his wife, Isobel Osler, *née* Fowler (Summerland, British Columbia): nephew to Sir Edmund B. Osler, Toronto, and Sir William Osler, Oxford, whose son (Lieut. Osler's cousin) 2nd Lieut. E.R. Osler, Royal Field Artillery, died of wounds, 30 August 1917: *b.* Winnipeg, 11 October 1891: Religion – Church of England: Occupation – Clerk: 5'7" tall; blue eyes, brown hair: serving member, 102nd Regt. (Militia); enlisted Victoria, British Columbia, 9 November 1914: proceeded to France, April 1915, and died 16 June 1916, of wounds received in action three days previously in the Sanctuary Wood – Observatory Ridge – Armagh Wood sector: Age 24. *unm.*

His cousin Edward 'Revere' Osler is buried in Dozinghem Military Cemetery (IV.F.21).

(VI.A.25) Lieut. Thomas Brehaut Saunders, 13th Bn. Canadian Infantry (Quebec Regt.), C.E.F.: *s.* of Dyce W. Saunders, K.C., of 72, Walmer Road, Toronto, and Amy Percival Saunders, *née* Brehaut, his wife: *b.* 4 June 1896:

Occupation – Farmer: previously served 6 months Canadian Forces, joined C.E.F. Toronto, 1 July 1915; apptd. Lieut.: served with the Expeditionary Force in France, and was killed in action, 13 June 1916, during the attack to recapture the Canadian trenches lost in the vicinity of Observatory Ridge during the Battle of Mount Sorrel one week previously: Age 20. *unm.*

Killed In Action Sanctuary Wood
Beati Mundo Cordia

(VI.A.26) Lieut.Col. Frank Albro Creighton, 1st Bn. Canadian Infantry (Western Ontario Regt.), C.E.F.: Legion D'Honneur, Croix de Chevalier (France): *s.* of Thomas Grassie Creighton, of Dartmouth, Nova Scotia, by his wife Avis Rebecca: Occupation – Waiter: enlisted Regina, Saskatchewan, 1 June 1915. Died of wounds, 19 June 1916, received at Hill 60 on the 13th when, moments before the battalion's relief, the headquarters dug-out was hit by a shell: Age 41. Capt. W.H.V. Van der Smissen was killed instaneously. Lieut. Col. Creighton leaves a wife, Rosalie (11, Lancaster Apartments, Winnipeg) in mourning for his loss.

Virtutis Gloria Merces

Capt. Van der Smissen has no known grave; he is commemorated on the Ypres (Menin Gate) Memorial (Panel 18).

(VI.A.27) Capt. Ross Penner Cotton, 19th Bn. Canadian Infantry (Central Ontario Regt.) attd. 3rd Inf. Bde. H.Q., C.E.F.: *yst. s.* of the late Maj.Gen. W.H. Cotton, by his wife Jessie (Pinehurst, Almonte, Ontario): and brother to Lieut. C.P. Cotton, Canadian Field Artillery, killed in action, 2 June 1916: On the outbreak of war was serving member of 72nd Seaforth Highlanders of Canada (Militia); volunteered and enlisted Valcartier, 23 September 1914: proceeded to France with Second Contingent, subsequently appointed (August 1915) A.D.C. to Brigdr.Gen. Leekie. Severely wounded in action, 13 June 1916 when, while leading a bombing attack with Lieut. R.T.S. Sachs (also killed), a number of the party were hit by a shell: Age 23. His sister Dorothy served as a Nurse; another brother Henry, was killed in the South African Campaign. (*Headstone records 16th Bn.*)

In The Beauty & Strength Of Early Manhood

His brother Charles is buried nearby (IX.A.7); also Lieut. Sachs (VI.A.32).

(VI.A.29) Lieut. 28818, William Norman McLennan, 16th Canadian Infantry (Manitoba Regt.), C.E.F.: *s.* of William G. McLennan, by his wife Mary Beatrice (c/o Vancouver Heights Post Office, British Columbia): *b*. Bootle, co. Lancaster, 13 November 1890: Religion – Presbyterian: Occupation – Accountant: 5"6½' tall, brown eyes, fair hair: a serving member (3 years) 72nd Seaforth Highlanders of Canada; joined C.E.F. Valcartier, 23 September 1914: proceeded to France with 1st Contingent, and was killed in action, 13 June 1916, in the attack to recapture lost trenches Observatory Ridge – Armagh Wood: Age 25. *unm*. Remains recovered 16–17 June; buried beside (and at the same time as) Capt. S.W. Wood in the Military Cemetery, Poperinghe, 4.15 p.m., on the 19th; battalion firing party (50 rifles), pipes and drums, under Capt. R. Bell-Irving's direction.

(VI.A.30) Capt. Stanley Willis Wood, 16th Bn. Canadian Infantry (Manitoba Regt.), C.E.F.: *s*. of Robert Whitney Wood, of Kansas City, United States, and Lillie Collins, his wife (Balboa Heights, Canal Zone, Panama): *b*. Clear Lake, Iowa, 29 July 1887: Religion – Church of England: Occupation – Soldier, 4 years, 7th U.S. Army: 5'8" tall; blue eyes, light brown hair: joined C.E.F. 24 March 1915: served with the Expeditionary Force in France, and was killed in action, 13 June 1916, on which date the battalion took part in the large scale Canadian attack which, while successful in the recapture of the trenches lost during the Battle of Mount Sorrel one week previously, cost 16th Battalion casualties of 5 officers – Capt. S.W. Wood, Lieuts. C.C.O.M. Adams, H.J. McLaurin, W.N. McLennan, R.T. Sachs – killed; 5 officers wounded (1 died; Capt. R.P. Cotton); and 257 other ranks killed, wounded and missing: Age 29. *unm*. Remains recovered 16–17 June.

2nd Lieut. 7th U.S. Infantry
A Gallant Soldier Under His Own And His Adopted Flag

Relieved by 10th Canadians (1 a.m., 14 June) the 16th moved back in small parties to Scottish Lines. The men – worn out and weary after the fighting, burdened down with rifle, pack, ammunition, etc. – not only managed to find the strength to carry back the bodies of several of their comrades and officers that they might be afforded a decent burial but – on two consecutive nights thereafter – volunteered to return to the front line to search for the dead and wounded, and it is to the credit of their efforts (both at the time and afterwards) that numerous of the wounded were brought in to safety and four of the officers killed are buried here. Despite extensive searches the remains of Lieut. C.C.O.M. Adams could not be found, he is commemorated on the Ypres (Menin Gate) Memorial (Panel 26).

(VI.A.32) Lieut. 29601, Roy Tessier Seaver Sachs, 16th Bn. Canadian Infantry (Manitoba Regt.), C.E.F.: *s*. of Frank (and Mrs) Sachs, of 33, Somerton Road, Cricklewood, London, NW.: *b*. Cricklewood, 9 November 1887: Religion –

Church of England: Occupation – Schoolmaster: 5'10" tall, blue eyes, auburn hair: serving member of the Militia, volunteered and enlisted Valcartier, 23 September 1914. Died of wounds, 13 June 1916. Buried in the Military Cemetery, nr. Poperinghe, 4.15 p.m., on the 20th; battalion firing party, pipes and drums, under Capt. R. Bell-Irving's direction: Age 28. *unm.* Canon H.D. Rawnsley wrote the following lines in his memory:

> In Memoriam
> Lieut. R.T.S. Sachs
> The Canadian Scottish, Seaforth Highlanders, Vancouver
>
> Queen of the snows, was ever purer heart
> Than this thy son's to help of Britain given?
> With fuller sacrifice have any striven
> To play for Europe's peace a warrior's part?
> Not from the thoughtless wrangling of the mart
> But from the student's cell uncalled, undriven
> He crossed the seas with one bright star in heaven –
> Duty, the pole-star of his patriot chart.
>
> Oh! Never pipes more sorrowfully played
> For one by life and deed to all endeared
> Their loud lament above a soldier's sleep;
> And every autumn bid its whispering shade
> Of his gold heart a golden memory keep.

(VI.A.33) Lieut. James Stokesbury Thorpe, 3rd Bde. Canadian Machine Gun Corps, 1st Canadian Divn., C.E.F.: *b.* Cedar Rapids, Iowa, U.S.A., 1889: emigrated to Canada in the pre-war years and became a Canadian citizen: volunteered and enlisted Vancouver, British Columbia on the outbreak of war: served with the Expeditionary Force in France and Flanders, and died at Remy Casualty Clearing Station, Poperinghe, 13 June 1916, of wounds received in action near Hill 60, Ypres. Buried there. In a letter to his mother and elder sister, Mary Augusta, he wrote, "6 March 1916: By the time you read this the Battle of Verdun will be finished, but the enclosed cutting from an English newspaper might be of interest to you as extraordinarily true to detail etc. We hear today that they are sending British troops there and it may be so, but the French seem to be able to handle the situation. If the Germans lose this battle the war will be over by next fall. Lately we have had a lot of cold and snowy weather, but it can't last much longer, and as I write the warm sun is on its way back and the snow is going fast. It is hell in the trenches for the men, but the officers are able to make themselves more comfortable. We don't get anything from stores that the men don't get in fact, not so much, but we buy a lot of stuff. The men are hardened now and it is wonderful the way they stay cheerful under these conditions. The machine guns are a little more interesting than ordinary infantry work, and not so much drudgery to it. It is considered much safer too. I have a friend in a howitzer battery near here, and was over there yesterday. I fired the guns, and also went up to the observation point to watch the effect on the German lines through my glasses. The guns were fired from behind hills, and they fire from the map without seeing the target. (We do the same with machine guns sometimes.) We fired at any old thing we liked for a while. Our target was 3 miles away, but the guns never missed a shot. Then we had tea down at the battery Mess, and after tea the chaplain came in and held a service. It was a funny church service. Almost every 'amen' was followed by a cracking salvo from the guns which were only a few yards away. They were engaged with a German battery 5 miles away. Our billet is surrounded by batteries, and they are banging away all day and night. We never notice them anymore. I suppose you want to know how I felt the first time under fire. Well I'll tell you what every man will if he speaks the truth, I was frightened. Everyone is frightened under shell fire, but the thing is not to show it. If an officer ducks and runs for cover he may as well quit, because he's through so far as his men are concerned. They always look to their officer, and if they trust him he can ask them to do anything and they'll do it. It doesn't take long to show up a quitter out here. There aren't many though. I've got to go up and take a trench building party now so must put on the high boots. Had a little sciatica and chilblains, that's all so far. With Love Jim." He was married to Olive I. Pettigrew, *née* Thorpe (Lucky Lake, Saskatchewan).

(VI.A.34) Lieut. Howard James McLaurin, 16th Bn. Canadian Infantry (Manitoba Regt.), C.E.F.: *s.* of John R. McLaurin Snr., of Vankleek Hill, Ontario, and his wife: and brother to Pte. 24856, D.C. McLaurin, 16th Canadian Infantry, died of wounds, 5 April 1916: *b.* Vankleek Hill, Prescott County, 26 July 1887: Religion – Congregationalist: *educ.* Public School and Collegiate there; Woodstock College; Royal College of Dental Surgeons, Toronto, 1905–09, D.D.S., Year Vice President, member of college Football and Hockey teams: Occupation – Dental Practitioner, Winnipeg: 5'8" tall, brown eyes, dark hair: enlisted Winnipeg, 18 December 1914; posted 43rd Battn.: proceeded to France, selected and transf'd. from first draft 43rd Battn. officers to 16th Battn. June 1915. Killed in action at Sanctuary Wood, Zillebeke sector 13 June 1916, on which date the battalion took part in the large scale Canadian attack which succeeded in recapturing the trenches lost during the Battle of Mount Sorrel one week previously. Immediately prior to the attack in which Lieut, McLaurin lost his life his unit were based in the vicinity of Reninghelst, supplying evacuation and burial parties to the forward area. During his year's service at the front Lieut.

McLaurin had been three times wounded, twice recommended for decoration, and four times Mentioned in Despatches; the last of these, March 1916, for his work in making a reconnaissance of a German listening post. His Captaincy was gazetted posthumously: Age 28. *unm.* (*IWGC record MacLaurin, 14 June*)

Greater Love Hath No Man

His brother Douglas is buried nearby (V.C.36A).

"June 22nd.... A number of aeroplanes are strafing to-day, and one of ours was shot down close to here. We walked up to look at it soon afterwards: it was smashed to pieces and the pilot killed, shot through the face..." *Wilfrid Ewart*.

(VI.A.35) Capt. Leonard Herbert Sweet, 1st Bn. (37th Foot) The Hampshire Regt. attd 29th Sqdn. Royal Flying Corps: *yst. s.* of the Rev. Charles Francis Long Sweet, Rector of Symondsbury, Bridport, co. Dorset, by his wife Edith Maud, eldest *dau.* of Col. Henry Walrond, Marquis de Vallado: *b*. Winterbourne, Kingston, Blandford, co. Dorset, 15 June 1891: *educ*. Sherborne, and Royal Military College, Sandhurst; gazetted 2nd Lieut. Hampshire Regt. 5 February 1913; promoted Lieut. 15 September 1914; Capt. 21 October following: served with the Expeditionary Force in France and Flanders: took part in the Battle of Le Cateau and subsequent Retreat; wounded at Forest Compiegne and invalided home: joined his regiment Gosport, November 1914: attd. Royal Flying Corps 18 December, which he joined at Farnborough: returned to France, February 1915, where for six months he was observer, came back to England, August, and obtained his pilot's certificate: joined 29th Sqdn. March 1916, with which he proceeded to France on the 29th, and was killed in action, 22 June following, while flying FE8 6378 on patrol over the British lines north-west of Ypres he was attacked and shot down by two hostile aircraft. Major Strange, 23rd Squadron, wrote, "Whilst under my command at Gosport your son rendered me most valuable assistance. Excelling as a pilot after little instruction, he became a good instructor to others training in the Squadron, and was a great organizer. When I recommended him for promotion to Flight Commander I had a vacancy in the Squadron for that rank, and hoped to keep him. This was filled up, however. I wish I could tell you how sorry everyone was to lose him," and Major Conran, 29th Squadron, "I must say it is a great blow to us all as he was a capable and very popular officer, both with officers and men." Lieut. G.F. Johnson also wrote: "It may perhaps interest you to know the particulars of the fight which resulted in the fall of a DeHavilland Scout at 11.29 a.m. on the 22nd inst. My section and myself were watching and observed every detail, and were admiring the skill and daring of the pilot. Two large German machines (probably L.V.G. and Albatross) were flying on parallel courses at about 10,500 feet. The DeHavilland, flying considerably higher, flew across them, and, so far as we could see, dived down over one and under the other. The one he went over turned left and fired broadside at him. From the way he fell I should think he was unconscious, for he fell absolutely vertically, and as far as I could see through my glasses, his plane was intact. My section joins me in an expression of high regard for this daring pilot.": Age 23. *unm.*

(VI.A.37) Lieut. Frank Joseph Corr, 20th Bn. Canadian Infantry (Central Ontario Regt.), C.E.F.: *s.* of Michael Corr, of 121, Brussels Street, St. John, New Brunswick: *b.* 9 August 1890: Occupation – Traveller: prior to enlistment and appointment Lieut. 20th Battn., 11 June 1915, served 3 years as Pte.: served with the Expeditionary Force, and was killed in action, 28 June 1916, when a shell landed in No. 1 Coy.'s dugout at The Bluff: Age 25.*unm.* Lieut. J.E.D. Belt (VI.A.41) was also killed.

"Shortly after 6 a.m. on the morning of 2nd June 1916, Major General M.S. Mercer and Brigadier General Williams (8th Canadian Infantry Brigade) were in the process of inspecting the condition of the Canadian trenches around Mount Sorrel and Tor Top, which had been heavily shelled the previous day, when an enemy bombardment commenced. "After a time the fire slackened and Mercer, who had miraculously escaped injury, determined to push his way back to his headquarters to organise resistance to the attack that the enemy would inevitably put over. He was still feeling the effects of the shock he had received, and as he went towards the rear, just before one o'clock, he had to be supported by Gooderham (his A.D.C.). The communication trenches had all been obliterated, and in this trip, made overland, there was but little shelter to be gained. Just as they reached Armagh Wood a chance shot hit Mercer in the leg, breaking a bone. His aide dragged him into a nearby ditch and did everything in his power to ease his suffering. Shortly after this event the bombardment lifted over Armagh Wood, and the Huns swarmed through the 4th Canadian Mounted Rifles. During the night eight attempts were made to recover the lost ground. While the fourth attack was on, a British shell burst close to Mercer and a piece of shrapnel pierced his heart. Gooderham, who had gallantly stood by him until this moment, remained alone in No Man's Land until the morning of 4 June when he was found by the Germans and taken prisoner." *Sir Max Aitken.*

(VI.A.38) Major General Malcolm Smith Mercer, C.B., Gen. Officer Comdg. 3rd Canadian Divn., Canadian Infantry, C.E.F.: 4th *s.* of the late Thomas Mercer (*d.*6 December 1889), of Dereham Township, Ontario, and Mary, *née* Smith (*d.*1883): and *gdson.* of Samuel Mercer (*b.* 30 May 1779), of Londonderry Township, Chester Co., Pennsylvania: *b.* Etobicoke, Township, York, Ontario, 17 September 1859: spent most of his boyhood on the family homestead Westwood, nr. Tillonsburg: *educ.* Delmer Public School, and University of Toronto (Law Graduate), where he was active in the Literary Society and the Glee Club. Always interested in the military, he succeeded Sir Henry Pellat (of

Casa Loma fame) as Commandant, Queen's Own Rifles: on the outbreak of war was a Barrister-at-Law, Toronto: subsequent to his medical examination – where he was noted as being 53 years, 11 months; 6' tall, of bronzed complexion, blue eyed, and dark haired – he completed his attestation form in his own hand at Valcartier, 22 September following; signing M.S. Mercer, O.C. 1st Inf.Bde.: next of kin Francis T. Mercer, 158, St. John's Road, Toronto. In June 1916 his brother John S. Mercer (d.1929) received notification that Malcolm (initially reported wounded, captured and held prisoner in Germany) had died in action. A Freemason Major Gen. Mercer was member of River Park Lodge No.356, Streetsville, and Victoria Lodge No.474, Toronto. Killed in action at Armagh Wood, nr. Ypres, 3 June 1916; partially decomposed remains recovered by battlefield clearance party, 24 June, and buried at Poperinghe 2.30 p.m. same day; firing party furnished by 58th Battn.: Age 56. Corpl. Reid, 4th Battn., assigned the task of searching No Man's Land (night of 21–22 June) to locate and bury soldiers killed during the German advance of 2–3 June, wrote of the recovery of General Mercer's body, "... I was examining bags of stuff that had been taken off the dead the night before when I came across a pass with 'General Mercer' signed on it. Just think of the excitement then, as we believed he was in the hands of the Hun. I called Pioneer Range, as we were together out searching the night before and he said that must be the spot where they opened the machine gun on us...The real excitement then started for we were spotted as soon as we left the dugout and thanks to some shell holes that we ever got there. They were not contented putting the machine guns on us. They even sent coal boxes over and some near ones too. Anyway, by six o'clock, we got the body dragged to a shell-hole about five yards from where we dug it out, where it had been buried except one boot and about four inches of a leather legging sticking out of the mud. That disinterring was really the worst part of the lot, as we had to lie face down and scratch until we got the General's body uncovered, and then we searched the body again and saw the epaulets with crossed swords and star. I then cut off the General's service coat and placed the body in a shell-hole till after dark..."

(VI.A.39) Capt. Edward Simpson Botterell, 'C' Coy., 15th Bn. (48th Highlanders of Canada) Canadian Infantry (Central Ontario Regt.), C.E.F.: s. of Henry H. (& Annie) Botterell, of Woodroffe, Ontario: b. Ottawa, 4 December 1892: Religion – Church of England: 5'9" tall, fair complexion, blue eyes, brown hair: Occupation – Salesman: serving member of the Militia, joined 48th Highlanders of Canada, Pte. 27312, Valcartier, 22 September 1914; subsequently gained rank Sergt.: served with the Expeditionary Force in France and Flanders from 18 February 1915; took part in the fighting at the Second Battle of Ypres: applied for a commission September 1915: detached 13th Bn. returned 15th Bn. temporarily apptd. Capt., Comdg. No.3 ('C') Coy., May 1916: took part in the fighting at Mount Sorrel, and was shot and killed by a sniper later that month, 23 June 1916, while passing a gap in the front-line trenches of his company: Age 23. *unm*.

He That Believeth In Me Though He Were Dead Yet Shall He Live
Jo.XI.25.

On the night of 27–28 June 1916 a party of bombers, under Lieut. Stewart, supported by a party of scouts under Lieut. Heron, left the 20th Canadian's trenches in the vicinity of The Bluff to raid the German trenches opposite and, at 12 midnight, deployed themselves close to the enemy parapet. Unfortunately for the Canadians, a German working party observed and opened fire on them killing Pte. 58189, F. Burns whereupon the party then prepared to advance and bomb. This was met by heavy rifle fire and counter-bombing by the Germans. 'At about this time Lieut. D.S. Anderson was killed and the party, knowing nothing of this, were awaiting his signal to enter the trench – the delay this caused made it necessary for the party to retire. This was done and they returned to our trench only after considerable difficulty and delay. Pte. Wright, although wounded himself, carried in Mr Anderson's body; it was impossible to recover Pte. Burns body – Pte. 58170, F. Baker is missing, Ptes. Andrus and Mitchell wounded. This experience only confirms that such enterprises cannot hope to be successful without a great deal of preparation. The enemy line along our front is apparently strongly held, and sentries very alert.'

(VI.A.40) Lieut. David Stewart Anderson, 20th Canadian Infantry (Central Ontario Regt.), C.E.F.: *s.* of Andrew Stewart Anderson, 25, Pine Avenue, Ontario, by his wife Mary Helen: and brother to E.A. Anderson Esq., Thomas Street, St. Mary's, Ontario: *b.* Sunderland, Co. Durham, England, 31 March 1892: Occupation – Traveller: previously served 4 years 16th (Queen's Westminster Rifles) Bn., London Regt. (T.F.), a serving member of the Militia, rank Lieut.: joined C.E.F., Toronto, 13 November 1914. Shot and killed, 28 June 1916; The Bluff: Age 24. *unm.* (*IWGC record age 23*)

Pte. 58189, F. Burns has no known grave and, with no trace found, Pte. 58170, B.H. Baker (struck off strength, 30 June 1916) also has no known grave; both are commemorated on the Ypres (Menin Gate) Memorial (Panel 26).

(VI.A.41) Lieut. James Edwin Devey Belt, 20th Bn. Canadian Infantry (Central Ontario Regt.), C.E.F.: *s.* of the late Rev. Alfred James Belt, Rector, (Grace Anglican) Church, Milton; Archdeacon of Niagara Diocese, by his wife Mary, *née* Farmer (808, Logan Avenue, Toronto): and brother to Pte. 507435, P.R. Belt, Canadian Divn. Signals Coy. (surv'd.): *b.* Arthur, Ontario, 6 July 1885: Occupation – Banker: enlisted Toronto, 13 November 1914: served with the Expeditionary Force in France where he was wounded (head), 19 April 1916, and after treatment for that wound and shell-shock returned to his battalion, 2 May following, and died of wounds received in action at The Bluff, 28 June 1916, when, during a period of heavy shelling, a shell entered No. 1 Coy.'s dugout killing Lieuts. Belt and F.J. Corr. Lieut. Belt was a Freemason of St. Clair Lodge No.135, Milton: Age 30.

We Beseech Thee Accept This Bounden Duty And Service

Lieut. Corr is buried nearby (VI.A.37).

(VI.A.42) Major Charles John Smith, 13th (Royal Highlanders of Canada) Bn. Canadian Infantry (Quebec Regt.), C.E.F.: *s.* of the late Col. W. Smith, V.D., and Mrs H. Smith (11, Rosewood Terrace, Dundee, Scotland): *b.* Dundee, 2 November 1884: sometime emigrated to Canada, finding employ as Traveller: previously served 12 years, 4th Black Watch, Scotland: enlisted Royal Highlanders, Valcartier, 23 September 1914: served with the Expeditionary Force in France and Flanders and was killed in action, 27 June 1916, when a large trench mortar shell scored a direct hit on the steel-lined dug-out in which he had established his Company Headquarters. His death on this occasion seemed a particularly hard stroke of fate, as he had just received his promotion (21 June) and was serving for the first time as a Major. Originally with No.3 Coy., then as Adjutant and finally as a company commander, he had worked faithfully and given of his best in a manner that was an inspiration to all who came in contact with him. With the deaths of Major Smith and Capt. Buchanan there passed from the Battalion Roll two very gallant officers and gentlemen.": Age 31. *unm.* *(IWGC record age 29)*

Blessed Are The Dead Who Die In The Lord

(VI.A.43) Capt. Fitz-Herbert Price Buchanan, Comdg. No.4 Coy., 13th (Royal Highlanders of Canada) Bn. Canadian Infantry (Quebec Regt.), C.E.F.: *s.* of Wentworth James Buchanan, and his wife, Agnes (26, The Linton, Sherbrooke, Montreal): *b.* 16 March 1875: *educ.* McGill University, from whence he graduated B.Sc.: Occupation – Civil Engineer: served 10 years, 5th Royal Highlanders of Canada, joined C.E.F., Valcartier, 23 September 1914: came over with 1st Canadian Contingent, October 1914. One of the original officers of the 13th, Capt. Buchanan had remained in England in command of the Base Company when the battalion proceeded to France, later rejoining the battalion at the front and serving there until late 1915 when illness compelled him to return to England for treatment and convalescence. On recovery he returned to France and died of wounds, 28 June 1916, after being struck on the head by a shrapnel shell at about 4 a.m. the previous day (Major C.J. Smith being killed in the same hour). Capt. Buchanan had just left his dug-out situated beneath the Observatory Ridge Road to check what effect the enemy bombardment was having and whether, or not, it was being used as a screen for an attack in force: Age 41. (*IWGC record age 42*)

(VI.B.13) Pte. 114061, Cyril Henry King Smith, 5th Bn. Canadian Mounted Rifles, C.E.F.: *s.* of John Chinery Smith, of Knodishall, Saxmundham, co. Suffolk, England, and Eleanor Mary Smith, his wife: and brother to Spr. 313039, C.W. Smith, Royal Engineers, died of wounds, 15 May 1918: *b.* Saxmundham, 12 April 1880: Occupation – Carpenter: previously served one year 22nd Saskatchewan Regt. (Militia): joined 9th C.M.R., Lloydminster, 4 January 1915; posted 5th Battn.: served with the Expeditionary Force, and died No.17 C.C.S. of wounds (G.S.W. L. leg, and compound fracture), 12 April 1916: Age 35. He was married to the late G.L. Smith (1809, 13th Avenue East, Vancouver, British Columbia).

Thy Will Be Done

His brother Claude is buried in Etaples Military Cemetery (LXVIII.B.1).

(VI.B.18A) Pte. 54292, William G. Davies, 18th Bn. Canadian Infantry (Western Ontario Regt.), C.E.F.: *s.* of Richard Davies, of 280, Egerton Street, London, Ontario: *b.* London, England, 24 April 1886: Occupation – Editorial Messenger, *London Advertiser*: enlisted London, Ontario, 11 March 1915. Died of wounds (G.S.W. head), 13 April 1916: Age 29. *unm.* Pte. Davies was a Freemason of St. Thomas Lodge No.44, St. Thomas, Ontario.

(VI.B.22) Pte. 475500, Edward Alfred Webb, Princess Patricia's Canadian Light Infantry (Eastern Ontario Regt.), C.E.F.: *s.* of Edward H. Webb: *b.* Brighton, co. Sussex, 28 March 1896: Religion – Presbyterian: *educ.* East Missouri Township Public School; St. Mary's Collegiate; Victoria College, University of Toronto, 1915: Occupation – Student: 5'8½" tall, medium complexion, brown eyes, dark brown hair: joined 4th Universities Coy., P.P.C.L.I., 15 October 1915 (shortly after entering college), and departed Canada the following month: went out February 1916 with a draft to the regiment in France; joined P.P.C.L.I., Mont des Cats, Flanders, 19 March, and was wounded in the 'Hooge Trenches' (Sanctuary Wood) nr. Ypres by a shell, 14 April following. Removed to the C.C.S., Poperinghe; he succumbed to his injuries three days later, 17 April 1916. Buried at Lyssenthoek: Age 20. *unm.*

(VI.B.22A) Pte. 56104, Ernest Belch, 19th Bn. Canadian Infantry (1st Central Ontario Regt.), C.E.F.: *s.* of Henry Belch, of 27, Ebury Road, Rickmansworth, co. Hertford, England, by his wife Annie 'Nellie' (86, Empire Avenue, Toronto): and brother to Pte. 522647/6014, H. Belch, C.E.F. (surv'd.): *b.* Rickmansworth, 17 July 1886: Occupation – Painter: joined 19th Battn. C.E.F. 5 March 1915: departed Montreal, 13 May 1915: trained West Sandling, Shorncliffe from the

23rd of the latter month; proceeded to France 12 September following, and died of wounds, 17 April 1916, received at duty on a working party to the front line, Voormezeele: Age 29.

(VI.B.23) L/Sergt. 28879, George Buchan, 16th (72nd Seaforth Highlanders) Bn. Canadian Infantry (Manitoba Regt.), C.E.F.: illegitimate *s.* of Mary Yule, Domestic Servant: *b.* co. Aberdeen, Scotland, 3 June 1887: some time removed to Canada where he was later engaged in practice as a Lawyer: volunteered and enlisted Vancouver, British Columbia, 1 September 1914; joining 72nd Seaforth Highlanders, Valcartier, Quebec, on the 23rd: left for Europe from the Bay of Gaspe with 1st Canadian Division, 3 October following: arrived Plymouth, 14 October, and was encamped at Enford, Salisbury Plain, undergoing training, 15 October 1914–9 February 1915: proceeded to France, moving into trenches in the Armentieres sector for indoctrination, 17 February, and died of wounds, 28 April 1916 received in action at Mount Sorrel: Age 27. *unm. (IWGC record age 28)*

(VI.B.23A) Pte. 401227, Henry Alfred Ingle Finch, 2nd Bn. Canadian Infantry (Eastern Ontario Regt.), C.E.F.: *s.* of George Ingle Finch, of Little Shelford, Cambridge, England, by his wife Bessie: *b.* Hammersmith, London, England: *educ.* St. Paul's School; and Trinity College, Cambridge, where he graduated B.A.: sometime engaged in farming, United States of America; prior to enlistment London, Ontario, 11 January 1915, was Book Keeper: served with the Expeditionary Force in France and Flanders, and died of wounds (G.S.W. left leg, head), 28 April 1916: Age 37.

The Lord Bless Thee And Keep Thee

>But sudden evening blurs and fogs the air.
>There seems no time to want a drink of water.
>Nurse looks far away. And here and there
>Music and roses burst through crimson slaughter.
>He can't remember where he saw blue sky ...
>The trench is narrower. Cold, he's cold; yet hot –
>And there's no light to see the voices by ...
>No time to ask ... he knows not what.
>
>*Wilfred Owen.*

(VI.C.8) Pte. 415293, Alexander Joseph Cameron, 'B' Coy., 2nd Bn. Canadian Pioneers, C.E.F.: *s.* of Alexander Cameron, of Bridgeport, Nova Scotia, by his wife Sarah: *b.* Bridgeport, Cape Breton, Nova Scotia, 4 June 1899 (attested 1897), by adding two years to his age: Religion – Roman Catholic: enlisted Sydney, Nova Scotia, 12 August 1915; apparent age 16 years, 2 months; the Medical Examiner noting he was 'somewhat pigeon-chested': 5'4½" tall, dark complexion, brown eyes, dark brown hair: departed Halifax, 6 December 1915: trained England, 14 December 1915–7 March 1916; disembarked Le Havre, France the following day, and died of wounds, 17 April 1916, received the previous evening while at duty trench clearing, drainage digging and trench-matting in the vicinity of Lille Road – Convent Lane: Age 16. At enlistment he stated he was a miner; 'minor' might have been more appropriate.

Rest In Peace

(VI.C.12) Pte. 10113, Henry Martin Abraham Dyer, 1st Bn. (3rd Foot) The Buffs (East Kent Regt.): *s.* of Henry Martin Dyer, of 192, Union Road, Dover, by his wife Johanna Louisa: and elder brother to Pte. L/9940, A.S. Dyer, The Buffs, killed in action, 20 October 1914, at Chateau de Flandres, Radinghem; and nephew to Sergt. T/504, E.G. Dyer, 4th The Buffs, a veteran of the South African Campaign, one of six men of his battalion who died of heatstroke, 25 September 1915, nr. Sheikh Othman, Aden: *b.* St. James, Dover: enlisted Canterbury: served with the Expeditionary Force in France and Flanders from 7 September 1914, and died of wounds (G.S.W., R. Leg, both feet), 19 April 1916: Age 26. *unm.*

His brother Albert has no known grave, he is commemorated on the Ploegsteert Memorial (Panel 2); their uncle Edward is commemorated on the Heliopolis (Aden) Memorial, Egypt.

(VI.C.19) Pte. 153013, Alexander Campbell, 43rd (Cameron Highlanders) Bn. Canadian Infantry (Manitoba Regt.), C.E.F.: *s.* of Malcolm Campbell, of Beechwood Farm, Inverness; and Jeannie Macleod, his wife: *b.* Monkstadt, Kilmuir, 27 September 1877: Occupation – Car Conductor: serving member of 79th Cameron Highlanders of Canada (Militia); enlisted Winnipeg, 19 June 1915: served with the Expeditionary Force in France and Flanders from 22 February 1916, and died of wounds (abdominal), 20 April 1916, consequent to being hit by machine-gun fire on the night of 18 April; Sanctuary Wood sector: Age 38. *unm.* Remembered on Kilmuir War Memorial, Isle of Skye.

(VI.C.20) Pte 65894, Henry Ernest Simkins, 24th (Victoria Rifles) Bn. Canadian Infantry (Quebec Regt.), C.E.F.: eldest *s.* of Ernest Simkins, of 115, Manor Road, Park Lane, Tottenham, by his wife Kate: *b.* Tottenham, co. Middlesex, 1896: *educ.* Coleraine Park School, there: went to Canada, July 1913; settled at Montreal: Occupation – Roofer: enlisted 24 January 1915: served in France and Flanders from the following September (1915). Wounded during a bombardment at St. Eloi 17 April 1916, and died at No.17 C.C.S. four days later. Buried at Poperinghe: Age 21. *unm.*

The Parting Was So Bitter The Meeting Will Be Sweet
From Mother

(VI.C.20A) Pte. 412912, Raymond Hill McConachie, 13th Bn. Canadian Infantry (Quebec Regt.), C.E.F.: s. of Robert McConachie, of Napanee, Ontario, by his wife Harriet Catherine: and brother to Pte. 454813, G.R. McConachie, 20th Canadian Infantry, died of wounds, 22 June 1917, in England: b. Brampton, Ontario, 24 February 1895: Occupation – Commercial Traveller: enlisted Napanee, 8 February 1915. Died of wounds (G.S.W. head), 21 April 1916, received in action two and a half hours previously: Age 21.

His brother George is buried in Brookwood Military Cemetery (IX.D.10).

(VI.C.29A) Corpl. 17121, Walter Randolph Fletcher; Sniper; 7th Bn. Canadian Infantry (British Columbia Regt.), C.E.F.: s. of J.W. Fletcher, of Sardis, British Columbia, by his wife Cora: b. Chilliwack, 9 June 1895: Occupation – Teamster: a member of 104th Regt. (Militia): enlisted Valcartier, 23 September 1914: came over with First Canadian Contingent: served with the Expeditionary Force in France from February 1915, wounded (G.S.W. wrist); and died of wounds (G.S.W. head), 6 May 1916: Age 20. *unm*. Remembered on Chilliwack War Memorial.

Only Beloved Son Of Mr And Mrs W. Fletcher Sardis B.C.

(VI.C.32A) Pte. 8323, Alfred Ring, 2nd Bn. Coldstream Guards: s. of John Ring, of 25, Orford Road, Park Road, Hockley, Birmingham, by his wife Hannah: enlisted Birmingham: served with the Expeditionary Force in France and Flanders from 12 August 1914, and died of wounds (G.S.W. abdomen) at No.17 Casualty Clearing Station, Lyssenthoek, 7 May 1916, received in action. Buried at Poperinghe: Age 32.

Greater Love Hath No Man

(VI.C.36) Pte. 1659, George William Skelton, 3rd Bn. Coldstream Guards: s. of Thomas Skelton, of 5, Wenlock Place, Church Street, Filey, co. York, by his wife Mary: enlisted Hull: served with the Expeditionary Force from 22 January 1915, and died of wounds (G.S.W. chest, abdominal), 9 May 1916, received in action: Age 23. *unm*.

(VI.C.36A) Dvr. 476603, Leland Wingate Fernald, 5th Bde. Canadian Field Artillery, C.E.F.: late of Victoria, British Columbia: s. of Frank F. Fernald, of 11, Nelson Street, Dover, New Hampshire, United States, by his wife Emma J.: and brother to Mrs M.E. Murphy (2616, H.Street, Bakersfield, California): b. Three Rivers, Quebec, 21 January 1889: Occupation – Painter: previously served 3 years, 1st California Cavalry; 1 week British Columbia Horse: enlisted Esquimalt, British Columbia, 11 November 1915: served with the Expeditionary Force in France from 19 January 1916, and died 8 May 1916, of wounds received in action at Dickebusch the previous day: Age 28. *unm.*

A Volunteer From The U.S.A. To Avenge The Lusitania Murder

For 9 May 1916, on which date 3rd Canadian C.C.S. began admitting at Lijssenthoek, the unit diarist recorded: '...Arrangements satisfactory.' 10 May: 'Statistics previous 24 hours. Admitted 71, Discharged 1, Susp. Paratyph. 3, Pneumonia other 2. Evacuated by A.T. 29, O.R. – 23, Lying 39 + 1, Sitting 23. To Hazebrouck, Lying 2, Sitting 10. Remaining 5 p.m., O.R. 14, For Evacuation Nil. In Hospital 84 (O.R.). Deaths 3. Lethbridge, Ramsden, Rothery.'

(VI.C.41) Pte. 20272, William John Rothery, 14th (Service) Bn. The Durham Light Infantry: late of Wheatloy Hill, Co. Durham: *b*. Willington: enlisted Sunderland: served with the Expeditionary Force in France from 11 September 1915, and died 10 May 1916, of wounds (S.W. shrapnel – back; compound fracture R. Tibia).

(VI.C.41A) Pte. 154146, Humphrey Ramsden, 1st Bn. Canadian Pioneers, C.E.F.: late of Victoria, British Columbia: *s*. of Rosina Ramsden (Dewsbury, co. York, England): *b*. 5 January 1885: Religion – Church of England: 5'4¾" tall, fair complexion, blue eyes, brown hair: Occupation – Miner: enlisted Victoria, 21 September 1915. Died (jaundice) 10 May 1916: Age 20. *unm.*

(VI.C.42A) Pte. 55650, George Henry Lethbridge, 19th Bn. Canadian Infantry (Central Ontario Regt.), C.E.F.: *s*. of Robert Lethbridge, of Owen Sound, Ontario, by his wife Rosa: *b*. Owen Sound, 18 June 1893: Religion – Wesleyan: Occupation – Railroad worker: 5'9½" tall, fair complexion, blue eyes, brown hair: enlisted Toronto, 12 November 1914. Died (volvulus of colon) No.3 Canadian C.C.S., 10 May 1916: Age 22. He was married to Pearl May Wigley, *née* Lethbridge (556, Wellington Street West, Saulte Ste. Marie, Ontario). (*IWGC record 9 May*)

Safe In The Arms Of Jesus

(VI.C.43) Corpl. 15403, Alexander Loughran, 14th (Service) Bn. The Durham Light Infantry: *s*. of Joseph Loughran, Farmer; of Killyharry Glebe Castlecaulfield, Co. Tyrone, by his wife Esther, *dau.* of George Davidson: *b*. Killyharry Glebe, 4 October 1890: *educ.* Kilnaslie Church School: Occupation – Mine Shot Firer: enlisted 10 September 1914, after the outbreak of war: served with the Expeditionary Force in France and Flanders from 10 September 1915, when he had charge of a company of bomb-throwers, and died at No.3 Canadian

Casualty Clearing Station, 10 May 1916. Buried in Lyssenthoek Soldier's Cemetery: Age 25. The Chaplain, Capt. W. Archer, wrote, "He was brought in this morning badly wounded and unconscious, and though everything possible was done he passed away about six o'clock this evening." He *m.* Presbyterian Church of St. Andrew, Blackhill, 24 March 1910; Charlotte Esther ('Inglenook,' Oakwood Road, Blackhill, co. Durham), widow of Tom Searth Young, of Blackhill, and *dau.* of Henry William Elsom, of East Law Farm, Ebchester, co. Durham.

(VI.D.2) Pte. 27325, John George Litherland, 2nd Bn. (106th Foot) The Durham Light Infantry: *s.* of Thomas Litherland, of 26, Station Avenue, Fence Houses, co. Durham, by his wife Francis: *b.* Jarrow, *c.*1900: enlisted Shiney Row, Houghton-le-Spring: served with the Expeditionary Force in France, and died of wounds, 22 April 1916: Age 16.

> *Greater Love Hath No Man Than This That*
> *He Lay Down His Life For His Friends*

(VI.D.5) Pte. 12543, James Enoch Shingler, 1st Bn. (53rd Foot) The King's (Shropshire Light Infantry): late of Westbury, co. Salop: *s.* of Richard Shingler, of 7, Lea Hall Cottages, New House Lane, Albrighton, Wolverhampton: and brother to Gnr. 79845, F. Shingler, 216th Siege Bty., Royal Garrison Artillery, who fell, 16 August 1917: *b.* Dawley, 1874: served in France from 25 March 1915, and died of wounds (G.S.W. head, chest), 23 April 1916, received in action; Morteldje Estaminet trenches: Age 42.

His brother Frederick is buried in Noeux-les-Mines Communal Cemetery (II.J.9).

(VI.D.25A) Pte. 22128, Robert Harrison, 1st Bn. Grenadier Guards: *b.* Manchester: enlisted there: served with the Expeditionary Force in France and Flanders from 5 October 1915; admitted No.3 Canadian C.C.S. wounded 13 May 1916, died the same day.

(VI.D.26) Pte. 24036, Edward Jones, 11th (Service) Bn. (Midland Pioneers) The Leicestershire Regt.: *s.* of Edward Jones, of 54, Upper Brook Street, Oswestry, co. Salop, by his wife Mary: served with the Expeditionary Force in France from March 1916; admitted No.3 Canadian C.C.S. wounded 13 May following, and died the same day: Age 33.

(VI.D.27) Pte. 1158, Stanley Allen, 1st Bn. Welsh Guards: *b.* Llanelly, co. Carmarthen: enlisted Swansea, co. Glamorgan: proceeded to France with 3rd Guards Bde.; disembarked Le Havre, 18 August 1915: took part in the fighting at Loos (September), and subsequent action at the Hohenzollern Redoubt (October): admitted No.3 Canadian C.C.S. wounded, 13 May 1916; died the same day: Age 29. He leaves a wife, Mary Ann Allen (2, Gorseinon Terrace,

Gorseinon, co. Glamorgan). Remembered on Ammanford Town War Memorial, Carmarthen.

Yr Hyn Allod Hwn Erl Ai Gwneath

Translation: He Loved All Things Bright And Beautiful

(VI.D.33) Pte. 10206, Albert Preece, 1st Bn. (53rd Foot) The King's (Shropshire Light Infantry): *s.* of the late William Preece, by his wife Alice (3, Limes Terrace, Maylord Street, Hereford): and brother to Pte. 6779, L. Preece, 5th King's Shropshire L.I., killed in action, 3 August 1915: *b.* Holmer: enlisted Hereford: proceeded to France, 10 September 1914, and died of wounds (G.S.W. both legs), 15 May 1916, No.17 C.C.S., Poperinghe. Buried in the cemetery there: Age 22.

Thy Will Be Done

His brother Leonard has no known grave, he is commemorated on the Ypres (Menin Gate) Memorial (Panel 49).

(VII.A.28A) Corpl. 457059, Isaac Philip Garlick, 'B' Coy., 60th Bn. Canadian Infantry, C.E.F.: *s.* of the late William (& Harriet) Garlick, of Richmond, co. Surrey, England: late *husb* to Daisy A. Garlick (46, May Road, Twickenham, co. Middlesex, England): previously served 12 years, Able Seaman, Royal Navy; also served in the Ashanti and Benin Expeditions, 1896–97: enlisted Montreal 4 June 1915: served with the Expeditionary Force in France from 22 February 1916, and died of wounds (G.S.W. both thighs, abdomen), 29 May 1916, received in action at Ypres: Age 39.

God Bless Thee Where-Ever Thou Art In His Great Universe To-Day

(VII.A.31A) Pte. 430276, Philip Butterfield, 31st Bn. Canadian Infantry (Alberta Regt.), C.E.F.: *s.* of Edward Butterfield, of Wynndel, British Columbia, by his wife Maria Amelia: *b.* London, England, 7 October 1888: Religion – Church of England: Occupation – Auto Driver: 5'11" tall, brown eyes, brown hair: a serving member of 109th Regt. (Militia); enlisted 48th (Pioneer) Bn., Victoria, Vancouver Island, 3 March 1915: departed Canada 1 July following: trained England, August 1915–March 1916: proceeded to France with a draft of reinforcements (transf'd.) 31st Battn., and died of wounds (S.W. head), 31 May 1916 received six days previously when 'eleven fellows in 'C' Company, located near Convent Wall, had a shell burst among them killing one and wounding the rest.'

He Being Dead Yet Speaketh

2 June 1916 started very quietly for No.3 Canadian C.C.S., one man died in the early hours of the morning:

(VII.A.32A) L/Corpl. R/6470, George Edward Seymour, M.M., 12th (Service) Bn. The King's Royal Rifle Corps: *s.* of George Seymour, of 13F, Kingwood Road, Fulham, London, S.W., by his wife Bessie. Died at No.3 Canadian C.C.S., Poperinghe, 2 June 1916, of intestinal wounds (G.S.W. multiple): Age 27. *unm.*

But as the day progressed, steadily increasing numbers of casualties from the German attack at Maple Copse started coming in amid rumours that ground as far back as No.10 Field Ambulance's A.D.S. had been taken. Between 8.30 p.m. and 3.40 a.m, 3 June (when No.10 started taking in), the numbers of casualties had steadily increased, until by the evening they were literally pouring into Remy Siding. Before darkness descended over the C.C.S. hurried preparations for the accommodation of 450 wounded were made by removing the furniture from the men's dining room and the hospital personnel from their tents into huts. By mid-night all the officers were on duty, two hours later so were all the nurses, and 526 cases had been safely accommodated under cover.

After incurring very little delay in transporting the casualties from Maple Copse back to the C.C.S. at Poperinghe, upon arrival the particulars of all the wounded were noted on cards by clerks with the assistance of the Chaplain and the dental officer. Many needed little more than their dressings changing, which was done in a room adjoining the reception area; some were redressed in tents on account of discomfort from their wounds. Those considered particularly urgent were passed straight through to the operating rooms where their condition could be assessed by the surgeons without loss of time before ultimately passing them on to the wards. And, there were those for whom the only mortal help that could be afforded was an injection of morphine to ease their last few hours.

(VII.A.35) Pte. 453150, Charles Wheeler, 2nd Bn. Canadian Infantry (Eastern Ontario Regt.), C.E.F.: *b.* England, 27 June 1892: Occupation – Farm Labourer: volunteered and enlisted Niagara, 29 June 1915: served with the Expeditionary Force in France and Flanders, and died 3 June 1916 in No.3 Canadian Casualty Clearing Station, Poperinghe, from a compound fractured leg: Age 23. Buried in the Lyssenthoek Military Cemetery, Remy Siding. All correspondence should be addressed to Miss Daisy Wheeler, c/o Mr Owen, Dr. Barnardos Home, Toronto. *unm.*

(VII.A.36) Sergt. 154871, George Alexander Milne, 1st Canadian Pioneers, C.E.F.: *s.* of James Milne, of R.R.2, Bellwood, Ontario, by his wife Ellen: *b.* Arthur, Co. Wellington, Ontario, 22 September 1897: Religion – Baptist: Occupation – Electrician: volunteered and enlisted Edmonton, 1 July 1915:

served with the Expeditionary Force in France and Flanders from 9 March 1916, and died at No.3 Canadian Casualty Clearing Station, 3 June 1916, from multiple abdominal bullet wounds received vicinity S.W. Corner; Maple Copse Wood. Buried at Poperinghe: Age 28. *unm.*

(VII.A.37) Pte. 147478, Robert Oliver Hughes, 10th Bn. Canadian Infantry (Alberta Regt.), C.E.F.: *s.* of John Hughes, of Café Cairch, Bettsw Cerwen, nr. Newton, co. Merioneth, by his wife Margaret: *b.* North Wales, 30 June 1892: Religion – Presbyterian: Occupation – Student: prior to enlistment served with 100th Winnipeg Grenadiers, and 34th Fort Garry Horse: volunteered and enlisted Winnipeg, 8 July 1915: served with the Expeditionary Force in France and Flanders, and died at No.3 Canadian Casualty Clearing Station, Remy, 3 June 1916, from bullet wounds to the left side of his body: Age 23. *unm.*

(VII.A.37A) Corpl. A/26903, William Robb, 10th Bn. Canadian Infantry (Alberta Regt.), C.E.F.: *s.* of William Robb, of Culzean Cottage, Dalrymple, co. Ayr, by his wife Jean Greig: *b.* Ayr, 28 August 1888: Occupation – Farmer: volunteered and enlisted Shorncliffe Camp, England, 9 August 1915: posted 46th Battn.: served with the Expeditionary Force in France and Flanders, transf'd. 10th Battn., and died at No.3 Canadian Casualty Clearing Station, 3 June 1916, from bullet wounds to the head and both arms: Age 27. *unm.*

Beloved Are The Pure In Heart For They Shall See God

Shortly after 7 p.m., 3 June 1916, both No.10 and No.17 C.C.S. were full to overflowing and No.3, already stretched beyond its capacity, began admitting again. By 8.30 a.m (4 June) No.3 had admitted between 700 and 750 cases, almost all of which belonged to 1st and 3rd Canadian Divisions. One of the wounded reported liquid fire had been used in the attack but there were no burn cases to corroborate this. The main concern of the C.C.S at this time was the onset of gangrene as many of the wounded had been lying out unattended for up to two days.

(VII.A.39) Pte. 81508, Arthur Leggott, 5th Bn. Canadian Infantry (Saskatchewan Regt.), C.E.F.: *s.* of Keal Leggott, of Horncastle Road, Boston, co. Lincoln, by his wife Harriet Ann: and brother to Pte. 81509, R.J. Leggott, 5th Bn. Canadian Infantry, who also fell: *b.* Brothertoft, Boston, 13 February 1886: Occupation – Farmer: volunteered and enlisted Winnipeg, 21 December 1914: served with the Expeditionary Force in France and Flanders from mid-1915, and died of gangrene poisoning, 4 June 1916, following the amputation of an arm: Age 30. *unm.*

His brother Robert has no known grave; he is commemorated on the Canadian National Memorial, Vimy.

(VII.A.39A) Sergt. 6089, John Hunter, 1st Bn. (14th Foot) The Prince of Wales's Own (West Yorkshire Regt.): *s.* of the late Alexander Hunter, of York, by his wife Mary (also dec'd.): *b.* Bowling, co. York, about 1883: a pre-war Regular, mobilised with his regiment on the outbreak of war, August 1914: served with the Expeditionary Force in France and Flanders from 10 September following, and died in the Canadian Hospital, Poperinghe, 4 June 1916, from multiple bullet wounds to the thighs and arm: Age 33. Sergt. Hunter leaves a wife, Florence Elizabeth (21, Darrington Terrace, South Kirkby, Wakefield, co. York).

Rest In The Lord

(VII.B.1) Pte. 3292, Edward Ford Abell, 3rd Divn. Supply Col., Canadian Army Service Corps, C.E.F.: *s.* of William J. (& Helen F.) Abell, of Kirkfield Park, Manitoba: *b.* Wolfe Island, Ontario, 10 February 1895: Religion – Presbyterian: Occupation – Chauffeur: enlisted Sewell, Manitoba, 8 July 1915. Died of wounds, 3 June 1916: Age 21. An officer said, "Pte. Abell was driving a motor ambulance loaded with patients from Transport Farm to the Advanced Dressing Station at the Asylum, Ypres, when, at Shrapnel Corner, an enemy shell burst about twenty yards from the vehicle. A fragment of the shell lodged in Pte. Abell's right thigh, another tore off three fingers of his right hand; a third fragment entered his right temple causing instant death. All the patients escaped injury, except one who received a slight wound."

All Gates Are Good Through Which We Pass To God

(VII.B.2) Pte. 428706, John Stewart, 7th Bn. Canadian Infantry (British Columbia Regt.), C.E.F.: *b.* Partick, Glasgow, 12 May 1876: Occupation – Labourer: prior to enlistment was a member of the local militia; volunteered and enlisted New Westminster, 18 March 1915; posted 47th Battn.: served with the Expeditionary Force in France and Flanders, transf'd. 7th Battn., and died 4 June 1916, from shrapnel wounds to his left leg and back. All correspondence should be addressed c/o his brother Andrew Stewart, of Broomhill Road, Partick, Glasgow, co. Lanark: Age 40.

(VII.B.2A) Pte. 66123, Samuel Kerr Wright, 24th Bn. Canadian Infantry (Quebec Regt.), C.E.F.: *s.* of Robert Wright, of 42, Sunnyside, Belfast, Ireland: *b.* Belfast, 13 March 1887: Occupation – Labourer: volunteered and enlisted Montreal, 8 March 1915: served with the Expeditionary Force in France and Flanders, and died, 4 June 1916, from bullet wounds to his right leg: Age 28.

(VII.B.3) Pte. 442239, Norman Allan Pope, 7th Bn. Canadian Infantry (British Columbia Regt.), C.E.F.: *s.* of Arthur N. Pope, of Melita, Manitoba, late of Peachland, Okanagan, by his wife Emma Ryland: *b.* Manitoba, 28 April 1887:

Occupation – Rodman: volunteered and enlisted Vernon, 29 May 1915: served with the Expeditionary Force in France and Flanders, and died of wounds (compound fracture right leg), 4 June 1916: Age 29. *unm. (IWGC record age 32)*

Greater Love Hath No Man Than This

(VII.B.7A) Pte. 11661, Christopher Parkinson, 2nd Bn. (106th Foot) The Durham Light Infantry: *b*. Durham: enlisted there: served in France from 24 August 1915. Died No.3 Canadian C.C.S., Poperinghe, 4 June 1916, of shrapnel wounds to the thighs. *(IWGC record 3/1661)*

(VII.B.8A) Pte. 418845, Thomas Alfred Williamson, 42nd Bn. Canadian Infantry (Quebec Regt.), C.E.F.: *s*. of Alfred Williamson, of Wybunbury, Nantwich, co. Chester: *b*. Crewe, co. Chester, 28 May 1875: Occupation – Clerk: previously served 1 year South Wales Borderers; 2 years 2nd Cheshire Railway Engineers: volunteered and enlisted Montreal, 13 May 1915: served with the Expeditionary Force in France and Flanders from October 1915, and died from abdominal bullet wounds, 4 June 1916, received in action at Maple Copse the previous day: Age 41.

(VII.B.9) Pte. 424105, Charles Burdett, 5th Bn. Canadian Infantry (Saskatchewan Regt.), C.E.F.: *s*. of the late George Burdett, by his wife Hannah (Little Stretton, nr. Leicester): *b*. Leicester, 18 May 1892: Occupation – Farmer: volunteered and enlisted, 45th Battn., Portage La Prairie, 12 February 1915: served with the Expeditionary Force in France and Flanders, transf'd. 5th Battn. (July 1915), and died in No.3 Canadian C.C.S., Remy, 5 June 1916 (S.W. shrapnel, Rt. arm, Rt. leg): Age 24. *unm. (IWGC record A/24105, age 25)*

Gone But Not Forgotten

(VII.B.9A) Pte. 8096, John Filtz, 15th Bn. Canadian Infantry (Central Ontario Regt.), C.E.F.: *s*. of P. (& Mrs) Filtz, of 79, Elm Street, Kingston, Ontario: *b*. Kingston, 1885: Occupation – Spinner: previously served 13 years Prince of Wales's Own Regt.: volunteered and enlisted Valcartier, 22 September 1914; posted 2nd Battn.: subsequently transf'd. 15th Battn.: came over with First Canadian Contingent, October 1914: trained Salisbury Plain, England, winter 1914–1915: served with the Expeditionary Force in France and Flanders from February 1915, and died at Poperinghe, 4 June 1916, of shrapnel wounds to the left side: Age 30. *unm.*

Asleep In Jesus

(VII.B.10) Pte. 21406, William Coleman, 1st Bn. (14th Foot) The Prince of Wales's Own (West Yorkshire Regt.): enlisted Leeds. Died 4 June 1916, of wounds (G.S.W. bullet; back).

(VII.B.12) Pte. 153322, George Haddon White, 43rd Bn. Canadian Infantry (Manitoba Regt.), C.E.F.: only *s.* of Cllr. John George White, of 'Red House,' Sutton-in-Ashfield, co. Nottingham, Miller & Corn Merchant, by his wife Annie Elizabeth, *née* Aked: *b.* 21 April 1891: Religion – Church of England: Occupation – Bank Clerk; Newark, before emigrating to Canada where, after a brief time farming, he returned to the banking profession in Winnipeg: 5'7" tall, brown eyes, black hair: a serving member of 79th Cameron Highlanders of Canada (Militia), enlisted Winnipeg, 18 June 1915: Died at No.3 Canadian C.C.S., Poperinghe, 5 June 1916 of wounds received in action the previous evening. Buried in the Military Cemetery there: Age 25. *unm.* A comrade, F.J. Fitter wrote, "…On the morning of June 3rd the Germans made an attack on the trenches held by various battalions in our (the 43rd) Division. The portion of the line held by the C.M.R. Brigade was broken and they were driven back into Sanctuary Wood and from there into Maple Copse, where the advance of the enemy was arrested, and he took up a position in Sanctuary Wood and along a trench communicating the two woods. The 43rd were several miles back in rest camp having, we understood, finished with the Ypres district, for we had done three months there, which was considered sufficient time for any troops to be stationed at that particular spot, but the word came through that our Division was in trouble and we were hurried into our equipment and taken into supports at Belgium Chateau where we rested the night and were hurried on again about 2.30 a.m. across the open country into the Zillebeke dugouts where we rested again for a few hours. George, along with a few others, spent this rest carrying wounded C.M.R.s. After the rest we were taken out of the dugouts and hurried up the line with the intention of relieving the Princess Pats, who had managed to hold their own during the attack, but it was found impossible to get up as far, so we were ordered to dig ourselves in, in a very battered trench running parallel to the enemy's trench between the woods. About five o'clock in the evening (the 4th) the Germans started a furious bombardment of our trench with both light and heavy artillery and a mixture of trench mortar shells as well. (The newspaper report said 82 shells per minute fell in each portion of the trench.) We were given the order to open up with rapid rifle fire across at the opposite trench to prevent the enemy coming over, which he started to do but retired again. George was next on my left and I caught a glimpse of him standing up above the parapet, the coolest one I believe of the whole lot of us, and he was laughing. The next time I looked his way he was lying on the bottom of the trench with a wound in the right side of the neck, which looked as though the jugular had been cut. He was bandaged up and placed in a little culvert for safety, to await the stretcher bearers coming up, our own bearers having by this time all been hit. He was in no pain, but fainted through loss of blood, and I imagine he must have slept his passage out. Any further information I am able to give you I shall be pleased to forward, so please write if there is anything else." "P.S. All George's effects were left behind at the Zillebeke dugouts, as we threw off our packs there when we made the last stage of our trip in. They would be most likely rifled by other troops who were stationed there."

He Died That We Might Live

(VII.B.14A) Pte. 432110, George William Shepherd Aspden, 49th Bn. Canadian Infantry (Alberta Regt.), C.E.F.: *s.* of Robert Aspden, of Carlton Hill, Alberta (c/o General Delivery, Edmonton South): *b.* Darwen, co. Lancaster, 5 July 1895: Occupation – Chauffeur: volunteered and enlisted Edmonton, 5 January 1915; posted 49th Battn.: served with the Expeditionary Force in France and Flanders, and died 4 June 1916 (G.S.W. multiple, both hips, Lt. leg): Age 20. *unm.*

(VII.B.16) Pte. 101096, Gordian Belcourt, 49th Bn. Canadian Infantry (Alberta Regt.), C.E.F.: *s.* of Magloire Belcourt, of Lac Sainte Anne, Alberta, by his wife Constance Letendre: *b.* Edmonton, 13 January 1891: Occupation – Packer: volunteered and enlisted Edmonton, 17 July 1915; posted 66th Battn.: served with the Expeditionary Force in France and Flanders, transf'd. 49th Battn., and died 4 June 1916, from shrapnel wounds to both legs and side: Age 29. *unm.*

Ave Maria For This Brave Son Of Canada

(VII.B.18) Pte. 44092, Charles Robert Gray, 'B' Coy., 3rd Bn. Canadian Infantry (Central Ontario Regt.), C.E.F.: *s.* of Alfred Gray, of 204, Rosethorn Avenue, Silverthorn, Toronto, by his wife Emily: *b.* co. Kent, 3 March 1891: Religion – Church of England: removed to Canada, 1913, finding employ as Labourer: enlisted Toronto, 4 April 1915: 5'8" tall, blue eyes, dark brown hair: posted 3rd Battn. 19 April: served with the Expeditionary Force in France and Flanders, and was killed in action, 3 June 1916, at Mount Sorrel. In a letter to their parents his brother Walter (*d.* 1974), serving in the same battalion and wounded in the same action, wrote, "10 July 1916: Just a few lines hoping to find you in the best of health as I am pleased to say I am feeling much better myself. The wound itself is quite better now, but my foot is just as bad as ever, but I expect to go under another operation soon, as the Doctor thinks there is something touching the nerves under my knee....They told me you had got the news of poor old Charlie. It was nearly three weeks before I knew. They would not tell me at first but I got the news through a lady writing to the Record Office, and I had an idea something had happened to him by the way the stretcher bearers spoke to me. They said he was alright, they had been speaking to him, but I thought different as no sooner had the shell exploded then those who was not hit ran for safety. So they never had the chance to speak to him, but I would have like to have known in a way so I could have said, Goodbye. But cheer up, we know he died for his King and Country, which every man out there is prepared to do or die. It was an awful place where we were. It was on the night of the 3rd, and the battle was going like fury and the Canadians were going to attack at dawn, and our Battn. was going up to supports in case we should be wanted, and we were on the Ypres road. Just before we got to the canal bridge a shell came over and either killed or wounded 12 to 15 of us. You asked how much my leg is wounded. Well a piece of shrapnel hit me above the knee cap and as it went through it cut the artery so as soon as I got to the cleansing station they operated on it and tied it together again. They could not treat me for 24 hrs as it would have proved fatal to my leg. I may have had to lose it if they had, but I have got over that now so don't worry.": Age 25. *unm.* (*IWGC record A/4092*)

May You Rest In Peace

Between 8.30 a.m., 2 June 1916, and 8.30 a.m., 6 June, No.3 Canadian C.C.S. had admitted and processed 1,663 casualties. During the last two days the wounds of many of them were found to have become so badly infected they had turned gangrenous; for these there was very little hope.

(VII.B.19) Pte. 3/10256, Harry Coverdale, 2nd Bn. (106th Foot) The Durham Light Infantry: *b.* Dinsdale, Darlington: enlisted Newcastle-on-Tyne. Died No.3 Canadian Hospital, Poperinghe, 6 June 1916; gangrene poisoning ensuing from shrapnel wounds to the hip and abdomen.

(VII.B.19A) Pte. 55673, Hubert Oldroyd, 19th Bn. Canadian Infantry (Central Ontario Regt.), C.E.F.: *s.* of John Oldroyd, of 19, Wellington Street East, Saulte Sainte Marie, Ontario, by his wife Ada: *b.* Bradford, co. York, 22 July 1885: Occupation – Labourer: volunteered and enlisted Toronto, 12 November 1914: proceeded to France with 2nd Contingent; served with the Expeditionary Force there and in Flanders, and died of multiple shrapnel wounds to the abdomen, neck, left arm and right leg, 5 June 1916: Age 30. *unm.* All correspondence should be addressed c/o Edith Casey, Saulte Sainte Marie, Ontario. (*IWGC record age 21*)

(VII.B.20) Pte. 419100, Percival 'Percy' George Maughan, 42nd Bn. Canadian Infantry (Quebec Regt.), C.E.F.: *s.* of the late Thomas James Maughan, of 1414, Marguerette Street, Montreal, by his wife Elizabeth: *b.* Toronto, 8 January 1895: Occupation – Electrician: previously served 1 year Highlander Cadets:

volunteered and enlisted Montreal, 8 June 1915: served with the Expeditionary Force in France and Flanders, and died 6 June 1916, of bullet wounds to the face and both arms: Age 21. *unm.*

> *Though Death Divides Fond Memory Clings*
> *Mother & Sisters*

(VII.B.20A) Pte. 8197, William McKenzie, 1st Bn. (14th Foot) The Prince of Wales's Own (West Yorkshire Regt.): *s.* of the late James Bell McKenzie, by his wife Fanny (20, Picadilly, Walmgate, co. York): a pre-war Regular, served on the North West Frontier, India, 1908, and with the Expeditionary Force in France and Flanders from September 1914, and died at Poperinghe, 6 June 1916, from a bomb wound in the perineum (between anus and external genitalia) received in action on the 4th.: Age 29. *unm.*

> *Though Lost To Sight To Memory Ever Dear*

During the course of the Great War 361 British and Commonwealth soldiers were executed for crimes contrary to military discipline. The first soldier to be tried by a Field General Court Martial and sentenced to death under the provisions of the Army Act and shot by firing squad on 8 September 1914 was Pte. Thomas Highgate who had enlisted in the Regular Army in 1913 aged 17 years. Less than two weeks after taking part in the fighting at Mons he deserted. Found hiding in a barn wearing civilian clothes he had removed from a scarecrow – his uniform was discovered hidden nearby – on apprehension he stated, "I want to get out of it, and this is the way I am doing it."

(VII.B.23A) Pte. L/10412, Joseph Highgate, 1st Bn. (3rd Foot) The Buffs (East Kent Regt.): *s.* of Alice Highgate (103, Brookdale Road, Catford, London, S.E.6): and brother to L/Corpl. 10395, R. Highgate, 2nd East Lancashire Regt., killed in action, 30 January 1915; and Pte. L/10061, T.J. Highgate, 1st Royal West Kent Regt., executed by firing squad, 8 September 1914: *b.* Shoreham, co. Kent: enlisted Woolwich: served with the Expeditionary Force in France and Flanders, and died from wounds, 6 June 1916; (G.S.W., Lt. side cranial).

His brothers Robert and Thomas have no known grave, they are commemorated on the Le Touret Memorial and La Ferte-Sous-Jouarre Memorial respectively. Joseph and Robert are recorded on the Shoreham War Memorial. Despite repeated campaigning by residents of the village Thomas is denied remembrance thereon. A local British Legion spokesman defended the decision thus: "Many men fought at Mons and stood their ground. Obviously, by deserting Highgate put his comrades at further risk. Should his name be honoured alongside those who stood and served their country bravely? I don't think so!"

(VII.B.24) Pte. 25647, Douglas Swindley, 14th Bn. Canadian Infantry (Quebec Regt.), C.E.F.: s. of Uriah Swindley, of 82, Lowell Avenue, St. Catherines, Ontario, by his wife Catherine: b. Swinton, co. Lancaster, 12 March 1882: resident Brighton, co. Sussex: went to Canada, finding employment as a Bottler: prior to the outbreak of war served 2 years 1st Canadian Grenadier Guards (Militia): volunteered and enlisted Valcartier, 22 September 1914: came over with First Canadian Contingent, October 1914: trained Salisbury Plain, England, winter 1914–1915: served with the Expeditionary Force in France and Flanders from February 1915, and died at No.3 Canadian Casualty Clearing Station, Remy, 6 June 1916, from multiple shrapnel wounds to the shoulders, both legs and left arm: Age 34. *unm.*

(VII.B.24A) Corpl. 26622, George Swift, 14th Bn. Canadian Infantry (Quebec Regt.), C.E.F.: b. Bolton, co. Lancaster, 18 July 1892: prior to enlistment served 4 years Territorial: Occupation – Furrier: volunteered and undertook Imperial Service obligations, Valcartier, 22 September 1914: came over with First Contingent, October following: underwent training on Salisbury Plain throughout the winter 1914–1915: went to France, February 1915: served with the Expeditionary Force there and in Flanders, and died of blood poisoning (gangrene) following shrapnel wounds and fractures to both legs, 6 June 1916. Buried in the Military Cemetery, Lyssenthoek: Age 23. *unm.* All correspondence should be addressed c/o Corpl. Swift's sister, Mrs Ann White (1232, Lanouette Street, Verdun, Quebec) late of 11, York Lane, Cote St. Paul, Ontario.

We Miss Him Most Who Loved Him Best

(VII.B.25) Pte. A/44233, Hanford Stanley Allaby, 14th Bn. Canadian Infantry (Royal Montreal Regt.), C.E.F.: eldest s. of James B. (& Hattie M.) Allaby, of Salt Springs, King's Co., New Brunswick: b. 29 August 1892: Religion – Baptist: *educ.* Hampton High School: Occupation – Mill Hand: joined C.E.F., St. John, 4 January 1915; apptd. 55th Bn.; transf'd. 14th Bn. 15 September following: served with the Expeditionary Force in France; took part in operations at Hill 63 and St. Eloi: on leave 11–19 May 1916. Reported missing and wounded, believed killed in action 3–6 June 1916, at Mount Sorrel; amended (25 September) died of wounds (GSW Lt. side), No.17 Casualty Clearing Station, Poperinghe, 5 June 1916: Age 23. *unm.*

John XV.13
Greater Love Hath No Man Than This

(VII.B.26) Pte. 432981, Felix Desmond MacSwiney, 49th Bn. Canadian Infantry (Alberta Regt.), C.E.F.: s. of Felix MacSwiney, of Wylde Green, Birmingham, co. Stafford, by his wife Mary: *b*. Croydon, co. Surrey, 27 October 1894: prior to going to Canada served 1 year Officer Training Corps, Birmingham: Occupation – Clerk: volunteered and enlisted Grouard, Alberta, 28 January 1915: went to France with Second Contingent and served with the Expeditionary Force there and in Flanders, and died 6 June 1916, of gangrene poisoning following shrapnel wounds to the left shoulder received in action at Mount Sorrel three days previously. Buried in the Soldiers Cemetery, Lyssenthoek: Age 21. *unm*. All correspondence should be addressed c/o his brother, Denis G.J. MacSwiney, Esq., Hudson Bay Co., Fort McMurray, Alberta.

Requiescat In Pace

(VII.B.30A) Pte. 40469, Patrick McTighe, 19th Bn. Canadian Infantry (Central Ontario Regt.), C.E.F.: *s*. of Julia McTighe (22, Woodsway, Galway, Ireland): *b*. Galway, 22 February 1885: Occupation – Labourer: volunteered and enlisted Toronto, 12 April 1915: served with the Expeditionary Force in France and Flanders, and died 6 June 1916; No.3 Canadian Casualty Clearing Station, Poperinghe, of gangrene poisoning consequent to bullet wounds in both legs and abdomen: Age 31. *unm*.

(VII.B.32) Pte. 23194, William H. Turner, 14th Bn. Canadian Infantry (Quebec Regt.), C.E.F.: *s*. of Ethel Turner (Smith Falls, Ontario): *b*. Liverpool, 2 August 1884: Occupation – Farmer: enlisted Valcartier, 23 September 1914: came over with First Canadian contingent, October 1914: served with the Expeditionary Force in France and Flanders from February 1915, and died 5 June 1916, of abdominal gunshot wounds received in action two days previously. Buried at Poperinghe: Age 31. *unm*.

(VII.B.32A) Pte. 434898, Raymond Matthews, 6th Coy., Canadian Machine Gun Corps, C.E.F.: *s*. of Alfred Matthews, of 533, 13th Avenue East, Calgary: *b*. Belleville, Ontario, 15 August 1895: Occupation – Clerk: enlisted Calgary, 8 February 1915: Religion – Presbyterian. Died at No. 10 C.C.S., Poperinghe, of septicaemia consequent to shrapnel wounds and amputation of leg, 7 June 1916. Buried in the Military Cemetery, Lyssenthoek: Age 20. A Freemason, Pte. Matthews was a member of Wellington Lodge No.46, Chatham.

(VII.B.33) Pte. A/454060, Ruben Belch, 2nd Bn. Canadian Infantry (Eastern Ontario Regt.), C.E.F.: *s*. of Hattie Belch (Belleville, Ontario): *b*. Belleville, 3 August 1894: Occupation – Farmer: previously served one season with 15th Battn. (Militia): volunteered and enlisted Belleville, 10 June 1915; posted 2nd Battn.: served with the Expeditionary Force in France and Flanders, and died 5 June 1916 of bullet wounds to the right thigh received in action near Sanctuary Wood two days previously: Age 21. *unm*.

(VII.B.33A) Pte. 54363, William H. Scobie, 18th Bn. Canadian Infantry (Western Ontario Regt.), C.E.F.: *b*. Kilbirnie, Scotland, 21 October 1883: volunteered and enlisted Windsor, 12 January 1915: Occupation – Plumber: served with the Expeditionary Force in France and Flanders from early 1915, and died of shrapnel wounds (left lung) 4 June 1916. All correspondence should be addressed c/o his brother Robert Scobie, of 3102, Ellery Street, Detroit, Michigan, United States (formerly of 90, Ludden Street): Age 32. *unm*.

He Died That We Might Live

(VII.B.34) Pte. 453696, Leonard Parkhurst, 58th Bn. Canadian Infantry (Central Ontario Regt.), C.E.F.: late *husb*. to Emma Parkhurst (101, Broad Street, Orillia, Ontario): *b*. Ontario, 11 May 1889: Occupation – Carriage Wood Turner: previously served 45th Regt. (Militia); serving member of 41st Regt., enlisted Niagara, 27 August 1915: served with the Expeditionary Force in France and Flanders from February 1916; severely wounded (G.S.W. head, multiple compound fractures both legs) during a continuous bombardment of the battalion's trenches – Rifle Pits, Maple Copse – died the same day, 6 June 1916: Age 27. Five other men were killed outright. See Pte. C.W. Cosseboom, Railway Dugouts Burial Ground (Transport Farm), (VI.D.40).

(VII.B.34A) Pte. 55850, Robert Herd, 19th Bn. Canadian Infantry (Central Ontario Regt.), C.E.F.: *b*. Wishaw, nr. Motherwell, co. Lanark, 17 October 1890: Occupation – Crane Operator: volunteered and enlisted Toronto, 12 November 1914: came over May 1915: served with the Expeditionary Force in France and Flanders from September 1915, and died 5 June 1916; multiple shrapnel wounds to both legs: Age 25. *unm*. All correspondence should be forwarded to Miss Agnes Hamilton, Burnside Place, Wishaw.

(VII.B.37A) Pte. 29520, McG/65, Stanton Emile Thomas McGreer, Princess Patricia's Canadian Light Infantry (Eastern Ontario Regt.), C.E.F.: *s*. of Fletcher E. McGreer, of 831, Lorne Crescent, Montreal, and Mrs V. de M. McGreer: and brother to A/Bmdr. 347452, M.L.A. McGreer, Canadian Field Artillery, died 7 October 1918, in England; Nursing Sister L. McGreer, (surv'd.); Gnr. 336860, E.D'A. McGreer, Canadian Field Artillery (surv'd.); and Pte. 234134, E.D. McGreer (surv'd). His adopted brother Pte. 670203, W.G.R. McGreer (*a.k.a.* McLaren), 47th C.E.F., was killed instantaneously by a shell, 11 August 1918, at the Battle of Amiens: *b*. Napanee, Ontario, 20 August 1891: Religion – Church of England: Occupation – Clerk: 5'7" tall, brown eyes, dark brown hair: served 1 year Grenadier Guards, and Militia; enlisted Niagara-on-the-Lake, 15 May 1915: served with the Expeditionary Force in France from September following, and died 7 June 1916, of septicaemia (blood poisoning) and shock following the amputation of his leg (6 June) consequent to wounds received at Sanctuary

Wood: Age 24. *unm*. His cousin, the Rev. Arthur H. McGreer, Chaplain to the Forces, attended him during his last hours.

His brother Maurice is buried in Basingstoke (Worting Road) Cemetery (A.9); adopted brother William, Cerisy-Gailly Military Cemetery (II.N.14). His cousin Arthur, his hat found beside the river at Lennoxville, was reported missing 10 December 1947; his body washed up downstream in April 1948. He is buried in Malvern Cemetery, Quebec.

(VII.C.5) Pte. A/40009, Sidney John Crook, 5th Bn. Canadian Infantry (Saskatchewan Regt.), C.E.F.: *s*. of Harry Crook, Farmer; of Overs Farm, East Harling, co. Norfolk, by his wife Mary Anne: and brother to Pte. 7253119, H.C. Crook, Royal Army Medical Corps, died of sickness, 22 August 1920, in Mesopotamia; and Sergt. 1649, Harry Crook, C.E.F., enlisted 21 August 1914, discharged 18 January 1919: *b*. 2 March 1892: Religion – Church of England: 5'10" tall, blue eyes, dark hair: removed to Canada (with brothers Harry and Frederick) early 1900's: enlisted 21 December 1914; after the outbreak of the European War, posted 53rd Battn.: came over with 2nd Canadian Contingent, transf'd. 5th Battn.: proceeded to France with a draft of reinforcements, and died at Remy Siding, Poperinghe, 7 June 1916, of wounds received in action: Age 25. *unm*. Remembered on Eccles (St. Mary's Church) War Memorial, Norfolk. One of six brothers; the youngest, Frank, died of wounds in the Second World War.

His brother Herbert has no known grave; he is commemorated on the Basra Memorial (Panel 42).

(VII.C.11) Pte. 73741, Henry B. Compton, D.C.M., 'B' Coy., 28th (North West) Bn. Canadian Infantry (Saskatchewan Regt.), C.E.F.: *s*. of J.W. Compton, of 1861, Retallie Street, Regina, Saskatchewan: *b*. Bangor, Prince Edward Island, 2 October 1889: Religion – Presbyterian: Occupation – Postal Clerk: 5'10" tall, dark complexion and hair, dark brown eyes: served 1 year 82nd Regt. (Militia); 1 year 29th Light Horse (Militia); enlisted Regina, 23 October 1914. Died of shrapnel wounds, 8 June 1916, received in action at Culvert Post the previous day: Age 26. *unm*. The first member of 2nd Canadian Divn. to be decorated, he was awarded the D.C.M. (*London Gazette*, 29 November 1915) "Kemmel, 8 October 1915: The enemy exploded mines and Compton was buried under the debris. Being dug out, he immediately volunteered to go forward as a member of a bombing party, and assisted in bombing the enemy from the crater in which they were advancing. He also assisted, under heavy shell and machine gun fire, to dig out four men buried by the explosion thus helping to save their lives." Pte. Compton was a member of the Grand Orange Lodge of Western Canada (7793, Regina).

(VII.C.21) Sergt. 80005, Albert Frederick Abbott, 31st Bn. Canadian Infantry (Alberta Regt.), C.E.F.: *s*. of Lemuel H. (& Mary) Abbott: late *husb*. to Charlotte

L. Abbott (2014, Noyes Street, Evanston, Illinois, United States): *b*. Chatham, New Brunswick, 27 December 1881: Religion – Wesleyan: Occupation – Building Superintendent: enlisted Edmonton, 12 December 1914. Died of wounds (GSW neck, Lt. shoulder) No.10 Casualty Clearing Station, 10 June 1916, received in action at Mount Sorrel, 6 June: Age 34.

Greater Love Hath No Man Than This That He Giveth His Life

(VII.C.21A) Pte. 404785, Charles Frederick Adams, 20th Bn. Canadian Infantry, C.E.F.: *s*. of William Francis Adams, of 1292, Danforth Avenue, Toronto, and his wife Elizabeth J.H. Adams: *b*. 23 September 1891: Religion – Wesleyan: *educ*. Harbord Collegiate School. Died of wounds, 10 June 1916: Age 20. An officer recorded, "Pte. Adams was one of a permanent working party, billeted in Dickebusch. At about 7 p.m., June 9th., 1916 a shell struck the billet, wounding Pte. Adams on the hip and in the abdomen. He died from the effect of these wounds the next day."

Mizpah
God Watch Between Thee And Me

(VII.C.38) Pte. 63041, Norman Leslie Allen, 3rd Bn. Canadian Infantry (Central Ontario Regt.), C.E.F.: *s*. of Annie Allen (Mount View, Great North Road, Dunston, co. Bedford, England): *b*. 26 November 1888: Religion – Church of England: Occupation – Clerk: joined C.E.F., Montreal, 21 November 1914: served with the Expeditionary Force: 'severely wounded in the back by shrapnel, 13 June 1916; evacuated to No.3 Canadian Casualty Clearing Station where he died the following day (14 June 1916)': Age 27. *unm*.

(VII.D.2A) Corpl. 141676, John Linn Graham, 13th Bn. Canadian Infantry (Quebec Regt.), C.E.F.: *s*. of the late James Linn Graham, by his wife Jane (29, Blacklands Row, Kilwinning, co. Ayr): *b*. Kilmarnock, 6 May 1894: removed to Canada, finding employ as Engineer/Machinist; Government Elevator Coy., Port Colborne, Ontario: volunteered for Foreign Service on the outbreak of war; enlisted St. Catherine's, Ontario, 27 July 1915. Died of wounds, (G.S. head) received in action at Ypres, at Remy Farm, Poperinghe, 22 July 1916. Buried in the Soldier's Cemetery, Lyssenthoek: Age 22. His relatives provided the following memoriam notice for publication in the *Ardossan & Saltcoats Herald*: 'So gentle in nature, so patient in pain, Our dear brother left us, heaven to gain.'

Faithful Unto Death

(VII.D.8) Corpl. A2547, William Utley Illingworth, 1st Bn. Canadian Infantry (Western Ontario Regt.), C.E.F.: *s.* of James William Illingworth, of Upper Sackville Street, Skipton, co. York, by his wife Elizabeth: and brother to Lieut. J. Illingworth, M.C., 6th West Yorkshire Regt., died 3 June 1918, of wounds: *b.* Skipton, 3 September 1889: removed to Canada 1913: Occupation – Watchmaker: joined C.E.F. 23 January 1915: served with the Expeditionary Force in France from late July 1915; wounded five days later (August), and returned to duty. Died at No.3 Canadian C.C.S., Poperinghe, 26 July 1916, of multiple extremity wounds (hands, arms, legs) received in action when, on 9 July, at duty in Halifax Trench, both his legs were fractured during a heavy bombardment: Age 26. *unm.* In a letter to his father the Chaplain wrote, "You will have had the sad news of your son's death soon after my last letter. He had been constantly getting worse and was quite unconscious. I am glad to tell you that he passed away so peacefully, and without pain. We have laid him away in our cemetery – in the Poperinghe-Boeschepe Road. A cross will mark his grave, while his personal effects will be sent to you. I pray that God may be your comfort. I know what a sad blow it is to you and Mrs. Illingworth, but he is in God's loving hands, and may He bring us together at the last."(*IWGC record 40257*)

Until The Day Breaks And The Shadows Flee Away

His brother John is buried in Hagle Dump Cemetery (I.B.3).

(VII.D.18A) Pte. 53827, Arthur John Parsons, 17th Field Ambulance, Royal Army Medical Corps: *s.* of Samuel Parsons, of 22, St. Michael's Road, Penn Mill, Yeovil, co. Somerset, by his wife Emily: *b.* Milborne Port, co. Somerset: Occupation – Cutter; Messrs Whitby, Glove Manufacturers, Yeovil. Drowned 2 August 1916, whilst bathing in a pond west of Lebbe Farm, Poperinghe: Age 25. *The Western Gazette* recorded: "Accompanying the notification was a letter signed by Mr. D. Lloyd George, Secretary of State for War, expressing the deep sympathy of the King and Queen with the family in their sorrow. The late Pte. Parsons, who was 25 years of age was a native of Milborne Port, where he actively identified himself with the Wesleyan Church, was a Sunday School teacher, and member of the Wesleyan Boys' Brigade; being a sergeant. On the family's removal to Yeovil he became a member of the Pen Mill Adult School, a movement in which he took a keen interest, and was also a member of the Vicarage Street Wesleyan Chapel. At the outbreak of war he was working in the North of England, but about six months afterwards patriotically offered his services to his King and country, and was accepted for the R.A.M.C. He subsequently went to France, and his frequent letters showed that he was doing excellent work amongst the wounded. His death will be regretted by his many friends in Milborne Port and Yeovil, by whom he was held in general respect and esteem."

God Is My Refuge

(VII.D.22) Pnr. 118140, David Caddy, 9th Labour Bn. Royal Engineers: late of Weymouth, co. Dorset: *s.* of John E. Caddy, of 1, Cameron Street, New Beckton, London, E.: enlisted London: served with the Expeditionary Force in France from 1 October 1915, and died, 4 August 1916, of accidental injuries (fractured skull): Age 50. All correspondence should be addressed c/o his son, John Edward Caddy, of 1, Cameron Street, New Beckton, London.

In The Midst Of Life We Are In Death

(VII.D.24A) Pte. 1758, Edward Jennings, 1st Bn. (6th Foot) The Royal Warwickshire Regt.: late of Ashted, Birmingham: served with the Expeditionary Force from 1 April 1915, and died of wounds (both arms, abdominal), 6 August 1916, sustained from the premature detonation of a bomb.

(VII.D.26) Pte. 153846, Hugh Livingstone, 43rd (Cameron Highlanders) Bn. Canadian Infantry (Manitoba Regt.), C.E.F.: 2nd *s.* of the late Hugh Livingstone, of Boularderie Island, Nova Scotia, by his wife Catherine (Black Brook, Cape Breton): and brother to Lieut. R. Livingstone, 1st Canadian Mounted Rifles (surv'd.); Major C.D. Livingstone, 1st Canadian Mounted Rifles, killed in action, 12 October 1916, at the Somme; and Lieut. D. Livingstone, 1st Canadian Motor Machine Gun Brigade, after whose death at Cambrai, 10 October 1918, their father passed away three weeks later: *b.* North Sydney, Nova Scotia, 1 January 1882: Religion – Presbyterian: Occupation – Lumberman: 5'11" tall, brown eyes, dark hair: a member of 79th Cameron Highlanders of Canada (Militia); enlisted Winnipeg, 22 September 1915: served with the Expeditionary Force in France and Flanders from 22 February 1916, and died 6 August 1916, of wounds received in action at Dormy House: Age 34. *unm.* Published 1916, Pte. Livingstone is recorded in *The Cameron Highlanders of Canada Roll of Honour.* His cousin L/Sergt. 222759, L. Livingstone, 85th C.E.F., was killed on 13 June 1917, at Arras.

He Giveth His Beloved Sleep

His brother Charles is buried in Pozieres British Cemetery (I.A.19); David, Haynecourt British Cemetery (III.C.3); cousin Lauchie, Cabaret-Rouge British Cemetery (XXIX.A.14).

(VII.D.26A) Pte. 2028, Alexander Jenkins, 6th Field Ambulance, Canadian Army Medical Corps: *s.* of Alexander Jenkins, of Hillhead, Black Hills, nr. Lhanbryde, Elgin, Scotland, by his wife Helen: *b.* Elgin, 16 February 1891: Religion – Presbyterian: Occupation – Clerk: 5'5½" tall, blue eyes, light brown hair: enlisted Montreal, 17 November 1914. Died of wounds (G.S.W. Head, Arms), 6 August 1916, No. 3 Canadian C.C.S., Poperinghe: Age 25.

Greater Love Hath No Man Than This

(VII.D.28) Pte. 487429, Henry Augustus Coit, Princess Patricia's Canadian Light Infantry (Eastern Ontario Regt.), C.E.F.: *s.* of Joseph Howland Coit, President, Moffatt, Yard & Co., Publishers, New York; of 52, Broadway, New York, by his wife Adeline Balch Coit: *b.* Concord, New Hampshire, 1887: Religion – Church of England: *educ.* St. Paul's; Harvard University: enlisted Montreal, Canada, December 1915: served with the Expeditionary Force in France. Wounded – hit by a motorised omnibus on the Vlamertinghe – Poperinghe road – 2 August 1916; conveyed to the P.P.C.L.I. lines (by the same vehicle) from whence, following examination, he was admitted to the Field Ambulance, thence to No.3 Canadian Casualty Clearing Station, Poperinghe, and died consequent to accidental injuries (amputation Rt. Leg, 4 August; amputation Lt. leg, 6 August;), 7 August 1916: Age 28.

Lead Us O Christ Our Life's Work Done Safe Home At Last

(VII.D.29) Pte. 21701, Alfred Henry Bale, 1st Bn. (13th Foot) Prince Albert's (Somerset Light Infantry): *s.* of Walter Bale, of Lillesdon, North Curry, Taunton, Somerset, by his wife Mary: *b.* Thurlberry: enlisted Taunton. Died of wounds (gas poisoning; G.S.W. Lt. arm), received on the Somme (*q.v.*), 9 August 1916: Age 27. Remembered on North Curry War Memorial.

(VII.D.30) Pte. 17734, Percy Keen, 2nd Bn. (67th Foot) The Hampshire Regt.: *s.* of Mrs M.A. Keen (6, Clarke's Cottages, Saxby Street, Lyham Road, Brixton, London): *b.* Streatham, London: enlisted Cockspur Street, London: served with the Expeditionary Force in Egypt (from December 1915); in France and Flanders (from March 1916), and died of wounds, 9 August 1916: Age 31.

(VII.D.31) Rfn. R/20989, William Housham, 8th (Service) Bn. The King's Royal Rifle Corps: late of Limehouse, London, E.: enlisted Whitehall. Died of wounds No.3 C.C.S. 9 August 1916; gas poisoning.

(VII.D.31) Pte. 19846, Frederick Kettlety, 1st Bn. (13th Foot) The Prince Albert's (Somerset Light Infantry): *s.* of Levi Kettlety, of 4, Shophouse Road, Twerton, Bath: and cousin to L/Corpl. 9219, F. Kettlety, 1st Somerset Light Infantry, killed in action, 28 March 1918: *b.* Twerton: enlisted Bath. Severely incapacitated by the inhalation of poisonous gas and died of asphyxiation enroute to No.3 C.C.S., Poperinghe, 9 August 1916: Age 35.

His cousin Frederick is buried in Haute-Avesnes British Cemetery (E.1).

(VII.D.32) Pte. 16058, Walter Edward Atkins, 'D' Coy., 1st Bn. (13th Foot) The Prince Albert's (Somerset Light Infantry): *s.* of Richard Atkins, of 29, Ordnance Road, Canning Town, London, by his wife Mary: enlisted Stratford, co. Essex. Killed in action, 9 August 1916; gas asphyxiation.

Peace Perfect Peace

(VII.D.32A) Pte. 4471, John Lynn, 1st Bn. (27th Foot) The Royal Inniskilling Fusiliers: *s.* of James Lynn, of Mousetown, Coalisland, Co. Tyrone, by his wife Elizabeth: served with the Expeditionary Force in France from 18 March 1915; died of wounds (gas), 9 August 1916: Age 26. One of four brothers who fell: Sergt. 5700, W.E. Lynn, 1st Royal Irish Fusiliers, killed in action at the Battle of the Somme, 17 July 1916, aged 21 years; Dvr. 45206, R. Lynn, Royal Field Artillery, killed in action, 6 August 1915, aged 30 years; and Sergt. EMT/57074, J. Lynn, 906th Coy., Royal Army Service Corps, died 7 August 1920.

Weep Not For Me My Parents Dear,
I Am Not Dead But Sleeping Here

His brother William is buried in Auchonvillers Military Cemetery (II.F.4); Robert, Hop Store Cemetery (I.E.9), and James, Haifa War Cemetery, Israel (C.3).

After the Battle of Albert 1st Royal Inniskillings were kept in the Somme sector until the end of July 1916; not taking part in any great attacks, they simply took their turn with tours in the front line and suffered 'the occasional casualties.' Moving up to the Ypres sector at the end of the beginning of August, 'for a time one of the quiet spots on the Western Front; defence work was the chief care of the troops.' However, as if to prove the evil reputation of salient, 'this lull before the storm was broken, on the night of 8–9 August a heavy gas attack caused severe casualties. The Regimental Historian recorded – "A concentrated discharge of phosgene gas by the enemy lasted nearly two hours. The 1st Inniskillings were in the front line in the Potijze area, and sustained the full force of the attack. Officers and men were on the alert and opened fire at once, and maintained steadily, heavy machine-gun fire on the enemy's parapet. If the enemy had had any intention of leaving his trenches for an assault, that intention was abandoned. But the battalion's losses were serious: 81 other ranks killed, 43 wounded. C Company was the worst sufferer. All the transport horses of the battalion perished from gas in this attack."

(VII.D.33) Pte. 3642, David Loftus Hanna, 1st Bn. (27th Foot) The Royal Inniskilling Fusiliers: *s*. of Henry Hanna, by his wife Elizabeth: *b*. Gilford, Co. Armagh: enlisted Belfast: served with the Expeditionary Force in France and Flanders from 25 March 1915, and died of wounds (gas), 9 August 1916: Age 32.

(VII.D.35) Pte. 3/6846, Charles Henry Henman, 1st Bn. (11th Foot) The Devonshire Regt.: *s*. of George Henman, of 3, Princess Street, London Road, Southwark, London, S.E., by his wife Amelia: enlisted Stratford. Died of wounds (gas), 9 August 1916: Age 19.

For His Voice We Listen And Yearn But Our Boy Will Never Return

(VII.D.36) Rfn. 936, Alfred Foster, 1st Bn. The Prince Consort's Own (The Rifle Brigade): *s*. of W. (& Mrs) Foster, of Leigh-on-Sea, co. Essex: volunteered and enlisted Warley, co. Essex, 6 August 1914: served with the Expeditionary Force in France and Flanders, and died of wounds (gas), 9 August 1916: Age 31.

Death Divides But Memory Clings

(VII.D.36A) Pte. 7838, James Hyman, 1st Bn. (13th Foot) The Prince Albert's (Somerset Light Infantry): *b*. Long Ashton, Bristol: enlisted Taunton, co. Somerset: served with the Expeditionary Force in France and Flanders from 21 August 1914, and was killed in action, 9 August 1916.

(VII.D.37) Rfn. C/7691, Frank Kershaw, 18th (Service) Bn. The King's Royal Rifle Corps: *s*. of M.H. Taylor, 9, Grove Street, Bolton Brow, Sowerby Bridge, co. York: *b*. Luddenden Foot, co. York. Died of wounds (gas), 9 August 1916: Age 19.

God Takes The Loved Ones From Our Homes But Never From Our Hearts

(VII.D.37A) Pte 17790, Leslie Arthur Guyatt, 2nd Bn. (67th Foot) The Hampshire Regt.: *b*. Eastleigh, 1900: served with the Expeditionary Force in Egypt (from December 1915); France and Flanders (from March 1916), and died of wounds (gas), 9 August 1916: Age 16. All correspondence should be addressed c/o his sister, Mrs G. Woodbridge (3, Barton Peveril Cottages, Eastleigh, co. Hants).

(VII.D.39) Pte. 24912, William Brindley Counsell, 1st Bn. (30th Foot) The East Lancashire Regt.: *s*. of William (& Sarah E.) Counsell, of 123, Johnston Street, Blackburn, co. Lancaster. Died of wounds (gas), 9 August 1916: Age 20.

Worthy Of Everlasting Love

(VIII.A.1) L/Corpl. 23578, Thomas Slater, 14th Bn. Canadian Infantry (Quebec Regt.), C.E.F.: *s*. of Harry Slater, of 3 (Back of 19), Hall Street, Bilston, co. Stafford: *b*. Bilston, 3 August 1896: Occupation – Farmer: previously served 1 year, 74th Regt. (Militia): enlisted Valcartier, 25 September 1914. Died from abdominal gun-shot wounds, 4 June 1916: Age 19. (*IWGC record age 21*)

(VIII.A.1A) Gnr. 51095, Edward Hemsworth, 94th Bty., 18th Bde., Royal Field Artillery: *b*. New Boultham, co. Lincoln: enlisted Lincoln: served with the Expeditionary Force in France and Flanders from 27 September 1914. Died at No.3 Canadian C.C.S., 3 June 1916, of concussion and gun-shot wounds to the head.

(VIII.A.9) Pte. 466318, Bernard Walter Northcott Cooke, 10th Bn. Canadian Infantry (Alberta Regt.), C.E.F.: *s*. of Charles Cooke, of 54, Palace Road, Crouch End, London, N.8: *b*. Brighton, co. Sussex, 2 October 1889: removed to Canada, 1913: Occupation – Stenographer, City Hall, Medicine Hat: enlisted Medicine Hat, 6 July 1915: arrived England, May 1916; promoted Corpl.: reverted to Pte. during training and joined a draft to France: previously wounded, 14 June 1915 at Ypres; one year later he was shot through the head at Mount Sorrel, and died en-route to the C.C.S., Poperinghe, 15 June 1916: Age 26. During his youth Pte. Cooke was a chorister, Westminster Abbey.

Steadfast & Undismayed He Gave His All

(VIII.A.13A) Pte. 23494, George Allen Bunnell, 16th (Canadian Scottish) Bn. Canadian Infantry, (Manitoba Regt.), C.E.F.: *s*. of Albert E. Bunnell, of 'Beechwood Farm,' Sussex, New Brunswick, and Mary J. Bunnell his spouse: and brother to L/Corpl. 23481, A.L. Bunnell, 14th Canadian Infantry, killed in action, 22 April 1915, at St. Julien: *b*. Sussex, 1 July 1892: Religion – Presbyterian: Occupation – Bank Clerk: a serving member (2 years) 8th Hussars (Sussex Militia); enlisted Valcartier, 23 September 1914. Died of wounds (GSW abdominal, both thighs) No. 17 C.C.S. 14 June 1916; Poperinghe: Age 24.

There Is No Death, What Seems So Is Transition

His brother Alfred has no known grave; he is commemorated on the Ypres (Menin Gate) Memorial (Panel 24).

(VIII.A.17A) Pte. A/26290, Aubrey Thomas James, 10th Bn. Canadian Infantry (Alberta Regt.), C.E.F.: *s*. of Walter Thomas James, of 112, Gladstone Street, Bedford, England, by his wife Sarah Ann: and brother to Pte. 38566, A.L. James, Norfolk Regt., killed in action, 29 September 1918: *b*. Bedford, 26 May 1893: Religion – Church of England: Occupation – Bank Clerk: 5'8½" tall, blue eyes, dark hair: enlisted Moosejaw, Saskatchewan, 8 January 1915: served with the Expeditionary Force in France and Flanders, and died 15 June 1916, of wounds (G.S.W. head): Age 23. *unm*. Remembered on the St. Martin's Church (Bedford) War Memorial.

His brother Arthur is buried in Gouzeaucourt New British Cemetery (X.A.19).

(VIII.A.36A) Pte. 622394, Clement Cowell, 27th (City of Winnipeg) Bn. Canadian Infantry (Manitoba Regt.), C.E.F: *s*. of Walter Cowell, of Castle Camps, co. Cambridge, England: and brother to Pte. 622395, W.G. Cowell, Canadian Infantry, killed in action, 11 June 1916, at Zillebeke: *b*. Castle Camps, 8 August 1895: Religion – Church of England: Occupation – Labourer: 5'7" tall, blue eyes, brown hair: previously served 1 year, King's Own Scottish Borderers: enlisted Portage la Prairie, apptd. 44th (Overseas) Battn., 24 April 1915: departed Quebec, S.S. 'Carpathia,' 17 May (transf'd. 27th Battn.); trained Dibgate, Shorncliffe, and Otterpool, England from the 28th of that month: served with the Expeditionary Force in France and Flanders from 19 September 1915, and died of wounds (S.W. [shrapnel] head, both legs), 18 June 1916: Age 20. *unm*.

His brother Walter has no known grave, he is commemorated on the Ypres (Menin Gate) Memorial (Panel 26).

(VIII.B.6) Pte. 12779, William Dick, 1st Bn. Scots Guards: late of Haddington: b. Broxburn: enlisted Edinburgh: served with the Expeditionary Force in France and Flanders, and died of wounds (S.W. head, Lt. leg, Rt. leg, Rt. arm) received in action at Ypres on the evening of 16 June 1916. Amputation of left leg (below knee) performed by Lieut. Crawford, 17 June; cause of death – shock consequent to amputation, and infection (gangrene) of right leg, 20 June 1916. Buried the following day. In a letter to Pte. Dick's widow the Chaplain wrote, "21 June 1916. Dear Madam, your husband, of the 1st Scots Guards, who has been here for some days in hospital received from me all the Sacraments, and was well prepared and resigned to die. He had the best of care and medical attention, and for some time we had good hopes of him recovering. I presided at his funeral this afternoon, and blessed his grave in the Military Cemetery, Remy Siding. Plot 8-B6. Praying God comfort you. I remain your humble servant, Frank L. French, Chaplain."

(VIII.B.6A) Corpl.41635, David Murray, 2nd Bde. Canadian Field Artillery, C.E.F.: *s*. of William Murray, of Forglen Villa, Queen Street, Huntly, co. Aberdeen, by his wife Margaret: *b*. Turriff, co. Aberdeen, 30 May 1883: Religion – Presbyterian: Occupation – Pharmacist: 5'8½" tall, blue eyes, dark hair: served No.3 Bde., Canadian Field Artillery, August -September 1914; thereafter 2nd Bde.; enlisted C.E.F., In the Field (Ouderdom), 6 May 1916: died of wounds (G.S.W. head) 20 June 1916: Age 33. *unm*.

Until The Day Break And The Shadows Flee Away

(VIII.B.11A) Pte. 154946, Hugh Stowell Hellings, 1st Canadian Pioneers, C.E.F.: s. of the late Robert Camal Hellings, by his wife Eliza, née Fisher (35, Clarence Square, Cheltenham, co. Gloucester): *educ*. Cheltenham Grammar School: enlisted Edmonton, Alberta, 14 August 1915. Died of shrapnel wounds (Rt. buttock), 23 June 1916, received in action at Mount Sorrel, Ypres. Pte. Hellings is commemorated on the Borough War Memorial, The Promenade, Cheltenham; Cheltenham Grammar School Memorial, and on the grave of his parents in Cheltenham Cemetery: Age 30.

He Loved Much

(VIII.B.13A) Pte. 81005, Henry James Alexander, 2nd Bn. Canadian Infantry (Eastern Ontario Regt.), C.E.F.: c/o Mrs W. McClelland (Carnegie, Manitoba): *b*. Middlesbrough, England, 20 June 1878: Religion – Church of England: Occupation – Farmer: previously served 12 yrs, 16th Lancers: joined C.E.F., Winnipeg, 29 December 1914. Died of wounds, 23 June 1916; No.10 Canadian Casualty Clearing Station, Poperinghe: Age 38.

(VIII.B.15) Pte. 13363, Herbert Arthur Figgis, 5th Bn. Canadian Infantry (Saskatchewan Regt.), C.E.F.: *s*. of Thomas Figgis, of Summerland, British Columbia, by his wife Zillah: *b*. Putney, London, 16 July 1886: Occupation – Miner: serving member of the Militia, enlisted Valcartier, 21 September 1914: served with the Expeditionary Force in France and died, 15 June 1916, of wounds received (nr. Railway Dugouts) in the early hours of the same day while carrying in wounded from Mount Sorrel: Age 29. *unm*.

Till The Roll Is Called In Heaven Lad Sleep On And Take Thy Rest

(VIII.B.17A) Pte. 57834, James Gaspe, 20th Bn. Canadian Infantry (Central Ontario Regt.), C.E.F.: *s*. of John Baptiste Gaspe, Chief of the Canadian Iroquois Indians, of Oka, County of Two Mountains, Quebec, by his wife Felecile Bonspille: *b*. Oka, Quebec, 11 December 1885: Religion – Wesleyan: Occupation – Fireman: enlisted Toronto, 12 November 1914. His Medical Examination notes record him as being 5'9¾" tall, dark complexioned, brown eyed, black haired, with a large birthmark (3½" x 4½") on his lower abdomen: served with the Expeditionary Force in France and Flanders from 1915, and died of wounds (G.S.W. Rt. thigh, compound fractures Rt. Arm, Rt. hand), Poperinghe, 25 June 1916; received in action at The Bluff. Buried in the Soldier's Cemetery, Lyssenthoek: Age 30. *unm*. (*IWGC record age 32*)

He Died But Not In Vain

(VIII.B.21A) Pte. 15492, Wilfrid Harrison, 2nd Bn. Coldstream Guards: *s.* of William Harrison, of 13, Ewart St., Bracebridge, nr. Lincoln, by his wife Elizabeth, *dau.* of the late Charles Wright, of Waddington, nr. Lincoln: *yr.* brother to Pte. 201868, W. Harrison, 2nd/5th West Yorkshire Regt., killed in action, 3 May 1917: *b.* Bracebridge, nr. Lincoln, 2 September 1893: *educ.* Bracebridge Board School: employee Foster's Foundry, Lincoln: enlisted Coldstream Guards, 23 February 1915: served with the Expeditionary Force in France and Flanders from 2 November following, and died at No. 17 Casualty Clearing Station, 28 June 1916, from wounds (G.S.W. head) received in action at Ypres two days previously. Buried in Lyssenthoek Military Cemetery. His Sergt. wrote, "He was a good, steady, upright, clean and good-living man, loved by all his comrades, always willing, and ever ready to do his best whenever called upon…and sadly missed by all of us." He was a keen footballer, and took great interest in all kinds of sport: Age 23. *unm.*

He Is Not Here He Is Risen

His brother William has no known grave; he is commemorated on the Arras (Faubourg d'Amiens) Memorial (Bay 4).

(VIII.B.22) Pte. 11682, George Leonard, 2nd Bn. Scots Guards: *s.* of George Leonard, of 42, Plover Street, Preston, co. Lancaster, by his late wife Hannah: and yr. brother to Pte. 4606, A. Leonard, Loyal North Lancashire Regt., died 30 December 1916, of wounds: *b.* Preston: enlisted there: served in France from 4 May 1915, and died of wounds (G.S.W. thigh), 28 June 1916, received in action at Ypres: Age 20.

On Whose Soul Sweet Jesus Have Mercy

His brother Arthur is buried nearby (X.C.44).

(VIII.B.27) Pte. 59252, Albert Le Mesurier De Lisle: 21st Bn. Canadian Infantry (Eastern Ontario Regt.), C.E.F.: *s.* of Charles A. De Lisle, of Quyon, Quebec, Canada, by his wife Helena Augusta: and yr. brother to Pte. 703999, A.W. DeLisle, died 10 September 1916, of wounds: *b.* 30 March 1894: Occupation – Banker: enlisted Kingston, Ontario, 13 November 1915. Died of wounds (fractured skull), 29 June 1916: Age 22.

His brother Alfred lies nearby (IX.D.19A).

(VIII.B.27A) Pte. A/15802, John Leo Lightizer, 13th Bn. Canadian Infantry (Quebec Regt.), C.E.F.: *s.* of Harry Lightizer, of Middleton, Annapolis County, Nova Scotia, by his wife Hannah: *b.* Middleton, 3 March 1900: Religion – Roman Catholic. Volunteering and enlisting in his home town of Middleton, 3 April 1915, John Lightizer gave his date of birth as 3 March 1897, and occupation Farmer. Dark complexioned, brown eyed, dark brown haired, at 5'8" in height he could easily have passed as being 18, but his chest measurement of 34" coupled with the fact that it was blatantly obvious he was barely literate might, under circumstances other than those which prevailed at the time, have given rise to doubt. At the time of his enlistment the lad had only just turned 15. Fourteen months later, on 28 June 1916, Pte. Lightizer died in No.3 Canadian Casualty Clearing Station, Remy Siding, of shrapnel wounds to the chest and abdomen; he was three months past his sixteenth birthday: Age 16. Remembered on Middleton War Memorial.

(VIII.B.29) Pte. 437688, Neil McPhail, 14th Bn. Canadian Infantry (Quebec Regt.), C.E.F.: *b*. Brandon, Manitoba, 2 February 1885: Occupation – Machinist: volunteered and enlisted Edmonton, 25 August 1915. Died of wounds (S.W. Lt. leg, gangrene), 26 June 1916: Age 31. A Freemason, Pte. McPhail was a member of Shuniah Lodge No.287, Thunder Bay.

(VIII.B.29A) Pte. 12880, Cyril William Comper, 3rd Bn. Coldstream Guards: *s*. of James Comper, of 40, Scarle Road, Wembley, co. Middlesex, by his wife Hettie Annie: *b*. Dalston: enlisted Whitehall: served with the Expeditionary Force in France and Flanders from 6 April 1915, and died of wounds (multiple machine-gun; abdominal, arm, leg), 30 June 1916: Age 20. *unm.*

Never Forgotten

(VIII.B.31) Pte. 415556, Stanley Herbert Clark, 13th Bn. Canadian Infantry (Quebec Regt.), C.E.F.: *s*. of Spurgeon A. Clark, of Mosher Corner, Nova Scotia: *b*. Boston, Massachusetts, June 1894: Occupation – Farmer: 5'7¼" tall, dark complexion, brown eyes, brown hair: Religion – Baptist: enlisted Middleton, Nova Scotia, 3 April 1915. Died of wounds (G.S.W. head), 1 July 1916: Age 20. *unm*. Remembered on Middleton Memorial Hospital Roll of Honour (Panel 1, Col.I), Nova Scotia.

(VIII.B.31A) Pte. 482063, Granvill Vincent Cleveland, 26th Bn. Canadian Infantry (New Brunswick Regt.), C.E.F.: *s*. of Joseph James Cleveland, of North West Cove, Lunenburg Co., Nova Scotia, by his wife Henrietta: *b*. North West Cove, 5 May 1896: Occupation – Fisherman: volunteered and enlisted Halifax, Nova Scotia, 26 August 1915; posted 26th Battn.: served with the Expeditionary Force, and died of bullet wounds (cranial), 1 July 1916: Age 22.

If The Lord Will We Shall Live

On 1st July 1916 7th D.C.L.I. were holding front-line trenches in the Potijze Wood sector where 'although there were no attacks on or by the enemy the Ypres salient lived up to its evil reputation, the guns of both sides were seldom silent and the trenches violently shelled, although with astonishingly small losses.' By close of day in the south the opening of the Battle of the Somme would cost the British Army some 60,000 casualties, in the north the salient's evil reputation cost the battalion 1 O.R. killed, 1 died of wounds.

(VIII.B.32A) Pte. 15489, George Thomas Gilbert, 7th (Service) Bn. The Duke of Cornwall's Light Infantry: *b*. Mile End, London: enlisted Stratford, co. Essex: served in France and Flanders from 23 April 1915. Died of abdominal wounds (G.S.) 1 July 1916. See also Pte. R.H. Simpson, Vlamertinghe Military Cemetery (IV.A.16).

(VIII.B.34) Pte. 16796, Ralph Cavanagh, 7th (Service) Bn. The Prince Albert's (Somerset Light Infantry): *s*. of Thomas (& Mrs) Cavanagh, of South Hetton, Sunderland: enlisted Easington, Co. Durham: served with the Expeditionary Force in France and Flanders from July 1915, and died of wounds (G.S.W. buttocks, scrotum), 1 July 1916: Age 21.

(VIII.B.34A) Pte. 6414, Walter Marnell, 1st Bn. Irish Guards: *s*. of John Marnell, of Dunamaggan, Callan, co. Kilkenny, by his wife Kate: volunteered and enlisted Kilkenny, September 1914, after the outbreak of war: proceeded to France with a draft of reinforcements May 1915, and died 1 July 1916, of wounds received in the Lancashire Farm – Canal Bank sector (28 June): Age 22.

Give Him O Lord Eternal Rest

(VIII.B.35A) Pte. 26231, Wilfred Smith Turton, 7th (Service) Bn. The King's Own (Yorkshire Light Infantry): *s*. of Walter Booth Turton, by his wife Georgina Grace: and brother to Pte. 702, S.B. Turton, Guards Machine Gun Regt., died 21 August 1918, of wounds. *b*. Ackworth, Pontefract, co. York, *c*.1882: enlisted Ackworth. Died of wounds (S.W. cranial, severe debridement Rt. arm), 1 July 1916: Age 34. He was married to Marion Turton (The Mount, Pontefract), to whom all correspondence should be addressed.

His brother Sydney is buried in St. Hilaire Cemetery Extension (M.3).

(VIII.B.36) Corpl. 112191, Harold Bales, 3rd Special Bde. Royal Engineers *s*. of Thomas Bales, of Toronto, Canada, by his wife Rebecca: *b*. Deal, co. Kent. Died of wounds (gas), 1 July 1916: Age 36.

Thy Kingdom Come O Lord Thy Rule O Christ Begin

(VIII.B.36A) Pte. 11913, William Greig Brown, 'C' Coy., 1st Bn. Scots Guards: *s*. of Hugh Brown, of Arniston, Gorebridge, co. Midlothian, by his wife Helen: served in France and Flanders from 23 April 1915; died of abdominal bullet wounds, 1 July 1916: Age 26.

(VIII.B.37) Pte. 79237, Pius Jos. Campbell, 31st Bn. Canadian Infantry (Alberta Regt.), C.E.F.: *s.* of C. Campbell, of Elmira, Prince Edward Island: *b.* King's Co., P.E.I., 10 April 1891: Occupation – Inspector; Canadian Pacific Railway Co.: member 103rd Calgary Rifles (Militia), previously served with St. John Artillery; enlisted Calgary, 17 November 1914: served with the Expeditionary Force. Died of wounds, 2 July 1916, received (22 June) while at duty on a work party to the front-line at St. Eloi: Age 25. *unm.*

(VIII.B.38) Pte. 8/3952, William John Mitchell, 2nd Bn. Otago Regt., N.Z.E.F.: *s.* of William (& Ellen Josephine) Mitchell, of Cromwell, Otago, New Zealand: *b.* Cromwell, 22 October 1895: Religion – Roman Catholic: Occupation – Compositor: 5'6" tall, dark complexion, brown eyes, dark hair: enlisted Trentham, 19 November 1915: departed Wellington, 4 March 1916; 10th Rfts., 'D' Coy: served with the Expeditionary Force, and was wounded (G.S.W. multiple, head, arms) Houplines, nr. Armentieres, 30 June; evacuated to No.8 C.C.S., Bailleul; transf'd No.14 Ambulance Train, died en-route to (dead on arrival) No. 3 Canadian C.C.S., 14.35 hrs, 1 July 1916: Age 20. The sole New Zealand burial in the cemetery plots relating to 1916.

(VIII.B.44) Pte. 2810, John Casey, 2nd Bn. Irish Guards: *s.* of James Casey: c/o R.H.Q. Irish Guards: *b.* Templemore, Co. Tipperary: enlisted Dublin: served in France from August 1914, and died of wounds (G.S.W. abdominal, Rt. arm), 3 July 1916, received during a large scale raid made by the battalion the previous day: Age 37. See Lieut. F.M. Pym, Ypres (Menin Gate) Memorial (Panel 11).

R.I.P.

(VIII.C.5A) Pte. 178060, Harold James Fox, 1st Bn. Canadian Infantry (Western Ontario Regt.), C.E.F.: *yst. s.* of the late John Fox, of Montreal, by his wife Mary Ann Burns: and brother to Irene Fox (420, Deszery Street, Montreal): *b.* Montreal, Quebec: Occupation – Clerk: enlisted Montreal, 9 November 1915; posted 87th (Grenadier Guards of Canada) Battn., subsequently transf'd. 1st Battn. in France, and died of wounds (G.S.W., Head & Back), 7 July 1916, No.3, Casualty Clearing Station, Poperinghe: Age 16.

His Warfare Over His Battle Fought
The Victory Won Though Dearly Bought

(VIII.C.8) Sergt. 422368, Thomas John Barr, 8th Bn. Canadian Infantry (Manitoba Regt.), C.E.F.: 2nd *s.* of John Barr, of The Maze, Lisburn, co. Down, by his wife Hannah Jane Carlisle: *b.* The Maze, 22 August 1882: joined North Ireland Imperial Yeomanry (later North Ireland Horse), 1900, aged

18 years: served against the Boers in the South African Campaign (King's Medal): thereafter served 3 years, South African Constabulary, and took part in operations in Natal against the Zulus, 1906: left South Africa for Canada and settled at Winnipeg, where he found employ as a Motorman, and joined 34th Fort Garry Horse (Militia): volunteered and enlisted Winnipeg, 18 March 1915; posted 8th Battn.: served with the Canadian Expeditionary Force in France: returned Belfast on leave April 1916. Wounded by shrapnel 5 July 1916, and died in the C.C.S., Poperinghe, 9 July 1916: Age 33. He was married to T.J. Barr (12½, Vinbourg Apartments, Agnes Street, Winnipeg).

(VIII.C.9) Pte. 177309, Joseph Armand Senecal, 1st Bn. Canadian Infantry, C.E.F.: *s.* of Joseph J. Eusebe Senecal, by his wife Virginie Ste. Marie (173, St. John's Street, Quebec); late of 317, Beaudry Street, Montreal: *b.* St. John Street, 11 January 1893: Religion – Roman Catholic: Occupation – Electrician: serving member 8th Royal Rifle Regt. (Militia); joined 87th (Overseas) Bn., C.E.F., Quebec, 26 October 1915; apptd. 1st Battn. 3 November: served with the Expeditionary Force in France and Flanders, and was wounded (shell fragment, abdominal) 'during the afternoon of July 8th., 1916. He was in a bombing post in the front line at the time, and was given First Aid by a stretcher bearer. He walked out to the Dressing Station, apparently suffering no pain, and evacuated to No.17 Canadian Casualty Clearing Station the following morning. Upon arrival an operation was performed immediately. He died 1.45 p.m. the same day (9 July 1916); 2½ hours after the operation.': Age 22. Buried Soldier's Cemetery, Lyssenthoek.

(VIII.C.14A) Rfn. S/14370, Herbert George Stillman, 12th (Service) Bn. The Prince Consort's Own (The Rifle Brigade): *s.* of William Stillman, of 7A, Robinson Road, Tooting, London, by his wife Jane: and yr. brother to Corpl. 91, W.E. Stillman, 5th Australian Machine Gun Corps, who fell 15 April 1917, aged 27 years: *b.* Hendon, co. Middlesex: enlisted London. Died 12 July 1916, of wounds received in action at Ypres: Age 24. *unm.*

His brother William has no known grave; he is commemorated on the Villers-Bretonneux Memorial.

(VIII.C.15) Spr. 500169, Cecil Beasley, 1st Army Troops Coy., Canadian Engineers, C.E.F.: *s.* of Mrs E. Beasley (St. John's College, North Vancouver, British Columbia): *b.* Leicester, England, 11 November 1895: Religion – Congregationalist: Occupation – Electrical Engineer: 5'10" tall, brown eyes, dark hair: serving member (18 months) 6th Field Coy., Canadian Engineers (Militia); volunteered for Overseas Service and enlisted North Vancouver, 20 July 1915: served with the Expeditionary Force in France and Flanders, and died of bullet wounds (back), 12 July 1916, received the same day while at duty at Quinton Siding. Buried the following day in the Military Cemetery, Poperinghe – Boeschepe road: Age 20. *unm.* (*IWGC record age 21*)

Missed By All Who Knew Him

(VIII.C.25A) Pte. 406558, William Jennings, Royal Canadian Regt., C.E.F.: *s.* of Thomas Jennings, of Tansley Hill Farm, Oakham Road, Dudley, co. Worcester: *b.* Broom, nr. Stourbridge, 11 June 1893: Religion – Church of England: Occupation – Iron Moulder: 5'6½" tall, blue eyes, light brown hair: serving member 44th Regt., Welland, Ontario (Militia); joined R.C.R. (No. A6558), Hamilton, Ontario, 15 April 1915: served in France and Flanders from 31 October following, and died of wounds, 16 July 1916, received in action; Roslyn Street, Menin Road on the 12th.: Age 23. *unm.* Chaplain A.B. Brooker wrote, "20 July 1916…I am very sorry, indeed, to tell you that your son, Pte. W. T. Jennings died in this station at 3.25 a.m. on July 16th. He was admitted four days before with serious shell wounds in the head, right arm and thigh. At first he was unconscious but the next day recovered a little, but we kept him very quiet. I was with him very often and prayed with him and did all I could to help and comfort him. I told him I would write to you. He sent you his dearest love. That was his only message but he was full of tender thoughts for you both. He was so good and patient and brave, and though he suffered very little pain yet the trial of lying there all those hours must have been great, but he bore it nobly. I administered Holy Communion to him the day before he died. It meant a great deal to him and he felt you very near to him in spirit and we did not forget you in our prayers together. The doctors and nurses spared no pains in their efforts for him and surrounded him with every care and comfort but they could not save his life. The evening before the end he once more became unconscious and later passed quietly away. We laid him to rest with the church ceremony in the Military Cemetery on the Poperinghe – Boeschepe Rd. at Lyssenthoek. His grave will be marked with his name and is numbered Plot VIII, Line C, Grave 25. Any personal effects of his will be sent to you later by the authorities. Please accept my deepest sympathy and I hope that you will feel that he was not alone but with friends that did their best to help him…"

(VIII.D.1) Pte. 445321, Edmond Joseph Simmons, 42nd Bn. Canadian Infantry (Quebec Regt.), C.E.F.: *s.* of Edward Simmons, of Bathurst, New Brunswick, by his wife Elizabeth: *b.* Bathurst, 24 May 1898 (attested 24 May 1896): Religion – Roman Catholic: Occupation – Labourer: 5'6" tall, grey eyes, dark brown hair: enlisted Sussex, 4 August 1915. Died of wounds (gas), 9 August 1916: Age 18.

(VIII.D.1A) Pte. 16644, John Downey, 1st Bn. (27th Foot) The Royal Inniskilling Fusiliers: *s.* of Patrick Downey, of 14, Stafford Street, Chester Road, Hulme, Manchester, by his wife Fanny: *b.* Manchester: served in the South African War, and with the Expeditionary Force in France and Flanders, and died of wounds (gas), 9 August 1916, received in action at Potijze: Age 39.

(VIII.D.2) L/Corpl. 18381, Harold Frank Stickland, 2nd Bn. (67th Foot) The Hampshire Regt.: *s*. of Jesse Stickland, of Sparr Farm, Wisborough Green, Billingshurst, co. Sussex, by his wife Amy: *b*. Ringwood, co. Hants. Died of wounds (gas), 9 August 1916: Age 20.

Rest In Peace

(VIII.D.2A) Sergt. 9029, Alexander Allen, 1st Bn. (13th Foot) The Prince Albert's (Somerset Light Infantry): *s*. of the late Mr (& Mrs) Allen, of Bristol. Killed in action, 9 August 1916: Age 23.

One Of The Dearest, One Of The Best
Ever To Be Remembered By His Brother Bert

(VIII.D.3) Pte. 14094, James Joseph McCoy, 'C' Coy., 1st Bn. (27th Foot) The Royal Inniskilling Fusiliers: *s*. of John McCoy, of Rosslea, Co. Fermanagh, by his wife Charlotte: enlisted Enniskillen. Died of wounds (gas), 9 August 1916: Age 21. (*IWGC record 11/14094*)

(VIII.D.3A) Pte. 14584, Frederick Douglas Burgess, 2nd Bn. (67th Foot) The Hampshire Regt.: *s*. of Mary A. Burgess (6, Dorien Road, Raynes Park, London): *b*. Southfields, co. Surrey: enlisted Merton: served in France from 25 April 1915, and died of wounds, 9 August 1916: Age 22.

Rest In Peace

(VIII.D.4) Corpl. 18524, John Clark, 1st Bn. (27th Foot) The Royal Inniskilling Fusiliers: late of Donaghadee: *b*. Cromer, co. Norfolk: enlisted Newtownards, Co. Down. Died of wounds, 9 August 1916, received in action at Potijze, Ypres.

(VIII.D.4.A) Sergt. 6844, Alexander McLaughlin, 1st Bn. (27th Foot) The Royal Inniskilling Fusiliers: *b*. Londonderry: enlisted there: served with the Expeditionary Force in France and Flanders with 2nd Bn. from 23 August 1914; promoted Sergt. 24 April 1915; subsequently transf'd. 1st Bn., and died of wounds (gas asphyxiation), 9 August 1916.

(VIII.D.5) Pte. 22723, Frederick Leonard Watts, 1st Bn. (37th Foot) The Hampshire Regt.: *b*. Boscombe, co. Hants. Died of wounds (gas), 9 August 1916.

(VIII.D.5A) Rfn. 3399, Charles Biggs, 1st Bn. The Prince Consort's Own (The Rifle Brigade): *b*. Sheerness, co. Kent: served with the Expeditionary Force in France and Flanders from 20 December 1914, and died of wounds, 9 August 1916.

(VIII.D.6) Pte. 22766, Percy William Read, 1st Bn. (37th Foot) The Hampshire Regt: *husb.* to Lucy Read (11, Royal Exchange, Newport, Isle of Wight): *b.* Newport, 1887. Died of wounds (gas), 9 August 1916: Age 29.

Thy Will Be Done

(VIII.D.6A) Pte. 23144, Arthur Stephen Atrill, 1st Bn. (37th Foot) The Hampshire Regt.: *s.* of Henry James Atrill, of 2, Oakfield Hill, Ryde, Isle of Wight, by his wife Mary Jane: *b.* Ryde: enlisted Newport. Died of wounds (gas), 9 August 1916, No.3 Canadian Casualty Clearing station, Poperinghe: Age 32.

God Shall Wipe Away All Tears From Their Eyes
And There Shall Be No More Death
Rev. XXI. 4.

(VIII.D.7) Pte. 12048, Robert Baker, 'B' Coy., 1st Bn. (13th Foot) The Prince Albert's (Somerset Light Infantry): *s.* of William Baker, of Minehead, co. Somerset, by his wife Jane: served in France from 24 March 1915, and died of wounds (gas), 9 August 1916: Age 44.

Gone But Not Forgotten

(VIII.D.7A) L/Corpl. 8954, Sidney Hayes, 2nd Bn. (67th Foot) The Hampshire Regt.: nephew to Ellen Budden (Trent Villa, Pine Road, Winton, Bournemouth): *b.* Wallace Down, co. Dorset: enlisted Winchester: served with the Expeditionary Force in France from March 1916, and died of wounds (gas), 9 August 1916.

Peace Perfect Peace

'No one cares less than I,
Nobody knows but God,
Whether I am destined to lie
Under a foreign clod,'
Were the words I made to the bugle call in the morning.

But laughing, storming, scorning,
Only the bugles know
What the bugles say in the morning,
And they do not care when they blow
The call that I heard and made words to early this morning.
                                                                Edward Thomas

At the bugle's call for England, he heard, cared and willingly answered.

(VIII.D.8) Sergt. 6101, Arthur Ernest England, 1st Bn. (13th Foot) The Prince Albert's (Somerset Light Infantry): *s.* of Sarah Ann England (Bristol): served with the Expeditionary Force in France and Flanders from 30 August 1914, and died of wounds (gas), 9 August 1916, en-route to the C.C.S. Poperinghe; pronounced dead on arrival: Age 30. He was married to Mrs E.K. Howard, *née* England (35, Gwilliam Street, Windmill Hill, Bedminster, Bristol). (*IWGC record 8101- VIII.H.17*)

Thy Will Be Done

(VIII.D.8A) Pte. 24297, Arthur Coles, 6th (Service) Bn. The Duke of Cornwall's Light Infantry: *s.* of Jessie Coles, of 56, Jewel Street, Barry, co. Glamorgan, by his wife Charlotte Ann: *b.* Penarth, co. Glamorgan: enlisted Barry. Died of wounds (gas), 9 August 1916. The only fatality recorded by his battalion for that day: Age 27.

Parted For A While

(VIII.D.9) Pte. 27899, Francis Patrick Hamill, 1st Bn. (27th Foot) The Royal Inniskilling Fusiliers: formerly no.32271, Highland Light Infantry: *s.* of Francis (& Elizabeth) Hamill, of 6, Ritchie Street, Glasgow: enlisted Glasgow: served with the Expeditionary Force in France, and died of wounds (gas), 9 August 1916: Age 19.

On Whose Soul Sweet Jesus Have Mercy
R.I.P.

(VIII.D.9A) Pte. 23067, John Rooney, 1st Bn. (27th Foot) The Royal Inniskilling Fusiliers: enlisted Omagh: served in the Dardanelles from 14 November 1915, France and Flanders from 18 March 1916, and died of wounds (gas), 9 August 1916.

(VIII.D.10) Pte. 24030, Matthew Carey, 1st Bn. (27th Foot) The Royal Inniskilling Fusiliers: enlisted Carlow. Died of wounds, 9 August 1916; Canadian Clearing Station, Remy. 'In Memoriam':

In far off Belgium the stars are shining.
Shining on a hero's grave,
Where the one we loved is sleeping,
He was a soldier brave.
In the prime of life death claimed him,

In the prime of manhood days,
None knew him but to love him,
None mentioned his name but with praise.
He bade us not a last farewell,
He said good-bye to none,
His spirit flew before we knew
He sleeps beside his comrades,
In a hallowed grave unknown
But memory is the only friend that grief can call its own.

Mother

(VIII.D.10A) Pte. 4/3630, Joseph Murray, 1st Bn. (27th Foot) The Royal Inniskilling Fusiliers: s. of Patrick Murray, of 28, Wallace's Row, Ravenhill Road, Belfast: and brother to Pte. 10722, J. Murray, Royal Inniskilling Fusiliers, died the same day: b. Ballymacarrett, Co. Down: enlisted Belfast: served with the Expeditionary Force in the Dardanelles from 4 May 1915; France and Flanders from 18 March 1916, and died of wounds, 9 August 1916: Age 17.

For The Holy Name Of Jesus,
For Their Country And For God

His brother James is buried in Bedford House Cemetery (IV.C.42/Enc.No.2).

(VIII.D.11) Pte. 3/6872, Michael James Lynch, 1st Bn. (13th Foot) The Prince Albert's (Somerset Light Infantry): of Ballymena, Co. Antrim. Killed in action (gas poisoning), 9 August 1916.

(VIII.D.11A) Pte. 461066, Alfred Freeman, 16th Bn. Canadian Infantry (Manitoba Regt.), C.E.F.: s. of Harry Freeman, of 14, Inkster Avenue, Winnipeg, by his wife Mary Ann: b. Skerton, Lancaster, England, 21 November 1891: Occupation – Silver Cleaner: previously served 4 years, King's Own (Royal Lancaster Regt.): joined C.E.F. Winnipeg, 16 January 1915. Died at No.17 C.C.S., 9 August 1916, of machine-gun wounds to the arm, thigh and abdomen: Age 25. Remembered on Lancaster War Memorial.

(VIII.D.12) Rfn. R/20870, Louis Walter George Bailey, 10th (Service) Bn. The King's Royal Rifle Corps: s. of Eliza Wheeler (99, Rutland Road, Forest Gate, London): b. Forest Gate: enlisted Bethnal Green. Died of wounds, 9 August 1916.

(VIII.D.12A) Pte. 22624, George Victor Gookey, 1st Bn. (37th Foot) The Hampshire Regt.: s. of George Gookey, of Southampton, by his wife Annie. Killed in action, 9 August 1916: Age 24.

(VIII.D.13) Sergt. 16731, William Daniel Nathaniel Cook, 1st Bn. (13th Foot) The Prince Albert's (Somerset Light Infantry): s. of Hobart N. Cook, of

Monte Carlo: enlisted Crown Hill, co. Devon: served in France from 11 January 1915, and died of wounds (inhalation of noxious gas), en-route to No.3 C.C.S., 9 August 1916; Dead on arrival: Age 35.

(VIII.D.13A) Rfn. C/7845, John William Holden, 18th (Service) Bn. (Arts & Crafts) The King's Royal Rifle Corps: *s*. of Samuel Holden, of Huddersfield, co. York, by his wife Florence: late *husb*. to Lizzie Holden (4, Roberts Yard, Church Lane, Moldgreen, Huddersfield). Died of gas poisoning and machine-gun wounds to the hand and thigh, 9 August 1916: Age 31.

Only Those Who Have Loved & Lost
Can Understand War's Bitter Cost

At the end of July 1916 the 1st Rifle Brigade found itself back again in the Zwaanhof Farm sector at Ypres where one year previously it had taken part in the attack on International Trench. On 1st August the battalion went into the line, relieving 1st Somerset Light Infantry. "On the 5th it returned to Canal Bank where, on the 8th, during the next relief of the Somersets, the enemy made a gas attack and put down a heavy bombardment which cut all telephonic communication to the rear, including the artillery line. The reply of the artillery and the steady fire of the Riflemen successfully held off the infantry attack for which, according to the statement of prisoners, a fresh brigade had been brought in by the enemy. The casualties however were severe. 4 Officers killed, 5 wounded, and over 200 Other Rank casualties, mostly killed. The bulk of the casualties were experienced in A Company which was not more than forty yards from the German line. The gas cloud was not observed until it had already passed over them."

(VIII.D.14) Rfn. S/6793, William Arthur Davidson, 1st Bn. The Prince Consort's Own (The Rifle Brigade): *s*. of Ellen E. Davidson (West Road, Histon, co. Cambridge): served with the Expeditionary Force in France and Flanders from May 1915, and died of wounds (gas), 10 August 1916.

(VIII.D.14A) Pte. Pte. 18045, Leslie Harold Gilbert, 2nd Bn. (67th Foot) The Hampshire Regt.: *b*. Newbury, co. Berks: enlisted Holborn, London: served with the Expeditionary Force in France from 20 March 1916, and died of wounds (gas), 10 August following.

(VIII.D.15) Pte. 21244, Ernest John Trill, 2nd Bn. (67th Foot) The Hampshire Regt.: formerly no. G/6995, Royal Sussex Regt.: *s*. of Jane Trill (9, Picton Street, Brighton, co. Sussex): served with the Expeditionary Force in France from 12 December 1915; transf'd. Hampshire Regt. 20 March 1916, and died of wounds, 9 August 1916: Age 22.

Not Dead But Gone Before

(VIII.D.15.A) Pte. 18392, William John Bass, 2nd Bn. (67th Foot) The Hampshire Regt. attd. Trench Mortar Bty.: late of Peckham, London, S.E.: enlisted Lambeth. Died of wounds (gas), 10 August 1916.

(VIII.D.16) Pte. 9588, Hugh McFadden, 1st Bn. (27th Foot) The Royal Inniskilling Fusiliers: *s.* of Jane McFadden (45, Long Tower Street, Londonderry): *b.* Templemore, Londonderry: served in the Dardanelles from 17 March 1915; France and Flanders from 18 March 1916, and died of wounds (gas), 9 August 1916: Age 32.

Queen Of The Most Holy Rosary Pray For Him
Rest In Peace

(VIII.D.16A) Sergt. 53, Harry Hetherington, M.M., 1/1st (West Riding Field Coy.) Royal Engineers (T.F.): enlisted Sheffield, co. York: served with the Expeditionary Force in France from 20 March 1915, and died of wounds, 9 August 1916.

(VIII.D.17) Private 15243 John White, 1st Bn Royal Inniskilling Fusiliers: *s.* of George White, of Letterkenny, Co. Donegal, by his wife Mary Jane: enlisted Finner Camp: served in the Dardanelles from 9 December 1915, France and Flanders from 18 March 1916, and died of wounds, 9 August 1916: Age 23.

(VIII.D.17A) Pte. 23177, Henry William Phillips, 1st Bn. (37th Foot) The Hampshire Regt.: *s.* of William Henry Phillips, by his wife Sarah Jane: *b.* Porstmouth, co. Hants. Died No.3 Canadian Casualty Clearing Station, 10 August 1916; gunshot wounds to the chest: Age 35.

We Mourn For You Dear Brother With Hearts Sincere With Loving Thoughts

(VIII.D.18) Pte. 3851, Oscar Bramble Kenyon Symonds, 1st Bn. (37th Foot) The Hampshire Regt.: *s.* of Frederick William Symonds, of 8, Osborne Road, Southampton, by his wife Fanny: served in France from 26 May 1915, and died of wounds (gas), 10 August 1916: Age 21.

(VIII.D.18A) Pte 19198, David Noble Mumford, 9th (Service) Bn. The Devonshire Regt.: *s.* of Sarah Ann Mumford (16, Pier Street, West Hoe, Plymouth, co. Devon): enlisted Plymouth: served in France from 16 December 1915, and died of wounds (gas), 9 August 1916: Age 27.

(VIII.D.19) Corpl. 9249, William Ernest Wiltshire, 1st Bn. (13th Foot) The Prince Albert's (Somerset Light Infantry): *s.* of William John Wiltshire, of 47, Lower Bristol Road, Bath, by his wife Amy Lucretia: enlisted Bath: served with the Expeditionary Force in France and Flanders from 21 August 1914, and was killed in action, 9 August 1916: Age 23.

In Memory Of Our Dear Son O Lord To Thee Myself I Give

(VIII.D.19A) Pte. 19863, Fred William Dampier, 1st Bn. (13th Foot) The Prince Albert's (Somerset Light Infantry): *s.* of John Dampier, of 'Athelney,' Boro' Bridge, Bridgwater, co. Somerset, by his wife Elizabeth Jane: *b.* Boro' Bridge: enlisted Taunton. Killed in action, 9 August 1916; dying of poisonous gas inhalation en-route from the Canal Bank, Ypres to No.3 Canadian C.C.S., Poperinghe: Age 32.

The Lord Giveth
The Lord Taketh Away

(VIII.D.20) Pte. 21112, Victor Harold James Coles, 2nd Bn. (67th Foot) The Hampshire Regt.: formerly no.G/7520, Royal Sussex Regt.: *s.* of Martha Maria Annie Coles (22, New Road, Shoreham-by-Sea, co. Sussex): served with the Expeditionary Force in France from 12 December 1915; transf'd. Hampshire Regt. March 1916, and died of wounds (gas), 9 August 1916: Age 18.

(VIII.D.20A) L/Corpl. 8089, George Warner, 2nd Bn. (67th Foot) The Hampshire Regt.: late of Blackmore, co. Hants: *b.* Ipswich, co. Suffolk: enlisted Winchester: a pre-war Regular, on the outbreak of war was at Mhow, India with his battalion: returned to England, 22 December 1914: served with the Expeditionary Force at Gallipoli (from 25 April 1915), Egypt, and in France from 20 March 1916, and died of wounds, 9 August 1916; received in action at Ypres.

(VIII.D.21) Pte. 3/4273, Thomas Brookes, 2nd Bn. (67th Foot) The Hampshire Regt.: late of Chichester, co. Sussex: enlisted Portsmouth: a pre-war member of the Reserve; joined his battalion on its return from India, December 1914; served with the Expeditionary Force at Gallipoli (from April 1915), Egypt, France (from 20 March 1916), and died of wounds, 9 August 1916, at Poperinghe.

(VIII.D.21A) Pte. 21285, James Crozier, 1st Bn. (27th Foot) The Royal Inniskilling Fusiliers: *s.* of J. (& Mrs) Crozier, of Bridge Street, Irvinestown, Co. Fermanagh: enlisted Randalstown, Co. Antrim: served in France from 6 October 1915, and died of wounds (gas), 10 August 1916: Age 29.

Asleep In Jesus Till The Dawn Breaks

(VIII.D.22) Pte 12201, Frederick Ernest Small, 1st Bn. (13th Foot) The Prince Albert's (Somerset Light Infantry): *s.* of Albert Small, of Worle, Weston-super-Mare, co. Somerset: *b.* Worle: enlisted Taunton: served in France from 7 April 1915, and died of wounds (gas), 9 August 1916 received in action – Canal

Bank, Ypres – when, during a relief by 1st Rifle Brigade the enemy released a heavy combined gas (chlorine, phosgene, prussic acid) discharge and artillery bombardment in preparation for an infantry assault which, due to a concentrated fire machine-gun and artillery fire, did not materialise: Age 24.

(VIII.D.22A) Pte. 15212, Herbert Cull, 2nd Bn. (67th Foot) The Hampshire Regt.: enlisted Southampton: served at Gallipoli from 25 April 1915, France from 20 March 1916, and died of wounds, 10 August 1916: Age 32. All correspondence should be addressed c/o his son, Joseph Cull, of Romsey, co. Hants.

(VIII.D.23) Pte 18735, William Roberts, 1st Bn. (30th Foot) The East Lancashire Regt.: *s.* of David Roberts, of 32, Kirkham Lane, Blackburn, co. Lancaster, by his wife Sarah: enlisted Darwen: served in France from 27 May 1915, and died of wounds (gas), 9 August 1916: Age 26.

Sweet Rest At Last

(VIII.D.23A) Pte. 18908, Frederick Spray, 1st Bn. (37th Foot) The Hampshire Regt.: late *husb.* to M.L. Girdlestone, *née* Spray (10, Glaucus Street, Devons Road, Bow, London, E.): *b.* Bromley-by-Bow: enlisted Stratford. Died of wounds (gas), 10 August 1916: Age 41.

(VIII.D.24) Pte. 17313, Frederick Collins, 1st Bn. (13th Foot) The Prince Albert's (Somerset Light Infantry): *b.* Newbury, co. Berks: enlisted Lambeth: served in France from 13 July 1915, and died of wounds (gas), 9 August 1916.

(VIII.D.24A) Pte. 17870, George Henry Antrim, 2nd Bn. (67th Foot) The Hampshire Regt.: *s.* of George Antrim, of Ossulton Street, Somers Town, London, by his wife Esther: enlisted St. Pancras, London: served with the Expeditionary Force in the Balkans, from 5 October 1915; France from March 1916, and died of wounds (gas), 9 August 1916, received in action at Potijze: Age 22.

Life's Work Well Done,
Life's Race Well Run,
Life's Crown Well Won.
R.I.P.

(VIII.D.25) Pte. 21067, Herbert Henry Pearce, 1st Bn. (37th Foot) The Hampshire Regt.: *b.* Berkhampstead, co. Hertford: enlisted Portsmouth, co. Hants. Died of wounds (gas), 9 August 1916.

Taking over a section of front-line trenches from the Scots Guards, 27 July 1916, 1st Somerset Light Infantry passed four 'uneventful days' before moving back into support on the Canal Bank, Ypres. "At the close of the second tour, however, just as the Battalion was being relieved by 1st Rifle Brigade (8 August), the enemy (about 10.30 p.m.) made a violent gas attack accompanied by heavy shelling. Dense clouds of the noxious fumes floated over the trenches and, although the Somerset men had only three casualties from the shell-fire, 12 Officers and 161 Other ranks became casualties from gas poisoning. Of these, 6 Officers (2nd Lieuts. R.P. Thompson, V.F. de Ritter, R.C. Roseveare, D.E. Sully, H.J. Griffiths, D.A. le Peton) and 27 Other ranks died from the effects of gas. H Company, closest to the enemy, lost most heavily – 5 Officers, 72 Other ranks. The gas, a mixture of chlorine, phosgene and prussic acid gas, was very insidious and clung to the ground and the men's clothes, so that if a man slept in his equipment he invariably developed gas poisoning and had to be evacuated to hospital."

(VIII.D.25A) Pte. 10739, Robert Richmond, 1st Bn. (13th Foot) The Prince Albert's (Somerset Light Infantry): *s.* of James Richmond, of Brislington, Bristol, by his wife Annie: served with the Expeditionary Force in France and Flanders from 21 April 1915, and was killed in action, 9 August 1916: Age 22.

2nd Lieuts. R.P. Thompson, V.F. De Ritter, H.J. Griffiths and D.A. Le Peton are buried nearby (IX.A.14, 17, 18 & IX.B.2); R.C. Roseveare and D.E. Sully are buried in Essex Farm Cemetery (III.A.6, III.B.8).

(VIII.D.26) Pte. 10668, Thomas Eugene Lush, 2nd Bn. (67th Foot) The Hampshire Regt.: *s.* of Silas Henry Herbert Lush, of 74, Brassey Road, Winton, Bournemouth, by his wife Augusta: *b.* Wareham, co. Dorset: served with the Expeditionary Force in the Balkans (from July 1915); France and Flanders from March 1916, and died of wounds (gas), 10 August 1916: Age 24.

Soldier Of Christ Well Done

(VIII.D.26A) Pte. 17774, Wilfred Robert Messer, 2nd Bn. (67th Foot) The Hampshire Regt.: *s.* of John Messer, of South Wood Farm, Preston Candover, Basingstoke, co. Hants, by his wife Emma: served with the Expeditionary Force in the Balkans; France (from March 1916), and died of wounds, 10 August 1916.

Jesus Said Come Unto Me And I Will Give You Rest

(VIII.D.27) Pte. 4069, Ernest Mark Ware, 2nd Bn. (67th Foot) The Hampshire Regt.: *s.* of Edward Ware, of 2, Widley Street, Cosham, co. Hants, by his wife Mary Elizabeth: served with the Expeditionary Force in the Dardanelles; Egypt, and in France and Flanders, and died of wounds (gas) received at Ypres, 10 August 1916: Age 18.

Sweetly Resting Till Jesus Comes

(VIII.D.27A) Pte. 8837, William Allford, 'C' Coy., 2nd Bn. (67th Foot) The Hampshire Regt.: *s.* of Mathew Allford, of 4, Robin Hood Street, Bartons Village, Newport, Isle of Wight, by his wife Mary Jane: enlisted Winchester, co. Hants: served in the Balkan Campaign from 15 June 1915; France and Flanders from March 1916, and died of wounds (gas), 9 August 1916: Age 24.

God Will Link The Broken Chain When In Heaven We Meet Again

(VIII.D.28) Pte. 21396, John Buckley, 1st Bn. (27th Foot) The Royal Inniskilling Fusiliers: formerly no.19573, Hussars: *s.* of John Buckley, of 11, Lower Dominick Street, Dublin, by his wife Bridget: enlisted Dublin: served in France from August 1915, and died of wounds (gas), 10 August 1916: Age 18.

Queen Of The Holy Rosary Pray For Him
In Memory Of Our Dear Son Jack

(VIII.D.28A) Pte. 26959, James Wilson, 1st Bn. (27th Foot) The Royal Inniskilling Fusiliers: *s.* of William Wilson, of 495, Coatbank Street, Coatbridge, co. Lanark, by his wife Mary: *b.* Oldmonkland, co. Lanark: enlisted Coatbridge. Died of wounds (gas), 9 August 1916: Age 33.

(VIII.D.29) Sergt. 8672, Henry Walter Doige, 1st Bn. (37th Foot) The Hampshire Regt.: *s.* of Mrs E. Doige (38, Mary Street, Arundell Street, Landport, Portsmouth): *b.* St. Luke's, Portsmouth, co. Hants: served with the Expeditionary Force in France and Flanders from 23 August 1914, and died of wounds (gas), 10 August 1916; No.3 Canadian C.C.S., Poperinghe.

(VIII.D.29A) Sergt. 5/7502, James Morris Hathorn, 1st Bn. The Prince Consort's Own (The Rifle Brigade): late of Kennington, London, S.E.: enlisted Woolwich. Died of wounds (gas), 10 August 1916.

(VIII.D.30) Pte. 29462, Harry Greenwood, 2nd Bn. (20th Foot) The Lancashire Fusiliers: *s.* of the late William Greenwood, by his wife Sarah Emma (Rochdale, co. Lancaster). Died of wounds (gas), 9 August 1916: Age 25.

(VIII.D.30A) Pte. 30122, James Hamilton Baldwin, 1st Bn. (13th Foot) The Prince Albert's (Somerset Light Infantry): formerly no.27944, Duke of Cornwall's Light Infantry: *s.* of Thomas Baldwin, of James Street, Woolwich, London, by his wife Mary: late *husb.* to Louise Cook (formerly Baldwin, Kingston Villa, Victoria Road, Freshwater, Isle of Wight): *b.* Aldershot: enlisted Whitehall. Died of wounds (gas), 9 August 1916: Age 20.

Rest In Peace Dear One

(VIII.D.31) Pte. 12081, Walter Gomm, 1st Bn. (13th Foot) The Prince Albert's (Somerset Light Infantry): *s.* of Mrs S. Gomm (Castle Street, Stoke-under-Ham, co. Somerset): enlisted Yeovil: served in France from 24 July 1915, and died of wounds (gas), 9 August 1916: Age 19.

(VIII.D.31A) Pte. 10410, George Vaughan Walton, 1st Bn. (30th Foot) The East Lancashire Regt.: *b.* Bradford, co. York: enlisted Stratford, co. Essex: served in France and Flanders from 22 August 1914, and died of wounds (gas), 10 August 1916.

(VIII.D.32) Pte. 441181, Arthur Edward Tatchell, 5th Bn. Canadian Infantry (Saskatchewan Regt.), C.E.F.: *s.* of Henry George Tatchell, c/o Box 683, Battleford, Saskatchewan; and his wife, Caroline Tatchell (11, South Street, Montacute, Somerset, England): and brother to Pte. 472284, J.E. Tatchell, 44th Canadian Infantry, killed in action 3 June 1917; and 88177, A.J. Tatchell, C.E.F. (surv'd.): *b.* Clapton, co. Essex, 26 December 1892: Occupation – Electrician: previously served 22nd Light Horse, Saskatchewan (Militia); enlisted C.E.F., Battleford, 30 March 1915, and died of wounds (gas), 9 August 1916: Age 22. (*IWGC record age 23*)

Gone From Us To Be With Jesus

His brother Joshua has no known grave; he is commemorated on the Canadian National (Vimy) Memorial.

(VIII.D.32A) Rfn. C/7694 Dick Sutcliffe, 18th (Service) Bn. (Arts & Crafts) The King's Royal Rifle Corps: *s.* of Lewis Sutcliffe, of Halifax, co. York, by his wife Sarah Esther. Died of wounds (gas), 9 August 1916: Age 26.

Rest In Peace

(VIII.D.33) Pte. 26951, William Handy, 1st Bn. (27th Foot) The Royal Inniskilling Fusiliers: *s.* of William Handy, of 54, Fenton Terrace, New Herrington, Fence Houses, Co. Durham, by his wife Margaret: enlisted Shiney Row, Co. Durham. Died of wounds (gas), 11 August 1916: Age 18.

Deeply Mourned For By Father, Mother, Sisters And Brother

(VIII.D.33A) Pte. 19614, William Perry, 'C' Coy., 1st Bn. (30th Foot) The East Lancashire Regt.: *s.* of Henry Perry, of 17, St. John's Road, Burnley, co. Lancaster, by his wife Mary Jane: *educ.* Rosegrove Wesleyan School: Occupation – Labourer; Towneley Brickworks, Burnley: enlisted Nelson, co. Lancaster, 13 March 1915. Died in No.10 C.C.S., of wounds (gas), 10 August 1916: Age 19. In a letter to Mrs Perry, the Chaplain, Rev. A.B. Brooker, wrote, "I am very sorry indeed to tell you that your son...died in hospital here at 6p.m. on the 10th of this month. He was admitted the day before suffering from the effects of gas poisoning. He was conscious for only a short time, and was not suffering much pain, but was very weak and exhausted, and unable to speak. I was with him and prayed with him, and did all I could to help and comfort him. I told him I would write to you, and he sent you his dearest love – that was his only message. Very soon he became unconscious, and remained so till the end, next day, when in spite of all the efforts of the doctors and nurses he passed quietly away. We laid him to rest with the Church service in the military cemetery. Please accept my deepest sympathy. I hope that you will feel that he was not alone, but with friends, who did their very best to help him."

Mercy Truth Honour
For These Things He Died

(VIII.D.34) Pte. 21065, Joseph Hunter, 1st Bn. (27th Foot) The Royal Inniskilling Fusiliers: *s.* of Joseph Hunter, of Dromore, Coleraine, Co. Londonderry, by his wife Margaret: served in France from 6 October 1915, and died of wounds, 10 August 1916: Age 28.

Welcome
Well Done

(VIII.D.34A) Pte. 26454, Arthur Halstead, 1st Bn. (30th Foot) The East Lancashire Regt.: *s.* of Alfred (& Mrs) Halstead, of Back Spring Terrace, Stacksteads, Bacup, co. Lancaster: employee Atherton Holme Mill: Religion – Wesleyan: enlisted Bacup. Died of wounds (gas), 11 August 1916: Age 27.

Too Far Away Thy Grave To See But Not Too Far To Think Of Thee
Peace Perfect Peace

(VIII.D.35) Rfn. R/3024, Samuel Grace, 8th (Service) Bn. The King's Royal Rifle Corps: *s.* of Daniel Grace, of 33, Balaclava Road, Sheffield, co. York, by his wife Ann Elizabeth: served in France from 21 July 1915, and died of wounds (gas), 9 August 1916: Age 19.

Worthy Of Everlasting Remembrance
Mother Father Sisters And Bros

(VIII.D.35A) Pte 17706, William Selway, 1st Bn. (13th Foot) The Prince Albert's (Somerset Light Infantry): *s.* of Albert (& Eliza) Selway, of Radstock, co. Somerset: enlisted Midsomer Norton, co. Somerset: served with the Expeditionary Force in France and Flanders from 20 July 1915, and died of wounds (gas asphyxiation), 11 August 1916 (received in action two days previously): Age 29.

(VIII.D.36) Rfn. S/9732, Edward Shadbolt, 1st Bn. The Prince Consort's Own (The Rifle Brigade): enlisted Hackney, co. Middlesex: served in France from 6 July 1915, and died of wounds (gas), 11 August 1916, received at Ypres on the 9th.

By the first week of August 1916, the Battle of the Somme had been raging for almost five weeks and the Allied High Command theorised that battle hardened German troops in the salient were being systematically removed to the Somme front and replaced by inexperienced and worn troops which had been bearing the British attack. To prove this theory and gain valuable information as to the disposition of German troops, and the effect the Somme battle was having on their morale, a series of raids on the enemy lines were arranged with the sole purpose of obtaining prisoners. In the St. Eloi sector the raid on the Canadian 31st Battalion front fell to 'A' Company who were informed that should they 'carry it out without assistance from the rest of the company it would redound to their credit.' Plans were carefully and meticulously drawn up to ensure success for the raid, and volunteers called for: "Buttress of our section volunteered without asking any questions...he had a novel and original idea for volunteering. He knew our company would be in the front line when the raid was pulled off and after it was over the raiders would retire to Headquarters and possibly the transport lines. Having been through the St. Eloi scrap and knowing that Fritz had our line well registered, he said our trenches would be subjected to particular Hell after the raid was over, consequently he reasoned he was taking the lesser risk if he volunteered..." The plan was for three raiding parties, each ten men strong, to hit three sections of the German front line trenches, the raiders "were armed to the teeth with bombs, revolvers and knobkerries. Their faces were blackened, badges removed and all correspondence left behind." Unfortunately the raid had to be aborted without success when the attacking parties were discovered within twenty yards of the German wire. "Fritz was prepared and waiting for the raid. He had men out in front of his wire..." Bombed and fired on by the enemy the Canadians were forced to retire to their own lines where it was found "about sixteen out of the thirty were wounded." "Buttress... got badly injured and succumbed later. It was believed he could have pulled through but the strain of the campaign marked its effect on him long before the raid and he was not physically the man he once was. Frank was the 'Adonis' of the platoon, six feet with thick, curly, black hair, quiet and uncomplaining, a very pleasant comrade. In his genial moments he used to hum 'Sunny Alberta of Mine' but he was destined never to see Sunny Alberta again."

(VIII.D.36A) Pte. 79243, Frank Buttress, 31st Bn. Canadian Infantry (Alberta Regt.), C.E.F.: s. of the late James Buttress, by his wife Caroline (32, Priory Road, Abbey Estate, Cambridge, England): and brother to Spr. 1879, C. Buttress (surv'd.): b. 7 August 1885: Occupation – Stenographer's Clerk: previously served 3 years, 3rd Suffolk Volunteers; enlisted C.E.F. Calgary, 17 November 1914. Died of multiple bullet wounds, 10 August 1916: Age 31.

In Loving Memory Of A Dear Son And Brother
Our Thoughts Are Ever With Thee

(VIII.D.37) Rfn. 811014, William Henry Geake, 1st Bn. Prince Consort's Own (The Rifle Brigade): s. of the late Robert Geake, by his wife Margaret (5, Gladwell Road, Crouch End, London): b. Bristol: qualified B.Sc. (Engineering): Occupation – Electrical Engineer: enlisted 1914, Holloway, co. Middlesex: served with the Expeditionary Force in France and Flanders from July 1915, and died of wounds (gas), 10 August 1916, received at Ypres on the night of the 8th – 9th; front line, Canal Bank: Age 29. See account (VIII.D.14).

He That Loseth His Life For My Sake Shall Find It

(VIII.D.37A) Pte. 16916, William Henry McCune, 7th Bn. Canadian Infantry (British Columbia Regt.), C.E.F.: c/o S. McCune ('Braniel,' Castlereagh, Belfast): b. Belfast, Ireland, 24 February 1889: Religion – Presbyterian: Occupation – Barrister: enlisted Valcartier, 23 September 1914. Died No.10 C.C.S., Poperinghe, of wounds received in action at Ypres, 10 August 1916: Age 27. *unm.*

(VIII.D.38) Pte. 18884, Thomas Errington, 1st Bn. (27th Foot) The Royal Inniskilling Fusiliers: b. Middlesbrough, co. York: enlisted Newcastle-on-Tyne: served with the Expeditionary Force in France and Flanders from 29 May 1915, and died of wounds, 11 August 1916, received in action at Potijze two days previously.

(VIII.D.38A) C.Q.M.S. 8632, Charles Henry Giblin, 1st Bn. (27th Foot) The Royal Inniskilling Fusiliers: s. of Charles Giblin, of Queenstown, Co. Cork, by his wife Margaret: served in France from March 1915, and died of wounds (gas), 11 August 1916, received in action at Potijze two days previously: Age 28.

Faithful Unto Death
Never Forgotten By Sisters Mary And Kate

(VIII.D.39) Rfn. R/20831, Thomas Spencer, 10th (Service) Bn. The King's Royal Rifle Corps: b. Newbridge, Co. Kildare. Died of wounds, 12 August 1916.

(VIII.D.39A) Rfn. R/7453, John Pratt, 17th (Service) Bn. The King's Royal Rifle Corps: *s*. of William Pratt, of 88, Broadwall, Lambeth, London: *b*. Southwark: served in France from 3 August 1915, and died of wounds, 12 August 1916.

(VIII.D.40) Pte. 147708, Charles William Stringer, 28th Bn. Canadian Infantry (Saskatchewan Regt.), C.E.F.: *s*. of Jeremiah Joseph 'John' Stringer, of 13 Manchester Building, East Street, London, by his wife Emma Maria, *née* Holt: *b*. London, England, 19 March 1892: Occupation – Milkman: member 106th Winnipeg Grenadiers (Militia); enlisted Winnipeg, Manitoba, 31 July 1915. Died of wounds, 11 August 1916: Age 24. *unm*.

Rest In Peace

(VIII.D.40A) Pte. 5984, Herbert Swatton, 1st Bn. (13th Foot) The Prince Albert's (Somerset Light Infantry): *b*. South Croom, co. Wilts: enlisted Devizes: served with the Expeditionary Force in France and Flanders from 1 June 1915, and died of wounds (gas poisoning), 11 August 1916.

(VIII.D.41) Pte. 435506, Edmund Chambers, 10th Bn. Canadian Infantry (Alberta Regt.), C.E.F.: *s*. of Clifford Chambers, of 'Haleworth,' Station Road, Knowle, Birmingham, by his wife Grace. Died of wounds (G.S.W., Neck, Chest) 11 August 1916, No.3 Canadian Casualty Clearing Station, Poperinghe. Buried in Lyssenthoek Military Cemetery: Age 26.

In Life In Death Lord Abide With Me

(VIII.D.41A) Pte. 418425, Horace Wren, 42nd Bn. Canadian Infantry (Quebec Regt.), C.E.F.: *s*. of James Wren, of Blechlingley, co. Surrey, by his wife Anne: *b*. Bletchingley, 29 March 1877: Occupation – Painter: previously served 12 years 1st Scots Guards; serving member (5 years) Royal Highlanders of Canada (Militia), enlisted Montreal, 11 March 1915. Died of wounds, 11 August 1916: Age 39.

(VIII.D.42) Pte. 25868, Thomas Earl, 1st Bn. (13th Foot) The Prince Albert's (Somerset Light Infantry): *s*. of Edwin (& Elizabeth) Earl, of 36, Charterhouse Road, Godalming, co. Surrey: and elder brother to Pte. G/7094, G.W. Earl, 10th Royal West Surrey Regt., killed in action, 20 September 1917: enlisted Godalming, May 1916. Died of wounds (gas poisoning), 11 August 1916: Age 35. He leaves a wife, Caroline Jessie Earl ('Seaton,' Peperharow Road, Godalming).

Loved & Remembered By All Relations & Friends Of Godalming

His brother George has no known grave; he is commemorated on the Tyne Cot Memorial (Panel 15).

(VIII.D.42A) Pte. 22540, Edward Harry Jenkins, 1st Bn. (13th Foot) The Prince Albert's (Somerset Light Infantry): *s.* of the late John George Jenkins, by his wife Fanny Helen (8, Prior Park Cottages, Prior Park Road, Bath): enlisted Bath, co. Gloucester. Died of wounds (gas), 11 August 1916: Age 26.

We Loved Him In Life
In Death Let Us Not Forget Him

(VIII.D.43) Pte. 428188, George Ramsay Barber, 7th Bn. Canadian Infantry (British Columbia Regt.), C.E.F.: *s.* of Dr. (& Mrs) John Barber, of 146, Grey Avenue, Notre Dame de Grace, Montreal: *b.* Nassagaweya, Ontario. Died of wounds, 12 August 1916: Age 30.

For Humanity's Sake

(VIII.D.43A) Pte. 439721, William James Allan, 52nd Bn. Canadian Infantry (Manitoba Regt.), C.E.F.: *s.* of William Allan, of 57, Dagmar Street, Winnipeg, by his wife Jane: *b.* 1 September 1894: Religion – Presbyterian: Occupation – Checker: joined C.E.F., Port Arthur, 8 September 1915; apptd. 52nd Bn. Died of wounds (S.W. [shrapnel] Rt. arm, Rt. leg), 13 August 1916. 'This soldier belonged to No.16 Platoon which was holding a strong-point near Hill 60 when the 52nd was in support to the 60th Battalion (Railway Dugouts). The officer in charge of the strong-point asked for two scouts to go out a short distance to get some information, Allan being one of the two. A shell burst near them, inflicting shrapnel wounds in Allan's arm and right leg from the effects of which he died.': Age 21.

Ever Fondly Remembered At Home

(VIII.D.44) Pte. 628991, Samuel 'Sam' Kennedy McEwan, 29th Bn. Canadian Infantry (British Columbia Regt.), C.E.F.: brother to Mrs Darragh (Princeton, British Columbia): *b.* co. Ayr, Scotland, 5 March 1889: Religion – Presbyterian: sometime removed to Canada: Occupation – Teamster: 5'4" tall, dark complexion, blue eyes, black hair; two vaccination marks on left arm, operation scar lower left abdomen: serving member 11th Irish Fusiliers of Canada (Militia); previously served 6 years 6th Cameronians (Sco.Rif.): enlisted Vernon, British Columbia, 18 June 1915; apptd. 29th Battn. 28 June. Died of bullet wounds to the thigh, 13 August 1916: Age 27. *unm.*

(VIII.D.44A) Pte. 153568, Charles Smith Laing, 43rd Bn. Canadian Infantry (Manitoba Regt.), C.E.F.: *s.* of Margaret (1329, Retallack Street, Regina, Saskatchewan): *b.* Slamannan, co. Stirling, Scotland, 28 June 1894: Religion – Presbyterian: removed to Canada with his parents; settled Regina: Occupation – Fireman: 5'7" tall, dark complexion, brown eyes, brown hair: prior to enlistment, Winnipeg, 31 July 1915, was a member of 79th Gordon Highlanders of Canada (Militia). Died of wounds (G.S.W. back, abdomen), 13 August 1916: Age 20. *unm.*

(IX.A.6) Capt. Benjamin Henry Rust, 13th Bn. Canadian Infantry (Quebec Regt.), C.E.F.: *s.* of Robert (& Amy Lillias) Rust, of Norwich Road, North Walsham, co. Norfolk: *b.* Holt, co. Norfolk, 18 May 1891: *educ.* Paston Grammar School, North Walsham; Christ's Hospital Scholl, co. Sussex: on graduation joined Bank of British North America, London; transf'd. Montreal Branch, Canada; June 1912: previously served 3 years, 3 months, 16th London Regt. (Queen's Westminster Rifles): enlisted Valcartier, 23 September 1914; Pte., 24681, 13th Battn.: came over with 1st Canadian Contingent, October following: served with the Expeditionary Force in France and Flanders from February 1915: apptd. Lieut. In the Field, after the 2nd Battle of Ypres, April – May 1915; in recognition of his gallant and efficient conduct throughout that fighting: subsequently promoted Capt., he was severely wounded by shellfire in action near Ypres, 19 July 1916, and died later the same day in the casualty Clearing Station, Poperinghe. Buried in the Canadian Military Cemetery there: Age 25. *unm.*

Faithful Unto Death

(IX.A.7) Lieut. Charles Penner Cotton, 2nd Bde. Canadian Field Artillery, C.E.F.: *s.* of the late Maj.Gen. W.H. Cotton, of Pinehurst, Almonte, Ontario, by his wife Jessie: *b.* Kingston, Ontario, 21 December 1890: *educ.* Ottawa Model School; Ashbury College, Ottawa (Applied Science), 1909–14, where he was a member of the Faculty Hockey team and won Second colours for Hockey; Alpha Delta Psi fraternity: enlisted 5th Bty., 2nd Bde., Canadian Field Artillery; came over with 1st Canadian Contingent, October 1914: served with the Expeditionary Force in France and Flanders from February 1915: obtained his commission, 8th Bty., June following: took part in all the major Canadian battles throughout 1915 and early 1916, and was killed in action, 2 June 1916. On which date he was in charge of the 'Sacrifice Guns' – two guns which had been brought up to the front line position at Sanctuary Wood, nr. Ypres for use in an emergency. Fire was opened on them when discovered and, assisted by his surviving gunners, he returned fire and continued firing until the enemy came over Observatory Ridge when he and his party were killed: Age 25. *unm.*

Remains recovered (25 June) and brought back to Poperinghe for burial. He was awarded the Order of St. George, IVth Class (Russia). His brother, Capt. R.P. Cotton, lies nearby (VI.A.27)

(IX.A.14) 2nd Lieut. Reginald Paul Thompson, 1st Bn. (13th Foot) The Prince Albert's (Somerset Light Infantry): *s.* of Edith Mary Twinberrow Thompson, and the late Paul Henry Thompson, her husband *b.* Cardiff. Died of wounds (gas), 9 August 1916: Age 28. See account (VIII.D.25A).

Dulce Et Decorum Est Pro Patria Mori

(IX.A.16) 2nd Lieut. George William Fletcher, 3rd (Reserve) attd. 1st Bn. (27th Foot) The Royal Inniskilling Fusiliers: *s.* of George Fletcher, of Hillside, Gourock, co. Renfrew, by his wife Ellen: *b.* Eltham, co. Kent. Died of wounds, 9 August 1916: Age 19.

All He Had Hoped For All He Had He Gave

(IX.A.17) 2nd Lieut. Frank Victor De Ritter, 1st Bn. (13th Foot) The Prince Albert's (Somerset Light Infantry): *s.* of the late W.H. De Ritter, and his wife Ada Lydia De Ritter (9, Wavertree Road, South Woodford, London). Died of wounds (gas), 9 August 1916: Age 19.

The Souls Of The Righteous Are In The Hands Of God

(IX.A.18) 2nd Lieut. Harry James Griffiths, 1st Bn. (13th Foot) The Prince Albert's (Somerset Light Infantry): *s.* of Henry Thomas Griffiths, of Calverley Mount, Tunbridge Wells, and Lillie Griffiths his spouse. Died of wounds (gas), 9 August 1916: Age 22.

He That Loseth His Life For My Sake Shall Find It

(IX.A.19) 2nd Lieut. Reginald Stuart Handford, 1st Bn. The Prince Consort's Own (The Rifle Brigade): *s.* of William Handford, of 'Barum,' Orchehill Avenue, Gerards Cross, co. Bucks, formerly of Barnstaple, co. Devon, by his wife Elizabeth: *educ.* West Buckland School, North Devon, where he was a Sergt., O.T.C.; was also sometime L/Corpl., Honourable Artillery Company (T.F.): served with the Expeditionary Force in France from 14 June 1916; died of wounds, 9 August 1916: Age 20.

West Buckland School, Devon Serjt O.T.C.
In Proud And Loving Memory

(IX.A.20) 2nd Lieut. Thomas Walter Doyle, 17th (Reserve) attd. 16th (Service) Bn. (St. Pancras) The Prince Consort's Own (The Rifle Brigade): *s.* of the late Thomas Doyle, by his wife Anne M. (Langley, co. Worcester): prior to enlistment was a student for Holy Orders of St. John's, Durham. Died of wounds (gas), 9 August 1916: Age 28. *unm.*

Not Dead But Living Unto Thee

(IX.B.2) 2nd Lieut. Desmond Alexander Le Peton, 1st Bn. (13th Foot) The Prince Albert's (Somerset Light Infantry): *s.* of Alfred Edward Le Peton, of Earlsfort House School, 3-4, Earlsfort Place, Dublin, and Rose Le Peton, his wife (44, Addiscombe Court Road, East Croydon, co. Surrey); and brother to Lieut. C.A. Le Peton, 8th Royal Inniskilling Fusiliers, killed in action, 15 August 1917: *educ.* Trinity College, Dublin where he was a member of the O.T.C.: served with the Expeditionary Force in France and Flanders from 20 July 1916, and died of wounds (gas poisoning), 9 August 1916, received in action at Canal Bank, Ypres the previous day: Age 19. Remembered on Trinity College War Memorial (Right Tablet, North Wall).

And In Memory Of Lieut. C.A. Le Peton
Royal Innis Fusiliers

His brother Clive has no known grave, he is commemorated on the Ypres (Menin Gate) Memorial (Panel 22).

(IX.B.6) Lieut. Alan William Russell Cowan, 73rd Bn. Canadian Infantry, C.E.F.: *s.* of Robert David Russell Cowan, of Bushley Vicarage, Tewkesbury, by his wife Catherine Florence. Died in the early hours of 20 August 1916, of wounds received shortly before his arrival at the C.C.S. when, as his battalion was nearing the Dressing Station, Vlamertinghe Mill, a shell landed in their midst killing Lieuts. F.R. Robinson, K. Turnbull, and seven other ranks. Remembered on the Salmon Arm & District (British Columbia) War Memorial. See account Brandhoek Military Cemetery (II.H.16-24).

"Dominus Pars Hereditatis Suae Requiescat In Pace"

(IX.B.8) Capt. Sidney Reginald Hockaday, 2nd Bn. The Monmouthshire Regt. (T.F.): *s.* of the late James Henry Hockaday (*d.*1902; drowned while attempting to save Sidney and his brother), of Sydney, New South Wales, and his wife Susan, *née* Holland (*d.*1904): adopted *s.* of Frank Step Hockaday, of 'Highbury,' Bledisloe, Lydney, co. Gloucester, and Jane Wansborough, his wife: and brother to Lieut. P.H. Hockaday, Monmouthshire Regt. (surv'd.): *b.* Woollahra, Sydney,

25 June 1892: *educ.* Monmouth Grammar School; Birmingham University, 1911–14: volunteered and enlisted Monmouth Regt., on the outbreak of war: given a commission 2nd Lieut. 20 August; served with the Expeditionary Force in France and Flanders from November following: took part in the fighting at Shell (Mouse) Trap Farm, nr. Wieltje; wounded (gas) 2 May 1915: apptd. Temp. Lieut. 5 May 1915; promoted Lieut. 25 September 1915; Temp. Capt. January 1916. Wounded while at duty with a day working party, Picadilly Trench, south of Potijze, and died No. 10 C.C.S., the following day, 2 September 1916: Age 24. 2nd Lieut. G.W. Greenland wrote, "I was going to write and tell you about… Capt. S.R. Hockaday…He took over 'B' Coy down South when Comley was wounded, a jollier fellow we have never had. Young, witty, happy, perfect in dress, 'Hock' as we called him was top-hole. The mess has been such a happy family after 'Hock' joined us. This morning he was very badly wounded. Besides night-work we always have a day party out and Hock & Lawlor had gone up to see the work this morning. A shell exploded just on the trench. Hock got two ghastly holes in the left shoulder, a Sergeant got it in the arm and a man got it in the thigh. I cycled down the shell-scarred road to the dressing station – a ruined chateau – this afternoon to see him. There he lay, white as death, and still on a stretcher, covered with blankets. His hair, always so immaculately parted, was ruffled and without the usual sheen. He was almost sleeping, but when I went he said in such a weak little voice, 'Good-bye, Greenland.' Oh! since then I have felt so very fed up! He was wounded at 11.30 this morning, but owing to that part being under observation by the Boche our ambulance will not take him from the dressing station until 10.30 tonight. The doctor says he will pull through with tremendous luck, but will probably lose his arm." The Medical Officer, 2nd Monmouths, wrote, "I'm so sorry to tell you that Sidney was seriously wounded yesterday. The same horrid piece of the line. He had only just been talking to the GOC over a trench. HE shrapnel. It has damaged his shoulder and chest badly – but has not injured his lung I think. He could not be moved till 10.30 pm. He was wounded at about 11.30 am. He was seen as soon as possible by 2 MDs who gave him morphia at once. I saw him as soon as possible afterwards and went with him down to the CCS. I have been with him all day today. The padre asked me to write to you as I knew all about him. I am so very sorry as I had begun to know him so well & we always went about together. I shall miss him dreadfully- he was one of the best officers we had I know- & alas- one of the few originals who can never be replaced. He was most extraordinarily brave and devoid of nerves. He won't be wanted any more for this war which is a blessing…" And in a letter to his brother Percy, the Chaplain, No.10 C.C.S., said, "Dear Sir, I thought perhaps you might like to hear from me…I have been with your brother since he was admitted early Friday morning. I have not written before as Capt. Sainsbury, M.O, has been writing and has been perfectly

splendid the whole time, practically never leaving your brother. He no doubt has told you he died yesterday, quite peacefully and quite happy...I need hardly add how much I liked him, he was a real brave unselfish English gentleman and died after having made his last Communion, at peace with both God and Man. There never was a chance for him – humanly speaking, tho' while he lived there was just a slight hope. You have my deepest sympathy...." Buried in the Soldier's Cemetery adjoining, 4 p.m. the following day; the Comdg. Officer, Medical Officer, Transport Officer, Adjutant, and Regtl. Quartermaster in attendance; Chaplain J.R. Hale, C. of E. officiating.

His Home – Highbury, Lydney
Gloucestershire

(IX.B.14) 2nd Lieut. William Bernard Bovey, 19th Bn. The London Regt.: *s.* of Alfred Bovey, of 165, St. John's Hill, Battersea, London, by his wife Jennie: served in France from September 1915; died of wounds received at Ypres, 15 November 1916: Age 23.

And So Make Life Death And That Vast For-Ever One Grand Sweet Song

(IX.B.15) Capt. Charles Kenneth McKerrow, Royal Army Medical Corps attd. 10th Bn. Northumberland Fusiliers: late of 14, Portinscale Road, East Putney, London, S.W.15: elder *s.* of the late Dr. George McKerrow, M.D. (*d.*1915), of 5, Barns Street, Ayr, and Jessie Cochrane Highet, his wife: and brother to Lieut. M. McKerrow, M.C., 11th Border Regt. & Royal Navy (surv'd.); and Miss E. McKerrow, Q.A.I.M.N.S. (surv'd.): *b.* Ayr, 2 June 1883: *educ.* Cargilfield Preparatory School, Ayr; Charterhouse (border); Clare College, Cambridge (scholarship student), obtained 1st Class, Natural Science Tripos (Pt.1), graduated M.B., B.C., M.R.C.S., L.R.C.P. (1908): thereafter held resident position St. George's Hospital, London, and extern 1st Frankenklinik, Vienna: later joined his father's practice in Ayr: volunteered his services as a doctor; enlisted R.A.M.C., May 1915; obtained a commission 2nd Lieut., June following: served with the Expeditionary Force in France and Flanders, apptd. Medical Officer, 10th Northumberland Fusiliers, from August 1915. Died of wounds (severe abdominal), 9 p.m., 20 December 1916, received from shellfire at Maple Copse at 10 a.m. that morning (severely wounded also, his Orderly, L/Corpl. Clark, died the following day): Age 33. His Commanding Officer wrote, "A few days before his death Capt. McKerrow read an excellent paper on Trench Fever before our Divisional Medical Society, giving proof of his clinical work even in the trenches. I formed a very high opinion of him, both as a gallant soldier and a skilful surgeon. He was absolutely fearless in the performance of his duty." He was married (January 1915) to Jean Bekewith Turnbull, *née* McKerrow (Hindhead, co. Surrey), only *dau.* of the late James Craik, and had a son, George Hamilton McKerrow, *b.* 19 November 1915.

Their Name Liveth For Evermore

(IX.B.16) 2nd Lieut. Harold Jameson, M.C., D.C.M., 42nd Sqdn. Royal Flying Corps: *s.* of William Storm Jameson, of 'Ryedale,' Chubb Hill, Whitby, co. York, by his wife Hannah Margaret: served with the Expeditionary Force in France and Flanders from 10 August 1914, and died of wounds, 5 January 1917, consequent to being shot down whilst directing artillery fire. At 07.45 on the day of his death, 2nd Lieut. Jameson took off from Abeele Aerodrome and shortly thereafter became engaged in combat over the enemy lines with two German aircraft and his aircraft (DH2 5946) was seen to nose dive and crash in the vicinity of Voormezeele. The crash site was later destroyed by shell fire. He also held the Medaille Militaire (France): Age 20. *unm.*

He Has Outsoared The Shadow Of Our Night

(IX.B.17) Lieut. William Davidson Thomson, Princess Patricia's Canadian Light Infantry (Eastern Ontario Regt.), C.E.F. attd. 6th Sqdn. Royal Flying Corps: only *s.* of the late John Thomson, by his wife Janet (714, Lansdowne Avenue, Saskatoon, Saskatchewan): *b.* North Gower, Carlton Co., 5 December 1885: *educ.* Salem Public School; Burk's Falls Public School; Guelph Collegiate; Regina Collegiate (& Normal School); University College, Toronto (Political Science), 1906–10, B.A.: between Regina and attendance at U.C. Toronto was Teacher, Radisson, Saskatchewan; and lately, Barrister, Messrs McCraney, Mackenzie & Hutchinson, Saskatoon: previously Lieut. 105th Regt. (Militia): enlisted 9 October 1915; apptd. 53rd Battn., Camp Hughes, 27th of that month: proceeded overseas March 1916: joined Princess Patricia's, France, June 1916, and served with that unit until transf'd. as Observer, Royal Flying Corps, August following: served with 6th Sqdn., 2nd Wing, on the Ypres front throughout the following months, and was killed in action, 5 January 1917, while directing artillery battery fire over No Man's Land, before Zillebeke: Age 31. *unm.*

He Gave His Life, Himself He Could Not Save

(IX.B.20) Major Henry Gorell Barnes, D.S.O., 19th (London) Bty., 47th Div. Royal Field Artillery: (served as Gorell): 2nd Baron Gorell, eldest *s.* of the late Rt. Hon. John Gorell Barnes, 1st Baron Gorell, by his wife Mary, *dau.* of Thomas Mitchell, of Arthurlie: *b.* 1882: *educ.* Summer Fields (1892–95); Winchester

(1895–1900); Trinity College, Oxford (1900–03), graduated B.A., 1903 (M.A. 1908), thence to Harvard University (1903–04, Law): called to the Bar, Inner Temple, 1906 (served as Secretary to his father), later appointed Secretary to Royal Commission (Divorce): volunteered his services, obtained a commission and enlisted on the outbreak of war, August 1914: joined 19th Bty., Capt., February 1915; proceeded to France early March; and died of wounds, 16 January 1917, received the previous day from shellfire in the Lankhof Farm – Marshall Walk; Verbrandenmolen sector. Buried with full Military Honours, his coffin was borne to the grave on a gun limber: Age 35. Mentioned in Despatches for his services in the Great War; he was awarded the D.S.O. for skilful reconnaissance under fire near High Wood, Somme, 1916. In his will he requested the sum of £50 be given to his groom, Dvr. Rayner; his servant, Gnr. Hill; Trmpr. Purchase and Gnr. Patterson; the latter in grateful recollection of many happy days spent together at the O.P. and especially on September 16th. last.'

Give Thanks For The Glory Of The Dead

(IX.C.13A) Pte. 117106, John 'Jack' Allan, 2nd Bn. Canadian Mounted Rifles (British Columbia Regt.), C.E.F.: s. of John Allan, of 14, Merkland Road East, Aberdeen, Scotland, and his late wife Maria: b. Aberdeen, 10 May 1890: Religion – Presbyterian: former employee Canadian Pacific Railway: joined C.E.F., Calgary, 21 January 1915; apptd. 2nd C.M.R.: proceeded overseas, October 1915: took part in the fighting at Mount Sorrel, 2 June 1916. Died of wounds (GSW multiple) No.17 Casualty Clearing Station, Poperinghe, 20 August 1916; received in action 4 p.m., vicinity Sanctuary Wood: Age 26.

For Ever With The Lord Amen
So Let It Be

(IX.D.3A) Dvr. 2662, Robert James Macgregor Barnet, 1st Australian Ammunition Sub. Park, Australian Army Service Corps, A.I.F.: s. of the Rev. Donald McKay Barnet, of 'The Manse,' Wollongong, New South Wales, by his wife Jessie Catherine: b. Illaroo, Nowra, New South Wales: Religion – Presbyterian: Occupation – Surveyor's Assistant: enlisted Marrickville, 4 January 1916, Gnr. 5th Rfts., 5th Field Artillery Bde.; subsequently apptd. Spr., 1st Mining Corps, 17 February: served in France from 17 June following; transfd. A.S.C., 1 July 1916; Awarded Forfeiture 7 Days Pay, 13 July 'Negligently driving a lorry (11 July) so as to cause damage to the radiator and fan'. Died of self-inflicted injuries (G.S.W. head), 27 August 1916 Dvr. 2017, C.A. Horne reported, "I saw this man, shot through the head, a rifle was lying near him. He had taken his own life. No one saw him do it, but we heard a shot and on going out found him dead. He had been punished for some mistake or neglect of duty and this preyed on his mind. He wrote some letters before taking this rash step. He was popular with his mates, civil and well-behaved. Sergt. H. Taylor (late of 1st Am.Sub-Park) now Royal Flying Corps, fixed up his grave and put a cross at the head of it. Mrs Barnet is acquainted with the above facts": Age 21. *unm.*

Beloved Son Of Rev. D.M. And J. Barnet Of Wollongong.
Abide In Me

(IX.D.10) Pte. 24649, George Armstrong, 1st Bn. (34th Foot) The Border Regt.: *s.* of Robert Armstrong, Farmer; of Carlatton Demesne Farm, Heads Nook, Cumwhitton, co. Cumberland, by his wife Ann: *b.* Moos Foot, Cumwhitton, 28 March 1892: *educ.* Cumrew Village School: joined 1st Border Regt. 8 April 1916: served with the Expeditionary Force in France and Flanders from 14 July following, and died at No.10 Casualty Clearing Station, France, 1 September of the same year, from wounds received in action at Ypres: Age 24. *unm.*

There Is A Link Death Cannot Sever
Sweet Remembrance Lasts Forever

(IX.D.16) Pte. 17668, James Arthur Arden, 'B' Coy., 1st Bn. (25th Foot) The King's Own Scottish Borderers: *s.* of Mr (& Mrs) Arden, of Sykes Street, Reddish: Occupation – Grand Central Railway worker: enlisted Stockport, January 1915. Admitted dead on arrival, 6 September 1916, consequent to wounds received from machine-gun fire while at work repairing and improving trenches in the Canal Bank sector: Age 25. He leaves a wife Annie Arden (3, Port Street, Princess Street, Stockport, co. Chester), and one child.

Never Forgotten

(IX.D.19A) Pte. 703999, Alfred Walter De Lisle, 102nd Bn. Canadian Infantry (Central Ontario Regt.), C.E.F.: *s.* of Charles A. De Lisle, of Quyon, Quebec, Canada, by his wife Helena Augusta: and brother to Pte. 59252, A.L. De Lisle, 21st Canadian Infantry, died of wounds, 29 June 1916: *b.* Bristol, Quebec, 26 September 1882: Religion – Church of England: Occupation – Carpenter: 5′10½″ tall, fair complexion, grey eyes, light brown hair; bullet scar right foot, bullet scar left index finger, little toe on right foot missing: enlisted Prince Rupert, 14 February 1916: disembarked Le Havre, 12 August 1916. Died of multiple shell wounds and amputation of right arm, 10 September 1916: Age 33. (*IWGC record age 34*)

His brother Albert lies nearby (VIII.B.27).

At 9 p.m., 23 January 1917, after a short but very intense barrage, a company of 8th K.O.Y.L.I. raided the German lines. Realising the barrage would be followed by a raid, the enemy vacated the trenches, and, although no prisoners were taken, valuable information was collected. Perfectly timed and finely led, the raiding party occupied the trenches for fifteen minutes under very heavy fire. Sadly, like many such actions, the casualty list was heavy, all three officers involved were wounded, forty-nine other ranks wounded and eight killed.

Following the raider's return to the company lines and subsequent roll-call, Capt. M.G. Donahoo and a number of volunteers crept out into no man's land in the early hours of 24 January to search for wounded men. Within moments Capt. Donahoo was mortally wounded by an alert German sniper.

(X.A.2) Capt. Malcomson Gardiner Donahoo, M.C., 8th (Service) Bn. The King's Own (Yorkshire Light Infantry): *s.* of Thomas Malcomson Donahoo, and Anna E.M., his wife: *b.* London: *educ.* Charterhouse School (1888–91), Clare College, Cambridge (1892–1901, BA.): Articled, Solicitor (February 1901), 28, St. Swithin's Lane, London, E.C.: served with the Expeditionary Force in France and Flanders from September 1915, and died of wounds, 31 January 1917, received one week previously being shot by a sniper while searching No Man's Land, vicinity Sanctuary Wood, for wounded and missing: Age 43. Awarded the Military Cross, November 1916; he leaves a wife, Annie Donahoo (The Cottage, Wonersh, Guildford, co. Surrey).

Virtutis, Gloria Merces

Translation: Glory Is The Reward Of Valour.

(X.A.6) Lieut. John Herbert Blackburn, 4th Bn. The King's Own (Yorkshire Light Infantry), (T.F.): *s.* of John Sheard Blackburn, of Bycroft, Leadhall Lane, Harrogate, co. York, by his wife Emma. Died of pneumonia, 7 February 1917: Age 21. *unm.* (*IWGC record 9th Bn., 8 February*)

Only Son Of John And Emma Blackburn Of Batley Yorkshire

(X.A.7) 2nd Lieut. Harold Eastly Gordon, 5th (City of London) Bn. (London Rifle Brigade) The London Regt. (T.F.) attd. 16th Bn. The Rifle Brigade: Occupation – Clerk; London Stock Exchange. Died of wounds, 23 February 1917, received nine days previously during the battalion's raid on 'The Mound.' He leaves a wife, Gwen Gordon (Avenue House, North Camp, Aldershot), to whom all correspondence regarding (and effects of) her late husband should be forwarded. See account re. 2nd Lieut. J.C. MacLehose, Brandhoek Military Cemetery (II.K.15).

Until We Meet Again

(X.A.10) 2nd Lieut. Walter Willox Steuart, 18th (Service) Bn. The Highland Light Infantry attd. 46th Sqdn. Royal Flying Corps: *yr. s.* of Walter Steuart, Iron Merchant; of Hillhead, Glasgow, by his wife Catherine, *dau.* of William Thomson Edmiston: *b.* Uddingston, *co.* Lanark, 12 March 1894: *educ.* Glasgow, and Southport: Occupation – Estate Factor's Assistant: joined Machine Gun Section 6th Cameron Highlanders, December 1914: served with the Expeditionary Force in France and Flanders from July 1915: took part in the Battle of Loos (September) and, in March 1916, was sent to Headquarters to train for a commission, being gazetted 2nd Lieut. Highland Light Infantry, April following: took part in the Battle of the Somme: attd. R.F.C., January 1917, and died at No.2 Canadian Casualty Clearing Station 5 March 1917, from wounds received in aerial action the previous day, while observing over the German lines. Buried in a Military Cemetery nr. Poperinghe: Age 23. *unm.*

I To The Hills Will Lift Mine Eyes

(X.A.11) Lieut. James 'Jim' Mahony, 9th (Service) Bn. The Queen's (Royal West Surrey Regt.): eldest *s.* of the late James Mahony, Schoolmaster, by his wife Ann Maria, *dau.* of the late William Evans: *b.* Portsmouth, co. Hants, 20 June 1882: *educ.* St. Aloysius College, Highgate, London, N.: thereafter employed for many years with Messrs Kodak Ltd.: volunteered for Foreign Service; joined Artists' Rifles, 5 September 1914, after the outbreak of war: gazetted 2nd Lieut. West Surrey Regt. 10 March 1915: promoted Lieut. 15 August 1916: took a draft of Hampshires to Egypt, November 1915, being attd. 1st Lancashire Fusiliers, 29th Divn., January 1916: served with the Expeditionary Force in France and Flanders from March 1916: wounded in the foot at Beaumont Hamel, 1 July 1916, and evacuated to England: returned to France, 29 January 1917, and died in No.2 Canadian Casualty Clearing Station, 4 March following, from wounds received in action at Ypres, 24 February, by a high explosive shell catching a tree and bursting over him while he was going to look at a ruined house with a brother officer. Buried in the Lyssenthoek Military Cemetery, Poperinghe: Age 35. His Commanding Officer wrote, "He had only been with us a comparatively short time, but not only was he very much liked by us, but he had also shown great capability. Almost as soon as he arrived he volunteered for, and went on, a raid in which he was not hurt, and the way he was hit later on was most unlucky," and his Company Commander, "Lieut. Mahony was my Second in Command, and we became great friends in the short time he was with us. He was of the greatest assistance to me in the line, as I could always implicitly rely on him. If I may be allowed, may I offer my most sincere sympathy at the death of a brave brother officer and friend held in the highest esteem by his men and the other officers of the battalion." The officer who was with him when he was wounded also wrote, "We were in reserve some thousand yards back from the line, and were going out to look at a ruined house behind our trench when we heard a shell coming. As we were commencing to lie down, it hit a tree nearby and burst, wounding your husband in the head and right leg. I had the stretcher-bearers on the spot at once and went down to the Dressing Station with him... We have lost a gallant officer and a keen soldier – one who knew his duty, and was ready at all times to perform it. In the short time he was with us I grew to know him as a real man – one of the few persons whom I had met whose example was worth following." He *m.* at St. Pancras, 28 October 1905, Lily Dora (360, Stanstead Road, Catford, London, S.E.), eldest *dau.* of Frank Ernest Barrett, of Catford, S.E., and had a *s.*, Bernard Charles, *b.* 18 November 1906.

In Proud And Loving Memory Of My Darling Husband Jim
R.I.P.

(X.A.13) Capt. the Hon. Eric Fox Pitt Lubbock, M.C., 45th Sqdn. Royal Flying Corps: Twice Mentioned in Despatches: 2nd *s.* of the late John Lubbock, P.C., F.R.S., 1st Baron Avebury, of Kingsgate Castle, co. Kent (*d.* May 1913), by his second wife, Alice Augusta Laurentia Lane, *née* Fox-Pitt-Rivers; Baroness Avebury, 2nd *dau.* of the late Lieut. Gen. Augustus H. Fox-Pitt-Rivers, D.C.L., F.R.S. (*d.* May 1900): and brother to Lieut. the Hon. H.F. Pitt Lubbock, 2nd Grenadier Guards, killed in action, 4 April 1918: *b.* 16 May 1893: *educ.* Eton College; Balliol College, Oxford: enlisted Motor Transport Sect., Army Service Corps on the outbreak of war; proceeded to France, September 1914: commissioned A.S.C., but chiefly employed attd. R.F.C. (Observer): returned to England 1916 where, after a course of instruction, he qualified as Pilot, and, after a period engaged in instructional work, returned to France, October 1916 as Flight Commander and was killed in aerial combat, 11 March 1917, being shot down by Leut. Paul Strähle, Jasta 18: Age 23. *unm.* Twice Mentioned in Despatches; awarded the Military Cross – "For conspicuous gallantry and skill when, on 26th October 1915, he attacked a German Albatross machine at a height of 9,000 feet with machine-gun fire. The hostile pilot was shot and the aeroplane was brought to the ground within our lines. The attack finished at a height of only 600 feet, and during an almost vertical dive, when the pilot was fully occupied, Lieut. Lubbock fired deliberately and with effect." In a letter written to his mother shortly before his death he said, "One is here confronted almost daily with the possibility of death, and when one looks forward to the next few months this possibility becomes really a probability. That is my purpose in writing for as my object in life is to comfort and help you, so it is my last hope, should I be taken from you, I may not cause you too great a grief...Also I know that if in my last hour I am conscious, my chief consolation will be to feel that these thoughts may reach you...So, with all my love my darling Mum I now say goodbye, just in case. Try to forget my faults and to remember me only as your very loving son." His Observer, Lieut. J. Thompson, is buried nearby (X.A.16).

No Work Begun Shall Ever Pause For Death

His brother Harold is buried in Boisleux-au-Mont Communal Cemetery (3).

(X.A.14) 2nd Lieut. Horace George Cecil Bowden, 45th Sqdn., Royal Flying Corps: elder *s*. of the late George Henry Bowden, of Sunningdale, Reigate, L.D.S., R.C.S. Eng., and Glasgow, by his wife Ada Crouch (55, Ladbroke Road, Redhill, co. Surrey), *dau*. of Adnett Wraight: *b*. Reigate, co. Surrey, 3 January 1897: *educ*. Oakshade Preparatory School; and Cranleigh School, Cranleigh, where he matriculated at the age of 16, being awarded the St. Nicholas Scholarship (July 1913); member of the O.T.C.; rank Sergt. (1912). He represented his school at Bisley for the Ashburton Challenge Shield, 1913–1914, being Captain of the school team during the latter year, and won the Surrey Rifle Association's Silver Medal offered for the best shot among the Surrey Cadets. Was subsequently apprenticed to his father, and registered at Guy's Hospital as a Medical Student: joined Royal Engineers as Despatch Rider, February 1915: served with the Expeditionary Force in France and Flanders from 29 May following: invalided home September with a broken collarbone; returned to France, January 1916, but was recalled almost immediately to act as Instructor at Dunstable, there to await his commission: subsequently gazetted 2nd Lieut. R.F.C., 3 June 1916: obtained his wings October following, and returned to France: invalided into hospital at Havre November, suffering from blood-poisoning and rheumatism; kept there three months, owing to an outbreak of diptheria: rejoined his squadron February 1917, and was killed in aerial combat, 11 March following, while on patrol over the lines north-east of Ypres. Buried in the Military Cemetery at Lyssenthoek, near Poperinghe. His Commanding Officer, Major L.R. Read, wrote, "Your son was pilot in one machine (Sopwith Strutter A1071) and another machine with him (A1082) was flying over our lines, when two German machines attacked, and both our machines were brought down. I am sure it will be some consolation to you to know your son died a very gallant airman's death...Capt. E.F.P. Lubbock (X.A.13) was brought down first, and your son put up a very brave fight against superior odds, until he also was brought down. His death is felt very much by the whole squadron, and he was one of the best pilots in my squadron." And another officer, "Bowden was liked by everyone, a jolly good pilot and fellow too. We all miss him awfully. He was shot and killed instantly before ever his machine began to fall.": Age 20. *unm*.

(X.A.16) Lieut. John Thompson, General List attd. 45th Sqdn. Royal Flying Corps: Observer: s. of John Thompson, of West Park, South Shields: joined 16th (Service) Bn. (1st Tyneside Commercials) Northumberland Fusiliers, September 1914; after the outbreak of war: applied for and obtained a commission Temp. Sub. Lieut. Royal Naval Volunteer Reserve; served in the evacuation at Gallipoli: subsequently promoted Lieut., attd. R.F.C., and was killed in aerial combat, 13 March 1917, by Leut. P. Strähle, Jasta 18. Lieut. Thompson's aircraft, Sopwith Strutter A1082, was piloted by Capt. E.F.P. Lubbock (X.A.13).

(X.A.17) Lieut. Basil Menzies Morris, Canadian Engineers, C.E.F. attd. 6th Sqdn. Royal Flying Corps: s. of James L. Morris, of Pembroke, Ontario, by his wife Mary A.: b. Pembroke, 19 May 1895: educ. Pembroke Public (& High) School; University of Toronto, 1911–15 (Applied Science), B.A.S.C. (Civil Eng.): member 42nd Regt. Lieut. attd. C.O.T.C., apptd. Machine Gun Officer, 59th Battn., May 1915: transf'd. No.1 Tunnelling Coy. late 1915; proceeded to France, February 1916: served with his unit in the Ypres salient until January 1917, when he was seconded to 6th Sqdn. R.F.C.: obtained his Observer's Wings the following month, and was killed, 17 March 1917. When flying over the Ypres sector, his machine was hit by anti-aircraft fire and collapsed. Buried at Remy Siding, nr. Poperinghe: Age 21.

(X.A.18) 2nd Lieut. Francis Gore, 23rd (Service) Bn. (2nd Football) The Duke of Cambridge's Own (Middlesex Regt.): s. of Lieut. Augustus Frederick Wentworth Gore, 7th Hussars (served in the Indian Mutiny), by his wife the Hon. Ann Emily Gore: late *husb*. to F.R.M. Gore ('The Elms,' 63, Thrale Road, Streatham, London, S.W.): died of wounds, 26 March 1917: Age 37.

Rest In Peace

(X.A.25) 2nd Lieut. Leonard Stanley Witt, 'A' Bty., 104th Bde. Royal Field Artillery: s. of William Charles Witt, Traveller; of Kildare, Hardwicke Rd., Palmer's Green, London N., by his wife Sarah Henrietta, *dau*. of Thomas Burt: and brother to Gnr. 201955 C.W. Witt, Royal Field Artillery, killed in action nr. Boesinghe, Belgium, 20 October 1917, while carrying despatches: b. Clapham, SW., 1 September 1888: *educ*. Clacton Grammar School: Occupation – Staff employee; Baltic Shipping Exchange: joined Honourable Artillery Company (no.289) 1911; mobilised on the outbreak of war, August 1914: served with the Egyptian Expeditionary Force from February 1915: returned to England May following and, after a period of training at Exeter and Shoeburyness, gazetted 2nd Lieut. Royal Field Artillery 2 September 1916: proceeded to France 3 January 1917, and died at No.2 Canadian Casualty Clearing Station, Poperinghe, 2 May following, from wounds received in action at Ypres the previous day. Buried in the Military Cemetery, Lyssenthoek. His Commanding Officer wrote, "His first thought when wounded was of others, and typified the gallant, unselfish officer he was, as he shouted that no one was to come near him as he could manage to reach a dug-out himself, although he knew himself that he couldn't, but didn't want to risk his comrades. He will not easily be forgotten by any of us," and another officer, "Your brother and myself were the greatest of friends. His persistent good spirits and the fact that he was always most jovial even under the most trying circumstances made him the very best fellow in the world. There was not a man in the battery who did not adore him and that speaks for itself.": Age 28. *unm.*

Died Of Wounds
Fearless, True And Beloved By All

His brother Claude is buried in Artillery Wood Cemetery (I.D.9).

(X.A.27) 2nd Lieut. Henry George Neville, 20th Sqdn. Royal Flying Corps: only *s.* of George Neville, of 25, Lopen Road, Upper Edmonton, London, N., by his wife Jane, *dau.* of James Hillyer: *b.* Hackney, London, E., 2 December 1894: *educ.* there: Occupation – Builder: gazetted 2nd Lieut. 6 December 1916: served with the Expeditionary Force in France and Flanders from 6 April 1917, and died at Poperinghe, 9 May, after receiving wounds in action two days previously. When on a bombing mission, the aircraft he was in was hit by anti-aircraft fire over Vlamertinghe and forced to land. The pilot, Lieut. F.J. Smart was also wounded: Age 22. *unm.* (*IWGC record 10 May, age 23*)

Sleep On Beloved Until The Dawn Breaks

(X.A.30) Lieut. Col. William Briggs Grandage, 235th Bde. Royal Field Artillery: *s.* of Abraham (& Ruth) Grandage, of Kent House, Rawdon, nr. Leeds: *educ.* Chevin Dell Boarding School, Otley; Sedbergh School; Clare College, Cambridge University (B.A.); St. Bartholomews Hospital, graduated M.D.: member of University of London O.T.C., in which he held a commission (Capt.): volunteered on the outbreak of war, apptd. Major, Royal Field Artillery, August 1914; promoted Lieut. Col. (Temp.) April 1916: proceeded to France 26 February 1917. Died of wounds, 14 May 1917, received from the bursting of a shell as he was walking from his headquarters to that of a nearby infantry brigade in the vicinity of Swan Chateau: Age 37. He was married to Helen Mary Gwatkin-Williams, *née* Grandage, *née* Landale (74, Gloucester Road, London, S.W.7).

(X.A.45) Capt. William Ernest Ind, M.C., Adjt., 1/15th (County of London) Bn. (Prince of Wales' Own Civil Service Rifles) The London Regt. (T.F.): *s.* of William Herbert Ind, of Duckmanton, Chesterfield, by his wife Martha Ann.

Died of wounds, 7 June 1917, received in action nr. White Chateau, before Hollebeke, in support to 140th Brigade's attack at the Battle of Messines. An able officer and a very gallant gentleman, his loss was keenly felt throughout the Division. Awarded the Military Cross, 1 January 1917: Age 25. *unm*. His friend and former Comdg. Officer, Lieut. Col. H.H. Kemble, O.C. 3rd London Regt., died in the same ward the same night.

(X.A.46) Lieut.Col. Henry Herbert Kemble, D.S.O., M.C., Comdg. 3rd (City of London) Bn. (Royal Fusiliers) The London Regt. (T.F.): c/o Miss M.E. Kemble (Lady Margaret Hall Settlement, 131, Kensington Road, London, S.E.11): *s*. of the late William Kemble, Indian Civil Service, by his wife Elizabeth Emma (Beechfield, Bathampton, co. Somerset): *b*. Purneah, India: Occupation – Tutor; Bath School. Died of wounds, 7 June 1917: Age 40. Remembered on Bathampton War Memorial.

(X.B.6) Pte. 33180, James Salisbury Price, 13th (Service) Bn. The South Wales Borderers attd. 21st Bn. The Welsh Regt.: *s*. of James Price, of Bristol House, 6, Queen Street, Nantyglo, co. Brecon (lately Surgery Road, Blaina), Horsekeeper, by his wife Eliza, *dau*. of William Salisbury: *b*. Purvin Hope, Leominster, co. Hereford, 3 July 1897: *educ*. there and Blaina: Occupation – Fitter: enlisted 24 September 1915: served with the Expeditionary Force in France and Flanders from 17 August 1916, and died at No.10 Casualty Clearing Station 15 September as a result of wounds received in action at Ypres. Buried on the Poperinghe Road, Lyssenthoek. His Captain wrote, "His coolness under fire was a great inspiration to the younger members of his platoon.": Age 19. (*IWGC record 32061*)

Peace Perfect Peace With Loved Ones Far Away

(X.B.1) Pte. 3095, Victor Charles Friberg, 8th Bn. Australian Infantry, A.I.F.: *s*. of Anders F. Friberg, of 'Mootala,' Locksley Road, Ivanhoe, Victoria, by his wife Amelia Bernadine: *b*. Canning Street, North Carlton, Victoria, May 1893: *educ*. Lee Street State School: 5'6" tall, fresh complexion, blue eyes, fair hair: Religion – Church of England: prior to enlistment – Melbourne, 22 August 1915–was 6 years apprentice Cabinetmaker to his father: posted 22nd Depot Battn. 3 September; 4th Depot Battn. 11 October; 1st Depot Battn. Seymour, 18 October; transf'd. 7th Rfts. 24th Battn. 16 November: departed Melbourne, HMAT A73 'Commonwealth,' 20 November 1915, proceeded to Alexandria, joined 8th Battn. Serapeum, 24 February 1916: served with the Expeditionary Force in France and Flanders from 31 March following: admitted 2nd Field Ambulance, 17 June (Pyrexia and Influenza), transf'd. 1st (Divisional Rest Station) the following day from whence he was discharged to duty 29 June. Severely wounded in action (G.S.W. both legs, Rt. thigh), 11 September 1916;

admitted No.10 C.C.S. where, after amputation of both legs, he died later the same day. Buried Lyssenthoek Military Cemetery, 1¼ miles S.W. of Poperinghe: Age 23. *unm*. His effects – Identity Discs (2), Letters, Wallets (2), Photos, Pouch, Pipe, Knives (2), Fountain Pen, Wristwatch & Strap, Belt, Hat Badge, Handkerchiefs, Pocket Diary, Draught Pieces, Fruit Fork – Victory Medal, Memorial Scroll and two photographs of his grave were received by his mother, Mrs Friberg (June 1917–February 1923); being unable to attend in person his father authorised a Mr & Mrs Cracken to collect his son's Memorial Plaque (February 1921).

In Memory Of Our Dear Son
The Lord Gave And The Lord Hath Taken Away

In her request for a photograph of Victor's grave Mrs Friberg would have been well aware that for many mothers there would be no possibility of such because their sons and husbands had no known grave; they were among 'the legions of the lost' remembered solely by name, rank and number somewhere on a memorial, perhaps buried beneath an anonymous headstone bearing the words 'A Soldier of The Great War – Known Unto God.' Thousands of relatives requested photographs; they served as keepsakes, proof positive their loved one was 'gone before,' and as an assurance to the bereaved that despite whatever distance might be involved, their son, husband, father, brother had a place that family members could always visit. A close relative placed a framed photograph of Victor on his grave with the lines "Son, brother and uncle, you lie under a Belgian sky but your memory and spirit lives on under the Southern Cross. Lest We Forget" – they had travelled over 12,000 miles to do so.

"No-one who was present at the memorial service at the Lijssenthoek Military Cemetery this morning will ever forget that slow-moving procession of a thousand lion-hearted bereaved parents, widows and orphans shuffling along the Poperinghe road under the hot sun, with shawls and rugs slung over their shoulders, artificial flowers and brown paper parcels in their arms, gathered from Ayr and Cornwall, Halifax and Lincoln, Balham and Barnstaple, to pay homage to their glorious dead." *Daily Express* reporting on the St. Barnabas Pilgrimage, 1923.

(X.B.8A) Pte. 414818, Gorden De Young, 60th (Victoria Rifles of Canada) Bn. Canadian Infantry, C.E.F.: *s*. of James De Young, of 24, West Street, Halifax, Nova Scotia, and his late wife Ellen: *b*. Halifax, 2 April 1899 (attested 1897): Religion – Roman Catholic: Occupation – Pipe Fitter: joined C.E.F., Halifax, 6 August 1915 (aged 16 years); apptd. 40th Bn. 11 August: proceeded overseas transf'd. 60th Bn. November following: served with the Expeditionary Force in France from 21 February 1916, and died of wounds (shellshock; internal trauma), No.3 C.C.S., 18

September 1916; attributable to the recent engagements (12–24 August) in which the battalion were involved at Hill 60: Age 17. (*IWGC record age 18*).

Gone But Not Forgotten

(X.B.11) Pte. 138559, Joseph Buchanan Duffie, 60th (Victoria Rifles of Canada) Bn. Canadian Infantry, C.E.F.: *s.* of William J. (& Sarah) Duffie: *b*. Londonderry, Ireland, 21 June 1891: Religion – Church of England: Occupation – Labourer: serving member of the Militia; joined 60th C.E.F. Toronto 15 July 1915; departed Montreal 5 November: served with the Expeditionary Force in France from 21 February 1916, and died of wounds (trench mortar shards; Anterior Lt. knee, Lt. leg) No.17 C.C.S., 26 September 1916; received Support Trench, Hill 60, night of 14–15 August inst.: Age 25. Correspondence to be addressed c/o his sister Mrs J. Mooney (40, Ballyclare Street, Belfast).

Peace Perfect Peace

For most of those who died in the war their graves would be too far away to visit, the expense of foreign travel prohibitive to all but the wealthy. After the war many of the bereaved chose to take advantage of pilgrimages organised voluntarily by the Church Army and the Salvation Army, who had assisted family members to visit critically wounded soldiers during the war. In the 1920's the St. Barnabas Society, founded by New Zealand Padre, Rev. A. Mullineux, took parties of pilgrims to Italy, Greece, Gallipoli and the Western Front; The War Graves Association, founded by Mrs S.A. Smith, of Leeds, who had lost her son in the war, organised a pilgrimage every Whitsuntide. The Ypres League, whose principal objectives were 'to commemorate the Immortal Defence of the Salient, and to keep alive that spirit of fellowship which was so powerful a lever and so beautiful an element in the war' also organised pilgrimages. By the late 1920's the British Legion played a significant role in organising what had become by then closely akin to battlefield tours. But, for many thousands who fell in the war their families would never see their graves; they would never receive the comfort of a visit from home. Many graves bear the epitaph: '*May some kind hand in that distant land place a flower on his grave for me, sorrowing mother.*' Sixteen year old Robert Murray's parents never chose an epitaph, perhaps because no words of sentiment could ever express their grief.

> And now they are sleeping their long last sleep,
> Their graves I may never see;
> But some gentle hand in that distant land
> May scatter some flowers for me.

(X.B.24A) Pte. 5747, Robert Cooper James Murray, 1st Bn. Australian Infantry, A.I.F.: late c/o Mrs F.A. Murray (Smithfield, nr. Fairfield, Sydney): *s.* of Reginald Edward Murray (late 17th Battn. A.I.F.), of Lloyd George Street, Oatley, New South Wales, by his wife Ada: and nephew to Pte. 236, H.C.M. Carter, 1st Australian Infantry, killed in action, 7 August 1915, at Lone Pine, Gallipoli: *b.* Penrith, New South Wales: *educ.* Petersham High School: occupation – Clerk: joined A.I.F. Casula 9 February 1916; posted 18th Rfts.: proceeded overseas, HMAT A55 'Kyarra,' 3 June 1916 (arrived Plymouth, 3 August): served with the Expeditionary Force in France and Flanders from 21 August, joining 1st Battn. In the Field, 5 September 1916. Capt. W.L. Archer wrote, "He was very badly wounded in both legs, and died on his way to 3rd Canadian Casualty Clearing Station on October 4th (1916). He was buried the following day in the Military Cemetery, Lyssenthoek, Map Location, Sheet 27, L22.D6.3, and the number of the grave is 10.B.24.": Age 16 years, 6 months. His attestation papers record age 18½, and were obviously completed on his behalf by a third party – possibly the attesting official – as Pte. Murray's signature bears no resemblance to any part of the other handwriting.

His uncle Hugh is buried in Lone Pine Cemetery, Anzac (II.B.12).

(X.B.37A) Pte. 8, Coulkchoue Azieff, 'A' Coy. 26th Bn. Australian Infantry, A.I.F.: late of Brisbane, Queensland: *s.* of Sergei Azieff, by his wife Katarno (Ferskaja Oblast, Vladikavkasky, Caucasus, Rossiia): *b.* Vladikavkasky Okrong, 1894: emigrated Australia, via Nagasaki, Japan, 1914: Religion – Russian Orthodox: Occupation – Labourer: enlisted Rockhampton, 25 February 1915: 5'7" tall, grey-brown eyes, dark hair: admonished by his Comdg. Officer, 24 April 1915, after being reported by Lieut. Hannay and Pte. P.J. Maher for 'Gambling;' and departed Australia aboard HMAT 'Ascanius' same day: posted 'A' Coy. 26th Battn. Enoggera, 23 May: served at Gallipoli, Egypt, and with the Expeditionary Force in France and Flanders from 21 March 1916, and died at No.17 C.C.S., France, 17 October 1916, of wounds (G.S.W. multiple) received in action the previous day: Age 20. *unm.* Buried in Lyssenthoek Military Cemetery, 1¾ miles south-west of Poperinghe, later the same day. *(IWGC record 25th Bn.)* See account re. Pte. W.G. Azerkoff, Messines Ridge British Cemetery (V.C.21).

(X.B.44A) Pte. 8015, Arthur Cambridge, 7th (City of London) Bn. The London Regt. (T.F.): formerly no.5492, 3/19th London Regt.: *s.* of Arthur Henry Cambridge, of 31, Olney Street, Walworth, London, by his wife Mary, *née* Boyens: and elder brother to Boy W.A. Cambridge, S.S. 'Aragon,' Mercantile Marine, lost when that ship was sunk by the German submarine U.54, 30 December 1917: enlisted Southwark: served with the Expeditionary Force in France and Flanders from March 1915, and died of wounds (G.S.W. chest), 29 October 1916: Age 20.

Gone Dear One But Not Forgotten

With no known grave but the sea, his brother William is commemorated on the Tower Hill Memorial, London.

(X.C.8) Pte. 7541, Graham Wellesley Hopper, 22nd (County of London) Bn. (The Queen's) The London Regt. (T.F.): formerly no.4692, 12th London Regt. (Rangers): *s.* of the late Henry Hopper, by his wife Jane (38, Elms Avenue, Muswell Hill, London): *b.* Croydon, co. Surrey, 1897: enlisted Holborn. Died of wounds, 12 November 1916: Age 19.

I Struck One Chord Of Music Like The Sound Of A Great Amen

(X.C.14A) Pte. 8193, Cecil Arthur Hallworth, 7th (Service) Bn. The Royal Fusiliers (City of London Regt.): only *s.* of John Hallworth, Railway Clerk; of 4, Canterbury Road, Watford, by his wife Harriet Eliza: *b.* Watford, co. Hertford, 27 February 1887: *educ.* St. Augustine's School, Kilburn, London, N.W.: Occupation – Railway Clerk: enlisted 25th Battn. London Regt. (Cyclists) 28 October 1915; transf'd. 7th Battn.: served with the Expeditionary Force in France and Flanders from 24 October 1916. Wounded (G.S.W. chest, Penet.) 27 December 1916, and died the following day at No.3 Canadian Casualty Clearing Station. Buried in Lijssenthoek Military Cemetery, Poperinghe: Age 29. *unm.*

God Gave Him A Work To Do And He Did It

(X.C.16A) Pte. 5217, Daniel Hugh Reynish, 23rd (County of London) Bn. The London Regt. (T.F.): late of Battersea, London, S.W.: *s.* of James Reynish, of 60, Barn Street, Haverfordwest, co. Pembroke, by his wife Elizabeth J.: and elder brother to Pte. 33510, S.J. Reynish, Devonshire Regt., killed in action, 4 September 1916, at Salonika: *b.* Haverfordwest, 1881: enlisted Battersea. Died of acute cardiac dilatation, 27 November 1916: Age 35.

Not Gone From Memory Nor From Love But To Our Father's Home Above

His brother Sidney has no known grave; he is commemorated on the Doiran Memorial.

(X.C.21A) Pte. 60111, Morton Bostwick Allen, 21st Bn. Canadian Infantry (Eastern Ontario Regt.), C.E.F.: *s.* of James (& Leona) Allen, of Kingston, Ontario: late *husb.* to Minnie B. Allen (425, Fell Street, San Francisco, California; c/o. British Consulate, San Francisco): *b.* 3 September 1878: Religion – Church of England: Occupation – Chauffeur: previously served 7 yrs. 14th P.W.O. Regt.; 3 yrs. Governor General's Body-Guard; 2 yrs. 47th Battn.; 9 months 2nd C.M.R.

(serving): joined C.E.F., Sandling Camp, Shorncliffe, co. Kent, England, 9 June 1915; apptd. 21st Bn. 2 July: served with the Expeditionary Force in France from 15 September 1915. Accidentally run over by an ambulance on the main road between Zillebeke and Lille Gate, Ypres, night of 2 December 1916; died from injuries received (contused scalp, five ribs fractured) No.2 Casualty Clearing Station, Poperinghe, 3 December 1916: Age 38. (*IWGC record age 37*)

Mortal Sacrifice...Is Immortal Service

(X.C.23) Rfn. 6492, Charles John Logan Surridge, 8th (City of London) Bn. (Post Office Rifles) The London Regt. (T.F.): formerly no.3653, 6th East Surrey Regt.: *s.* of Charles Surridge, of 153, Amesbury Avenue, Streatham Hill, London, S.W., by his wife Mary Ann: *b.* 1896: Occupation – Clerk; London County Council: enlisted Streatham, 6 February 1915: served with the Expeditionary Force in France and Flanders from 1 September 1916, and died at No.2 Canadian C.C.S., Poperinghe, 6 December 1916, of blood poisoning (septicaemia) consequent to a wound in the hand received in action at Ypres: Age 20. *unm.*

He Laid His Joys Aside For Us

(X.C.24A) Pte. 25262, Frank Collins, 12th (Service) Bn. (Bermondsey) The East Surrey Regt.: formerly no.23322, Middlesex Regt.: *b.* Stratford: enlisted Tottenham. Mortally wounded by a sniper in No.1 Crater, St. Eloi, died 7 December 1916.

Always In The Memory Of His Loving Wife

Although highly disputed, the resurgence of cerebrospinal meningitis in Great Britain in 1915 is widely believed to be directly attributable to the arrival of a particularly virulent strain of the virus brought over by the Canadian contingents in the late autumn of 1914. With several cases of the disease diagnosed in their home camps before embarkation, further cases aboard the overcrowded troop ships enroute to England, and a sharp outbreak recorded on their arrival on Salisbury Plain; it was several weeks before it was first noticed among British troops. At Eastney Barracks, Portsmouth, it began on 15 January 1915 among men who had come into contact with a visiting Canadian football team six days previously; at Caterham the first victim was a man who had travelled down overnight by train from Scotland sharing a compartment with three Canadian soldiers.

Due in no small measure to investigations carried out by bacteriological specialists within the military medical services the disease mortality rate diminished towards the latter part of 1915 and seemed to be under control throughout most of 1916, but in early 1917 it rose again claiming civilian and military personnel in equal numbers.

(X.C.27A) Rfn. R/25457, Ernest Augustus Ottley, 21st (Service) Bn. (Yeoman Rifles) The King's Royal Rifle Corps: *s*. of the late George Ottley, by his wife Mary (Alben Road, Binfield, Bracknell, co. Berks): *b*. Sherborne, St. John, co. Hants, *c*.1887: enlisted Lambeth, London. Died of cerebrospinal meningitis, 14 December 1916: Age 29. He leaves a wife, Rose Violet (8, Milbrook Road, Brixton, London). (*SDGW record Ernest Austin*) See also Rfn. N. Derwent (XIV.E.4A)

Gone But Not Forgotten

(X.C.36A) L/Corpl. 6271, George Thomas Clark, 10th Bn. The Northumberland Fusiliers: *b*. Newcastle-on-Tyne. Died 9 p.m., 21 December 1916 of wounds, (severe abdominal) received from shellfire while at duty with Capt. McKerrow at Maple Copse the previous morning.

Capt. McKerrow is buried nearby (IX.B.15).

(X.C.38A) Pte. 4062, John Henry Clarke, 1/4th Bn. The King's Own (Royal Lancaster Regt.), (T.F.): *s*. of James Clarke of Wigan, by his wife Maggie: volunteered and undertook Foreign Service obligations, Bolton, August 1914: served with the Expeditionary Force in France and Flanders from 5 May 1915, and died in the Casualty Clearing Station, Poperinghe, of multiple bullet wounds, 23 December 1916, being shot in the arm and through the chest and lung in the early hours of the same day while taking part in a raid on the German trenches in the St. Julien sub-sector. Buried in the Military Cemetery on the Lyssenthoek – Boeschepe Road: Age 27. He was married to Mrs E. Pilkington, *née* Clarke (136, Holland Street, Bolton). See L/Sergt. M.Caddy, Ypres (Menin Gate) Memorial (Panel 12).

(X.C.39) Pte. 2783, Arthur Akred, 1/4th Bn. The King's Own (Royal Lancaster Regt.), (T.F.): a pre-war Territorial, volunteered and undertook Foreign Service obligations, Ulverston, co. Lancaster, August 1914: served with the Expeditionary Force in France and Flanders from 5 May 1915, and died of wounds, Christmas Day, 25 December 1916, received in action in the early hours of the 23rd while taking part in a raid on the German trenches in the St. Julien sub-sector: Age 26. He leaves a wife, Annie (94, Lonsdale Road, Millom). See L/Sergt. M.Caddy, Ypres (Menin Gate) Memorial (Panel 12).

Rest In Peace

From Wife & Family

(X.C.39A) L/Corpl. 2658, James Little, 1/4th Bn. The King's Own (Royal Lancaster Regt.), (T.F.): *s.* of Robert Little, of 9, Nelson Street, Millom, co. Cumberland, by his wife Elizabeth Mary: *b.* Millom, 1894: a pre-war Territorial, volunteered and undertook Foreign Service obligations, Ulverston, co. Lancaster, August 1914: served with the Expeditionary Force in France and Flanders from 5 May 1915, and died of wounds (G.S.) at Poperinghe, 26 December 1916, received in action in the early hours of the 23rd while taking part in a raid on the German trench – Cameron Support – in the St. Julien sub-sector: Age 22. *unm.* See L/Sergt. M.Caddy, Ypres (Menin Gate) Memorial (Panel 12).

Peace Perfect Peace

(X.C.40) Pte. 4900, Thomas Ashton, 1/4th Bn. The King's Own (Royal Lancaster Regt.), (T.F.): *s.* of Nathaniel Ashton, of 750, Oldham Road, Bardsley, Ashton-under-Lyne, co. Lancaster, by his wife Sarah Ann: *b.* 1895: a pre-war Territorial, volunteered and undertook Foreign Service obligations, Bolton, co. Lancaster, on the outbreak of war August 1914: served with the Expeditionary Force in France and Flanders from 5 May 1915, and died of wounds, 26 December 1916, received in action three days previously while taking part in a raid on the German trenches in the St. Julien sub-sector: Age 21. *unm.* See L/Sergt. M.Caddy, Ypres (Menin Gate) Memorial (Panel 12).

Asleep In Jesus

(X.C.42A) Sergt. 1948, Harold Brushett, 'X' 41st Trench Mortar Bty., Royal Field Artillery: formerly 2nd Dragoon Guards: late of Elmsdale Avenue, Foles Hill, Coventry: *yst. s.* of the late George Sidney Brushett, and his wife Sarah, *née* Pearce: c/o A.S. Brushett Esq., 86, Camden Street, Walsall, co. Stafford: *b.* Kidderminster, co. Worcester: former employee Coventry Chain Co. Ltd.: enlisted Coventry: served with the Expeditionary Force in France from April 1916: died of wounds, 28 December 1916, received consequent to a bombardment of the German lines the previous evening. In a letter to Mrs Brushett Lieut. G. Tilley, R.F.A. wrote, "For the last six months he had served under me and, during all that time, I could not have wished for a better or more cheerful worker. I feel that in losing him the Battery has lost its best man.": Age 24. (*IWGC record age 28*)

To Know Him Was To Love Him

After the war scientific examination of hospital records showed that nephritis, after frostbite and venereal disease, was one of the biggest causes of admission for sickness, and concluded that the fatigue of trench life aggravated by exposure to the elements and infestation by lice and other vermin were the main causes of the condition which in a considerable number of cases proved fatal. The onset of the condition – breathlessness, severe headaches, coughing spasms, vomiting, pains in the extremities and chest – could continue over a period of several months or just a few weeks and in severe cases a combination of uraemia and rapid weight loss led to enlargement of the heart, cerebral haemorrhage and kidney failure.

(X.C.43) Rfn. C/12324, George Stephenson, 21st (Service) Bn. (Yeoman Rifles) The King's Royal Rifle Corps: *s.* of Isabella Stephenson (Great Ryde, Whittingham, co. Northumberland). Died of nephritis, 28 December 1916: Age 36.

(X.C.44) Pte. 4606, Arthur Leonard, 1/4th Bn. The Loyal North Lancashire Regt. (T.F.): *s.* of George Leonard, of 42, Plover Street, Preston, co. Lancaster, by his late wife Hannah: and elder brother to Pte. 11682, G. Leonard, Scots Guards, died of wounds, 28 June 1916: enlisted Preston. Died of wounds, 30 December 1916, received in action at Ypres: Age 24. *unm.*

On Whose Soul Sweet Jesus Have Mercy

His brother George is buried nearby (VIII.B.22).

(X.D.11A) Rfn. 3697, George Henry Joy, 17th (County of London) Bn. (Poplar & Stepney Rifles) The London Regt. (T.F.): *s.* of William Nicholas (& Elizabeth Margaret) Joy, of Old Ford, Bow, London, E.: volunteered and enlisted Tredegar Road, Bow: served with the Expeditionary Force in France and Flanders from 12 July 1915. Died of wounds, 9 January 1917: Age 19. First afforded the comfort of a visit from home, 10 November 2014; his family recorded;- "George, We cannot shake your hand, Nor look you in the eye, But we will remember. Stay forever young in everlasting peace."

(X.D.17A) Rfn. 6406, Sidney William Corner, 21st (County of London) Bn. (First Surrey Rifles) The London Regt. (T.F.): *s.* of William Corner, of Battersea, by his wife Eliza: late *husb.* to L. Winifred Corner (30, Ursula Street, Battersea, London). Died of albuminuria (kidney disease), 11 January 1917: Age 28.

Gone From Our Sight But Not From Our Hearts

(X.D.26A) L/Corpl. G/24255, William Abrey, 10th Bn. The Queen's Own (Royal West Kent Regt.): eldest *s.* of the late William (& Mrs) Abrey, of High Street, Ingatestone, co. Essex: *b.* Ingatestone: enlisted Norwich, co. Norfolk.

Died of wounds (G.S.W. Back, Fractured Spine) at No.3 Canadian C.C.S. 19 January 1917. Buried in the cemetery Poperinghe: Age 23. He leaves a wife, Agnes M. Abrey (80, Russell Street, Peterborough, co. Northampton), to whom he had been married for but a short time. Remembered on Ingatestone & Fryerning Roll of Honour.

In Loving Hearts He Lives For Evermore

(X.D.33) Pte. 35346, Robert Marsden, 8th (Service) Bn. The King's Own (Yorkshire Light Infantry): *s.* of Mary Ellen Marsden (61, Grimshaw Park, Blackburn): *b.* Withnell, co. Lancaster: enlisted Pontefract. Died of wounds, 24 January 1917, received during a raid on the enemy lines the previous evening. See account re. Capt. M.G. Donahoo (X.A.2).

(X.D.34A) Pte. 38330, George Nelson, 8th (Service) Bn. The King's Own (Yorkshire Light Infantry): formerly no.20289, King's Own Scottish Borderers: *s.* of George Nelson, of 10, Strathallan Terrace, Dowanhill, Glasgow: *b.* Barony, co. Lanark: *educ.* Hillhead High School; Glasgow University (Medicine): enlisted Glasgow, May 1915: served in France from 29 September following; wounded November (sniper bullet); invalided home: returned to France, June 1916; transf'd. 8th K.O.Y.L.I. in consequence of losses incurred during the Somme Offensive. Died of wounds, 24 January 1917, received the previous evening during a raid on the enemy lines: Age 24. A quiet unassuming, reserved and thoughtful man, the sights and sounds of war were altogether hateful to his nature and it was only his compelling sense of right and duty that brought him to the battlefield. He was married to Barbara Cuthbertson, *née* Nelson (102, Kenmure Street, Pollokshields, Glasgow). See account re. Capt. M.G. Donahoo (X.A.2).

(X.D.37) Pte. 2292, John Backhouse, 8th (Service) Bn. The King's Own (Yorkshire Light Infantry): foster *s.* of Jane Brownlow (51, Nelson Street, Otley, co. York): *b.* Barrow-in-Furness, co. Lancaster: enlisted Keighley: served in France and Flanders from 26 August 1915, and died of wounds, 26 January 1917, received during a raid on the enemy lines three nights previously: Age 46. See account re. Capt. M.G. Donahoo (X.A.2).

In Loving Memory
Died In Action
Sadly Missed But Fondly Remembered

(XI.A.11A) Coy.Sergt.Major 320045, John Thomas Graysmark, 6th (City of London) Bn. (Rifles) The London Regt. (T.F.): *s.* of George Graysmark, of 44, Brookehouse Road, Bellingham; formerly of Forest Hill, London, S.E., by his wife Emily: and brother to Pte. 249984, E.J. Graysmark, 58th Canadian Infantry, killed in action, 7 August 1918; and Pte. 164246, W. Graysmark, 75th Canadian Infantry, killed in action, 9 April 1917, at Vimy: *b*. Lewisham: enlisted London: served in France from 18 March 1915, and died, 9 February 1917, of wounds received in action vicinity The Bluff – Hill 60: Age 37. Mentioned in Despatches and awarded the Croix de Guerre (with palms), France; he was married to Florence R. Walters, *née* Graysmark (24A, Ewart Road, Forest Hill).

His brother Ernest is buried in Longueau British Cemetery (II.E.8); William lies in Canadian Cemetery No.2, Neuville-St. Vaast (5.D.1).

(XI.A.21) Pte. 6598, Henry George Jupp, 3/1st Bn. The Cambridgeshire Regt. (T.F.): eldest *s*. of George Jupp, by his wife Mary Ann, *dau*. of T. Gaylor: *b*. Brighton, co. Sussex, 5 May 1875: *educ*. Dorman's Land: Occupation – Nursery Gardener: enlisted New Barnet, 24 June 1916: served with the Expeditionary Force in France and Flanders from 10 December following, and died in No.10 Casualty Clearing Station, 14 February 1917, from wounds received in action. Buried on the Poperinghe Road, Lyssenthoek: Age 42. His Captain wrote, "He was on duty with a working party behind the firing lines, the same shell wounding a comrade. Nothing, I know, will console you in your hour of grief but, as his Company Officer, I might say that he was a good and well-liked soldier, and died nobly for his country." He *m*. Hoddesdon, 6 May 1899, Alice Margaret (40, Brunswick Crescent, New Southgate), *dau*. of William Henry Seabrook, and had four children – George, *b*. 29 October 1899; Dora, *b*. 24 March 1901, and Ralph and Eliza (twins), *b*. 24 March 1901.

Gone But Not Forgotten By His Loving Wife And Children

(XI.A.35) Pte. 25479, Walter Henry Charman, 12th (Service) Bn. (Bermondsey) The East Surrey Regt.: formerly no.2997, Surrey Yeomanry: *s*. of Richard Charman, of 88, High Street, Purley, co. Surrey, by his wife Clara J.: *b*. Purley: enlisted Clapham: served in France from May 1916, and died of wounds, 22 February 1917: Age 21. *unm*.

Thy Will Be Done

(XI.A.36) Pte. G/11471, Thomas James Cecil, 10th (Service) Bn. The Queen's Own (Royal West Kent Regt.): *s*. of the late Thomas James Cecil, by his wife Sarah (27, Quaker Street, Spitalfields, London, E.): *b*. Quaker Street, 25 November 1896: Occupation – Carman: enlisted Royal West Kent Regt., 12 November 1915: served with the Expeditionary Force in France and Flanders from March 1916, and died at No.10 Casualty Clearing Station, 22 February 1917, consequent to multiple shrapnel wounds and being severely crushed (multiple contusions, compound fractures) when a portion of the company's trench was hit and collapsed by shellfire. Buried in Lyssenthoek Military Cemetery, nr. Poperinghe: Age 20. *unm*.

Dearly Loved So Sadly Missed

(XI.B.13A) Pte. 633030, Arthur Edwin Bronsdon, 20th (County of London) Bn. (Blackheath & Woolwich) The London Regt. (T.F.): *s*. of the late Charles Bronsdon, Builder, of 8, Grotes Place, Blackheath, London, S.E., by his wife Laura, *dau*. of Alfred Postle: *b*. Blackheath, 11 November 1890: *educ*. St. Michael's School: Occupation – Clerk; London Stock Exchange: enlisted Woolwich, 9 June 1916: served with the Expeditionary Force in France and Flanders, and died 1 March 1917, from wounds (G.S. abdominal, facial) received in action the previous day. Buried at Poperinghe: Age 26. *unm*.

Rest In Peace

By August 1914 over a decade had passed since the war against the Boers in South Africa, but a series of blunders and costly lessons learned in that conflict remained fresh in the national consciousness and, among the public, the image of the Army and its efficiency was the subject of much speculation. But, for a considerable number of the thousands of young men who rushed to enlist, the Army held a certain romantic attraction. Raised on tales of high adventure and deeds of daring performed throughout the Empire, standing in remembrance of Trafalgar, Waterloo, Balaclava, Rorkes Drift, celebrating public holidays on the anniversaries of Mafeking and Ladysmith; imaginings of performing acts of bravery and winning medals were in no small measure responsible for inducing many to enlist, and if this should bring reward in the form of female admiration or the respect of one's peers – then so be it.

For some, the Army provided a refuge, an escape from the problems of everyday life and, besides its fair share of runaways and recruits from the margins of criminality, it also drew in those who had no family and few friends. A veteran of the Seaforth Highlanders recalled a man in his unit to whom the Army was his family; he had come from a Barnardo's background, had no relatives, never received any mail and had little contact outside of the regiment.

Although very little is known about William Crabbe, he would, in all probability, have fitted into the same category. His early life would not have been particularly happy or stable; an Enfield Barnardo's orphan, at some time prior to enlistment, he had been boarded out to someone unknown fifty miles away in the village of Penn, near High Wycombe. The only ascertainable difference between William and the case of the Seaforth Highlander is that after William's death the unknown Penn villager obviously mourned his loss, evidenced by the simple choice of sentiment in his epitaph.

(XI.B.18A) Pte. 632176, William Crabbe, 20th (County of London) Bn. (Blackheath & Woolwich) The London Regt. (T.F.): *b.* Enfield, co. Middlesex, *c.*1896: an orphan from Dr. Barnardo's Home, boarded out to someone unknown in the village of Penn, near High Wycombe: enlisted Lewisham, London, S.E. Died of wounds (G.S.W. back), No.3 Canadian Casualty Clearing Station 4 March 1917: Age 20. *unm.* Remembered on Tylers Green (St. Margaret's Churchyard) War Memorial.

Peace Perfect Peace

Gentle Jesus, meek and mild, Pray for me an orphan child.
Be my strength, be my friend; Stay with me until the end.

Anon.

(XI.B.32) Coy.Sergt.Major 241167, Charles Lamb, 1/5th Bn. The King's Own (Royal Lancaster Regt.), (T.F.): *s.* of the late Fred Lamb, by his wife Jane Anne (16, Norfolk Street, Skerton, co. Lancaster): and brother to Pte. 62612, A. Lamb, Welch Regt. (Depot), died 15 October 1918, in Northampton Hospital, of wounds received in France: *b.* Lancaster: enlisted there: served in France from 4 June 1915, and died of wounds, 13 March 1917: Age 31. He leaves a wife, Mrs A. Lamb (102, Prospect Street, Lancaster). Three other brothers also served.

One I Loved But Could Not Save

His brother Alfred is buried in Lancaster (Skerton) Cemetery (A.CE.547).

(XI.B.34) L/Corpl. G/4539, John Enticknap, 13th (Service) Bn. (3rd South Down) The Royal Sussex Regt.: *s.* of Charles Enticknap, of Collins Marsh, Wisboro' Green, Billinghurst, co. Sussex: *b.* Kirdford, co. Sussex, 12 January 1896: *educ.* Plaistow and Kirdford Schools: enlisted 16 November 1914: served with the Expeditionary Force in France and died at No.2 Canadian Casualty Clearing Station, 14 March 1917, from bomb wounds (legs, face) received in action. Buried in Lyssenthoek Military Cemetery, Poperinghe. His Commanding Officer wrote, "I am sure it will be some slight comfort for you to know your boy died game, and, from what I know of your boy, I am convinced he was a good true son to you. On one occasion when the enemy made a bombing attack on our trenches, your son carried himself with the utmost coolness and bravery; he threw his bomb to such good effect that his splendid conduct was largely responsible for frustrating the enemy's attack. It was at this time that I myself so thoroughly appreciated his sterling qualities for his prompt and determined action which completely inspired his comrades. I ask you to accept our sincerest sympathy, and I would like to add my own personal appreciation of his manliness. He stood out among his comrades as a man who was without fear; I cannot say more. England can ill afford to lose such men, for by their example, they encourage others to do likewise." His Chaplain wrote, "He was a brave boy, and I can truthfully say he had no suffering, and his end was very peaceful. John died as he lived – a brave young fellow.": Age 21. *unm.*

Rest In Peace

(XI.B.36) Rfn. C/6565, John Thomas Greenwood, 18th (Service) Bn. The King's Royal Rifle Corps: *s.* of John Henry Greenwood, of 89, Oak Leigh, Mytholmroyd, co. York, by his wife Mary. Died of meningitis, 14 March 1917: Age 21. *unm.*

Gone But Not Forgotten

(XI.B.37) Rfn. 322074, William Arthur Woollams, 6th (City of London) Bn. (Rifles) The London Regt. (T.F.): *s.* of Joseph Woollams, of 231, New Road, Croxley Green, Rickmansworth, co. Hertford, by his wife Mary Rose: and brother to L/Corpl. 16097, J. Woollams, 4th Bedfordshire Regt., killed in action 30 September 1918: *b.* Croxley Green: enlisted London. Died of abdominal bullet wounds, 13 March 1917: Age 22. *unm.* Dedicated 'And The Leaves Of The Tree Were For The Healing Of The Nations,' the brothers Woollams are remembered on the Croxley Green War Memorial.

His brother Joseph has no known grave; he is commemorated on the Vis-en-Artois Memorial.

(XI.C.2) Sergt. 1224, Walter Edward Bastable, 6th Sqdn. Royal Flying Corps: *s.* of Walter John Bastable, of 13, Eldon Terrace, Swanage, co. Dorset, by his wife Alice: and *yr.* brother to L/Corpl. 28300, G.H. Bastable, 56th Field Coy., Royal Engineers, who fell 15 November 1916, at the Somme: joined R.F.C. 11 May 1914: apptd. Air Mech. (2nd Class), No.6 Sqdn. France, October 1914: obtained his Aviator's Certificate, 26 November 1916. Died of wounds, 17 March 1917, received when returning from an artillery observation patrol, aircraft Be2D (no.6238) broke up, crashed and was completely destroyed. The observer, Lieut. B.M. Morris also died: Age 24. *unm.* The brothers Bastable are recorded on Swanage War Memorial, Purbeck.

Jesus Called Him Unto Himself

His brother George is buried in Courcelles-au-Bois Communal Cemetery Extension (C.5). Lieut. Morris is buried nearby (X.A.17).

(XI.C.4) Pte. 204194, Herbert Edwards, 1/9th Bn. The King's (Liverpool) Regt. (T.F.): *s*. of Frederick Matthew Edwards, Master Mariner; by his wife Margaret: *b*. Liverpool, 12 March 1883: *educ*. Garston National Schools: Occupation – Licensed Victualler: joined King's Liverpool Regt. 3 November 1916: served with the Expeditionary Force in France and Flanders, and was killed in action, 17 March 1917: Age 34. He *m*. 26 December 1906, Helen Minnie (8, Modred Street, Liverpool), *dau*. of Frank Puzay, and had four *daus* – Esther May, *b*. 4 May 1910, Phyllis Margaret, *b*. 18 November 1913, Helen Mary, *b*. 17 April 1915; Amy Marjorie, *b*. 18 February 1917. (*IWGC record age 35*)

He Endured All He Gave, All That Honour And Freedom Might Prevail

(XI.C.13A) Pte. 243809, Albert Ward, 1/5th Bn. The Loyal North Lancashire Regt. (T.F.): formerly no.4566, East Lancashire Regt.: *s*. of Thomas (& Emma Jane) Ward, of 22, Shale Street, Burnley, co. Lancaster: Occupation – Weaver: served with the Expeditionary Force in France from February 1915, and died of wounds (Shrapnel, head) No.17 Casualty Clearing Station, 27 March 1917. Buried in the Military Cemetery, Lyssenthoek; Rev. S.W. Allen officiating: Age 21. 'In Memoriam,' *Burnley Express*, 14 April 1917: '*Somewhere abroad in a soldier's grave, Lies our dear brother amongst the brave. Oh God! How mysterious and strange are Thy ways, To take our dear brother in the best of his days.*' From brothers Tom and James and sisters Annie and Ada.

He Gave Up His Own Life That Others Might Live In Freedom

(XI.C.32A) Rfn. 531891, William Comber, 1/15th (County of London) Bn. (Prince of Wales's Own Civil Service Rifles) The London Regt. (T.F.): late of Spring Grove House, Isleworth, London: *s*. of William J.B. Comber, Carpenter; late of 'Mervale,' Kingswood Way, Sanderstead; resident 44, Cotford Road, Thornton Heath, co. Surrey, and Clara L. Comber, his wife: and brother to Pte. 1907, J. Comber, 15th London Regt., missing believed killed, 20 December 1915: *b*. New South Wales, Australia, 23 April 1897: *educ*. Whitgift Grammar School (Mason's House, 1908–14); O.T.C. member (Pte.): Occupation – Clerk; Messrs Stephens, White & Co., Lloyd's Brokers, London: joined 15th London Regt. October 1915: served with the Expeditionary Force in France and Flanders, took part in the fighting at Vimy Ridge, Souchez, the Somme, Arras and Ypres. Died of wounds (G.S. back, Rt. thigh) No.3 Canadian Casualty Clearing Station, 10 April 1917: Age 19. "On the night of 7 April 1917 the 15th London Regt. relieved 18th London Regt. in the trenches at Ypres. At 6.30 p.m., 9 April, the Germans attacked the positions to the immediate left of 15th Londons and continuously bombarded the sector throughout the night. Although not directly involved in the fighting on their flank the battalion suffered 13 killed, 18 wounded of whom several subsequently died."

Also His Brother Pte. Jack Comber
Missing December 1915, Age 21.
Resurgent

His brother John has no known grave; he is commemorated on the Loos Memorial (Panel 132).

(XI.C.34) Pte. G/9904, William James Drewett, 11th (Service) Bn. (Lewisham) The Queen's Own (Royal West Kent Regt.): *s.* of Walter Drewett, by his wife Eleanor 'Ellen,' *née* Howard: *b.* Bromley, co. Kent: Occupation – Carman: enlisted Lewisham, London, S.E.: served in France from May 1916. Killed in action, 10 April 1917: Age 51. Pte. Drewett had recently returned to France from his first home leave; he leaves a wife, Mary Jane (Bird-in-Hand Cottages, Dartmouth Road, Forest Hill, London, S.E.), and nine children – Annie, *b.*1892; Eleanor Gertrude, *b.* 1895; William Walter James, *b.* 1897; Frederick Charles, *b.* 1900; Dorothy Kate, *b.* 1902; twins Arthur Henry & George Thomas, *b.* 1905; Lily Margaret, *b.* 1909; William Francis, *b.* 1913.

(XII.A.25) Pte. 17959, William Shooter, 11th (Service) Bn. The Sherwood Foresters (Notts & Derbys Regt.): *s.* of William Shooter, of 56, Skegby Road, Annesley Woodhouse, co. Nottingham, by his wife Clara: and elder brother to 23 year old twins Pte. 14200, J. Shooter, 2nd Lincolnshire Regt., killed in action, 9 May 1915; and Pte. 14196, J. Shooter, 2nd Lincolnshire Regt., killed in action, 13 March 1915, and Pte. 141493, J. Shooter, 46th Machine Gun Corps (Inf.), who died of wounds, 30 October 1918, at Rouen, aged 21 years: *b.* Kirkby Woodhouse, nr. Mansfield, *c.*1886: enlisted Mansfield: served in France and Flanders from 27 April 1915, and died of wounds (G.S.W. neck and legs), 29 April 1917: Age 31. One of four brothers who fell, two of whom were twins.

Until The Day Break And The Shadows Flee Away

Twins Jonathan and James have no known grave, they are commemorated on the Ploegsteert Memorial (Panel 3) and the Le Touret Memorial (Panel 8) respectively; Joseph is buried in St. Sever Cemetery Extension (S.II.EE.5).

(XII.B.14) Pte. 11777, Robert William Buss, 10th (Service) Bn. The Queen's Own (Royal West Kent Regt.): *s.* of Robert Markham Buss, Farm Labourer; of Fuller's Corner, Wateringbury, nr. Maidstone, co. Kent; by his wife Flora Edith, *née* Newman: Occupation – Labourer: enlisted Tonbridge, 10 December 1915:

served with the Expeditionary Force in France and Flanders from 23 January 1916, and died, 20 May, 1917 of wounds consequent to being accidentally shot by a comrade, 4 May inst.: Age 22. The circumstances being: 'Between 06.30 and 07.00 hrs, on the 4.5.17, Pte. 11777, R.W. Buss (Actg.Siglr.) was making his way along the trench to fetch his breakfast when he was shot in the right thigh by a bullet accidentally discharged by Pte. G/41115, F. Martin. L/Corpl. H. Philpot (I/C. No.9 Sentry Post) said he had ordered two of the sentries (one being Pte. Martin) to clean their rifles, and had seen Martin remove the magazine from his rifle and place it on the ground; it was about a minute later he heard a report and, on turning about, saw Pte. Buss had been hit. Pte. Martin stated that when he squeezed the trigger he was unaware of there being a round in the breech.' Questioned shortly after being shot, Pte. Buss submitted a statement; it closed "It was quite an accident." Tried (25 May) by F.G.C.M. and convicted, Pte. Martin received 42 Days Field Punishment No.1 without remission. Pte. Buss *m*. St. Mary's Parish Church, Hadlow, 27 November 1915; Edith Ellen, *née* Bassett (Hadlow Stair, Tonbridge), and leaves a daughter.

From His Loving Wife And Daughter

(XII.B.16) Pte. 23873, Charles Ambrose Pearce, 8th (Service) Bn. The Queen's Own (Royal West Kent Regt.): formerly no.20894, Duke of Cornwall's Light Infantry: *s*. of Charles Pearce, of Rowse Farm, Pillaton, St. Mellion, co. Cornwall, by his wife Eliza Ann, *dau*. of William Hodge: *b*. Pillaton, 19 December 1895: *educ*. Church of England School, there: enlisted 4 November 1915: served with the Expeditionary Force in France and Flanders from 30 November 1916: took part in successful operations with 24 Divn. 12–17 April 1917, and died 24 May 1917, of shell wounds received in action nr. Poperinghe. Buried in Lyssenthoek Military Cemetery. His Commanding Officer wrote, "He was in my platoon for several months, and on several occasions he accompanied me on dangerous patrols, displaying at all times great courage and devotion to duty. His place will be very difficult to fill .. I regarded him as one of my bravest and best men.": Age 20. *unm*.

(XII.B.29A) Pte. 32086, Charlie Dewhirst, 8th (Service) Bn. The York & Lancaster Regt.: formerly no.4000, Queen's Own Yorkshire Dragoons: *s*. of Eliza Dewhirst (Four Lane Ends, Midgley, Luddenfoot, co. York): attended Midgley United Methodist Church & Sunday School: enlisted Halifax; subsequently transf'd York & Lancaster Regt. and proceeded to France; served with the Expeditionary Force there, and died in No.3 Canadian Casualty Clearing Station; Remy Siding, nr. Poperinghe – shrapnel wounds, back and left leg and buttock – 28 May 1917: Age 22.

Rest In Peace

(XII.B.31) Pte. 20543, Albert George Efemey, 13th (Service) Bn. The Duke of Cambridge's Own (Middlesex Regt.): only *s*. of Albert Frederick Efemey, of 12, Pears Road, Hounslow, by his wife Jane, *dau*. of George Saunders: *b*. Windsor, co. Berks, 22 September 1893: *educ*. Town Boys School, Hounslow: Occupation – Grocer's Assistant: joined 8th (Territorial) Bn. Middlesex Regt. 8 December 1911: called up on the outbreak of war, undertook Active Service Obligations; proceeded to Gibraltar, September 1914: returned home, February 1915: served with the Expeditionary Force in France and Flanders from the 8th of the following month: wounded at Ypres, 11 May 1915, repatriated home: rejoined his regiment 26 June 1916: wounded again, at Hebuterne, attd. Machine Gun Section: returned to France, May 1917, transf'd. 13th Battn. of his regiment. Died at No.3 Canadian Casualty Clearing Station on the 28th of wounds received in action: 28 May 1917: Age 23. He *m*. Holy Trinity Church, Hounslow, 31 December 1916; Kathleen A. Grimms, *née* Efemey (Glan Ely Hospital, Fairwater, nr. Cardiff), *dau*. of John Smith.

Greater Love Hath No Man Than This

(XII.B.40A) Pte. 43515, Arthur William Helsdown, 7th (Service) Bn. The Northamptonshire Regt.: *s*. of Herbert Helsdown, of 37, Sartoris Road, Rushden, co. Northampton, by his wife Fanny: and cousin to Pte. 1960, L.W. Helsdown, 1/4th Northamptonshire Regt., killed in action at Gallipoli, 10 October 1915, by the explosion of a mine: *b*. Rushden: Occupation – Boot & Shoe worker; Messrs B. Ladds, Boot Manufacturers, Rushden: enlisted Northampton, September 1914, aged 16 years: served with the Expeditionary Force in France from August 1916, and died at Poperinghe, 30 May 1917, of wounds (S.W. abdominal, legs) received in action earlier the same day: Age 19. In a letter to Pte. Helsdown's parents the Chaplain, Capt. J.O. Murray attd 3rd Canadian C.C.S., wrote, "I deeply regret to have to inform you that your son, Pte A.W. Helsdown, died this morning here, a few hours after admission. He was suffering from severe shell wounds in the abdomen, and from the first his case was practically hopeless. Everything possible, however, was done for him, and he wanted for no care or attention. At first he was conscious, and gave me your address, with a request to write to you. Afterwards he became unconscious, and so was mercifully spared any further suffering. I prayed for him, and I think he knew that his end was near, and accepted it with brave and quiet resignation. He has fought a good fight and is at rest. He will be buried in a quiet cemetery near here, with all due respect and military honours, and I will send you the number of his grave. I pray that God may comfort and sustain you in your great trouble."

Rest In Peace

His cousin Leonard is buried in 7th Field Ambulance Cemetery (IV.E.13).

(XII.B.41A) Rfn. 71110, Cyril Dennis, 16th (Service) Bn. (Chatsworth Rifles) The Sherwood Foresters (Notts & Derbys Regt.): formerly no.54110, North Staffordshire Regt.: s. of James Dennis, Coal Miner; of 62, Stoney Street, Sutton-in-Ashfield, by his wife Sarah Jane, née Newton: b. 9 March 1897: Died of wounds (G.S.W. abdominal, facial), 29 May 1917: Age 22. unm.

(XII.B.44A) Pte. 20943, Frederick Denton, M.M., 7th (Service) Bn. The Northamptonshire Regt.: s. of Frederick (and Mrs) Denton, of 6, Station Road, Rushden, co. Northampton: and brother to Pte. 8558, A. Denton, 2nd Northamptonshire Regt., killed in action 8 July 1916: b. Rushden: Occupation – Boot & Shoe worker; Messrs C.W. Horrell, Rushden: enlisted September 1914: served with the Expeditionary Force in France and Flanders from August 1915; took part in the Battle of Loos, the Somme, Vimy. Died 30 May 1917 of wounds (loss of one arm and both legs) received from shellfire the previous day in the build up to the Battle of Messines: Age 30. Awarded the Military Medal for distinguished service at Guillemont, Somme. He leaves a widow to mourn his passing. Two other brothers Bert, Royal Army Medical Corps, and Len, Northamptonshire Regt., are currently (June 1917) on active service somewhere in France.

His brother Arthur has no known grave; he is commemorated on the Thiepval Memorial.

(XII.C.2) L/Corpl. P/5750, James Lewis Bailey, 1st Traffic Control Coy., Military Foot Police Corps: s. of Alfred E. Bailey, of 7, Houghton, King's Lynn, by his wife Elizabeth: b. South Creake, Fakenham, Norfolk: enlisted Wroxham. Died (multiple bullet wounds; abdominal, chest), 30 May 1917, received at duty: Age 26. Remembered on South Creake War Memorial.

At Rest

(XII.C.5) Dvr. 960303, John Gustaves Green, 'C' Bty., 7th London Bde., Royal Field Artillery (T.F.): formerly no.1104: eldest s. of John Green, Artist & Photographer; of 63A, Chalk Farm Road, Camden Town, London, N.W.1, by his wife Helen, dau. of John Brett: b. Camden Town, 23 August 1889: educ. Holloway, London, N.: joined 7th London Brigade Royal Field Artillery, 1907: volunteered for Foreign Service on the outbreak of war, August 1914: served with the Expeditionary Force in France and Flanders from 17 March 1915, and was killed in action at Messines, 1 June 1917: Age 27. He m. Tottenham, London, N., 25 December 1911; Rebecca (19, Almington Street, Finsbury Park, London, N.), dau. of William Matsill, and had a son – Leslie William. Dvr.

Green's widow has since remarried; now Mrs Wilson ('Harringay', Newcastle Road, Midland Junction, Western Australia). (*IWGC record 236th London Bde. Age 28*)

(XII.C.11A) Dvr. 80631, Henry Mosley, 'B' Bty., 102nd Bde., Royal Field Artillery: *s.* of Mrs Mosley (Langley Mill, co. Derby): and *yr.* brother to Pte. 17780, H. Mosley, 20th (Tyneside Scottish) Bn. Northumberland Fusiliers, died two months previously, 11 April 1917: *b.* Langley Mill, 1898: enlisted Ilkeston: trained Newcastle and Whitburn, thereafter proceeded to France; served with the Expeditionary Force there and in Flanders, and died 3 June 1917 of wounds (G.S. multiple; buttocks, Lt. femur) received in action the previous day. The Church of England Chaplain wrote, "I am indeed sorry to tell you that your son died at an early hour this morning. He was admitted last evening suffering from a number of severe shell wounds, including one which had fractured his thigh. He will be buried with all due respect and military honours in a quiet cemetery near here. May He who wept by the grave of Nazareth be with you and all who suffer in these dark days, making you realise that He is the resurrection and the life." Henry Mosley had been an enthusiastic football player in civilian life, turning out for both Langley Mill Wesleyan and Eastwood Rangers Clubs: Age 19. One of six brothers who served.

His brother Herbert is buried in Aubigny Communal Cemetery Extension (I.L.63).

(XII.C.22A) Pte. 32663, Tom Wheeler, 2nd Bn. (99th Foot) The Duke of Edinburgh's (Wiltshire Regt.): Died of wounds, 3 June 1917, received the previous night while taking part in a bombing attack on the German positions opposite No.2 Canadian Tunnelling Coy. in the Hedge Street sector: Age 32. He was married to Mrs R. Marks, *née* Wheeler (4, Ansties Court, Mortimer Street, Trowbridge, co. Wilts). See Ramparts Cemetery (J.8-11); Hop Store Cemetery (I.A.24,26,30).

God Be With You Till We Meet Again

(XII.C.32) Gnr. 101496, David Arthur Nelson, 'C' Bty., 102nd Bde., Royal Field Artillery: *s.* of the late James Nelson, Farmer, by his wife Alice (Longfield, Carrickmacross, Co. Monaghan), *dau.* of George Spink: *b.* Tarrowingee, Victoria, Australia, 10 December 1896: *educ.* Viscount Weymouth's Grammar School, Carrickmacross: Occupation – Farmer: enlisted 8 November 1915: served with the Expeditionary Force in France and Flanders from 31 July 1916, and died at Remy, nr. Poperinghe, 4 June 1917, from wounds received in action there, 27 May previously. Buried at Remy: Age 21. *unm.*

(XII.C.43A) Corpl. (Actg. Sergt.) 16000, John Thomas Johnson, M.M., 8th (Service) Bn. The King's Own (Yorkshire Light Infantry): *yst. s.* of George

Johnson, of 11, Day's Croft, Monk Bretton, nr. Barnsley, by his wife Ann, *dau*. of James Kitchen: *b*. Monk Bretton, co. York, about 1894: *educ*. there: Occupation – Collier: enlisted 4 September 1914: served with the Expeditionary Force in France and Flanders from 8 March 1915, and died of wounds, 6 June 1917. Buried in Lyssenthoek Military Cemetery, Poperinghe. Awarded the Military Medal 'for gallant and distinguished service in the field on 1 July 1916': Age 22. *unm*. (*IWGC record Pte*.)

(XIII.A.1) Lieut. John Ernest Hartington, M.C., 5th Bn. The Lancashire Fusiliers (T.F.) attd. 164th Coy. Machine Gun Corps: late of Highfield House, Manchester Road, Hopwood: *s*. of George A. Hartington, of Heywood, co. Lancaster, by his wife Mona Gertrude: *educ*. Bury Grammar School (School Captain, 1914): Died 13 July 1917, of abdominal wounds received in action: Age 21. *unm*. Awarded the Military Cross (23 November 1916), for 'gallantry in the field by continuously passing through enemy bombardments to supervise the efficient working of field guns;' decorated one week before his death by H.M. King George, at Buckingham Palace, he was the first Heywood man to receive this award.

In 2004, as part of Bury Grammar School's '10th Annual Visit to the Battlefields of France and Flanders', School Captain William Webster laid a wreath and placed the 1911 Captain's Medallion on the grave of Lieut. Hartington; the same one that he had worn when he held that office.

(XIII.A.4) 2nd Lieut. Harry Norbury Nuttall, Army Service Corps attd. H.Q. Heavy Bde., Machine Gun Corps: elder *s*. of Harry Nuttall, of 'Briarfield,' Walton-on-the-Hill, Tadworth, co. Surrey, M.P. for Stretford Division of Lancashire, by his wife Edith Mary, *dau*. of Wm. Smith, J.P.: *b*. Southport, co. Lancaster, 31 May 1887: *educ*. Harrow, and Lincoln College, Oxford; graduated B.A. (Hons. Law): on the outbreak of war was engaged in business as an India and China Merchant Trader: obtained a commission 2nd Lieut. Army Service Corps, October 1915: served with the Expeditionary Force in France and Flanders, being there attd. Heavy Bde. Machine Gun Corps from 14 July 1916, and died on 5 July 1917, as a result of wounds received whilst attached to that corps. Buried in Remy Cemetery, Poperinghe: Age 30. He *m*. Bowdon, co. Chester, 10 June 1914, Meryll (since re-married, now Mrs Gillies-Reyburn), elder *dau*. of William Nield, of Hart Hill, Bowdon, co. Chester, and had a son, Michael Vernon, *b*. 17 July 1915.

(XIII.A.5) Capt. John Norman Wilson, 1/6th (Perthshire) Bn. The Black Watch (Royal Highlanders), (T.F.): only *s*. of the late Sir James Wilson, K.C.S.I., I.C.S., of 19, Coates Gardens, Edinburgh, by his wife Anne Campbell ('Annieslea', Crieff), *dau*. of the Rev. Norman Macleod, D.D., of The Barony, Glasgow: *b*. Shahpur, Punjab, India, 11 December 1891: *educ*. Ardvreck School, Crieff; Winchester, and Balliol College, Oxford (1910–1914): volunteered for

Active Service on the outbreak of war; gazetted 2nd Lieut. 6th Black Watch August 1914: subsequently promoted Lieut. and Capt.: served with the Expeditionary Force in France and Flanders from May 1915: invalided home, suffering from fever January following, and on recovery was employed for some months under the Ministry of Munitions, Gretna Munitions Factory: rejoined his battalion in France, March 1917, and died at a Canadian Casualty Clearing Station 4 July, as a result of wounds received in action at Ypres on the 2nd, while engaged in getting his men out of danger; Yser Canal Bank sector. Buried in Remy Cemetery, nr. Poperinghe. His Commanding Officer wrote, "He was a great favourite in the regiment, and although by his nature he would not have chosen a military career, he never for one moment tried to shirk his duty, and always showed the best example to all ranks;" and his Major, "He was the essence of everything that was upright, noble and brave." A brother officer also wrote, "I never knew a more conscientious officer, or one whose influence was so beneficial to those amongst whom he lived, merely from the unostentatious goodness of his life;" and another, "If ever there was a white man through and through, that man was Jack Wilson. His men were all fond of him, and are much distressed at his death. One of them, badly wounded himself, burst into tears when he heard of it.": Age 25. *unm.* See account Vlamertinghe New Military Cemetery.

An Only Son He Did His Duty

(XIII.A.6) Capt. Robert Baird Rowley Orr, 4th Sqdn. Royal Flying Corps and 9th Bn. Princess Louise's (Argyll & Sutherland Highlanders): *s.* of James Rowley Orr, Solicitor; of Leddriegreen, Strathblane, nr. Glasgow, co. Lanark, by his wife Annabelle: *educ.* Glasgow University; graduated B.A. (Law): Died of wounds received 3 July 1917, when, while flying (as observer) on an Artillery Observation Patrol, shortly after taking off from Abeele the aircraft's engine stalled which forced it into a nose dive and fall, spinning out of control, to earth: Age 26. Remembered on Glasgow Academy Roll of Honour; dedicated – "These Former Members Of This School Left All That Was Dear To Them, Endured Hardship, Faced Danger And Finally Passed Out Of The Sight Of Man By The Path Of Duty And Self Sacrifice; Giving Up Their Own Lives That Others Might Live In Freedom. Let Those Who Come After See To It That Their Names Are Not Forgotten;" over 300 former students and staff of the academy are recorded thereon. Capt. Orr's pilot (2nd Lieut. F. Moore) also died.

Who Had Done His Work And Had No Fear To Die

(XIII.A.7) 2nd Lieut. Frederick Moore, 4th Sqdn. Royal Flying Corps: only s. of Frederick Moore, of 2, Malvern Road, Acock's Green, Birmingham, and Rose Moore his spouse: gained his Flying Certficate, London & Provincial Flying School, Hendon, 30 May 1916. Died in No.3 Canadian Casualty Clearing Station 3 July 1917 of wounds (fractured skull, fractured Rt. hip) received when, shortly after taking off for the purpose of an Artillery Observation Patrol, his aircraft stalled at altitude and crashed: Age 22. The observer (Capt. R.B. Orr) also died.

Only Son
To Know Him Was To Love Him

(XIII.A.14) 2nd Lieut. Reginald Samuel Harris, 13th (Service) Bn. The Duke of Cambridge's Own (Middlesex Regt.): *s*. of Samuel Harris, and Louisa Laura; his spouse: served with the Expeditionary Force in France from 7 October 1915. Died of wounds 24 July 1917, consequent to being hit by a shell (22 July), Battle Wood – Ypres-Comines canal sector: Age 24. *unm*. 2nd Lieut. Webb, hit by the same shell, survived. Married for but a short while, 2nd Lieut. Harris leaves a wife and son Geoffrey.

(XIII.A.17) 2nd Lieut. Bernard Tootell, 3/7th Bn. (Robin Hood) The Sherwood Foresters (Notts & Derbys Regt.), (T.F.) attd. 4th Sqdn. Royal Flying Corps: *s*. of the late Frederick James Tootell, by his wife Gertrude (now wife of William J. Hibblitt, of 2, Oxford Villa, Colwick Vale, Nottingham), *dau*. of G.R. Smith: *b*. Netherfield, co. Nottingham, 14 June 1896: *educ*. Nottingham Boys' College: enlisted Sherwood Foresters, September 1914: obtained a commission, gazetted 2nd Lieut. 8 October 1915: served with the Expeditionary Force in France and Flanders from the latter month: twice wounded: attd. R.F.C., April 1917; obtained his 'Wings,' May, and was killed when his aircraft RE8, No.A3473, after taking off on a photographic reconnaissance patrol was accidentally (mistakenly) engaged and, forced to land, crashed at the aerodrome near Poperinghe on 23 June of the same year. Buried in the Lyssenthoek Hospital Military Cemetery: Age 21. *unm*.

Thou Wilt Keep Him In Perfect Peace Whose Mind Is Stayed On Thee

(XIII.A.18) 2nd Lieut. Lawrence Allan Davis, 4th Sqdn. Royal Flying Corps: *s*. of H. (& Mrs) Champneys Davis, of 'Maskee,' Golf Road, Budleigh Salterton, co. Devon: *b*. Boston, Massachusetts, U.S.A.: obtained his Flying Certificate, Military School, Catterick Bridge, 22 June 1916. Killed in a flying accident (incident) 23 June 1917: Age 23. His observer 2nd Lieut. Tootell was also killed.

To Live In Hearts We Leave Behind Is Not To Die

(XIII.A.20) Lieut. Cuthbert Farrar Savage, 'A' Coy., 10th (Service) Bn. The Northumberland Fusiliers: s. of the Rev. Canon Edwin Sidney Savage, M.A., Rector of Hexham Abbey, at present on special service with the Serbian Red Cross, by his wife Sybil (The Rectory, Hexham Abbey, co. Northumberland), *dau.* of Dean Farrar: and cousin – by his aunt, Maud Farrar (wife of the Revd. Henry Montgomery) – to Capt. Bernard Law Montgomery, 2nd Royal Warwickshire Regt. (see account re. Meteren Military Cemetery): *b.* St. Mark's Vicarage, Barrow-in-Furness, co. Lancaster, 27 July 1890: *educ.* Aysgarth School, Rugby, and New College, Oxford: went to Vancouver 1913, and was studying for the Bar: volunteered for Foreign Service on the outbreak of war; enlisted 72nd Seaforth Highlanders of Canada, 11 August 1914: returned to England with 1st Canadian Contingent: obtained a commission; gazetted 2nd Lieut. Northumberland Fusiliers, 25 January 1915; promoted Lieut. 12 June 1917: served with the Expeditionary Force in France and Flanders from 25 August 1915: wounded at Bulley Grenay, 4 April 1916, and invalided home: rejoined his regiment September following, and died at No.10 Casualty Clearing Station, Poperinghe, 20 June 1917, of multiple shrapnel wounds to the synovial hinge and patella (elbow, knee) received the same day by the explosion of a shell outside the battalion headquarters at Dickebusch. Buried in Lyssenthoek Military Cemetery, Poperinghe. He was keenly interested in ski-ing, and at age 14 was first in the Alpine Public School Ski-ing Competition: Age 25. *unm.* (*IWGC record age 26*)

So He Passed Over & The Trumpets Sounded For Him On The Other Side

(XIII.A.21) Rev. Cecil Herbert Schooling, Chaplain 4th Class, Army Chaplains' Dept. attd. 122nd Infantry Bde.: *s.* of Frederick Schooling, of 'Hollydene,' Bromley, co. Kent, by his wife Lily: and brother to Capt. E.C. Schooling, 2nd Royal Warwickshire Regt., killed 31 October 1914: *b.* Wandsworth Common, London, S.W., *c.*1885: *educ.* Tonbridge School, and Pembroke College, Cambridge (elected University Guild, February 1902), graduated B.A. (1906), thereafter went up to Theological College, Wells (obtained his M.A., 1910): Occupation – Curate, All Saints Parish Wakefield (1907–10); thereafter St. John's, Croydon: volunteered his services as Chaplain to the Armed Services, 5 December 1916: proceeded to France early 1917, and died of wounds (S.W. [shell]) 21 June 1917, received at Dickebusch the previous day: Age 32. Visited on the 100th anniversary of the outbreak of the Great War, a wreath on his grave recorded;- "With gratitude on behalf of the Chaplain General and serving members of the R.A.Ch.D. 'Since we have died with Christ we believe we shall also live with him.' 'Romans 6.8.'"

> Also Capt. E.C. Schooling
> Royal Warwickshire Regt.
> Killed At Gheluvelt
> 31st October 1914

His brother Eric has no known grave; he is commemorated on the Ypres (Menin Gate) Memorial (Panel 8).

(XIII.A.23) 2nd Lieut. Louis John Bailey, General List attd. 41st Sqdn. Royal Flying Corps: *s.* of the late William Bailey, of 126, Norbury Crescent, London, S.W.1, and Ellen Bailey, his wife: *b.* Thornton Heath, co. Surrey. Died of accidental injuries received whilst on patrol duty, 17 June 1917: Age 24.

> *Here Loyal Hearts And True Stand Ever In The Fight*

(XIII.A.25) Lieut.Col. George Eric Burroughs Dobbs, Signal Corps (A.D.Signals), Royal Engineers: Brevet Major: 2nd *survg. s.* of Joseph Dobbs, of The Chalet, Temple Road, Dublin, J.P., by his wife Mary Augusta, *dau.* of William Harte, C.E.: *b.* Castlecomer, co. Kilkenny, 21 July 1884: *educ.* St. Stephen's Green School, Dublin, and Shrewsbury: gazetted 2nd Lieut. 1904: served in South Wales, Devon, Singapore, and Limerick: on the outbreak of war served with the Expeditionary Force in France and Flanders: promoted Capt. 1914; Brevet Major 1915; Temp. Lieut.Col. November 1916: apptd. to Assistant Director (A.D.) of Signals with a corps, and died in a casualty clearing station, 17 June 1917, having been hit by a shell when returning from inspecting a new cable trench in the front line. Buried at Poperinghe. He was awarded the Legion of Honour for valuable services in keeping up communication during the Retreat from Mons, and was three times Mentioned in Despatches (*London Gazette*, 19 October 1914; 1 January 1916) by F.M. Sir John (now Lord) French, and (*London Gazette*, 15 May 1917) by General Sir Douglas Haig, for 'gallant and distinguished service in the field.' A well-known Rugby football player; he played for England in 1905–06 against Wales and Ireland: Age 32. *unm.*

> *We Asked Thee For Life And Thou Hast Given It*
> *Yea Life For Evermore*

(XIII.A.26) Capt. Alexander Falkand Gulland, 3rd (Reserve) Bn. The Buffs (East Kent Regt.): *s.* of the late Surgeon-General Alexander Dudgeon Gulland, by his wife Margaret (Malvern Hill House, Albert Road, Cheltenham): *b.* 1891: *educ.* Cheltenham College: served in France and Flanders from 2 October 1915, and died of wounds, 16 June 1917, received in action at Messines. Recording 41 names and inscribed 'Pray for the souls of the men from this parish who gave their lives for their country in the Great War 1914-1918. Jesu Mercy;' Capt. Gulland's name can be found on the Prestbury War Memorial, High Street, Prestbury. He is also commemorated on the St. Mary's Church Roll of Honour, Prestbury; Holy Trinity Church Roll of Honour, Portland Street, Cheltenham, and Cheltenham College Roll of Honour: Age 26.

(XIII.A.30) Lieut. John Edward Raphael, 18th (Service) Bn. The King's Royal Rifle Corps, A.D.C. & Camp Commandant, 41st Divn.: only *s.* of the late Albert Raphael, by his wife Harriette (5, Wild Hatch, Hendon): *b.* Brussels, Belgium, 30 April 1882: *educ.* Streatham School, Merchant Taylors' School, and St. John's College, Oxford: Occupation – Barrister: gazetted 2nd Lieut. 9th Duke of Wellington's (West Riding) Regt., September 1914: subsequently transf'd. 18th King's Royal Rifle Corps; raised by his cousin, Sir Herbert Raphael: promoted Lieut. December 1914: served with the Expeditionary Force in France and Flanders from May 1916: apptd. A.D.C., Major-General Sir Sydney Lawford, K.C.B., 41st Divn., October 1915: Died No.10 Casualty Clearing Station, 11 June 1917, from wounds received in action at St. Eloi, during the attack on the Damnstrasse, Wytschaete-Messines Ridge on the 7th of that month. Buried in the Military Cemetery, Lijssenthoek, nr. Poperinghe. A Staff Officer, who was with him when wounded, wrote, "I have seen many men in many parts of the world under all sorts of conditions, but never in my experience have I been so impressed by such a magnificent display of pluck and unselfishness. During the three days he lived he was bright and cheerful, never talked about himself, but was very concerned about his servant, his groom, his horses, and everything but himself." In 1909 he contested the Croydon Division in the Liberal interest, but without success, although his charm and characteristic straightforwardness won the admiration of his most decided opponents. Lieut. Raphael achieved a high reputation as a cricketer and Rugby Union International three-quarter back. He was captain of the Merchant Taylors' Cricket XI, establishing a public school record for the runs he made. At Oxford he played in the University XI, and Rugby XV, 1903–06. In 1904 he accomplished his best performance with the bat against the Yorkshire XI, at Oxford, scoring 201 out of a total of 374. He was a member of the Surrey County XI for four seasons, commencing in 1903, and in 1904 acted as captain. Lieut. Raphael's last cricket appearance in Yorkshire was for an England XI, against the county at Harrogate, August 1913, when he and Mr H.D.G. Levenson-Gower saved the Englanders from defeat by a plucky stand in the last half-hour of the match. Between 1902 and 1906 Lieut. Raphael played in nine international matches for England as a Rugby centre three-quarter back, distinguishing himself by powerful running. He also captained, in 1910, an English team on a visit to the Argentine. Besides cricket and rugby football John Raphael was an expert fencer and swimmer, being president of the Oxford University Swimming Club in 1904. Under his leadership the Old Merchant Taylors' Football Club became one of the most renowned sides in the country. It was often said of him that he was the most versatile and one of the best sportsmen who have come down from Oxford in the present century. He found, however, his vocation in the Army, where his gift for dealing with men came into play. All his energies were given to promoting their sports, organizing canteens, seeing to the catering and cooking for his units; the men wrote of him, "He was to us a father." He was very often to be found in the front-line trenches, where his cheery presence heartened the men; it was thus he got his death wound. A rising young politician, a writer for the Press, a traveller, sportsman and soldier, one of the most chivalrous and devoted of sons, an ardent worker for social reform, a loyal friend, of him it may be said: "If character be destiny, then his is assured.": Age 35. *unm.*

Character Is Destiny

Footnote: On a cold autumnal afternoon in 1929, Walter Sutherland (Head Gardener, Lijssenthoek) was approached by a finely dressed woman who had just arrived in a chauffeur driven car. More than a decade had passed since the end of the war, and pilgrimages by grieving wives and mothers were commonplace. However, there was something about this woman's demeanour and purposeful stride as she approached Walter that made him think this was no ordinary visitor. Introducing herself as Harriette Raphael, the mother of Lieut. John Raphael, she requested Walter accompany her to her son's grave where she revealed to Walter that she was, in fact, seriously ill and although totally in agreement with the IWGC's rulings regarding civilian burials in military cemeteries, she dearly wished to be laid to rest beside her only beloved son. Exactly what was said between Walter and Harriette is not known. A kindly and sympathetic man, Walter had witnessed the sadness of countless mothers who had suffered the tragic loss of their loved ones and, when thirteen months later a package arrived at the cemetery addressed to him, he knew exactly what the contents were and what he had to do. Making sure no one could witness what he was about to do (it could have cost him his job) he made his way to the grave where he dug a hole of sufficient size to accommodate the package, reverently buried it, and carefully replaced the turf which, after a few weeks gave no indication of disturbance.

This secret act of kindness was related to his son George who said, "My father was moved by her determination. He showed me where he had cut out an area of grass and slipped the urn beneath. He knew what he did was in defiance of the rules, so he knew he could not mark her name on the grave but he said a short prayer and always said he had 'done the right thing.' For years whenever I was planting or cutting the grass near the grave I would always think about Mrs Raphael who, like all those mothers, never recovered from losing a son in the

Great War. I swear that the actions of my father allowed Harriette and her son to rest together in peace. "

(XIII.B.1) 2nd Lieut. William Gerald Wright, 8th (Princess Beatrice's) Bn. (Isle of Wight Rifles) The Hampshire Regt. (T.F.): *s.* of William James Wright, of 'Roycroft,' Harold Road, Upper Norwood, London, by his wife Catherine Mary: *educ.* Alleyn's School, Dulwich (Spurgeon's House). Died of wounds, 8 June 1917. His Colonel wrote, "He was hit in the throat and head by pieces of shell, and in spite of the fact that he knew he was dying, had nothing but praise for his men and satisfaction at our victory. He was most gallant throughout the entire action, and was commanding his company at the time of his death. He was a most capable officer, thoroughly deserving the confidence we all felt in his judgment, capability and personal gallantry.": Age 24. *unm.*

Sunshine And Youth And Laughter, All He Gave In Sacrifice

(XIII.B.12) Lieut. William Jackson Horner, 'V' 39 Heavy Trench Mortar Bty., Royal Field Artillery: only *s.* of William Horner, of No.2 Flat, Second Avenue, Hove, co. Sussex, by his wife Emmeline. Died of wounds, 15 July 1917: Age 30. Employed in the Electrical Dept. (Buenos Aires & Pacific), Central Argentine Railways on the outbreak of war, he gave up that appointment to answer his country's call, and returned to England to offer his services.

After All Is Told His Was A Glorious Death And He Still Lives

(XIII.B.14) 2nd Lieut. Edgar Churcher, 3rd Bn The Prince Consort's Own (The Rifle Brigade) attd. 32nd Sqdn. Royal Flying Corps: *s.* of Herbert Churcher, of 31, Meadow Road, South Lambeth, London, S.W., by his wife Isabella *née* Harnot. Killed 14 July 1917 when, returning from a patrol over the German lines, his machine nose-dived and crashed: Age 25.

"On five consecutive nights, between 8 and 13 July 1917, this officer supervised the filling up of gun pits with ammunition in the vicinity of Zillebeke. The entire work was admirably carried out – invariably under heavy shellfire – and the full amount of ammunition was delivered three days in advance of the time allowance for the purpose. On the night of 12/13 July, he was mainly responsible for the organisation and supervision of an ammunition convoy – consisting of 64 wagons and 384 animals – which came under a very heavy barrage of enemy fire, involving casualties to the extent of 16 personnel and 44 animals. On the night of 17/18 July, he was in charge of a further ammunition convoy, which suffered seven casualties, including himself. He died from his wounds on 19 July and never lived to receive the Military Cross which had been previously awarded to him."

(XIII.B.15) Lieut. William Atkinson, M.C., 25th Divn. Ammunition Column, Royal Field Artillery: *s.* of the late G. (& M.A.) Atkinson, of Newcastle-on-Tyne: late *husb.* to M.A. Atkinson (4, Lynchford Terrace, South Farnborough, co. Hants): served in France and Flanders, and died of wounds (G.S. multiple), 18 July 1917, being hit by machine-gun fire on the night of the 17th while leading a munitions convoy: Age 40.

Ever In Our Thoughts

(XIII.B.22) Lieut. Christian Creswell Carver, 'A' Bty., 83rd Bde., Royal Field Artillery: eldest *s.* of Frank Carver, of Weatherbury, Harborne, Birmingham, by his wife Annie, *dau.* of Edmund (& Mary) Creswell, of Gibraltar: *b.* Birmingham, 5 July 1897: *educ.* Naish House, Burnham, co. Somerset; Rugby School, and Royal Military Academy, Woolwich (passed out April 1915): gazetted 2nd Lieut., R.F.A., 22nd of the aforementioned month: served with the Expeditionary Force in France and Flanders for two full years (from 27 July 1915), and died of wounds, 23 July 1917, received (15 July) when the battery dugout on the Menin Road, nr. Zillebeke Lake, received a direct hit. Buried in the Military Cemetery, nr. Poperinghe: Age 20. *unm.*

Lighten Our Darkness We Beseech Thee O Lord

(XIII.B.23) Capt. James Hosking Sandall, 229th Siege Bty., Royal Garrison Artillery: 2nd *s.* of the late Frederick Sandall (*d.* 6 February 1917), by his wife Emerentia Maria Petronella, *dau.* of Professor Schneither: *b.* Dulwich, London, S.E., 11 July 1882: *educ.* Forest Hill House School (Rev. Ryder Bird, M.A.): employee Lloyd's Shipping Register: joined Royal Naval Air Service, Spring 1915: gazetted 2nd Lieut. R.G.A. July 1916; promoted Capt. December 1916: served with the Expeditionary Force in France and Flanders from the 15th of the latter month, and died 23 July 1917 from wounds received in action the previous day. Buried in Lyssenthoek Military Cemetery, nr. Poperinghe. His Commanding Officer wrote, "The men who brought him in when wounded were full of admiration for his fine courage, as he never made a moan the whole time, and even thanked them each separately for their trouble.": Age 35. *unm.*

Greater Love Hath No Man Than
That He Lay Down His Life For His Friends

(XIII.C.7) Pte. G/33416, John Riley, 23rd (Service) Bn. (2nd Football) The Duke of Cambridge's Own (Middlesex Regt.): late *husb.* to Alma Harriet Hubbard, *née* Riley (73, Rangemoor Road, Broad Lane, Tottenham, London): *b.* Newington:

enlisted Woolwich. Died 7 June 1917, of wounds received the previous evening; vicinity Voormezeele Switch – Old French Trench: Age 31.

Gone From Us But Not Forgotten Never Shall His Memory Fade

(XIII.D.7) Pte. 33742, Joseph Harries, 'D' Coy., 9th (Service) Bn. The Welch Regt.: *s.* of Josiah Harries, of St. David's Cottages, Incline, Dafen, Llanelly, by his wife Mary: and brother to Pte. 5728, J. Harries, 2/7th Royal Warwickshire Regt., killed in action, 17 July 1916: *b.* Llanelly, co. Carmarthen: enlisted there. Died 8 June 1917, of wounds: Age 20.

Too Far Away Thy Face To See But Not Too Far To Think Of Thee

His brother Josiah is buried in Laventie Military Cemetery (II.A.24).

(XIII.D.10) Gnr. 147828, Alfred Leonard Cowdrill, 'C' Bty., 149th Bde., Royal Field Artillery: eldest *s.* of Alfred Cowdrill, Gun Worker; of Guildford Street, Birmingham, by his wife Emma, *dau.* of Thomas Kemp: *b.* Birmingham, 3 May 1884: *educ.* Cowper Street School: Occupation – Brass Finisher; employee to Mr Peakman, New Street, Aston: enlisted 6 June 1916: served with the Expeditionary Force in France and Flanders, and died of wounds (shrapnel) and gas poisoning, 8 June 1917: Age 33. He *m.* Lyells, 25 December 1914; Emily Edith, *dau.* of the late Harry Horton. (*IWGC record Fitter*)

(XIII.D.10A) Pte. 13864, George Church, 6th (Service) Bn. The Duke of Edinburgh's (Wiltshire Regt.): formerly no.14137, Oxford & Bucks Light Infantry: *s.* of Thomas Church, Farm Labourer; of 129, Stony Stratford, co. Buckingham, by his wife Ada: and brother to Pte. 13224, H. Church, 7th Oxford & Bucks Light Infantry, died of wounds, 22 May 1917; Salonika; and Pte. 17581, W. Church, 5th Oxford & Bucks Light Infantry, killed in action, 17 October 1915: *b.* Stony Stratford, 1890: Occupation – Rail Worker, Wolverton, co. Buckingham: enlisted Wolverton: served with the Expeditionary Force from 21 September 1915, and died of wounds, 8 June 1917: Age 27. *unm.* Remembered on Stony Stratford (Horsefair Green) War Memorial.

Though Death Divides Fond Memories Cling
Three Loved Ones Gone Forever
R.I.P.

His brother Herbert is buried in Salonika (Lembet Road) Military Cemetery, Greece (1046); William has no known grave, he is commemorated on the Ypres (Menin Gate) Memorial (Panel 39).

(XIV.A.4) Lieut. Algernon Edward Le May, 'A' Bty., 235th Bde., Royal Field Artillery: *s.* of Edward Le May, Hop Factor; of Denmark House, Tonbridge, by his wife Mary Ann, *dau.* of Martin Deavin: *b.* Capel, co. Kent, 27 November 1882: *educ.* Tonbridge School: obtained a commission 2nd Lieut. 4 August 1915; promoted Lieut. 1 June 1916: acted as Gunnery Instructor, Luton Artillery Training School from January 1916: served with the Expeditionary Force in France and Flanders. Wounded 23 July 1917, and died at No.2 Canadian Clearing Station the following day. Buried in the Military Cemetery, Lyssenthoek, Poperinghe: Age 34. His Colonel wrote, "The Brigade and the country has lost a brave and efficient officer, and his brother officers have lost a comrade whose place it will be very hard to fill;" and a brother officer wrote, "He was very much valued by me as a battery officer, and very brave, and was most successful at battery work. He was specially applied for to come to the battery." He *m.* Lee, co. Kent, 1 June 1906; Constance Mabel (Cage Lodge, Tonbridge, co. Kent), *dau.* of Herbert Le May, of Bromley, and had three children – Ian Edward, *b.* 21 April 1907; Kenneth Herbert, *b.* 26 January 1911; Anthony Deavin, *b.* 3 March 1914.

Beloved Husband Of Constance & Eldest Son Of L. & M.A. Le May
Tonbridge, Kent

(XIV.A.7) Major George Eustace Summers Bowen, M.C., Comdg. 'A' Bty. 83rd Bde., Royal Field Artillery: *s.* of the Rev. Thomas James Bowen, of St. Nicholas Vicarage, Bristol, co. Gloucester, by his marriage to the late Susan Elvina Bowen: and brother to Lieut. C.E.L. Bowen, East Africa Military Police Corps attd. K.R.R.C., killed 1 December 1914; Kissi, British East Africa: *educ.* Royal Military College, Sandhurst: awarded the Military Cross (*London Gazette*, 1 July 1916). Died of wounds, 29 July 1917, received in action near Zillebeke Lake: Age 29.

Until The Day Dawns
Younger Son Of The Vicar Of St. Nicholas, Bristol

His brother Cuthbert is buried in Kisumu Cemetery (II.B.2).

(XIV.A.13) Brigdr. Gen. Alister Fraser Gordon, C.M.G., D.S.O., The Gordon Highlanders, Comdg. 153rd Infantry Bde. Staff, 51st (Highland) Divn.: 3rd *s.* of William Grant Gordon, of Drumdevan, co. Inverness, by his wife Louisa, *dau.* of John Fraser, of Achnagairn, co. Inverness: *b.* 1 February 1872: *educ.* The College, Inverness, and Royal Military College, Sandhurst: gazetted Royal Highlanders, 8 October 1890: transf'd Gordon Highlanders, 12 November 1890: promoted Lieut. 1 September 1893: served with Chitral Relief Force, 1895 (Medal with clasp), and on the North-West Frontier of India, 1897–98, including the actions of Chagru Kotal and Dargai, where, as a Lieut., he commanded a company and was first in successfully leading it across a zone of fire: present at the capture of the Sampagha and Arhanga Passes: operations in the Waran Valley, and actions of 16 November 1897: operations in the Bara Valley, 7–14 December 1897: Mentioned in Despatches (*London Gazette*, 5 April 1898) awarded two clasps: promoted Capt. 28 May 1899: employed with Central African Rifles, and King's African Rifles, 12 April 1899–11 April 1902: served with 2nd British Central African Regt. in the Ashanti Campaign, 1900: Mentioned in Despatches (*London Gazette*, 8 March 1901): created Companion of the Distinguished Service Order (*London Gazette*, 26 April 1901) 'In recognition of services during the recent operations in Ashanti.' Invested by H.M. The King, 24 October 1902: served in the South African War, 1901–02, as Railway Staff Officer, and Station Staff Officer: took part in operations in the Transvaal, September 1901–31 May 1902 (Queen's Medal, three clasps): G.S.O., 3rd Grade, Coastal Defences, Northern Command, 18 February 1908–17 February 1912: promoted Major 4 July 1908: D.A.A. and Q.M.G., Highland Division, Scottish Command, 6 June 1913–20 January 1914: served as D.A.A. and Q.M.G. in the European War, 5 August – 17 September 1914: A.A. and Q.M.G., 18 September 1914–9 April 1915: promoted Lieut.Col. Gordon Highlanders, April 1915: severely wounded in the leg at the Battle of Festubert, 16 May following: G.S.O., 2nd Grade, War Office (temp.) 1 December 1915–12 February 1916: Brigade Commander, 13 February 1916. Six times Mentioned in Despatches for his services in the European War; created C.M.G. (1915), Brevet Col. (1917). Wounded south-east of Langemarck, 3.50 a.m., 29 July 1917, he died at Poperinghe on the morning of the 31st.: Age 45. He was a highly scientific and brilliant officer – a loss to the Army and the nation. The following account was given of his death: "On the Sunday morning, 29 July 1917, General Gordon, was visiting the frontline trenches, as was his custom, when the (51st Divn.) assembly trench that he was in was hit by a direct German shell, which killed his Brigade Major (Capt. H.H. Lean), two Gordon Highland N.C.Os. and one other rank, (Corpl. E.M. Pope, L/Corpl. W. Lockerby, Pte. A. Whannell) on the spot, and mortally wounded him. He died (just as the Gordons were going 'over the top') two days later, in No.10 Casualty Clearing Station, to which he had been carried, and was buried in the Cemetery at Poperinghe." By Special Order of the King, a printed copy of General Gordon's six Mentions in the European War was sent, 18 December 1917, from the War Office to his widow, with a kind message of 'high appreciation of these services,' by His Majesty. He *m*. January 1908, Pilar Mary (10, Onslow Gardens, London) *dau*. of the late C.E.H. Edmondstoune Cranstoun, of Corehouse, and had three children – Alastair Joseph Edgar; Margaret Collette Mary, and Elizabeth Pilar Mary.

Jesus Mercy
Mary Help

Capt. Lean lies in Poperinghe New Military Cemetery (II.G.35); Corpl. Pope, L/Corpl. Lockerby and Pte. Whannell have no known grave, they are commemorated on the Ypres (Menin Gate) Memorial (Panel 38).

(XIV.A.14) 2nd Lieut. James Clifford Lee, 2nd Bn. (66th Foot) Princess Charlotte of Wales's (Royal Berkshire Regt.): *s*. of Howard Westerman Lee, of Springvale, nr. Redditch, by his wife Henrietta Maud Mary, *dau*. of the late William Gibbs, of Crosslea, Redditch, J.P.: *b*. Redditch, co. Worcester, 23 March 1898: *educ*. Ellesmere College, co. Salop, where he was a Sergt. in the O.T.C.: in Bermuda on the outbreak of war; returned home to England and passed into the Royal Military College, Sandhurst, August 1915: gazetted 2nd Lieut. 15 April 1916; held First Class Bombing Certificate: served with the Expeditionary Force in France and Flanders, and was wounded (G.S. abdominal, head and legs) at Ypres, 31 July 1917, and died at No.17 Casualty Clearing Station nr. Poperinghe, 1 August following. Buried in the adjoining Lyssenthoek Military Cemetery. His Commanding Officer wrote, "It is with deep emotion that I have to inform you of Clifford's death, on 1 August, of wounds received on the morning of 31 July 1917, whilst in action. I have been closely associated with your son for nearly two months, and knew him to be fearless and ever strongly devoted to duty. He was a most promising officer, and extremely popular with his brother officers, and also with the regimental signallers; of whom he was in command. His Brigade Signal Detachment, which he had been specially chosen to command, ask me to include their sincerest sympathies." A brother officer wrote, "Those who knew him loved him for his purity of character, and his entire devotion to what he chose as his life's work. His was a truly dedicated life." While at school he gained his football, cricket and hockey colours: Age 19.

Faithful Unto Death
Dulce Et Decorum Est Pro Patria Mori

(XIV.A.17) Capt. Richard Wellington Shegog, Royal Army Medical Corps attd. 1/4th Bn. The Loyal North Lancashire Regt. (T.F.): elder *s*. of the Rev. Richard William Ashe Shegog, late Rector of Holmpatrick, Skerries, co. Dublin, by his wife Mary Backas, *dau*. of the Rev. R. Hemphill: *b*. Dublin, 6 July 1886: *educ*. Mountjoy School, where he took several Exhibitions, and Trinity College, Dublin, becoming a Scholar and Moderator in Classics: obtained a commission Lieut. Royal Army Medical Corps, 7 September 1915; promoted Capt. September 1916: served with the Expeditionary Force in France and Flanders from 7 January 1916. Wounded by shellfire at the Dressing Station, Pommern Castle,

Ypres 31 July 1917, and died of his wounds and shock the following day at No.17 Casualty Clearing Station. Buried in the Military Cemetery at Poperinghe: Age 31. He *m.* at Skerries, 27 July 1915, Florence Margaret (Salcombe, Skerries), *dau.* of Dr. William Sandham Symes, and had a son, Richard Francis Albert, *b.* 6 June 1916.

Faithful Unto Death

(XIV.A.19) 2nd Lieut. Andrew Mitchell, 2nd Bn. (109th Foot) The Leinster Regt. (Prince of Wales's Royal Canadians): *s.* of James (& Mrs) Mitchell, of 'The Cottage,' Fahan, Co. Donegal: served with the Expeditionary Force in France from 1 June 1917, and died 2 August following, of wounds received in action (31 July) in the attack on Jehovah Trench, nr. Shrewsbury Forest: Age 23. *unm.*

He Sleeps, One of Ulster's Loyal Sons, Far From His Loved Ones

(XIV.B.17) L/Corpl. 36262, Samuel Trick, 88th Coy., Machine Gun Corps (Inf.): formerly no.21033, Devon Regt.: *s.* of John Trick, of Larksbear Cottage, Barnstaple, by his wife Elizabeth, *dau.* of Richard Piper: *b.* Westleigh, co. Devon, 15 November 1896: *educ.* Barnstaple Grammar School, and St. John's College, Battersea, London, S.W.: joined 3rd Devonshire Regt. December 1915: transf'd. Machine Gun Corps December 1916: offered a commission, but declined, not wishing to delay his departure for the Front: served with the Expeditionary Force in France and Flanders from March 1917, and died at a Casualty Clearing Station, 10 July following, of wounds received in action during the attempt to recapture the French coast for the Allied Forces. Buried in Lyssenthoek Military Cemetery, south-west of Poperinghe. He was a most promising scholar, with a fine record both at school and at college: Age 20. *unm.*

He Hath Fought The Good Fight

(XIV.C.18) Gnr. 50559, Harold Dibb, 'D' Bty., 107th Bde., Royal Field Artillery: *s.* of Arthur Dibb, of 11, Pool Road, Otley, co. York, by his wife Jane: and elder brother to Gnr. 1809, A.C. Dibb, Royal Field Artillery, died of gas poisoning 19 March 1916; and Pte. 36227, J.C. Dibb, 6th King's Own Yorkshire Light Infantry, killed in action, 12 October 1917: *b.* Yeadon: enlisted York: served with the Expeditionary Force in France and Flanders from 30 August 1915, and was killed in action, 26 June 1917: Age 24.

Duty Nobly Done

His brother Arthur lies nearby (V.D.5A); Joseph has no known grave, he is commemorated on the Tyne Cot Memorial (Panel 109).

(XIV.D.5A) Pte. G/6220, William George Richardson, 9th (Service) Bn. The Royal Sussex Regt.: *s.* of Samuel Richardson, of 'Rodmell,' Lewes, co. Sussex, by his wife Harriet: *husb.* to R.M. Richardson (95, St. George's Road, Kemp Town, Brighton): *b.* Brighton: enlisted Guildford. Died of wounds, 23 June 1917: Age 39.

Until The Day Dawns When We Shall Meet Again
R.I.P.

(XIV.D.8) Pte. G/19365, Ernest Cheesman, 8th (Service) Bn. The Queen's Own (Royal West Kent Regt.): *s.* of Henry Cheesman, Farm Labourer; of Oak Tree Cottage, Wadhurst, late of Shovers Green Cottage, by his wife Martha: and brother to Gnr. 81025, A. Cheesman, Royal Garrison Artillery, died 7 July 1917: *b.* Hackwoods, Salehurst, co. Sussex, 29 December 1884: *educ.* Wadhurst School: Occupation – Gamekeeper, in the employ of Major Courthope, M.P.: previously served four years Royal Garrison Artillery: re-enlisted Hastings, co. Sussex, 18 November 1915, 3rd Royal Sussex Regt. (no.12235), placed on the Reserve: mobilised 31 May 1916, but remained in England: served with the Expeditionary Force in France and Flanders from 8 May 1917, being transf'd. 8th Queen's Own: took part in the Battle of Messines and, while in the Mount Sorrel sector, 24 June 1917, was seriously wounded in the back by shellfire – shot through the right thigh and both legs – and died later the same day in No.3 Casualty Clearing Station, Poperinghe: Age 32. He *m.* St. Mary's Church, Ticehurst, 10 April 1912; Laura, *née* Puxty, and had a *s.* Frederick Ernest, *b.* January 1913.

Ever In Our Thoughts

His brother Arthur is buried in Vlamertinghe New Military Cemetery (III.E.21).

(XIV.E.3) Corpl. 35455, Trevor Anwyl Jones, 72nd Field Ambulance, Royal Army Medical Corps: *s.* of Daniel R. Jones, Mining Engineer; of Maesyberllan, Pontypridd, co. Glamorgan: *b.* Treherbert, co. Glamorgan, 25 February 1895: *educ.* Intermediate School, Porth, Rhondda Valley: joined Royal Army Medical Corps, Newport, co. Monmouth, 7 September 1914; after the outbreak of war: served with the Expeditionary Force in France and Flanders and, hit in the body and face by traversing machine-gun fire while loading provisions for the trenches, died shortly after arrival at No.3 Canadian C.C.S., Remy Siding, Poperinghe, 18 June 1917. Buried in Lyssenthoek Military Cemetery, Poperinghe: Age 22. *unm.* (*IWGC record Pte.*).

It is generally accepted that at any given time approximately 2% of the population are carriers of the bacteria which causes cerebrospinal meningitis, and the prime reason in at least 95% of infected cases results not from being exposed to another person suffering from the disease but from being in close proximity to a carrier – an apparently healthy person who shows no symptoms of the disease.

In 1907 an outbreak of cerebrospinal meningitis of almost epidemic proportions claimed thousands of lives among the tenement populations of Glasgow, Edinburgh and Belfast. Between 1912 and 1914 compulsory registering of the disease in England and Wales showed an annual toll of approximately 300 lives. In 1915 the incidence of cases – 2,343 civilian and 1,136 military – raised considerable alarm among the authorities as the mortality rate soared and a serum, which had been effective in combating the 1907 and subsequent outbreaks, was having little effect on what was proving a more virulent strain of the disease.

At the outbreak of the Great War the necessity to rapidly raise a large armed force was, without doubt, the primary cause of the resurgence of the disease in Great Britain. The severe overcrowding of camps and depots with large numbers of recruits, the effect of entering into a new way of life, nostalgia, fatigue from training, the cold winter weather; all combined to provide the ideal conditions in which the disease would flourish. On the western front the atmosphere of overcrowded and ill ventilated billets, hutments, tents and dug-outs – where the resistance of the individual was greatly lowered, men lived in extremely close proximity to one another, and catarrhal infections were rife – played a significant part in ensuring the meningococcal bacteria success in attacking the meninges. The bacteria, sprayed out in droplets by the acts of sneezing, coughing or just speaking loudly, were sure to give any susceptible individual a massive dose of the organism.

With an incubation period of three to four days cerebrospinal meningitis is symptomatic of the sudden onset of intense headaches, vomiting, variable degrees of fever, a comparatively slow pulse, stiffness of the muscles and neck, and a rash over certain parts of the body; particularly the buttocks, back, hands and feet. In no disease is the rapid diagnosis of greater importance.

(XIV.E.4A) Rfn. C/12207, Norman Derwent, 21st (Service) Bn. (Yeoman Rifles) The King's Royal Rifle Corps: *yst. s.* of Henry Casaubon Derwent, J.P, of 3, Farcliffe Terrace, Bradford, co. York, Managing Director *Bradford Telegraph & Argus*, by his wife Ann Maria: and brother to 2nd Lieut. R.I. Derwent, West Yorkshire Regt., who fell 1 July 1916 at the opening of the big offensive: *b.* Birmingham, 1893: Occupation – Assistant Clerk; Official Receiver's Office, Scarborough: enlisted King's Royal Rifle Corps, Scarborough: served with the Expeditionary Force in France and Flanders from 5 May 1916; wounded 15

September following; his left ear being shot off and neck lacerated: returned to England for treatment and convalescence, contracting rheumatism during the winter of 1916–17 while stationed at Northampton: returned to France 1 May 1917, and died of cerebrospinal meningitis in No.2 Canadian Casualty Clearing Station, Poperinghe, 18 June following. Buried in the Soldier's Cemetery there. Prior to enlistment Rfn. Derwent had an experience of war which nearly proved fatal when, during the Zeppelin bombardment of Scarborough, December 1914, the house in which he was staying was wrecked. On hearing the sound of the shells exploding he hurriedly left his bedroom, and three or four minutes later the house was in ruins, and, when he was standing in the street his clothing was pierced by pieces of the shell: Age 24. *unm.* See also Rfn. E.A. Ottley (X.C.27A).

Youngest Son Of Ann Maria And Henry Casaubon Derwent J.P
Bradford, Yorkshire, England

His brother Robert is buried in Euston Road Cemetery, Colincamps (I.B.27).

(XIV.E.6A) Pte. 47643, Frederick William Laurisch, 12th (Service) Bn. The Royal Fusiliers (City of London Regt.): *s.* of Julius Laurisch, of 30, Princess Street, Manchester, Chemical Merchant, by his wife Sarah Elizabeth, *dau.* of John Simpson, of Clayton-le-Woods, co. Lancaster: *b.* Oak House, Grange Avenue, Levenshulme, Manchester, 9 June 1896: *educ.* South Manchester Grammar School, Rossall (O.T.C. member); and Germany: enlisted Universities & Public Schools (20th) Battn., November 1914: volunteered as Bomb Thrower; served with the Expeditionary Force in France and Flanders in that capacity: wounded 14 March 1916; sent on sick leave to England, rejoined his regiment on recovery; wounded (G.S.W. legs, arms) in the attack on Battle Wood, nr. Ypres, 14 June 1917, and died four days later (18 June), No.3 Casualty Clearing Station, Poperinghe. Buried at Lyssenthoek Cemetery. A keen sportsman, while at Rossall School he won many cups for long-distance running, in which he excelled: Age 21. *unm.*

Died Of Wounds
Son Of Mr & Mrs Laurisch, Manchester

(XIV.E.7A) Sergt. 265738, James William Wharton, 1/7th Bn. The King's (Liverpool) Regt. (T.F.): *s.* of James Wharton, of 30, Shaftesbury Road, Great Crosby, Liverpool, by his wife Margaret: and yr. brother to Pte. 307133, F.J. Wharton, Tank Corps, killed in action, 9 August 1918: *b.* Great Crosby: enlisted Liverpool. Died of multiple bullet wounds (abdominal, thoracic), and severely fractured arm, 18 June 1917: Age 24. *unm.*

*Sacred Heart Of Jesus Have Mercy On Him May He Rest In Peace,
Amen*

His brother Frederick has no known grave; he is commemorated on the Vis-en-Artois Memorial (Panel 11).

(XIV.E.8) A/Bmdr. 315377, Leonard Kingswell, 1st (Wessex) Heavy Bty., Royal Garrison Artillery (T.F.): *s.* of George Kingswell, by his wife Mary, *née* Richardson: *b.* South Wallington, Fareham, 19 November 1887: *educ.* Fareham, co. Hants: Occupation – Fishmonger: enlisted 12 October 1915: served with the Expeditionary Force in France and Flanders, and died, 19 June 1917, from wounds received in action. Buried in the Military Cemetery on the Poperinghe-le-Boeschepe Road: Age 29. His Major wrote, "He did very well out here, and I looked on him as one of my most reliable N.C.O.'s." His Captain wrote, "Both officers and men are dreadfully sorry to lose him, as he was always so willing and trustworthy, and we shall feel his loss very much." He *m.* at Fareham, 26 August 1914, Evelyn Mary Ann (32, York Street, Gosport, co. Hants), *dau.* of Alfred Smith, and had a son – Leonard Bert, *b.* 23 August 1915.

(XIV.E.16) L/Corpl. 132934, William Austin, 254th Coy., Royal Engineers: *s.* of William Austin, by his wife Eliza: *b.* Chesterton, co. Stafford, 15 May 1889: *educ.* there: Occupation – Miner: enlisted 8 October 1914: served with the Mediterranean Expeditionary Force at Gallipoli from 21 November 1915: wounded and invalided to Malta, and later to Egypt: proceeded to France, 5 June 1916, and died at Poperinghe, 19 June 1917, from wounds received in action. Buried in the Lijssenthoek Military Cemetery: Age 28. An officer wrote, "I had full opportunity of appreciating his conscientious hard work and stout heart. Had he only been spared he was noted for early promotion when chance offered. His loss is deeply felt by all who knew him." He *m.* at Chesterton, 1911, Martha Annie (34, Silver Street, Dodworth), *dau.* of Albert Speed, and had three children – Charles, *b.* 22 March 1912; Ivy May, *b.* 24 June 1913; Lily, *b.* 17 April 1915.

Death Divides But Memory Clings

(XIV.F.19) Dvr. 129556, Charles Henry Moakes, 'D' Bty., 149th Bde. Royal Field Artillery: *s.* of William Moakes, of 124, Sutton Road, Huthwaite, Mansfield, co. Nottingham: and yr. brother to Pte. 956, R.W. Moakes, 1/8th Sherwood Foresters, who fell 15 June 1916, during an enemy attack near Wytschaete: *b.* Hucknall-under-Huthwaite, 1897: enlisted Sutton-in-Ashfield. Died of wounds, 16 June 1917, at Poperinghe: Age 19.

His brother Robert is buried in Kemmel Chateau Military Cemetery (D.69).

(XIV.G.1) Bmdr. 127462, Allan Weatherhead, 505th Bty. Royal Field Artillery: s. of John Weatherhead, of Pannal, Harrogate, co. York, by his wife Sarah Ann: and elder brother to L/Corpl. 200516, A. Weatherhead, 1/5th West Yorkshire Regt., killed in action, 28 September 1916, aged 20 years: b. Burnbridge: enlisted Harrogate. Died 9 June 1917, of accidental injuries: Age 23.

His brother Arthur is buried in Connaught Cemetery, Thiepval (I.B.16).

(XIV.G.2A) Pte. 723472, John Henry Gibson, 24th (County of London) Bn. (The Queen's) The London Regt. (T.F.): formerly no.3030, 2/5th Bn. The Buffs (East Kent Regt.), (T.F.): s. of John Gibson, of 145, Tower Gardens Road, Tottenham, London, N.17, by his wife Eliza: b. Tottenham, about 1881: Occupation – Clerk; London Stock Exchange: enlisted Tottenham. Died of wounds, 10 June 1917: Age 36.

Rest In The Lord

(XIV.G.11A) Pte. 47712, Harold Barton Perris, 26th (Service) Bn. (Bankers) The Royal Fusiliers (City of London Regt.): formerly no.5122: s. of the late George Henry Perris, of Manchester, by his wife Annie: and yr. brother to Actg. S/Sergt. S4/045458, C.H. Perris, Army Service Corps, died 6 October 1917: enlisted Manchester. Died of wounds, 10 June 1917, received in the attack on the Damnstrasse: Age 33.

His brother Charles lies nearby (XXI.B.5A).

With the exception of New Zealand, none of whose headstones bear any epitaph, one of the last acts performed by many families and relations of the dead was to request a personal inscription for addition to the headstone detail. The epitaphs found on C.W.G.C. headstones are extremely varied and thought provoking. Often biblical in context: *Greater Love Hath No Man Than This That He Lay Down His Life For His Friends* – to a mother's request: *Will Some Kind Hand In That Far Off Land Lay A Flower On His Grave For Me* – Few perhaps could be both as poignant and pertinent as that chosen by the family of Dudley Mitchener.

Just A Soldier
They are grouping there, in the barrack square,
On a sunlit afternoon;
And proud they stand, a gallant band,
Awaiting orders soon.
There's one lad shy, who hurrying by,
Leaves home for far away.
Yet he bravely smiles, as watching at whiles,
You whisper soft and say.

Chorus: He's just a simple soldier
With a number to his name,
He's out to fight for all that's right
And dear old England's fame.
He wants to do his duty,
Break the Kaiser's iron rod,
He'll strike with nerve to proudly serve,
His Country, King and God.

One night at dark, to himself says, "Hark!
I think I hear a tread!"
And forward creeps, whilst his comrades sleep,
Then stops as if struck dead.
In the darkness there, in the midnight air
Comes the sound of a steady tramp.
He gives a low shout, the warning goes out,
And that's how he saves the camp. *Chorus:*

In the papers at home, across the white foam,
They tell how he fought and won;
How at the bitter start he was shot to the heart,
Ere the battle had begun.
Now his comrades stand by a mound of sand
With the enemy's guns their gain.
And in voices low, as laying him low,
Comes the sound of this sad refrain. Chorus:

*S. Ashley / T. Gray,
Chappell & Co. 1900.*

(XIV.H.3A) Pte. 350501, Dudley William Arthur Mitchener, 'C' Coy., 7th (City of London) Bn. The London Regt. (T.F.): formerly no.2134: late of Enfield, co. Middlesex: *s.* of William Mitchener, of 99, Muswell Avenue, London, N.10, and his wife, Annie: *b.* Hove, co. Sussex: a pre-war Territorial, volunteered and enlisted Sun Street, Waltham Abbey, August 1914: proceeded to France 17 March 1915. Died, 9 June 1917, of wounds received in action two days previously from hostile machine-gun fire before White Chateau in the attack at Hollebeke: Age 21.

Just A Simple Soldier With A Number To His Name

On the night of 2 August 1917 C.S.M Handley, 1/6th King's (Liverpool) Regt., and a handful of men took shelter in a captured German pillbox which, being utilised as an aid post, was crowded with wounded, stretcher-bearers, and men from all manner of units. He wrote, "About midnight Rifleman Peet, an officer's servant, stumbled into the pill-box badly wounded and saying that Lieut. Burton was 'out there' also wounded, but trying to get shelter. I ordered two stretcher-bearers to come with me. They objected so I threatened them with my pistol and out we went on what I feared was a hopeless quest. The only illumination was from exploding shells and rocket lights. Eventually we saw him, a crouching figure, silhouetted by a shell burst. 'Thank God, Sergeant Major!' he said, as I got hold of his arm, but he groaned and said, 'The other one.' On getting him into the pillbox, I found his left shoulder blown away revealing a bloody mess that looked like his lung. He died on his way to the first aid station. This officer was acting as 'Liaison Officer' – keeping touch between our companies and the regiments on either side of us. He carried with him as much rum as he could, which he shared out to the men he met on his rounds, in his sympathy for them in their terrible conditions. This 'errand of mercy' he had just performed at the trench full of water in front of my pillbox. It was his last good deed in this world."

(XV.A.2) Lieut. Geoffrey Bunnell Burton, 1/6th Bn. (Rifles) The King's (Liverpool) Regt. (T.F.): *s.* of George Lewis Burton, of Blundellsands, Liverpool, by his wife Katherine Mary: served with the Expeditionary Force in France from 12 July 1915, and died in the early hours of 3 August. 1917, of wounds received in action on the 2nd.: Age 21.

Dulce Et Decorum Est Pro Patria Mori

Rfn. 109320, W. Peet died at home, 18 February 1919, consequent to wounds received in action on the Western Front; he is buried in Bickerstaff (Holy Trinity) Churchyard, Lancs (New S.E.51).

(XV.A.14) 2nd Lieut. Ifor Griffiths Gibson, 11th (Service) Bn. The Prince of Wales's Own (West Yorkshire Regt.) attd. 6th Sqdn. Royal Flying Corps: only *s.* of Frederic Gibson, Architect & Surveyor, of 22, Llantwit Road, Treforest, Pontypridd, by his wife Mary May, *dau.* of Edgar Treharne, of Abercynon: *b.* Pontypridd, co. Glamorgan, 30 May 1895: *educ.* Colston School, Stapleton, Bristol: Occupation – Articled Architect to his father: enlisted 5th Bn. Welsh Regt., August 1914, and sent to Gallipoli: took part in the landing at Suvla Bay, and hard fighting before being wounded by a bullet through the chest and invalided home: on recovery joined the recruiting staff at Pontypridd: obtained a commission January 1916: served with the Expeditionary Force in France and Flanders: volunteered and requested attachment Royal Flying Corps (June

1916); returned to England and underwent training at Hendon; proceeded back to France the following month. Wounded in the chest and legs, 10 August 1917, and died at No.3 Canadian Casualty Clearing Station the following day. Buried in Lyssenthoek Military Cemetery, Poperinghe. His pilot Lieut. Pickett wrote, "We had gone up to do a shoot rather a long way over the lines, and low clouds and bad visibility made the target very difficult to see. Whilst we were busy we were suddenly attacked from above by nine Albatross Scouts. Their machines were twice as fast as ours, and they simply made rings round us. I knew that it was useless to attempt to fly straight for even a second. I don't know how long the scrap lasted, but your son got off 100 rounds. I don't know how the machine managed to get home – the propeller, wings and engine were shot through, and so badly wrecked, that it had to be 'walked off.'": Age 22. *unm.*

(XV.A.15) Lieut. Douglas Arthur Leamon, 8th (Service) Bn. The Norfolk Regt.: *yst. s.* of Philip Augustus Leamon, of 195, Parkview Street, St. James-Assiniboia, Headingley, Manitoba, by his late wife Lucy: and brother to Pte. 25987, G.M. Leamon, 1st Norfolk Regt., killed in action, 9 October 1917, aged 33 years: *b.* Neatishead, Norwich, England, 11 June 1890: *educ.* Beccles College, co. Norfolk: removed to Canada, 1912: Occupation – Real Estate Rental Manager: joined 43rd Bn. C.E.F. (Pte., No.420951), Winnipeg, 16 January 1915. Mortally wounded by the explosion of a gas shell at Railway Dugouts, 14 August 1917; died in the ambulance en-route to No.17 C.C.S., Poperinghe. Buried in the cemetery there: Age 27. *unm.* (*IWGC record age 22*)

A Most Loving Son And Devoted Brother

His brother Grantley has no known grave; he is commemorated on the Tyne Cot Memorial (Panel 35).

(XV.A.16) Lieut. James Andrew Lewton-Brain, 8th (Service) Bn. The Norfolk Regt.: 3rd *s.* of James Lewton-Brain, of The Mill House, Toftwood, Dereham, by his wife Clare, *dau.* of William Andrew Lawrence: *b.* Swanton Morley, co. Norfolk, 25 March 1888: *educ.* King Edward VII Grammar School, King's Lynn: Occupation – initially Clerk; London & Provincial Bank (Great Yarmouth Branch); removed to Canada for a similar appointment with the Bank of Montreal, Vancouver; and thereafter Victoria Branch: previously served 2 years, 6 months, 6th Norfolk Regt. (Cyclists): enlisted Canadian Highlanders, Pte., no.77579, Victoria, British Columbia, 5 November 1914; after the outbreak of war: served with the Expeditionary Force in France and Flanders until January 1916, when he returned to England for officer training – transf'd. British Expeditionary Force – commissioned 2nd Lieut. attd. 8th Norfolk Regt. 23 January 1916, and returned to France: promoted Lieut., apptd. Machine Gun Officer, 18 March 1917. Severely wounded and poisoned by the detonation of a gas shell at Railway Dugouts, Zillebeke, he was removed to the Casualty Clearing

Station at Poperinghe where he died a few hours after arrival, 14 August 1917. Buried there. His Commanding Officer wrote, "I can hardly express to you what a loss he is to all of us, both officers and men of this battalion. He was a splendid stamp of officer, and a good leader, and was my Battalion Machine Gun Officer, and of great value to me. And as we are in action at the moment of writing, it is difficult for me to give you many particulars; but he died a few hours after his attack, so, please God, he did not suffer too much. He was so popular with us all, we shall miss him terribly;" and a brother officer, "He was very popular amongst us all, not only the officers but all the men knew him well. I can assure you that your loss is shared by us all; his place will be hard to fill in our midst." He was well-known in the Dereham and Yarmouth districts as an enthusiastic football player and cricketer.": Age 29. *unm*.

Requiescat In Pace

(XV.C.2) Gnr. 926515, Charles William Brunsden, 'A' Bty., 150th Bde., Royal Field Artillery: *s*. of the late James Henry Brunsden, and his widow, Elizabeth Emma Bettis, *née* Brunsden (28, Lismore Road, Kentish Town, London): *b*. Hampstead: enlisted London, S.E.: Died of wounds, 2 July 1917: Age 20. (*Headstone records Brunsdem*)

Ever In My Thoughts My Darling Boy
Mother

(XV.C.18A) Pte. 266499, George Knowles, Lewis Gun Sect., 6th Bn. The Cheshire Regt. (T.F.): late of 54, Brady Street, Stockport, co. Chester: *s*. of James Knowles, and Frances his spouse: *b*. Portwood, Stockport: Occupation – Millworker; Messrs Vernon Cotton Spinning Co., Portwood: enlisted Stockport, 1915. Died of wounds (G.S.W. head, arms) 6 July 1917, received when the battalion's front line was attacked by enemy aircraft earlier the same day. The Chaplain said Pte. Knowles was unconscious on arrival at the Casualty Clearing Station and despite the best possible attentions he passed away peacefully within a few hours: Age 25. He was married to Edith Pickersgill, *née* Knowles (10, Colonial Road, Heaviley, Stockport), and had one child. *Stockport Express*, In Memoriam:

Oh! God, how mysterious and strange are Thy ways,
To take from me my loved one in the best of his days.
Could I have been there at the hour of his death,
To have caught the last sigh of his fleeting breath.
"One of the best."

Sorrowing Wife & Child.

He Gave His Life That We Might Live

(XV.C.20) Pte. 266498, John Madden, 6th Bn. The Cheshire Regt. (T.F.): formerly no.3963: *s.* of John Madden, of 71, Heaward Street, Stockport, co. Chester, and Mary, his wife: enlisted Stockport 1915. Died of wounds, 6 July 1917, received from retaliatory fire following a successful raid on Caliban Trench, north of Wieltje (opposite Hill Top) made by a large number of the battalion (and a R.E. demolition party) on the night of 4–5 July: Age 22. *Stockport Express*, In Memoriam:

> *Sleep on, dear friend, in a soldier's grave,*
> *Your life for your country you nobly gave,*
> *We could not stand by you to say Good-bye,*
> *But safe in God's keeping now you lie.*

His chum L/Corpl. Geo. Bradbury.

(XV.D.3A) Gnr. 65571, Frank Seal, 160th Siege Bty., Royal Garrison Artillery: *s.* of James (& Eliza) Seal, of Shingle Cottage, Edenbridge, co. Kent: and brother to Rfn. S/14455, J. Seal, 1st Rifle Brigade, died of wounds, 24 January 1917, received in action nr. Albert: *b.* Edenbridge: *educ.* National School, Limpsfield: enlisted Guildford, co. Surrey. Died of wounds, 26 June 1917: Age 20. *unm.*

Oh How We Miss Him
Jesus Said I Am The Light Of The World

His brother James is buried in Hem Farm Military Cemetery (I.E.3).

(XV.D.11) Pte. 28170, George Price, 9th (Service) Bn. Alexandra, Princess of Wales's Own (Yorkshire Regt.), (The Green Howards): *s.* of William Price, of Stockton-on-Tees, by his wife Harriet: enlisted Stockton. Died of wounds, 25 June 1917, received earlier the same day when the battalion's camp at Dickebusch was subjected to long-distance enemy shellfire: Age 27. He was married to Margaret A. Price (6, Wedgwood Street, Thornaby-on-Tees, co. York).

(XV.E.6A) Pte. 19572, Martyn Beresford Gieve, 12th (Service) Bn. The Durham Light Infantry: *s.* of Percy Parnall (& Sarah Emma) Gieve, of 75, Ferney Park Road, Stroud Green, London: *b.* London: enlisted, joined 14th D.L.I., 1914: served with the Expeditionary Force in France and Flanders from 11 September 1915: wounded late 1915; on recovery rejoined 12th Battn. D.L.I., 1916, and died of wounds, 20 June 1917 (shot through the lungs) at Messines: Age 21.

(XV.H.15) Pte. 2690, Herbert Beswick, 2nd Bn. (96th Foot) The Manchester Regt.: late *husb.* to Mary Beswick (10, Buckley Street, Stalybridge, Manchester):

served with the Expeditionary Force in France from March 1915, and died of wounds (gas), 13 June 1917: Age 41. Remembered on the War Memorial, Trinity Street, Stalybridge.

Christ Will Clasp The Broken Chain Closer When We Meet Again

(XV.J.6A) Pte. G/9136, Ernest Thomas Wayling, 10th (Service) Bn. (Kent County) The Queen's Own (Royal West Kent Regt.): *s.* of Mrs Wayling (104, Corleylands Road, Sidcup, co. Kent): and brother to Dvr. 177394, H.R. Wayling, 317th Bde., Royal Field Artillery, killed in action, 17 November 1917: *b.* Abbey Wood, co. Kent: enlisted Woolwich, London, S.E.: served with the Expeditionary Force in France and Flanders, and died of wounds, 9 June 1917.

The Lord Giveth & The Lord Taketh Away
Blessed Be The Lord

His brother Henry is buried in Duhallow A.D.S. Cemetery (II.C.9).

(XV.J.7) Pte. 285014, Benjamin Williams, 9th (Service) Bn. The Welsh Regt.: formerly no.201472, King's (Liverpool) Regt.: late of Wavertree, Liverpool: eldest *s.* of Peter Williams, of Cross Street, Prescot, by his wife Elizabeth: *b.* 1886: *educ.* Prescot: left school aged 14, finding employ in coal mining; later joined Mercantile Marine and attained grade Able Seaman from which profession he enlisted at Liverpool. Died 8 June 1917, of wounds (multiple GS), received in the vicinity of Grand Bois, Wytschaete the previous day: Age 32. He *m.* 1908; Annie Rose Williams (St. Charles' House, Lower Bullingham, co. Hereford), and leaves a *dau.* Doris.

The British Journal Of Nursing
September 8, 1917

Nurse Nellie Spindler

Miss Nellie Spindler, Staff Nurse, Q.A.I.M.N.S.R., was killed in the bombardment of the hospital at Abbeville (*q.v.*) by the Germans on August 21, 1917. Letter and telegram from the War Office state that she was 'killed in action.'

Private communications from Abbeville state that the hospital was shelled all day, that Miss Spindler was struck at 11 am., became unconscious immediately and died twenty minutes later in the arms of Nurse Wood of Wakefield, which is also Miss Spindler's native city; her father being Inspector of Police.

She was given a full military funeral and the 'Last Post' was sounded over her grave, which is quite near the hospital and will be well looked after.

Miss Spindler was 26 years of age, and was trained at the Townbridge Infirmary, Leeds, from 1912 to 1915.

From November 1915 to May 1917 she was Staff Nurse at Whittington Military Hospital, Lichfield. Since May 1917, Staff Nurse at Stationary Hospital, Abbeville, France.

She was right in the danger zone, but while recognising it her letters were hopeful and cheery.

She is the second member of the Leeds Infirmary to die on Military Service. The first was the A.M.O. Capt. William Crymble, R.A.M.C., who died of enteric fever at Suez, after ten months' interment in Germany. He had been taken prisoner at the Battle of Le Cateau.

At present there are over 100 nurses of the L.T. Infirmary on active service.

Miss Spindler was very popular during her training and her loss is deplored by the many friends she made who deeply sympathise with her family in their sorrow.

(XVI.A.3) Staff Nurse Nellie Spindler, Queen Alexandra's Imperial Medical Nursing Service: *dau.* of George Kealey Spindler, of Wakefield, co. York, and Elizabeth, *née* Snowden, his wife. The only woman buried at Lijssenthoek. She was killed on 21 August 1917 while attached to 44 CCS at Brandhoek – the only woman to be killed that close to the front at Ypres. The CCS War Diary records – "Yesterday morning the enemy began to shell the railway alongside the camp and the third or fourth shell killed S/Nurse Spindler. She was hit in the chest and died in about five minutes." 4 other nurses were concussed by the same blast and, as a consequence of this, next day 44 CCS evacuated all its nurses to St. Omer. 44 CCS moved back to Remy Sidings where the officers and men from the unit held a burial service for S/Nurse Spindler. Her funeral was attended by over one hundred Officers, four Generals and the Surgeon-General. The diary records that during the bombardment the Nursing Sisters behaved splendidly and one of them, Sister M. Wood, was awarded the MM – one of only a handful of women to win the award.

A Noble Type Of Good Heroic Womanhood

The only other British female member of nursing staff buried in Belgium is Sister Elsie Kemp, who is buried in nearby Godewaersvelde British Cemetery, France (I.M.1).

(XVI.A.10) 2nd Lieut. Geoffrey Nicholson, 6th Sqdn. Royal Flying Corps: *s*. of Joseph Shield Nicholson, of 3, Belford Park, Edinburgh, Professor of Edinburgh University, by his wife Jeanie Walmsley: *educ*. Merchiston, and Edinburgh University (History, Hons); member of the O.T.C.: studying Law for the Bar on the outbreak of war, August 1914: obtained a commission 2nd Lieut. Black Watch, February 1915: much interested in flying he gained his certificate, Beatty's, Hendon, November 1915: subsequently (February 1917) transf'd. Royal Flying Corps. Died of wounds, 22 August 1917, received in action the previous day when, whilst flying escort to a photographic mission, his aircraft was attacked and disabled. He brought his aircraft and wounded observer (Lieut. F.L. McLeary) safely back to the aerodrome at Abeele. At the time of his death 2nd Lieut. Nicholson had been six weeks qualified as pilot: Age 23.

Beloved

(XVI.A.11) 2nd Lieut. Benjamin Brayshaw Victor McCracken, 9th (Service) Bn. (Co. Tyrone) The Royal Inniskilling Fusiliers: eldest *s*. of the late George McCracken, of Dromore, Co. Tyrone, Manager of the Ulster Bank, Dromore, by his wife Emma Frances (now wife of J.J.H.. Waddell, M.A., LL.B., of Ardnachree, Dalkey, Co. Dublin), *dau*. of Spencer Binns, of Manchester: *b*. Stretford, Manchester, 14 June 1897: *educ*. Masonic School, Clonskeagh, Dublin: enlisted 12th Inniskilling Dragoons, 28 August 1915: transf'd. Cadet Corps; gazetted 2nd Lieut., Royal Inniskilling Fusiliers, December 1916: served with the Expeditionary Force in France from 2 January 1917, and died at Poperinghe 23 August following. Buried in the Military Cemetery, Remy, Poperinghe. His Chaplain wrote, "I came to this battalion in May last, and soon got to know your boy; I took to him at once. During the day he behaved with great courage and altogether splendidly, and you have great reason to be proud of his memory. In mine he will always be associated with what is brave and noble;" and his Major, "Your son formed one of a very happy family here, who worked and played together. I feel I must tell you that he was hit leading his men, and though you have lost him for a while, you will always be proud of a son who gave his life for his country." A nurse wrote, "Everything we could do for your son we did, he was so bright and cheerful through it all. Though the wounds were so severe, he was such a brick, and never complained at all;" and the day before he died he wrote, "I am lying on a nice bed with nice nurses, and all the rest of it." Concluding with his love he made a mention of all in the home to which he was deeply attached: Age 20. *unm*.

Till The Day Dawns And The Shadows Flee Away

(XVI.A.12) Capt. James Ernest Studholme Wilson, M.C., Royal Army Medical Corps attd. 2/1st (Buckinghamshire) Bn. Oxford & Bucks Light Infantry (T.F.): elder *s*. of the late Rev. Studholme Wilson, formerly Rector of Millbrook, Southampton, by his wife Helen Louisa (Stoneleigh, Newport, co. Salop), *dau*. of the late Samuel Rawlins: *b*. Burley Rectory, co. Hants, 25 July 1886: *educ*. Summerfields, nr. Oxford; Radley College, and London Hospital: became M.R.C.S. and L.R.C.P. autumn 1911, and went into practice at Iver, co. Buckingham: volunteered for Foreign Service; gazetted Lieut. R.A.M.C. December 1915: served with the Expeditionary Force in France and Flanders attd. Oxford & Bucks Light Infantry from May 1916: promoted Capt. 4 June following. Awarded the Military Cross (*London Gazette*, 23 September 1916) for 'conspicuous gallantry, and devotion to duty during operations' – at the Battle of Fromelles, 19 July 1916 – 'He went up to the front line from his Aid Post through a very heavy barrage in order to assist the wounded. By his pluck and skill he undoubtedly saved many lives. He afterwards controlled the evacuation of the wounded under heavy fire.' Capt. Wilson died at the Canadian C.C.S., Poperinghe, 23 August 1917: Age 31. Of the circumstances of his death, Major C. Miller wrote, "On August 20th, in the evening, the battalion moved forward into the Support Line, just forward of Wieltje with HQ at Uhlan Farm. It was a pretty grim business, with many casualties, but the greatest tragedy that night was the fate of Wilson. When the battalion was put in the Support Line, about 7 p.m. to wait until dark to take over the front, he insisted in going up to his Aid Post at once without waiting for HQ. His objective was to get in before night, put his runners and representatives of companies in touch with his Dressing Station and Company HQ in daylight and erect directing signs. He relied on finding his way with a map, and rejected the Colonel's advice to go up to HQ who had guides who could be trusted to find the way. He lost his way after leaving Warwick House and with his party (consisting of his batman, Rupert Hayers, and Jack Baker) wandered about this wilderness for some hours, eventually halting in a large shell hole to wait for dawn. But, as luck would have it, this was in the neighbourhood of the Hun's barrage line and he was wounded in the stomach by a small piece of high explosive. This must have occurred about 11.00 p.m., but was only discovered some hours later when he collapsed and his Corporal found the wound when he examined him. When dawn broke it was discovered that the party was only a few hundred yards from the Regimental Aid Post for which they had been searching. Trying to find one's way with a map and no guides in the Ypres or Somme areas was hopeless as all the features except hill, valleys and rivers ceased to exist. Houses, roads and woods are blotted out, new tracks are formed and all features by which one would expect to find the way are removed or distorted, so the task becomes impossible. Poor

Wilson reached the Aid Post at about 6 a.m. the next day, and the hospital at Brandhoek (on the Poperinghe – Ypres Road) soon after. He was operated upon in the afternoon, while the hospital was being shelled. The hospital had to be evacuated the same afternoon and he was removed to a Casualty Clearing Station at Remy Siding, behind Poperinghe, where he died two days later. He was buried at Lyssenthoek Cemetery, adjoining the Casualty Clearing Station. In Wilson the Battalion lost one of its most valuable officers. He was devoted to the Battalion, studied its interests before all else, realised the value of esprit de corps and fostered it in all he did. He had the deepest insight into the feelings of all ranks. He knew what an asset cheerfulness is in a Battalion, and he exceeded his brilliant wit as a writer, as an artist and as an organiser to promote it. He had an instinctive knowledge of the minds of the officers and men that was often of great value to his Commanding Officer. When it is realised how many M.O.'s are 'Field Ambulance' men, the value of a man like Wilson, who lived for the Regiment, can be fully appreciated. Also, to the sorrow of all, he was to die for it." And Lieut.Col. J.B. Muir, Comdg. 2nd O.B.L.I., "Our Medical Officer, Capt. J.E.S Wilson, M.C., was hit while proceeding to the Aid Post. With characteristic pluck he did not disclose the fact for several hours and this, coupled with the fact that the enemy shelled the hospital during his operation, resulted in his death; one of the greatest disasters the Battalion has had since its landing in France. We are left only with the memory of a cheerful and greatly loved companion and with the visible fruits of his untiring efforts for the good of the Battalion as a whole. We have all lost many friends in the last two or three years, but none, I feel certain, is more regretted than this." He *m.* at St. Michael's, Paddington, London, W., 3 July 1912, Marjory, *dau.* of the late Thomas Ircland, of Mossley Hill, Liverpool, and had a son, Geoffrey Studholme, *b.* 5 June 1913.

(XVI.A.15) 2nd Lieut. James Thomas 'Ginger' Jones, 20th (County of London) Bn. (Blackheath & Woolwich) The London Regt. (T.F.): *s.* of David Rees (& Mary) Jones, of 13, Amersham Grove, New Cross, London, S.E.14: *b.* Aberaeron, co. Cardigan, 1897: *educ.* Brockley School, and St. Olave's Grammar School (Scholarship Student), 1912–15. Died 24 August 1917, of wounds received in action at Ypres: Age 20. *unm.* 2nd Lieut. Jones is remembered on the Brockley School War Memorial, and St. Olave's.

Hyn A Allodd Hwn Efe Ai Gwnaeth

Translation: He Hath Done What He Could.

(XVI.A.18) 2nd Lieut. Oswald Matthews Holmes, 6th (Service) Bn. The King's Own (Yorkshire Light Infantry): only *s.* of Harry Holmes, of 72, Chatsworth Gardens, Acton Hill, London, W., by his wife Clara, *dau.* of Samuel

Matthews, of Halifax: *b*. Bristol, 2 April 1895: *educ*. Balham Modern School, London: on leaving there was engaged in business with Messrs Charles Morgan & Co., Stationers, London: joined Inns of Court O.T.C. 2 August 1915: obtained a commission October following: trained at Ripon, passing the Veterinary Examination; thereafter sent to Pontefract as Transport Officer: served with the Expeditionary Force in France and Flanders from June 1916: took part in the operations on the Somme; gassed 16 September: returned to England on sick leave; apptd. Commandant, Shooting Ranges, Hornsea, co. York, on recovery: rejoined his regiment in France, 27 June 1917 and, wounded nr. Ypres, 23 August 1917; died two days later at No.17 Casualty Clearing Station. Buried at Lyssenthoek Military Cemetery, Poperinghe: Age 22. The Hospital Chaplain wrote, "Your son came in on the evening of 25 August, and died at 11.20 p.m that night of wounds in the shoulder, body and hand. He had acute gas gangrene and nothing could be done for him. He suffered very little owing to weakness and the great shock. He was too weak to speak or understand much. His body lies in the Lyssenthoek Military Cemetery (Plot 16, A18), south-west of Poperinghe;" and Capt. B. Hettler, "My Commanding Officer has asked me to write to you and give you what details I can about the death of your son, 2nd Lieut. O.M. Holmes...It is a most painful duty to perform, for by the loss of 2nd Lieut. Holmes I miss a real good helper and officer, one who was most conscientious in the performance of his duties, most thorough in all that he undertook, and a real friend to the men under his command. I knew his value as an officer, as an only son I can conceive the greatness of the loss you have sustained...On the morning of Wednesday, 22 August, we went into action, your son commanding one of the platoons of my company. He was quite all right until Thursday morning at eleven o'clock when he was hit by a fragment of shell on the left hip. He was promptly attended to by the stretcher-bearers who dressed his wound, and then carried him to a place of safety, ready to be despatched to hospital. I saw him in the afternoon and he seemed rather cheerful for one in his condition, and I really believed that he would pull through all right. However, news came through that he had died in the evening of the 25th." He *m*. Leeds, 23 June 1917; Marjorie Jessie (27, Cambridge Road, Lee, London, S.E.), *dau*. of Charles Henry Holden, of Leeds.

And He Was Not For God Took Him
Gen. 5.24

(XVI.B.8A) Corpl. 120586, Erick Wilkinson Knowles 'N' Special Coy. (Gas), Royal Engineers: *s*. of George Mason Knowles, of Ben Rhydding, co. York, by his wife Laura: *b*. Baildon: enlisted Royal Army Medical Corps, 1915: transf'd. Royal Engineers, Chatham, September of that year, and left immediately for the

Front: served with the Expeditionary Force in France and Flanders, and died at Lyssenthoek, nr. Poperinghe, 14 July 1917, from gunshot wounds to the left side (shoulder, arm) received in action at Zillebeke four days previously: Age 21. Dedicated – *'Let Those Who Come After See To It That Their Names Be Not Forgotten'* – Corpl. Knowles is remembered on Ilkley War Memorial (Panel 3).

(XVI.C.16) Pte. 34373, Leslie Matthew Revell, 8th (Service) Bn. The Loyal North Lancashire Regt.: formerly no.23134, Royal Fusiliers: *s*. of Matthew (& Frances Elizabeth) Revell, of Haytor View, Totnes, co. Devon: *b*. Totnes, 5 November 1895: *educ*. King Edward VI Grammar School: Occupation – Bank Clerk: joined 5th Devonshire Regt. (T.F.), 2 September 1914: discharged shortly afterwards, suffering from appendicitis; rejoined – Bankers' Battn. Royal Fusiliers, 8 December 1915: served with the Expeditionary Force in France and Flanders from December 1916; transf'd. Loyal North Lancashire Regt., and died at No.2 Canadian Casualty Clearing Station 23 July 1917, from wounds received in action nr. Ypres on the 20th of that month. Buried in the Military Cemetery, Lijssenthoek, nr. Poperinghe. His Commanding Officer wrote, "The officers and men much regret having lost the services of so good a soldier and comrade as he proved himself to be." He was a keen athlete; in 1909 he won the cross-country race (four miles) and many other prizes at different times at the annual school sports sports: Age 21. *unm*.

*Until The Easter Morn Farewell
One Of The Best*

(XVI.C.17A) Pte. 12781, George Edward Lloyd, 'C' Coy., 9th (Service) Bn. The Sherwood Foresters (Notts & Derbys Regt.): *s*. of Elizabeth Lloyd (28, Trinity Street, Belle Vue, Shrewsbury): *b*. Wellington, co. Salop: Occupation – Footman to Mrs M.E. Arkwright, Oak Hill, Cromford: enlisted Derby, 1914: served with the Expeditionary Force at Gallipoli, August – December 1915; and in France and Flanders from July 1916. Died 24 July 1917, of multiple (Left leg, Mid-Upper abdominal, Left arm) machine-gun wounds: Age 21. *unm*. Remembered on Bellevue (Holy Trinity Church) Roll of Honour (Addenda). Oak Hill (Alison House), was (1920) a Toc H Holiday Centre.

(XVI.D.1) Gnr. 143200, Alfred Matson, 'D' Bty., 107th Bde., Royal Field Artillery: 3rd *s*. of Thomas Matson, Labourer; of 6, Wilson Street, Darlington, by his wife Mary: and elder brother to Corpl. 18/113, C. Matson, Durham Light Infantry, died of wounds, 2 March 1917: *b*. Aycliffe: Occupation – Teacher; Durham Education Committee: enlisted Darlington. Died 17 July 1917, of wounds (G.S.W. multiple abdo-thoracic [Penet.]; humerus, compound fracture): Age 23. *unm*. Remembered on Aycliffe War Memorial.

Dearly Loved Son Of Thomas & Mary Watson, Aycliffe, Darlington

His brother Charles is buried in Sailly-au-Bois Military Cemetery (II.A.12).

(XVI.D.1A) Pte. G/1515, Charles Humphreys, 7th (Service) Bn. The Queen's (Royal West Surrey Regt.): foster *s*. of Miss H. Hill (10, Wandle Road, Beddington, Croydon): *b*. At sea, about 1894: served with the Expeditionary Force in France and Flanders from 27 July 1915, and died 17 July 1917, No.3 Canadian C.C.S., of wounds (SW Head [Penet.] Rt. mastoid) received from the detonation of a shell at Sanctuary Wood the previous day: Age 23. *unm*. L/Sergt. S.J.A. Palmer and two other men were killed by the same shell.

L/Sergt. Palmer has no known grave; he is commemorated on the Ypres (Menin Gate) Memorial (Panel 11).

(XVI.F.6) Gnr. 170891, Frank Albert Shelford, 'B' Bty., 180th Bde., Royal Field Artillery: *s*. of the late Frank Warner Shelford, by his wife Annie (14, Letchmore Road, Stevenage, co. Hertford): and yr. brother to Corpl. 91574, H.J. Shelford, Tank Corps, killed in action 23 July 1918, aged 23: enlisted Hertford. Died of wounds (G.S. Rt. thigh), 16 July 1917: Age 20. *unm*. Remembered on Stevenage War Memorial.

Thy Will Be Done

His brother Henry is buried in Roye New British Cemetery (III.F.15).

(XVI.F.14) L/Corpl. 533445, Albert Bannister Parsons, 'D' Coy., 15th (County of London) Bn. (Prince of Wales's Own, Civil Service Rifles) The London Regt. (T.F.): *s*. of Albert Parsons, of 77, Hazelbank Road, Catford, London, S.E.6, by his wife Martha: *b*. Plumstead: *educ*. Brockley School, Hilly Fields, London, S.E.4: enlisted Lewisham. Died at No.3 Canadian Casualty Clearing Station, 16 July 1917, of gun-shot (bullet) wounds; left arm, right leg: Age 20. *unm*. Dedicated 'In Memory Of The Old Scholars Of Brockley School Who Fell In The Great War 1914-1918;' L/Corpl. Parsons is one of twenty-eight former students recorded on the Brockley School War Memorial.

Greater Love Hath No Man

(XVI.F.18) Pte. S/18846, Daniel Galt, D.C.M., M.M., 6th (Service) Bn. The Queen's Own (Cameron Highlanders): *s*. of the late Peter Galt, by his wife Elizabeth (55, Kirkgate, Leith, Edinburgh): and yr. brother to Pte. S/6794, P. Galt, 2nd Seaforth Highlanders, killed in action, 26 April 1915: *b*. North Leith, *c*. 1885: proceeded to France, October 1915, and died 17 July 1917 of pneumonia following gas poisoning: Age 32. Awarded the Distinguished Conduct Medal (*London Gazette*, 4 June 1917) "For conspicuous gallantry and devotion to duty (at Arras). He displayed great courage in going over open ground under heavy fire to attend wounded men, and carrying one man back.' Remembered on Gretna Memorial, Rosebank Cemetery, Leith.

His brother Peter is buried in Seaforth Cemetery, Cheddar Villa (B.1/A.4).

(XVI.H.5A) Gnr. 29160, Charles Matthew Duncan St. Clair, 3rd Bty. 1st Bde., Australian Field Artillery: *s*. of Matthew John St. Clair, Inspector of Stock; of 'Nangoorie,' Glen Innes, New South Wales, by his wife Charlotte Fraser, *dau*. of D.M. Sinclair: *b*. Glen Innes, Gough Co., New South Wales, 2 March 1886: Religion – Church of England: *educ*. Private tutorship: Occupation – Private Secretary: 5'9¾" tall, brown eyes, light brown hair; 'a tendency to flat feet': enlisted Moore Park, 6 June 1916; posted 116th Howitzer Bty., 3 July; departed Sydney, HMAT 'Aeneas,' 30 September: trained England from 19 November: served with the Expeditionary Force in France and Flanders from 9 January 1917; transf'd. 1st Field Artillery Bde. 28 January. Wounded (G.S.W. Lt. side, both thighs, elbow) 21 July 1917, while making his way back to his battery position after delivering a message to an officer at Zillebeke Lake, and admitted 55th Field Ambulance; died at No.10 Casualty Clearing Station on the 24th. (July 1917): Age 31. *unm*. Correspondence, in the first instance, to be addressed c/o the deceased's sister, Miss Violet Jane Hamilton St. Clair (Lambeth Street, Glenn Innes).

The Beloved Son Of M. & C. St.Clair
Be Thou Faithful Unto Death

(XVI.H.10A) Sergt. 43461, David Ireland Meikle, 12th (Service) Bn. The Highland Light Infantry: formerly no.258, Royal Scots: *yst*. *s*. of Thomas Meikle, of Longridge, Fauldhouse, co. West Lothian, and Elizabeth Meikle, *née* Lindsay, his wife: enlisted Royal Scots, Fauldhouse, 1908: on the outbreak of war promoted Sergt., posted Home Defence, Berwick-on-Tweed: volunteered for Overseas Service July 1916; proceeded to France, August, transf'd. Highland Light Infantry: took part in the latter stages of the Somme Offensive, 1916: hospitalised late autumn (rheumatism), and removed to England for treatment and convalescence: returned to France May 1917, and died of wounds (G.S. Head) at Remy Siding 25 July 1917, received in action during an attack on Iberia Trench, nr. Verlorenhoek, the previous day: Age 42. 'Erected In Proud And Grateful Memory Of The Men Of This District Who Fell In The Great War 1914–1919' the Fauldhouse War Memorial records the names of 111 men who marched away to war and never returned; among their number David Meikle (Panel 1).

(XVI.I.3A) Pte. 39816, Fred Bone, 2nd Bn. (16th Foot) The Bedfordshire Regt.: late of Hemel Hempstead: *b*. Redbourn, co. Bedford: enlisted Bedford.

Died of wounds, 26 July 1917, received from the bursting of a shell while returning to Chateau Segard from a raid on the enemy trenches.

(XVI.I.4A) Pte. 18731, Richard Walldock, 2nd Bn. (16th Foot) The Bedfordshire Regt.: *b*. St. Alban's, co. Hertford: enlisted Watford. Died of wounds, 26 July 1917, received in action the same day when a shell landed in the midst of 17 men of the battalion returning to the reserve position at Chateau Segard, after taking part in a raid in the Zillebeke sector with 2nd Yorkshire and 18th Manchester Regt. He was married to L.E. Worrell, *née* Walldock (45, Church Road, Watford).

Peace Perfect Peace To Our Loved One Far Away

(XVI.J.3A) Gnr. 1482, John Leslie Opie, 'Y' (Medium) Bty. 5th Divn., Australian Trench Mortar Bde., A.I.F.: *s*. of the late John Ivey Opie, by his wife Lucy ('Poperinghe,' Military Road, Henley Beach, South Australia): Occupation – Farmer: enlisted 26 July 1915, departed Melbourne, 27 October: served in France from 25 June 1916; died No.17 C.C.S. 31 July 1917, of bullet wounds received in action the same day. Buried Lyssenthoek Cemetery, Poperinghe, 1 August and his grave duly marked: Age 29. A comrade, Gnr. 1121, E.W. Wearne recalled seeing Gnr. Leslie wounded by shrapnel, which hit him in the side, whilst standing beside his battery.

Father In Thy Gracious Keeping Leave We Now Thy Servant Sleeping

On 31 July 1917, 6th Seaforth Highlanders lost Capt. J. Bliss, 2nd Lieut. C.N. Lipp, and 58 other ranks killed; the following day Lieut. H.B. Lendrum, Ptes. Barron, Wilson and Keith died of wounds:

(XVI.J.7) Pte. S/43169, Edward Robert Keith, 1/6th (Morayshire) Bn. The Seaforth Highlanders (Ross-shire Buffs, The Duke of Albany's), (T.F.): *s*. of Mr W. Keith, of Lybster, Wick, Caithness: *b*. Latheron, Caithness: enlisted Army Service Corps, no.061394, Wick: subsequently transf'd. Seaforth Highlanders: served with the Expeditionary Force in France and Flanders. Wounded 31 July 1917, and died the following day at the Casualty Clearing Station, Remy Siding, Poperinghe.

Sadly Missed

Capt. Bliss is buried in Gwalia Cemetery (I.G.32); 2nd Lieut. Lipp has no known grave, he is commemorated on the Ypres (Menin Gate) Memorial (Panel 38); Lieut. H.B. Lendrum is buried in Dozinghem Military Cemetery (II.H.1), and Ptes.Wilson and Barron lie in Brandhoek New Military Cemetery (II.C.1 and II.C.6).

(XVI.J.13) Pte. 13629, George Samuel Pretlove, 2nd Bn. (77th Foot) The Duke of Cambridge's Own (Middlesex Regt.): *s.* of A.M. (& Mrs) Pretlove, of 125, Granville Road, Lordship Lane, Wood Green, London, N.: and elder brother to Dvr. 169183, C. Pretlove, Royal Field Artillery, died 22 August 1917: *b.* Old Southgate: enlisted Mill Hill, London, N.W.7.: served in France from 7 November 1914, and died of wounds, 1 August 1917: Age 23.

Sleep Peacefully Sleep

His brother Charlie is buried nearby (XVIII.D.1).

(XVI.J.18A) Sergt. 100393, Thierman Bryant Murray, D.C.M., M.M., 'D' Bty., 277th Bde., Royal Field Artillery: late of Main Street, Central Wyalong, Australia: *s.* of George Murray, of 22, Silver Street, Marrickville, Sydney, New South Wales: enlisted Cork, Ireland. Died No.3 Canadian C.C.S. of wounds (S.W. Chest [Penet.] Rt. Leg.), 2 August 1917: Age 25. Buried in the Soldiers Cemetery, Lyssenthoek. A posthumous recipient of the Distinguished Conduct Medal (*London Gazette*, 25 January1918) 'For conspicuous gallantry and devotion to duty at a time when his battery was suffering heavily from an intense bombardment. On his own initiative he crawled across the open under heavy fire and rescued the wounded, making several journeys, although wounded himself. He displayed a magnificent disregard of danger and splendid devotion to duty;' he was also awarded the Military Medal.

He Shall Be My Son Rev.21-7
I Will Raise Him Up At The Last Day Jn. 6-40

(XVI.K.18A) Corpl. SD/718, George William Porter, 11th (Service) Bn. (1st South Down) The Royal Sussex Regt.: *s.* of Richard Porter, by his wife Alice Mary, *née* Bridge (24, Canning Street, Brighton, co. Sussex): and brother to Corpl. 46637, S.C. Porter, 98th Field Coy., Royal Engineers, missing (believed killed) in action, 22 March 1918: *b.* Franklin Road, Brighton, 1 November 1891: previously served 4 years 1st (Sussex) Coy., R.G.A. (T.F.), and, from July 1913 until shortly before taking up employ as a Hall Porter (Gwydyr Mansions, Hove), was a member of West Sussex Constabulary: enlisted Horsham, September 1914. Died of wounds, 29 July 1917, received in action at Railway Wood: Age 25. He leaves a wife, Daisy Harriet Porter (20, Sutherland Road, Brighton), to whom he had been married two years and six months.

Our Dear One Not Forgotten

His brother Sydney has no known grave; he is commemorated on the Pozieres Memorial.

Between 19 and 27 August 1917 a series of minor attacks in the St. Julien sector resulted in the capture of several key enemy positions and a large number of prisoners. Prior to (and during) these attacks 1/5 Duke of Cornwall's were the designated Pioneers of 61st Division. Working in the vicinity of Wieltje Dump, the battalion suffered several casualties as they toiled under 'the most unfavourable conditions of ground and weather,' through thick cloying mud, flooded shell holes, and hostile fire, to keep the troops in the front line supplied. On the night of 14 August the bursting of an enemy shell severely wounded L/Corpls. Doidge and Hodge, and Pte. Raddon; all three died the following day:

(XVII.AA.4) L/Corpl. 240713, Samuel Longford Doidge, 1/5th Bn. (Pioneers) The Duke of Cornwall's Light Infantry (T.F.): *s.* of Longford Doidge, of 'Trehnow,' Tintagel, co. Cornwall, by his wife Martha: and brother to Dvr. 109421, W.J. Doidge, Royal Field Artilery, died 28 October 1918, in the Base Hospital, Boulogne: enlisted The Keep, Bodmin. Died 15 August 1917, of wounds received in action at Wieltje.

Asleep In Jesus
Mother & Father, Brothers & Sisters

His brother William is buried in Etaples Military Cemetery (LXXI.F.10).

(XVII.AA.5) Pte. 240972, Sydney Raddon, 1/5th Bn. (Pioneers) The Duke of Cornwall's Light Infantry (T.F.): *s.* of George Frederick Raddon, of Town End, Bodmin, by his wife Mary Jane: *b.* Penzance, co. Cornwall, 1895: Occupation – Staff Member, Bodmin Mental Asylum: enlisted Herne Bay, co. Kent. Died of wounds, 15 August 1917 received at Ypres: Age 32. Remembered on Bodmin War Memorial.

L/Corpl. Hodge lies in Brandhoek New Military Cemetery (II.AA.9).

On 16 August 1917, 2nd Lincolns lost 33 men killed, and 1 died of wounds:

(XVII.AA.7) Pte. 41478, Frank Mansell, 2nd Bn. (10th Foot) The Lincolnshire Regt.: formerly no.35809, South Staffordshire Regt.: *s.* of Albert Mansell, of 75, Corngreaves Road, Cradley Heath, co. Stafford, by his wife Mary: enlisted Birmingham. Died of wounds, 16 August 1917, received during an attack on the German lines nr. Bellewaarde the same day: Age 19. Of the 33 killed only one – Pte. 25116, A. Holt – has a known grave; Bedford House Cemetery (III.E.9/Enc. No.4) – the remainder are recorded on the Tyne Cot Memorial (Panel 35–37).

Dearly Beloved By All

(XVII.A.13A) Pte. 17957, Sydney Mackness, 2nd Bn. (58th Foot) The Northamptonshire Regt.: *s.* of George E. Mackness, of 26, Denmark Road, Rushden, co. Northampton, by his wife Elizabeth: and brother to Pte. G. Mackness, Northamptonshire Regt., shortly (August 1917) to return to France after recovery from wounds received at the Battle of Loos; Pte. E. Mackness, Northamptonshire Regt., wounded in the hand on the same day as his brother was killed and currently (August 1917) in hospital at St. Albans; and Gnr. C. Mackness, Royal Horse Artillery, on active service somewhere in France: *b.* Rushden: Boot & Shoe worker; Messrs Nurrish & Pallett, Boot Manufacturers, Rushden: enlisted April 1915, posted 3rd Northamptonshire Regt.: served with the Expeditionary Force in France and Flanders from 25 August following, transf'd 2nd Battn. (Pigeon Section). Reported missing/believed killed in action 31 July 1917, since confirmed, died 1 August 1917 of wounds: Age 22. *unm.* In a letter to Pte. Mackness' parents, his commanding officer wrote, "It is with the deepest sympathy that I am writing to inform you that your son, No. 17957, Pte S. Mackness, has been missing since July 31st, and has unofficially been reported killed. It is indeed very sad, and we all know what a terrible blow this must be to you. The last time I saw your son was in a captured trench. As you know, he looked after the pigeons, and as they had all flown, I told him he could go back with another man. Since then nothing has been heard of him. We all feel the loss very much. He has been with us for a long time, and being a very popular fellow we all liked him immensely. He was also a very brave fellow and a hard worker. He would do anything that was required of him. You have one consolation, however. It is small, it's true, but he died fighting for his country, being a brave fellow and doing his duty until the last, I trust the blow will not be too overbearing." His 'In Memoriam' card bore the following verse:

>Another man down 'over there,'
>Another shortened life,
>Another hero lost for e'er
>In dark and bloody strife;
>Another heart with grief is stilled,
>A head bowed down with woe,
>Another mother's eyes are filled
>With tears that overflow.
>
>His mind was fired with passion deep,
>His heart was strong and brave,
>And though we mourn his loss and weep,
>We see his glorious grave –

> He fought for God, tho' now he's gone
> And this the heart must ease.
> God bless the mothers, everyone !
> Of heroes such as these.

> *Victor Vane.*
> *God Be With You Until We Meet Again*
> *From Father, Mother, Sisters And Brothers*

After moving forward from Halfway House on the night of 30 July 1917, 3rd Worcesters took over a section of trenches on the Bellewaarde Ridge from 8th Division on 1st August, remaining there until the 5th. During this period the battalion 'was to experience a trial equal to almost any other in its history...heavy rain fell continuously and enemy shellfire was equally continuous. At night the front of the ridge was plastered with gas shells of a new type, mustard gas, which caused many casualties. The removal of the wounded was extremely difficult through the deep mud and slime into which the sodden clay was fast being converted.' The position on the Menin Road held by 'D' company suffered particularly heavily losing half its strength in killed and wounded and, when at last they were relieved at 9 p.m on the Sunday evening, nearly a quarter of the battalion had been put out of action: 22 killed, 3 officers and 103 N.C.O.'s and other ranks wounded.

(XVII.B.9A) Pte. 40744, Ernest Wall, 3rd Bn. The Worcestershire Regt.: formerly no.24338, Oxford & Bucks Light Infantry: *s.* of James Wall, of Harborne, by his wife Harriet: *b.* Birmingham, *c.*1881: conscripted 1916: served in France, and died of wounds, 6 August 1917, received in action on the Bellewaarde Ridge, nr. Hooge, four days previously: Age 36. He was married to Elizabeth 'Lizzie' Cottom, *née* Wall (11, High Brow, Harborne, Birmingham), and had two children, Norman and Constance. See also Pte. W.T. Banford (XVII.C.13).

> *Duty Well Done*

(XVII.B.20A) Pte. 34749, Enos Barker, 8th (Service) Bn. The Loyal North Lancashire Regt.: formerly no.54288, Cheshire Regt.: c/o Miss Sarah Edwards (1, Dyson Yard, Shaw Road, Oldham): enlisted Ashton-under-Lyne. Died of wounds (mustard gas), 7 August 1917: Age 37.

> *Never To Be Forgotten*

(XVII.C.13) Pte. 41426, William Thomas Banford, 3rd Bn. The Worcestershire Regt.: *s.* of Joseph Banford, of Holland House, Malvern, co. Worcester, by his wife Maria: *b*. Malvern: enlisted Worcester. Died of wounds (G.S. back), 3 August 1917: Age 19. See Pte. E. Wall (XVII.B.9A).

After moving up to the front near Klein Zillebeke 32nd Bn. Royal Fusiliers 'had a strange experience on 5 August 1917. The Germans had delivered counter-attacks on various parts of the front, and on that day the blow fell to the left of the battalion front. At 4.10 a.m. the enemy barrage lifted and the Germans advanced under cover of fog and smoke bombs. Only half the front was involved; and there the attack was held up by rifle and machine-gun fire. But the Germans broke through the right flank of the battalion further north and a party of them got to the rear of 32nd Royal Fusiliers. At midday it was ascertained that the enemy were holding 100 yards of Jehovah Trench, which was in a strip of wood lying north of the Klein Zillebeke road and some 500 yards east of the village.' A bold and decisive attack made by three officers and a handful of men on the German detachment in the centre of the forward-most zone killed some of the enemy, dispersed the rest, and restored the situation. This 'strange experience' and the action taken incurred surprisingly few casualties; 1 Officer killed, 1 died of wounds, 3 O.R. died of wounds: 2nd Lieut. C.F. Cook, Capt. J.M. Thorburn, Ptes. H. Hart, E. Tompsett, and M. Heap.

(XVII.D.4A) Pte. 66918, Maurice Fleming Heap, 32nd (Service) Bn. (East Ham) The Royal Fusiliers (City of London Regt.): formerly no.31432, Duke of Wellington's (West Riding Regt.): brother to Mrs S. Rawnsley (Clough Head, Norland, Sowerby Bridge, Yorkshire): enlisted Duke of Wellington's, Halifax, with his friends Fred Jagger (killed in action, 3 August 1917) and Clement Haigh (killed in action, 7 August 1917). All transferred to 32nd Bn. Royal Fusiliers in early 1917 and died within three days of each other. Maurice died in the Casualty Clearing Station at Remy Siding, 6 August 1917, of wounds received in action at Ypres the previous day.

Worthy Of Everlasting Love From Those He Left Behind

John Thorburn and Henry Hart are buried in Godewaersvelde British Cemetery (I.C.33 & I.C.31 respectively). Edward Tompsett and Maurice's friends, Fred Jagger and Clement Haigh, have no known grave; all three are recorded on the Ypres (Menin Gate) Memorial (Panel 6).

(XVII.D.10A) Pte. 22791, Alfred David Sutton, 7th (Service) Bn. The Northamptonshire Regt.: *yst. s.* of the late Thomas Sutton, by his wife Julia (4, Denny Road, Lower Edmonton, London, N.): *b*. Feltham, co. Middlesex, 19 April 1885: *educ*. there: enlisted Northamptonshire Regt. 1 January 1916: served with the Expeditionary Force in France and Flanders from the following June, and died at No.3 Casualty Clearing Station, 7 August 1917, from bullet wounds and fractured right femur: Age 32. *unm*. (*IWGC record age 30*)

In Ever Loving Memory Of My Dear Son
Abide With Me

(XVII.D.13) Spr. 269540, John Rees Davies, 343rd Road Construction Coy., Royal Engineers: *s.* of J. (& Mrs) Davies, of Oakfield House, Llanafon, co. Brecon: *b.* Llanotonfaur, co. Brecon: enlisted Llandrindod Wells, co. Radnor. Died 8 August 1917, of wounds: Age 39. He was married to Mrs M. Davies, *née* Stedman (33, Wye View Terrace, Builth Road, Builth Wells, co. Brecon). One of eleven parishioners remembered on Cwmbach Llechryd (St. John The Divine) Parish Church War Memorial.

Tread Softly And Doff Thy Cap For Such As He Stopped The Gap

(XVII.D.15A) A/Bmdr. 82159, John Turton, 'C' Bty., 82nd Bde., Royal Field Artillery: c/o Mrs G. Butland (31, Barrett Street, Shipley, co. York): *s.* of Thomas (& Elizabeth) Turton, of Ackworth, co. Lancaster. Died of wounds, 8 August 1917 (concussion / gas) received in action on the 5th.: Age 27. In a letter to his sister, the Chaplain said that Bmdr. Turton had attempted to limit the effect of the shell blast and protect his comrades by placing his body in the dug-out entrance. He continued, "Such a deed is worthy of the Victoria Cross, in my opinion. He is seriously ill but I hope he will be able to pull through..." Written in two parts the letter closes, "He succumbed to bronchial pneumonia which came as a result of gas poisoning at 2 a.m. to-day. He was conscious until nearly the last but had been unable to speak more than a word or two since he came. His death was a merciful deliverance, for his sufferings were great. He will be buried at Lijssenthoek military cemetery in Belgium and his personal belongings will be returned to his next of kin through the War Office. He left no last message."

(XVII.D.20A): Pte. 28026, Jasper McCleery Warke, 9th (Service) Bn. (County Tyrone) The Royal Inniskilling Fusiliers: *s.* of John Warke, of 52, Abercorn Road, Londonderry, by his wife Elizabeth: and brother to Rfn. 22758, S. Warke, London Irish Rifles, killed in action, 5 September 1918: *b.* Londonderry: enlisted Newtownards. Died 8 August 1917, of wounds: Age 20.

Peace Perfect Peace

His brother Samuel is buried in Peronne Communal Cemetery Extension (III.I.26).

(XVII.E.1A) Sergt. 25788, Frederick Cecil Newall, 18th (Service) Bn. (2nd City) The King's (Liverpool) Regt.: late of Poulton, co. Chester: *s.* of James Newall, of 26, Lonsborough Road, Somerville, Seacombe, co. Chester, by his wife Eleanor: and yr. brother to L/Corpl. 17081, H.J. Newall, 18th King's (Liverpool) Regt., killed in action, 1 July 1916, at the Battle of the Somme: *b*. Runcorn, 1887: enlisted Liverpool: served with the Expeditionary Force in France from 7 November 1915; died of wounds, 2 August 1917, at the Third Battle of Ypres: Age 30.

Father In Thy Gracious Keeping Leave We Now Our Dear One Sleeping

His brother Harold is buried in Dantzig Alley British Cemetery, Mametz (VIII.U.5).

(XVII.E.12) Pte. 11822, Frederick Arthur Brown, 7th (Service) Bn. The Queen's Own (Royal West Kent Regt.): *s*. of Frederick Arthur Brown, Fisherman; of 6, Wellington Road, Pakefield, Lowestoft, by his wife Florence Ellen, *dau*. of William Canham: *b*. Chelsfield, co. Kent, 14 March 1894: *educ*. Farnborough, and Morton Road School, Lowestoft: enlisted Bromley, 20 January 1916: served with the Expeditionary Force in France and Flanders from the following May, and died of wounds, 3 August 1917: Age 23. He *m*. Lowestoft, Hilda, *dau*. of J. Boyce, of Lowestoft, and had a *dau*. Gladys Evelyn, *b*. 20 March 1916.

Peace Perfect Peace

(XVII.F.3A) Pte. G/22878, Richard Barton, 7th (Service) Bn. The Queen's (Royal West Surrey Regt.): formerly no.40655, King's Own Yorkshire L.I.: *s*. of the late William Barton, of Thornsett, Sheffield: *b*. New Mills, co. Derby, *c*.1879: employee Birch Vale Printworks, Derby: enlisted Buxton. Died of wounds (G.S. thoracic), 11 August 1917, received in action the previous day: Age 38. Pte. Barton was a member of Thornsett Prize Band.

(XVII.F.7A) Pte. G/12641, Percy Nicholas Bassett, 8th (Service) Bn. The Buffs (East Kent Regt.): *s*. of John Allen Bassett, Labourer; of 6, Scotts Row, Newtown, Ramsey, co. Kent, by his wife Elizabeth, *dau*. of Mathew Scott: *b*. Ramsey, 1897: *educ*. there: enlisted 1 April 1916: served with the Expeditionary Force in France and Flanders from the following August, and died of wounds (G.S. thoracic), 12 August 1917: Age 20. *unm*. Remembered on Ramsey War Memorial.

(XVII.G.5) Pte. G/17058, John Clayton, 10th Bn. The Queen's Own (Royal West Kent Regt.): late of Palmers Green, co. Kent: *s*. of the late Thomas Clayton, and Jemima, his wife (1, Teviot Row, Hawick, co. Roxburgh): late *husb*. to Mrs A.M. Clayton (87, Tennyson Avenue, Scarborough): and brother to Pte. S/12389, J.W. Clayton, 8/10th Gordon Highlanders, killed in action, 17 June 1916; and Pte. 7767, J. Clayton, 2nd Highland Light Infantry, killed in action,

14 November 1914: *b*. Hawick: enlisted Palmers Green. Died of wounds, 4 August 1917: Age 41. One of three brothers who fell.

His brother James is buried in Vermelles British Cemetery (II.C.9); Joseph has no known grave, he is commemorated on the Ypres (Menin Gate) Memorial (Panel 38).

(XVII.H.7A) Pte. 34347, Willie Hartley, 2nd Bn. (59th Foot) The East Lancashire Regt.: *s*. of Harry Hartley, of Greetland: *husb*. to Martha Ellen (31, Ashfield Terrace, Greetland) formerly of Shutts Lane: Occupation – Postman; G.P.O.: enlisted Elland, co. York. Died of wounds, 17 August 1917: Age 40.

Gone But Not Forgotten

(XVII.H.9A) Rfn. 651393, Arthur Robert Ashby, 21st (County of London) Bn. (First Surrey Rifles) The London Regt. (T.F.) attd 17th C.C.S.: *s*. of Anne Ashby (23, Trafalgar Road, Old Kent Road, Camberwell, London). Killed in an aerial bombing attack on the night of 17 August 1917: Age 18.

The Lord Hath Given And Hath Taken

(XVII.J.3A) Gnr. 12359, Robert Emmanuel Davis, 33rd Bde., Royal Field Artillery: *s*. of William Davis, of 48, Pontrhondda Road, Llwynypia, Rhondda, by his wife Alice Rosina, *dau*. of George Bolt: *b*. Rhondda, 1 May 1893: *educ*. Llwynypia Schools: enlisted July 1910: served with the Expeditionary Force in France and Flanders, and died at the Canadian Casualty Clearing Station, 10 August 1917, of shrapnel wounds (back) received in action. Buried in Lyssenthoek Cemetery. His Chaplain wrote, "He was picked up unconscious on the battlefield, and died without regaining consciousness. He was buried with all due respect and military honours in a cemetery nearby.": Age 25. *unm*. (*IWGC record 108th Bde.*)

Thy Will Be Done
The Beloved Son Of William And Alice Rosina Davis

(XVII.J.12) Pte. 52661, William Pimblott, M.M., 11th (Service) Bn. The Cheshire Regt.: *b*. Cheadle, Cheshire: resident with his wife at 8, Bank Street, Cheadle: enlisted Chester 1915, after the outbreak of war: served with the Expeditionary Force in France and Flanders: Awarded the Military Medal, *Stockport Advertiser*, 24 August 1917, 'for dressing the wounded under heavy fire during the June push.' On 6/7 June 1917, at the Battle of Messines, the 11th Battn. had left their trenches at 6.50 a.m. and succeeded in capturing and securing their main objectives by 9 a.m. One party, having pushed further ahead than they were supposed to, found themselves in front of the British creeping artillery barrage; their officer, realising their predicament, ordered the men to find whatever shelter they could in shell holes and wait for the bombardment to pass over. During the course of the day the Germans launched two counter-attacks which were beaten off and, although subjected to violent enemy shelling throughout the following day, few casualties were sustained. On 1 August the battalion went into support trenches in front of Westhoek Ridge where they stayed until the night of the 6th when they were relieved to dug-outs at the Esplanade, Ypres. The War Diary for the six days tour of duty records the weather was extremely bad, the trenches 'where they existed' were knee deep in water, and the battalion lost 22 men killed. On the 9th the battalion was further relieved and moved back to Halifax Camp. During this relief Private Pimblott was wounded and evacuated to the Canadian Casualty Clearing Station at Remy Siding where he died the following day. The Chaplain, in writing to Mrs Pimblott, said, "It grieves me deeply to tell you that your husband succumbed to his wounds at 8.20 this evening. He made a brave fight for life but a penetrating wound to the chest made it unavailing. I saw him just before he died, but he was too far gone to leave any message.": 10 August 1917: Age 34. Remembered on Cheadle War Memorial.

(XVII.K.4A) Pte. G/13259, John Weeding, 'D' Coy., 7th (Service) Bn. The Buffs (East Kent Regt.): s. of George Weeding, of Edgemount, Coleman's Hatch, co. Sussex, by his wife Sarah: and yr. brother to Tpr. 1548, G. Weeding, Household Battn., killed in action, 3 May 1917: b. Hatfield: enlisted East Grinstead: proceeded to France mid-1916, served with the Expeditionary Force there, and died 20 August 1917, of appendicitis. At the time of his death the battalion were undergoing training at Eringhem, north-west of Steenvoorde: Age 20. unm.

Peace Perfect Peace With Loved Ones Far Away
In Jesus Keeping

His brother George is commemorated in Roeux British Cemetery (Sp. Mem.H.7).

(XVII.K.11A) Pte. G/52447, Frank Bottomley, 2nd Bn. (77th Foot) The Duke of Cambridge's Own (Middlesex Regt.): late of 108, Thornhill Road, Rastrick, co. York: formerly no.41925, York & Lancaster Regt.: s. of Prenn (& Hannah) Bottomley, of 112, Thornhill Road, Rastrick: late employee to Messrs Lister Brook & Co., Brighouse: enlisted Halifax: served with the Expeditionary Force in France and Flanders, transf'd. 2nd Middlesex Regt., and died in an Australian Casualty Clearing Station in France from an abdominal gunshot wound, 22 August 1917: Age 32. He leaves a widow, Martha Eleanor (21, Tofts Grove, Rastrick) to mourn his loss.

Until The Day Dawns
Rastrick

(XVIII.A.8A) Pte. 17343, Alfred Reynolds, 5th (Service) Bn. The Oxford & Bucks Light Infantry: *s*. of Eliza Reynolds (90, Arthur Street, West Bromwich), and the late John Reynolds: *b*. West Bromwich: served with the Expeditionary Force in France and Flanders from 1 October 1915; took part in the fighting at Railway Wood, nr. Ypres later the same month: took part in operations at Arras and the Somme. Died of wounds, 24 August 1917, received in action at Glencorse Wood: Age 25. His Memoriam Card recorded: "Sleep on dear brother in a far off land, In a grave we may never see. But as long as life and memory last, We will remember thee. We think of him in silence, And his name we oft' recall, But there's nothing left to answer But his photo on the wall. A Devoted Brother, a Faithful Friend, One of the best that God could lend. He bravely answered duty's call, His life he gave for one and all, But the unknown grave is our bitterest blow, None but an aching heart can know. I often pause to think dear one, And wonder how you died, With no one near who loved you dear, Before you closed your eyes; You've nobly done your duty, And like a hero fell, Could I have held your drooping head, And heard your last farewell."

(XVIII.A.16) Pte. 242514, William Miller, 2/6th Bn. The Royal Warwickshire Regt. (T.F.): *s*. of Joseph Miller, of 46, Bridge Street, Chatteris, co. Cambridge, by his wife Sarah: and brother to Pte. 203572, J. Miller, 9th Royal Warwickshire Regt., died of malaria, 4 October 1918, in Mesopotamia: enlisted Atherstone. Died of wounds, 25 August 1917: Age 38. He leaves a wife, Nellie Miller (11, Long Street, Dordon, nr. Tamworth, co. Warwick).

Death Divides But Memory Ever Clings
From His Loving Wife And Children

His brother John is buried in Tehran War Cemetery (IV.B.13).

(XVIII.B.4) L/Corpl. 265982, Alexander Harrold Falconer, 8th (Service) Bn. The Seaforth Highlanders (Ross-shire Buffs, The Duke of Albany's): formerly no.2738: 4th *s*. of the late James Falconer, Dairyman; by his wife Elspet, *née* Taylor (Flower Cottage, King Street, New Elgin): *b*. New Elgin, 17 May 1883: *educ*. East End School, New Elgin: Occupation – Tailor: enlisted 18 November 1914 and was, for some time, employed in the training of new recruits at the Drill Hall, Elgin: proceeded to France, joined the Expeditionary Force there and in Flanders 5 December 1915, and died at No.17 Casualty Clearing Station, 22 August 1917, of wounds received in action. Buried in Lyssenthoek Military Cemetery, Poperinghe: Age 34. He *m.* Elgin; Maggie McMurran, *née* Falconer (214, High Street, Elgin), *dau.* of Alexander McKerron, Builder, and had three children – Alexander, *b.* 31 March 1911; Jessie, *b.* 9 November 1912; James, *b.* 8 September 1914.

(XVIII.C.3A) Sergt. 240117, William Porter, M.M., 4/5th Bn. The Black Watch (Royal Highlanders): *s.* of the late James Porter, of 16, Jamieson Street, Arbroath, and his wife Helen, *née* Hutchison: *b.* Arbroath: Occupation – Mechanic; Dens Iron Works: joined Royal Highlanders, Pte., 1909; subsequently attained rank Sergt.: mobilised on the outbreak of war, August 1914; proceeded to France November following. Died of heart failure night of 29–30 August 1917, at Poperinghe, having gone to bed, apparently in his usual health, he was found dead the following morning. A comrade said, "All the boys liked and admired Bill, as they called him. His death was the last thing we looked for – it was the hardest of misfortunes, coming through all that he did that he should pass away so quickly." He was awarded the Military Medal for gallant conduct in the face of the enemy; afterwards distinguishing himself in organising and consolidating work.: Age 24. *unm.*

Until The Day Dawns

Prior to September 1917 the first row in the majority of plots in the cemetery contained the grave of at least one officer. Buried in a coffin in an individual grave, the distance between the graves in the 'A Rows' is noticeably greater than the following rows. Wrapped in army blankets the bodies of soldiers were buried closely together and marked with individual crosses, however, when the headstones were erected these had to be placed close together to ensure the graves were properly marked; this in turn gave rise to the necessity to number the graves with the suffix 'A'. (ie. Plot I. Row A. Grave 1A) The utilisation of the first row for officers was abandoned in late August; 2nd Lieut. R.R. Ross was the first officer to be buried within a plot between two privates.

(XVIII.C.11) 2nd Lieut. Ronald Ross Douglas, 7/8th Bn. King's Own Scottish Borderers: formerly Pte. no.1928, Royal Scots: *s.* of Rev. John Douglas, of West Manse, Bothwell Road, Hamilton, co. Lanark; formerly of Nagpur, India: *educ.* Edinburgh University, Arts (1909–13): served with the Expeditionary Force in France and Flanders from 4 April 1915, and died of wounds (jaw, facial), 30 August 1917, received in action at Square Farm, Frezenberg, on the 28th.: Age 25.

A Lover Of Men A Good Soldier Of Jesus Christ

(XVIII.C.16) 2nd Lieut. Lachlan Seymour Graham, 7/12th (Service) Bn. The Highland Light Infantry: only *s.* of the late Duncan Graham, of Glasgow, Leather Merchant, by his wife Isabella MacLachlan (also predeceased), *dau.* of the late Lachlan MacLachlan: *b.* Glasgow, 19 September 1882: *educ.* Glasgow Collegiate, and Glenalmond: graduated Arts and Law, M.A. and B.L., Glasgow University: Occupation – Writer; being sole partner in the firm of Messrs Hubbard & Seymour Graham, Writers, Glasgow: joined Inns of Court O.T.C., 7 February 1916: obtained a commission, January 1917: served with the Expeditionary Force in France and Flanders, from 17 May following. Wounded in action near Ypres 23 August 1917, and died in the Casualty Clearing Station, Lyssenthoek, Poperinghe on the 29th of that month. Buried in the adjoining cemetery: Age 34. *unm.* He was secretary of the City Business Club; Hon. Secretary and Treasurer, West of Scotland Lawn Tennis Association; and Manager, Renfield Street United Free Church. Correspondence and effects to be marked for the attention of his cousin and forwarded – Miss J.H. MacLachlan, c/o J.W. Taylor Esq., 75, St. George's Place, Glasgow.

In His Will Is Our Peace

(XVIII.D.1) Dvr. 169183, Charlie Pretlove, 122nd Bty., Royal Field Artillery: *s.* of A.M. (& Mrs) Pretlove, of 125, Granville Road, Lordship Lane, Wood Green, London, N.: and yr. brother to Pte. L/13629, G.S. Pretlove, Middlesex Regt., died 1 August 1917: enlisted Mill Hill, London, N.W.7. Killed in action, 22 August 1917: Age 17.

Sleep Peacefully Sleep

His brother George is buried nearby (XVI.J.13).

(XVIII.D.12) Pte. 235408, Thomas Smith, 6th (Service) Bn. The King's Own (Yorkshire Light Infantry): formerly no.49190, Sherwood Foresters: late *husb.* of eighteen months to Mrs H. Smith (66, Elnor Street, Langley Mill, co. Derby): *b.* Langley Mill, 1891: enlisted Nottingham. 'Pte. Smith's career as a soldier was altogether an unlucky one, for whilst undergoing training he was accidentally shot through the leg by one of his comrades during firing practice, and on another occasion he received injuries to an eye by a bayonet during a battle rehearsal.' In a letter to his widow his Company Commander wrote, "He died from wounds received in action during an enemy attack. It may console you to know that he received his injuries fighting for his country like a true Britisher." Pte. Smith was a man of strong religious belief, a regular churchgoer and member of St. Andrew's Church since boyhood: 24 August 1917: Age 26. (*IWGC record age 27*)

Ever In My Thoughts The One Who Was So Dear

(XVIII.D.14A) Pte. 267534, James Savory, 2/6th Bn. The Gloucestershire Regt. (T.F): *b*. Ripple, co. Worcester, 1883: enlisted Cheltenham: served with the Expeditionary Force in France and Flanders, and died of wounds, 24 August 1917, at Poperinghe: Age 34. He leaves a wife, Ethel Mary (41, Queen Street, Cheltenham), and children. Unveiled 10 October 1920, and inscribed 'Lest We Forget 1914–1919. Greater Love Hath No Man Than This,' Pte. Savory's name is recorded on the St. Peter's Church War Memorial, Tewkesbury Road, Cheltenham. He is also remembered on the grave of his son Frederick James Savory; Cheltenham Cemetery.

Peace Perfect Peace

(XVIII.E.14) Corpl. 241130, Reginald Ivo Rimell, 2/5th Bn. The Gloucestershire Regt. (T.F.): *s*. of Ivo Rimell, of 3, Ivy Terrace, The Meddings, Cheltenham, by his wife Kate: *b*. Cheltenham, 1897: enlisted Gloucester: served with the Expeditionary Force, and died of wounds, 12 September 1917, received from shell fire nr. Hill 35 (Kansas Cross) the same day. Corpl. Rimell is remembered on St. Catherine's Roll of Honour, Staverton, and Holy Trinity Church Roll of Honour, Badgeworth: Age 20. *unm*.

Nothing In My Hand I Bring, Simply To Thy Cross I Cling

(XVIII.E.15A) Rfn. 320645, Thomas Henry Hewitt, 1/6th (City of London) Bn. (Rifles) The London Regt.), (T.F.): *s*. of Albert Hewitt, of South Woodford, London, E.18, by his wife Elizabeth: and elder brother to L/Corpl. 2358, C.A. Hewitt, 1/6th London Regt., killed in action, 8 October 1916, at the Somme: enlisted London. Died 12 September 1917, of wounds: Age 27. *unm*.

The Labours Of A Well Spent Life End In A Great Reward

(XVIII.F.11) Lieut. Frederick Clifton Dawkins, M.C., 'A' Bty., 8th Bde., Royal Field Artillery: formerly no.7, Honourable Artillery Company: Occupation – Clerk; London Stock Exchange: enlisted H.A.C., Artillery House: served Egypt (from 21 April 1915), subsequently obtained a commission R.F.A. (Special Reserve): served in France and Flanders from 1916, and died of wounds, 2 September 1917: Age 27. Awarded the Military Cross (*London Gazette*, No.30111, 4 June 1917). Promotion to Lieut. gazetted posthumously (*London Gazette*, No.30283, 14 September 1917); Lieut. Dawkins leaves a wife, Louise G. Dawkins (2, High Street, Shoeburyness, co. Essex) to whom Lieut.

Dawkins' undisposed income of £7.10/- should be made transferable, and all correspondence addressed.

Out Of The Stress Of The Doing Into The Peace Of The Done

(XVIII.F.13) Gnr. 3479, Raymond Cary, 114th (Howitzer) Bty., 14th Bde. Australian Field Artillery, A.I.F.: s. of Sarah Cary (8, Sheffield Street, Coburg, Victoria): b. Coburg, February 1897: Religion – Presbyterian: Occupation – Pastry Cook: 5'6¾" tall, blue eyes, fair hair: a serving member (3 years) Senior Cadets; joined A.I.F., Melbourne, 19 July 1915: posted 8th Rfts., 21st Battn., Broadmeadows, 17 December: departed Melbourne, HMAT 'Wiltshire,' 29 December 1915: served in Egypt (from 26 February 1916), transf'd. 60th Battn.: apptd. Gnr. 25th Bty., 17 March following: served in France and Flanders from 25 June; transf'd. 14th F.A. Bde., 8 July. Severely wounded (both legs blown off, abdomen shattered) by a shell burst in the battery dugout, St. James Trench, nr. Ypres, 4 September 1917, and died in No.3 Canadian Casualty Clearing Station the same day: Age 20. Gnr. Scadden, also in the dugout, was killed outright.

Gnr. V.A. Scadden is buried in Brandhoek New Military Cemetery No.3 (I.E.13).

(XVIII.F.19A) Gnr. 46969, Norman Bartholomew, 14th Ammunition Sub. Park, Royal Field Artillery: s. of Edwin George Bartholomew, of 74, Brompton Street, Oldham, co. Lancaster, by his wife Sarah Jane Elizabeth. Killed in an enemy air raid, 5 September 1917. Age 27.

(XVIII.G.8A) Dvr. 311321, William Henry Kraus, 111th Northumbrian (North Riding) Heavy Bty., Royal Garrison Artillery (T.F.): b. Middlesbrough, co. York, c. 1886: husb. to Betsy Kraus (2, Britannia Place, Darmanstown, Redcar): served with the Expeditionary Force, and was wounded in action by an enemy air raid on the afternoon of 26 August 1917: Age 31.

Still To Memory Dear

See Huts Cemetery – Sergt. R. Boast, R.A.V.C.; A/Bmdr. W. Ashwood, and Gnrs. A. Barlow, G. Scholey, W. Owens, W.E. Ballam, A. Hudson, and A. Legg, R.G.A.. Also Corpl. M. Stephenson, R.G.A. – Dozinghem Military Cemetery (III.H.23).

(XVIII.H.8) Lieut. William Edwin Sandys, 32nd Sqdn. Royal Flying Corps: c/o Messrs Grindley & Co., 54, Parliament Street, London: s. of Francis Edwin Sandys, of Wemyss Road, Blackheath, London, by his wife Mary, née Llewellyn: b. Calcutta, 20 December 1888: Occupation – Life Assurance Agent: enlisted Valcartier, British Columbia, 22 September 1914: posted 'A' Sqdn. Lord Strathcona's Horse, 26 September: came over with 1st Canadian

Contingent, October 1914: subsequently transf'd. Army Service Corps; later R.F.C. (obtained Flying Certificate, September 1916): returned to France 1 August 1917, and was killed in action, 5 September 1917, when his DH5 aircraft (no.9374) was engaged in aerial combat, shot down and crashed in the Ypres canal. His body, later retrieved, was brought back to Poperinghe and buried by members of the R.F.C. that evening: Age 28. Married to Elsie C.V. Sandys (58, Ansell Road, Tuffnell Park, London); he was killed on her birthday. Dedicated 'To The Memory Of Brave Men Who Fought In The Great War 1914-1918 Their Name Liveth Forevermore;' Lieut. Sandys is remembered on Blackheath (All Saints Church) War Memorial.

Greater Love Hath No Man Than This
Chpt. 15. Vrs. 13. St. John

(XVIII.H.11) Pte. 243807, George Stoneley, 13th (Service) Bn. The Cheshire Regt.: *s.* of the late Herbert Stoneley (*d.*1900), by his wife Mary (The Shop, Tattenhall, co. Chester): *b.* 1898: *educ.* Church of England School, Tattenhall: sometime Telegraph Messenger, Tattenhall Post Office; lately Railway Station Porter: enlisted 10 January 1917: proceeded to France, April following, and died of wounds, 6 September 1917: Age 19. In a letter to Mrs Stoneley the Chaplain, G.A. Ambrose, wrote, "…was brought in to us this morning. He had suffered a very bad wound in the abdomen, and had expired before reaching us; probably about 9 a.m. I found your address in a letter in his pocket. He will be buried in the military cemetery at Lyssenthoek, and the few things that were in his pocket when he came in (a wrist watch, purse and badge, and a few coins) will be forwarded through the War Office. With deepest sympathy…" The sudden and sad news of his death cast quite a gloom over the village of Tattenhall where he was well-known and respected by all classes. Two other brothers also served; both survived.

Until The Day Break And The Shadows Flee Away

(XIX.A.2) Pte. 18810, Henry Groark (*a.k.a.* Rourke), 8th (Service) Bn. The King's Own (Yorkshire Light Infantry): 3rd *s.* of Patrick Rourke, Farm Labourer; of Wooller Houses, Batley, co. York, by his wife Bridget: and brother to Pte. 19677, J. Groark, York & Lancaster Regt.; and Pte. 6093, M. Rourke, Royal Scots Fusiliers, killed in action, 16 June 1915: *b.* Batley, 1892: enlisted Dewsbury: served with the Expeditionary Force in France and Flanders, and died of wounds, 19 September 1917: Age 25. All three brothers are recorded on the Batley and St. Mary's (Roman Catholic) Church War Memorials and on individual brass plaques in St. George's Memorial Church, Ypres in the name

Groark. A fourth brother, Frederick, served with King's Own (Yorkshire Light Infantry); he survived. One of three brothers who fell. (*Headstone records Groak*)

Brothers James and Michael have no known grave; they are commemorated on the Ploegsteert Memorial (Panel 8) and Ypres (Menin Gate) Memorial (Panel 19) respectively.

(XIX.A.3) Pte. 3250, Hans Casper Caspersen, ANZAC Provost Corps: *s.* of Edward Casperson, of Vogts Gate 29, Moss, Norway, by his late wife Marie Sofie: *b.* Norway, 1892: Religion – Church of England: Occupation – Sail maker: 5'8" tall, blue eyes, fair hair: volunteered and joined A.I.F., Melbourne, 6 July 1915; posted 11th Rfts., 5th Battn., Broadmeadows, 11 September: transf'd. Anzac Police Corps, 11 March 1916. Wounded at duty (S.W. abdominal, penetrating) 1st Anzac Provost Unit, Menin Road, 20 September 1917; admitted and died No.17 C.C.S. the same day. Interred Remy Siding Cemetery, 1¾ miles S.W. of Poperinghe: Age 25. *unm.*

(XIX.B.2) 2nd Lieut. Noel Charles Whittall, 7th (Extra Reserve) Bn. The Royal Fusiliers (City of London Regt.), attd. 6th Sqdn. Royal Flying Corps: *s.* of the late Frederick James Whittall, by his wife Catherine Mary ('Cairo,' 11, Torridon Road, Hither Green, co. Kent), *dau.* of John Henry Dines: *b.* London, 23 January 1896: *educ.* St. Dunstan's College, Catford, London, S.E.6: Occupation – Electrical Engineer: gazetted 2nd Lieut. Royal Fusiliers, 3 June 1915: served with the Expeditionary Force in France and Flanders from 23 July 1916, being employed as Signalling Officer: detached/attd. Royal Flying Corps, 1917: returned to England to complete training July: rejoined his squadron in France 14 August following, and was killed in aerial action while carrying out observation duties, 13 September 1917. Buried in Lyssenthoek Military Cemetery, nr. Poperinghe. Col. Hesketh wrote, "Your gallant son was not only a charming boy, but a most keen and capable officer, and a great loss to the battalion when he went to the Flying Corps; I am sure no one could say more in his praise than he deserved." And his Squadron Commander, Major James, Royal Flying Corps, "He was one of the greatest losses my Squadron could have sustained. Although he had been with us for such a short time, I realised what an excellent fellow he was. His zeal reflected itself in his work, and he was getting on exceptionally well." Lieut. Glashier also wrote, "I assure you no words of praise can be too generous in describing Noel's work and our appreciation of him. He was much liked by all of us, even in the comparatively short time he was here. He died as a man would wish, doing his duty and facing big odds. You knew, perhaps, that I was piloting his machine when he brought down one of the four enemy machines that attacked us, some distance over their lines, where we had gone to get some photographs. This is a feat which makes all of us out here very proud of him, particularly myself, quite apart from his other fine work.": Age 21. *unm.* (*IWGC record age 22*)

Brave Heart
Too Dearly Loved Ever To Be Forgotten
Au Revoir

(XIX.B.8) Pte. 905153, Herbert Wallace Kiernan, 8th Bn. Canadian Railway Troops, C.E.F.: *b*. Mansfield, Dufferin Co., Ontario, 29 August 1885: Occupation – Farmer: enlisted Edmonton, 1 September 1916; posted 194th Edmonton Highlanders Battn., transf'd 211th Overseas Battn.: transf'd. 8th Railway Troops, England: served with the Expeditionary Force in France and Flanders, and died, 15 September 1917, of wounds (left hand shot off, G.S.W. base of skull): Age 32. Three men – Sprs. Andrichuk, Donly and Donchuk – were killed, and six wounded of whom two others – Sprs. Drobaha and Chernuck – also died. Pte. Kiernan leaves a widow, Grace Violet Kiernan (West Peace River Crossing, Alberta), to whom all correspondence regarding her late husband should be addressed.

Sprs. Andrichuk and Chernuck are buried in the Huts Cemetery (VI.A.11 / IV.D.17); Sprs. Donly and Donchuk, Belgian Battery Corner Cemetery (I.N.2 / I.N.3); Spr. Drobaha lies nearby (XIX.B.13A).

(XIX.B.11) Corpl. 11613, Percy Edmund Clements, 104th Howitzer Bty., 4th Bde. Australian Field Artillery, A.I.F.: *s*. of Edith Clements (Freemason's Beach, New South Wales). Died of wounds (multiple shard), 16 September 1917, received in action the previous day, left hand side Menin Road, nr. Birr Cross Roads and Hell Fire Corner. "…They were just about to fire their last shell when an enemy shell, a 5.9, got a direct hit on the gun, and the whole crew were wiped out. Gnr. Martin was blown to pieces…Clements was the only one not killed outright. He died of wounds next day…Buried in the cemetery beside the Canadian Casualty Clearing Station, Poperinghe, cross erected with full particulars."

Gnr. J.S. Martin is buried in Birr Cross Roads Cemetery (I.G.1).

(XIX.B.12A) Pte. 240334, John Langstreth, 1/5th Bn. The King's Own (Royal Lancaster Regt.), (T.F.): *s*. of John Langstreth, of Cark-in-Cartmel, Carnforth, by his wife Francis Ann: *b*. Ulverston: enlisted Lancaster: served in France and Flanders from 14 February 1915, and died of wounds, 15 September 1917: Age 26.

His Memory Is As Fresh Today As In The Hour He Passed Away

(XIX.B.13A) Spr. 279374, Sergy Drobaha, 8th Bn. Canadian Railway Troops, C.E.F.: late of Edmonton: *b*. Kiev, Russia, 7 October 1884: Religion – Russian Orthodox: Occupation – Labourer: enlisted Edmonton, 25 March 1916. Died 15 September 1917, of wounds (SW multiple, Rt. femur, thigh, genitalia, Rt.

arm. head), received whilst engaged in railway construction nr. Dickebusch: Age 32. Three men – Sprs. Andrichuk, Donly and Donchuk – were killed, and six wounded of whom two others – Pte. Kiernan and Spr. Chernuck – also died.

Sprs. Andrichuk and Chernuck are buried in the Huts Cemetery (VI.A.11 / IV.D.17); Sprs. Donly and Donchuk in Belgian Battery Corner Cemetery (I.N.2 / I.N.3); Pte. Kiernan lies nearby (XIX.B.8).

(XIX.C.3) Lieut. Col. Stanley Gordon Gibbs, D.A.Q.M.G., 1st ANZAC attd. 2nd Divn. Train, Australian Army Service Corps, A.I.F.: *s.* of Hugh Frederick Gibbs, of 17, Abingdon Court, Kensington, London, by his wife Sarah: *b.* Southampton, co. Hants. Killed by shell-fire, 20 September 1917, while assisting Lieut.Col. Nicholas in directing the loading of wounded onto transports across the road from the A.D.S., Menin House: Age 31.

Until The Day Breaks And The Shadows Flee Away

(XIX.C.4) Lieut. Col. James Joachim Nicholas, A.D.M.S., 2nd Divn., 5th Field Ambulance, Australian Army Medical Corps, A.I.F.: s. of William John Nicholas, of Moama, New South Wales: *b.* Picola, Victoria, 17 November 1890: Occupation – Medical Practitioner: volunteered his services and joined Australian Army Medical Corps, Capt. 18 August 1914; apptd. Major, 1st Light Horse Field Ambulance, 20 August: departed Australia, A27 'Southern,' 18 October: apptd. D.A.D.M.S., 1st Australian Divn., 8 December: Mentioned in Sir Douglas Haig's Despatch, 9 April 1917: apptd. to command No.5 Field Amb. 22 July: promoted Lieut.Col. 19 September, and was killed by shell-fire (in company with Lieut.Col. Gibbs) the following day while directing the loading of wounded onto transports across the road from the A.D.S., Menin House: 20 September 1917: Age 26. *unm.*

(XIX.C.5) Major Frederick Harold Tubb, V.C., 7th Bn. Australian Infantry: *s.* of the late Harry Tubb, and his spouse Ellen E. Tubb ('St. Helena,' Longwood East, Victoria): *b.* Longwood, 28 November 1881: *educ.* Merit State School: previously served 14 years, 3 months (including 1 year, 9 months commissioned rank); joined A.I.F. 12 April 1914; volunteered for Overseas Service, 12 August: served in Egypt, Gallipoli, France and Flanders, and was killed in action, 20 September 1917: Age 36. The *London Gazette,* 15 October 1915, cites: "…For most conspicuous bravery and devotion to duty at Lone Pine trenches on the Gallipoli Peninsula, on 8th August 1915. In the early morning the enemy made a determined counter-attack on the centre of the newly-captured trench held by Lieutenant Tubb. They advanced up a sap and blew in a sandbag barricade, leaving only one foot of it standing, but Lieut. Tubb led his men back, repulsed the enemy and rebuilt the barricade, supported by strong bombing parties in the barricades, but on each occasion

Lieut. Tubb, although wounded in the hand and arm, held his ground with the greatest coolness, and finally succeeded in maintaining his position under very heavy bomb fire." In 1917 a newspaper correspondent reported, "Major Frederick Harold Tubb, V.C., Australian Infantry, whose death from wounds is officially announced today, won the Victoria Cross, one of seven Australians to be awarded that honour, during the fighting at Lone Pine trenches in Gallipoli 8–9 August 1915. He then held the rank of Lieutenant. He was mortally wounded during the fighting on the Ypres front on Saturday. The gallant officer had been wounded, and was being carried back on a stretcher when he was struck by a British shell...". His brother Capt. F.R. Tubb served with 7th Battn. A.I.F., awarded the Military Cross (surv'd).

Our Dearly Loved Son And Brother Called To Higher Service

(XIX.C.17A) Pte. 290285, Frederick Allingham, 2nd Bn. (12th Foot) The Suffolk Regt.: formerly no.28333, Suffolk Regt.: *s*. of Walter Allingham, of Hopper Farm, Faygate, Horsham, by his wife Grace Annie: and yr. brother to Sergt. 75377, W. Allingham, Tank Corps, died of wounds, 22 August 1917, at the Base Hospital, Boulogne: *b*. Redhill, co. Surrey: enlisted Pinner, co. Middlesex. Died of wounds, 26 September 1917, at Poperinghe: Age 31. He leaves a wife, Mrs H.K. Allingham (East End Cottages, Moss Lane, Pinner). (*IWGC record age 37*) Remembered on Pinner War Memorial (Panel 1), and St. Saviour's Parish Church Memorial, Colgate, West Sussex.

For My Beloved Husband
Until The Day Breaks And The Shadows Flee Away

His brother Walter is buried in Boulogne Eastern Cemetery (VIII.I.12).

(XIX.C.18A) Pte. 2742, Johannes Tois, 53rd Bn. Australian Infantry, A.I.F.: *s*. of Hans Tois, of Zeitenhof, Parnu: *b*. Parnu, Russia, 1895: Occupation – Russian Seaman: joined AI.F. Bathurst, New South Wales, 3 March 1916: departed Sydney, 7 October following: trained 1 month, England; proceeded to France, 21 December 1916: transf'd. Tactical Works Party, 9 September 1917, and died of wounds (S.W. head) on the 26th of that month, received at duty the same day: Age 22: *unm*.

(XIX.D.4A) Pte. 73146, William Augustine Mossop, 1st Bn. (45th Foot) The Sherwood Foresters (Notts & Derbys Regt.): formerly no.11299, South Staffordshire Regt.: *s*. of Edward Mossop, of Eccleshall, co. Stafford, by his wife Ellen, *née* Hall: and brother to Corpl. 15835, B.A. Mossop, Gloucestershire Regt., killed in action, 11 October 1915; and Gnr. V. Mossop, Royal Field Artillery (surv'd.): *b*. Eccleshall, 13 November 1884: enlisted Smethwick:

served in France from December 1915, and died 16 September 1917, of wounds: Age 32. He was married to Emily Mossop, *née* Andrews, and leaves five children.

His brother Bernard has no known grave; he is commemorated on the Loos (Dud Corner) Memorial.

(XIX.D.12) Sergt. 240228, John Wilkinson, D.C.M., 5th Bn. The East Lancashire Regt. (T.F.): *s.* of David Wilkinson, of 117, Hurley Wood Road, Burnley, co. Lancaster, by his wife Mary Ellen, *dau.* of John Bullock: *b.* Burnley, 8 December 1893: *educ.* Hurley Wood School: Occupation – Weaver: joined East Lancashire Regt. 10 March 1914: mobilised on the outbreak of war, August following: served with the Egyptian and Mediterranean Expeditionary Forces: proceeded to France, May 1915, and died at No.17 Canadian Casualty Clearing Station, 17 September 1917, from a bullet wound (chest) sustained while asleep in a rest billet nr. Ypres on the 12th. Buried in the Military Cemetery, Lyssenthoek. Awarded the D.C.M. (*London Gazette*, 5 January 1918) "For conspicuous gallantry and devotion to duty. He has rendered excellent service during the past year, and his devotion to duty has been most meritorious. On several occasions he has afforded the men of his section a splendid example of endurance and self-sacrifice.": Age 24. *unm.* (*IWGC record age 23*)

God Takes Our Loved Ones From Our Homes But Never From Our Hearts

At 9.20 p.m., on the night of 17 August 1917, four bombs were dropped on the C.C.S. at Lijssenthoek by enemy aircraft. Twenty-three personnel and patients were killed, a further thirty-nine badly wounded; nine of the dead were German prisoner patients:

(XX.B.1 Coll) Deutsche Krieger, Graf, Johann, Bayer 19 R.J.R: *s.* of Lorenz (& Margarete) Graf, Dobereiner, Schumachermeister-in-Kirchenlamitz. Wounded Frezenberg, 16 August: Deutsche Krieger, Mau, Johannes, (Ersatz Reservist) J.R. 84. Wounded Frezenberg.

(XX.B.2 Coll) Deutsche Krieger, Neumann, Hans, (Musketier) J.R. 84. Wounded Frezenberg: Deutsche Krieger, Warnecke, Willi, (Musketier) J.R. 84. Wounded Frezenberg.

(XX.B.3 Coll) Deutsche Krieger, Kleine-Kollmeier, Heinrich, (Gefreiter) J.R. 145. Wounded Westhoek-Bellewaarde Ridge: Deutsche Krieger, Paulsen, Willy, (Musketier) J.R. 84. Wounded Frezenberg.

(XX.B.4 Coll) Deutsche Krieger, Driessen, Theodor, (Musketier) J.R. 145. Wounded Westhoek-Bellewaarde Ridge: Deutsche Krieger, Ehrich, Friedrich, (Schutze) J.R. 84. Wounded Frezenberg: Deutsche Krieger, Vollrath, Hugo, (Musketier) R.J.R. 127. Wounded Frezenberg.

(XX.C.13A) Pte. 36253, Cyril Frank Roper, 2nd Bn. (36th Foot) The Worcestershire Regt.: *s.* of Frank Roper, of 2, Spring Villas, Worcester Road, Malvern Link; formerly of 'The Laurels,' Worcester Road, by his wife Edith Jessie: *b.* Great Malvern, 1898: prior to enlistment was 4½ years member Malvern (St. Matthias') Church Lad's Brigade, attained rank Corpl.: enlisted Worcester: served with the Expeditionary Force, and died of wounds, 30 September 1917; being shot through the chest while at duty as a signaller: Age 19.

He Gave His Life For Us

(XX.C.18) 2nd Lieut. Lawrence Arthur Joscelyne, M.C., 7th (Service) Bn. Prince Albert's (Somerset Light Infantry): only *s.* of Dr. Arthur Joscelyne, of Salisbury House, Taunton, co. Somerset: *b.* Greenwich, London, S.E., 16 December 1897: *educ.* Epsom College, and Trinity College, Oxford: gazetted 2nd Lieut. Somerset Light Infantry, November 1916: served with the Expeditionary Force in France and Flanders from January 1917, and was killed in action at Poperinghe, 1 October following. Buried at Lyssenthoek Cemetery, Poperinghe. His Colonel wrote, "He is a great loss to the battalion, being one of our best subalterns. His courage and cheerfulness were a splendid example to all ranks." Awarded the Military Cross (*London Gazette*, 7 March 1918) "For conspicuous gallantry and devotion to duty in command of a mopping-up party. Finding the attacking line had lost all their officers, and were held up by machine-gun fire, he left his 'mopping-up' party to carry on. He led the attacking line forward and kept direction over very boggy ground, reaching and consolidating the first objective.": Age 19.

Christ Our Redeemer Passed The Self Same Way

(XX.D.14A) Spr. 7133, William Hopkins Abbott, 2nd Field Coy., Australian Engineers, A.I.F.: *s.* of Henry James Abbott, of 'Avon,' Olola Avenue, Vaucluse, Sydney, New South Wales, by his wife Rebekah. Died of wounds (GSW right leg), 3.15 p.m., 3 October 1917: Age 26. *unm.* Pte. 16514, B. Lamb recorded, "On September 20th/17 at Ypres, an officer was killed and 4 lads volunteered to go and bring his body down, Pte. W.H. Abbott, 7133, being one of them on October 1st. They got the body down to Chateau Wood when Abbott was hit by a bit of shrapnel and died of wounds 2 days later at the C.C. Station, and was buried at Poperinghe. The boys erected a very decent Cross with his name engraved upon it." Cross erected by Corpl. G. Wallace.

Fondly Remembered

The officer, Lieut. J. Darbyshire, is buried in Hooge Crater Cemetery (III.A.11).

(XX.D.17A) Gnr. 88144, Robert Charles Long, 147th Heavy Bty., Royal Garrison Artillery: s. of Henry Long, of Woodford, by his wife Rosa (née Davidson): husb. to Ethel A. Long (17, Marlborough Road, South Woodford, co. Essex): b. Holborn: enlisted London. Died of abdominal bullet wounds, 4 October 1917: Age 31.

R.I.P.

(XX.F.8) Pte. 39293, Archibald McNeil, 3rd Bn. Otago Regt., N.Z.E.F.: s. of Archibald McNeil, of Benhar, Dunedin, Otago, by his wife Grace: and brother to Pte. 8/2088, D. McNeil, Otago Regt. (surv'd.); and Rfn. 26/193, J. McNeil, N.Z. Rifle Brigade, killed in action, 12 October 1917, nr. Wolf Copse: b. Larkhall, co. Lanark, c.1882: Occupation – Coal Miner: enlisted Balebutcha, 7 October 1916: departed Wellington, HMNZT 75, 'Waitemata,' 19 January 1917; Rfn. Rfts., N.Z. Rifle Brigade: disembarked Plymouth, 27 March following: served with the Expeditionary Force in France and Flanders transf'd. Otago Regt. from 28 May 1917, and died 5 October 1917 of wounds (G.S. back, abdomen) received in action at Broodseinde the previous day: Age 35.

His brother John has no known grave, he is commemorated on the Tyne Cot (New Zealand) Memorial (Panel 7).

(XX.F.13) L/Corpl. 8/4159, John George Laidlaw, 3rd Bn. Otago Regt., N.Z.E.F.: s. of the late John Laidlaw, by his wife Hannah (Otautau, Southland): and elder brother to Pte. 8/3938, F.A. Laidlaw, 2nd Otago Regt., killed in action, 15 September 1916: enlisted Trentham, 15 December 1915: departed Wellington, 1 April 1916; served in France from May 1917, and died of wounds, 4 October 1917, received in action at Broodseinde: Age 22. *unm.*

His brother Francis has no known grave; he is commemorated on the Caterpillar Valley (New Zealand) Memorial.

(XX.F.15A) Pte. 51575, Orlando Cyril Garnett, 22nd (Service) Bn. The Manchester Regt.: eldest s. of John William Garnett, of Burnt Mill, Cautley, Sedbergh. co. York, by his wife Ellen: enlisted Sedbergh. Severely wounded in action at Passchendaele, 3 October 1917, and died at No.2 Canadian C.C.S., Poperinghe the following day without regaining consciousness: Age 19. Buried with full military honours in the military cemetery beside the Boeschepe Road on the afternoon of the 5th.

A Brave And Loving Son Never Forgot

(XX.F.19) Pte. 6737, Leslie Athol Drayton, 5th Bn. Australian Infantry, A.I.F.: s. of Frederick William Drayton, of 'Lesgoelen,' Clarke Avenue, Caulfield,

Victoria, and Annie Drayton, *née* Stewart, his spouse: and elder brother to Pte. 3382, G.F. Drayton, 60th Australian Infantry, killed in action, 2 September 1918, aged 17 years: *b*. Port Melbourne, July 1894: Occupation – Grocer: enlisted A.I.F., August 1916: served with the Expeditionary Force in France from 15 March 1917; wounded (G.S.W. Rt. leg) 17 May, and evacuated to England: returned to France, 27 July, and died at No.2 Casualty Clearing Station, Poperinghe of wounds (G.S. head), 2 October 1917 received in action at Zonnebeke, before Passchendaele: Age 23. He leaves a widow, Amelia P. Drayton (20, Watt Street, Spotswood, Melbourne, Victoria).

Too Far Away Thy Grave To See But Not Too Far To Think Of Thee

His brother George is buried in Peronne Communal Cemetery Extension (IV.E.6).

(XX.G.16) L/Corpl. 3665, Samuel Jones, 22nd (Service) Bn. The Manchester Regt.: *yr. s.* of John Jones, of 4, Model Farm Cottages, Mill Lane, Liscard, Wallasey, by his wife Mary, *dau.* of James Roberts: *b*. Egremont, Wallasey, co. Chester, 7 July 1881: *educ*. St. Mary's Church School, Liscard: Occupation – Bricklayer: enlisted 19 August 1914: served with the Mediterranean Expeditionary Force in Gallipoli from July 1915: wounded at Suvla Bay, 6 August, while serving with 11th Manchester Regt., and invalided home: proceeded to France, April 1916, and was again invalided home in November suffering from trench fever: returned to France, 14 June 1917, and died in No.2 Canadian Clearing Station, 5 October following, from wounds received in action on the 3rd. Buried in Lyssenthoek Military Cemetery: Age 36. He *m*. St. Mary's Parish Church, Birkenhead, 23 July 1900; Emily Mercer (formerly Jones, of 6, Cecil Road, Liscard, co. Chester), 3rd *dau.* of John Davies, of Birkenhead, and had seven children – Ida Alexandra, *b*. 24 April 1902; Lillian Maria, *b*. 3 August 1904; Emily Frances, *b*. 12 February 1906; John Owen, *b*. 27 October 1907; Marie Elizabeth, *b*. 7 April 1909; Samuel Joseph, *b*. 18 August 1913; Edna Mary, *b*. 24 June 1916.

Time Changes Many Things But Loving Memory Always Clings

(XX.H.1) Pte. 5787, William Henry Rickard, 'C' Coy., 28th Bn. Australian Infantry, A.I.F.: late of Smith's Mill, Western Australia: *s*. of William Henry Rickard, Snr., of Glen Forest, Western Australia, and Emma Rickard, his late wife (*d*.1901): *b*. Footscray, Victoria, 1891: Religion – Church of England: Occupation – Engine Driver: 5'5" tall, blue eyes, fair hair: joined A.I.F., Black Boy Hill, 25 April 1916; apptd. 16th Rfts. 28th Battn., 4 October; departed Fremantle, 10 October: trained England, 2–21 December: joined 28th Battn.

In the Field, 23 January 1917: wounded in action at Lagnicourt, 26 March (GSW Rt. hand – thro' tip middle finger; slight); evacuated 1st Southern General Hospital, England, transf'd. Harefield (8–16 May), for treatment, convalescence; thereafter proceeded on leave, on return from which he was admonished (28 June) by Lieut. Crampton (and awarded forfeiture of two day's pay); 'Being Absent Without Leave mid-night 25 June – 6.45 a.m. 27 June': returned France, 26 July, and died No.10 C.C.S., Poperinghe, 4 October 1917, of wounds (SW head) received in action at Broodseinde the same day: Age 25.

It Is Men Of My Age And Single Who Are Expected To Do Their Duty

(XX.H.4) Sergt. 189, Reginald William Muddle, 1st Bde. Australian Field Artillery, A.I.F.: *s.* of William Edward Muddle, by his wife Minnie Elizabeth Gertrude: *b.* Dungog, July 1890: Occupation – Greengrocer: serving member 44th Bty. Field Artillery, enlisted Sydney, 28 August 1914: departed Australia, 18 October: served at Gallipoli (from 4 April 1915), wounded 22 April (G.S.W. Lt. ankle), transf'd. convalescent camp, 28 June: thereafter was (until 9 April 1917) almost continuously hospitalised for various minor ailments: served in France and Flanders from 27 March 1916, wounded (G.S.W. Lt. arm), 31 July 1917: returned to duty, 17 August, and died of wounds (S.W [shrapnel] Lt. side, face and head), 12.15 p.m., 4 October 1917, received in action at Anzac Ridge, Westhoek, earlier the same day: Age 27. He leaves a wife, Florence Annie E. Muddle (71, Marian Street, Enmore, New South Wales).

He Died As He Lived, Noble And Brave

(XX.H.5) Pte. 39428, Erick Curties, No.4 Coy., New Zealand Machine Gun Corps, N.Z.E.F.: *s.* of the late Walter William (& Elizabeth) Curties, of Ipswich, England: c/o Charles Edward Watts, Motor Specialist; 45, Layard Street, Invercargill, New Zealand: *b.* London, England, 10 August 1895: Religion – Church of England: Occupation – Labourer; Messrs J. McLeod: joined N.Z.E.F., October 1916; apptd. 22nd Rfts. 'F' Coy. (Canterbury): departed Wellington, HMNZT 77 'Mokoia', 17 February 1917: trained England from 2 May; transf'd. 'B' Coy, Canterbury Regt.: transf'd. N.Z.M.G.C., 6 June: proceeded to France 23 July; joined No.4 Coy., 9 September. Died of wounds (GSW Rt. buttock & leg), No.10 C.C.S., 5 October 1917, received in action at Broodseinde Ridge two days previously. Buried 1 ¾ miles S.W. of Poperinghe: Age 22. *unm.* His brother Cyril (Pte. 39429) and sister Emily (Nurse, 22/23, *a.k.a.* Wilson) also served.

(XX.H.21A) L/Corpl. 32763, James Henry Furmidge, 12th (Service) Bn. (Bermondsey) The East Surrey Regt.: only *s*. of Henry William Furmidge, of 6, Park Rd., Ryde, Isle of Wight, by his wife Harriet, *dau*. of James Sheath, of Stroud Wood, nr. Ryde, Isle of Wight: *b*. Ventnor, Isle of Wight, 10 June 1895: *educ*. St. Helen's National School: Occupation – Drapers Assistant: enlisted East Surrey Regt., June 1915: served with the Expeditionary Force in France and Flanders from 1 January 1917: took part in several engagements; invalided home suffering from illness, 1 November 1917: returned to France, 30 March 1918, and died at No. 10 Casualty Clearing Station, 9 August following, of wounds received in action at Mont Kemmel the same day....His Commanding Officer, Capt. Barry, wrote, "Your son was one of those soldiers we can least afford to lose. He leaves a stainless record and gave promise of doing good service as a L-Corporal...he was always ready to undertake all that was required of him;" and the Chaplain, "...All his friends speak highly of him, and you have every reason to be proud of his bravery and faithfulness.": Age 23: *unm*.

Greater Love Hath No Man Than This

(XX.I.5A) L/Corpl. 24/1602, Francis Brogan, 2nd Bn. Auckland Regt., N.Z.E.F.: *s*. of Edward Patrick (& Alicia) Brogan, of 1, Seddon Street, Dannevirke, Hawke's Bay: and elder brother to Pte. 4/1025, W.A. Brogan, Samoan Relief Force, died, 30 July 1919, of sickness contracted while on Active Service: *b*. Australia, 1894: Occupation – Labourer: departed New Zealand, 8 January 1916. Died 8 October 1917, of wounds (G.S. abdomen) received in action at Broodseinde two days previously: Age 23. *unm*. Correspondence to be forwarded c/o his friend, R. Calvert Esq., Hamilton Hospital.

His brother Wilfred is buried in Wellington (Karori) Cemetery (150.Q.R.C.).

(XX.I.16A) Pte. 12/3042, Lionel Balmer Hayward, 2nd Bn. Auckland Regt., N.Z.E.F.: *s*. of Frederick Hayward, of Maungakaramea, Whangerai, New Zealand, by his wife Rhoda. Died of wounds (G.S. head), 7 October 1917, received in action at Broodeseinde: Age 20. *unm*. Pte. Hayward is one of twelve local men recorded on the Maungakaramea War Memorial, the first memorial to be erected in the north honouring those locals who had died in the Great War; a further three names were added in memory of those who fell during the Second World War. See Pte. E.C. Cook, N.Z. Army Medical Corps, The Huts Cemetery (XV.A.18).

Thousands of boys falsified dates of birth in order to meet the minimum age requirement to enlist. Desperate for soldiers, recruiting officers did not always check a boy's details as carefully as they might. One sixteen year old later told how he was able to join the Army: "The recruiting sergeant asked me my age, and when I told him he said, 'You had better go out, come back in again, and tell me different.' I went out, came back, told him I was nineteen, and I was in." By adding 4 years to his age Herbert West managed to enlist aged 14 years and 1 month, and his application to enlist purports to have been supported by a signed document of consent from his parents!

(XX.I.19A) L/Corpl. 5914, Herbert Austin West, 20th Bn. Australian Infantry, A.I.F.: *s.* of Edwin West, of Darleyoak, Rylstone, New South Wales, by his wife Margaret: and brother to C.Q.M.S. 116, H.W. West, 54th Bn. A.I.F. (surv'd), and Pte. 4281, C.S. West, 56th Bn. A.I.F. (surv'd): *b.* Leichardt, Botany, Sydney, N.S.W., April 1901: employee to Messrs Anthony Hordern & Sons Ltd., Department Store, Sydney: enlisted, Sydney, 13 May 1916: left for France aboard H.M.A.T. 'Ceramic,' 7 October 1916: served in the trenches from February 1917; promoted Corpl. sixteen years of age: wounded (shrapnel, Rt. arm) 3 May 1917, returned to duty within one week and died, No.2 Canadian Casualty Clearing Station, 8 October 1917, of wounds (shrapnel, back, upper Rt. arm) received in action before Passchendaele two days previously (6 October): Age 16.

Peace Perfect Peace

(XX.I.23) Capt. 109309, Thomas William Eric Dixon, M.C., M.M. (*a.k.a* T. Baylis Dixon), 4th Canadian Mounted Rifles (Central Ontario Regt.), C.E.F.: 2nd *s.* of William Arthur Dixon, of Hatfield Lodge, Devon's Road, Babbacombe, co. Devon, by his wife Grace Adelaide Maunsell; *dau.* of George Roche Smith, Surgeon, 2nd Queen's Royal Regt.: and brother to Lieut. Gerald B. Dixon, C.E.F. (surv'd.): *b.* Torquay, co. Devon, 8 January 1893: *educ.* Berkhampstead Grammar School: went to Canada with his brother 1910, where they were adopted by Mr (& Mrs) F.W. Baylis, of Toronto: volunteered for Active Service soon after the outbreak of war, and enlisted (with his brother) as Troopers, 4th Canadian Mounted Rifles, September 1914: served with the Expeditionary Force in France and Flanders, 1915–18; took part in many engagements, and did much valuable reconnaissance work, for which he was given a commission in the field June 1916, at the 2nd Battle of Ypres (*q.v.*). During the engagement at Mount Sorrel, 2 June 1916, Capt. Dixon crept into No Man's Land with his brother and took shelter in a shell hole. Throughout the next twenty-four hours they crept back and forward through the German lines with valuable information. For this gallantry, Capt. Dixon and his brother both received commissions the next day and Capt. Dixon received the Military Medal: promoted Capt. June 1917: fought in most of the battles of the Somme Campaign, and, at Vimy Ridge, as Scout Officer, received the Military Cross: apptd. Adjutant, Divisional Training School, June 1917: recalled to the battalion December following, given command of a company, and, while in a dugout being used as

Battalion Headquarters, nr. Kemmel, was hit in the head by shrapnel and killed instantaneously; 3 August 1918. Buried in Lyssenthoek Cemetery, nr. Abeele. His Commanding Officer, Lieut.Colonel W.R. Patterson, D.S.O., wrote, "I have always taken a keen personal interest in him, and considered him one of my best officers, and his loss is irreparable...his comrades in the regiment join with me in mourning the loss of a brave soldier and a true friend." He was Mentioned in Despatches by F.M. Sir Douglas Haig, for 'gallant and distinguished service in the field.': Age 25. *unm.*

Beloved Son Of W. Arthur Dixon And Ada His Wife Of Torquay
R.I.P.

(XX.J.1A) Pte. 2450A, Thomas Mallion, 51st Bn. Australian Infantry, A.I.F.: *s.* of the late George William Mallion, Farm Labourer; by his wife Hannah: and brother to Rfn. 1179, A. Mallion, M.M., Rifle Brigade, died of wounds (gas), 9 August 1916: *b.* 'The Tanyard,' Heathfield, co. Sussex, 29 October 1882: *educ.* Burwash School: was a Builder prior to emigrating to Australia, 1911; settled at Perth, finding employment as a Hospital Orderly: enlisted Perth, 20 March 1916: left for England, 20 September 1916, arriving Plymouth, 15 November following: served with the Expeditionary Force in France and Flanders from 13 December 1916: hospitalised (septic heel) Dartford, co. Kent, January 1917: returned to France, 24 September 1917: took part in the fighting at Polygon Wood, and, during the assault on Passchendaele Ridge, 11 October 1917, was wounded by a rifle bullet to the head, dying the next day at No.2 Canadian Casualty Clearing Station, Poperinghe. Buried in the Military Cemetery, Lyssenthoek, Plot 20: Age 34. He *m.* St. George's Cathedral, Perth, 18 March 1916; Emily Anne (South Crescent, Bayswater, Perth, Western Australia), *dau.* of John Chester.

Thy Will Not Mine O Lord

His brother Albert is buried in Essex Farm Cemetery (III.B.25).

(XX.J.6A) Pte. 2947, Charles Leonard Lockhart, 51st Bn. Australian Infantry, A.I.F.: *s.* of John Charles Ernest Lockhart, of Gornell's, nr. Perth, Western Australia, by his wife Rosannah: and elder brother to Pte. 2676, E.E. Lockhart, 16th Australian Infantry, died of wounds (GSW, cranial), 12 August 1916, aged 20 years: *b.* Blakeville, Victoria, 1893: Occupation – Teacher: enlisted Perth, 1 June 1916: departed Fremantle, 10 November: trained England; hospitalised greater part February – May 1917 for various ailments: proceeded to France, 9 May: joined 51st Battn. In the Field on the 13th.: severely wounded (GSW Lt. thigh, abdomen) before Passchendaele, 10 October 1917, and died No.10

Casualty Clearing Station, Poperinghe, two days later (12 October). Buried at Lyssenthoek: Age 24. 'In Memoriam,' his father wrote, "One by one they're going from us, To that heavenly home of love, Where they wait for us to join them, When this earthly race is run." For 95 years, Pte. Lockhart's family were totally unaware that shortly before his departure for Europe he had become engaged to be married to Miss Amy Richards, of Armadale. This became known – purely by coincidence – when, on the anniversary of his death his descendants chose to put up a plaque to his memory in King's Park, Perth and some descendants of Miss Richards turned up to pay their respects.

Till We Meet Again

His brother Ernest is buried in Puchevillers British Cemetery (I.F.66).

(XX.J.22A) Pte. 47344, George Palmer, 'Z' Coy., 18th (Service) Bn. The Lancashire Fusiliers: *s*. of the late Frederick Palmer; Publican (*d*.1903), 'The Red Lion, Brafield-on-the-Green, co. Northampton, by his wife Jane (78, Cedar Road, Northampton): and brother to Pte. R. Palmer (surv'd.): *b*. 'The Cock Inn,' Kingsthorpe, co. Northampton. Died 5 August 1918, of accidental wounds received from the careless mishandling of an unexploded artillery shell: Age 23. *unm*. His father Frederick died of septicaemia, after being cut by a glass while trying to break up a fight which had broken out in the bar of 'The Red Lion.'

Till We Meet Again In The Resurrection Morn

(XX.K.12A) Pte. 675, Arnold Middleton, 21st Bn. Australian Infantry attd. 6th Light Trench Mortar Bty., A.I.F.: 4th *s*. of Jacob Middleton, of 2, Oldham Terrace, Acton, London, W., by his wife Eliza Ann, *dau*. of Robert Sutcliffe: and brother to Pte. J. Middleton, Royal Fusiliers, reported missing after the fighting at Arras, 3 May 1917: *b*. Sheffield, co. York, 18 February 1892: *educ*. Osborne Road School, Acton: removed to Australia (1913); settled Victoria: Occupation – Stores Manager; John Hall's Universal Emporium, Yinnar: volunteered for Foreign Service on the outbreak of war; joined Australian Infantry, 11 January 1915: served with the Mediterranean Expeditionary Force at Gallipoli: proceeded to France, 24 May 1916, and died in No.2 Canadian Casualty Clearing Station of bullet wounds to the head, 4 October 1917. Buried at Remy Siding, Poperinghe. His Commanding Officer, Capt. Hogg, wrote, "We are all very sorry to lose him, as he was such a splendid soldier, always so willing to do his best under any circumstances…it is a very small consolation to you to know that he was one of the best, and gave his life for others.": Age 25. *unm*. (*IWGC record 5 October*)

His brother Jacob has no known grave; he is commemorated on the Arras (Faubourg d'Amiens) Memorial (Bay 3).

Plot 21, AA to HH lies adjacent to A to H
(XXI.AA.9A) L/Corpl. 37938, Edward Bell, M.M., 24th (Service) Bn. (1st Tyneside Irish) The Northumberland Fusiliers: formerly no.1298: *s.* of Robert Bell, of New Delavel: *husb.* to M.J. Bell (65, New Road, New Delavel, Newsham, Northumberland): enlisted Blyth. Died of bomb wounds to the legs and right side received in an enemy air raid, 31 October 1917: Age 26.

Remembered By All

(XXI.AA.17A) Pte. 70399, George Smith, 1st Bn. (23rd Foot) The Royal Welsh Fusiliers: formerly no.31270, South Wales Borderers: *s.* of the late Thomas Smith, by his wife Mary, *dau.* of John Thomas, of Aberdare: *b.* Ystrad, Rhondda, co. Glamorgan, 20 December 1879: *educ.* Tylorstown Board School: enlisted South Wales Borderers, 13 June 1917: served with the Expeditionary Force in France and Flanders from 10 October following, being transf'd. Royal Welsh Fusiliers on the 19th., and died at No.2 Canadian General Hospital, Poperinghe, on the 31st, of shrapnel wounds received in action. Buried in Lyssenthoek British Military Cemetery: 31 October 1917: Age 37. He *m.* at Holy Trinity Church, Tylorstown, 26 October 1899, Ceridwen (16, Stanley St., Senghenydd), since re-married, now Mrs Desmond, *dau.* of William Harris, and had six children – Mary Lizzie, *b.* 26 September 1900; Margaret, *b.* 7 December 1904; Thomas, *b.* 28 October 1906; Ceridwen, *b.* 22 July 1908; Myfanwy, *b.* 21 July 1910, and Ethel, *b.* 27 November 1912.

(XXI.BB.11) Capt. Herve Murray Grant, M.C., 'B' Coy., 52nd Bn. Canadian Infantry (Manitoba Regt.), C.E.F.: *s.* of W.S. Grant, c/o Messrs Allan, Killam & McKay, Winnipeg, Manitobae: *b.* Winnipeg, 29 August 1891: *educ.* Queen Victoria Preparatory School; Upper Canada College (1905–07): employee Messrs Robinson & Black: serving member Lieut. 90th Regt. ('Little Black Devils'), Militia: enlisted Winnipeg, Lieut. 144th Bn., 24 February 1915: proceeded overseas, 13 September 1916: trained England; Physical Training & Bayonet Fighting Instructor, Seaford; apptd 18th (Res.) Bn., Seaford, January 1917: joined 52nd Bn., France, 26 April 1917: promoted Capt. September: took part in the fighting at Fresnoy (April), Hill 70 (August), Lens (September), and Passchendaele where, following the successful assault on Bellevue Spur (26 October), he was inspecting the position with his Commanding Officer when he was shot by a German sniper. First Aid was immediately rendered. Removed to No.2 Casualty Clearing Station, Poperinghe, and operated on the following day, he died 28 October 1917: Age 26. Awarded the Military Cross (*London Gazette*, 15 March 1918) "For conspicuous gallantry and devotion to duty in a raid on the enemy's position. His excellent leadership and gallantry materially contributed to the complete success of the undertaking, during which the entire objective was captured, the garrison were destroyed or taken prisoners, and four machine-guns were captured. Owing to casualties he took command of his company and carried out the plan of operations with great success." He leaves a widow Marjorie F. Grant (484, River Avenue, Winnipeg), to mourn his loss.

"Greater Love Hath No Man Than This"
John 15.13

(XXI.BB.14) Pte. 245284, Martin Henry Grey, 10th (Service) Bn. The Durham Light Infantry: *s.* of Thomas Grey, Miner; of 6, Blackwood Street (formerly of Panhaven Road), Amble, by his wife Margaret Isabella, *dau.* of Martin Archbold: *b.* Craster, co. Northumberland, 23 June 1898: *educ.* Church of England School, Dunstan, nr. Craster: Occupation – Miner: enlisted Durham Light Infantry, 17 April 1917: served with the Expeditionary Force in France and Flanders from 17 July, and died at the No.3 Canadian Casualty Clearing Station, 29 October following, from shrapnel wounds received in action. Buried in the Military Cemetery, Lyssenthoek: Age 19.

Ever Remembered By His Father, Mother, Sister And Two Brothers

(XXI.BB.18) Lieut. James Mansfield Reid, M.C., 2nd Field Coy., Australian Engineers, A.I.F.: *s.* of George Watson Reid, of 'Clyde,' Sackville Street, Kew East, Victoria, by his wife Lillian Margaret: *b.* Williamstown, Victoria. Died of wounds, 30 October 1917: Age 29. Lieut. W. Collins recorded, "Following operations near Passchendaele Lieut. Reid was engaged on strongpoint work with his section, and it was after completing his task that he was hit. It is fairly conclusive that he was shot by a sniper; the bullet struck his prismatic compass and entered his abdomen, coming out on the right side. He was immediately attended to by his boys and they carried him to a Canadian First Aid Post where he was dressed properly by an M.O. From the advanced post he was carried to Zonnebeke where he was placed on board a motor ambulance which conveyed him to Poperinghe, where he died a few days later in the 10th C.C.S. He was buried in the graveyard there. The Coy., before leaving the Flanders front, erected a beautiful oak Cross over his last resting place." Cross erected by Corpl. G. Wallace, 2nd Field Coy. Posthumously awarded the Military Cross for the above action (*London Gazette*, No.4238, 6 April 1918).

Beloved Son Of Mr & Mrs G.W. Reid
Kew Vic. Australia
"Pro Patria"

(XXI.CC.3) L/Sergt. 18902, Joe Hewitt, 21st (Service) Bn. (6th City) The Manchester Regt.: *s.* of Joseph (& Annie) Hewitt, of 50, Brook Street, Hyde, co. Chester: and brother to Pte. 9866, W.H. Hewitt, 18th Manchester Regt., killed in action, 30 July 1916: *b.* Hyde, *c.*1895: enlisted Manchester: served with the Expeditionary Force in France and Flanders from 10 November 1915, and died 31 October 1917 of shrapnel wounds to his side and scrotal region: Age 22. *unm.*

Fight The Good Fight

His brother William has no known grave; he is commemorated on the Thiepval Memorial, Somme.

(XXI.CC.8A) Pte. 1015939, Edward Burdett Garrard, Observer, 72nd (Seaforth Highlanders) Bn. Canadian Infantry (British Columbia Regt.), C.E.F.: 4th *s.* of the late Major Francis Thomas Garrard, 27th Madras Native Infantry, by his wife Eliza Mary (21, Eler's Road, Ealing, London, W.), *dau.* of Capt. Sir Charles Burdett, 41st Madras Native Infantry: *b.* Colerne, co. Wilts, 17 November 1875: *educ.* Bedford Grammar School, and Wantage Grammar School: subsequently went to British Columbia: settled at Port Alberui, Vancouver Island, as Postmaster, Dominion Government Telegraph Agent & Collector (H.M. Customs): joined Canadian Seaforth Highlanders: served with the Expeditionary Force in France and Flanders, and died at No.10 Casualty Clearing Station, 31 October 1917, of multiple shrapnel wounds received in action. Buried in the Military Cemetery at Lyssenthoek: Age 41. His Commanding Officer wrote, "I cannot speak too highly of his work in every action in which he has been engaged since coming to France; his work as Battalion Observer in the initial stages of the action in which he received the wounds from which he died was of the greatest importance to the success of the same, and he and his N.C.O.'s died splendidly." He *m.* at Vancouver Island, British Columbia, Eleanor M. (Port Alberui, Vancouver Island), *dau.* of Dr. Watson, and had three children.

I Have Fought A Good Fight I Have Kept The Faith

Whilst thousands of young boys were adding years to their ages in order to join up, large numbers of older men were deducting years from theirs that they might pass as being younger men and thereby do likewise. To avenge the death of his brother, ex-New Zealand All Blacks captain, David Gallaher enlisted by deducting three years from his age; Irish-Canadian Shipping Clerk John Fishbourne deducted nine years!:

(XXI.CC.13) Gnr. 349279, John Fishbourne, 5th Bde. Canadian Field Artillery, C.E.F.: late *husb.* to Mary Elizabeth Fishbourne (45, Andover Road,

Twickenham, co. Middlesex, England): and brother to William Charles Fishbourne, 461, Merton Avenue, St. Lambert's, Quebec: *b.* Dublin, Ireland, 5 July 1864 (on attestation, Kingston, Ontario, stated 5 July 1873): enlisted Royal Artillery (11th Field Bty.), 1879, aged 15 years, served 10 years in India; discharged 1893, re-enlisted 1900: removed to Canada, 1905: joined C.E.F., 21 August 1916, posted 'C' Bty., Royal Canadian Horse Artillery: coat of arms tattoo on right forearm, anchor chain heart on left: served in France and Flanders from January 1917; court-martialled 27 February for 'permitting the escape of a person in custody': Died of wounds, 1 November 1917: Age 53.

Greater Love Hath No Man Than This

Sergt. D. Gallaher is buried in Nine Elms British Cemetery (III.D.8).

(XXI.CC.19A) Pte. 424641, James Robert Calder, 78th Bn. Canadian Infantry (Manitoba Regt.), C.E.F.: *s.* of George Calder, of 1, Ash Grove, Elgin, co. Moray, by his wife Margaret: and brother to Pte. 266465, A. Calder, 6th Seaforth Highlanders, killed in action, 9 April 1917; and Corpl. 1898, P. Calder, 2nd Seaforth Highlanders, killed in action, 8 August 1918: *b.* Aberlour, co. Banff, 10 September 1877: Occupation – Farmer: joined C.E.F., Dauphin, Manitoba, 22 April 1915: served with the Expeditionary Force in France from 15 August 1916, and died, 1 November 1917, of shrapnel wounds to the head and left arm received in action (30–31 October) at Passchendaele: Age 40. He was married to Florence Helen Calder (988, Erin Street, Winnipeg). One of three brothers who fell. (*IWGC record age 33*)

Not Lost But Gone Before

His brother Alexander is buried in Highland Cemetery, Roclincourt (I.C.9); Patrick is commemorated in Pont-du-Hem Military Cemetery, La Gorgue (Sp. Mem.3).

(XXI.DD.7) Lieut. John Murray, 6th Bn. (Renfrewshire) Princess Louise's (Argyll & Sutherland Highlanders): *s.* of the late John Murray, Junior, of Paisley, Writer, by his wife Elizabeth R., *dau.* of Robert Macintyre, of Paisley: *b.* Paisley, co. Renfrew, 7 November 1891: *educ.* Paisley Grammar School: employee Coats Central Agency: volunteered for Active Service on the outbreak of war; joined 9th Highland Light Infantry (T.F.), Pte., 7 September 1914: served with the Expeditionary Force in France and Flanders from 25 January 1915, where he saw much service and took part in the fighting at Festubert and Loos: returned home, December 1915; gazetted 2nd Lieut. Argyll & Sutherland Highlanders, on the 5th of that month: after training at Ripon, joined his regiment in France, 4 July 1916, fighting in the Battle of the Somme in July of that year, also at

Arras, 9 April 1917, in which he was Acting Capt.; promoted Lieut. 8 October 1917, and died at No.17 Casualty Clearing Station, nr. Poperinghe, 30 October 1917, from the effects of gas poisoning received at Passchendaele. Buried in Lyssenthoek Military Cemetery. His Major wrote, "We will all miss him very much, he was always so cheery and full of spirits and quiet humour. He was a good soldier, always keen on his work, and thoroughly reliable;" and his Captain, "I appreciated to the full his unfailing good humour and true gentlemanly bearing under all conditions out here. He did his share in helping others, and so lightened the load we all had to bear.": Age 25. *unm*.

*The Day Thou Gavest Lord Has Ended
The Darkness Falls At Thy Behest*

(XXI.DD.13A) Pte. 16243, William Henry Pluck, 1st Bn. (31st Foot) The East Surrey Regt.: *s*. of William Henry Pluck, Builder & Decorator; of 18, Date Street, Walworth, London, S.E., by his wife Amy Matilda: *b*. Walworth, 6 July 1895: *educ*. Penrose Street School: Occupation – Assistant Painter & Decorator: enlisted East Surrey Regt., 21 November 1915; posted 3rd (Reserve) Battn.: served with the Expeditionary Force in France from February 1916, transf'd. 1st Battn.: thrice previously wounded. Died No.2 Canadian Dressing Station, Lyssenthoek, 30 October 1917, of wounds received in action. Buried there. A lieutenant wrote, "I was very sorry to lose your son, as he was an excellent soldier and friend to his comrades, and everyone he came in contact with.": Age 22. *unm*.

Peace Perfect Peace

(XXI.EE.13A) Gnr. 2038, George Leonard Illingworth, 13th Bty., 5th Bde. Australian Field Artillery, A.I.F.: *s*. of Joe Illingworth, of Bullawa Creek, Narrabri, New South Wales, and his spouse Alice Mary Illingworth: and brother to Gnr. 2039, L.G. Illingworth, 13th Bty. (surv'd.), and Pte. 1682A, A.E. Illingworth, 4th Australian Light Horse (surv'd.): *b*. October 1889: Religion – Church of England: Occupation – Farmer: 6' tall, grey eyes, brown hair: enlisted Narrabri, 13 September 1915; posted 14th Rfts., 1st Australian Light Horse, 10 January 1916; departed Sydney, 15 January: served in France from 27 March following; transf'd. 13th Bty. 5th F.A. Bde., 28 January 1917: on leave, England, 4–16 September: wounded (GSW shoulder, neck) ,15 October, returned to duty on the 19th of that month. Died No.10 C.C.S. of wounds, 4 November 1917, received on the night of 1–2 November when, while asleep in a sand-bag lean-to beside a pill-box on Westhoek Ridge (nr. Anzac), the enemy shelled the region heavily with gas. A shell entered the lean-to and although suffering badly from inhalation of the poisonous fumes he attempted to walk to the dressing station about three hundred yards away, but did not get very far before collapsing: Age 28.

God Rest His Soul Till We Meet Again

(XXI.FF.4) Lieut. 410948, Cluny James Lightbody, Princess Patricia's Canadian Light Infantry (Eastern Ontario Regt.), C.E.F.: s. of Mrs A. Lightbody (25, Upper Grove Place, Edinburgh, co. Lothian, Scotland): b. Edinburgh, 26 August 1884: Religion – Presbyterian: Occupation – Divinity Student: 5'8½" tall, brown eyes, dark brown hair: member McGill University C.O.T.C., enlisted as Pte., Montreal, 8 March 1915; posted 1st (University) Coy. P.P.C.L.I.; joined the regiment in France 28 July 1915: wounded Sanctuary Wood, 2 June 1916: promoted Lieut. 11 October 1917. Severely wounded in action, 1 November 1917 at Pommern Castle, nr. Ypres, and died en-route to No.2 C.C.S., Poperinghe. Buried there: Age 33. *unm.*

(XXI.FF.6) Corpl. 252599, Elmer Ellsworth Rosa, 102nd Bn. Canadian Infantry (Central Ontario Regt.), C.E.F.: s. of Charles Edward Rosa, of Kincaid, Saskatchewan, by his wife Annie Elizabeth: and brother to Pte. 252889, E.G. Rosa, 102nd Battn., killed in action, 9 April 1917 in the attack west of Vimy: b. Gravelbourg, Saskatchewan, 13 December 1895: Religion – Presbyterian: Occupation – Farmer: enlisted Swift Current, 24 March 1916. Died of shell wounds to the back, 1 November 1917, received in action at Passchendaele: Age 21.

In Loving Memory Of A True And Faithful Son
His Mother

His brother Edward is buried in Givenchy Road Canadian Cemetery, Neuville-St.Vaast (A.46).

(XXI.FF.6A) T/Sergt. 1153, Edward Alexander Keid, 9th Bn. Australian Infantry, A.I.F.: s. of Charles George Keid, of Malonga Terrace, Graceville, Brisbane, Queensland, by his wife Mary Elizabeth: and brother to Lieut. L. Keid, 49th Australian Infantry, killed in action, 3 September 1916; Sergt. 3909, B.W. Keid, 49th Australian Infantry, killed in action the following day; and Tpr. 170, W. Keid, 2nd Australian Light Horse, killed in action, 23 June 1915, at Gallipoli: b. Brisbane, 1889: Religion – Baptist: Occupation – Farmer: enlisted Townsville, Queensland, 5 October 1914: 5'11" tall, grey eyes, dark brown hair: apptd. 1st Rfts. 9th Battn., Enoggera, 22 October: served in Egypt and Gallipoli (1915–16), and with the Expeditionary Force in France and Flanders, 27 March – October 1916 and, after almost nine months back in England, returned to

France, June 1917: attended Corps School, 25 August – 15 September, on which latter date he rejoined his battalion. Died No.10 Casualty Clearing Station, 2 November 1917, of wounds (shrapnel, head) received in action at Broodseinde Ridge the previous day. Buried in the Military Cemetery nearby: Age 28. *unm.* One of four brothers who fell; two other brothers also served – Pte. 61, Harold G.W. Keid, 3rd Field Ambulance, and Pte. 1154, Henry C. Keid, 9th Australian Infantry – both survived.

Rejoicing In Hope

The brothers Leonard, Bennett and William have no known grave; they are commemorated on the Villers-Bretonneux Memorial and Lone Pine Memorial (2), respectively.

(XXI.FF.7) Pte. 22101, John Brown, 2nd Bn. (36th Foot) The Worcestershire Regt.: *b.* Wolverhampton: employee Monmore Green (Victoria Iron) Works, Wolverhampton. Died of wounds, 1 November 1917.

(XXI.FF.13) Capt. Walter Douglas Aston, 1/1st Bn. The Cambridgeshire Regt. (T.F.): *s.* of Walter (& Mrs) Aston, of 'Riversdale,' Shelley Road, Worthing, co. Sussex: *b.* Tarporley, co. Chester: *educ.* Downing College, Cambridge, LL.M; held offices of Steward, Librarian and Lecturer in Law: later *husb.* to C.O. Aston (1228, Ohio Street, Lawrence, Kansas, U.S.A.): served with the Expeditionary Force in France and Flanders from September 1917, and died of bullet wounds (neck), 2 November 1917: Age 35.

Greater Love Hath No Man Than This
John 15.13.
R.I.P.

(XXI.GG.13A) Pte. 5161, Wilfred Worsley Kent, 20th (Service) Bn. The Royal Fusiliers (City of London Regt.) attd. no.G/17268, 11th (Service) Bn. Royal Sussex Regt.: elder *s.* of William Worsley Kent, Jeweller & Silversmith; of 24, Chandos Road, Chorlton-cum-Hardy; and 92, Deansgate, Manchester, by his wife Maragret, *dau.* of Peter Hooker: *b.* Chorlton-cum-Hardy, Manchester, 10 June 1898: *educ.* St Margaret's Schools, Whalley Range, Manchester: joined Universities & Public Schools Battn. Royal Fusiliers, December 1914: served with the Expeditionary Force in France and Flanders attd. 11th Sussex Regt. from 7 September 1917, and was killed in action at Gheluvelt, 7 November following. Buried in Lyssenthoek Military Cemetery: Age 19.

(XXI.GG.19) Pte. 75500, Hereward 'Harold' Henderson, 29th Bn. (Tobin's Tigers) Canadian Infantry (British Columbia Regt.), C.E.F.: *s.* of John Baptist Henderson, of 1246, Robson Street, Vancouver, by his wife Mary C.: nephew to

Dr. J.C. Henderson, Chilliwack: *b*. 9 July 1891: as a student, sometime worked in the offices of Messrs R.A. Henderson, Surveyors & Railway Construction Engineers, Chilliwack: Occupation – Surveyor: serving member of 104th Regt. (Militia); enlisted Vancouver, 12 November 1914. Died of wounds (G.S. head), 6 November 1917, received in action in the front line earlier the same day; Abraham Heights, Passchendaele: Age 24. *unm*.

Love Can Never Lose Its Own

Lieut. R.A. Henderson, 54th Bn. Canadian Engineers, died 11 April 1917; buried Villers Station Cemetery (VII.J.34).

(XXI.HH.3) Pte. 9543, Frederick Peach, 1st Bn. (10th Foot) The Lincolnshire Regt.: *s*. of George Peach, of Holbeach St. John's, Holbeach, co. Lincoln, by his wife Mahalah: and yr. brother to Pte. 13881, W. Peach, 1st Lincolnshire Regt., killed in action, 16 June 1915, at Ypres: *b*. Holbeach: enlisted there: served in France and Flanders from May 1915, and died of wounds, 2 November 1917 at Poperinghe: Age 20. *unm*.

Peace Perfect Peace
From His Loving Parents
Holbeach, St. Johns

His brother William has no known grave, he is commemorated on the Ypres (Menin Gate) Memorial (Panel 21).

(XXI.HH.5) Pte. 291010, Henry Adams, 1st Bn. Canadian Mounted Rifles (Saskatchewan Regt.), C.E.F.: *s*. of Henry Adams, by his wife Jane: late *husb*. to Elizabeth R. Adams (281, Harbison Avenue, Elmwood, Winnipeg): *b*. Sydenham, London, England, 13 April 1889: Religion – Church of England: Occupation – Caretaker: joined C.E.F., Winnipeg, 11 December 1915. Died, No.2 Canadian C.C.S., 2 November 1917, of wounds received in action before Passchendaele: Age 28. (*IWGC record age 27*)

Gone From Us But Not Forgotten By His Loving Wife And Children

(XXI.HH.7) Gnr. 27205, Wilfred Heard Beer, 3rd Bty. 1st Bde. Australian Field Artillery, A.I.F.: *s*. of Charles Heard Beer, of 64, Railway Street, Rockdale, Sydney, New South Wales, by his wife Amelia: *b*. Stanmore, New South Wales, March 1895: Occupation – Clerk: enlisted A.I.F., Sydney, 8 May 1916; posted 20th Rfts., 1st F.A. Bde.: departed Australia, 30 September: trained England (from 19 November): proceeded to France, 24 January 1917; hospitalised on the 30th (scabies), returned to England for treatment: returned to France, 5 June

1917. Wounded (poisonous gas inhalation), 3 November 1917; admitted 3rd Australian Field Ambulance, transf'd. No.2 Canadian C.C.S.; died the same day: Age 22.

A Young Life Nobly Ended

(XXI.HH.8) Temp.Bmdr. 808, Andrew Scott, M.M., 101st (Howitzer) Bty., 1st Bde. Australian Field Artillery, A.I.F.: *s*. of Robert Scott, of 'Framerville,' Williams Avenue, Newstead, South Australia, and Jessie Mitchell Scott, his spouse: *b*. Delamere, South Australia: Occupation – Labourer: enlisted, 18 December 1914: departed Melbourne, HMAT 'Armadale,' 12 January 1915. Died of wounds (gas poisoning), 2 November 1917: Age 22. Awarded the Military Medal, 9 October 1917 (*London Gazette*, 28 January 1918), 'On 7 and 8 October 1917 the road leading to the batteries of the 1st AIF Brigade near Zonnebeke was heavily barraged with all calibres of Howitzer fire. Temp Bombardier Scott fearlessly lead his ammunition pack train through the barrage on both days and succeeded in getting the ammunition to his battery which at the time was urgently in need of it. His courage and devotion to duty set a magnificent example to all ranks under him.'

His Duty Done

(XXI.HH.12) Sergt. 117225, David Dick, 2nd Canadian Mounted Rifles (British Columbia Regt.), C.E.F.: 2nd. *s*. of David Dick, of 'Foreland,' Bruichladdich, Isle of Islay, co. Argyll, by his wife Isabella, *dau*. of James (& Euphemia) Thomson: *b*. Islay, 4 September 1888: *educ*. there: went to Canada 1907: Occupation, Farmer; Calgary, Alberta: enlisted November 1914: served with the Expeditionary Force in France and Flanders from January 1916, and died at No.2 Canadian Casualty Clearing Station, 4 November 1917, from wounds received in action at Passchendaele. Buried in the Military Cemetery, Lyssenthoek. A Sergt. wrote, "His loss is keenly felt by all who knew him, as he had endeared himself to all under him by his kindly interest and consideration; I had the honour to be his junior sergeant, and to me the loss is a very personal one.": Age 29. *unm*.

Tis Sweet To Know We'll Meet Again Where Partings Are No More

(XXI.HH.20A) Pte. 6725, Nathan Douglas Barrett, 11th Bn. Australian Infantry, A.I.F.: late of 4, Wade Street, Perth: late *husb*. to Evelyn Cooper, *née* Barrett (100, Coogee Street, Mount Hawthorn, Western Australia): *b*. Southern Cross, 1891: Religion – Church of England: Occupation – Cycle Mechanic: joined A.I.F.,

Perth, 31 May 1916; apptd. 22nd Rfts., 11th Bn., Blackboy Hill, 1 November: departed Fremantle, 9 November 1916: served with the Expeditionary Force in France from 6 April 1917; joined 11th Bn., 24 April, and died of wounds (SW abdominal) No.17 Casualty Clearing Station, Poperinghe, 4 November 1917, received nr. Zonnebeke the previous day: Age 26. His effects – Silver Watch & Strap, Silver Matchbox, Pipe, Purse, Electric Torch, Testament, Metal Cigarette Case, Letters, Photos, Gold Ring, Bone Ring, 3 Coins, Crucifix, Cards, Silver Watch (marked S.C. Smith) – were received by his widow, 1918. It is highly probable the personalised watch belonged to Sydney Clyde Smith, 11th Bn., killed in action six weeks previously.

Sydney Smith has no known grave; he is commemorated on the Ypres (Menin Gate) Memorial (Panel 17).

(XXI.A.9) Dvr. 249, Thomas Joseph Hurley, 2nd Bn. Australian Pioneers, A.I.F.: s. of Denis Hurley, of Henty, Victoria, South Australia, by his wife Mary Jane: and brother to Pte. 3869, D. Hurley, 46th Bn. Australian Infantry, who fell at the Battle of the Somme, 13 August 1916; and Sergt. 2392, J. Hurley, 46th Bn. Australian Infantry, who fell at the Battle of the Somme, 13 July 1918: b. Colac, Victoria, June 1891: educ. Pirron Yallock State School: enlisted 13th Light Horse, Melbourne, 12 December 1914: served in Egypt, Gallipoli, and in France and Flanders from 26 March 1916; transf'd. 2nd Pioneer Battn. June following. Died of wounds (G.S.W. head) received in action at the Battle of Ypres, 12 October 1917: Age 26.

2 Other Bros Also Fell

His twin brother Denis is buried in Sunken Road Cemetery, Contalmaison (I.A.2); Jeremiah, Crouy British Cemetery, Somme (IV.A.6).

(XXI.A.21A) Rfn. 44004, Alfred Mumford, 4th Bn. 3rd New Zealand Rifle Brigade, N.Z.E.F.: late of 38, Howard Street, Spreydon, Christchurch: s. of the late William Robert Mumford, and Mary, his wife: and brother to Pte. 54067, A. Mumford, 27th Rfts. (surv'd.); and Rfn. 44005, H.E. Mumford, N.Z. Rifle Brigade, killed in action, 12 October 1917: Occupation – Storeman: proceeded overseas, 26 April 1917; arrived Plymouth, England via Cape of Good Hope, 28 July following. Died 14 October 1917, of multiple bullet wounds to both legs received in action two days previously at Passchendaele: Age 28. He leaves a wife, Elsie Anderina Mumford (20, Madras Street, Sydenham, Christchurch).

His brother Henry has no known grave, he is commemorated on the Tyne Cot (New Zealand) Memorial (Panel 7).

(XXI.B.1A) Sergt. 752, Stuart Norman Spence, 41st Bn. Australian Infantry, A.I.F.: 2nd s. of Stuart Spence, J.P., Wholesale Stationer; of 11, West Regent Street, Glasgow, by his wife Catherine Horgan (Abertay, Bothwell, co. Lanark), *dau.* of James Donaldson, of Mansfield, Tayport, J.P.: *b.* Glasgow, 27 August 1876: *educ.* Public School, Bothwell; and Hutcheson's Grammar School, Glasgow: went to Australia, January 1908; settled in Sydney: Occupation – Fruit Grower: volunteered for Imperial Service; joined Australian Imperial Force, Brisbane, March 1916: served with the Expeditionary Force in France and Flanders from 24 November following. Wounded (shrapnel; shoulder, hip), Passchendaele Ridge, 5 October 1917, and died (7 October), at No.10 Casualty Clearing Station. Buried in Lyssenthoek Military Cemetery, Poperinghe: Age 41. *unm.*

'Tis Sweet To Die For One's Country

(XXI.B.5A) Actg. S/Sergt. S4/045458, Charles Hind Perris, 1st Coy., 7th Divn. Train, Army Service Corps: *s.* of the late George Henry Perris, of Manchester, by his wife Annie: and elder brother to Pte. 47712, H.B. Perris, 26th Royal Fusiliers, died 10 June 1917, of wounds: *b.* Sheffield, co. York: enlisted Belfast: served in France from October 1915, and died, 6 October 1917, of wounds: Age 37. He leaves a wife, Margaret Perris (22, Powerscourt Street, Belfast), and family.

His brother Harold lies nearby (XIV.G.11A).

(XXI.B.17) Gnr. 18693, Edward John Luck, 7th Bde. Australian Field Artillery, A.I.F.: *s.* of Edward John Luck, of 6, Essex Road, Westgate-on-Sea, by his wife Caroline: and brother to Sergt. G/469, F. Luck, 6th The Buffs, killed in action, 7 October 1916; and L/Corpl. G/452, G. Luck, D.C.M., 6th The Buffs, died of wounds, 3 July 1916: *b.* Westgate-on-Sea: served with the Expeditionary Force in France from 30 December 1916, and died of wounds, 9 October 1917; Shrapnel, multiple (Lt. arm, Lt. leg, torso, facial): Age 33.

His brother Frank has no known grave; he is commemorated on the Thiepval Memorial. George is buried in Millencourt Communal Cemetery Extension, Somme (A.21).

(XXI.C.3) Pte. 6/2080, William Smith Bruce, 1st Canterbury Regt., N.Z.E.F.: *s.* of John Bruce, of Woodland Cottage, Inverurie, Aberdeen, ex-Police Constable; Glasgow Force, by his wife Eliza Ann, *dau.* of John Lendrum, of co. Aberdeen: *b.* Glasgow, 8 January 1897: *educ.* Provanside School: Occupation – Clerk; District Superintendent's Office, North British Railway Company, Glasgow: went to New Zealand, June 1914, and obtained an appointment, Christchurch Branch, Bank of Australia: enlisted Trentham, 19 February 1915: served with the Mediterranean Expeditionary Force at Gallipoli; afterwards in France and Flanders. Severely wounded (S.W. abdominal, both legs, Lt. hand) at Bellevue, Third Battle of Ypres, 12 October 1917, and died two days later (14 October) at No.2 Casualty Clearing Station. Buried at Lyssenthoek Military Cemetery, nr. Poperinghe. His Commanding Officer wrote, "The fine qualities of your son were appreciated by his comrades; he was very popular among the men of his company. He was a sportsman and a fine soldier, and it is the loss of such as he that carries the sympathy of the company to which he belonged.": Age 20. *unm.*

(XXI.C.4A) Spr. 5685, George Frederick Gilbert, 2nd Field Coy., Australian Engineers, A.I.F.: *s.* of Peter Gilbert, of Bendigo, Victoria, by his wife Elizabeth Ann: *b.* 1871: Occupation – Labourer: enlisted, 22 February 1916: served with the Expeditionary Force in France from 15 May 1917. Admitted No.10 C.C.S. (SW penis, hip, head), 12 October 1917, and died the following day (13 October): Age 46. Buried Lyssenthoek Military Cemetery, 1¾ miles s.w of Poperinghe; Cross erected by Corpl. G. Wallace, 2nd Field Coy. He was married to Elizabeth A. Gilbert (8, Watkin's Street, Fitzroy North, Victoria).

There Is A Link Death Cannot Sever, Sweet Remembrance Lasts For Ever

(XXI.D.10) 2nd Lieut. George Herbert Berry, 'D' Bty., 315th Bde., Royal Field Artillery *s.* of George Thomas Berry, of Strathmore, Alberta, Canada, by his wife Ada: *b.* Pincher Creek, Alberta, 18 May 1894: *educ.* Detroit University School, Michigan; Upper Canada College, Toronto (1910–12); University College, Toronto (1912–16): enlisted April 1915; proceeded overseas same month: joined No.3 Canadian Stationary Hospital, England, June 1915, proceeded with that unit to Island of Lemnos – Gallipoli Expedition Hospital Base – served there June 1915–March 1916: on transfer to France served with the hospital throughout 1916: applied (and began training) for a commission, Royal Field Artillery; gazetted 2nd Lieut, December of that year: returned to France, April 1917 where, on 6 October 1917, in his capacity as Forward Observation Officer, he was in the process of locating a new Observation Post (near Hooge Crater), when he was severely wounded by shellfire. Died at Lyssenthoek, nr. Poperinghe 9 October 1917. Buried in the cemetery there: Age 23. Shortly before his death 2nd Lieut. Berry had been recommended for the Military Cross (Sepember 1917); it was not awarded.

Bert

(XXI.F.1) Lieut. Henry Scott Manisty, M.C., 24th Field Coy., Royal Engineers attd. XVIII Corps H.Q.: *s.* of Edward Manisty, M.I.C.E.: served in France from July 1915. Killed in action, 11 October 1917: Age 31. Awarded the Military Cross for "Excellent work during a raid on the enemy's trenches at 0.29-central (Sheet 28) in front of Ypres on the night of 25th -26th June; when with one N.C.O. and three sappers he destroyed two dugouts and an Observation Post. Owing to a slight hitch with the 3rd charge, touch with the infantry was lost and the party left the enemy's trenches after the infantry. A small attempt at a counter-attack was made by the enemy round a traverse on this small party. Lieut. Manisty shot the leader and the party brought in four prisoners after loading one with pack, bandolier, two helmets and a rifle. One sapper was killed and Lieut. Manisty and a sapper wounded, but not till their return to our own trenches. This officer also brought back some very clear notes of the enemy's trenches, and showed great coolness and courage throughout." A brass plaque erected in Thorpe Abbott (All Saints) Parish Church by his widow, Mrs G. Manisty; is dedicated 'Greater Love Hath No Man Than This That A Man Lay Down His Life For His Friends.' (*IWGC record age 33*)

Elder Son Of Edward Manisty M.I.C.E.

(XXI.F.2A) Pte. 18516, Edward Louis Warren, 2nd Bn. Canterbury Regt., N.Z.E.F.: late of Christchurch: *yst. s.* of the late T.R. Warren, of Auckland, and M.J. Warren (Post Office, Gisborne): enlisted Trentham, 14 April 1916; departed Wellington, 26 July; 6th Rfts., 'G' Coy., 3rd N.Z. Rifle Brigade: subsequently transf'd. 2nd Canterbury Regt. Died somewhere in France, 14 October 1917, of a bullet wound to the head received in action at Bellevue two days previously: Age 24. *unm.* The *Auckland Weekly News*, 28 February 1918, recorded:

> *The sad news has reached me, young Ted has been killed,*
> *He died like a hero on a foreign battlefield.*
> *In a land far away, across the deep blue sea,*
> *He sleeps in a grave that I may never see – Only a boy.*
> *New Zealand is now giving the flowers of the land,*
> *When young lads of twenty-two in the trenches they stand.*
> *Though just but a boy, he played a brave part,*
> *For honour of his country he had at his heart – Only a boy.*
> *What more could he give to his Country and King,*
> *A life that's so young but yet dear to him.*
> *No stone marks the grave of that hero so true*
> *Who died for his country and the Belgians too – Only a boy.*
> *Sleep on in peace, lad, your work is now done*
> *And your comrades will finish the task you begun.*
> *Like all New Zealand soldiers, they will never say die*
> *Until peace is declared in the sweet bye and bye – Only a boy.*

(XXI.F.4) 2nd Lieut. William Thomas Walsh, 'A' Coy., 51st Bn. Australian Infantry, A.I.F.: *s.* of William Lovell Walsh, of Guildford, Western Australia, by his wife Margaret Elizabeth. Died of wounds (shrapnel), 2nd. Canadian C.C.S., 3 p.m., 13 October 1917, received in the vicinity of Daisy Wood, Broodseinde, the same day: Age 28. *unm.* Pte. 5085, N.V. Collins, reported, "He was hit by a shell at Passchendaele, having his left leg blown off at the base, a big gash in the right knee and his thumb blown off, and a wound in the left arm and part of his right foot blown away...." Carried to 13th Dressing Station by the battalion stretcher bearers, one of whom Pte. 2909, C.C. Gast (subsequently promoted Corpl. and awarded the Croix De Guerre) reported, 'it was a long carry;' Lieut. Walsh was taken back through the casualty evacuation chain to Remy Siding where he died shortly after arrival.

In Memory Of The Dearly Beloved Son Of Mr & Mrs Walsh
Guildford W.A.

Charles Gast died of wounds, 26 April 1918, he is buried in Longpre-les-Corps Saints British Cemetery (A.18).

(XXI.F.5A) Pte. 6454, Robert George Gregg, 26th Bn. Australian Infantry, A.I.F.: *s.* of Charles Henry Gregg, of Grace Street, Arthur Terrace, Ithaca, Brisbane, Queensland, by his wife Mary Ann: enlisted Roma, 25 October 1915: served in France from 24 July 1917. *The Western Star*, 31 October 1917 reported, "The sad news has just been received to the effect that two more Roma volunteers have been killed in action. They are Pte. Ern Kupfer, son of a well-known farming family at Yingerbay, killed October 4 in France, and Pte. Bob Gregg, killed October 14 in France. Pte. Gregg worked in Roma for Mr C. O'Malley, and we understand his parents live in Brisbane. Recent casualty lists are making a heavy toll of volunteers from this district, and since our last issue word has been received of two more having been wounded, Ptes. Quinliven and Hadwen." Pte. Gregg died at Remy Siding, 14 October 1917, of wounds received in action at Ypres; Ptes. Quinliven and Hadwen survived.

Rest In Peace

Pte. Kupfer has no known grave; he is commemorated on the Ypres (Menin Gate) Memorial (Panel 27).

(XXI.F.8A) Gnr. 24090, Walter Rawsthorne, 38th Bde., Royal Field Artillery: eldest *s.* of Joseph Henry Rawsthorne, of 24, London Road, Oldham, co. Lancaster, by his wife Nanny, *dau.* of Edwin (& Elizabeth) Travis: *b.* Oldham, 4 December 1894: *educ.* Derker Council School, Oldham: Occupation – Piecer; Woodstock Mill: enlisted, 17 May 1915: served with the Indian Expeditionary Force in Mesopotamia from 27 February 1916; contracted enteric fever and invalided home: joined the Expeditionary Force in France, 29 March 1917, and died at No.3 Canadian Casualty Clearing Station, 16 October following, from multiple bullet wounds to both legs and feet received in action the previous day. Buried in the Lijssenthoek Military Cemetery, 1¾ miles south-west of Poperinghe: Age 22. *unm.*

Dearer To Memory Than Words Can Tell Are The Thoughts Of Him We Loved So Well

(XXI.F.9) Pte. 12997, John Joseph 'Jack' Duggan, 'C' Section, 9th Field Ambulance, Australian Army Medical Corps, A.I.F.: *s.* of John Joseph Duggan, of 'Rosslare,' Christie Street, St. Leonard's, Sydney, New South Wales, by his wife Ethel Dora: departed Australia aboard 'Marathon,' 5 May 1916: served with the Expeditionary Force in France and Flanders, and died of wounds – shell fragment, right leg and thigh – 5.15 p.m., 14 October 1917. Pte. 12995, F.E. Dennison wrote, "At the time of meeting his fatal wounds Pte. Duggan was working as a stretcher bearer, carrying from a German pill-box that was being used as an aid post, and was situated just in front of Passchendaele Ridge and Village. Most of the aid posts had distinguishing names such as Berlin Wood, Otto Farm, Lett House, and Leine Farm, but the one from which Pte. Duggan was working was not so named. The shell that wounded Pte. Duggan also killed another of his party (Pte. J.D. Nankivell) and wounded a third. The only remaining member of this stretcher squad, Pte. Wagstaffe, also 9th Field Ambulance, was the man who obtained assistance and carried Pte. Duggan back to safety, after his wounds had been seen and dressed by the Medical Officer. At this stage he passed through the hands of the unit to which he belonged, receiving further surgical attention at the Advanced Dressing Station known as the White Chateau, which was located at what had once been the village of Potijze. From here he was carried by one of our motor ambulances to Ypres, where he passed out of the 9th Field Ambulance, and was evacuated to No.3 Canadian Casualty Clearing Station, situated at Remy Siding, near Poperinghe, near Ypres. It was here that Pte. Duggan died after having one leg amputated at the knee. He was not buried on the field, but in the Cemetery attached to the C.C.S., and under those circumstances he would have received the last rites of the Church to which he belonged. Map Location, Sheet 27, L22. D6.3. Plot 21F." Pte. Duggan was 5'6" tall, of stout build, and fair complexion. He was a keen cricketer and good football player: Age 20–22. *unm.*

He Died As He Lived, Nobly

Joseph Nankivell has no known grave; he is commemorated on the Ypres (Menin Gate) Memorial (Panel 31).

(XXI.F.16) Gnr. L/26599, Ralph Blackwell, 'D'Bty., 232nd Bde., Royal Field Artillery: eldest *s.* of Cope Blackwell, of 21, New Street, Uttoxeter, and Lucy, his wife: and brother to Pte. 1823, J. Blackwell, 1/6th North Staffordshire Regt., killed in action, 13 October 1915: *b*. Uttoxeter, co. Stafford, 1892: Occupation – Grocery Assistant; Messrs Hunter's, Uttoxeter: enlisted Rotherham, co. York, May 1915: served in France from December following. Died of wounds (gas), 14 October 1917: Age 24. He leaves a wife, Gladys Blackwell (101, Wath Road, Mexborough, co. York) to whom he had been married for a short time before his departure for France; and one child.

May His Reward Be As Great As His Sacrifice

His brother Joseph has no known grave; he is commemorated on the Loos Memorial.

(XXI.G.4A) Pte. 14804, Joseph Squires, 20th Coy., Machine Gun Corps (Inf.): formerly no.12591, 95th T.R. Bn.: late of Princes Risborough: *s*. of Herbert Squires, of 71, Park Street, Thame, co. Oxford, by his wife Amelia: and brother to Pte. 22664, B. Squires, 2nd Grenadier Guards, killed in action, 28 March 1918, aged 21; and Corpl. 27854, G. Squires, 7th Bedfordshire Regt., killed in action, 16 August 1917: *b*. Thame: enlisted Aylesbury. Died 27 October 1917, of wounds: Age 25. *unm*.

I.H.S.
Loved But Lost

His brother Benjamin has no known grave, he is commemorated on the Arras Memorial (Bay 1); George is buried in Tyne Cot Cemetery (XLV.E.2).

(XXI.G.6) Lieut. Henry Richard Thomson, 58th Bn. Canadian Infantry (Central Ontario Regt.), C.E.F.: *s*. of George C. Thomson, of Hamilton, Ontario, by his wife Mona L.: *b*. Hamilton, 30 May 1894: *educ*. Highfield School, Hamilton; Trinity College, University of Toronto, 1914–15; member C.O.T.C.: apptd. 58th Battn. June 1915: served with the Expeditionary Force in France from Spring 1916: wounded nr. Ypres, May 1916; evacuated to England, thence to Canada from whence, after a period of leave, he returned to England and served for a time at Headquarters, Shorncliffe: returned to France, and rejoined his battalion, June 1917. Ordered to return for duty in England, after serving on the Lens and Passchendaele fronts, he was proceeding to the transport lines when he was struck in the head by a shell fragment, and died one hour later, 25 October 1917. Buried Remy Siding, Poperinghe: Age 23.

Beloved Son Of George And Mona Thompson
Hamilton, Canada

(XXI.G.8) Pte. 27472, William James Anger, 2nd Bn. (55th Foot) The Border Regt.: formerly no.5881, Essex Regt.: no.5564, Border Regt.: *s.* of Frederick W. (& A.M.) Anger, of High Street, Ingatestone, co. Essex: *b.* Ingatestone: enlisted Chelmsford. Died at a Canadian Casualty Clearing Station in France, 27 October 1917, from wounds received in action nr. Hooge, Ypres. Buried Lyssenthoek Military Cemetery, Poperinghe: Age 23. *unm.* His Memoriam card bore the following – In Loving Memory Of Our Dearly Loved Son: 'Greater Love Has No Man Than This, That He Gave His Life For His Friends': 'His heart was good, His spirit brave, His resting place a soldier's grave. We loved him in life, he is dear to us still, But in grief we must bend to God's holy will. Our sorrow is great our loss hard to bear, Angels will tend you dear William with care. He was one of the best that God could lend, A loving son and brother; a faithful friend.': 'Jesus said: "He that believeth in Me though he were dead yet shall he live and whosoever liveth and believeth in Me shall never die."': 'Sleep on dear lad, in a far-off grave, In a grave we may never see: But as long as life and memory last, We shall always remember thee.' Remembered on the Ingatestone & Fryerning Roll of Honour.

We Loved Thee Well Christ Loved Thee Better

(XXI.G.10A) Pte. 60204, John Gunning, Scout Section, 9th (Service) Bn. The Royal Welsh Fusiliers: formerly no.1312, Royal Engineers: only *s.* of John Gunning, Schoolmaster; of 48, Queen's Drive, Walton, Liverpool, by his wife Catherine Prudence, *dau.* of the late William Swift, Farmer: *b.* Liverpool, co. Lancaster, 7 March 1895: *educ.* Liverpool Institute: Occupation – Clerk; Mersey Dock & Harbour Board; also Organist, Speke Parish Church: joined Lancashire Fortress Engineers, Royal Engineers (T.F.), 14 February 1916: became Pte., Royal Welsh Fusiliers, 17 December 1916: served with the Expeditionary Force in France from May 1917, and died at the 2nd Canadian Casualty Clearing Station, 28 October following, from wounds received in action nr. Ypres on the 27th. Buried in the Lyssenthoek Military Cemetery: 28 October 1917: Age 22. *unm.*

(XXI.G.12A) Pte. 41749, Reginald Eustace Kilpin, 1st Bn. (38th Foot) The South Staffordshire Regt.: late of Preston Deanery, co. Northampton: brother to Pte. 40335, F. Kilpin, 6th Leicestershire Regt., killed in action, 22 March 1918: *b.* Stoke Goldington, co. Buckingham: enlisted Northampton. Died 29 October 1917, of wounds.

His brother Frederick has no known grave; he is commemorated on the Pozieres Memorial.

(XXI.G.16) Pte. S/18294, Archibald Davidson, 2nd Bn. (92nd Foot) The Gordon Highlanders: *s.* of William (& Bella) Davidson, of Orchardstown

Cottage, Udny, co. Aberdeen: *b.* Udny, 24 July 1898: *educ.* there: Occupation – Farm Labourer: enlisted 13 June 1917: served with the Expeditionary Force in France, and died at No.10 Casualty Clearing Station, 27 October 1917, from wounds received in action. Buried in the Military Cemetery, Lyssenthoek, west-south-west of Ypres: Age 19. (*IWGC record 28 October*)

They Miss You Most Who Love You Best

At the end of September 1917, after an arduous series of tours in and out of the trenches before Ypres, 7th King's Royal Rifles were withdrawn to the Neuve Eglise sector where – expecting this to be their quarters for the winter – they spent a good deal of time and trouble making themselves as comfortable as possible. However, 'Somebody must have got wind of this, as on the 6th October, we were moved to good huts in Reninghelst and three days later again found ourselves in Dickebusch Trenches, 4th Middlesex on our right, 7th R.B. on our left. This tour was most unpleasant, communications, especially to the rear, were very difficult, and the Menin Road, which was the chief approach, was freely shelled. The Battalion suffered a severe loss in the death of three C.Q.M.S. – Ellis, Steward (*q.v.*), and Johnson; these Warrant Officers were amongst the oldest members of the battalion, and had done splendid work. R.S.M. Oxley was also severely wounded. These casualties occurred through a shell landing on the dump, a most wretched piece of ill luck. ... Relieved on the 16th, Casualties during six days – 27 OR killed, 59 wounded, 4 missing.'

After treatment at the Regimental Aid Post C.Q.M.S. Johnson was evacuated back to the Casualty Clearing Station at Remy Siding where, due to the severity of his wounds, he passed away within a few hours of arrival.

(XXI.H.6) Coy.Q.M.Sergt. R/277, Ernest Ralph Johnson, 7th (Service) Bn. The King's Royal Rifle Corps: eldest *s.* of Herbert Johnson, of Broadmead Lane, Norton-sub-Hamdon, by his wife Merci: *b.* July 1891: Religion – Church of England: Occupation – Attendant; Horton Asylum: 5'9¾" tall, fair complexion, blue eyes, light brown hair: enlisted Winchester, 29 August 1914; aged 23 years, 30 days: underwent training, 9 September 1914–May 1915: apptd. L/Corpl. (paid) 13 February 1915; promoted Corpl. 27 May 1915, proceeded to France same day: took part in the fighting at Hooge, nr. Ypres, and apptd. L/Sergt. 30 July 1915: promoted Sergt. 20 August following. Died of wounds (abdominal), No.17 Casualty Clearing Station, 16 October 1917, received in action the previous day: Age 27. In writing to his widow, the Chaplain, Rev. Salmon, said, 'I deeply regret to say that your husband, C.Q.M.S., E.R. Johnson, 277, died here at 6.30 a.m. October 16th of wounds in the abdomen. He was only with us a few hours. He suffered little owing to weakness and shock. He sent his fondest love to you and wished you to write. He did not realise he was dying, and could not think or speak much. I commended his soul to God and he passed away very peacefully. His effects will be sent to you in due course. His body is in the Lyssenthoek Military Cemetery, 2 miles south-west of Poperinghe. God bless you and sustain you in this great sorrow.' The local press reported, 'The sad news has come within the last few days that C.Q.M.S. Ernest Ralph Johnson, K.R.R., has made the great sacrifice. It is indeed a terrible blow to Mrs Guy and the young widow, her daughter, coming so soon after all the anxiety and suspense they have gone through of late. He was killed on the field of honour on October 16th, having been at the Front since May 1915; it is only a fortnight or so since he was home on leave, thoroughly enjoying his brief stay among those who were so near and dear to him. But they will bear their desolating sorrow and loss bravely, we know; it is what he would have wished. May all Christian hope and comfort be granted to them from the Source that never fails.' He *m*. Bishops Sutton; Esme Francis Lillian 'Lilly,' *née* Guy, of Alfresford, co. Hants, and had a *dau*. Esme Florence Mary, *b*. 16 October 1915.

He Died That We Might Live

After C.Q.M.S. Johnson's death, Lilly was awarded twenty-two shillings and sixpence a week Widows' Pension. On 19 February 1918 she received his effects as promised; they comprised: a haversack, his watch, one identity disc, a bundle of photographs and photo-case, his cigarette case and tobacco pouch, a pocket knife, notebook, purse, two German five mark notes, his Post Office Savings book and a 19 carat gold ring.

C.Q.M.S. Sidney Ellis and C.Q.M.S. William H. Stannard have no known grave; both are recorded on the Tyne Cot Memorial (Panel 115).

(XXI.H.17) Pte. M2/114698, Reginald King, Mechanical Transport Coy., Army Service Corps attd. 25th Siege Bty., Royal Garrison Artillery: *s*. of John King, of 65, Belgrave Road, Longton, Stoke-on-Trent, co. Stafford, by his wife Susan: and brother to Pte. 209559, H.A. King, United States Army, died 20 September 1918, of pneumonia: *b*. Winchmoor Park, co. Stafford. Died of multiple shrapnel wounds to the face, left elbow, wrist and compound fracture of left leg, 17 October 1917: Age 23.

Thy Way Not Mine Oh Lord

His brother Harry lies nearby (XXXII.A.11)

Plot 22, A to H lies adjacent to AA to HH
(XXII.B.2A) Pte. 1515, Eugene Sullivan, 9th Field Ambulance, Australian Army Medical Corps, A.I.F.: *s*. of Maurice Sullivan, of 'Dunboy,' Wyrallah

Road, Lismore, New South Wales, Australia, Solicitor; by his wife Margaret, *dau.* of Capt. O'Sullivan, of Heather Brae, North Sydney: godson of the late Timothy Daniel Sullivan (1827–1914), Poet, Historian, and Editor of the *Nation* (Dublin); wrote the Irish national hymn *God Save Ireland* (1867): *b.* Lismore, New South Wales, Australia, 28 May 1894: *educ.* Nudgee College, Queensland: Occupation – Managing Clerk; Messrs. Sullivan & McDermott, Solicitors, of Lismore: volunteered for Foreign Service, and enlisted Australian Army Medical Corps, 28 October 1915: served with the Expeditionary Force in France and Flanders. Admitted to No.17 Casualty Clearing Station, in the early hours of 16 October 1917, suffering from severe shell wounds in the chest – received in action near Zonnebeke on the 12th – and in a critical condition, and died at 6.10 a.m. Buried the following day. Sergt. R.J. Watts said, "I was told by Sergt. Southam, 9th Field Ambulance, that he had seen 1515, E. Sullivan, 12084, C.J. Walshe, and 4489, C.O.D. Edser, lying out in no man's land; Edser and Sullivan being dead on October 12th." His Officer Commanding wrote, "Throughout the whole time your son served with us he did exceptionally good work...Nothing was a trouble to him, and he never once failed to do his very utmost to help the men. He was one of the best known, and the best beloved of the whole battalion. For his manly and honourable bearing, his unselfishness and patience, and his high sense of duty, he set us all a splendid example. In action he distinguished himself by his coolness and devotion to duty. We mourn more than any words of mine can express the loss of such a noble and gallant comrade," and the members of the Army Medical Corps Detail, "He was respected and loved by the members of the 33rd, whom he served so well. At all times he played the game, and was a white man, a noble man to the very core.": Age 33: *unm.*

He Giveth His Beloved Rest

Charles Walshe is buried in Tyne Cot Cemetrey (LIII.D.10), Charles Edser has no known grave; he is commemorated on the Ypres (Menin Gate) Memorial (Panel 31).

(XXII.B.17) 2nd Lieut. Douglas St.George Pettigrew, 14th (Reserve) attd. 17th (Service) Bn. (Wellbeck Rangers) The Sherwood Foresters (Notts & Derbys Regt.): *yr.* & only *survg. s.* of Robert William Pettigrew, of Penarth, Cardiff, by his wife Ella Elizabeth Leman, 2nd *dau.* of the late George Frederick Hare, of Limerick: and *gdson.* to the late William Pettigrew, of Warrenpoint, Co. Down: *b.* Tranmore, Co. Waterford, 8 August 1892: *educ.* Monkton Combe School, Bath (O.T.C. member): D.St.G. Pettigrew came of a fighting stock, his great-great-grandfather having fought through the Peninsular War and at Waterloo: volunteering immediately war was declared, enlisted Public Schools

Brigade, 15 September 1914: went to France, November 1915, and, as one of the Scouts of his Battn. – 19th Royal Fusiliers (2nd Public Schools) – took part in much patrol work between the trenches in Flanders during the winter 1915–16: sent home for a commission, Spring 1916: gazetted 2nd Lieut. 4th Sherwood Foresters, 22 July: returned to France in September, and was severely wounded in the fighting between the Ancre and the Somme, outside Thiepval, 7 October 1916. After a complete recovery from his wounds, at the end of seven months, he made his third, and last, journey to the Front, 5 May 1917, and from that date was fighting on the stricken field of Ypres until he fell, mortally wounded in action nr. Gheluvelt, while leading his men, 22 October 1917. Died No.10 Casualty Clearing Station the following morning. All through the summer and into the autumn he had wonderful luck, never being hit; he came through the hard fighting which started on 20 September (and in which the Sherwoods, in a few days, lost over fifty officers, killed and wounded) without a scratch, but the end came shortly afterwards; the Sherwoods were holding that part of the line known as the Tower Hamlets sector, and, on Monday 22 October, he and his platoon were specially picked to take a couple of German 'pill-boxes' on the side of the Ypres-Menin Road, between Hooge and Gheluvelt, west-north-west of the latter place: in leading the attack he was mortally wounded, and died at four o'clock the following morning (Tuesday 23 October 1917). Buried in Lyssenthoek Military Cemetery, Poperinghe, in sure and certain hope of the Resurrection to eternal life, through our Lord Jesus Christ. He played the game. "In Flanders are the fields of fair renown." Only twenty-five, he was beloved by everybody; he had a genius for friendship, and had the affection and esteem of young and old, rich and poor together. His first Commanding Officer wrote, "I cannot tell you how grieved I was to hear he had been killed; he was one of those sure to be hit, the best always are." His Chaplain wrote,"He was one of the best loved officers I have ever met; he was beloved, almost worshipped, by his men." His old Company Commander wrote, "I was fortunate enough to have him in my company of the 19th Battn. Royal Fusiliers in France, he was in every way a splendid fellow, quite one of the best in A Coy., which I am proud to think contained a very large number of good fellows;" And his servant, "He was idolized by his men, for he studied their every comfort, and always tried to better their condition, and cheer them." Very keen on flying (having been 'up'), he was accepted for the Royal Flying Corps in August 1916, and would have been transferred to it that autumn but for his going out to the front in September, the Sherwoods having been badly cut up in the fighting on the Somme at that time. He put in again for it in the summer of 1917, and was expecting his transfer when he met his death. In the last letter he wrote home, Sunday 21 October 1917, the day before he was mortally wounded, he said, "My application for the R.F.C. has gone past the Brigadier; it has now been sent on to the division, so I am hoping to get my transfer any day now." "Dulce et decorum est pro patria mori.": Age 25. *unm.*

Tramore 1892 Ypres 1917
Only Surviving Son Of R.W. And Ella Pettigrew

(XXII.C.11) Pte. 25735, Thomas Bickle, 9th (Service) Bn. The Devonshire Regt.: *s.* of James (& Maria) Bickle, of Liddaton Green, Lewdown, co. Devon: and brother to Pte. M/274278, A. Bickle, Royal Army Service Corps, killed in action, 20 July 1918, in Mesopotamia: *b.* Colyton, co. Devon: enlisted Tavistock. Died 26 October 1917, of wounds: Age 33. He leaves a widow, Mary Jane Bickle (Holster Yard, Marystowe, Lewdown), to lament his loss.

Greater Love Hath No Man Than He
That Layeth Down His Life For His Friends

His brother has no known grave, he is commemorated on the Tehran Memorial (Panel 5, Col. I).

(XXII.C.15) Lieut. George Edward James Williams, 2nd Field Coy., Australian Engineers, A.I.F.: stepson of Mrs. G.H. Williams (5, Military Road, Dover, co. Kent): *b.* Battersea, London, *c.*1892: Religion – Church of England: Occupation – Mechanical & Motor Engineer: 5′4½″ tall, hazel eyes, brown hair: joined A.I.F. Brisbane, 2 June 1915; Dvr., Army Service Corps: transf'd. 10th Rfts. 3rd Field Coy. Engineers, August 1915, as Spr.: apptd. L/Corpl. (Serapeum) March 1916: served with Mediterranean Expeditionary Force, November 1915–27 March 1916; France and Flanders from 4 April: returned to England to attend Engineers School, Wales, October 1916 from whence, after completing all courses and passing the relevant examinations, he returned to France, May 1917: promoted Lieut. 5 August following. Admitted No.10 C.C.S., 25 October 1917, dead on arrival. (S.W. penetrating, chest left side): Age 25. Cross erected by Corpl. G. Wallace, 2nd Field Coy. Lieut. Williams leaves a wife, Gleasant Williams (17, Templar Street, Dover, co. Kent).

(XXII.D.9) Pte. 126, Bernard Joseph Gilliman, Stretcher-bearer; 'C' Coy., 4th Field Ambulance, Australian Army Medical Corps, A.I.F.: *s.* of George (& Florence Maud) Gilliman, of 259, Dandenong Road, Windsor, Victoria: *b.* Melbourne. Killed in action, 21 October 1917.

Beloved Son Of Mr & Mrs Geo. Gilliman Of Windsor, Victoria
R.I.P.

(XXII.D.10) Pte. 5512, Edwin Augustus Esdaile, Stretcher-bearer; 'C' Coy., 4th Field Ambulance, Australian Army Medical Corps, A.I.F.: *s.* of William David (& Ada) Esdaile, of Wonga Park, Croydon, Victoria: *b.* London, England. Killed in action, 21 October 1917: Age 25. A comrade, H.S. Smith, said, "He was in a squad of four carrying a patient on their shoulders down the Corduroy Road from Zonnebeke to Ypres. The whole squad were hit by a whizz-bang, and the back of Esdaile's head was carried away. We brought him down and buried him at Poperinghe. The whole of the squad and the patient they were carrying were killed." His 'Memoriam Card' recorded: "We have no mark of his resting place, We did not see him die, We only heard he had passed away, 'Twas hard not to say goodbye. Sleep on dear Edwin in your lonely grave, In a grave we may never see, But as long as life and memory last, We will remember thee. His loving smile and friendly clasp Are pleasant to recall, He had a kindly word for each, And died beloved by all. Those who have loved alone can tell, How we grieve for him we loved so well, Not dead to us but gone before, He'll live in memory evermore."

Only A Stretcher Bearer

(XXII.D.10A) Pte. 15649, Leslie Robert Stirling, Stretcher-bearer; 'C' Coy., 4th Field Ambulance, Australian Army Medical Corps, A.I.F.: *s.* of Alfred (& Mary Ann) Stirling: late *husb.* to E.E. Stirling (Cleve, Arno Bay, South Australia): *b.* Point Lincoln. Killed in action, 21 October 1917: Age 25. Ptes. Esdaile, Stirling and Pritchard were also killed.

He Giveth His Beloved Sleep

Pte. Pritchard has no known grave; he is commemorated on the Ypres (Menin Gate) Memorial (Addenda Panel 58).

(XXII.E.16A) Pte. 100106, William Henry Turner, 31st Bn. Canadian Infantry (Alberta Regt.), C.E.F.: *s.* of Edward Turner, of 'Malvern View,' Croft Road, Charlton Kings, nr. Cheltenham, co. Gloucester, by his wife Mary. Seriously wounded while taking part in the battalion's attack on Passchendaele, 7 November 1917, and died in the Casualty Clearing Station at Poperinghe the following day (8 November). Unveiled 4 August 1920, inscribed 'To the undying memory of the men from Charlton Kings who, in defence of their country, sacrificed their lives in the Great War 1914-1919;' Pte. Turner is one of 116 names recorded on the Charlton King's War Memorial, Horsefair Street: Age 21.

Thy Will Be Done

(XXII.F.8) Pte. 859354, Alexander Walker, 43rd Bn. Canadian Infantry (Manitoba Regt.), C.E.F.: late of Outlook, Saskatchewan: *s.* of John Walker, of Knowepark, Bo'ness, co. Linlithgow: *b.* Bo'ness, 5 July 1894: Religion – Presbyterian: 5'9" tall, blue eyes, fair hair: on completion of his education took employ with Union Bank of Scotland Ltd. (1910); removed to Canada (1913), to appointment as Clerk, Bank of Montreal and, on the outbreak of war was Accountant, Outlook, Saskatchewan branch: serving member 79th Cameron Highlanders of Canada (Militia): enlisted 43rd Battn., Winnipeg, 22 November 1915: proceeded overseas late 1915 and, after a brief period of training in England, went to France with his unit, early 1916: took part in all the major operations in which the Canadian Corps were involved and, severely wounded early in the attack for the capture of Passchendaele, died at the Canadian Hospital, Poperinghe, 26 October 1917. Buried in Lyssenthoek Cemetery: Age 23. *unm.*

He Hath Done All Things Well

(XXII.F.10) Pte. 38042, John Avery, 8th (Service) Bn. The Devonshire Regt.: *s.* of William Avery, of Boldventure, Germansweek, co. Devon, by his marriage to the late Mary Jane Avery: *b.* Broadwood Widger, 1886: enlisted Okehampton. Died of wounds, 27 October 1917, received in action nr. Hooge: Age 31. He leaves a wife, Emily Avery (Eworthy, Germansweek, Beaworthy). Dedicated – 'In commemoration of peace 1919 this plot of land was enclosed as a pleasure ground and also this memorial erected by the parishioners in perpetual memory of those of this parish who served their King and country during the Great War 1914–1918,' the Germansweek War Memorial records the names of three men killed in action, three died of wounds, and twenty-eight who served. Rightly or wrongly John Avery's name heads the first category.

Thy Will Be Done

(XXII.F.14) Spr. 2000006, William Frank Karr, 10th Canadian Railway Troops, C.E.F.: c/o Earl Karr, of 720, Chandler Street, Topeka, U.S.A.: *b.* Des Moines Co., Iowa, United States, 30 August 1863 (attested 1873): Occupation – Removals Contractor; North Topeka: enlisted Regina, Saskatchewan, 31 October 1916: departed Nova Scotia, 22 March 1917: trained in England and worked on the completion of the Military Dockyards railway system, Purfleet: served with the Expeditionary Force in France from 19 June 1917, and died 28 October 1917, of wounds (shrapnel, Rt. underarm) received at duty on railway maintenance and construction in the vicinity of Spoil Bank: Age 54. A widower with a grown up family, William crossed the border into Canada, deducting ten years from his true age that he might enlist in the Overseas Force. He is commemorated in the Shawnee County (Kansas) Honour Roll.

(XXII.G.7) 2nd Lieut. Robert Harold Richardson, 18th (County of London) Bn. (London Irish Rifles) The London Regt. (T.F.) and 6th Sqdn. Royal Flying Corps: *s.* of Lieut.Col. Thomas William Richardson, late 7th (Volunteer) Battn. King's Royal Rifles; of 104, Tollington Park, Wood Green, London, N., Seventh Day Baptist Minister, by his wife Gertrude Elizabeth, *dau.* of Robert Crosby: *b.* Wood Green, London, N., 27 August 1892: *educ.* Public Schools: Occupation – Architect/Surveyor; Somerset House: joined Artists' Rifles, no.5285, November 1915: gazetted 2nd Lieut. London Irish Rifles, 10 July 1916: served with the Expeditionary Force in France and Flanders from October following: joined R.F.C.: returned to England, July 1917 and, after a period of training at Brooklands, returned to the Front the following month, and was killed in aerial service at Dickebusch Lake, Ypres, 6 November following. Buried in the Military Cemetery, Lijssenthoek. His Squadron Commander wrote, "Your son's death was most sincerely lamented by the whole squadron. He was gallant and efficient, and had done very well indeed during the recent operations." And a brother officer, "It came as a great shock to me to read his name in the Gazette… He was always extremely cheerful and keen on any work he was given to do. He was one of my best friends. He was very popular with all the officers and men while he was with the battalion, and we were very sorry to lose him when he went to the R.F.C. I cannot express my grief at the loss of such a good friend." Another wrote, "He always played the game like a soldier and a man, and gave his life for his country. Your dear boy was popular alike with officers and men, and his death is deplored by all." Attested as a Special Constable, October 1914; his colleagues wrote, "We can always remember him as we knew him, kind and thoughtful for others, fearless and brave … became exceedingly fond of your son; in all weathers and at all times he was so bright and cheerful, always ready with a jest or a laugh.": 6 November 1917: Age 25. *unm.*

Beloved Son Of Lt.Col. & Mrs T.W. Richardson, London

(XXII.G.11A) Pte.267104, Robert Franklin Allen, 28th Bn.Canadian Infantry (Saskatchewan Regt.), C.E.F.: *s.* of Sarah Allen (Quill Lake, Saskatchewan): *b.* Marlborough, Ontario, 5 May 1896: Religion – Methodist: Occupation – Farmer: joined C.E.F., Wadena, 19 January 1916, apptd. 214th Overseas Bn. Died of wounds (GSW multiple, both legs, Lt. arm), No.3 Canadian Casualty Clearing Station, 7 November 1917. Buried in the Soldier's Cemetery: Age 21.

He Gave His Life For Others

(XXII.G.16A) Corpl. 1201, Gordon Adam, M.M., 4th Field Ambulance, Canadian Army Medical Corps, C.E.F.: *s.* of Mrs Elizabeth Adam, c/o (his brother) William J. Adam Esq., of Cummingston, Burghead, co. Moray, Scotland: *b.* Dufus, Scotland, 3 September 1889: Religion – Presbyterian: Occupation – Carpenter: joined C.E.F., Winnipeg, 10 November 1914: served with the Expeditionary Force in France from 14 September 1915. Died "On 6 November 1917, at Passchendaele, while in charge of a squad of stretcher bearers, on duty at an Advanced Dressing Station, which was located in a pill-box recently vacated by the enemy, Corpl. Gordon received multiple shrapnel wounds in the arms and abdomen from enemy fire. He lived for only a few minutes after being hit.": Age 28.

(XXII.G.18) L/Corpl. 31683, Philip Dicker, 1st Bn. (32nd Foot) The Duke of Cornwall's Light Infantry: *s.* of William George Dicker, of London House, Beaminster, co. Dorset, by his wife Laura Charlotte, *dau.* of William Salisbury Cox: and brother to Engr. E. Dicker, R.N. (surv'd.): *b.* Bridport, co. Dorset, 3 May 1889: *educ.* Beaminster Grammar School: Occupation – Draper's Assistant: enlisted 4 April 1916: served with the Expeditionary Force in France and Flanders from 19 July following, and died at No.2 Canadian Casualty Clearing Station, 8 November 1917, from wounds received in action two days previously, during the attack on Polderhoek Chateau, north of the Menin-Ypres Road. Buried in the Lijssenthoek Military Cemetery: Age 28. *unm.* Dedicated – "Remember In God The True And Faithful Sons Of Beaminster Who Gave Their Lives In The Cause Of Justice And Honour;" L/Corpl. Dicker is remembered on Beaminster (St. Mary of the Anunciation) Church War Memorial.

A Good Soldier Of Jesus Christ

(XXII.G.20A) Pte. 808603, George Frederic Furley, 31st Bn. Canadian Infantry (Alberta Regt.), C.E.F.: c/o General Dely., Calgary: eldest *s.* of Rev. Henry Furley, late Rector, Kingsnorth, co. Kent, England; resident Mount Sandford, Southborough, and Helen Mary Furley, his spouse: nephew to Major B.E. Furley, 6th The Buffs (East Kent Regt.), killed in action, 13 October 1915; and elder brother to 2nd Lieut. R.B. Furley, Oxford & Bucks Light Infantry (T.F.), killed in action, 25 January 1916; being shot by a sniper: *b.* Heydor, co. Lincoln, 31 December 1875: *educ.* Tonbridge School (School House), 1892–94: removed to Canada 1903: Occupation – Farmer; Virden, Manitoba: volunteered and enlisted Calgary, 16 February 1916; posted 137th (Overseas) Battn. Served with the Expeditionary Force in France, and died of wounds (shrapnel, both arms), 8 November 1917: Age 41.

Dulce Et Decorum Est Pro Patria Mori

His uncle Bernard has no known grave, he is commemorated on the Loos Memorial; brother Robert is buried in Hebuterne Military Cemetery (I.A.10).

(XXII.H.2) 2nd Lieut. Alexander Edward Croockewitt, 3rd attd. 1st Bn. (16th Foot) The Bedfordshire Regt.: (Special Reserve of Officers): formerly no.T4/058235, Army Service Corps: *yr. s.* of John Henry Croockewitt, of 'Menin', 32, Leyburn Road, Dover, formerly of 'The Mount', Shepherdswell, co. Kent, by his wife Fanny M. *dau.* of Dr. Edward Rapp: *b.* Dover, co. Kent, 8 December 1885: *educ.* Grammar School, Bedford: went to Canada, 1905; was there engaged on Rail Transport work: returned to England, 1910: underwent a serious operation to qualify for Active Service: joined Army Service Corps, February 1915: served with the Expeditionary Force in France and Flanders, August 1915–January 1917, when he returned home and, after a period of training at Fleet, was gazetted 2nd Lieut. 3rd (Special Reserve) Bn. Bedfordshire Regt.: returned to France July1917, and died of wounds received in action on the Menin Road, Ypres, 26 October 1917. Buried Lyssenthoek Military Cemetery, nr. Poperinghe. His Commanding Officer wrote, "He was greatly liked by all his officers as well as N.C.O.'s and men. We are all more than sad that we shall never see his cheery face again, and shall never be able to replace him. He died a soldier's death in a manner reflecting the highest credit both to himself and the regiment to which he had the honour to belong.": Age 31. *unm.*

His Life For His Country His Soul To God

(XXII.H.14A) Pte. 202912, Arthur Thomas Hollex, 1st Bn. (9th Foot) The Norfolk Regt. *s.* of Charles S. Hollex, of Lower Green, Felsham, Bury St. Edmunds, and Elizabeth, his wife: and brother to Pte. 9469, J.R. Hollex, 1st Suffolk Regt. died of wounds, 24 July 1915: *b.* Felsham: enlisted Bury St. Edmunds. Died of wounds, 27 October 1917.

Gone But Not Forgotten

His brother John is buried in Locre Churchyard (II.B.16).

(XXII.BB.2) Pte. 26328, Robert Henry Booth, 1st Bn. (31st Foot) The East Surrey Regt.: *b.* Wimbledon, London, S.W.: enlisted Kingston-on-Thames, co. Surrey. Died 12 November 1917, of pneumonia: Age 41. He leaves a widow, Mrs R. Booth (12, Edna Road, Raynes Park, West Wimbledon, London).

Until The Day Break And The Shadows Flee Away

(XXII.BB.21) 2nd Corpl. 156543, John Davies, 254th Tunnelling Coy., Royal Engineers: formerly no.26205, Royal Welsh Fusiliers: *b.* Higher Neath, co.

Glamorgan, 1867: enlisted Neath: served with the Expeditionary Force in France from 5 December 1915, and died of wounds, 12 November 1917: Age 51. Correspondence regarding the deceased should be addressed c/o his son, Edgar John Davies, of 8, Roman Road, Banwen, Onllwyn, Glamorgan.

(XXII.DD.7) Capt. Richard Austin Brown, M.C., 15th Bn. Canadian Infantry (Central Ontario Regt.), C.E.F.: s. of T. Albert Brown, of 181, Crescent Road, Toronto, Ontario, by his wife Jennie: b. Toronto, 21 October 1896: *educ.* Rosedale School, Toronto; St. Andrew's College (1908–14); University College, Toronto University (Zeta Psi, 1914–15): during his time at St. Andrew's he won the Cross Country Run, 20 November 1913; Senior Championship, Spring Term 1914, and gained his Second Rugby Colours at University College: member St. Andrew's, and Toronto University Cadet Corps, attaining rank of Corpl., C.O.T.C. in the latter: enlisted Niagara, 6 July 1915, posted 58th Battn.: served with the Expeditionary Force in France and Flanders, joining 15th Battn. (48th Highlanders of Canada) In the Field, November 1915: served in the Ploegsteert sector, St. Eloi and was wounded near Zillebeke, Ypres salient, 1916: after recovery returned to Canada on leave, rejoining his battalion in Flanders, October 1916: took part (as Lieut.) in the fighting at Vimy Ridge, 9 April 1917, for his part in which he received the Military Cross; also at Lens and Hill 70, and died at Poperinghe, 14 November 1917, after being mortally wounded in the head while commanding his company in the vicinity of Otto Farm, Passchendaele, five days previously. The Battalion War Diary recorded, "9 November 1917: Our artillery and that of the enemy continued a constant bombardment. A shell exploded in the doorway of No.3 Company Headquarters and wounded Capt. R.A. Brown, M.C. and Lieut. J.H. Creighton, both in the head. Capt. Brown died a few days later in No.2 Canadian C.C.S. at Poperinghe." He was awarded the Military Cross (*London Gazette*, 26 July 1917) for 'conspicuous gallantry and devotion to duty. With great courage and ability he led his Company during the advance, and was instrumental in silencing an enemy machine gun which was causing casualties.': Age 21. *unm.*

(XXII.EE.19) Pte. 766315, John Charles 'Jack' Adams, 'A' Coy., 3rd Bn. Canadian Infantry (Central Ontario Regt.), C.E.F.: s. of Charles Adams, of 107, Uxbridge Avenue, Toronto, and the late Mrs Adams: b. Bradford, Ontario, 22 January 1897: Religion – Church of England: Occupation – Farmer. Died No.17 C.C.S., 10 November 1917, of wounds (S.W. head, shoulder, thigh) received in action at Passchendaele: Age 20. On returning from a brief period of leave in London, his brother Dave wrote to his sisters informing them Jack had been wounded and died, "…I got a pass and permission to go and find out a few particulars and make sure…He was one of a machine-gun crew, and they were all wounded or killed except one, and he was pretty well shaken up I was told. I found out from one of the stretcher-bearers that Jack was wounded alright, and was carried out to the Dressing Station. It is pretty hard to find out in a case like that and all his Coy. Officers were either killed or wounded and the casualties of the Coy. were very heavy. It is a great consolation to one to know he got admitted to a hospital but he must have suffered something awful, poor kid. I will try to find out more as soon as possible…Your loving brother, Dave."

Thy Will Be Done

(XXII.EE.20) Pte. 117018, Firman Frederick Myatt, 13th Coy., Machine Gun Corps (Inf.): formerly no.203700, Leicestershire Regt.: *b*. Coalville, co. Leicester: employee Stableford Wagon Works, Coalville: enlisted Birmingham, May 1917: served in France for three weeks, and died 6.15 p.m., 10 November 1917, from an abdominal wound received in action at the Battle of Passchendaele; only four hours after joining his Company: Age 23. He leaves a wife, H. Myatt (47, North Street, Whitwick).

Greater Love Hath No Man
He Laid Down His Life For His Friends

(XXII.FF.7) Pte. 799197, Joseph William Whyles, 19th Bn. Canadian Infantry (Central Ontario Regt.), C.E.F.: *b*. Whitwell, co. Derby, 10 March 1883: removed to Canada, found gainful employ as Engineer, Canadian Pacific Railway Co.: late *husb*. to Mary Whyles (661, Annette Street, Toronto): enlisted Toronto, 16 December 1915: served with the Expeditionary in France and Flanders from 1916, and died 14 November 1917, of multiple shell wounds in the Casualty Clearing Hospital situated at Remy Siding, Poperinghe. A Freemason, he was a member of Teeswater Lodge No.276, Teeswater, Ontario: Age 34.

(XXII.GG.2A) Dvr. 116149, Levi Davies, 'C' Bty., 331st Bde., Royal Field Artillery: *yst. s*. of Levi Davies, 71, Llantrisant Road, Pontypridd, by his wife Elizabeth Ann, *dau*. of Thomas Thomas: *b*. Pontypridd, co. Glamorgan, 3 December 1897: *educ*. Graig Board School: was employee Great Western Colliery: enlisted 1 January 1916: served with the Expeditionary Force in France, from 1 March 1917, and died at Ypres, 14 November following, from wounds received in action there. Buried at Poperinghe: Age 19.

His Name Liveth For Ever

(XXII.HH.26) Pte. 452, Percy Goddard Garraway, 8th Bn. Canadian Infantry (Manitoba Regt.), C.E.F.: *s*. of James Garraway, Blacksmith & Sub. Post Master; The Post Office, Little Missenden, co. Buckingham, by his wife Susan: *b*. Little Missenden, October 1886: enlisted Valcartier, September 1914: served in France from 13 February 1915. Seriously wounded by machine-gun fire in front of Passchendaele, 11 November 1917, and died in a Casualty Clearing Hospital the following day: Age 31. Remembered on the St. John the Baptist, Little Missenden; St. Paul's Church, and Cheltenham Borough War Memorials; he left a wife, Maud Daisy Garraway (77, Marle Hill Parade, Cheltenham, co. Gloucester).

In His Presence Is Fullness Of Joy

(XXII.HH.29) Sergt. 9183, Edgar Robert Smith, 2nd Bn. (69th Foot) The Welsh Regt.: *s.* of William Hogarth Smith, Decorator; of 64, Marston Road, Frome, co. Somerset, by his wife Annie, *dau.* of Edward Thompson: *b.* Salisbury, 31 March 1889: *educ.* Frome: enlisted, 7 December 1906: served seven years with the Colours in South Africa, and at Khartoum: discharged time expired 19 February 1914, but rejoined on mobilisation August following: served with the Expeditionary Force in France and Flanders from the middle of that month, and died near Poperinghe, 11 November 1917, from wounds received in action the previous day. Letters from officers and comrades testify to Sergt. Smith's conscientiousness and cheerfulness: Age 28. *unm.*

Loved Long Since And Lost Awhile
God Grant To Him Eternal Rest

(XXIII.A.2) Lieut. Edgar Boyd Clouston, 4th Coy., Australian Machine Gun Corps, A.I.F.: *s.* of the late Rev. Thomas Edward Clouston, B.A., D.D. (*d.*1913), by his 2nd wife Mary Eliza, *née* McKaughan (3, Croyland Flats, McKye Street, North Sydney, New South Wales): *b.* 21 September 1895: prior to enlistment was studying at Sydney University, for the profession of Schoolmaster. Died of wounds 10.30 p.m., 26 September 1917; No.10, C.C.S., Poperinghe: Age 22. *unm.* A member of No.4 Company said, "I was in the front line at the time, to the left of Polygon Wood, and Mr Clouston was in supports examining an old German three compartment dug-out. Fritz got onto the dug-out just when Mr Clouston was there and sent over a number of shells. Mr Clouston's leg was blown off and other men were wounded or killed. He died from the effects of his wounds as soon as he reached the dressing station. He was never strong. His grave is near a C.C.S. near Poperinghe. We lost a fine officer in him." He had just returned from celebrating his twenty-second birthday on leave in Paris.

Beloved Son Of Mary & Thomas Clouston B.A. D.D. Sydney

(XXIII.A.11A) Sergt. 146, Francis Paget Hewkley, M.M., Signal Coy., 4th Australian Division, A.I.F.: *s.* of Frank Hewkley, of 37, Walbrook, London, E.C., and St. James', Hatcham, London, S.E., M.B., F.R.C.S. Eng., by his wife Dorothy, *dau.* of John Brewis, of Tynemouth, co. Northumberland: *b.* Stoke Newington, London, N., 10 March 1894: *educ.* Merchant Taylors' School, and Scouts' Farm, Buckhurst Place, co. Kent: went to Western Australia, June 1912, and settled at Perth as an officer of the Bank of Australasia: enlisted 9 August 1914: was in first section sent to Melbourne for further special instruction: left Australia with 1st Division: landed Egypt, November 1914: served with the Mediterranean Expeditionary Force at Gallipoli from 25 April 1915, taking part in the landing and evacuation of the Peninsula: returned Egypt, 6 January 1916, when he was transferred to 4th Australian Division, then being formed, and with which he then proceeded to France, June 1916. Sergt. Hewkley was wounded by a shell fragment in his left shoulder at Tokio, on the Zonnebeke Ridge, 26 September 1917, and whilst walking away to the Dressing Station another shell burst in close proximity fracturing his skull. Immediately thereafter he was taken to No.2 Casualty Clearing Station, but, such were the severity of his wounds, he died within a few hours. Buried at Lyssenthoek Cemetery, 1¾ miles southwest of Poperinghe; a cross has been erected to his memory. Sir Robert Baden-Powell wrote, 'I remember your boy so well at Buckhurst Farm, and know he was a universal favourite there. He has left behind an example of service and self-sacrifice which will be an inspiration to the Boy Scouts who knew him in carrying out their duty – as he did – at no matter what personal cost.' His Officer Commanding wrote, 'He was previously wounded while holding a position with conspicuous bravery, and showing the most heroic examples to his comrades. Your boys' memory will ever be revered by his comrades;' and his Major, 'Paget, as he was generally known, even among the officers, was a true soldier boy, one that the Australian Army can ill afford to lose; his experience, his bravery, his total indifference to fire of any kind, his Christian-like character, all went to make the lad one of the most popular in the unit.' A comrade also wrote, 'The boys of the section and battalion runners speak of him as if he were still alive but absent elsewhere. He will always be to us all a fond memory of someone better in every way than any of us, and in the Signal Companies (1st & 4th) his name and spirit will be a tradition." Awarded the Military Medal (*London Gazette*, 9 December 1916) for 'gallantry in mending lines under fire at Pozieres on 3–4 September 1916: Age 23. *unm.*

We Thank Our God For Every Remembrance Of Him
R.I.P.

(XXIII.A.14) Maj. Conrad Hugh Dinwiddy, 13th Siege Bty., Royal Garrison Artillery: 5th *s.* of Thomas Dinwiddy, the Manor House, Blackheath, SE., and St. Margaret's-at-Cliffe, F.R.I.B.A., R.S.I., by his wife Eliza Charlotte, *dau.* of Philip Rooke: *b.* Greenwich, co. Kent, 11 February 1881: *educ.* Private Tutorship: Occupation – Junior Partner; Messrs Thomas Dinwiddy & Sons, Architects & Surveyors, Westminster, SW.: joined OTC, Exeter, June 1916; gazetted 2nd Lieut. October 1916; promoted Capt. April 1917 and, within six months of joining, promoted Major: served with the Expeditionary Force in France and Flanders from December 1916, and died No.2 Canadian Casualty Clearing Station, Belgium, 27 September 1917, from wounds received in action near Ypres the previous day. Buried at Poperinghe: Age 36. Early in the war he voluntarily studied gunnery: invented the Dinwiddy Aircraft Range Finder, which after severe official tests was patented, and is now installed in the London Defences. He also invented a gunnery slide rule. After six months in an Officer's Training Corps, went to France in December 1916 as junior subaltern in a 6-inch Siege Battery: was shortly promoted Capt. without serving the intermediate rank, and within six months of joining became Major in command of the battery. He was gassed and reported wounded, but remained at duty: he, however, asked to be relieved of the first command, and was appointed second in command of a 9.2 Siege Battery. Whilst serving he invented new methods of night firing – submitted a scheme for barge mounted batteries, and improved methods of ammunition supply. Major Dinwiddy took an active interest in political and municipal affairs, was Councillor of the Borough of Kensington; a prolific journalist and a capable speaker, he was invited to become a candidate for Parliament at the next General Election. He *m.* All Saints,' Margaret St., London, W., 26 July 1910; Winifred (3, Oakdale Rd., Tunbridge Wells), *dau.* of Ashby Pochin, Lieut., The Buffs, and had a son, Hugh, *b.* 16 October 1912. (*IWGC record age 35*)

Until The Day Break And The Shadows Flee Away

(XXIII.A.16) Pte. 5841, Alfred Eager McGill, 18th Bn. Australian Infantry, A.I.F.: *s.* of Arthur McGill, by his wife Margaret: and yr. brother to Pte, 2934, J.E. McGill, 58th Battn. A.I.F., who died the previous day: *b.* Sydney, New South Wales, Australia: enlisted there May 1916: served in France from 10 April 1917. Died of multiple bullet wounds, 26 September 1917, received in action at Polygon Wood: Age 21.

He Gave His Best He Gave His Life

His brother James lies nearby (XXIII.C.18)

(XXIII.B.5) 2nd Lieut. William Keith Seabrook, 17th Bn. Australian Infantry, A.I.F.: s. of William George Seabrook, of Great North Road, Five Dock, Sydney, New South Wales, by his wife Fanny Isabel: and brother to Pte. 6174, G.R. Seabrook, and Pte. 6147, T.K. Seabrook, who were both killed the previous day: held rank of Lieut. in Australia, but gave up his commission and took rank of Sergt. Major to proceed to France, and died of wounds, 21 September 1917, received between 1 and 2 a.m. in the vicinity of Bordon Dump, about one mile beyond Hell Fire Corner, on the way up to Glencorse Wood. It was Lieut. Seabrook's first time in the line and he was leading his men to their positions (in readiness for their part in the Battle of the Menin Road) across a duckboard track when a phosphorous shell exploded among them badly wounding Lieut. Seabrook, killing eight other men, and setting fire to the duckboards. He was carried out by Pte. R. Cullen and Corpl. J.C. Abbey, Australian Army Medical Corps. Corpl. Abbey later reported, "11 November. 1917...He was very badly wounded on the night of 19th – 20th September whilst going up the line. I personally dressed his wounds but they were of such a nature I do not think it advisable to let his people know what they were. He was taken away and reached the 10th C.C.S. where he died. He was buried in the soldiers cemetery attached thereto.": Age 21. *unm.*

A Willing Sacrifice For The World's Peace

His two brothers, George and Theo, have no known grave; both are recorded on the Ypres (Menin Gate) Memorial (Panel 17).

(XXIII.B.9) Pte. 6471, Lawrence James Brooks, 9th Bn. Australian Infantry, A.I.F.: s. of John H. Brooks, of Mainside-via-Winton, Queensland: b. Tambo, Queensland, 1898: Religion – Roman Catholic: Occupation – Stockman: enlisted Charters Towers, 26 June 1916; apptd. 21st Rfts., 9th Bn.: departed Brisbane, 21 October: joined 9th Bn., France, 1 May 1917: severely wounded (S.W. abdominal) Menin Road, Ypres, 20 September 1917, died No.10 C.C.S., Poperinghe the following day: Age 19.

(XXIII.C.3) Pte. 1654, Arthur William Baldwyn, 2nd Bn. Australian Pioneers, A.I.F.: s. of Florence Baldwyn (Up Green, Eversley, Basingstoke, co. Hants): and brother to Pte. V78385, H. Baldwyn, A.I.F. (surv'd.); and Pte. 3118, F.C. Baldwyn, 1/4th Hampshire Regt., killed in action, 21 January 1916, in Mesopotamia: b. Gonderton, Tewkesbury, co. Gloucester, c.1890: Religion – Church of England: Occupation – Salesman: 5'4¾" tall, blue eyes, fair hair: enlisted A.I.F., 31 January 1916: joined 2nd Pioneers, France, 14 July 1916: wounded in action (G.S.W. Lt. arm), 2 August; hospitalised and removed to England: returned France, 1 January 1917. Wounded in action (S.W. Head,

Hand) 25 September 1917, and died at No.10 C.C.S., Poperinghe, the following day. Buried in Lyssenthoek Military Cemetery: Age 27. *unm.*

His brother Frederick has no known grave; he is commemorated on the Basra Memorial (Panel 21).

(XXIII.C.8A) L/Corpl. 27552, Wallace Rawson Guise, 'D' Coy., 2nd Bn. (36th Foot) The Worcestershire Regt.: *s.* of Rawson Guise, of Church Cottage, Himbleton, Droitwich, co. Worcester, by his wife Martha: enlisted Worcester. Died of wounds (G.S. Rt. buttock, Rt. thigh), 26 September 1917: Age 23.

Peace Perfect Peace With Loved Ones Far Away
Mother

(XXIII.C.12) Lieut. Wilfred Norman Beaver, 60th Bn. Australian Infantry, A.I.F.: *s.* of the late Albert Beaver, by his wife Evelyn (48, Leinster Square, Bayswater, London, W.), *dau.* of the late T. Bloomington: *b.* Melbourne, Australia, 11 May 1882: *educ.* Scotch College, and Melbourne University, Australia: was 12 years Resident Magistrate; Papua, being a Fellow of the Royal Geographical Society, also of the Royal Anthropological Society, and author of many articles on Tribal Research: volunteered for Foreign Service, and joined Australian Imperial Force, January 1916: obtained 2nd Lieutenancy, 60th Battn. February following: promoted Lieut. March 1917: served with the Expeditionary Force in France and Flanders, from November 1916, and died at No.17 Casualty Clearing Station, 26 September 1917, from wounds (abdominal) received in action at Polygon Wood. Buried in the Military Cemetery at Poperinghe. His Colonel wrote praising the way in which he brought his men through Polygon Wood on the day he was wounded: Age 35. *unm.*

(XXIII.C.18) Pte. 2934, James Edward McGill, 58th Bn. Australian Infantry, A.I.F.: *s.* of Arthur McGill, by his wife Margaret: and yr. brother to Pte. 5841, A.E. McGill, 18th Australian Infantry, died the following day: *b.* Sydney, New South Wales, Australia: enlisted there, 4 September 1916: served in France from May 1917, and died of multiple shell wounds, 25 September 1917: Age 18.

He Was Only A Boy But He Did His Duty

His brother Alfred lies nearby (XXIII.A.16).

(XXIII.D.6A) Pte. 8194, Norman Kenneth McDowell, 14th Field Ambulance, Australian Army Medical Corps, A.I.F.: *s.* of Alexander McDowell, of 186, North Road, Brighton, Victoria; late of Garnet Street, South Preston; by his wife Elizabeth: and yr. brother to Sergt. 3194, A.H. McDowell, 60th Australian Infantry, reported missing (28 July 1916) after the fighting on the 19th of that month, since confirmed (5 September) killed in action, aged 26 years: *b.* Gordons,

Ballarat, 1895: Occupation – Clerk: served 4 years Senior Cadets; joined A.I.F., Melbourne, 16 July 1915 (with parental consent); posted 2nd Australian Field Ambulance (Reinforcements), Broadmeadows Camp, 7 October: departed Melbourne, 15 October; served Egypt, 2nd Australian General Hospital from 7 November 1915, transf'd. attd. Ras-el-Tin Convalescent Depot, 15 March 1916: subsequently transf'd. Australian Army Medical Corps, departed Alexandria, 15 September and proceeded to France, 12 October 1916: joined 14th Field Ambulance In the Field, 13 November 1916. Wounded (G.S.W. head) 21 September 1917 at duty; evacuated 6th Australian Field Ambulance, transf'd. No.3 Canadian C.C.S. where he died and was buried later the same day: Age 20. *unm.*

Our Thoughts Are Ever With Thee

Buried at the time by the Germans his brother Athol's remains were recovered from one of a number of mass graves discovered in 2009 and, after extensive investigations, positively identified and re-interred the following year in Fromelles (Pheasant Wood) Military Cemetery (III.B.4).

(XXIII.D.17A) Coy.Sergt.Major 970, John William Schwarer, 7th Bn. Australian Infantry, A.I.F.: *s.* of the late John Schwarer, by his marriage to Agnes Rasmussen, *née* Schwarer (666, Grady Street, Clifton Hill, Victoria): *b.* Rutherglen, Victoria: served at Gallipoli and in France and Flanders, and died of wounds, 21 September 1917, received the previous day from artillery fire dropping short at Black Watch Corner, Polygon Wood: Age 25.

In Loving Memory Of My Darling Son Jackie

(XXIV.A.1) Pte. 1889, Leslie Raswell Elton Coleman, 55th Bn. Australian Infantry, A.I.F.: *s.* of the late Charles William Coleman, by his wife Maria ('Woodview,' Wheeo, Crookwell, New South Wales); and brother to Pte. 2535, C,C, Coleman, Australian Provost Corps; and Lieut. S.W. Coleman, 29th Australian Infantry, believed killed in action, 9 August 1918, nr. Vauvillers: *b.* Wheeo, 1895: Religion – Church of England: Occupation – Confectioner: 5'10" tall, grey-brown eyes, light brown hair: enlisted Holdsworthy, 23 August 1915; discharged (Varicocele) October following; re-enlisted Goulburn, 24 January 1916; posted Depot Battn. (no.13034): departed Sydney, 23 June: hospitalised Salisbury Plain (Rheumatism), 19–26 September: proceeded to France, 12 November; joined 55th Battn. In the Field, 1 December: wounded (G.S. Rt. Foot, Self-Inflicted), 10 December; and hospitalised. F.G.C.M. convened 28 December 1916, Charged (1) Wilfully maiming himself with intent thereby rendering himself unfit for service; Alternatively (2) An act to the prejudice of good order and military discipline in that he by carelessly discharging his rifle wounded himself in the foot. Found Not Guilty, 1st Charge; Guilty 2nd Charge. Sentenced to 18 months hard labour, commuted (3 January 1917) to 90 days F.P. No.1: on discharge to duty (1 May 1917) awarded Forfeiture 143 Days Pay: rejoined 55th Battn. 17 May: detached Pigeon School, 25–27 June. Wounded (Facial Abrasions, Fractured Skull, Shock) Polygon Wood, 23 September 1917, admitted 6th Field Ambulance, transf'd. 10th Casualty Clearing Station; died shortly after arrival. Buried Lyssenthoek Military Cemetery, 1¾ miles S.W. of Poperinghe: Age 21. *unm.* Remembered on the Crookwell War Memorial, New South Wales.

In Memory Of The Dearly Loved Son Of Mr & Mrs Coleman Of Wheeo

His brother Spencer is buried in Heath Cemetery, Harbonnieres (I.D.14).

(XXIV.A.14) Pte. M2/114701, Archibald Arthur Douglas Bentley, Mechanical Transport Coy. (11th Motor Ambulance Convoy), Army Service Corps: *s.* of Joseph Bentley, Sergt., Royal Field Artillery, by his wife Jane, *dau.* of James Tall: *b.* Secunderabad, India, 30 April 1881: *educ.* there, and Plymstock, nr. Plymouth: Occupation – Taxi Driver: enlisted 28 June 1915: served with the Expeditionary Force in France and Flanders from 10 July following. Wounded by a bomb, 18 October 1917, and died the following day at No.10 Casualty Clearing Station. Buried in Lyssenthoek British Soldiers' Cemetery, nr. Poperinghe: Age 36. His Commanding Officer wrote, "He was wounded by an aerial bomb, while boarding his car on the night of the 18th, and died shortly after. He was a willing and thoroughly satisfactory soldier, popular alike with his comrades and officers, by whom his death is deeply felt." He *m.* at Buckland, 1902, Matilda Elizabeth (122, Phillimore Street, Devonport), *dau.* of the late Richard Andrews, R.N., and had three children.

Into Thy Hands O God

(XXIV.A.18) 2nd Lieut. Simon Van der-Linde, 6th (Service) Bn. The Bedfordshire Regt.: *s.* of S.H. Van der-Linde, of Highbury New Park: and brother to 2nd Lieut. M.J.T. Van der-Linde, Queen Victoria's Rifles, killed in action, 30 August 1918; and uncle to Pte. 43756, M.S. Van der-Linde, Royal Army Medical Corps, died 18 August 1915, in England: *educ.* Northern Polytechnic Institute: gazetted 2nd Lieut. Bedfordshire Regt., from London University O.T.C.: proceeded to France 1917 and died 18 October of that year, of wounds received from an aerial bomb dropped on the battalion whilst training in a camp north-east of Ypres; 5 other men were also wounded. (*IWGC record Vander-Linde & Vanderlinde*)

His brother Maurice is buried in Hem Farm Military Cemetery (I.B.21), nephew Mark is buried in Willesden Jewish Cemetery (CX13.8).

(XXIV.A.23) Sergt. M2/100291, Thomas Armstrong, D.C.M., Mechanical Transport Coy., Army Service Corps attd. 85th Siege Bty., Royal Garrison Artillery: *s.* of Christopher Armstrong, by his wife Caroline: *b.* West Ham, London: served in France from August 1915, and was killed in an enemy air raid, 15 August 1918: Age 34. Awarded the Distinguished Conduct Medal (*London Gazette*, 21 October 1918): 'For conspicuous gallantry and devotion to duty. He has done extremely good work in charge of tractors, remaining at duty and carrying out gun shifts under continuous fire. He showed a splendid example of perseverance and courage.' He leaves a wife, Elizabeth Armstrong (19, Penge Road, Upton Park, London).

We Are Proud Of You

(XXIV.A.26) Bmdr. 283315, Reginald Albert Sefton, 212th Siege Bty., Royal Garrison Artillery: eldest *s.* of the late Ernest Sefton, by his wife Clara (10, Highbury Road, Wimbledon, London, S.W.): *b.* Malvern Link, co. Worcester, December 1880: *educ.* Malvern C.E. School: served in the South African Campaign with 'M' Bty., Royal Horse Artillery: obtained his discharge 1906: Occupation – Warehouseman: conscripted June 1916: posted to 212th Bty., R.G.A., and left for France, February 1917: apptd. Actg. Bmdr. May 1917; Bmdr. September following: rejoined his unit after two weeks home leave, February 1918, and died No.140 Field Ambulance, 24 August following, of wounds received in action the same day. He *m.* St. Mary's Church, Honley, co. York, August 1904; Rose Mildred, *née* Phipps ('Laburnum,' Leamington Place, Quest Hills Road, Malvern), and had four children – Lilian Beryl, *b.* April 1905; Clarence, *b.* 1909; Jack, *b.* 1911; Joan, *b.* 1913. His personal effects – letters, photographs, two South African Campaign medal ribbons – were returned to his widow. Bmdr. Sefton's death was reported in the *Malvern News*, 28 September 1918, and memorial plaques bearing his name installed in both St. Mathias's Church, Malvern Link, and Holy Trinity Church, North Malvern: Age 37.

Faithful Unto Death

(XXIV.B.8) Lieut. John Edward Turnour, 59th Bn. Australian Infantry, A.I.F.: *yst. s.* of Keppel Arthur Turnour, of Black Rock, South Australia, by his wife Margaret A.: and brother to Pte. 673, A.W. Turnour, 38th Australian Infantry, killed in action, 13 October 1917, at Passchendaele; Pte. V/60176, D. Turnour (surv'd.) Pte. 5099, J.O. Turnour (severely wounded, lost leg, surv'd.); and Pte. 26626, K.E. Turnour (surv'd.): *b.* Brighton, Victoria, 1893: Occupation –

Divinity Student; Theological Hall, Bendigo, Victoria: enlisted 'G' Coy. 7th Bn. A.I.F., 1 September 1914: departed Melbourne, 19 October: wounded at Gallipoli landing, 25 April 1915: promoted Corpl. 22 January 1916; transf'd. 59th Battn., 11 March, promoted QMSergt. 14 April: served in France from 29 June 1916: slightly wounded (G.S. head), 5 August: gazetted 2nd Lieut. 59th Battn., 9 August: wounded (S.W. Rt. arm), 6 March 1917, evacuated to England: returned to France, 9 June 1917. Died of shrapnel wounds to the upper right arm and abdomen, 28 September 1917, received in action 5.50 a.m. on the 26th. Mentioned in Despatches: 'For conspicuous gallantry and devotion to duty. In the attack at Polygon Wood on 26th September he commanded 'C' Company. In the advance some men were held up by a large Pill Box. Lieut. Turnour took charge and gave the order to prepare to charge, and then led the charge on to the Pill Box which was then captured. Lieut. Turnour was badly wounded and subsequently died of his wounds." Posthumously (30 October 1917) congratulated for his 'gallant services in recent operations.' Buried with full military honours, Rev. Sulman officiating: Age 26.

Although his parents requested John and his brother be buried together the request was denied; Arthur is buried in Tyne Cot Cemetery (XXII.G.14).

(XXIV.B.20) Capt. Reginald Henry Gill, M.C., 28th Bn. Australian Infantry, A.I.F.: *s.* of George Gill, by his wife Agnes. Killed by the explosion of a bomb dropped from a German aircraft beside 28th Battn. H.Qrs. Tent, Reninghelst on the night of 28 September 1917: Age 35. H.Q.rs Officers Col. Read, Majors Brown and Darling (plus 10 other officers and men) were wounded, and three other men killed. Capt. Gill leaves a wife, Laura J. Gill ('Valhalla,' Essex Street, Fremantle, Western Australia).

Semper Fidelis

(XXIV.E.19) Major. Charles Elles Stuart Beatson, M.C., 105th Bty., 22nd Bde., Royal Field Artillery: *s.* of Major-Gen. Sir Stuart Brownlow Beatson, K.C.B., K.C.S.I., K.C.V.O., Bengal Lancers, of 75, Portland Court, London, by his wife Lady Edith Cecil Beatson, *née* Kidston-Elles: *b.* 1891. Died of wounds, 3 October 1917: Age 26. *unm.* Major Beatson is remembered on the Slaugham (Parish Church) War Memorial, Sussex.

Through The Door Of Sacrifice And Victory They Have Passed On

(XXIV.E.20) Dvr. 3907, David Mason, 1st Divn. Ammunition Col., Australian Field Artillery, A.I.F.: *s.* of Thomas Mason, of 14, Chapel Street, Silsden, co. York: *b.* Skipton, nr. Keighley, 2 December 1893: emigrated to Australia about 1913; took up Dairy Farming: previously served 4 years Territorial Force (England);

joined A.I.F. Victoria, 16 November 1914: proceeded to join Mediterranean Expeditionary Force, 30 April 1915: Awarded 7 Days Confinement aboard troopship *Minneapolis*, 7 May 1915, for 'Being absent from piquet parade': Awarded 7 Days Confinement, Cleopatra Camp, Alexandria, 15 September 1915, for 'Leaving stables without being properly relieved, and insubordinate language to an N.C.O.': served with the Expeditionary Force in France from 2 April 1916: Awarded 21 Days F.P. No.2, 19 August 1916, for 'Ill-treating a horse, and conduct to the prejudice of good order and military discipline': Awarded 14 Days F.P. No.2, 18 September, for 'Neglect of duty, and insolence to an N.C.O.': several times hospitalised (sick) from May 1917: rejoined his unit, 17 August 1917, and died of wounds (Bomb, abdomen, head), 30 September following, received in action the same day: Age 23. *unm*. In a letter to a Miss Bancroft a comrade wrote, "I am sure the news concerning Driver Mason's death will be a great blow to his people as it is likewise to me. I had been camping with him for some time, and had become very much attached to him. How he met his death I will try to explain. It was Sunday night, the 30th September. We were all in the dugout together. David and I were busy writing on some cards when he was called out into the horse lines for some reason – I don't exactly know what. However, while he was out a German Taube came over and dropped bombs in the camp. We soon learned that David had been badly wounded. I quickly went out to dress his wounds; he having been hit in both legs, and a fairly large piece of shrapnel had entered his back. This, he said, he could feel on his stomach, as he was continually complaining about his stomach. He died after being admitted to hospital, which was done in all good haste. Poor David was always talking about his sisters, of whom he was very fond. I trust they will accept my sincerest sympathy in their sad bereavement. He was thought well of by all who knew him."

(XXIV.F.2A) Pte. 41123, Harry Anderson, 11th (Service) Bn. The Prince of Wales's Own (West Yorkshire Regt.): *husb*. to Mary Anderson (1, Drury Lane, Horsforth, Leeds): *b*. Horsforth: enlisted there. Died of bullet wounds to both legs, and fractured femur, 22 September 1917: Age 36.

(XXIV.G.14) Pte. 1306, Thomas Waugh, 'C' Coy., 1st Bn. Australian Infantry, A.I.F.: *s*. of the late William Alexander Waugh, by his wife Augusta (Richmond Grove, Invercargill, New Zealand): *b*. Paddington, Sydney, 1888: Occupation – Coal Lumper: previously served 2 years Invercargill City Guard, 2 years Invercargill Defence Cadets: enlisted Liverpool, New South Wales, 4 November 1914: proceeded to Gallipoli, 5 April 1915; wounded (G.S.W. Hip, Thigh), on the 30th of that month, and removed to Base Hospital, Egypt: returned Gallipoli, 24 August 1915: took part in the evacuation; disembarked Alexandria, 28 December 1915: served with the Expeditionary Force in France and Flanders from 28 March 1916; and was killed in action, 22–25 July 1917, by the bursting of a shell in a trench at Ypres. Buried where he fell: Age 28. *unm*. In response to a letter of enquiry from the Red Cross, L/Corpl. W. Bradley reported, "Concerning the death of 1306 Pte. T. Waugh...As I was a pal of his and knew him well I am able to inform you he was killed early on the morning of the 25.7.16, and was buried in the field, and presume his grave would not be registered as it was not in a cemetery, though a small wooden cross is generally placed at the head of any grave when a soldier is buried in the field to mark the place where the body lay. Pte. Waugh was of fair complexion and stood about 5'8" or 10" high. Any other mark of identification I am unable to give as it is almost a year since he left us. (*q.v.*)' Directorate of Graves reported '12 December 1917, Buried Lyssenthoek Military Cemetery, 1¾ miles S.W. of Poperinghe.' Pte. Waugh's identity disc was received by Corpl. Bradley's mother, 26 February 1918. (*IWGC record 25 July 1917*)

(XXIV.H.7A) Pte. 54796, Albert Edward Crassweller, 15th (Service) Bn. (2nd Portsmouth) The Hampshire Regt.: *s*. of Frederick Crassweller, of 18, Clarendon Road, Brockhampton, Havant, co. Hants, and Sarah Crassweller his spouse: and yr. brother to Pte. 20711, A.J. Crassweller, 15th Hampshire Regt., killed in action, 7 October 1916, aged 18 years: *b*. Brockhampton, Havant: enlisted Winchester. Died of wounds, 4 October 1918: Age 18.

His brother Alfred has no known grave; he is commemorated on the Thiepval Memorial, Somme.

(XXIV.H.8A) Pte. 6819, Albert Edward Collis, 12th Bn. Australian Infantry, A.I.F.: *s*. of Nickols E.R. Collis, of Brighton Junction, Tasmania, by his wife Mary Jane: and yr. brother to Pte. 6818, F.J. Collis, 12th Australian Infantry, died 24 March 1918, of generalised tuberculosis consequent to trench fever and wounds received in action in France: *b*. Broadmarsh, Brighton, March 1895: Religion – Roman Catholic: Occupation – Labourer: 5'11" tall, brown eyes, dark hair: joined A.I.F. Claremont, 19 September 1916; posted 22nd Rfts., 12th Battn.: departed Melbourne HMAT A38 'Ulysses,' 25 October: trained Durrington Camp, England, December 1916–April 1917: joined 12th Battn., France, 12 April 1917: hospitalised 4–16 May (Inflenza): rejoined battalion on the 23rd of that month. Admitted 6th Australian Field Ambulance; transf'd. No.3 Canadian C.C.S. and died of wounds (multiple G.S.W. Lt. leg and forearm fractured, chest), 21 September 1917, received in action on the night of 19–20 September. Buried in the cemetery, Lyssenthoek, 1¾ miles south-west of Poperinghe: Age 22. *unm*. His effects – Disc, Photos, Pipe, 2 Souvenir bullets, Metal Cigarette Case, Purse, 2 Rosaries, Metal Wristwatch (Damaged) & Strap, Cards, Note Case – were received by his mother, May 1918; his British War (and Victory) Medals, Memorial Plaque and Scroll, by his father 1921–1923.

Known locally as the Australian Graveyard, his brother Francis is one of 167 (143 Australian) First World War casualties buried in Sutton Veny (St. John's) Churchyard (329.D.19).

(XXIV.H.16) Capt. James Alfred Daniels, 15th (Service) Bn. (2nd Portsmouth) The Hampshire Regt.: *s.* of James Alfred (& Minnie Kate) Daniels, of 43, Main Avenue, Bush Hill Park, Enfield, co. Middlesex: *b.* 1896: *educ.* Enfield Grammar School: Occupation – Clerk; London Stock Exchange: served in France from 30 July 1915, and died of wounds, 21 September 1917: Age 21. *unm.*

In God's Keeping He Is Sleeping Till We Meet Again

(XXIV.H.25) Sergt. 15986, James Roulston, M.M., 10th (Service) Bn. The Royal Inniskilling Fusiliers: 3rd *s.* of David S. Roulston, of 'Glen Lower,' Ramelton, Letterkenny, Co. Donegal: *educ.* Ramelton: volunteered for Active Service soon after the outbreak of war, enlisted Royal Inniskilling Fusiliers, 4 September 1914: served with the Expeditionary Force in France and Flanders, from October 1915: previously wounded three times and, during the Battle of Cambrai, was taken prisoner, but escaped March 1918, and died at No.10 Casualty Clearing Station, 5 October following, of wounds received in action on the 1st. His Commanding Officer wrote, "He was my Platoon Sergt. for the past two months, and during that time I never found a fault with him. I had a great liking for him, and would certainly have recommended him for a further decoration, but I knew it was no use, as he was very badly wounded...The men in his platoon loved him, and always looked up to him." Awarded the Military Medal for 'conspicuous bravery and devotion to duty on the field.': Age 21. *unm.*

(XXV.AA.17) Spr. 7149, Claude Harmon Chegwidden, 1st Field Coy., Australian Engineers, A.I.F.: *s.* of Harmon Jacob Spearshot Chegwidden, of Merredin, Western Australia, by his late wife Dorothy: *b.* Birdsville, Queensland, 1893: Religion – Roman Catholic: Occupation – Blacksmith: 5'4¾" tall, grey eyes, fair hair: joined A.I.F., Blackboy Hill, 17 November 1915: posted 5th Rfts., 4th (Depot.) Battn., Engineers, 16 December 1915: departed Australia, April 1916: trained Egypt: served with the Expeditionary Force in France from 15 June 1916: Awarded Forfeiture 1 day's pay 'Parading for R.C. Church Parade in a filthy condition,' Etaples, 23 July following: transf'd. 1st Field Coy, 12 August 1916. Died at No. 10 C.C.S. 30 September 1917, of wounds (Bomb; hands, legs, abdomen), received in action on the 28th.: Age 24. *unm.* Buried at Lyssenthoek; Memorial Cross erected Belgian Battery Corner. Distraught by the death of her son, his mother died, 1 November 1917.

(XXV.A.12) Gnr. 23100, Frederick Voase, 16th Bty., 6th Bde., Australian Field Artillery, A.I.F.: *s.* of the late George (& Mrs T.) Voase (5, Carlton Avenue, Cliff Lane, Hornsea, co. York, England): *b.* Hull, co. York, 1888: Religion –

Church of England: Occupation – Cook: previously served 7 months Territorial Force, 1908: joined A.I.F., Brisbane, 30 December 1915; apptd. Pte., 11th Depot Bn.; transf'd. apptd Gnr., 1st Rfts, 9th F.A. Bde., 12 April 1916: Awarded (10 April) 119 Hours Confinement, Forfeiture 5 Days Pay 'Absent Without Leave, Enoggera, 4–9 April': departed Sydney, HMAT A8, 11 May: hospitalised (at sea; influenza) 19–21 May: trained England from 10 July: Awarded 48 Hours Detention, 4 Days Forfeiture Pay 'Absent Without Leave When On Active Service, 17 November,' Larkhill, 25 November 1916: Awarded 168 Hours Detention 'Hesitating to Obey an Order given by a NCO, 21 January,' Larkhill, 27 January 1917: hospitalised (mumps), 31 March – 18 April: proceeded to France 5 June; transf'd. England Under Escort 20 June; Awarded (22 June) Forfeiture 4 Days Pay 'Being Absent Without Leave 4–5 June, until reporting to Conducting Party; Folkestone, and being placed on Draft Roll;' returned France same day: joined 16th Bty., 4 August. Severely wounded (SW abdominal, both legs) in action nr. Chateau Wood; died later the same day, 1 October 1917, 17th C.C.S., Poperinghe: Age 39. Married (11 September 1902) to Minnie Voase, *née* Bradshaw (9, Witney Street, Highfield, Sheffield, England); he bequeathed all his monies and possessions to his sister Julia Johnson, *née* Voase (High Street, Hull).

(XXV.A.22) 2nd Lieut. Eric Oswald Mansfield, 8th (Service) Bn. The King's Royal Rifle Corps: *s.* of Horace Rendall Mansfield, formerly M.P., Spalding, co. Lincoln: and yr. brother to 2nd Lieut. R.H. Mansfield, 121st Bty., Royal Field Artillery, died of wounds, 1 October 1918, aged 26 years: *b.* Church Gresley, Burton-on-Trent, co. Stafford, 1892: *educ.* Leys School, Cambridge, where he was a Prefect and won Second Colours for Football and Lacrosse: joined Public Schools Battalion on the outbreak of war; later obtaining a commission K.R.R.C., and was killed in action, 24 August 1918: Age 25. *unm.*

Rest With Honour And In Peace

His brother Reginald is buried in Grevillers British cemetery (XV.B.12).

(XXV.B.11) Pte. 1714, Frederick Nicoll Herron, 'B' Coy., 2nd Bn. Australian Pioneers, A.I.F.: *s.* of the late James Nicoll Herron, Blacksmith; of 49, East Abbey Street, Arbroath, Scotland: *b.* Arbroath: Religion – Presbyterian: Occupation – sometime Moulder; Dens Iron Works; removed to Melbourne, Victoria, 1911: joined A.I.F., Prahan, Victoria, 5 February 1916; apptd. 2nd Rfts., 2nd Pnr. Bn., Broadmeadows, 6 April: trained England, 11 June – 12 July 1916. Died of wounds (compound fracture, both legs), No.10 C.C.S., 29 September 1917, received 4 p.m. the same day, after preparing roads for the forward movement of artillery, he was drinking cocoa at the Comfort Funds Station, Menin Road, when he was struck by a fragment of shell dropped from an enemy Gotha aircraft: Age 29.

Ptes. 2667, A. Gerkens and 2686, W. Hall were both killed by the same bomb; Pte. 2480, C. Kennedy, seriously wounded, died at Poperinghe four days later.

Albert Gerkens and Walter Hall are buried in Menin Road South Military Cemetery (II.I.8); Pte. Kennedy is buried nearby (XXV.E.5A).

(XXV.B.21) Rfn. A/203858, Mark Glover, 18th (Service) Bn. (Arts & Crafts) The King's Royal Rifle Corps: eldest *s.* of Arthur Alfred Glover, of 11, Queen's Road, Mitcham, co. Surrey, by his wife Elizabeth, *née* Kenning: and brother to Rfn. A/203833, W. Glover, 18th K.R.R.C., who died of wounds exactly three months previously: *b.* Mitcham, 1887: enlisted Army Service Corps, subsequently transf'd. K.R.R.C., Wimbledon, London, S.W. (on the same day as his brother): served in France from July 1915. Died of wounds (concussion), 11 August 1918: Age 31.

His brother William is buried in Brandhoek New Military Cemetery No.3 (III.D.3).

August 1918 saw the highest number of executions on the Western Front for that year – 10 soldiers and 1 Chinese labourer shot by order of the British Army. With the exception of May (9 shootings) no other month had seen more than six. Volunteer, Pte. William Baker, 26th Bn. Royal Fusiliers – a prolific deserter – was under arrest, pending Field General Court Martial for desertion, when he absconded from custody, 22 April 1918. On 8th May he presented himself at the Army Post Office, Boulogne, informing the N.C.O. he had been told to report for duty there. Ten days later his motives became apparent when he was arrested, loitering near the mail boat at Boulogne Docks where, in an attempt to evade being returned to his regiment, he gave a false name and details. Later that month he again escaped from custody and, using another false name, tried unsuccessfully to gain admittance to a hospital at Etaples. He was shot at Poperinghe on 14 August 1918.

(XXV.B.22) Pte. G/22635, William Baker, 26th (Bankers) Bn. The Royal Fusiliers (City of London Regt.): *s.* of Elizabeth Baker (13, Russell Street, Plaistow, London): Executed – 14 August 1918.

(XXV.C.11) Pte. 22802, Alfred Frank Hodgson, No.1 Coy., New Zealand Machine Gun Corps, N.Z.E.F.: *s.* of William Charles Hodgson, of Rawhitiroa Road, Eltham, late of 64, Oriental Parade, Wellington, by his wife Miriam Ann: and *yr.* brother to Pte. 10/3908, H.F. Hodgson, 1st Wellington Regt., killed in action, 16 September 1916, at the Somme: enlisted February 1916: served in France from August following, and died of wounds, 6 October 1917, received in action at Broodseinde: Age 20. *unm.*

His brother Henry is buried in Serre Road Cemetery No.2 (XLI.D.8).

(XXV.C.17) L/Corpl. 2214, David McNamara; Lewis Gunner, 'A' Coy., 21st Bn. Australian Infantry, A.I.F.: *s.* of David (& Mary) McNamara, of 10, Irving Street, Malvern, Victoria: *b.* Numurkah, Victoria, 1894: Religion – Roman

Catholic: Occupation – Clerk: serving member Senior Cadets, Light Horse (Numurkah); previously rejected 'Defective Eyesight;' joined A.I.F., Melbourne, 20 July 1915; apptd. 4th Rfts. 21st Bn. Broadmeadows, 10 September: proceeded overseas, 27 September 1915: joined 21st Bn. Tel-el-Kebir, 21 January 1916: hospitalised (bronchial influenza), Ismalia, 12–29 February: proceeded to France, 19 March: wounded slight (GSW abdominal, embedded & Rt. thigh) 26 August; hospitalised Rouen, transf'd. England, 30 August; discharged to Depot, 15 September 1916: returned to France, 8 February 1917; rejoined 21st Bn., Warlencourt Sector, 12 February: apptd. L/Corpl., Campagne, Somme, 4 August. Died of wounds (SW neck; both legs; severe blood trauma) No.17 Casualty Clearing Station, Poperinghe, 7 October 1917, received 6–6.30 a.m., 'resultant from the enemy's pre-zero bombardment,' 4 October; Passchendaele: Age 23.

R.I.P.

(XXV.C.17A.) Pte. 1883, David Pratt, 41st Bn. Australian Infantry, A.I.F.: *s.* of David Pratt, of Town Common Road, Mackay, Queensland: *b*. Mackay, 1894: Religion – Presbyterian: Occupation – Labourer: 5'11½" tall, hazel eyes, dark brown hair: joined A.I.F., Mackay, 1 April 1916: posted 2nd Rfts., 41st Battn., Bells Paddock, Enoggera, 10 May: departed Brisbane, A.42 'Boorara,' 16 August: underwent training, England from 14 October: proceeded to France 28 February 1917 and, after further training, Etaples, joined 41st Battn. In the Field, 22 March. Wounded in action (G.S.W. hand, right hip perforating iliac vein), 5 October 1917, and admitted 3rd Australian Field Ambulance, transf'd. No.3 C.C.S., Lyssenthoek (pronounced dead on arrival) the same day: Age 21. In response to a request from his father (September 1921) that the Burning Bush be inscribed on the permanent headstone, he was notified this 'can not be complied with' and accepted the 'Presbyterian Cross.'

Our Tears Are Mingled With Our Pride
He Died That All May Live

(XXV.C.23A) Pte. G/71766, Percy John Kitchener, 23rd (Service) Bn. (2nd Football) The Duke of Cambridge's Own (Middlesex Regt.): *s.* of Charles Kitchener, Grocer, of The Post Office Stores, Bennington, co. Hertford, by his wife Sarah: *b*. Bennington: Occupation – Carpenter: enlisted Hertford: served with the Expeditionary Force, and died of wounds, 19 August 1918, received during a relief of American troops near Kemmel.

(XXV.C.27A) Pte. G/60119, James Albert Wigley, 23rd (Service) Bn. (2nd Football) The Duke of Cambridge's Own (Middlesex Regt.): eldest *s.* of James Alexander Wigley, Ship Rigger; of 30, Seymour Road, Chatham Hill, Chatham, by his wife Sarah Betsy, *dau.* of Thomas (& Mary) Bundock: *b.* Rochester Common, co. Kent, 5 May 1899: *educ.* Troytown Board School, Rochester: employee Chatham Post Office: enlisted 5 May 1917: served with the Expeditionary Force in France and Flanders from 1 April 1918, and was killed in action at Ypres, 21 August following. Buried in the Military Cemetery, Lyssenthoek, 1¾ miles south-west of Poperinghe: Age 19.

God Shall Wipe All Tears From Their Eyes
And Their Shall Be No More Death
Rev. 21.4

(XXV.E.5A) Pte. 2480, Charles Kennedy, 'B' Coy., 2nd Bn. Australian Pioneers, A.I.F.: *s.* of Neil Kennedy, of Croveagh, Dungloe, Donegal, Ireland, by his wife Mary, *née* Doolan: *b.* Croveagh, Donegal: Religion – Roman Catholic: Occupation – Miner: joined A.I.F., Melbourne, Victoria, 12 May 1916; apptd. 4th Rfts. 2nd Pnr. Bn. Seymour, 20 July: trained England, 11 September – 12 November 1916. Died of wounds (SW multiple), No.10 C.C.S., Poperinghe, 3 October 1917, received at the Comforts Fund Station, Menin Road (29 Sepember), from the explosion of an aerial bomb: Age 35. Ptes. 2667, A. Gerkens and 2686, W. Hall were both killed by the same bomb.

Albert Gerkens and Walter Hall are buried in Menin Road South Military Cemetery (II.I.8 & 13). See also Pte. 1714, F.N.Herron (XXV.B.11).

(XXV.D.8A) Pte. 3223, Leslie Montgomery Prowd, 59th Bn. Australian Infantry, A.I.F.: *s.* of John Prowd, of 19, Poplar Street, Caulfield, Melbourne, Victoria, by his wife Catherine Maud Charlotte: *b.* March 1888: Religion – Church of England: Occupation – Contractor: 5'8" tall, fresh complexion, brown eyes, black hair: enlisted Warragul, 24 November 1916: posted 8th Rfts. 59th Battn. Royal Park, 8 December, embarked Melbourne, HMAT A7 'Medic,' on the 16th of that month: underwent four months training in England, thereafter went to France, joining his battalion In the Field, 28 June 1917. Wounded (shellfire – both legs), 26 September 1917 at Polygon Wood, admitted 3rd Australian Field Ambulance, transf'd. 17th C.C.S. where he died the following day. The R.A.M.C. Officer Comdg. Wrote, "He was admitted to this hospital suffering from severe shell wounds – leg – and in a critical state. His condition did not improve, and he died at 7.30 a.m, 27-9-17, as a result of these wounds. He was buried the same day in the Soldier's Cemetery near to the hospital by the Rev. Salmon, his grave being duly marked and registered.": Age 27. *unm.* In his will, with the exception of a 'pony mare and foal' which he left to Miss Ivy Allott, Welshpool, South Gippsland, Pte. Montgomery bequeathed all his possessions to his mother; in October 1918 she received his effects – belt, metal wrist watch and strap, electric torch, pipe, wallet, photos, cards, letters, receipts, map, 3 violin strings and 2 coins. His Memorial Plaque, Scroll, War (54628) and Victory (53752) Medals were received by his father in 1923.

> *In Memory Of Our Dear Son And Brother Leslie*
> *At Rest With The Lord*

"The great Duke of Wellington stood on the path which runs round the ramparts of Walmer Castle on a sunny day in July 1843. Near him, standing at attention, was a young Staff Officer of the Adjutant General's Department. He had just asked a question on a small matter of detail which the War Office thought should, as a courtesy, be referred to the Commander of the Forces. A name typical of the British private soldier was required, for use on the model sheet of the soldier's accounts to show where the men should sign.

The Duke stood gazing out to sea while the young officer waited, searching in a long memory stored with recollections for a man who typified the character of Britain's soldiers. He thought back to his first campaign in the Low Countries where he had fought his first action with his old Regiment, the 33rd Foot.

When the battle was over and won, Wellesley rode back to where little groups of wounded men were lying on the ground. At the place where the right of his line had been, lay the right-hand man of the Grenadier Company, Thomas Atkins. He stood six foot three in his stockinged feet, he had served for twenty years, he could neither read nor write and he was the best man at arms in the Regiment. One of the bandsmen had bound up his head where a sabre had slashed it, he had a bayonet wound in the chest, and a bullet through the lungs. He had begged the bearers not to move him, but to let him die in peace. Wellesley looked down on him and the man must have seen his concern. 'It's all right, Sir,' he gasped. 'It's all in the day's work.' They were his last words.

The Old Duke turned to the waiting Staff Officer. 'Thomas Atkins,' he said."

The Ypres Times, April 1929.

Throughout the Great War the British soldier was typically known as Tommy Atkins, the Commonwealth War Graves Commission record twelve T. Atkins of whom only two are to be found within the confines of the Ypres Salient. The first T. Atkins to be killed in the Great War is recorded on the Menin Gate Memorial to the Missing, Ypres – the last:

(XXV.D.12A) Pte. G/37874, Thomas Atkins, 'B' Coy., 1st Bn. (2nd Foot) The Queen's (Royal West Surrey Regt.): *s*. of T. (& A.) Atkins: late *husb*. to Jane Atkins (Botleys Lane, Chertsey, co. Surrey): *b*. Chertsey, *c*.1882. Died of wounds, 26 September 1917, received the previous day in the vicinity of Tower Hamlets Ridge when, at 3.30 in the morning, the enemy opened a bombardment of hitherto unparalleled intensity. The Official History records 'So vicious was this bombardment, and in such great depth upon our rear communications, that it was impossible to move transport or troops along the roads. Following up their bombardment, the enemy counter-attacked in massed formation upon our lines, no less than six divisions being used in this attack upon our divisional front. On the right the posts of 1st The Queen's were overwhelmed, the enemy debouching from the village of Gheluvelt armed with flame-throwers; the stream of burning oil thrown from these devilish weapons reached a length and height of 100 yards and set fire to the trees, which, being as dry as tinder, immediately took fire.." By 7.30 a.m. the front line, held by B and D companies, had been practically obliterated; both companies had almost ceased to exist.: Age 35.

> ... Then it's Tommy this, an' Tommy that
> an' Tommy, 'ow's your soul?
> But it's 'Thin red line of 'eroes'
> When the drums begin to roll ...
>
> ... For it's Tommy this an' Tommy that,
> an' 'Chuck him out, the brute!'
> But it's 'Saviour of 'is country'
> When the guns begin to shoot ...
>
> *Rudyard Kipling*

At Rest

Pte. Thomas Henry Atkins, 1st Lincolnshire Regt., killed in action, 1 November 1914, is recorded on the Ypres (Menin Gate) Memorial (Panel 21).

(XXV.E.4) Pte. 37838, Philip James Kelly, 7th (Service) Bn. The Leicestershire Regt.: formerly Spr. 3851, East Lancashire Royal Engineers (T.F.): eldest *s*. of the late Joseph Kelly, by his wife Margaret, *dau*. of the late James Hulme: *b*. Stockport, 1 May 1885: *educ*. Edgeley Roman Catholic School, there: Occupation – Apprentice Stonemason: joined East Lancashire R.E, Stockport, 2 March 1916: transf'd. Leicestershire Regt. 18 December following: served with the Expeditionary Force from January 1917, and died at No.10 Casualty Clearing Station, 2 October following, from wounds received in action at Polygon Wood. Buried in Lyssenthoek Military Cemetery, 1¾ miles south-west of Poperinghe: Age 31. One of his officers wrote, 'We were very sorry to lose him as he was a good soldier, and popular with both officers and men.' He *m.* St. Mary's Parish Church, Stockport, 4 August 1909; Elizabeth Hannah (5, Mahood Street, Edgeley, Stockport), *dau.* of William Jackson (& Elizabeth Ann) Downs, and had five children – Nora, *b.* 26 May 1911; Philip & Doris (twins), *b.* 24 April 1913; Margaret, *b.* 18 December 1915; Vera, *b.* 7 October 1917 (five days after the death of her father).

Until The Day Break And The Shadows Flee Away

(XXV.E.12) Spr. 146183, Joseph Armitage, 95th Field Coy., Royal Engineers: 2nd *s.* of William Armitage, Gamekeeper; of 'The Coppice Cottage,' Poynton, nr. Stockport, co. Chester, by his wife Annie, *dau.* of Thomas Bennett: *b.* Poynton, 4 November 1893: *educ.* Poynton Church School: Occupation – Joiner: enlisted 7 February 1916: served with the Expeditionary Force in France and Flanders from 20 July following, and died No.2 Canadian Clearing Station, 1 October 1917, from wounds (S.W. head, buttocks, abdomen) received in action at Polygon Wood the previous day (30 September). Buried in the Military Cemetery at Lyssenthoek: Age 24. *unm.* Remembered on Poynton War Memorial.

The Dearly Loved Son Of William And Annie Armitage,
Boynton, Cheshire
Thy Will Be Done

(XXV.F.2) 2nd Lieut. Theodore Milton Pflaum, 25th Coy., Australian Machine Gun Corps, A.I.F.: *s.* of Theodor (& Mary Jane) Pflaum, of Birdwood (Blumberg), South Australia: and elder brother to Pte. 161, R.H. Pflaum, 32nd Australian Infantry, severely wounded/believed died in enemy hands, 19 July 1916, at Fromelles: *b.* Birdwood, September 1895: *educ.* Birdwood High School: Occupation – Clerk: previously served Senior Cadets; Machine Gun Sect. 79th Inf., enlisted Keswick, 16 July 1915, assigned 32nd Battn.: departed Adelaide, 19 November: trained Egypt, 16 December – 16 June 1917 (promoted Corpl. 1 June): served in France and Flanders from the 23rd of the latter month; promoted Sergt. 1 September: transf'd. 25th A.M.G.C., February 1917: trained for, and obtained, a commission, England; returned to France, 7 September. Severely wounded (S.W., shrapnel, Lt. thigh, compound fracture of) while supervising the sending forward of supplies and ammunition from St. James' trench, Battle of the Menin Road, 24 September 1917, died shortly thereafter en-route to No.10 C.C.S. Poperinghe: Age 22. *unm.*

Loved Son Of T & M J Pflaum Of Birdwood, South Australia

His brother Raymond, commemorated on the Villers-Bretonneux Memorial, is buried in Fromelles (Pheasant Wood) Military Cemetery (I.B.11).

(XXV.G.2) Pte. 10/3067, Thomas Henry Reynish, 1st Bn. Wellington Regt., N.Z.E.F.: c/o H.D. Buchanan, Gisborne: *s.* of the late George Crowther Reynish, by his marriage to Avis Jane Le Brun, *née* Reynish, *née* Giles (Greymouth, Westland): and brother to Tpr. 7/1887, A.F. Reynish, Canterbury Mounted Rifles (surv'd.); Pte. 1989, R.S. Reynish, Australian Infantry, died 3 July 1921; and Pte. 10/3066, R.C. Reynish, Wellington Regt., killed in action, 30 November 1917: *b.* Geraldine, New Zealand, 1891: enlisted 17 June 1915; departed Wellington, 7th Rfts., 9 October 1915: served at Egypt, thereafter (April 1916) proceeded to join the Expeditionary Force in France and Flanders. Pte. Reynish died of a self-inflicted wound (S.I.W.); Suicide, shot himself through the forehead with his rifle – Mill Camp, 19.45 hrs., 30 September 1917: Age 26. *unm.* All correspondence regarding the deceased should be addressed c/o J. Reynish, Esq., Little River, Canterbury. (*IWGC record 20 September*)

His brother Robert is buried in Christchurch (Bromley) Cemetery (2.17.A); Roger has no known grave, he is commemorated on the Buttes New British Cemetery (New Zealand) Memorial.

War Diary, 2nd Canadian C.C.S. Remy: "29 September 1917. 8.00 p.m. Beautiful moonlit night and the air is alive with enemy aeroplanes which are dropping bombs all over the area. One has just passed over us, caught in the glare of the searchlights amid a shower of our anti-aircraft shells. The angry hum of their machines can be heard in the depths of the sky. One waits with a feeling of utter helplessness for the crash of bombs, and draws a sigh of relief when the sound of the machine recedes. Poperinghe seems to be the centre of the attack. No such raid has occurred in this area before. 9.15: Began admitting. The victims of the bomb raids are beginning to arrive. They are the worst mangled casualties one can imagine. Several have already died. Others will soon follow. 10.40: Completed admitting (110 Lying + 81 Sitting) 191. Of these, 96 were bomb casualties. The Resuscitation Ward is overflowing and such a mangled mass of humanity I have seldom, if ever, seen. 11.15: Evacuated 81."

"30 September 12.10 a.m. Another bombing plane over. Picked up by search lights and fled after dropping bombs near Poperinghe. Most of the casualties admitted are from camps around Poperinghe. Some bombs fell in a Chinese compound and the collies are 'hiking' down the rail tracks like mad. Our N.Y.D.N. cases are also in a sorry plight. 12.45: Another terrific bombing raid between here and Poperinghe. The machine was picked up by search-lights directly over our compound; turned back amidst a fusillade. 30 September 8.30 p.m. Enemy planes dropped bombs within 100 yards of officers and sisters quarters, which were splattered with falling debris. The crater was 8' deep x 15' in diameter. 9.00: Another plane passed in searchlights directly over our heads, bombs are falling all around the area especially to the north and west. The air is filled with the buzz of their machines, which have quite a distinctive 'double' hum. Full moonlight. 10.30: Continued bombing towards Ouderdom. It is impossible to keep our N.Y.D.N. cases in their tents; most of them (40–50) are over in a neighbouring field, taking shelter under some wheat stacks. 11.45: Began admitting. 12.00: Terrific fusillade of bombs close by. There have been 17 deaths from bomb wounds in this station in the last 24 hours." Signed Capt. J.E. Davey.

(XXV.G.7) Dvr. 13874, Hector Lawrence Brown, 'K' Supply Col., Australian Army Service Corps, A.I.F.: late *husb.* to Jessie Elinor Brown (66, Carlton Street, Carlton, Victoria): *b.* Fitzroy, August 1894: Occupation – Motor Transport Driver: previously served 12 months Junior Cadets, 3 months Citizen Forces, 15 months Guard Duty, 6 weeks A.I.F. (discharged 1914 – Unfit): re-joined A.I.F., Melbourne, 15 July 1916: departed Australia, A.7 'Medic,' 16 December: trained England from 18 February 1917: Awarded (22 March 1917) 168 hours Detention; Parkhouse – (1) Not complying with an order (2) Insolence to a N.C.O.: proceeded to France, 29 March: joined 1st Base M.T. Depot; subsequently detached (18 April) 6th Bde. Australian Field Artillery Park: Awarded (8 September) Forfeiture 7 Days Pay – 'When on Active Service, Absent without leave from 4 p.m. 4-8-17 until apprehended by the Military Police, 9 p.m., 4-8-17': Died of wounds (bomb, penet. abdominal & cranial) 1.20 p.m., 30 September 1917. A comrade Dvr. E.J. Bury, 1st M/T. Coy., reported, "...at Poperinghe, four of us, Brown, Hinds, Brewer and myself were walking in the streets of the town at about 8.30 p.m. The Huns planes came over and dropped bombs; we scattered for cover. In the morning we found Brown absent. We made enquiries and found at the C.C.S. that Brown had been carried there the previous night, and had died there from wounds caused by bombs. He was buried at the cemetery at the C.C.S. I did not see the grave...." And S/Sergt. Scanlan, "Brown was about 5′9″, hair – fair, eyes – grey, markings – gravel on arm, build – slight, between 10 and 11 stone, clean shaven, dark complexion, heavy eyebrows, teeth plate with one tooth missing right upper jaw, slightly knock-kneed."

(XXV.G.9) Major Power MacMurrough Maxwell, M.C., 'B' Bty., 95th Bde., Royal Field Artillery: *yr. s.* of the late Col. Robert James Maxwell, War Office Intelligence Branch; by his wife Harriet Fanny (Hampton Court Palace, Hampton Court), *dau.* of Col. W.A. Middleton, Deputy Adjutant-General Royal Artillery: *b.* The Walls, Hampton Court, 12 April 1892: *educ.* Bedford Grammar School: gazetted 2nd Lieut. R.F.A., 19 July 1912: promoted Major, November 1916: served with the Expeditionary Force in France and Flanders from August 1914, and died in No.10 Casualty Clearing Station, Poperinghe, 1 October 1917, from wounds received in action whilst reconnoitring for his battery position during the advance from Ypres. Buried in Lyssenthoek Military Cemetery, Poperinghe. Awarded the Military Cross (*London Gazette*, 3 June 1916) for 'gallant and distinguished service in the field,' and a Bar to the M.C. in July 1917, being also three times Mentioned in Despatches by F.M. Sir Douglas Haig: Age 25. *unm*.

(XXV.G.19A) Sergt. 207, George Mace, M.M., 16th Bn. Australian Infantry, A.I.F.: *s*. of James Mace, of King Street, Brimington, Chesterfield, co. Derby: Occupation – Farmer: joined A.I.F., Helena Vale, 9 September 1914: departed Melbourne, 22 December: served with the Expeditionary Force in France from 9 June 1916. Died of wounds (Shrapnel, abdominal; perf.), 22 October 1917: Age 31. Awarded the Military Medal "For bravery and gallant conduct on the night of the 10th – 11th April 1917. He volunteered for patrol duty in 'No Man's Land' prior to the attack on the Hindenburg Line near Reincourt. He patrolled 'No Man's Land' from our Outpost Lines to the line held by the enemy, on the night of the 9th – 10th April and secured valuable information. He accompanied several Officers up to the enemy's wires for the purpose of ascertaining to what extent they had to be cut by our Artillery fire, and in his patrol duties on that occasion displayed great enterprise and bravery. Again on the night of 10th – 11th April he assisted the Intelligence Officer in placing the jumping off tapes in 'No Man's Land.' Before dawn on the 11th April he rendered valuable assistance in guiding the several companies of the Battalion on to their jumping off tapes. On the morning of the 11th April after the attack had been launched he went out into a veritable hail of Machine gun bullets and attended to and assisted to bring in wounded men."

(XXV.H.8A) Pte. 6721, Evert Isidor Backman, 16th Bn. Australian Infantry, A.I.F.: late of Morgan Hills, Western Australia: *s*. of Erick Hendrick Backman, of Paskmark-by-Kristinestad, Finland, Russia, by his wife Selma Josephina: *b*. Kristinestad, 5 September 1880: Religion – Lutheran: emigrated to Australia, via South Africa, 1898: employee Lumber Industry, Western Australia: 5'9" tall, fair complexion, blue eyes, fair hair: enlisted Black Boy Hill, 5 July 1916: posted 22nd Rfts. 16th Battn. 4 September: departed Fremantle, 9 November, H.M.A.T. A.29 'Argyllshire': served with the Expeditionary Force in France, joining his battn. at Noreuil, 10 April 1917, and died in No.2 Canadian C.C.S. of wounds (Shrapnel, right thigh and chest penetration), 25 September 1917, received in action at Polygon Wood earlier the same day. Buried Lyssenthoek Military Cemetery, 1¾ miles south-west of Poperinghe: Age 37. *unm*. See account re. Pte. W.G. Averkoff, Messines Ridge British Cemetery (V.C.21).

(XXV.H.15) 2nd Lieut. Albert Edward Ballard, 42nd Bn. Australian Infantry, A.I.F.: 2nd *s*. of John Nelson Ballard, Boot Salesman; of 185, Kilburn Park Road, Paddington, London, W.2, by his wife Florence E.: *b*. Kilburn, London, N.W.6, 1889: Occupation – Railway Porter: enlisted Brisbane, 20 October 1915: served in France and Flanders from 12 July 1917, and died at Poperinghe, 19 October 1917, of abdominal gun-shot wounds received two weeks previously (3–4 October) when his battalion was heavily shelled and fired on as it approached its assembly position for the Battle of Broodseinde. Buried the same day in the Military Cemetery, Lyssenthoek: Age 28. He was married to Bertha May Ballard (Thistle Estate, Kedron, Brisbane, Queensland), to whom all correspondence should be addressed.

Thy Will Be Done

(XXV.H.27) Capt. Atherton Harold Chisenhale-Marsh, 9th (Queen's Royal) Lancers attd. 34th Divn. General Staff: *s.* of William Swaine Chisenhale-Marsh, of Gaynes Park, Theydon Gamon, Epping, co. Essex, by his wife Esther Eleanora Mary, eldest *dau.* of Edward Byrom, of Culver: and brother-in-law to Major A.D. Bell, 4th (Q.O.) Hussars, died 8 April 1918; and Lieut. H.C.M. Lucas, 2/2nd K.E.O Gurkha Rifles, killed in action, 2 November 1914, at Neuve Chapelle: *b.* Theydon Gamon, 20 August 1883. Killed 28 September 1918, by a shell which fell whilst he was proceeding on the road from Wytschaete to Ypres: Age 35. He *m.* 1914, Lorna, *dau.* of Capt. Francis Charrington, of Pishiobury Park, Sawbridgeworth. Inscribed 'Who Died Far From Here Before Their Time, But As Soldiers And For Their Country,' Capt. Chisenhale-Marsh and his brothers-in-law are three of 27 men recorded on the Theydon Gamnon Church War Memorial; a brass plaque to both his and Major Bell's memory is sited in the nave.

Major Bell is buried in Blargies Communal Cemetery Extension (I.C.3); Lieut. Lucas has no known grave, he is commemorated on the Neuve Chapelle Memorial

(XXV.J.9A) Bdsmn. 9760, James Francis Basil Adkins, 3rd (Reserve) attd. 2nd Bn. (12th Foot) The Suffolk Regt.: 2nd *s.* of James Edward Adkins, Mus. Bac., F.R.C.O., Organist, Preston Parish Church; of 30, Bairstow Street, Preston, Lancashire, by his wife Louisa, *dau.* of the late William R. Day (former Governor of Millbank): *b.* Preston, 4 April 1898: *educ.* Preston Grammar School, and St. Paul's Cathedral Choir School: apptd. Chorister; St. Paul's Cathedral when 10 years of age, 1908, becoming their soloist 1911–14. On his voice breaking he was awarded the Merchant Taylor's Musical Scholarship by the Dean and Chapter of St. Paul's: studied to become Organist, under his father, and at the same time acted as Organist of Christ Church, Preston: enlisted May 1916, for the express purpose of becoming a Line Bandmaster: served with the Expeditionary Force in France and Flanders from early May 1917. Wounded 29 September during an enemy air raid while acting as stretcher-bearer with 7th Field Ambulance at Ypres, and died, 1 October 1917, No.17 Casualty Clearing Station. His Adjutant wrote, " He was a great loss to the battn., did fine work during the operations as a stretcher-bearer, and everyone spoke highly of his devotion to duty." He was awarded the King George V Coronation Medal for singing at the Coronation, Westminster Abbey, June 1911: Age 19.

He Sang God's Praises In St. Paul's Choir 1908 1914

Plot 26, A to H lies adjacent to AA to HH.
(XXVI.A.1) Pte. 532362, John Brown, 12th Canadian Field Ambulance, Canadian Army Medical Corps, C.E.F.: 4th *s.* of the late Hamilton Brown, Coal Master; by his wife Jane (Garrell House, Kilsyth, Glasgow), *dau.* of Alexander Cullen: *b.* Kilsyth, co. Stirling, 27 March 1891: *educ.* Kilsyth Academy, and Glasgow High School: apprenticed as Farmer; went to Canada, 1911, with the intention of gaining experience; took a farm and settled there: enlisted Winnipeg, 31 May 1916; came to England with 12th Canadian Field Ambulance, August following: proceeded to France, and died No.17 Casualty Clearing Station, 24 November 1917, from wounds received at Passchendaele Ridge on the 15th. Buried in the Military Cemetery, Poperinghe: Age 27. *unm.*

Greater Love Hath No Man

(XXVI.A.2A) Pte. 267397, Fred Chapman, 'A' Coy., 1/6th Bn. The Duke of Wellington's (West Riding) Regt.: *s.* of A. (& Mrs) Chapman, of 9, Victoria Terrace, Bradley, Keighley, co. York: *b.* Bradley, *c.*1892: enlisted Crosshills, 1 March 1916: proceeded to France, July following, and died 24 November 1917, of wounds: Age 29. *unm.* Chaplain J.A. Townson, No.17 C.C.S., wrote, "It is with deep regret and sympathy I send you the sad news of the death of your son, Pte. F. Chapman, West Riding Regt. He received shell wounds in right arm and both legs, and was admitted on the 23rd inst. to this Casualty Clearing Station, where he passed away at 11 a.m. on the 24th inst. He was buried in the cemetery near. I pray that in your loss and sorrow you may be comforted of God our Heavenly Father, and may confide in him your refuge and strength and present help in trouble." On the day of his being fatally wounded, Pte. Chapman had been two days returned from leave.

There Is No Death, Love Lives For Ever

(XXVI.A.6A) Rfn. S/26587, Edward Aslett, 2nd Bn. The Prince Consort's Own (The Rifle Brigade): formerly R/27411, King's Royal Rifle Corps: late *husb.* to Margaret Aslett (53, Catherine Street, Tidal Basin, London): *b.* Goodmayes, co. Essex, 1881: enlisted Canning Town. Died of wounds, 25 November 1917, received at Cambrai: Age 36.

Greater Love Than This Hath No Man
He Died For Us

(XXVI.A.9) Bmdr. 107925 Francis 'Frank' Edward Hall, 'D' Bty., 311th Bde., Royal Field Artillery: *s*. of Helen Hall (Avington, Winchester): and cousin to Pte. 10634, E.G. Hall, 1st Hampshire Regt., killed in action, 26 April 1915, aged 22; and Pte. 45014, S.H. Hall, died 6 October 1918, aged 19: *b*. Alresford, co. Hants: enlisted Winchester. Died of wounds, 27 November 1917: Age 20. Six men of Avington gave their lives in the Great War; they are remembered on the war memorial situated in the village (St. Mary's) churchyard.

God Chooses Those He Loves The Best

His cousin Edward has no known grave, he is commemorated on the Ypres (Menin Gate) Memorial (Panel 35); Sidney is commemorated in Cross Roads Cemetery, Fontaine-Au-Bois (Landrecies Com.Cem.Mem.21).

(XXVI.A.14) Spr. 636250, Thomas Wilson Deremo, 3rd Tunnelling Coy., Canadian Engineers, C.E.F.: *s*. of George (& Nellie) Deremo, of Trenton, Ontario: *b*. Consecon, Prince Edward Co., Ontario, 9 January 1897: Religion – Methodist: Occupation – Labourer: joined C.E.F., Wellington, 8 January 1916; apptd. 155th (Overseas) Bn., 10 January; apptd. 4th Pioneers, 27 June: transf'd. 3rd Tunnelling Coy., France. Wounded, 17 November 1917, by a gas shell, while on a ration party on the Menin Road at Birr Cross Roads. Admitted 2/2nd East Lancashire Field Ambulance, transf'd. 2nd Canadian C.C.S. Poperinghe the same day, and died nine days later (26 November) from the effects of mustard gas poisoning: Age 20. (*IWGC record age 19*)

When Pte. John Cheesewright, 2/9th Manchester Regt., arrived in the Salient in October 1917 it was a desolate, shell-pitted bog contaminated by mustard gas and decomposing bodies. On 8 November the battalion moved up from their bivouacs at Ypres for their part in 198th Brigade's attack at Poelcapelle. Unremitting heavy rain had created a quagmire and, under the weight of battle equipment, many men sank into the mud as they tried to reach their assembly position. In the inky blackness, they made painfully slow progress along narrow tracks already torn up by pack animals, while shell storms burst around them. Despite orders forbidding them to stop for any reason, frequent halts, made to rescue men blown off the slime-covered duckboards into the waterlogged waste, put them hopelessly behind schedule, forcing the battalion to abandon this work and slog onward with the pitiful cries of comrades drowning in mud filled shell-holes going unheeded.

After eleven hours, struggling through driving rain, knee deep in mud – for the final two miles there were no tracks at all – the Manchesters reached their jumping-off lines. At 5.20am, 9 October, barely able to see their feeble barrage, let alone follow it, the Manchesters attacked with every movement pitilessly observed by the enemy on the Passchendaele Ridge. What followed rapidly descended into tragic chaos as German artillery and machine-gun fire picked them off.

By the end of the Battle of Poelcapelle 2/9th Manchesters casualties numbered 18 officers and 322 men. The four territorial battalions of the Lancashire Fusiliers counted 307 dead, of whom 247 have no known grave. Though the Canadians went on to liberate Passchendaele on 6 November, when they got there they found the dead bodies of Lancastrians from the 66th Division who, on 9 October, had fought their way through, in ever-dwindling numbers. Relieved by the Anzacs in the early hours of 10 October, the ravaged Manchesters struggled back to a camp in the vicinity of Vlamertinghe. Lieut. Wilfred Owen wrote to his mother: "I have suffered seventh hell...the ground was an octopus of sucking clay...I allow myself to tell you all these things because I am never going back to this awful post. It is the worst the Manchesters have ever held."

John Cheesewright also wrote home, but neither of his surviving letters give the slightest indication of what he had been through. In a letter to his mother, Floretta, from their training base 4 November, fretting about not having heard from his wife, hoped "Father's knee will soon be quite well again," and added, "Parcels will be very acceptable. Any sort of tobacco will do. Thick socks are also very useful." One week later, from a dugout in Ypres that was under constant artillery bombardment and where 10 of his comrades were killed or wounded, he apologetically wrote, "I know I don't let you have a letter as often as I should like to, but we have to write under such disadvantageous conditions that letter-writing is horrible." Disadvantageous conditions! Life above ground in Ypres was virtually impossible and below ground squalid beyond imagination, yet he assured his mother, "I am quite well so far." By the time this assurance reached her he was dead.

2/9th Manchesters returned to the front on 19 November; the Passchendaele offensive was over but the shelling and killing continued unabated and on 28 November, a day for which the Battalion War Diary simply records, 'No special activity,' a dawn strafe near Zonnebeke severely wounded Pte. Cheesewright, twelve of his comrades were killed outright.

(XVI.A.20A) Pte. 53310, John Francis Cheesewright, 2/9th Bn. The Manchester Regt. (T.F.): formerly no.48320, North Staffordshitre Regt.: 4th *s*. of Joseph Cheesewright, of Boston, co. Lincoln, Manager, National & Provincial Union Bank of England, by his wife Floretta, *dau*. of the late John Meech, of Blandford, co. Dorset: *b*. North Ormesby, co. York, 15 November 1877: *educ*. Moulton, and Boston Grammar Schools: Occupation – Bank Accountant: enlisted Ferry Hill, Co. Durham, June 1917: served with the Expeditionary

Force in France and Flanders from 11 October, and died at No.3 Canadian Casualty Clearing Station, 29 November 1917, from wounds received in the Zonnebeke sector the previous day: Age 40. He *m.* at Spennymoor, Co. Durham, June 1917, Jane Ann 'Jennie' Watson (43, Clyde Terrace, Spennymoor), *dau.* of the late Thomas Farthing, of Whitley Bay, co. Northumberland. *s.p.* In a letter to his wife Nurse Annie Coulter, No 3 Canadian C.C.S., said her husband had been brought in, wounded but in a 'fair' condition, and had asked her to write and send his love. The Regimental Chaplain wrote of Pte Cheesewright's cheerfulness, but was unable to disguise the truth that both his legs had been shattered and he had died in the night after what must have been a double amputation. "Afterwards he seemed to have lost his strength for he sank very rapidly and died peacefully in two hours, hardly, I think, being conscious." And his Officer, K. Lund, wrote, "He was hit about dawn on the morning of the 28th, his left foot being blown off by a shell splinter. There was a very heavy strafe on at the time, but he was attended to immediately and sent down to the dressing station on a stretcher."

Recquiescat In Pace

In May 1923 Pte. Cheesewight's two sisters, Hilda and Mabel, visited their brother's grave and sent a sepia coloured postcard showing the hundreds of rows of simple wooden crosses at Lijssenthoek home to his widow Jennie. Hilda had a G.R.U. photograph of his grave, she wrote, "We found it looking very lovely. Much nicer than on this card. We tried to get some photos of it as it looked but couldn't. We are having a lovely time." Almost ninety years would pass before he again received the comfort of a family member's visit. His great-niece Elizabeth Grice visited in 2007; her account of this was published in *The Telegraph*, 16 June 2007.

(XXVI.B.1) Pte. 18611, Henry Ward, 10th (Service) Bn. The Gloucestershire Regt.: *b.* Nancegollan, nr. Helston, co. Cornwall, 1878: enlisted Cheltenham: served with the Expeditionary Force in France and Flanders. Wounded (G.S.W. cranial, Lt. knee) in the Kronprinz Farm sector, 18 November 1917; died in the hospital at Poperinghe, almost two weeks later, 30 November 1917, and was buried in the soldiers cemetery at Remy Siding: Age 39. He was married to Louisa Ward (50, Queen Street, Cheltenham).

(XXVI.B.6) Gnr. 92711, Donald Bears, 1st Siege Bty., Canadian Garrison Artillery, C.E.F.: *s.* of Benjamin Bears, of Brooklyn, Prince Edward Island, by his wife Mary, *née* Compton: *b.* 29 April 1882: Religion – Methodist: Occupation – Farmer: 5'6¾" tall, brown eyes, dark brown hair: enlisted Charlottetown, 23 September 1915, proceeded overseas, 11 October. Died of heart failure (myocardial infarction), 30 November 1917: Age 24. He leaves a wife Mabel

Bears, *née* Bradford, to whom he had been married for but a short time prior to his departure for France.

It Is Sweet And Honourable To Die For One's Country

After a difficult and protracted relief over two nights (26–27 November 1917) New Zealand Rifle Brigade were removed from the Zonnebeke sector and, after moving back into camps near Dickebusch, became Division Reserve providing large working parties under the direction of the Divisional Salvage Officer. Scattered over the entire Divisional area was an incredible quantity of valuable material of all kinds, such as rifles, machine-guns, harness, wagons and limbers; cartridges, bombs, shell-cases and live shells of all calibres; coils of barbed-wire, stakes and tools; discarded clothing and web-equipment – the flotsam and jetsam of recent battles. Every officer and man moving towards the rear from any part of the area was expected to carry back to special dumps at least one article of equipment or clothing salvaged from the mud of the Salient. This, indeed, was a standing order, but so framed as to make obedience a point of honour. The Divisional commander set the example by carrying out his own orders to the letter, and, serving as a prick to the conscience if one should be careless or forgetful, there were staring posters everywhere on lorries and buildings asking the pointed question, "What Have You Salved Today?" How thoroughly the work was done may be judged from the statements published from time to time, that for the week ending 30th November giving the estimated value of stores salvaged by the Division at £141,768. Unfortunately, the saving was not without cost.

(XXVI.B.8) L/Corpl. 25/180, Leonard Aubrey Gudgin, 'B' Coy., 3rd Bn. 3rd New Zealand Rifle Brigade, N.Z.E.F.: *s.* of Frederic (& Florence Annie) Gudgin, of 'Wigton,' Julian's Road, Wimborne, co. Dorset: *b.* 113, Sydenham Road, Croydon, co. Surrey, 1890: Occupation – Sheep Farmer: enlisted 20 October 1915: departed Wellington, 5 February 1916; trained Egypt, thereafter proceeded to France and died of wounds, 1 December 1917, received while attached Divisional Salvage Dept.: Age 27. *unm.*

(XXVI.B.17) Pte. 45998, Julian Anthony Christophers, 1st Bn. Canterbury Regt., N.Z.E.F.: *s.* of Anthony Christophers, of 258, Tweed Street, Invercargill, New Zealand, by his wife Juliet Mary: and brother to Capt. 24/7, H.H. Christophers, 2nd Bn. 3rd N.Z. Rifle Brigade, died of wounds, 2 June 1916; 2nd Lieut. 60286, R.G. Christophers, 1st Otago Regt., killed in action, 13 October 1918; and Tpr. 9/549, V.J. Christopher, Otago Mounted Rifles, killed in action, 31 May 1915, at Gallipoli: departed Wellington, 26 April 1917: served in France from 5 August; wounded by machine-gun fire, back and abdomen, died 5 December 1917, No.10 Casualty Clearing Station the same day: Age 33.

He leaves a wife, Earle F. Christophers (7, Rossmore Crescent, Wellington). One of four brothers who fell.

His brother Herbert is buried in Cité Bon Jean Military Cemetery, Armentieres (I.B.7); Reginald, Beaulencourt British Cemetery (I.B.1); and Victor, No.2 Outpost Cemetery (A.7).

(XXVI.B.20A) Pte. 38733, Bernard McQuillan, 2nd Bn. Auckland Regt., N.Z.E.F.: *s.* of the late Peter McQuillan, of Leagh, Ballybay, Co. Monaghan, Ireland, by his wife Kate (Wairiki Road, Mount Eden, Auckland): and brother to Pte. 12/1479, A.W. McQuillan, Auckland Regt., died in Egypt, 7 May 1915, of wounds received in action at Gallipoli: Occupation – Telegraph Lineman: enlisted Auckland, 9 October 1916; proceeded overseas, 13 February 1917. Died 5 December 1917, of wounds (G.S. cranial) received in action before Passchendaele on the 3rd.: Age 35. Correspondence should be addressed c/o his uncle, John McQuillan, Post Office, Matamata, New Zealand.

His brother Arthur is buried in Alexandria (Chatby) Military And War Memorial Cemetery (C.158).

(XXVI.D.4) Pte. 267712, Arthur Foster, 1/6th Bn. The Duke of Wellington's (West Riding) Regt. (T.F.): *s.* of M.A. Foster, of Cockshott Fold, Addingham, co. York: *b.* Addingham, 1879: Occupation – Carter; Addingham Co-operative Society: enlisted Keighley, 26 August 1916: served with the Expeditionary Force in France, and died of wounds (multiple fractures both legs), New Year's Eve, 31 December 1917, received in action on the night of the 29th – 30th.: Age 38. He was married to Edith Foster (109, School Bridge, Addingham, Ilkley), and had two children. In a letter to his wife his commanding officer said that her husband, after having both his legs broken, had been treated in the field almost immediately before being removed to the Casualty Clearing Station where, despite the best possible attention, he succumbed to his injuries the following day. Recently returned to duty after a period of hospitalisation due to trench foot, he had been expected home at Christmas; he had been allocated leave commencing 2 January 1918.

Rest After Strife

(XXVI.E.2) Pte. 307808, Fred Lightowler, 1/7th Bn. The Duke of Wellington's (West Riding) Regt. (T.F.): *s.* of David Lightowler, of Low Moor, Bradford, co. York, by his wife Sarah Jane: late *husb.* to Florrie Lightowler (25, Worthing Head Road, Wyke, Bradford): enlisted Bradford. Died of wounds, 17 March 1918: Age 24. See also (IV.B.27).

He Rests In God's Beautiful Garden In The Sunshine Of A Perfect Day

It is well documented that during both World Wars British soldiers often encountered German soldiers who in happier times had resided and worked in England. An infantry officer, Lieut. J.D. Wyatt, tells of an incident which befell a patrol: "A Bedford patrol went out and very bravely crawled close to the German barbed wire. After a long time spent listening the patrol were just about to make their way back when a German voice, in impeccable English, said, "If you don't go away soon, we really shall have to shoot you." Understandably the patrol hastily withdrew. Back in the British lines this incident would probably have been elaborated on and exaggerated by the participants of the patrol, and no doubt raised a few smiles. Similarly, Fred Germany, probably nicknamed 'Fritz,' 'Wilhelm' or perhaps even 'Kaiser' would probably have been subjected to a good deal of leg-pulling by his mates, and raised more than a few smiles. No doubt those same mates mourned his passing when, after being severely wounded in the face and back while on patrol, 18 March 1918, the following day he was simply recorded as '1 O.R. died of wounds.'

(XXVI.E.4) L/Corpl. 28095, Frederick William Germany, 6th (Service) Bn. The Bedfordshire Regt.: *s.* of Thomas Germany, of Stow Bridge, co. Norfolk, by his wife Sarah Ann: *b.* Stow Bardolph, co. Norfolk, 1896. Died of wounds (twisted spine, G.S.W. facial), No.10 Casualty Clearing Station, Remy Siding, 19 March 1918, received in action the previous day. Buried there: Age 21. *unm.*

(XXVI.E.12) Pte. 202261, Frank Hewitt, 1/4th Bn. The Duke of Wellington's (West Riding) Regt. (T.F.): *s.* of William E. Hewitt, of 19, Halifax Lane, Luddenden, Yorkshire, by his wife Emma: employee Messrs Law & Crossley, Halifax; a member of St. James Church, Luddenden, and Secretary of the Sunday School there. His parents received a letter from the chaplain notifying them of his death; it stated that he died in Number 10 Casualty Clearing Station after having been badly burnt and blinded by gas. Buried there: 2 April 1918: Age 24.

(XXVI.E.17A) Pte. 39859, James McNelis, 5th (Service) Bn. (Pioneers) The South Wales Borderers: formerly no.4053, Monmouthshire Regt.: 3rd *s.* of Patrick McNelis, Labourer; of 172, Brook Street, Birkenhead, by his wife Mary Jane, *dau.* of the late James McCunningham: *b.* Newtowncunningham, Co. Donegal, 15 November 1891: *educ.* Our Lady's School, Birkenhead: Occupation – Metal Dealer: enlisted South Wales Borderers, 16 March 1916: served with the Expeditionary Force in France and Flanders from 6 September of the same year, and died at No.2 Canadian Casualty Clearing Station, Poperinghe 12 April 1918, of wounds received in action west of Ypres. Buried in the Military Cemetery, Lyssenthoek: Age 28. *unm.* (*IWGC record 11 April*)

R.I.P.

(XXVI.F.10A) Pte. 42405, Richard Henry Stevens, 2nd Bn. (67th Foot) The Hampshire Regt.: *s.* of Thomas Henry Stevens, Farm Labourer; of 'Perrandowns,' Goldsithney, Marazion, co. Cornwall: *b.* St. Hilary, co. Cornwall, 26 October 1899: *educ.* St. Hilary Board School: enlisted Hampshire Regt., Penzance, 28 February 1917: served with the Expeditionary Force in France and Flanders, and died 13 April 1918 of wounds received in action. Buried in St. Bartholomew's British Military Cemetery, Lyssenthoek, west of Poperinghe: Age 18. (*IWGC record age 19*)

(XXVI.F.20A) Spr. 526225, Frank Cowell, 94th Field Coy., Royal Engineers: formerly no.42332, King's Own (Yorkshire Light Infantry): T/3097, Royal Fusiliers: *s.* of Matilda Cowell (136, St. Leonard's Road, Far-Cotton, Northampton): and brother to Pte. 305220, T.G. Cowell, Royal Air Force, died of influenza at Blandford Camp, co. Dorset, 30 October 1918, aged 24; Pte. 55280, G. Cowell, 2nd Northamptonshire Regt., killed in action, 23 October 1918, aged 19; and Sergt. 5289, P. Cowell, 59th Machine Gun Corps, died of wounds, 9 February 1918: *b.* Hardingstone, Northampton, 1897. Died of wounds, 14 April 1918: Age 21. One of four brothers who fell.

> *Not Dead To Those Who Loved Him*
> *Not Lost But Gone Before*
> Mother

His brothers Thomas and George are buried in Towcester Road Cemetery, Northampton (446.4.17325), and Valenciennes (St. Roch) Communal Cemetery (II.D.28) respectively. Percy is buried nearby (XXVII.FF.12A).

(XXVI.H.7) Dvr. T4/124243, Alfredo Henry Duff, Army Service Corps, posted 2nd Field Survey Coy., Royal Engineers: *s.* of John Duff, of Savana Grande, Trinidad: and brother to Pte. 144504, A.J. Duff, 87th Canadian Infantry, killed in action, 16 November 1917: *b.* Princes Town: enlisted 16th Rifle Brigade: served with the Expeditionary Force in the Balkans (from August 1915), France and Flanders, and died 11 April 1918, of wounds.

His brother Arthur has no known grave; he is commemorated on the Ypres (Menin Gate) Memorial (Panel 30).

(XXVI.AA.7) Dvr. 2114933, Cecil William Gardiner, 2nd Reserve Park, Canadian Army Service Corps, C.E.F.: 2nd *s.* of the late James Gardiner, of 95, Wellsway, Bath, by his wife Mary Rachel (8, Devonshire Villas, Bath, co. Somerset), *dau.* of Alfred B. Barnett: *b.* 3, Malvern Villas, Camden Road, Bath, 24 February 1891: *educ.* High School, Weston-super-Mare, and Technical School, Bath: removed to Canada, 1910, and took up farming, subsequently owning a farm of his own in Monitor, Alberta: joined C.E.F., Calgary, 15 December 1916; apptd. Dvr., Canadian Army Service Corps, 22 January 1917:

returned to England with the Contingent early in the same year: served with the Expeditionary Force in France from 10 August following, and died 29 November 1917, of wounds (S.W. back; penet.) received in action the previous day. On 28 November 1917, a party sent out to attempt to salvage wagon No.50, on the Zonnebeke-Westhoek road, found it had been completely demolished by shellfire during the night of the 27th. On the return journey the party was caught in a bombardment and the road was heavily shelled. Dvr. Gardiner was seriously wounded and one of his horses, wounded, bolted and was lost. Buried in the Military Cemetery, Lyssenthoek, nr. Poperinghe. He was highly commended by his Commanding Officer for his courage and devotion to duty: Age 26. *unm.* Remembered on the War Memorial, Royal Victoria Park, Bath.

(XXVI.AA.7) Pte. 352577, William Dawbarn, 2/9th Bn. The Manchester Regt. (T.F.): *s.* of Albert Yelverton Dawbarn, M.A., of 31, Argyll Street, Birkenhead, by his wife Edith Annie, *dau.* of John Elliott, of Thakenham: *b.* Thakenham, co. Sussex, 19 February 1899: *educ.* At Home: Occupation – Hotel Assistant: joined Manchester Regt., Birkenhead, co. Chester, 13 May 1916: served with the Expeditionary Force in France and Flanders from March 1917, and died in Lyssenthoek Military Hospital, 30 November 1917, of penetrating wounds to the chest received in action from machine-gun fire. Buried in the hospital cemetery: Age 18.

(XXVI.BB.8) Pte. 46776, Patrick O'Rourke, 3rd Bn. Otago Regt., N.Z.E.F.: late of Tuturau, Mataura: *s.* of Michael O'Rourke, of Gore, Southland, Invercargill: and brother to Pte. 9/1343, S.W. O'Rourke, Otago Regt., killed in action 12 October 1917: Occupation – Farmer: departed Wellington, HMNZT 83 'Tofua,' 26 April 1917. Died 6 December 1917, of wounds (G.S. cranial; penetrating): Age 30.

His brother Stephen has no known grave, he is commemorated on the Tyne Cot (New Zealand) Memorial (Panel 3).

(XXVI.BB.8A) L/Corpl. 13022, Alexander Hyland, 1st Bn. 3rd New Zealand Rifle Brigade, N.Z.E.F.: *s.* of Julia Hyland (73, Havelock Street, Ashburton, New Zealand): and brother to Sergt. 6/1319, 4th Bn. 3rd N.Z. Rifle Brigade, died of wounds, 6 October 1918: Occupation – Labourer: enlisted, 15 December 1915: departed Wellington, 6 May 1916: proceeded to France, 20 August following. Died 6 December 1917, of wounds (Lt. leg and foot, Rt. hand) received from machine-gun fire: Age 27.

His brother Francis is buried in Caudry British Cemetery (IV.A.9).

(XXVI.BB.11A) Pte. 42230, George Alfred Thornton, 1st Bn. Wellington Regt., N.Z.E.F.: *s.* of George William Thornton, by his marriage to the late Margaret Thornton: enlisted 4 November 1916: departed Wellington, 2 April 1917: proceeded to France, 6 July following. Died of wounds, 6 December 1917, received in action: Age 29. Erected by the residents of Maungakaramea,

Whangerai, Pte. Thornton is one of twelve local men remembered on what was the first war memorial in northern New Zealand.

(XXVI.CC.9A) Spr. 18752, Edwin Leonard Bowden, 5th N.Z. Railway Troops, Light Railway Op. Serv., New Zealand Engineers, N.Z.E.F.: late of 30, Picton Street, Ponsonby: *s.* of John Henry Bowden, of 22, Tivoli Street, Cheltenham, co. Gloucester, by his wife Elizabeth: and brother to Pte. G.W. Bowden, Gloucestershire Regt. (surv'd.); and Sergt. L. Bowden, South Lancashire Regt. (surv'd.): *b.* Cheltenham, 14 September 1894: *educ.* Christchurch School: Occupation – Grocer's Assistant: enlisted Trentham, 5 April 1916: departed Wellington, 26 July; 15th Rfts. 'A' Coy, Auckland Regt.: proceeded to France, 20 December; served with the Expeditionary Force there and in Flanders, Wounded (G.S.W., shoulder, wrist) at the Battle of Messines, June 1917 and evacuated to England (also required treatment for trench feet and influenza); returned to France where, due to the nature of his previous wounds, he was unable to continue further active service and transf'd. N.Z. Light Railway Op. Serv. and, after accidentally being run over by a motor vehicle on which he was working on 13 December 1917, died of his injuries, 17 January 1918, at Poperinghe: Age 23. *unm.* He is remembered on the Cheltenham Borough War Memorial, and (St. Stephen's Church) Roll of Honour.

Nephritis is one of the highest causes of human death. Commonly caused by auto-immune diseases which affect the major organs; it can also be caused by prolonged periods of marching, severe physical exertion and abnormal stress, all factors associated with life in the trenches. To these, due to the unsanitary conditions in which men were forced to live must be added one of the biggest, and under the circumstances most likely causes – bacterial or viral infection of the urinary tract. Whatever the disorder's cause, it invariably leads to inflammation of the kidneys which in turn leads to reduced blood flow, reduced urine output and retention of waste products. As the kidneys inflame, they begin to excrete needed protein from the body into the urine stream, one of these is the protein which stops blood from clotting. The loss of this protein will bring about a sudden fatal stroke.

(XXVI.CC.10) Rfn. 13719, William Almond, 'F' Coy., 2nd Bn. 3rd N.Z. Rifle Brigade: late of Millers Point, Wellington: *s.* of the late Thomas Almond, of 44, Salisbury Road, Preston, co. Lancashire, England, by his wife Jane (9, Lauderdale Street, Preston): *b.* 22 January 1883: Occupation – Labourer: enlisted Trentham, 7 March 1916; posted 'F' Coy. 14th Rfts. (Inf.): departed Wellington, 26 June 1916; 8th Rfts. 'F' Coy., 2nd N.Z.R.B.: disembarked Devonport, 22 August: served with the Expeditionary Force in France, and died of nephritis, 16 January 1918: Age 34. (*IWGC record age 35*)

Numerous accounts regarding the high-ranking staff-officers and Generals of the British Army in the Great War refer to them as 'butchers and bunglers' and the troops under their command – 'lions led by donkeys.' Indeed, the commonly held conception of the British Generals is one of men who, despite the lessons of past experience and a blatant refusal to learn from them, were convinced large scale frontal attacks were the only way to win the war. Obsessed with killing as many Germans as possible, regardless of how many of their own troops would be slaughtered in the process.

The British General of the day is invariably envisaged as an elderly, grey, overweight, handle-bar moustached, pompous, bumbling, ex-cavalryman, dressed in breeches and boots, quaffing copious quantities of port or sherry, punctuating every sentence with 'I Say Old Man!, Absolutely Spiffing!, Don't you know!, Top Ho!, Jolly Fine Show!, What!' and numerous other totally inane and meaningless remarks; seemingly at every possible opportunity. Comfortably ensconced in their Chateaux miles behind the lines, dining on gourmet foodstuffs, totally oblivious to the miserable existence the men in the trenches were enduring, the 'donkeys' whiled away their time devising, planning more ways by which they could send men across machine-gun and artillery-swept expanses of open ground, through impenetrable and unbroken belts of barbed wire – which for some strange reason their own artillery had once again failed to destroy – enter the enemy trenches where any German belligerent enough to put up or show the slightest resistance would be quickly and soundly dealt with and the war would be over.

Sadly, despite these conceptions being based on misinformation, greatly exaggerated and biased opinion, they have nonetheless been widely accepted by many as the truth. In reality General staff officers were highly trained, extremely competent and experienced men, totally cognisant of the ever changing tactics the war demanded, and mindful of the lessons and suffering past experienced. Frequent visitors to the front-line for the purpose of observing conditions there for themselves, they regularly commanded from the front, led by example and a great many of them paid the ultimate price.

(XXVI.FF.1) Brigdr.General Robert Clements Gore, C.B., C.M.G., 1st Bn. (91st Foot) The Princess Louise's (Argyll & Sutherland Highlanders); Comdg. 101st Inf. Bde., 34th Divn.: Mentioned in Despatches: 2nd *s.* of Nathaniel Gore, of Clifton, Bristol, co. Gloucester, by his 3rd wife Frances Louisa, only *dau.* of Samuel Page, of Hadley House, Barnet, London, E., and Louisa Wallis, his spouse: *b.* Clifton, 3 February 1867: *educ.* Haileybury (Melville, 1880–83): served in the South African Campaign; Dum Dum, India (from 13 December 1912); France from 20 December 1914, and was killed in action, 14 April 1918, nr. Fleurbaix: Age 51. He *m.* 1899, Rachel Cecilia Gore (27, Lowndes Street, Belgrave Square, London, S.W.1), 3rd *dau.* of the late Llewellyn Traherne Bassett-Saunderson, of Kingstown, Co. Dublin, and his wife Lady Rachel Mary Scott (Dromkeen House, Co. Cavan), and leaves one child, Adrian Clements

Gore (mistakenly thought to have been still-born and put aside for burial until a nurse noticed he was, in fact, alive), *b*. 14 May 1900. (*IWGC record 13 April, age 50*)

> *In Loving Memory Of My Husband*
> *In This Death He Lies Content*

One of 13 Brigadier-Generals who made the supreme sacrifice, buried/ commemorated in Ypres Salient: Brigdr. General C. Fitzclarence, Ypres (Menin Gate) Memorial (Panel 3); A.C. Lowe, Ypres Reservoir Cemetery (I.C.7); F.A. Maxwell, Ypres Reservoir Cemetery (I.A.37); J. Hasler, White House Cemetery (III.A.5); J.F. Riddell, Tyne Cot Cemetery (XXXIV.H.14); C.G. Rawling, The Huts Cemetery (XII.C.20); C.W. Gordon, Reninghelst New Military Cemetery (III.D.16); N.R. McMahon, Ploegsteert Memorial (Panel 1); R.C. MacLachlan, Locre Hospice Cemetery (II.C.9); A.F. Gordon, Lijssenthoek Military Cemetery (XIV.A.13); H.G. Fitton, Lijssenthoek Military Cemetery (II.A.27); F.J. Heyworth, Brandhoek Military Cemetery (II.C.2). Major General, M.S. Mercer, Lijssenthoek Military Cemetery (VI.A.38); W. Holmes, Trois Arbres Cemetery (I.X.42).

(XXVI.FF.5) Capt. 30, Charles St.Clair Strong, 1st Bn. Newfoundland Regt, B.E.F.: *s*. of William G. Strong, of 309, South Side, St. John's, Newfoundland, by his wife Elizah: enlisted 2 September 1914, Pte. no.30, apptd. Sergt. on the 21st; Colour-Sergt., 3 October: departed St. Johns, HMT 'Florizel,' 4 October 1914: continued to rise through the ranks, being promoted Coy.Sergt.Major, 6 May 1915; commissioned 2nd Lieut., 9 October 1915: served in the Balkans from December 1915; wounded while engaged in raiding the German trenches at Beaumont-Hamel, Somme, 28 June 1916: promoted Lieut. 9 October 1916; Capt. 16 August 1917. Wounded during the fighting at Neuve Eglise, 12 April 1918, and died in the Casualty Clearing Station, Poperinghe, the following day (13 April). Buried in the Military Cemetery there: Age 28. *unm.*

> *His Toils Are Past, Work Is Done, He Fought The Fight The Victory Won*

(XXVI.FF.9) Rev. Charles Ivo Sinclair Hood, Army Chaplain 4th Class, Royal Army Chaplain's Dept. attd. 41st Bde., Royal Garrison Artillery: formerly Rector of Sidestrand, Cromer, co. Norfolk: *s*. of the late Sinclair Frankland Hood, of Nettleham Hall, Lincoln, by his wife Grace Elinor: late *husb*. to Christobel M. Hood (Sidestrand, Cromer): and brother to Lieut.Col. E.T.F. Hood, D.S.O., Household Cavalry, Comdg. 38th Bde. Royal Field Artillery, died of wounds, 15 May 1915: formerly Head of the Magdalen College Mission, Euston, London; served as Chaplain to the Forces at Gallipoli and Egypt (1915–1916), and with the Expeditionary Force in France and Flanders, and died of wounds, 15 April 1918: Age 31. Remembered on the Royal Army Chaplain's Memorial, Royal Garrison Church (All Saints), Aldershot.

Right Dear In The Sight Of The Lord Is The Death Of His Saints

His brother Edward is buried in Ebblinghem Military Cemetery (II.B.19).

(XXVI.HH.1A) Pte. 61725, Charles Henry Revill, 15th (Service) Bn. The Prince of Wales's Own (West Yorkshire Regt.): *s.* of the late Pte. 16064, William 'Bill' Henry Revill, 6th Lincolnshire Regt., killed in action at Gallipoli, 22 September 1915; by his wife Sarah (21, Spencer Street, Mansfield), *dau.* of Charles Hack, of 25, Padley Hill, Mansfield: *b.* Mansfield, co. Nottingham, 20 May 1899: *educ.* Rose Mary School: Occupation – Stage Manager; Mansfield Empire: enlisted Mansfield, 21 May 1917: served with the Expeditionary Force in France and Flanders from 31 March 1918, and died at No.10 Casualty Clearing Station, 13 April following, from wounds received in action during the defence of Calais the previous day. Buried in Lyssenthoek Military Cemetery, south-west of Poperinghe: Age 18.

A Life Long Sorrow Too Deep For Time To Heal
Asleep With The Brave

His father Bill has no known grave; he is commemorated on the Helles Memorial, Gallipoli.

Plot 27, A to H lies adjacent to AA to HIII.
From 6th October 1917 until the close of the Third Battle of Ypres (10th November) 1st Lincolnshires 'had a most unenviable time.' When not in the front line in the Polygon Wood sector they were called upon to furnish large working parties for digging purposes, and when in camp enemy air raids were a continual nuisance. On 26 October they moved up to the front line – about 1,500 yards east of the Butte, Polygon Wood – where the trenches were knee-deep in water and, after five days of misery, the battalion came out of the line having lost nine men killed, thirty-two wounded, and fifty-nine evacuated sick to hospital suffering from trench-feet. Several days were then spent in Railway Dugouts, Zillebeke, before moving back up the line again at 4.15 p.m, 8 November. The trenches were, as before, knee-deep in mud and water and the relief – carried out under heavy artillery fire – a costly affair: Lieut. R.L. de Brisay (Comdg. 'A' Coy.) and Asst. Adjt. 2nd Lieut. L.C. Williams were wounded; five other ranks killed, seventeen wounded, and two were missing.

(XXVII.A.3) 2nd Lieut. Leonard Charles Williams (Asst. Adjt.), 3rd attd. 1st Bn. (10th Foot) The Lincolnshire Regt.: *s.* of Harry Williams, of Waldon House, Torquay, co. Devon, by his wife Mary. Died of wounds, 10 November 1917, received during a relief in the early hours of the 9th.: Age 19. Remembered on Torquay (Princess Gardens) War Memorial.

(XXVII.A.17A) Pte. 805002, John Arthur Aldcroft, 2nd Bn. Canadian Infantry (Eastern Ontario Regt.) attd. 1st Canadian Machine Gun Corps, C.E.F.: late of Bowmanville, Ontario: *s.* of William (& Mary Jane) Aldcroft, of 32, Chapel Street, Altrincham, co. Chester, England: *b.* 30 April 1897: Religion – Methodist: Occupation – Rubber Worker: enlisted Bowmanville, 22 November 1915. Died of wounds (GSW. Rt. leg, arm; Lt. leg), 12 November 1917; No.3 Casualty Clearing Station: Age 20. (*IWGC record age 19*)

The Call Was Short The Shock Severe, To Part With One We Love So Dear

(XXVII.A.21) Pte. 54306, James Abbott, 5th Bn. The Prince of Wales's Own (West Yorkshire Regt.), (T.F.): formerly no.1908, Army Service Corps: *s.* of William James Abbott, by his wife Jane: *b.* Pencombe, co. Hereford, 17 December 1880: *educ.* Pencombe School: Occupation – Miller's Loader: enlisted A.S.C., 11 March 1915; transf'd. to a training battalion, thereafter West Yorkshire Regt.: served with the Expeditionary Force in France from September 1917, and died at No.3 Canadian C.C.S. of wounds (G.S.W. back [penet.]) 13 November following, received in action at Ypres. Buried in the Lyssenthoek Cemetery: Age 39. He *m.* Leominster; Ellen Elizabeth (1, Pember's Court, Etnam Street, Leominster), *dau.* of Charles Pocknell, and had four children – Winifred Beatrice, *b.* 9 November 1900; Edith Mary, *b.* December 1902; Ethel, *b.* 27 March 1905; Arthur, *b.* 23 March 1907.

(XXVII.B.1) Corpl. 274258, William Oliver Thomas, 343rd Road Construction Coy., Royal Engineers: eldest *s.* of the Rev. Lewis Thomas, Wesleyan Minister; of Boroughbridge, co. York, by his wife Elizabeth Anne (59, Bannister Street, Withernsea, Hull), *dau.* of William Rowlands, of Llanelly: *b.* Cardiff, co. Glamorgan, 23 August 1890: *educ.* Kingswood School: thereafter articled to Mr Robert Browning, J.P., Surveyor & Estate Agent, Wells, co. Somerset: served 6 years, Valuation Department, Inland Revenue, Harrogate & Skipton; Member, Surveyors' Institution, and an Under Estate Agent: enlisted Royal Engineers, Leeds, 24 April 1917: served with the Expeditionary Force in France and Flanders from 4 May, and died at No.3 Canadian Casualty Clearing Station, France, 18 November 1917, of bullet wounds received in action the same day. Buried in the Lyssenthoek British Military Cemetery: Age 27. *unm.*

The Sun Is Rising With God Behind It

(XXVII.B.5) Pte. 1057335, George Sansom, 87th Bn. Canadian Infantry (Quebec Regt.), C.E.F.: s. of James Sansom, of Blenheim Cottage, Chandler's Ford, Southampton, by his wife Emma: b. Chandler's Ford, 24 July 1896: Religion – Church of England: Occupation – Farmer: 5'11½" tall, blue eyes, light brown hair: enlisted Montreal, 23 January 1917: served with the Expeditionary Force in France and Flanders, admitted No.17 C.C.S. Poperinghe 'dangerously ill,' and died, 19 October 1917, of shrapnel wounds (cranial, arm) received at Passchendaele the previous day. Buried at Lyssenthoek: Age 21. *unm.*

He Died That We Might Live

(XXVII.C.4) L/Corpl. 9/939, Albert Edward Johnson, 3rd Bn. Otago Regt., N.Z.E.F.: s. of Seldon Johnson, of 8, Pentland Avenue, Mount Eden, Auckland, late of 'Hillside,' Anne Street, Devonport, by his wife Harriett: and brother to L/Corpl. 7/219, W.J.P. Johnson, 10th Sqdn. Canterbury Mounted Rifles, died May 1915, at Gallipoli; and Pte. 54886, A.J. Johnson, 3rd Auckland Regt., died New Year's Eve, 31 December 1917: b. Westport, 1892: enlisted Trentham, 14 December 1914: departed New Zealand, 17 April 1915; Tpr., 4th Rfts., Otago Mounted Rifles: served at Suez, Egypt (from 25 May following); with the Expeditionary Force in France and Flanders from 9 April 1916, and died No.10 Casualty Clearing Station, Poperinghe, 19 December 1917, of bullet wounds to the left side and chest: Age 25.

His brother Walter is buried in No.2 Outpost Cemetery (E.19); Arthur lies in Polygon Wood Cemetery (G.20).

(XXVII.C.9) Pte. 34730, Edwin John Rankin, 'A' Coy., 3rd Bn. Canterbury Regt., N.Z.E.F.: late of Kingsley Street, Christchurch: s. of John Rankin, of 106, Mary Street North, East Invercargill, New Zealand, by his wife Agnes: b. Wyndham, Southland, 3 April 1893: Occupation – Salesman: enlisted 23 August 1916: departed Wellington, HMNZT 71, 'Port Lyttleton,' 7 December following; arrived Plymouth, 18 February 1917: served with the Expeditionary Force in France and Flanders, and died of wounds, 21 December 1917: Age 24. *unm.*

(XXVII.C.11A) L/Corpl. 4/288, Neil McLeod Matheson, 2nd Bn. 3rd New Zealand Rifle Brigade, N.Z.E.F.: s. of Mrs M. Matheson (7, Oates Street, Roslyn, Dunedin): and brother to Pte. 9/1580, C. Matheson, Otago Regt., killed in action, 5 November 1918; and Pte. 1214, N. Matheson, Australian Infantry, who also fell: b. 1891: *educ.* Kaikorai School: Occupation – Clerk: enlisted Otago prior to the outbreak of war: departed Wellington aboard either HMNZT 1 'Moeraki' or HMNZT 2 'Monowai' with Samoan Advance Party, Railway Engineers, 15 August 1914, rank of Sergt.: re-embarked Wellington, 25th Rfts. 26 April 1917, aboard HMNZT 83 'Tofua,' arriving Plymouth, via

Cape of Good Hope, 19 July: served with the Expeditionary Force in France and Flanders from 28 September 1917, and died of wounds (S.W. neck, perf.) 29 December 1917: Age 26. *unm*. All correspondence should be addressed c/o his brother George Stafford Matheson Esq., 7, Oates Street, Roslyn.

His brother Charles is buried in Cross Roads Cemetery, Fontaine-au-Bois (I.C.1), Neil lies in Shrapnel Valley Cemetery (IV.B.6)

(XXVII.C.19) Pte. 39240, Ernest Victor Hunt, 3rd Bn. Otago Regt., N.Z.E.F.: *s*. of Charles Hunt, of 58, Forth Street, Invercargill, by his wife Catherine: and *yr*. brother to Pte. 8/398, C. Hunt, Otago Regt., killed in action, 1 October 1916: enlisted, 10 October 1916: departed Wellington, 19 January 1917; proceeded to France, 23 July, and died of wounds Christmas Day (25 December) 1917, No.2 C.C.S., Poperinghe (G.S.W. abdominal; Lt. arm comp.frac): Age 20. *unm*.

His brother Charles has no known grave; he is commemorated on the Caterpillar Valley (New Zealand) Memorial.

(XXVII.D.2) Pte. 22401, Samuel Anthony Gospodnetich, 1st Bn. Canterbury Regt., N.Z.E.F.: *s*. of T. Frank Gospodnetich, c/o Tarakohe Cement Works, Nelson; by his wife Sarah Elizabeth (Waimangaroa): and brother to Pte. 6/1299, F.J. Gospodnetich, Canterbury Regt. (surv'd.): *b*. 1898: Occupation – Labourer: enlisted Trentham, 7 May 1916: departed Wellington, HMNZT 63 'Navua,' 20 August; proceeded to France, 20 November following. Died No.10 C.C.S., 7 December 1917, of wounds received from shellfire before Polderhoek Chateau two days previously: Age 19. Correspondence regarding the deceased may be addressed c/o Sister Frances Gospodnetich (Roman Catholic Convent, Westport).

(XXVII.D.17A) Rfn. 14063, James Campbell, 4th Bn. 3rd New Zealand Rifle Brigade, N.Z.E.F.: *s*. of Robert Campbell, of Waituna, Waimate, South Canterbury, by his wife Helena, *née* Westphal: and brother to Tpr. 7/27, J.R. Campbell, Canterbury Mounted Rifles, died (and buried) at sea, 30 June 1915, consequent to wounds received in action at Gallipoli: Occupation – Teamster: enlisted 3 March 1916: departed New Zealand 26 June; proceeded to France, 19 September 1916, and died, 7 December 1917, of wounds (G.S. both legs): Age 24. *unm*.

With no known grave but the sea, his brother John is commemorated on the Lone Pine Memorial (71).

(XXVII.D.18A) Gnr. 2/2600, Walter Richard Costar, M.M., 11th Bty., 3rd Bde., New Zealand Field Artilery, N.Z.E.F.: *s*. of Matoaka Atlantic Costar, of Manurewa, Auckland, by his wife Sarah Caroline (Karaka, via Papakura): and elder brother to Pte. 48457, R.E. Costar, 1st Auckland Regt., died of wounds, 13 September 1918, aged 24 years: Occupation – Electrician: enlisted Trentham, 20 October 1915: embarked Wellington, HMNZT 37 'Maunganui,' 8 January 1916: underwent training in Egypt: served with the Expeditionary Force in France and

Flanders, and died 9 December 1917, of wounds (G.S.W. leg) received in action at Ypres. He was awarded the Military Medal (*London Gazette*, 28 January 1918) for bravery in the field: Age 24.

His brother Reginald is buried in Serre Road Cemetery No.2 (XXIX.H.16).

(XXVII.E.4) Pte. 39222, William John Guise, 1st Bn. Otago Regt., N.Z.E.F.: *s.* of J.T. Guise, of 15, George Street, North Invercargill, and Mrs H. Guise (Post Office, Drummond, Southland): and brother to Pte. 56924, N.A. Guise, Otago Regt. (surv'd.): Occupation – Farm Labourer: departed Wellington, HMNZT 76 'Aparima,' 22nd Rfts. 'D' Coy. Otago Regt. and 14th Rfts. Maori, 16 February 1917: arrived Plymouth via Cape of Good Hope, 2 May: underwent training at Sling Camp, thereafter proceeded to France, took part in the fighting at Passchendaele, and died of wounds (G.S. Rt. & Lt. thigh, facial [jaw], hand) at No.3 Canadian Casualty Clearing Station, Remy Siding, 20 February 1918, received at Polygon Wood on the night of 18–19 February: Age 22. Buried in the Military Cemetery, Boeschepe – Lyssenthoek Road.

(XXVII.E.8A) L/Corpl. 32499, William John Albert Bell, 1st Bn. Otago Regt., N.Z.E.F.: *s.* of the late John Bell (ex-Sergt. Royal Irish Constabulary), of Ballygoney, Coagh, Co. Tyrone, by his wife Margaret Ann: Occupation – Police Constable: enlisted Trentham, 24 July 1916, apptd. L/Corpl.; promoted Sergt. October following: departed Wellington, HMNZT 77 'Mokoia' (as Sergt. Major), 22nd Rfts. 'F' Coy., 13 February 1917: arrived Plymouth via Cape of Good Hope, 2 May: underwent training at Sling Camp (reverted L/Corpl., 1st Otago Regt.); proceeded to France, June 1917, where he was wounded on two occasions, and died of wounds (G.S. thoracic [penet.], lung, Lt. forearm) 21 February 1918, received at Polygon Wood on the night of 18–19 February: Age 29.

(XXVII.E.11A) Pte. 49063, Henry Baverstock, 2nd Bn. Auckland Regt., N.Z.E.F.: *s.* of Charles Best Baverstock, by his wife Mary: late *husb.* to Ruth Irene Baverstock (Ohakune Junction, New Zealand): *b.* East Tamaki, Auckland, N.Z.: Occupation – Farmer: enlisted, 26 April 1917. Died 27 February 1918; pneumonia: Age 34.

(XXVII.F.1A) Rfn. 23/2281, Charles Hadden Simpkin, 2nd Bn. 3rd New Zealand Rifle Brigade, N.Z.E.F.: late of 11, Dunedin Street, Ponsonby: eldest *s.* of William Simpkin, of Rehia, Northern Waeroa, Auckland, by his wife Rose Alice: and brother to Rfn. 75265, J.A. Simpkin, N.Z.E.F. (surv'd., *d.*1970); and Pte. 33620, W.G. Simpkin, Auckland Regt. (surv'd., *d.*1962): *b.* 29 January 1894: Religion – Methodist: *educ.* Rehia; Aratapu Secondary School, and Auckland Teaching College (*c.*1913): Occupation – School Teacher, Ngaruawahia and Waingaro: previously served 4th Waikato Mounted Rifles: enlisted 15 December 1915: departed New Zealand, 1 April 1916; 5th Rfts. 1st Battn. 'E' Coy.: underwent training in Egypt and England: served with the Expeditionary

Force in France and Flanders from May 1916; wounded (Lt. leg), 30 September 1916. Died in No.3 Canadian Casualty Clearing Station, Poperinghe, 19 January 1918, of wounds (left forearm blown off, multiple [machine-gun] bullet wounds to both legs) received in action the previous day: Age 22. *unm*. The *Auckland Weekly News*, 7 February 1918, carried the following lines:

> *God's ways are always right and perfect, love is o'er them all, though far above our sight.*
> *Beloved, it is well –*
> *Tho' deep and sore the smart, the hand that wounds knows how to bind and heal the broken heart.*

(XXVII.F.2A) Rfn. S/32112, Charles 'Horace' William Guilford, 2nd Bn. The Prince Consort's Own (The Rifle Brigade): *s*. of Charles Guilford, of London, E., by his wife Hannah: enlisted Woolwich. Died 21 January 1918, of wounds (G.S.W. Rt. hip) received in action at Bellevue: Age 29. He leaves a wife, Rebecca Guilford ('Kentville,' Park Avenue, Westmead, New South Wales).

> *In Life I Loved You Dearly In Death I Do The Same*
> *From Your Loving Wife*

(XXVII.F.3) Pte. 41067, Edward Alexander Bertram Barber, 1st Bn. Canterbury Regt., N.Z.E.F.: late of Clarks Flat, Lawrence: *s*. of Stephen Barber, of 42, Richmond Street, South Dunedin, New Zealand, by his wife Margaret Alice: and *yr*. brother to Pte. 9/2045, T. Barber, 2nd Bn. Otago Regt., killed in action, 12 October 1917, aged 22: *b*. 15 October 1896: Occupation – Farm Hand: a serving member of 14th Regt. (Militia); enlisted Lawrence, 28 October 1916: departed New Zealand, 2 April 1917, Rfts. 'J' Coy.: proceeded to France, 23 July 1917. Died of wounds, 22 January 1918: Age 21. *unm*.

His brother Theophilus has no known grave; he is commemorated on the Tyne Cot (New Zealand) Memorial (Panel 3).

In accordance with orders received 6 January 1917, for 2nd N.Z. Infantry Briagde to relieve 3rd (N.Z. Rifle) Brigade in the left sub-sector of the New Zealand Divisional front, 1st and 2nd Otago Regiment moved up and took over the Noordemdhoek sector (the extreme left of the Divisional frontage); 2nd Otago the Reutel sector, on the evening of 8 January. Both lay immediately to the east of Polygon Wood.

The state of the two sectors was such that all available manpower had to be employed in the hope of effecting some kind of improvement; the lack of shelters of any kind was particularly noticeable and keenly felt by all ranks. Heavy snow made the conditions infinitely worse and, following an almost immediate thaw, the trenches were reduced to a state impossible to describe. Further heavy falls of snow completely inundated large areas of the countryside; trenches either flooded or fell in, and many of the avenues were waist deep in mud. Relieved on the 14th and moved back to rest in dug-outs at Halfway House and Railway Wood (1st Bn.), Otago Camp (2nd). It had been a very hard and trying tour and the regiment's 'rest' proved exceedingly short lived. With the continuance of exceedingly heavy weather and the Ypres area living up to its winter reputation – a combination of a large number of men medically classified as 'excused duty' or 'light duty' and several suffering from various stages of trench foot – caused an immediate and insistent call for working parties great difficulty in procuring the requisite numbers; a state of affairs which, while not to be wondered at, had to be accomplished.

The regiment returned to the line on 20 January – the trenches were in an even worse condition than formerly, there was no possibility of any improvement by drainage until a return of fair weather – and shortly after midnight the support and reserve areas were heavily shelled by the enemy.

(XXVII.F.4) Pte. 8/4020, William Sinclair, 2nd Bn. Otago Regt., N.Z.E.F.: late of Awarua, Invercargill: *s.* of William Sinclair, of Timaru, by his wife Sarah: *b.* Lyttleton, Canterbury: Occupation – Farm Labourer: proceeded overseas, 4 March 1916: served in Egypt; France and Flanders, and died of wounds (severe cranial fracture), 22 January 1918, received from shellfire on the night of 20–21 January; Reutel sector: Age 24. *unm.*

(XXVII.F.4A) Pte. 45125, William John Paul, 1st Bn. Otago Regt., N.Z.E.F.: late of Winton, Southland: *s.* of William Paul, of Belfield, Geraldine: Occupation – Labourer: enlisted 25 November 1916: proceeded overseas, 5 April 1917: served in France from 27 September, and died of wounds (cranial), 22 January 1918, received from shellfire on the night of 20–21 January; Noordemhoek sector: Age 26. *unm.*

(XXVII.F.5) Pte. 56950, John Andrew Stewart Pickens, 2nd Bn. Otago Regt., N.Z.E.F.: late of Invercargill, Southland: *s.* of Thomas Pickens, of Richardson Road, Mount Albert, Auckland, by his wife Annie: Occupation – Farmer: enlisted Invercargill, 29 March 1917: proceeded overseas, 26 July 1917: served in France from 26 October 1917, and died of wounds (S.W. [shrapnel] multiple), 22 January 1918, received on the night of 20–21 January; Reutel sector: Age 21. *unm.*

(XXVII.F.10A) Pte. 55811, Lewis Alexander Tavendale, 2nd Bn. Otago Regt., N.Z.E.F.: *s.* of the late James Tavendale, by his wife Annie (Derwent Street, Oamaru): and brother to Pte. 8/3087, J. Tavendale, Otago Regt. (surv'd.): *b.* co. Aberdeen, Scotland, 1896: Occupation – Coachbuilder: enlisted Oamaru, 27 March 1917: departed Wellington, HMNZT 90 'Ulimaroa,' 26 July 1917: arrived Plymouth via Cape of Good Hope, 24 September following. Died 24

January 1918, of bullet wounds to the right shoulder (penetrating [thoracic] chest cavity) received on the night of the 22nd when about 100 of the enemy, in four parties, unsuccessfully attempted to raid the company front east of Polygon Wood: Age 21. *unm.*

(XXVII.F.16A) Spr. 2204272, Francis Trevor King, 10th Bn. Canadian Railway Troops, C.E.F.: elder *s.* of the late Thomas Harper King, author of *The Study Book of Mediaeval Architecture & Art*, and other works, by his wife Fanny (124, Elm Park Mansions), *dau.* of John Scott, Barrister-at-Law: and brother to Q.M.Sergt. 11/511, L.H. King, 2nd Wellington Mounted Rifles, N.Z.E.F., died at home in New Zealand, 9 November 1918, of cardiac failure following influenza: *b.* London, 20 May 1870: Occupation – Salesman: over-age to qualify for an Active Service battalion, Francis joined Canadian Railway Reconstruction Contingent, Vancouver, British Columbia, 10 July 1917; and died at Remy Siding Hospital, Poperinghe, 31 January 1918, from albuminuria and broncho-pneumonia. Buried in St. Bartholomew's Cemetery, Lyssenthoek: Age 47. He leaves a wife, Abbie-Jane King (2907, College Avenue, Berkeley, California).

His brother Louis is buried in Hamilton East Public Cemetery Soldiers Area (E4.245).

(XXVII.F.18A) L/Corpl. S/17522, Charles Frederick Bell, 12th (Service) Bn. The Prince Consort's Own (The Rifle Brigade): *s.* of Charles Richard (& Alice) Bell: late *husb.* to Cicely Florence Bell (22, Arundel Square, Barnsbury, London), and father to one child: enlisted Marylebone, London. Died of wounds (GSW cranial [Penet.] Rt. eye and face), No.3 Canadian C.C.S., 2 February 1918, received in action at Inverness Copse: Age 24.

Daddy Dear I Did Not See You But Mummy Has Taught Me To Love You

(XXVII.F.19A) Pte. 12/735, Arthur Gordon Fish, 1st Bn. Auckland Regt., N.Z.E.F.: *s.* of Joseph Fish, of 41, Grange Road, Mount Eden, Auckland, by his wife Henrietta, *née* Brown: and yr. brother to Pte. 27803, S.H. Fish, who, after being discharged and returned to New Zealand, died, 20 July 1918, consequential to wounds received on Active Service in France: enlisted Auckland, 18 August 1914; departed New Zealand, 16 October following: served at Samoa, Gallipoli, and in France and Flanders from October 1916, and died of wounds (G.S. Rt. thigh, Lt. buttock), 1 February 1918: Age 29. He was married to Eleanor Kate Andrews, *née* Fish (Tarrant Monkton, Blandford, co. Dorset, England).

His brother Samuel is buried in Waikaraka Park Cemetery (Area 1, Block K, Grave 154).

(XXVII.G.4A) Pte. 15512, Harry Gibson, Stretcher-bearer; 10th (Service) Bn. The Cheshire Regt.: *s.* of William Gibson, of Dods Marsh, Prestbury, Macclesfield, co. Chester, by his wife Sarah, *dau.* of James Smith, of Poynton:

b. Poynton, co. Chester, 3 April 1896: *educ.* Church of England School, Prestbury: prior to enlistment Macclesfield, 9 September 1914 (posted Cheshire Regt.), was employee Messrs L.C. Slater, Paper Stainer, Bollington: served with the Expeditionary Force in France and Flanders from 23 September 1915: wounded at Ypres, January 1916, and invalided home: rejoined his regiment in France, 10 December following, and died in 1/3rd Field Ambulance, 18 April 1918, of wounds received at Messines the previous day whilst acting as Regimental Stretcher-bearer. Buried in Lyssenthoek Military Cemetery, Poperinghe. His Commanding Officer wrote, "Your son was a fine soldier, ever ready to do his duty faithfully to his King and country. His unfortunate end, after such good service, at so youthful an age, is much to be regretted.": Age 22. *unm.*

He Fought The Fight The Victory Won And Entered Into Rest

(XXVII.G.6) Pte. 269093, Albert Joseph Campkin, 1st Bn. The Hertfordshire Regt. (T.F.): *s.* of John Campkin, of 19, Kibes Lane, Ware, co. Hertford, by his wife Charlotte: and brother to Pte. 36275, A. Campkin, 6th Royal Berkshire Regt., killed in action, 12 October 1917; and Pte. 266739, E.R. Campkin, 1st Hertfordshire Regt., killed in action, 23 August 1918: *b.* Ware: enlisted Bedford. Died of wounds, 18 April 1918: Age 33.

His brother Alfred has no known grave, he is commemorated on the Tyne Cot Memorial (Panel 105); Edward is buried in Bucquoy Communal Cemetery Extension (B.15).

(XXVII.G.20) Major Hugh Alexander Leslie Rose, D.S.O., 9th Divn. Artillery Staff Hd.Qrs., Royal Field Artillery: formerly Capt., 3rd Divn. Ammunition Park: *s.* of the late Hugh Rose, by his marriage to Mrs Drysdale, *née* Rose (2, St. Aubyn's, Hove, co. Sussex): proceeded to France, August 1914. Killed in action nr. Bde. H.Q., nr. Scherpenberg, 18 April 1918, by the detonation of a high explosive shell: Age 36. Lieut.Col. R. Horn and Rev. Chaplain C.G.C. Meister were killed by the same shell; severely wounded, Capt. R. Somers-Cocks, M.C., Somerset Light Infantry died six days later.

Till The Day Breaks And The Shadows Flee Away

Capt. Somers-Cocks is buried nearby (XXVII.H.21); Rev. Chaplain Meister, La Clytte Military Cemetery (IV.E.1).

(XXVII.G.21) Lieut. Col. Robert Horn, D.S.O. & Bar, M.C., Comdg. 1st Bn. (72nd Foot) The Seaforth Highlanders (Ross-shire Buffs, The Duke of Albany's): eldest *s.* of the late William Horn, M.A. (Oxon), of Woodcote, Midlothian, Advocate, by his wife Myra, *dau.* of the late John Macandrew, W.S.: *b.* Edinburgh, 30 May 1881: *educ.* St. Ninian's Preparatory School, Moffat, and

Winchester College: gazetted 2nd Lieut. 1900; promoted Lieut. 1901; Capt. 1906; Major 1915; Colonel 1916: served with his regiment in Egypt and India: took part in the Zakka Khel and Mohmaund Expeditions, 1908: served with the Expeditionary Force in France and Flanders from October 1914–April 1918: severely wounded at Neuve Chapelle, 1915, and again in 1916: gassed at Passchendaele, 1917, and was killed in action, 18 April 1918 when Brigade Head Quarters, vicinity Scherpenberg – Ouderdom, was hit by a high explosive shell. Buried at Poperinghe. Lieut. Col. Horn was four times Mentioned in Despatches (*London Gazette*, 17 February; 22 June 1915), by F.M. Sir John (now Lord) French, and (*London Gazette*, 25 May; 21 December 1917), by Gen. Sir Douglas Haig. He was awarded the M.C. in 1915, and the D.S.O. (& Bar), 1917, 'For conspicuous gallantry and devotion to duty. He led his Battalion with great ability and courage. It was largely due to his personal reconnaissance that many difficulties were overcome, and the objectives gained with complete success. He served for eighteen years with the Seaforth Highlanders, and refused other regiments, and other deferments in order to do so: Age 31. *unm.*

Eldest Son Of William And Myra Horn Of Woodcote
Lest We Forget

(XXVII.H.20) 2nd Lieut. Bennet-Edmund Hoskyns-Abrahall, 242nd Siege Bty., Royal Garrison Artillery: eldest s. of Bennet Hoskyns-Abrahall, C.B.E., of 'Rubers Law,' West Byfleet, co. Surrey, by his wife Edith Louise, *dau.* of the Rev. W. Egerton-Tapp.: *gdson.* to Theophilus Bennet Hoskyns-Abrahall, and Helena Kingsmill, his wife: *b.* 30 October 1899: *educ.* St. Edmund's, Hindhead, and Repton College. Died of wounds, 25 April 1918, received in action at Ypres: Age 18. Remembered on Byfleet War Memorial.

R.I.P.

(XXVII.H.21) Capt. Reginald Somers-Cocks, M.C., 7th (Service) Bn. The Prince Albert's (Somerset Light Infantry) attd. (Staff Capt.) 26th Bde. Hd.Qrs.: *s.* of the Rev. Henry Lawrence Somers-Cocks, of Eastnor Rectory, Ledbury, and Deas Thusnelda Haskell, his spouse; only child of Llewellyn Haskell: *b.* 24 July 1894. Severely wounded by a high explosive shell nr. 26th (Infantry) Bde. Hd.Qrs., Ouderdom, 18 April 1918; died at Lijssenthoek six days later (24 April 1918): Age 23. He was married (16 January 1918) to Flora Margaret, *dau.* of Henry King Sturdee, of Norton Manor, Taunton, co. Somerset. Awarded the Military Cross, 1918. Lieut.Col. R. Horn, D.S.O. & Bar, M.C. and the Rev. G.G.C. Meister, M.C., were killed by the same shell.

Love Is Stronger Than Death In Christ's Presence

Lieut.Col.Horn is buried nearby (XVII.G.21): Rev. Meister, La Clytte Military Cemetery (IV.E.1).

(XXVII.BB.4) L/Corpl. 201505, Arthur Garlick, 1/4th Bn. The Duke of Wellington's (West Riding) Regt. (T.F.): formerly of 15, Castle Terrace, Rastrick, co. York: *s.* of William Garlick, of Rastrick, by his wife Annie: *educ.* Rastrick Grammar School, 1909–1911: Occupation – Office Clerk; Brighouse Co-operative Society: enlisted February 1915: went to the Front where, after receiving multiple wounds on Anzac Ridge, Ypres, 19 November 1917, he was removed to the Casualty Clearing Station, Poperinghe, where, 36 hours after being operated on, he died: 21 November 1917: Age 20. *unm.*

(XXVII.BB.15A) Sergt. 25/162, Edmund Bassett, M.M., 'B' Coy., 3rd Bn. 3rd New Zealand Rifle Brigade, N.Z.E.F.: *s.* of Francis Bassett, of High Street North, Dannevirke, Hawkes Bay, by his wife Sarah: *b.* Bunnythorpe, Manawatu, 23 June 1886: Occupation – Labourer: enlisted, 12 October 1915: departed Wellington, 5 February 1916. Died of wounds, 23 November 1917, received in action at Polygon Wood the previous day: Age 31. He was awarded the Military Medal (*London Gazette*, 9 December 1916) "For great courage during the attack 15th September 1916, at Flers. When the Company was prevented from advancing, by heavy rifle and machine gun fire, L/Corpl. Bassett left cover and kept up a constant rifle fire. By his courage and example he got others to follow him and so enabled the advance to be continued." He was married to Mrs A.E. Bassett (High Street North, Dannevirke).

(XXVII.BB.19A) Pte. 267890, George Frederick Raven, 1/6th Bn. The Duke of Wellington's (West Riding) Regt. (T.F.): late of 28, Smithy Carr Lane, Brighouse, co. York: *s.* of John William Raven, of Brighouse, by his wife Emma: and *yr.* brother to Sergt. 10364, C. Raven, West Yorkshire Regt., who fell, 19 June 1918; and Pte. 34605, J.F. Raven, 9th Loyal North Lancashire Regt., killed in action, 22 March 1918: Occupation – Silk-Dresser; Messrs Wood Robinson & Co., Wilkin Royd Mills; attended St. James Church, and member of the Wheelers Club: enlisted Halifax, August 1915: served with the Expeditionary Force in France and Flanders, and died in No.17 Casualty Clearing Station, nr. Poperinghe, Belgium, 25 November 1917, of wounds received in action at Ypres: Age 23.

Ever In Our Thoughts

His brother Charlie is buried in Etaples Military Cemetery (LXVI.F.2); John has no known grave, he is commemorated on the Arras Memorial (Bay 7).

(XXVII.BB.21) Rfn. 48512, Jack Everard Kayes, 1st Bn. 3rd New Zealand Rifle Brigade, N.Z.E.F.: s. of Benjamin Arthur Kayes, of 67, Belle Vue, Mount Eden, Auckland, New Zealand, by his wife Annie Demaris: and yr. brother to Sergt. 2/3029, E.A. Kayes, New Zealand Field Artillery, killed in action, 2 October 1918: enlisted Auckland, 18 January 1916. Died of wounds, 24 November 1917: Age 20. unm.

His brother Eric is buried in Flesquieres Hill British Cemetery (V.B.6).

(XXVII.CC.2) Pte. 49438, Duncan McDermid, 2nd Bn. Otago Regt., N.Z.E.F.: s. of Peter McDermid, of Queen's Street, South Invercargill, by his wife Caroline: and brother to Pte. 71068, A. McDermid, N.Z.E.F. (surv'd.); Pte. 8/2069, W. McDermid, Otago Regt. (surv'd.); and Pte. 67526, P. McDermid, Otago Regt., killed in action, 8 October 1918: Occupation – Carter: enlisted Invercargill, 28 August 1916: proceeded overseas, 12 June 1917: served in France from 14 October following, and died in No.10 Casualty Clearing Station from multiple shrapnel wounds, 27 December 1917: Age 35. Correspondence should be addressed c/o D.J. McDermid, Esq., Queen's Street, South Invercargill, New Zealand.

His brother Peter is buried in Marcoing British Cemetery (II.B.19).

(XXVII.CC.6) Lieut. Frank Green, 'C' Coy., 5th Bn. Alexandra, Princess of Wales's Own (Yorkshire Regt.), (The Green Howards), (T.F.): yst. s. of William Green, of Keld Gate, Beverley, co. York, by his wife Martha: and brother to Capt. R. Green, Yorkshire Regt. (surv'd.); and 2nd Lieut. P. Green, 1/4th East Yorkshire Regt., killed in action, 28 March 1918: b. Beverley, 1894: educ. Beverley Grammar School, and Gotha, Thuringia, Germany: a Staff member of the Beverley Guardian news, and pre-war member of 'B' Sqdn., East Riding Yeomanry (T.F.), mobilised on the outbreak of war, August 1914: obtained his commission, 2nd Lieut. Green Howards, 1915. Died of wounds, 28 December 1917, resultant from a direct hit on 'C' Company's headquarters the previous day which killed Lieut. F.G. Danby, 2nd Lieut. W.H. Coles, and Pte. 201822, J.W. Mudd outright: Age 23. unm.

His brother Philip has no known grave; he is commemorated on the Pozieres Memorial, Somme; Lieut.Danby, 2nd Lieut. Coles and Pte. Mudd are buried in Tyne Cot Cemetery (I.F.1, I.F.2, II.F.5).

(XXVII.CC.19A) Pte. 252001, Fred Hoyes, 6th Bn. The Manchester Regt. (T.F.): only s. of Fred Hoyes, of Milton Cottage, Milton Place, Pendleton, Manchester, by his wife Edith, dau. of William F. Walker: b. Salford, Manchester, 6 August 1897: educ. Pendleton: employee Messrs Kay Brothers, Brazil Street, Manchester: enlisted 3 May 1916: served with the Expeditionary Force in France and Flanders from 5 March 1917, and died at the General Canadian Casualty Clearing Station, 30 December 1917, from shrapnel wounds to his back and right thigh received in action at Ypres. Buried in the Lyssenthoek

Military Cemetery, one and three quarter miles south-west of Poperinghe. An officer wrote, "Fred was without exception one of the most popular men I know, and all the company officers said what a good, reliable and hard-working fellow he was. He was called at all hours of the day and night, and he always turned out in a very willing manner. Nothing gave me greater pleasure than to send his name before the Commanding Officer for a reward." Mentioned in Despatches, by Gen. Sir Douglas Haig, for 'gallant and distinguished service in the field.': Age 20. *unm.*

Into Thy Hands O Lord

(XXVII.DD.2) Lieut. John Crichton Kirkpatrick, 11th (Service) Bn. The Cameronians (Scottish Rifles) attd. 20th Sqdn. Royal Flying Corps: elder *s.* of John Kirkpatrick, Mechanic; of 'Bellfield,' Kirkintilloch, co. Dumbarton, by his wife Jeanie, *dau.* of Thomas Grant: *b.* Kirkintilloch, 1 March 1890: *educ.* Glasgow University: Occupation – Teacher; Onslow Drive School, Dennistoun, Glasgow: volunteered for Active Service on the outbreak of war, enlisted Cameron Highlanders, September 1914: received his commission 2nd Lieut. Scottish Rifles, November following; proceeded to France, August 1915: subsequently attd. Royal Flying Corps; promoted Lieut. 13 April 1917. Killed in action on (northern sector) offensive patrol duty, 10 December 1917; his aircraft being hit by anti-aircraft fire: Age 26. *unm.*

Happy Is He Who Heareth His Chimes Of Eternal Peace

(XXVII.DD.10A) Pte. 49670, Andrew Costin, 1st Bn. Otago Regt., N.Z.E.F.: *s.* of the late Thomas Costin, by his wife Mary E. (16, Huxford Street, Heretaunga): and brother to Pte. 37917, D. Costin, 1st Otago Regt., killed in action the previous day (11 December): enlisted Wellington, 23 February 1917: proceeded overseas 14 July: served in France from 26 October 1917, joined his battalion in the field, 11 November, and died of wounds (S.W. severe trauma Lt. hand), 12 December 1917, received in action the previous day: Age 24.

His brother David has no known grave; he is commemorated on the Buttes New British Cemetery (New Zealand) Memorial.

(XXVII.DD.14A) Corpl. 23/1661, Charles Harvey, 2nd Bn. Canterbury Regt., N.Z.E.F.: *s.* of Frederick John Harvey, by his wife Fanny Jane: and elder brother to Pte. 7/209, P. Harvey, Canterbury Regt., died of wounds, 28 September 1916, at Etaples: enlisted, 28 October 1915: departed New Zealand, 8 January 1916; served with the Expeditionary Force in France and Flanders from April 1916. Died of wounds (G.S. cranial, penet.), 14 December 1917: Age 25. *unm.*

His brother Percy is buried in Etaples Military Cemetery (XI.D.16A).

(XXVII.DD.15) Pte. 45810, Charles Herbert Etridge, 15th Infantry Labour Coy., The Queen's Own (Royal West Kent Regt.) transf'd. no.126823, 10th Coy., Labour Corps: *s.* of Thomas Etridge, of 42, Brunswick Road, Tottenham, London, N., by his wife Eliza, *dau.* of Charles Southey: uncle to Pte. F. Etridge, Middlesex Regt., killed in action, 10 October 1917: *b.* Tottenham, N., 1885: *educ.* Woodberry: enlisted, 24 February 1917: served with the Expeditionary Force in France from March, and died there, 14 December 1917, of heart disease, contracted while on military service. Buried 1¾ miles south-west of Poperinghe: Age 32. *unm.*

His nephew Frederick is buried in Chester Farm Cemetery (III.G.14).

(XXVII.DD.15.A) Pte. 6/3653, John Leslie Churchill, M.M., 2nd Bn. Canterbury Regt., N.Z.E.F.: *s.* of Robert Churchill, of 12, Compton Avenue, Brighton, co. Sussex, by his wife Anne: Occupation – Farm Labourer: enlisted Trentham, 20 October 1915; departed Wellington, 8 January 1916: served in Egypt, and with the Expeditionary Force in France and Flanders (from April 1916), and died, 14 December 1917, of bullet wounds to the face and ankle. Awarded the Military Medal (*London Gazette*, 17 December 1917) Re. Operations Gravenstafel: 1st – 5th October 1917; "For conspicuous gallantry and devotion to duty. On the night of 2nd – 3rd October 1917, this man, a Company Runner, repeatedly carried messages from Company Headquarters to the Front line, thus keeping constant communications despite heavy enemy artillery fire. His conduct throughout the operation was worthy of great praise and set a fine example to the Company.": Age 23. *unm.* (*Archives N.Z. record L/Corpl.*)

(XXVII.DD.19) Pte. 6/2345, John James Skilton, 3rd Bn. Canterbury Regt., N.Z.E.F.: late of French Pass, South Island: *s.* of Thomas Mark Skilton, of Puramahoi, Takaka, Nelson, by his wife Florence Octavia: and brother to Pte. 68848, N. Skilton, 35th Rfts. (surv'd.); Pte. 6/2346, P.R. Skilton, Canterbury Regt. (surv'd.); Pte. 6/722, R.G. Skilton, Canterbury Regt. (surv'd.); and Tpr. 7/782, S.T. Skilton, Canterbury Mounted Rifles, died 11 August 1918, aged 33 years: *b.* Collingwood, Golden Bay, 1889: enlisted Collingwood: departed Wellington, 13 June 1915: served in Egypt (24 July–6 August 1915), and with the Expeditionary Force in France and Flanders from 7 April 1916. Wounded by machine-gun fire, 16 December 1917, and died en-route to the Casualty Clearing Station, Poperinghe. Buried in the Military Cemetery there: Age 28. *unm.*

His brother Sydney is buried in Collingwood Cemetery.

(XXVII.EE.17) Rfn. 47497, Herman Bollinger, 2nd Bn. 3rd New Zealand Rifle Brigade, N.Z.E.F.: *s.* of the late Max H. Bollinger, of Omata, Taranaki, and Margaret Isabella Smith, *née* Sproule (Bracken Street, New Plymouth): and elder brother to 2nd Lieut. G.W. Bollinger, 2nd Wellington Regt., died of wounds, 10 June 1917: *educ*. New Plymouth Boy's High School: Occupation – Clerk: enlisted, 3 May 1917; departed Wellington, 12 June: served in France and Flanders from February 1918, and died 15 March following, consequent to multiple machine-gun wounds to the thighs, pelvis, upper body, shoulder and face received in action at Ypres: Age 28.

His brother George is buried in Bailleul Communal Cemetery Extension (III.C.106).

(XXVII.FF.2A) Sergt. R/3755, Joseph Stapleton, 11th (Service) Bn. The King's Royal Rifle Corps: *s*. of Stephen Stapleton, of Doddington, Lincoln, by his wife Harriet: *b*. Alford, co. Lincoln, 12 March 1890: *educ*. Scopwick, co. Lincoln: Occupation – Farm Servant: enlisted, 5 September 1914: served with the Expeditionary Force in France and Flanders from 20 July 1915, and died at No.3 Canadian Casualty Clearing Station, 4 February 1918, from bullet wounds (neck, Lt. shoulder) received in action, 27 January. Buried in the Military Cemetery, Lyssenthoek, south of Ypres. Major-General B. Matheson, Commanding 20th Division, wrote to him, "The Major-General, 20th Division, has received a report of the gallant conduct of R.3755, L/Corpl. J. Stapleton, with Battn. The King's Royal Rifle Corps on 4 April 1917, for tending to the wounded under heavy fire at Metz, and he wishes to congratulate him on his behaviour.": Age 27. *unm*. (*IWGC record L/Sergt*.)

(XXVII.FF.8) 2nd Lieut. Francis Alexander Lewis, 53rd Sqdn. Royal Flying Corps: formerly no. 37543, Royal Army Medical Corps; Corpl. 30289, Royal Engineers: 2nd *s*. of James Lewis, of The Priory, Larkhall Rise, Clapham, London, S.W., by his wife Ada: served with the Expeditionary Force in France and Flanders from 31 December 1914. Killed, 5 February 1918 when, flying on a photographic mission, his RE8 aircraft (no.B6446) was hit by ground machine-gun fire and crashed: Age 25. Remembered on Holy Trinity War Memorial, Clapham Common.

Dearly Loved Second Son Of James & Ada Lewis Of Clapham

(XXVII.FF.9) Lieut. Thomas McKenny Hughes, 53rd Sqdn. Royal Flying Corps and King's Royal Rifle Corps: *s*. of Professor T. McKenny Hughes, of Cambridge, by his wife Mary Caroline: *b*. 1884: *educ*. Eton (Edward Impey's house): Twice Mentioned in Despatches. Killed 5 February 1918, while flying as Observer to 2nd Lieut. F.A. Lewis.: Age 34. (*IWGC record 6 February*)

(XXVII.FF.12A) Sergt. 5289, Percy Cowell, 59th Coy. Machine Gun Corps (Inf.): formerly no.9617, 2nd King's Own (Royal Lancaster Regt.): *s*. of Matilda Cowell (136, St. Leonard's Road, Far-Cotton, Northampton): and brother to Pte. 305220, T.G. Cowell, Royal Air Force, died of influenza at Blandford Camp, co. Dorset, 30 October 1918, aged 24; Pte. 55280, G. Cowell,

2nd Bn. Northamptonshire Regt., killed in action, 23 October 1918, aged 19; and Spr. 526225, F. Cowell, Royal Engineers, died of wounds, 14 April 1918: *b*. Far-Cotton, 1891: served with the Expeditionary Force in France and Flanders from 16 January 1915; subsequently transf'd. M.G.C. (Inf.). Died of multiple bullet wounds (G.S. abdominal, upper body) and compound fracture of the right knee, 9 February 1918: Age 26. One of four brothers who fell.

Although The Sea And Death Divide
Fond Memory Ever Clings
Mother

Brothers Thomas and George are buried in Towcester Road Cemetery, Northampton (446.17325), and Valenciennes (St. Roch) Communal Cemetery (II.D.28) respectively; Frank is buried nearby (XXVI.F.20A).

(XXVII.FF.19) Pte. 52619, James Joseph Kent, 2nd Bn. Wellington Regt., N.Z.E.F.: *s.* of John Kent of 41, King Street, Timaru, by his wife Catherine: *b*. Dunedin, 20 November 1888: enlisted Timaru, 3 January 1917: departed Wellington, July: proceeded to France, 18 December 1917, and died of wounds (shattered tibia, fibula, cranial, hands), 12 February 1918, received from the bursting of a shell while at duty in the front line at Ypres the previous day: Age 29. Ptes. 27248, W. Duval, 44495, R.L. Langdon and 15779, P.A. Rook were killed outright. See Oxford Road Cemetery (III.C.2 / G.3 / J.12).

(XXVIII.A.3) Lieut. Thomas Henry Thriscutt Bale, 3rd attd. 2nd Bn. (19th Foot) Alexandra, Princess of Wales's Own (Yorkshire Regt.), (The Green Howards): *s*. of the late Thomas Henry Thriscutt Bale, by his wife Emma (4, Trematon Terrace, Mutley, Plymouth): served with the Expeditionary Force in France from September 1917, one of sixteen junior officers to join Yorkshire Regt. In the Field – White Mill Camp – 20 April 1918; he was killed in action five days later, 24 April 1918: Age 33.

(XXVIII.A.18A) Pte. 242874, Herbert Siddle, 1/4th Bn. The King's Own (Yorkshire Light Infantry), (T.F.): formerly no.3383: *s*. of Charles Siddle, of Hardy Croft, Wakefield, co. York, by his wife Emma, *née* Mills: and cousin to 2nd Lieut. J. Siddle, 1/5th K.O.Y.L.I., died of wounds, 14 October 1917: *b*. Wakefield: a pre-war Territorial, volunteered for Active Service on the outbreak of war, August 1914: served in France from 15 April 1915 and, mortally wounded at Kemmel, 26 April 1918, died en-route to the C.C.S. Poperinghe: Age 26. Three brothers also served; all survived.

Too Dearly Loved To Be Forgotten
From His Loving Mother And Family

His cousin Joe is buried in Nine Elms British Cemetery (IV.F.8).

(XXVIII.A.19A) Dvr. 92185, John Dobson, (Sh./Smith) 90th Field Coy., Royal Engineers: *s.* of the late Thomas Dobson, by his wife Sophia (Church Hill, Ringmer, co. Sussex): *b.* Ringmer, *c.*1881: *educ.* there: enlisted 14th Royal Sussex Regt., Brighton, September 1915: transf'd. Dvr., Royal Engineers, France, 1916; attd. Transport Section (Horses): took part in the Battle of the Somme, Arras, Third Ypres, The Lys, and was mortally wounded by shellfire, 25 April 1918, during a heavy bombardment of the back areas in the vicinity of the Scherpenberg; he died at the C.C.S., Poperinghe the following day: 26 April 1918: Age 37.

In Loving Memory Of Our Dear Brother

(XXVIII.C.2A) Gnr. 5187, Albert Sprudd, 'B' Bty., 50th Bde., Royal Field Artillery: *s.* of Harry Sprudd, of 6, Davies Terrace, Whitchurch, co. Glamorgan, by his wife Emily: and elder brother to Bmdr. 5185, A.A. Sprudd, Royal Field Artillery, died 9 October 1918: *b.* Whitchurch: enlisted Cardiff. Killed in action, 2 May 1918: Age 27. *unm.* Remembered on Whitchurch War Memorial.

Gone But Not Forgotten

His brother Alec is buried in Awoingt British Cemetery (V.C.2).

(XXVIII.D.6A) Corpl. 69987, Harold Valentine Dancy, 11th (Service) Bn. The Queen's (Royal West Surrey Regt.): *yr. s.* of William Albert Dancy, of 32, Florence Rd., Brighton, by his wife Annie Maude, *dau.* of Benjamin Hallett, of Bedford: *b.* Brighton, co. Sussex, 14 February 1899: *educ.* Brighton, Hove, and Sussex Grammar School (member of the OTC): on leaving was Articled Pupil to a firm of Land Agents & Auctioneers: member Royal Sussex Volunteers; enlisted Queen's Royal West Surrey Regt., March 1917: served with the Expeditionary Force in France and Flanders from 1 April 1918, and died at the 140th Casualty Clearing Station, 14 July following, of wounds received in action in the Ypres sector the same day. His Commanding Officer wrote, "He was a general favourite with the officers and men, and one of the smartest N.C.O.'s in the company, and one who it is very difficult to replace.": Age 19.

For King And Country Great Love Hath No Man Than This

(XXVIII.D.12A) Spr. 48505, William Mainwaring, 237th Field Coy., Royal Engineers: *s.* of Daniel D. Mainwaring, of 'Gwangili Villa,' Cross Hands, Lanelly, co. Cramarthen, by his wife Hannah: and twin brother to Pnr. 48405, D. Mainwaring, 93rd Field Coy., Royal Engineers, died of wounds nr. Ploegsteert,

16 December 1915: *b.* Llanon, co. Carmarthen, 1889: served in France from mid-July 1915, and was killed in action, 17 July 1918: Age 26. *unm.*

Nid Hawddfyd Ond Heddwch Ir Ryd Oedd Ei Nod

Translation: 'Not Ease But Peace For The World Was His Desire'
His twin brother Dan is buried in Bedford House Cemetery (IV.C.24/Enc. No.2).

(XXVIII.E.3A) Sergt. 38857, Alfred Frank Saunders, 11th (Service) Bn. (Cambridgeshire) The Suffolk Regt.: formerly no.1215, Gloucestershire Regt.: late of 1, Gratton Street, Cheltenham: *b.* Cheltenham, 1893: *educ.* St. James' School, Merestone Road: served in France and Flanders from April 1915, and died of wounds, 29 April 1918. He leaves a wife, Elizabeth Hannah (1, Riverview, Capelulo, Penmaenwawr, North Wales), and two children. He is remembered on the Borough War Memorial, Cheltenham, and – unveiled 20 May 1920, recording 50 names – the St. James' School Roll of Honour: Age 25.

Peace Perfect Peace

(XXVIII.E.4A) L/Sergt. 29321, John Henry Ure, New Zealand Entrenching Battn., N.Z.E.F.: formerly 3rd Bn. Canterbury Regt.: *s.* of Robert Ure, of Herbert, North Otago, by his wife Mary: and brother to Pte. 8/3780, J. Ure, Otago Regt. (surv'd.); Rfn. 24/1506, R. Ure, N.Z. Rifle Brigade (surv'd.); and Pte. 58941, H.D. Ure, Otago Regt., died of wounds, 29 August 1918; age 21: Occupation – Labourer: enlisted Trentham, 28 June 1916: departed Wellington, HMNZT 67 'Tofua,' 11 October; L/Corpl., 18th Rfts. Canterbury Regt.: served in France and Flanders from late May 1917; transf'd. Entrenching Battn., and died, 29 April 1918, of wounds: Age 22. *unm.* Commemorated on the Herbert War Memorial, North Otago. (*IWGC record 3rd Bn. Canterbury Regt.*)
His brother Hugh is buried in Shrine Cemetery, Bucquoy (II.B.2).

(XXVIII.E.13A) Pte. 268523, Jess Lawson, M.M., 'A' Coy., 1/6th Bn. The Duke of Wellington's (West Riding) Regt. (T.F.): *s.* of William T. (& Mrs S.) Lawson, Farmer; of Crow Trees Farm, Tosside, Long Preston, co. York: was employee to his father: enlisted Settle, co. York, 1916: served with the Expeditionary Force in France from November 1916, and was killed in action, 28 April 1918. In a letter to his parents Capt. Dixon said, "Your son was in his post when a shell dropped into it and he was killed almost instantaneously. The loss of a man of his kind is far more than words of mine can express. He has done most excellent work since the recent fighting commenced. On April 10th, your son, by great courage and devotion, saved a wounded comrade from falling into the enemy's hands and carried him to a place of safety while enemy machine guns were firing at him. Such men as these we can ill spare. Please accept the deepest sympathy of all officers, N.C.O.'s and men of the Company in your great loss," and Lieut. C.H.E. Lowther, "It will be some consolation to you in your great loss to know that he passed away without pain. I have been his platoon officer for a long time, and I can say with absolute truth that there was no one in the platoon who did his duty better, or who was more reliable than your son. He was always very quiet and never bragged about his own doings. He was buried in a cemetery behind the fighting area, and his grave marked by a regimental cross.": Age 25. *unm*. Recommended for the Military Medal 'for conspicuous gallantry and devotion to duty' (prior to his death), the medal was awarded (and forwarded to his parents) posthumously. Pte. Lawson was well-known and highly respected by the local community, and great sympathy is felt for his bereaved parents.

Thy Will Be Done

(XXVIII.E.20A) 2nd Lieut. Robert Philips Greg, 11th (Service) Bn. The Cheshire Regt.: 2nd *s*. of Col. Ernest William Greg, C.B., of Norcliffe Hall, Handforth, co. Chester, by his wife Marian, *née* Cross: *b*. Bolton: *educ*. Rugby School: commissioned 2nd Lieut. 4th (Reserve) Battn. Cheshire Regt.: proceeded to France, 16 April 1918; posted 11th Battn. upon arrival, and was killed in action, 3 May 1918, by a H.E. shell bursting directly upon his dug-out: Age 19.

Thy Memory Is Enshrined In Our Hearts Forever

(XXVIII.F.1) Rfn. 52443, William Leslie Mills,12th (Service) Bn. (Central Antrim) The Royal Irish Rifles: formerly no.38513, Royal Warwickshire Regt.: *b*. Rochester, co. Kent: enlisted Maidstone. Died 6 June 1918, of wounds received earlier the same day when, while at duty on a working party behind the front line, a shell exploded close by; Rfn. T.A. Evered, also wounded, died at Brandhoek. Nine were killed instantly:

(XXVIII.F.1A) Rfn. 50142, George Quinlan, 12th (Service) Bn. (Central Antrim) The Royal Irish Rifles: formerly no.324820, London Regt.: *s*. of Frederick Quinlan, of 2, Corunna Place, South Lambeth, and his late spouse: *b*. Battersea: enlisted Camberwell. Died 6 June 1918, of wounds received earlier the same day when, while at duty on a working party behind the front line, a shell exploded close by: Age 18. Also wounded, Rfn. T.A. Evered, died at Brandhoek; nine were killed instantly.

Peace Perfect Peace

Rfn. Evered is buried in Hagle Dump Cemetery (I.A.3); eight of the nine killed are buried in Klein-Vierstraat British Cemetery (V.A.17); Rfn. A.J. Evans has no known grave and is commemorated on the Tyne Cot Memorial (Panel 139).

(XXVIII.F.7A) Spr. 58680, Frederick George Avis, 255th Tunnelling Coy., Royal Engineers: eldest *s.* of Philip Aguila Avis, of Priory Mill House, 14, Garden Road, Tonbridge, by his wife Violet, *dau.* of William Card: *b.* Tonbridge, co. Kent, 28 January 1891: *educ.* National School, Tonbridge: Occupation – Bootmaker: enlisted Royal Engineers, 28 December 1914: served with the Expeditionary Force in France and Flanders from 10 July 1915, taking part in the Battle of Loos, 25 September following, and many other engagements: wounded February 1916, invalided home: rejoined his regiment in France, 28 June following, and was killed in action nr. Ypres, 31 May 1918. Buried in Lyssenthoek Military Cemetery, south-west of Poperinghe. The Adjutant wrote, "His loss will be very keenly felt by his officers and comrades," and another officer, "You have the consolation of knowing he died doing a man's work. He was a really nice boy.": Age 27. *unm.*

In Loving Memory Of Our Dear Son
They Miss Him Most Who Loved Him Best

(XXVIII.F.12) Pte. 3127, James Henry Whiting, 18th (Service) Bn. (1st Public Works Pioneers) The Duke of Cambridge's Own (Middlesex Regt.): Occupation – Gas Worker; South-Eastern Gas Co., Port Greenwich, London, S.E.: enlisted Canning Town, January 1915: served in France and Flanders from 15 November 1915, and died, 25 June 1918, of wounds: Age 43. He leaves a wife Mrs J.H. Whiting (47, Mary Street, Canning Town, London), and family to lament his passing.

(XXVIII.G.1) Lieut. Robert Amor Edwards, 1st Bn. (14th Foot) The Prince of Wales's Own (West Yorkshire Regt.): *yst. s.* of Dr. Eben Henry Edwards, Capt., Royal Army Medical Corps, of Old Falinge, Rochdale, co. Lancaster (and formerly of North China), by his wife Susannah Florence, *dau.* of the late George Tawke Kemp, of Rochdale: *b.* Taiyanfu, Shansi, North China, 18 November 1897: *educ.* Ecole Nouvelle, Lausanne, Switzerland; Merchiston Castle School, Edinburgh; and R.M.C. Sandhurst: gazetted 2nd Lieut. 1st West Yorkshire Regt. 16 August 1916; promoted Lieut. 16 February 1918: served with the Expeditionary Force in France and Flanders from March 1917: wounded at Loos in the following April, and invalided home: rejoined his regiment in France, April 1918, and died in No.17 Field Ambulance, Abeele, 14 July following, of wounds received in action at Dickebusch the same day. Buried in Lyssenthoek Military Cemetery, nr. Poperinghe. His Commanding Officer wrote, "Your son had endeared himself to all, and I heard it remarked that he was just 'a white man' to his fingertips. He died doing his duty nobly in the cause of justice and freedom." And his Coy. Officer Comdg., "I was in command of C Coy. in the attack, and the success of our operations was mainly due to the very gallant and determined leading of your son and my other platoon officer. The company and the regiment have lost a very gallant officer, but it will be a comfort to you to know that it was while leading his men to victory that he was mortally hit." The Chaplain also wrote, "I had seen a good deal of your son. .. I think he was one of the best examples of a Christian amongst us, and one of the best of the junior officers.": Age 19.

In Thy Presence Is Fullness Of Joy

(XXVIII.G.7) Pte. 42103, James Henry Trevis, 6th (Service) Bn. The York & Lancaster Regt.: *s.* of Henry Samuel (& Martha Ann) Trevis, of 10, Joiner Street, Masborough, Rotherham, co. Lancaster: late *husb.* to Edith Evelyn Trevis (20, Edmund Street, Holmes, Rotherham), and father to Hilda Edith: *b*. Rotherham, 1891: served with the Expeditionary Force in France from July 1916, took part in the fighting at the Somme; wounded and repatriated to England: returned to France after treatment and convalescence, and died of wounds (GSW abdominal), 22 July 1918: Age 27.

Memories Still Cling
Mother

(XXVIII.G.12) Pte. G/86194, Frederick Bowman Angood, 19th (Service) Bn. (2nd Public Works Pioneers) The Duke of Cambridge's Own (Middlesex Regt.): late of Park Road, Raunds, co. Northampton: *s.* of Frederick Angood, of Mepal, co. Cambridge, by his wife Jane: apprenticed as Shoemaker, St. Ives; sometime held a position with Messrs C.E. Nicols; at enlistment was employee Messrs Tebbutt & Hall Bros., Thrapston, nr. Kettering: enlisted Northampton. Killed in action, 23 July 1918: Age 35. He was married to Lilian A. Angood, *née* Kirby (High Street, Thrapston), and had two children. Remembered on Raunds (St. Peter's) Parish Church Memorial.

A Loving Husband, A Father So Kind, A Beautiful Memory Left Behind

(XXVIII.G.15) Pte. 133964, Sidney George Keeler, 41st Bn. Machine Gun Corps (Inf.): *s.* of John Keeler, Publican; of Cooke's Road, Bergh Apton, by his wife Martha: and brother-in-law (by his sister Louise's marriage) to Pte. 15008, H.G.V. Greenacre, 1st Coldstream Guards, killed in action, 27 March 1916, at Ypres; and Pte. 16520, C.W. Greenacre, 2nd Norfolk Regt., killed in action,

25 July 1916, in Mesopotamia: *b*. Thurton, 1899: enlisted Norwich, co. Norfolk, 3 August 1915, aged 16 years; discharged – Underage – December following: re-enlisted Wroxham: proceeded to France, May 1918: trained Etaples, joined 41st M.G.C. In the Field, 21 July 1918, and was killed in action four days later, 25 July 1918: Age 19. Remembered on Bergh Apton War Memorial.

Brother-in-law Henry is buried in Menin Road South Military Cemetery (III.E.16); Charles has no known grave, he is commemorated on the Basra Memorial (Panel 10).

(XXVIII.G.20) Pte. G/68425, James Frederick Oswald Thorp, 10th (Service) Bn. The Queen's (Royal West Surrey Regt.): *s*. of Frederick Thorp, of 130, Ardgowan Road, Catford, London, S.E., by his wife Kate, *dau*. of Richard Norburn: *b*. East Brixton, Camberwell, co. Surrey, 14 March 1899: *educ*. Ardgowan Road London County Council School: Occupation – Clerk: enlisted 100th Training Corps, subsequently (from September 1916) 52nd (Graduated) Battn. Royal Sussex Regt., Aldershot, 1 May 1917: served with the Expeditionary Force in France and Flanders from 1 April 1918, being there drafted to Royal West Surrey Regt., and was killed while on a night working party at Kemmel Hill, 27 July following. Buried in a Military Cemetery at Lijssenthoek, nr. Poperinghe. The Chaplain wrote, "You have much reason to be proud of him, for the fine way in which he has given himself in life and in death." The Oswald Thorp Dormitory in the Home for Fatherless and Orphan Girls at 64–72, Lewisham Road, Greenwich, London, S.E., is so named in commemoration of his services there in the Sunday School, which was carried on by the Mission Band from Brownhill Road Baptist Church, Catford, London, S.E., of which he was a member and assistant treasurer: Age 19.

He Gave Himself To Christ And His Life At Duty's Call Willingly

(XXX.A.5) Gnr. 216472, Arthur Thomas 'Tommy' Saye; Officer's Servant, 'D' Bty., 157th Bde., Royal Field Artillery: 5th *s*. of Walter Saye, of Great Wigborough, Tolleshunt D'Arcy, co. Essex, by his wife Sarah: and brother to Pte. 16031, E. Saye, 3rd Coldstream Guards, killed in action at the Battle of Flers Courcelette, Les Boeufs, 15 September 1916: *b*. 28 April 1898: *educ*. Tolleshunt D'Arcy School: Occupation – Butler/Personal Valet; Richmond, co. Surrey: enlisted Colchester, co. Essex: served with the Expeditionary Force in France and Flanders, and died of wounds, 5 October 1918, received in action at Zandvoorde four days previously: Age 20. *unm*. In a letter written to his mother on the eve of his death, Gnr. Saye said, "My dearest Mother, Just a few lines to let you know I got wounded in a barrage four days ago. I got it in the leg, so you must not worry, but keep smiling as I was rather bad the first three days but I am going on alright. I suspect to be back in Blighty by the time you receive this so it has got me out of it alright. Well dear I won't try to write more. I hope the other boys are alright...Your ever loving son. I will write again tomorrow." Sister L.M. Clebe, 62nd C.C.S. wrote, "I regret to tell you, your son died at 11.30 this morning. Everything possible was done for him, but his condition was most serious from the first. He died quite peacefully, and was not in pain. He wished me to give you his love, he did not know he was dying. I am sorry you have this great sorrow. I enclose letter your son wrote yesterday. With much sympathy..." His death card bore the lines "Sick, dying in a far off land, No mother by him to take his hand, A loving son closed his eyes, Far from his native land he lies. – Yet again we hope to meet him, When the day of life is fled, Then in Heaven we hope to greet him, Where no farewell tears are shed." Deeply lamented by all who knew him.

God Is Love

His brother Ernest has no known grave; he is commemorated on the Thiepval Memorial, Somme.

In Memory of Thomas and Ernest: "We would not wish to call them back, To such a world as this, But trust one day that we shall join them in the realms of bliss." Sarah Saye (Mrs).

According to official statistics, over 500,000 horses owned by the British Army are believed to have died in the First World War, mostly from exposure, disease, starvation and while carrying men, ammunition and equipment. In the latter three cases, the majority of fatalities were as a direct consequence of shell fire and, if not killed outright, many animals were so badly wounded there was no alternative but 'to put them out of their misery.' 2nd Lieut. Denis Wheatley, R.F.A., described an incident which occurred in December 1915: "When the bombs had ceased falling we went over to see what damage had been done...we had not sustained many human casualties. The horses were another matter. There were dead ones lying all over the place, and scores of others were floundering and screaming with broken legs, terrible neck wounds or their entrails hanging out. We went back for our pistols and spent the next hour putting the poor, seriously injured brutes out of their misery by shooting them through the head. To do this we had to wade ankle deep through blood and guts. That night we lost over 100 horses." After almost three years in France, this scenario would have been all too familiar to Harry Glasspool. His job required him to care for – to aid and assist – the animals employed by the Army; sometimes the only assistance he too could administer was a bullet.

(XXX.A.11) A/Sergt. SE/11270, Harry Glasspool, Royal Army Veterinary Corps attd. 150th (Heavy) Bty., Royal Garrison Artillery: *s.* of Mrs A. Glasspool (Steventon Warren, Overton, co. Hants): and brother to Pte. 6859, F. Glasspool,

D.C.M., 1st Hampshire Regt., killed in action, 9 May 1915, and Pte. 7167, J. Glasspool, Hampshire Regt., killed in action, 11 October 1915: *b*. Overton, 1891: volunteered and enlisted Woolwich on the outbreak of war, August 1914: served with the Expeditionary Force in France and Flanders from 1915, and died 5 October 1918, of wounds received in action at Ypres.: Age 27. *unm.*

From His Sorrowing Mother, Dad, Brothers And Sisters

His brother Frank has no known grave, he is commemorated on the Ypres (Menin Gate) Memorial (Panel 35); John is buried in Hamel Military Cemetery, Beaumont Hamel (I.C.16).

The last British Officer to die in the Salient:

(XXX.B.14) Lieut.Col. George Ernest Beaty-Pownall, D.S.O., 2nd Bn. (55th Foot) The Border Regt. attd. 1st Bn. (25th Foot) The King's Own Scottish Borderers, 20th Bde., 7th Divn.: *s.* of Lieut.Col. G.A. Beaty-Pownall, by his wife Susan: and elder brother to Lieut. T.T. Beaty-Pownall, 2nd attd. 3rd Border Regt., killed in action, 24 March 1917: *b*. Campbeltown, co. Argyll: *educ*. St. Paul's School; and Royal Military College, Sandhurst: joined R.A. from Special Reserve, as Capt. 1 July 1908; apptd. Adjt., 3rd Battn. 7 March 1913: served with the Expeditionary Force in France from 1914 and – the last British officer to die in the Ypres Salient – is buried with those of his men who fell during the September and October fighting. Died of wounds, 10 October 1918: Age 41. He was awarded the D.S.O. (*London Gazette*, 4 June 1917), 'for distinguished services in the field.'

Greater Love Hath No Man

His brother Thomas is buried in St. Leger British Cemetery (A.4).

The most decorated Isle of Man soldier:

(XXX.C.16) Capt. Temp. Lieut.Col. William Anderson Watson Crellin, D.S.O. & Bar, 2nd Bn. (95th Foot) attd. 15th (Service) Bn. The Sherwood Foresters (Notts & Derbys Regt.): 3rd *s.* of the late John Christian Crellin, of Ballachurry, Andreas, Isle of Man, J.P., M.H.K., by his wife Sophia Harriet, *dau*. of Lieut.Col. W.J. Anderson, Receiver General of the Isle of Man: *b*. Ballachurry, Isle of Man, 10 December 1892: *educ*. King William's College, Castletown, Isle of Man, and Royal Military College, Sandhurst: gazetted 2nd Lieut., Sherwood Foresters, February 1912: promoted Lieut. 21 November 1914; Capt. February 1916: served with the Expeditionary Force in France and Flanders from 4 September 1914; as 2nd Lieut. 2nd Bn. Sherwood Foresters: wounded in both hands on the 20th of that month: apptd. Adjt., 11th Sherwood Foresters, November 1915; attd. 15th Battn. of that regiment the same year:

apptd. Temp. Major 1916; Lieut.Col. May 1918, and died at No.10 Casualty Clearing Station, 8 October following, of shell wounds received in action; Doll's House, south of Ypres, the previous day (7 October). Buried in Lyssenthoek Cemetery, Poperinghe. Capt. Crellin was three times Mentioned in Despatches (*London Gazette*, 25 May, 21 December 1917; December 1918) by F.M. Sir Douglas Haig, for 'gallant and distinguished service in the field,' and was awarded the Distinguished Service Order and Bar. He *m*. St. Olave's Church, Ramsey, Isle of Man, 1 November 1916; Valerie (Myrtle Hill, Ramsey), *dau*. of Frederick Malcolm La Mothe, J.P. Capt. Crellin was the most decorated Isle of Man soldier: Age 25. *s.p*.

(XXX.C.17) Pte. 13301, George Jones, 1/4th Bn. The Cheshire Regt. (T.F.): 2nd *s*. of Henry Jones, Labourer; of 30, Mill Street, Higher Tranmere, Manchester, by his wife Mary Jane, *dau*. of George Corrie: *b*. Higher Tranmere, 8 November 1896: *educ*. St. Luke's Schools, Lower Tranmere: Occupation – Carter: volunteered for Active Service soon after the outbreak of war: enlisted 12th Cheshire Regt., Birkenhead: served with the Salonika Army from August 1915: transf'd. 4th Battn. of his regiment, July 1918: proceeded to France, and served with the Expeditionary Force there from 21 August 1918, and died No.62 Casualty Clearing Station, Remy Siding, 9 October following, of wounds received in action the previous day. Buried in Lyssenthoek Military Cemetery, Poperinghe: Age 21. *unm*. (*IWGC record age 22*)

Gone But Not Forgotten
Ever Remembered By All At Home

(XXX.D.18) Sergt. 200788, William Shells, 1/5th Bn. The Durham Light Infantry (T.F.): 3rd *s*. of Charles France Shells, by his wife Elizabeth, *née* Barker: and elder brother to Pte. 24779, H. Shells, 2nd Duke of Wellington's Regt., killed in action, 15 April 1918: *b*. Armitage Bridge, Huddersfield, 1893: enlisted Huddersfield: served in France from April 1915: took part in the fighting at Hill 60. Died of bomb wounds (groin, Rt. hip), 15 October 1918, received nr. Gullegem the previous day: Age 25. In a letter to his sister Ida, written one week prior to his death, Sergt. Shells informed her he had come through the 'big push safely' and was in the 'very best of health.' For whatever reason, circumstances dictated the same post would deliver to his mother, "Dear Mrs Shells, I am very sorry to have to say your son passed away yesterday afternoon. I will write again as soon as possible. With much sympathy. Yours Sincerely, H.J.J. Clarke (Padre)"

At Rest

His brother Herbert has no known grave; he is commemorated on the Ploegsteert Memorial (Panel 6).

(XXX.E.5) Pte. TF/201068, Frank Fuller, 4th Bn. The Royal Sussex Regt. (T.F.): *s*. of John Fuller, of 14, Caryll's Cottages, Faygate, Horsham, co. Sussex, by his wife Louise: Occupation – Gardener: *b*. Colgate, 1896: a pre-war Territorial (no.4/3452), enlisted Horsham, 13 July 1915, aged 19 years. Died of wounds, 15 October 1918, received in action six days previously: Age 22. *unm*. Remembered on St. Saviour's Parish Church Memorial, Colgate, West Sussex.

Gone From Us But Not Forgotten

(XXX.F.2) Gnr. 122194, Peter McKenzie Jones, 35th Bn. Machine Gun Corps (Inf.): formerly no.029162, Royal Army Ordnance Corps: *s*. of George Jones, Auctioneer; of Old Bridge, Haverfordwest, by his wife Mary: and brother to Lieut. J.D. Jones, Royal Field Artillery, died of wounds, 21 February 1916; and Pte. G/29321, C.D. Jones, 21st Middlesex Regt., killed in action, 24 November 1917: *b*. Haverfordwest, co. Pembroke, 1888: *educ*. there: conscripted August 1917, posted R.A.O.C., Woolwich, where he was, for a time, engaged on munitions work, subsequently transf'd. Machine Gun Corps: served with the Expeditionary Force in France and Flanders, and died at Poperinghe, 16 October 1918, of wounds received in action the same day: Age 30. *unm*. The brothers are remembered on Haverfordwest World War 1 Memorial, and St. Martin of Tours Church Memorial.

Waiting For The Dawn

His brother John is buried in Ste. Marie Cemetery, Le Havre (Div.19.S.2); Clement has no known grave, he is commemorated on the Cambrai Memorial, Louverval (Panel 9).

(XXX.F.6) Pte. 56578, John Devenport, 15th (Service) Bn. The Sherwood Foresters (Notts & Derbys Regt.): *s*. of James Devenport, of Langley Mill, co. Derby, by his wife Hannah: *b*. Langley Mill, about 1892: enlisted Ilkeston, July 1916: served with the Expeditionary Force in France, and died of wounds, 16 October 1918: Age 26. In a letter to his parents, the Chaplain wrote, "I am sorry to say your son passed away on October 16th. He was a dear, sweet patient lad." Pte. Devenport leaves a wife, Alice (44, Holbrook Street, Heanor), to whom he had been married for but a short time.

Too Dearly Loved To Be Forgotten By His Ever Loving Wife Alice

The Military Service Act, introduced by the British Government, 27 January 1915, brought about an end to voluntary enlistment; from that date onward any man resident in the British Isles (excluding Ireland) who had not already joined up was now automatically deemed 'enlisted.' Aged between 18 and 41, single or widower (extended to married men, May 1916), these were the 'conscripts;' men with no choice of which regiment, unit or arm of the services they joined and – from September 1916 – with the traditional regimental means of training unable to cope with the large numbers of men passing through the depots, after 'call up' they were assigned to a unit of the 'Training Reserve.'

Citing the defeat of the Fifth Army in March 1918 and the subsequent forced extension of the British section of the Western Front as the prime reasons, a serious crisis regarding the provision of manpower necessitated a further extension of the Act on 10 April 1918, whereby the minimum age of recruitment was reduced to 18.

Tom Norris had to go war; he didn't want to but, as a result of the April 1918 extension of the Military Service Act, he had no choice and, when the time came, he duly reported at Preston Police Station along with his best friend. No one knew the war now had only a matter of months to run – it was generally believed victory was finally in sight – but for Tom, despite protestations by his parents, there was no evading the issue, he would have to go; his only consolation being that it just might be over before he got there.

(XXX.H.6) Pte. 67414, Thomas 'Tom' Norris, 1/4th Bn. The Cheshire Regt (T.F.): *s*. of William (& Elizabeth) Norris, of 122, Gordon Street, Preston, co. Lancaster: *b*. Preston, 1900: served with the Expeditionary Force in France and Flanders from June 1918, and died of abdominal wounds, 19 October 1918, received in the advance on Menin six days previously. In a letter to his parents, the nurse who attended him in his last hours wrote, "He was the dearest patient and we all became very much attached to him for his sweet aspirations. Yesterday, when much worse, I told him he was a very sick boy. He asked me if he would get better and I told him I could not say he would. I asked him if there was any message I could send home. First he said tell them I'm fine. Later he told me to tell his mother he was thinking of her and loved her. 'Do tell Aunt Emily and Uncle Jack,' his thoughts were of them too and to fire them his best regards. He spoke little after, and died 10 a.m. this morning. He just slept away. The end was very peaceful.": Age 18. (*IWGC record age 19*)

Cherished Memories Of One So Dear Oft Recalled With A Silent Tear

(XXXI.AA.2) Pte. 141051, Charles Henry Knott, 47th (Garrison) Bn. Royal Fusiliers attd. Graves Registration Unit: *s*. of the late James (& Elizabeth) Knott, of Salford, Manchester: served in the South African Campaign, 1899–1902: 25 years in H.M. Forces: Died of pneumonia, 23 January 1920: Age 57.

(XXXI.AA.3) Pte. 51299, J.E. Lally, The King's Own (Royal Lancaster Regt.) attd. No.5 Group, Directorate of Graves Registration & Enquiries: *s.* of Mrs J.E. Lally (73, Cranworth Street, Ardwick, Manchester): Died of heart failure, 28 January 1920.

(XXXI.BB.5) Pte. 692272, David Arthur Jefferies, 126th Coy. Labour Corps attd. Graves Registration Unit: *s.* of Thomas John Jefferies: late *husb.* to Eleanore F.E. Jefferies (7, Cromer Road, Tooting Junction, London). Died of pneumonia, 13 August 1920: Age 57.

Gone But Not Forgotten

(XXXI.BB.7) Pte. 6454288, Simpson Meldrum, Exhumation Coy., Directorate of Graves Registration & Enquiries: late 47th (Garrison) Bn. Royal Fusiliers: Mentioned in Despatches: *s.* of George (& Mrs) Meldrum, of 7, Ballantine Place, Perth: Died of haemorrhage, 18 June 1921: Age 47. The last person to die and be buried at Lijssenthoek; only exhumations and reburials were performed after this date.

The earliest 'dated' French burial in Lijssenthoek Military Cemetery:

(XXXI.C.24) Soldat 2me Classe, Jean Baptiste Leon Jarland, 3rme Bn. Chasseurs à Pied.: *s.* of Antoine Jarland, and Marie Giboulot, his wife: *b.* St. Pierrre-en-Vaux, Côte d'Or, France, 21 April 1889: enlisted Auxonne, Burgundy: *Mort Pour la France*; *blessures* (died of wounds), 6 November 1914: Age 35.

(XXXI.D.4) 2nd Lieut. Sterling Maurice, 1st (Wessex) Field Coy., Royal Engineers: 6th *s.* of the late Major-Gen. Sir Frederick Maurice, K.C.B., and his wife Lady Maurice (Highland View, Camberley, co. Surrey): *gdson.* to the late Denison Maurice, and brother to Brigadier-Gen. F. Maurice, C.B., and Capt. L. Maurice, Royal Engineers: *b.* Highland View, 12 November 1886: *educ.* St. Paul's School, and King's College, London – obtained his degree of B.Sc. from the latter – and London University: a student member of the Institute of Civil Engineers; passed his examination – A.M.I.C.E. – just prior to joining the Army. He was a member of Inns of Court O.T.C. for eight years, and had worked as an Engineer in both England and West Africa; on the outbreak of war he was assistant to Fearnside Irving, Esq., of 1, London Wall Buildings, and 'Ach-na-Cree,' Ridgway, Horsell: volunteered on the outbreak of war; obtained his commission, Wessex Engineers, August 1914: served with the Expeditionary Force in France from December following: wounded April 1915, but remained at duty. In the early morning of 11 May 1915 he was wounded by a sniper at Hooge, and died a few hours later in the Casualty Clearing Hospital, Poperinghe. Buried in the Military Cemetery there: Age 28. The General Officer Commanding his Division, in writing of him, said, "He was a most promising young officer, and has since his arrival in this country done as hard and as good work for his country as anyone out here. We shall miss him in the Division," and an Officer Commanding another battalion, "He worked with me in many a difficult and dangerous situation, and I learnt to appreciate most fully his capacity and gallantry in helping us to improve and render tenable positions that had become difficult. We were always glad when he came on duty; we knew he would give us good and practical advice and assistance. His death is indeed a dreadful loss to the Service." Mentioned in Sir John (now Lord) French's Despatch, 30 November 1915. He *m.* November 1914; Hope, only child of Fearnside Irving.

The earliest dated British burial in Lijssenthoek Military Cemetery:

(XXXI.D.19) Capt. William Arthur Mould Temple, 1st Bn. (28th Foot) The Gloucestershire Regt.: eldest *s.* of Lieut.Col. William Temple, V.C., late Army Medical Service, by his late wife Anne Theodosia (*d.*1914), *dau.* of Major-General T.R. Mould, C.B., Royal Engineers: *b.* The Officer's Quarters, Woolwich Arsenal, London, S.E., 14 June 1872: *educ.* Portsmouth Grammar School; Brussels, Belgium, and Royal Military College, Sandhurst: winning medals for running while at school, and being a good football player: gazetted 2nd Lieut. Gloucestershire Regt. 19 July 1893, joining 1st Battn. of his regiment at Aldershot the following month: served in Malta, Egypt, India and Ceylon: promoted Lieut. 15 March 1897, Capt. 27 May 1903: served in the South African War 1899–1900: took part in the operations in Natal 1899, including actions at Rietfontein and Lombard's Kop: operations in the Transvaal, June 1900, and those in the Orange River Colony, July – August 1900 (Queen's Medal, three clasps): served with the Expeditionary Force in France and Flanders. Shot through the right chest and shoulder at Koekuit, north of Langemarck, Belgium, while attempting to repulse a German attack from the direction of Mangalaere, 21 October 1914, and died two days later (23 October 1914) at Chateau D'Hondt (No.4 Casualty Clearing Hospital), Poperinghe. Buried there: Age 42. 'In him the battalion lost a most gallant and efficient officer, beloved by all ranks and most sincerely mourned.' He *m.* Rhoda Mary Hebe, *dau.* of J.P.L. Hazeldine Esq., Barrister-at-Law, Inner Temple, of Bragborough Hall, co. Northampton, one time M.P., co. Carnarvon. Capt. Temple left one daughter, Hazel Rhoda, *b.* Kasauli, India, May 1908. All correspondence should be addressed c/o Mrs Vaughan (Burlton Hall, nr. Shrewsbury, co. Salop). (*IWGC record 21 October*)

He Was Called Faithful And True

Capt. Temple was the first British officer to die of wounds in Poperinghe; originally buried in the town cemetery after the war his remains were exhumed and reburied at Lijssenthoek.

The only civilian burial in Lijssenthoek Military Cemetery:

(XXXI.D.20) Thomas McGrath, Imperial War Graves Commission: formerly Sergt. 8902, 2nd Bn. (59th Foot) East Lancashire Regt., and Chinese Labour Corps: Occupation – Gardener; Imperial War Graves Commission, Lijssenthoek. Died of sickness, 23 April 1920: Age 31. He was married to Maria McGrath, Café Remy, Poperinghe. His headstone carries the East Lancashire regimental crest and, unlike most I.W.G.C. staff headstones, is not of the chamfered corner design.

I Have Fought The Good Fight My Reward Is In Heaven

(XXXI.D.21) Rev. Robert Wilson Hopkins, Chaplain 4th Class, Army Chaplain's Dept.: late of 'Glascoed,' Clifford Road, New Barnet: *s.* of Joseph H. (& Mary) Hopkins: late *husb.* to Helena B. Hopkins (Applegarth Road, West Kensington, London): Religion – Wesleyan: Died while out on the battlefields with an exhumation unit, 24 April 1920. The Royal Army Chaplain's Memorial, Royal Garrison Church, Aldershot, dedicated 31 October 1923, contains (in mosaic) the line: The Righteous Live For Evermore, Their Reward Is Also With The Lord, And The Care Of Them Is With The Most High: Wisdom Vs.15." It records the names of 172 Army Chaplains who lost their lives in the Great War; the Rev. Hopkins is remembered among them.

> He is that fallen lance that lies as hurled,
> That lies unlifted now, come dew, come rust,
> But still lies pointed as it ploughed the dust.
> If we who sight along it round the world,
> See nothing worthy to have been its mark,
> It is because like men we look too near,
> Forgetting that as fitted to the sphere,
> Our missiles always make too short an arc.
> They fall, they rip the grass, they intersect
> The curve of earth, and striking, break their own;
> They make us cringe for metal point on stone.
> But this we know, the obstacle that checked
> And tripped the body, shot the spirit on
> Further than target ever showed or shone.
>
> *Robert Frost.*

Robert Frost, of American/Scots parentage, moved to America in 1885. From 1912 to 1915 he lived and farmed in England, where he became a friend of Edward Thomas, who encouraged him to take up writing poetry. A visitor left the above poem *A Soldier* with the simple – yet appropriate – request it stand in memory of Harry King, David Beattie, James Pigue and all American servicemen who made the supreme sacrifice, wherever they may lie.

(XXXII.A.11) Pte. 1st Class, 209559, Harry Arthur King, Troop 'F', 3rd Cavalry, United States Army: New York: *s.* of John King, of 11, Maple Place, Meir, Stoke-on-Trent, co. Stafford, by his wife Susan: and brother to Pte. M2/114698, R. King, Army Service Corps attd. R.G.A., died of wounds, 17 October 1917: *b.* Heybridge, Tean, Stoke-on-Trent. Died at Bourbonne-les-Bains, France, of bronchial pneumonia, 20 September 1918. Originally buried in the Argonne American Cemetery, Romange-sous-Montfaucon, in compliance to a request by his mother, his remains were removed to Lijssenthoek in October 1921; she also chose the epitaph:

The Best Of Sons And Brothers
Also Reggie Buried Close By

His brother Reginald is buried nearby (XXI.H.17).

(XXXII.A.14) Pte. 131428, George Godfrey Earnshaw, 34th Bn. Machine Gun Corps (Inf.): *s.* of the late George Henry Earnshaw (*d.*1919), of Stannington, Sheffield, by his marriage to Florence Brocklehurst, *née* Earnshaw, *née* Fisher (The Nook, Stannington): *b.* Stannington, 1898: enlisted Sheffield. Killed in action, 25 October 1918: Age 20. Remembered on Stannington War Memorial.

God Shall Wipe Away All Tears From Their Eyes

(XXXII.C.14) Sergt. 120274, David Stanley Beattie, 27th Div., 105th Infantry, United States Army: late of New York: only *s.* of David Beattie, of Troy, New York, and Isabel his wife: *educ.* Troy High School: Occupation – Bank Clerk: member 2nd Infantry Regt., New York National Guard, served with his unit in the Mexican border conflict, 1916: departed United States and proceeded to join the European War, May 1918: served in France from 14 July following, the division being the first United States troops to take over a sector of the line in Belgium, being responsible for the Dickebusch Line, nr. Poperinghe. Killed in action by one of the last long range enemy shells fired in the salient, being hit in the temple by shrapnel while on traffic control duty in the nearby village of Watou: 31 August 1918: Age 20.

He Lived By Faith
He Still Lives

In June 1919 the mortal remains of Lieut. J.A. Pigue were removed from nearby Gwalia Cemetery and reinterred here. After the reburial his surviving family received assurance from the British Government that Lijssenthoek would be 'his final rest' and his grave would not be disturbed again.

(XXXII.E.9) 1st Lieut. James Aaron Pigue, 'A' Coy., 117th Infantry Regt., United States Army: late of Tennessee: *s.* of Edward Hicks Pigue, of Tennessee, and Fannie Pigue, his wife: *b.* Nashville, Tennessee: *educ.* Virginia Military Institute (1901–02), joined U.S. Marine Corps, 1904; Annapolis: obtained his Lieutenancy; seconded to Special Duty – Construction, Panama Canal: granted Honourable Discharge 1909: joined 1st Tennessee National Guard, 1916, took part in the fighting in Mexico: promoted 1st Lieut. and rejoined 1st Tennessee N.G., reassigned 3rd Tennessee N.G. (re-designated 117th Infantry Regt. for service in the European War): proceeded to France, 4 May 1918, and was killed in action, 18 July 1918, being shot through the heart by a sniper while on observation duty; Poperinghe Defences: Age 37. He was married to Jane Weller, *née* Pigue, and leaves one son.

Gave His Life For Humanity

(XXXV.A.11) Pte. 9738, John Daniel Macnaughton, 1/5th Bn. Princess Louise's (Argyll & Sutherland Highlanders), (T.F.): *yst. s.* of the late John Macnaughton, Builder, by his wife Isabella ('Carn-Dhu,' Aberfeldy), *dau.* of James Smith, of Birse: and brother to Pte. 438737, A. Macnaughton, 52nd Canadian Infantry, died Ninette Sanatorium, Canada, 1 April 1919, from the combined effects of exposure and wounds received in action near Ypres, 5 June 1916: *b.* Aberfeldy, co. Perth, 21 October 1893: *educ.* Breadalbane Academy: Occupation – Architect: enlisted 1/14th Argyll & Sutherland Highlanders, about mid-June 1915: served with the Expeditionary Force in France and Flanders from 6 June 1916, transf'd. 1/5th Battn. and died at No.62 Casualty Clearing Station, 15 October 1918, of wounds received in action on the River Lys two days previously. Buried in Lijssenthoek Military Cemetery: Age 24. *unm.*

God Takes Our Loved Ones From Our Homes But Never From Our Hearts

His brother Alexander is buried in Belmont Hillside Cemetery, Manitoba (3).

(XXXV.A.21) Pte. 56577, John William Perry, 18th Bn. The Lancashire Fusiliers: eldest *s.* of William John Perry, Freeman (General) Carter; of 25, Baddow Road, Chelmsford, co. Essex, by his wife Emily Mary, *née* Coe: *b.* Roxwell, 1899: enlisted Witham: served with the Expeditionary Force in France from the summer of 1918, and died of wounds, 20 October 1918, at Poperinghe: Age 19.

Loving Memory Of Our Dearly Beloved Son
Hope To Meet With Jesus

(XXXV.A.32) Pte. 63508, Ernest Henry Parton, 14th Bn. Machine Gun Corps (Inf.): formerly no.4681, Monmouthshire Regt.: s. of Thomas Barton, of Bringsty, co. Worcester, by his wife Anne: and elder brother to 2nd Lieut. R.T. Parton, Oxford & Bucks Light Infantry attd. 1/10th London Regt., died of wounds, 21 November 1917: enlisted Leominster. Died of accidental injuries, 25 October 1918: Age 36. He was married to May Sarah Lloyd, née Parton (Bringsty).

Until The Day Breaks

His brother Roland is buried in Alexandria (Hadra) War Memorial Cemetery (B.30).

(XXXV.A.45) L/Sergt. R/23990, Arthur Thomas Exeter, M.M. & 2 Bars, 18th (Service) Bn. (Arts & Crafts) The King's Royal Rifle Corps: b. Dartford, co. Kent: enlisted there. Died of wounds, 22 October 1918, the only fatality recorded by his battalion on that day Mentioned in Despatches for his services in the Great War.

(XXXV.A.49) Pte. 77463, William Ireland, 'B' Coy., 15/17th (Service) Bn. The Prince of Wales's Own (West Yorkshire Regt.): s. of the late Thomas Ireland, by his wife Fanny (23, Station Road, Steeton, nr. Leeds): Occupation – Tailor; Messrs J.W. Whitaker, Sutton Mill: b. Keighley: enlisted Halifax, June 1917: served with the Expeditionary Force in France from 1 October 1918, and died in the early hours of the 23rd of that month, of wounds (G.S. arm, leg, abdomen) received in action the previous day: Age 27. A founder member of St. Stephen's Church Lad's Brigade, prior to the outbreak of war, Pte. Ireland was well-known as a half-back for St. Stephen's C.L.B. and Steeton Association football teams. (*IWGC record 22 October*)

In Loving Memory Of Our Dear One At Rest

(XXXV.A.58) Sergt. 19206, Richard Phillipson, 15th (Service) Bn. (1st Birkenhead) The Cheshire Regt.: s. of James Phillipson, of 9, Croft Street, Preston, co. Lancaster, by his wife Susannah: and elder brother to Pte. G/76687, S. Phillipson, 24th Royal Fusiliers, died 27 October 1918, of wounds received in action during the fighting north of Courtrai ten days previously: b. Christchurch, Preston, c.1896: enlisted Preston. Died 21 October 1918, of wounds: Age 22. He leaves a wife, Lillian Phillipson (24, Talbot Road, Preston).

He Died That Others Might Live

His brother Sidney is buried in Awoingt British Cemetery (II.B.26).

(XXXV.B.12) Pte. M2/119185, Thomas Hyland, 884th Mechanical Transport Coy. Army Service Corps attd. XIXth Corps Heavy Artillery: late *husb.* to Gertrude Campion, *née* Hyland (2, Mansfield Villas, Thornaby-on-Tees, Stockton-on-Tees): enlisted West Hartlepool: served in France and Flanders from 25 August 1915, and died of accidental injuries, 3 November 1918: Age 32.

Valley Of The Shadow
God, I am travelling out to death's sea,
I, who exulted in sunshine and laughter,
Thought not of dying – death is such a waste of me!
Grant me one comfort: Leave not the hereafter
Of Mankind to war, as though I had died not –
I, who in battle, my comrade's arm linking,
Shouted and sang – life in my pulses hot
Throbbing and dancing! Let not my sinking
In dark be for naught, my death a vain thing!
God, let me know it the end of man's fever!
Make my last breath a bugle call, carrying
Peace o'er the valleys and cold hills, for ever!

John Galsworthy

(XXXV.B.16) Rfn. R/33386, Albert Bogg, 18th (Service) Bn. (Arts & Crafts) The King's Royal Rifle Corps: formerly The Rifle Brigade, no.S/18250; TR13/13230, 19th T.R. Bn.: *s.* of John Bogg, by his wife Florence Emily: *b.* Plumstead, co. Kent, *c.*1892: Occupation – Munitions Worker; Woolwich Arsenal: enlisted Woolwich, June 1915: proceeded to France, 6 May 1916: wounded 1917; returned to England; returned France: wounded (shrapnel, lung) nr. Grammont, River Dender (East Flanders) during the fighting there on the 10th. and, removed (over fifty miles) to Lyssenthoek, died in the C.C.S. there the following day (11 November 1918): Age 26. He leaves a widow, Winifred A. Bogg, *née* Nainby (30, Coxwell Road, Plumstead) and a baby daughter Joy, in mourning. His last letter home, written late October 1918, read, "My Darling Win, I am just attempting a few lines after all the letters you have written to me. Many happy returns of the day dear, I must make it all up to you when I come home. Yes dear, it is hard lines about the arsenal moving but I know you will keep smiling. Thanks for the books dearie, but you needn't send any more as I can borrow plenty here. I am so glad to hear Joy is in the pink, and I hope you are yourself dear. I received a letter from Rich with yours dear. Well dearie, I must pack up now. With fondest love to all at home, and tell mum I am often thinking of her, not to mention Little Joy. With heaps of love and kisses, I remain your Ever Loving Hubby Bert. xxxxxxxxx. xxx For Joy. Hope Ma is improving in health."

(XXXV.B.17) Capt. Percy James Belcher, 'D' Coy., 49th Bn. Canadian Infantry (Alberta Regt.), C.E.F.: *s*. of Lieut.Col. Robert Belcher, of 9846, 107th Street, Edmonton, Alberta, by his wife Maggie: *b*. 1 March 1891: Occupation – Banker; Merchant Bank of Canada: previously served 19th Alberta Dragoons (Militia); enlisted Edmonton, 21 January 1915. Killed in action at Passchendaele, 30 October 1917: Age 26. (*IWGC record age 27*)

Not Forgotten
Mother

By early 1919 the effectiveness of the medical services had been seriously affected by staff shortages due to demobilisation. At Lyssenthoek newly sited No.54 C.C.S. had lost a third of its strength due to this process and was heavily reliant on German prisoners of war for the day to day running of the facility. The unit diary, for its first month (from 4 February), records the majority of admissions to the hospital were predominantly victims of influenza and German (357). Other nationalities admitted included Chinese, Canadian, British – after treatment some passed through, some did not.

(XXXV.B.27) Sergt. WR/125840, Edmund Devine, 34th Light Railway Operating Coy., Royal Engineers: formerly no.251348, formerly no.8415, King's Own: *b*. Manchester: Occupation – Railway Labourer: a pre-war Reservist returned to the Colours on mobilisation, August 1914.; proceeded to France on the 23rd of that month. Died of influenza, No.54 C.C.S., 3 March 1919. Cross erected. He leaves a widow, Sarah Ellen Devine (14, Woodland Terrace, Salford), and *dau*. Helen Frances (*b*.1918).

(XXXV.B.39) Pte. 30442, William Lampe, 2nd Inf. Labour Coy. The Duke of Cambridge's Own (Middlesex Regt.): *s*. of Mr (& Mrs) Lampe: late *husb*. to Y.H.A. Lampe (2, Rue Warein, Hazebrouck, France). Died of cerebral abscess, 15 August 1919: Age 24.

Not Forgotten By His Loving Wife, Baby And Family

(Sp.Mem.AL034) Labourer, 46564, Kao Ch'ing Lin, Chinese Labour Corps: Shot and killed by Henri Tailleu, Publican, Hollebeke, on suspicion of breaking and entering, 28 September 1919.

(Sp.Mem.AL034) Labourer, 62638, Chang T'ung Sheng, Chinese Labour Corps: Shot and killed by Henri Tailleu, Publican, Hollebeke, on suspicion of breaking and entering, 28 September 1919.

On 2 January 1918, 76 year old local blacksmith/innkeeper Karel Dewachter was knocked down by a motor car in the Rue de Cassel, Poperinghe. Admitted to the hospital at Remy Siding, Lyssenthoek with his right arm broken in two places, he died here later the same day. He has no known grave, but is believed to be buried here.

UK -7,350. Aust.-1,131. NZ- 291. Can.- 1,053. NF-5. SAfr.-29. BWI -21. India-2.
KUG-3. Fr.-658. US-3. IWGC-1. Chinese Labour Corps-32. Ger.-223.

The cemetery was designed by Sir Reginald Blomfield.